Our police protectors : history of the New York police from the earliest period to the present time.

Augustine E Costello

Our police protectors : history of the New York police from the earliest period to the present time.
Costello, Augustine E
collection ID ocm20683561
Reproduction from Harvard Law School Library
Published for the benefit of the Police Pension Fund.
New York : The author, 1885.
xix, 574 p., [19] leaves of plates : ill., facsims., ports. ; 26 cm.

The Making of Modern Law collection of legal archives constitutes a genuine revolution in historical legal research because it opens up a wealth of rare and previously inaccessible sources in legal, constitutional, administrative, political, cultural, intellectual, and social history. This unique collection consists of three extensive archives that provide insight into more than 300 years of American and British history. These collections include:

Legal Treatises, 1800-1926: over 20,000 legal treatises provide a comprehensive collection in legal history, business and economics, politics and government.

Trials, 1600-1926: nearly 10,000 titles reveal the drama of famous, infamous, and obscure courtroom cases in America and the British Empire across three centuries.

Primary Sources, 1620-1926: includes reports, statutes and regulations in American history, including early state codes, municipal ordinances, constitutional conventions and compilations, and law dictionaries.

These archives provide a unique research tool for tracking the development of our modern legal system and how it has affected our culture, government, business – nearly every aspect of our everyday life. For the first time, these high-quality digital scans of original works are available via print-on-demand, making them readily accessible to libraries, students, independent scholars, and readers of all ages.

The BiblioLife Network

This project was made possible in part by the BiblioLife Network (BLN), a project aimed at addressing some of the huge challenges facing book preservationists around the world. The BLN includes libraries, library networks, archives, subject matter experts, online communities and library service providers. We believe every book ever published should be available as a high-quality print reproduction; printed on-demand anywhere in the world. This insures the ongoing accessibility of the content and helps generate sustainable revenue for the libraries and organizations that work to preserve these important materials.

The following book is in the "public domain" and represents an authentic reproduction of the text as printed by the original publisher. While we have attempted to accurately maintain the integrity of the original work, there are sometimes problems with the original work or the micro-film from which the books were digitized. This can result in minor errors in reproduction. Possible imperfections include missing and blurred pages, poor pictures, markings and other reproduction issues beyond our control. Because this work is culturally important, we have made it available as part of our commitment to protecting, preserving, and promoting the world's literature.

GUIDE TO FOLD-OUTS MAPS and OVERSIZED IMAGES

The book you are reading was digitized from microfilm captured over the past thirty to forty years. Years after the creation of the original microfilm, the book was converted to digital files and made available in an online database.

In an online database, page images do not need to conform to the size restrictions found in a printed book. When converting these images back into a printed bound book, the page sizes are standardized in ways that maintain the detail of the original. For large images, such as fold-out maps, the original page image is split into two or more pages

Guidelines used to determine how to split the page image follows:

• Some images are split vertically; large images require vertical and horizontal splits.
• For horizontal splits, the content is split left to right.
• For vertical splits, the content is split from top to bottom.
• For both vertical and horizontal splits, the image is processed from top left to bottom right.

PAGINATION INCORRECT

TREASURER'S OFFICE,
Police Department of the City of New York,
No. 300 Mulberry Street.

New York, October 29th 1883

To Whom it may Concern

This is to certify that the proceeds of the book, "Our Police Protectors" will be devoted to the Police Pension Fund.

S. B. French
Pres't Police Board

J. P. Nichols
Treasurer Police Board

Police Department,
of the City of New York,
300 Mulberry Street,
New York, Feby 14th 1885

To whom it may Concern

I do hereby certify to the accuracy of the certificate signed by J. P. Nichols, Treasurer and S. B. French President — dated October 29= 1883 relative to the book "Our Police Protectors"

Wm S Kipp
Chief Clerk

Our Police Protectors.

HISTORY OF THE

NEW YORK POLICE

FROM THE

EARLIEST PERIOD TO THE PRESENT TIME.

PUBLISHED FOR THE BENEFIT OF THE

POLICE PENSION FUND.

SECOND EDITION.

BY

A. E. COSTELLO.

ILLUSTRATED WITH OVER TWO HUNDRED CHOICE ENGRAVINGS.

PUBLISHED BY THE AUTHOR.
1885.

TREASURER'S OFFICE,
Police Department of the City of New York,
No. 300 Mulberry Street,

New York, June 12th 1885

A. E. Costello Esq
Dear Sir

It is due to you that the Board of Police Commissioners should give an expression of their appreciation of your services to the department as author and publisher of the volume "Our Police Protectors". The book we are free to say, reflects credit upon you and on the department. Its literary and artistic merits alone should demand for it a large sale. When however there is added to these attractive features the fact that the book "Our Police Protectors" is published for the benefit of the Police Pension Fund, its financial success should not be a debatable question. It is to be hoped that the members of the force will aid you within the sphere of their duty in accomplishing this desired result.

Very truly yours
S. B. French
John McClave
John R. Voorhis
Fitz John Porter

Copyrighted 1884,
By A. E. Costello.

JUN 28 1921

PREFACE.

IN the fall of 1883 fears were entertained that the Police Pension Fund would soon have become depleted. Under the decision of the Court of Appeals in the case of John Ryan against the Board, money to the amount of $77,420.29 was paid for judgments obtained against the Board for sick time deducted from the pay of Policemen for six years prior to 1883. Had not the Legislature opportunely stepped in and provided the remedy, within ten months a dollar of the Pension Fund would not have remained. It was during this period of depression—in October, 1883—that the writer conceived the idea of doing something which, while helping the Police Pension Fund, would serve to perpetuate in durable form the historical achievements of the Police force. The writer was then a reporter in charge of the *Herald* Police Bureau, an office that is located opposite Police Headquarters, and, day and night, collects the news that comes over the Police wires, or through Police channels, for publication. He had been so employed for a number of years, and such employment necessarily brought him a great deal in the society of Police officials and Policemen. After thinking the matter over carefully, he made known his views to the late Sidney P Nichols, who was then a Police Commissioner and Treasurer of the Police Pension Fund. Mr Nichols entered heartily into the project, and encouraged the writer to go ahead. With his characteristic promptitude, he waited on Commissioner French, in whose presence the writer again unfolded his plans Mr. French also cordially approved of the scheme It was then decided to put those ideas into practical shape, and it was also settled that the book should be published for the benefit of the Police Pension Fund. Permission to this effect was granted by the Board

The writer continued his connection with the *Herald*, and, when opportunity offered, he went about the collection of his material for the book. But the work was slow and tedious, and, at the end of some six months, the writer found that if the book was to be published within a reasonable period he should devote all his time to it, and "take off his coat" to the task. Work on the book was thenceforward shoved with all proper diligence.

Mr. Nichols' interest in the book never abated. He kept a constant and intelligent supervision on the progress made, and, by his kindliness, encouraged the writer to press on, to be industrious, and to fear not. The compiler was naturally diffident of his ability to do justice to so important an undertaking; and, now that the book is printed, his diffidence has not in the least abated. He is well aware that in more able and experienced hands the story of "OUR POLICE PROTECTORS" would have been more pleasantly, accurately and intelligently told. But he has done his best to do justice to the subject, and for this, if for nothing else he is, perhaps, entitled to a little praise.

"Who does the best his circumstance permits, does well, acts nobly; angels could no more."

Mr. Nichols, early in the fall of 1884, was stricken down with a fatal illness, which, to some extent, retarded the progress of the work, as it was usual to consult him a good deal, particularly on business and financial affairs, in connection therewith. Had he survived, we are satisfied that he would have continued his friendly and fostering interest in the book.

It is usual for a writer to gratify the curiosity of his readers by making known to them, either in foot-notes or in some other form, the sources of his information. Well, this is proper, but in the present case it would be somewhat difficult to comply with this rule, as the authorities consulted are not exclusively such as are to be found in libraries. However, it may be stated that the early historical facts were mostly obtained from the Dutch and English manuscript records in the City Hall library; also, the following authorities were, among a number of others, consulted: The Proceedings of the Common Council, City Ordinances, State Laws, various Histories, Hand-books, Guide-books, and Gazetteers of New York; Valentine's Manuals, O'Callahan's Documentary History of New York, and such other facts were gleaned as were to be obtained by diligent study in the Astor and Historical Libraries.

The writer is under many deep obligations to George P. Gott, Treasurer's Bookkeeper of the Police Department; Captain Kipp, Chief Clerk; Superintendent Walling, and Inspectors Murray Dilks, Thorne and Byrnes. He also desires to extend his acknowledgments to Mrs. Frank Leslie, who kindly allowed the use of a number of valuable cuts; to the Messrs. D. Appleton & Co., for electrotypes of cuts from their "New York Illustrated"; and to The Century Publishing Company for similar favors. His thanks are likewise due to George B. Taylor, of the *Times*, who has aided the writer in the compilation of the chapters on Inspector Byrne's Staff of Detectives, and "The Duties of a Policeman," and who has also supplied a portion of the material used in the description of the various precincts.

PREFACE

Mr. Thomas Nast, by permission of the Messrs. Harper Brothers, has kindly furnished the clever drawing which forms the frontispiece of this book. M... C de Grimm, the *Telegram* artist, by kind permission of Mr. James Gordon Bennett, has also supplied us with the clever sketches which are so readily distinguishable

Valuable tables of arrests and other police statistics had been prepared, but these have been crowded out, owing to the unexpected size to which this volume has grown and the desire to go to press. In a subsequent edition these statistics will be inserted.

A E COSTELLO.

NEW YORK,
    Sept 1, 1885

PRESS NOTICES.

[THE SUNDAY STAR, June 7, 1885.]

SELDOM has a labor of love been so ably and acceptably performed as that which now appears before the New York public in the shape of a handsome volume entitled "Our Police Protectors." The author and publisher is Mr A E Costello, and as the proceeds of the sales are to be devoted to the augmentation of the Police Pension Fund, it is certain to be the means of putting a very handsome sum into the treasury of that worthy organization

But, apart from these considerations, Mr Costello has produced a work which deserves to rank with the best historical and biographical volumes having relation to the Empire City or State From the first to the last page it is replete with interest, and its literary features are enhanced by the addition of over two hundred choice engravings, embracing many incidents prominent in the history of the city, the noted riots of a century, the famous police officials of olden times, and the superintendents, inspectors, captains and best known officers of a more recent period, down to date.

Of the genesis of the book Mr Costello speaks modestly It was in 1883 that the idea of writing a history of the police first occurred to him, and after thinking the matter over, he consulted with the late Commissioner Sidney P Nichols, who entered heartily into the project

"Mr Nichols' interest in the book," he writes, "never abated He kept a constant and intelligent supervision on the progress made, and, by his kindness, encouraged the writer to press on, to be industrious, and to fear not Mr Nichols, early in the fall of 1884, was stricken down with a fatal illness, which, to some extent, retarded the progress of the work, as it was usual to consult him a good deal, particularly on business and financial affairs in connection therewith Had he survived, we are satisfied that he would have continued his friendly and fostering interest in the book"

Concerning a volume embracing a multitude of events, and covering almost the entire period of the growth and development of our city, it is impossible to give an adequate idea in the columns of a newspaper The opening chapters deal with the primitive police regulations from 1609 to 1664, events during the period of British occupancy up to 1783, the old system of watching which prevailed in the early part of the present century up to 1830, and the repeal in 1844 of the old system—which proved altogether insufficient

Coming down to later times, the provisions of the consolidation act and the model system of the police force of the present day are discussed, the operations of the Central Office Bureau of Detectives and its able chief, Inspector Byrnes, are explained, and the general government and discipline of the entire department made clear to the mind of the reader Each inspection district is the subject of a special chapter, embracing its personnel and the records of its present and past chiefs A sketch of the organization and objects of the Police Pension Fund is given, and the volume fitly closes with a chapter explanatory of the methods governing our criminal courts, showing the multifarious operations of justice and how vice is beset on every side by the safeguards and precautions erected for the protection of virtue, the suppression of crime, and the apprehension and punishment of the criminal

[SUNDAY DEMOCRAT, June 7, 1885]

"OUR POLICE PROTECTORS" is the title of a royal octavo volume just published The author is Mr Augustine E Costello, a well known journalist Mr Costello may be congratulated on writing a very readable and instructive book It is not a dry historical narrative of police proceedings so much as a historical review of city affairs in general, from the foundation of New Amsterdam to the present time

The book is elegantly illustrated throughout with many interesting views of old New York Thomas Nast, C de Grimm, and other well known artists, have contributed to make the artistic merits of the work equal to the subject. There are in all about two hundred and fifty choice and appropriate engravings in the volume

The book will undoubtedly secure a large sale, as it is, apart from its general interest, a valuable work of reference A vast amount of information has been diligently collated by the author and pleasantly narrated His style is clear, expressive and entertaining The volume reflects credit on the author and the subject of which it treats The book is published by the author, and is sold by subscription only, the proceeds being devoted to the Police Pension Fund The names of the subscribers, it is understood, and the amounts subscribed, will, in due time, be published in the newspapers A considerable part of the first edition has been already disposed of, and it is expected that a large amount of money will—in this manner—be realized for this praiseworthy object

[THE MORNING JOURNAL, June 8, 1885]

A HISTORY of the New York police force from the earliest time has just been published under the title of "Our Police Protectors" by the author, A E Costello, and the proceeds from its sale will be devoted to the benefit of the Police Pension Fund

The narrative of the suppression of the draft riots in 1863 is a graphic description of the most terrible work the police of New York were ever called upon to undergo. The illustrations of the trying situations in which they were then placed, as well as others of an older as well as a more recent date, lend an additional attraction to the work

Among the two hundred fine engravings with which it is embellished are many portraits of deceased and living officers who have earned the respect and esteem of their fellow citizens

In a word, the work is a valuable addition to local history, and the object for which it has been compiled ought to secure for it a wide list of subscribers among the people whose persons and property the beneficiaries have protected

[DAILY NEWS, June 16, 1885]

"OUR POLICE PROTECTORS" is the title of a history of the police of this city from the Dutch occupancy of Manhattan Island to the present time The author is Mr Augustine E Costello, the well known journalist The publication is a royal octavo volume of about six hundred pages It is impossible in a brief notice to give an adequate idea of this highly meritorious work Mr Costello sketches graphically in the opening chapter the primitive system of "watching" that prevailed under the old Dutch burgomasters, another chapter being devoted to the period of British rule

The book contains over two hundred engravings, Nast and de Grimm having furnished some remarkably bright sketches. The exploits of the leading officials, from the time of High Constable Hays, are mentioned in detail, namely Matsell, Walling, Acton, Carpenter, Kennedy, Murray Byrnes, etc The book, finally, is an encyclopedia of police affairs It is published under the auspices of the police commissioners for the benefit of the Police Pension Fund

[SUNDAY DISPATCH, June 7, 1885]

WE commend "Our Police Protectors" as a book worth the attention of all New Yorkers, more especially as the proceeds from it are to be devoted to the aid of the Police Pension Fund The book contains over five hundred pages, is handsomely printed and bound, and very profusely illustrated

[THE NATION, June 11, 1885]

THE laborious and praiseworthy compilation entitled "Our Police Protectors History of the New York Police from the Earliest Period to the Present Time," is published by the author, Mr A E Costello, for the benefit of the Police Pension Fund It is a mine of information on a subject in which every city in the country has a vital interest—the development of a constabulary force equal to the demands of increasing population and increased facilities for crime, disorder and destructiveness The chapters on the draft riots of 1863 connect this work with the political history of the republic Great numbers of portraits and other illustrations add much to the value of the record

[THE SUN, June 7, 1885]

Mr A E COSTELLO is the author of a handsome octavo volume of nearly six hundred pages, entitled "Our Police Protectors," giving a history of the New York police from the earliest period to the present time It is illustrated with many engravings, including a series of faithful and life like portraits of the various police commissioners and police captains It is published for the benefit of the Police Pension Fund

[SUNDAY NEWS, June 7, 1885]

A E Costello has added to the already large number of works on New York City a highly interesting, and at the same time reliable, historical and biographical encyclopædia, entitled "Our Police Protectors History of the New York Police from the Earliest Period to the Present Time Published for the Benefit of the Police Pension Fund" The book is thorough Everything in connection with it is well done It commences with the primitive police regulations in 1609, and, in twenty three chapters, brings the history of the city down to its present period It contains two hundred and fifty-seven illustrations, of which nineteen are full-page engravings The portraits of the police commissioners, superintendents, inspectors, captains and sergeants, from the day of Jacob Hays to the present time, Mayors Harper and Wood, Chief Matsell, important points of interest, incidents that have occurred at various times and particularly during the draft riots, a reproduction of localities as they existed long ago, and a thousand other useful, instructive and entertaining facts and pictures are set forth The portraits, as a rule, are remarkably correct The proceeds of the sale of the book go to swell the Police Pension Fund, and there is no doubt that there will be an eager demand for it Those wishing to obtain copies can do so by addressing Superintendent Walling.

[DAILY TRIBUNE, June 29, 1885]

"OUR POLICE PROTECTORS" is the title of an attractive volume reciting the history of police organization and work in this city, recently published in this city The profits derived from the sale of the book are to be devoted to the Police Pension Fund It is written by A E Costello, whose practical experience as a newspaper police reporter gave him many advantages in the accomplishment of the task He has gone back to the first appearance of a police system in the earliest Dutch settlement or Manhattan Island, and has traced its gradual growth and development to the present time The story of the progress and repeal of the old watch system and the organization of a municipal police, in the twenty five years subsequent to 1830, is well told and in fuller detail than is perhaps to be found in any other single publication The charter of 1853 provided for the entire reorganization of the police force Mr Costello thinks that the greatest benefit to the community that resulted from this law was the separation of the department from political influences The police commissioners at this time first put in force the rule that no officer would be permitted to connect himself directly or indirectly with any political society, club, or similar organization The history of the riots in New York is given at considerable length, as well as of all the changes and chief events affecting the police department since the rebellion The whole work is interspersed with amusing or pathetic incidents illustrating the varied and exciting life of the average policeman Considerable space is given to brief sketches of various officers who have distinguished themselves by particularly good work in the department The illustrations by Nast and de Grimm are spirited and appropriate

[GRAPHIC, July 5, 1885]

This useful book, embellished with over two hundred engravings, is a history of the city's protectors from the earliest period to the present time It gives an account of the primitive police regulations, beginning with 1609, and those during the period of British occupancy, the organization of a municipal police in 1844-'53, two interesting chapters relate to the draft riots and their suppression, the era of organization and development is dwelt upon, the detective department is discussed, the Police Pension Fund sketched, and the duties of the policeman defined Full and accurate lists of the present force are embodied in this comprehensive work, and a vast deal of other information

[WORLD, June 21, 1885]

"OUR POLICE PROTECTORS" is the title of a book of nearly six hundred pages just issued Mr A E Costello, the author, has been closely associated with the police for many years The book contains much interesting matter, beginning with the establishment of a primitive police force on Manhattan Island in 1621 up to the beginning of the present year It is profusely illustrated with portraits and sketches by Thomas Nast and other well-known artists. The proceeds from the sale of the work are to be given to the Police Pension Fund

[BROOKLYN STANDARD, July 21, 1885]

UNDER the title "Our Police Protectors," a very interesting and elaborate history of the New York police, by Mr A E. Costello, has been published for the benefit of the Police Pension Fund As a journalist of ability and experience, especially as a police reporter, Mr Costello was well equipped for the task, which he commenced in October, 1883 The history begins with the primitive police regulations of 1609, and deals with the various methods of police government in the metropolis from that remote period to the present time The old watch system, its progress and ultimate abolishment, is the subject of a very interesting narrative The organization of a municipal police, appointment of a board of commissioners, and finally, the establishment of the Metropolitan police district, supply material for three readable chapters The eighth chapter is devoted to a graphic sketch of the draft riots in July, 1863, and the next chapter presents in detail the methods adopted by the police in suppressing the rioters. The five hundred and odd pages abound with striking incidents—horrors and heroisms alike being presented throughout with the utmost fidelity to truth In addition to the historical portion of the work, which is profusely illustrated, there is an appendix containing a complete list of the members of the police force up to May 1, 1885, and the date of their appointment. Elegantly printed, substantially bound, and containing much valuable information Mr Costello is to be congratulated upon the completion of his laborious work

[SUNDAY MERCURY, June 14, 1885]

"OUR POLICE PROTECTORS"—This is the title of a work of five hundred and seventy royal octavo pages, illustrated with over two hundred engravings, compiled and published by Mr A E Costello, the well known journalist The book gives a complete and most interesting history of the police protective system of New York from the days of the Dutch Governors, Peter Minuet and Wouter Von Twiller down to the first of May last It is literally packed with facts and figures, and at the same time is as interesting in many portions as a romance Mr Costello has done his work well and produced a book of great historical value, fit to take its place beside Mary J Lamb's "History of New York" It is, in fact, itself a history of New York, for the progress and growth of the police department marks, step by step, the progress and growth of the city The book is published for the benefit of the Police Pension Fund, and may be had at Police Headquarters

[TELEGRAM, July 8, 1885]

Mr A E COSTELLO has compiled an extremely interesting, informing and valuable work It is entitled "Our Police Protectors History of the New York Police from the Earliest Period to the Present Time" It is published for the benefit of the Police Pension Fund It is admirably complete, including two hundred illustrations and nearly six hundred pages It also contains a full table of contents to its twenty-three chapters, a list of the illustrations, and an adequate index—a feature too often lacking in works of this kind A year and a half's hard and steady labor has been concentrated upon this volume The wood engravings are extremely happy in reproducing the spirit of the scenes wherewith they are concerned The more ambitious illustrations fulfill their ambition —an arduous task seldom satisfactorily performed The information is immense, dating from 1609 to the present day He tells us all about primitive police regulations, the period of British occupancy, the city's condition when outgrowing the old system of watching the progress and repeal of that system, the organization of a municipal police, the appointment of a board of police commissioners, the Metropolitan police districts and the draft riots of 1863 and their suppression History of this kind is continued until he acquaints us with the Detective Department, Inspector Byrnes' command, the Police Central Office, the duties of a policeman, and the history of the Police Pension Fund In all the necessary statistics of crime there is nothing to please the prurient In the many faithful portraits of police officials there is everything to please all who esteem what is estimable in those servants of the public The late Sidney P Nichols was deeply interested in the success of this work, and Mr Costello's personal experience peculiarly qualified him for his well performed task.

CONTENTS.

CHAPTER I—1609-1664—PRIMITIVE POLICE REGULATIONS.

Charter Establishing the Dutch West India Company (1621.)—Director-General Minuet's Council—Duties of the Schout-Fiscal—First Trace of a Penal or Police System (1632.)—The Island Assuming an Aspect of Permanent Settlement (1639)—A Reason why Justice was Administered with Great Promptitude—Erection of a Stadt Huys (1642)—Regulations for the Better Observance of the Sabbath—Establishment of a Burgher Guard (1643)—New Regulations Contemporaneous with the Arrival of Governor Stuyvesant.—A Career of Reform—Ordinance Regulating the Sale of Liquor—Appointment of a Rattle-Watch (1651)—The City Incorporated (1652)—The Police of the City Chiefly Centered in a Schout.—Regulations of the Burgher Watch.—Dirk Van Schillwyne, First High Constable (1655.)—Organization of a Paid Rattle-Watch (1658)—Instructions for the Burgher Provost—Records of Court Cases.—Capture of the Province by the British

CHAPTER II—1664-1783—PERIOD OF BRITISH OCCUPANCY

Obe Hendrick, First Constable under the English—Lighting the City by Night (1668.)—Watchmen ordered to provide themselves with "a Lanthern and a Stick of Firewood"—A Strict Police established throughout the City—Orders to be observed by the Constables' Watch, etc.—Rules governing the Watch—New Police Regulations (1684)—Dongan's Charter (1686)—First Uniformed Policeman—Appointment of a Civil Watch—New City Hall, Wall Street.—Modes of Punishment Inflicted on Criminals.—Montgomerie Charter (1730)—First main Watch-house.—Citizens ordered to Watch or find Substitutes—First Poor-house erected (1734)—"Insurrection and the Plot of Slaves"—Quakers exempt from serving on the Watch—Petitioning against a Military Watch—The old Jail—Bridewell.—Occupation of the city by the British—Evacuation

CHAPTER III.—1783-1830—THE CITY OUTGROWING THE SYSTEM OF WATCHING

The City divided into Seven Wards—New York described as "A Strange Mosaic of Different Nations"—The Force and the Pay of the Men Increased—Progress of the Police System very marked—Establishing a Police Office in the City Hall—Places of Confinement· State Prison, Penitentiary, Bridewell and Jail—The Watch doubled on account of the increase of Crime—Example of

"A Good Arrest"—An Act establishing Courts of Justices of the Peace and Assistant Justices —A Law for the better regulating of the City Watch —Petition for an Increase of Pay —A perfect Police of extreme importance.—Watchmen declared not eligible to act as Firemen.—The Humane Society.—Result of the Watch Committee's Investigation.

CHAPTER IV.—1831-1844 —PROGRESS AND REPEAL OF THE OLD WATCH SYSTEM

Watchmen Dissatisfied with their Pay.—The Duty of Captains at the Breaking out of a Fire —Inquiring into the Expediency of Re-organizing the Police Department.—Increasing the Number of Police Justices.—"The Year of Riots"—Erection of New Watch-houses —The Five Points.—Necessity of an Increase in the Number of the Watch —First Attempt at Forming a Detective Squad —The Flour Riots —Re-organization of the Watch —Powers of the Mayor over the Watch Revoked and Transferred to the Common Council —The Mayor Re-invested with Supreme Police Authority —Mayor Morris' plan of Forming the Marshals into a Day Police —Report of the Special Committee in Relation to the Re-organization of the Watch.—Battery Park in Former times —High Constable Hays —His Remarkable Career —How he Suppressed Crime and Scourged Criminals

CHAPTER V —1844-1853 —ORGANIZATION OF A MUNICIPAL POLICE

A Turning Point in the System of Policing the City —The Old Watch Department Abolished —Establishment of a Day and Night Police —Chief Matsell.— A man who Played an Important part in Police Affairs —Harper's Police — First effort to Introduce a Uniform —The new System not Satisfactory — Changes in the Law —Astor Place Riot —Battery Park —Growing Boldness of Criminals —Citizens Alarmed —The whole Force Directed to Patrol Day and Night —Detailment of Policemen a Growing Evil —Measures taken to Suppress it.—Table of Arrests

CHAPTER VI.—1853-1857 —APPOINTMENT OF A BOARD OF POLICE COMMISSIONERS

Ex-Superintendent Walling —His Long and Honorable Connection with the Department —Charter of 1853 —Re-organizing the Police Force —Tenure of Office to Remain During Good Behavior —The Recorder, City Judge, and Mayor Appointed as a Commission —A Reserve Corps Established —An Improvement in the Efficiency of the Force —Introduction of a Police Uniform.— Hostility thereto.—The "Star" Police —Efforts made to Induce the Men to wear the Uniform.—Judgment Speedily Rendered in Trial Cases —Beneficial effects.—Appointment of a Drill Sergeant —Salaries Increased.—Tables of Arrests.—Sanitary Matters.

CONTENTS

CHAPTER VII—1857–1863.—THE METROPOLITAN POLICE DISTRICT

The Law Designating the Mayor, Recorder, and City Judge, Police Commissioners, Repealed.—Appointment of Five Commissioners.—The Counties of New York, Kings, Westchester and Richmond made to Comprise the New District—Opposition to the Change—A Year of Riots and Financial Failures.—The Metropolitan Police District Act Declared to be Constitutional.—Conflict Between Mayor Wood and the Newly-Appointed Commissioners.—The Municipal Police and the Metropolitan Police Arrayed in Open Battle.—Intervention of the Military.—The Act Amended by making the District to consist of the Counties of New York, Kings, Westchester and Richmond, and the Towns of Newtown, Flushing and Jamaica.—The Number of Commissioners Reduced to Three.

CHAPTER VIII—JULY, 1863—SKETCH OF THE DRAFT RIOTS

The City in the Hands of a Frenzied Mob.—An Emergency in which the Police covered themselves with Glory.—Popular Discontent growing out of a latent sympathy with the Southern Cause.—The Method adopted for the Enforcement of the Draft not the most judicious one.—Superintendent Kennedy's arrangements in anticipation of trouble.—Growing Desperation of the Mob.—Firing of the Buildings in which the Provost Marshal had his Office.—Superintendent Kennedy Attacked and Brutally Beaten.—His Miraculous Escape from Death.—Commissioner Acton assumes Command of the Force.—His Energy and Promptitude more than a Match for the Mob, who Fight Furiously.—The Rioters beat back the Police, but are in turn overcome and routed.—Clubs versus Stones, Bricks and Bullets.—"By the Right Flank, Company Front, Double Quick, Charge!"—Mob Desperation and Police Heroism.—"Up Guards, and at 'em"—Action of the Military.—End of the First Day's Fighting

CHAPTER IX—JULY, 1863—SUPPRESSION OF THE DRAFT RIOTS.

The City Saved from Pillage and Arson.—A Defiant and Unterrified Mob.—Negroes Hanged from Lamp-posts and their Bodies Burned.—Station Houses and Private Dwellings Fired and Sacked.—Stones, Bricks, and other Missiles Showered on the Heads of Policemen from the Housetops.—Police Retaliation—Arrival of the Military.—Col O'Brien's Frightful Death.—The Battle on Second Avenue and Twenty-first Street.—The Mob Taught some Severe Lessons.—Erecting Barricades.—Fired upon by the Troops.—The Police ply their Clubs on the Heads of Rioters with Unbounded Liberality.—Children from the Colored Orphan Asylum Protected by the Police.—Hard Hand-to Hand Fighting.—Backbone of the Riot Broken.—A Reign of Mob Law Averted.—Valuable Services Performed by the Detective Force and Telegraph Bureau.—Suppression of the Riot.—The Board of Police Issue a

xii　　　　　　　　　　CONTENTS.

Congratulatory Address to the Force —Governor Seymour bears Willing and Appreciative Testimony to the Gallant Services Performed by the Police. —Arraignment and Conviction of Rioters

CHAPTER X —1864–1866 —THE METROPOLITAN POLICE DISTRICT.

Organizers of Police Victory —Acton, Bergen, Hawley, Carpenter, Leonard, etc. —The Law of 1864 —Establishment of the House of Detention.—Boundaries of the Metropolitan Police District.—Division Commands —Uniform of the Metropolitan Police —Appropriations for the Building and Repairing of Station Houses —A Marked Tendency to Crimes of Violence towards the Person. —List of Policemen who were Killed or Wounded at the hands of Desperate Ruffians —President Acton favors the Passage of a Law rendering it a Crime to carry Concealed Weapons —Lost Time —Tables of Arrests.—An Act to Regulate and Increase Police Salaries —The Jurisdiction of the Board extended over the Rural Districts of Yonkers, West Farms and Richmond County.—An Act to Regulate the Sale of Intoxicating Liquors —Increased Duties of the Police Board

CHAPTER XI —1866–1870.—AN ERA OF ORGANIZATION AND DEVELOPMENT

New Station Houses Erected and old ones Renovated.—Improvement in the Discipline and Efficiency of the Force —Establishment of a Central Police Office in New York —Death of John G. Bergen —Appointment of a Metropolitan Fire Marshal and Assistant.—House of Detention for Witnesses.— Table of Arrests for a Series of Years —Time Lost by Sickness —Re-organization of the Board of Metropolitan Police —Resignation of Commissioner Acton.—Average Length of Posts —Amounts Paid for Sick Time —Value of Lost or Stolen Property Recovered.—The Sanitary Company —Lost Children. —Buildings found Open and Secured —Tables of Arrests —Salaries —Location of Station Houses —An Era of Organization and Development —" The Tweed Charter "—Death of Superintendent Jourdan

CHAPTER XII —1871–1876 —CLUBS MORE TRUSTWORTHY THAN LEADEN BALLS.

Orange Riots —Police and Military called out.—The Streets of New York again the Scene of Riot and Bloodshed —The Militia, unauthorized, Fire upon the Mob.—Eleven Killed and Thirty Wounded —Cleaning of the Streets charged to the Board of Police.—Completion of the Building of the House of Detention —Tables of Arrests.—Time Lost to the Department by Reason of Sickness —Property Clerk's Returns —Presentation of the Flag of Honor —An Act to Re-organize the Local Government of New York.—The Board of Police to consist of Five Members.—A Revised Manual Issued to the Force. —Duties of the several Heads of the Department and of the Force Generally.

CONTENTS

—Regulation Uniforms —Qualifications for Appointment as a Patrolman.—Measures of Economy Introduced.—Board of Surgeons.—Police Salaries.—The Board made to Consist of Four Members.—Changes in the Board.

CHAPTER XIII —1875-1880 —"New York Says, Stop!"

New York Fast Becoming a Law-abiding City.—Proceedings and Report of the Select Legislative Committee on the Causes and Increase of Crime.—Government of the Police Force —Demoralization and Inefficiency —All the Blame for these Evils not Attributable to the Police —Convictions Hard to Gain —Legal Loop-holes of Retreat for Criminals —Lottery and Policy —The Detective Police not Properly Remunerated for their Services —Salary and Duties of Patrolmen, etc —The Board of Police Commissioners.—Evil Effects of Political Intermeddling with the Force.—Too few Policemen.—The Great Railroad Strikes —Scenes of Riot and Bloodshed —The Tompkins Square Meeting —"New York Says, Stop"—New Rules for the Guidance of the Force

CHAPTER XIV —1880-1885 —Provisions of the Consolidation Act

Central Office Bureau of Detectives —Government and Discipline of the Police Department —Powers Invested in the Board of Police —Bureau of Elections —Board of Health —Police Surgeons —Special Patrolmen —Police Life Insurance Fund —Powers of the Police Force —Pawnbrokers —The Sanitary Company —Duties of Captains and Sergeants; of Physicians.—The Telegraph System —An Act Amendatory of the Consolidation Act —Roosevelt Committee —Lottery and Policy

CHAPTER XV.—First Inspection District

Superintendent William Murray —A Brilliant Record.—What a Policeman may become by Honesty, Perseverance and Ability.—A Model Police Official.—Methodical, Keen, and Devoted to his Profession —The First Precinct, Captain Caffry.—"The Iron Man"—The most Important Police District in the World — Fourth Precinct, Captain Webb —Sixth Precinct; Captain McCullagh —Seventh Precinct; Captain Hedden —Tenth Precinct; Captain Allaire —Eleventh Precinct; Captain Meakim —Thirteenth Precinct; Captain Petty —Fourteenth Precinct, Captain Murphy.—Seventeenth Precinct, Captain McCullagh.—Eighteenth Precinct; Captain Clinchy —Twenty-first Precinct; Captain Ryan.—Twenty-sixth Precinct; Sergeant Stewart.

CHAPTER XVI.—Second Inspection District.

The Late Inspector Thorne.—A Veteran Officer, whose Experience was Coeval with the Existence of the Police Department —Intelligence, Energy and Zeal.—A Notable Record —Fifth Precinct; Captain Eakins.—Eighth Precinct;

Captain McDonnell.—Ninth Precinct, Captain Copeland.—Fifteenth Precinct, Captain Brogan—Sixteenth Precinct, Captain McElwain.—Twentieth Precinct; Captain Washburn.—Twenty-fifth Precinct, Captain Garland.—Twenty-seventh Precinct; Captain Berghold.—Twenty-ninth Precinct; Captain Williams

CHAPTER XVII.—THIRD AND FOURTH INSPECTION DISTRICTS

Inspector Dilks.—Enjoying a rare Privilege, namely, reading his own Obituary—An Officer who has Distinguished Himself by his Bravery and Vigilance—A Veteran with a highly honorable Record.—Second Precinct; Captain Conlin.—Twelfth Precinct; Captain Hooker.—Nineteenth Precinct; Captain Mount.—Nineteenth Sub-precinct, Captain Schultz.—Twenty-second Precinct; Captain Killilea.—Twenty-third Precinct; Captain Sanders.—Twenty-eighth Precinct; Captain Gunner.—Thirtieth Precinct, Captain Siebert—Thirty-first Precinct, Captain Leary.—Thirty-second Precinct, Captain Cortright—Thirty-third Precinct; Captain Bennett.—Thirty-fourth Precinct; Captain Robbins.—Thirty-fifth Precinct; Captain Yule

CHAPTER XVIII.—DETECTIVE DEPARTMENT

Its Origin, Progress and Development.—Detectives called " Shadows" in Chief Matsell's Time.—Inspector Thomas Byrnes.—A Record that Reads like a Romance.—His Re-organization of the Detective Force.—The Wall Street Bureau.—Detective Sergeants.—Inspector Byrnes' Methods.—How Detectives Detect Criminals.—Inspector Byrnes and "The Crook".—Their Chance Meeting in the Street.—How Inspector Byrnes Reasons out a Case.—Decrease of Crime Among Professional Criminals.—Criminals and Their Methods.—New York a Difficult City to Protect against Thieves.—Forgers, Pickpockets, Sneak Thieves, Bank Thieves, Bunco Steerers, Etc.

CHAPTER XIX.—INSPECTOR BYRNES' COMMAND

The Men who Protect the City from the Depredations of Knaves of High and Low Degree.—Forty Quick-witted, Wide-awake Detectives.—Their History and Record of Arrests.—How they Make the City a Safe Abiding-place for Honest People.—Interesting Tales of Some Celebrated Cases.—The Romance and Reality of Crime.—Truth Stranger than Fiction.—A Devoted Band of Police Officers.—Their Struggles and Triumphs.—The Men who Make it Possible for Inspector Byrnes to Retain his Well-earned Laurels.

CHAPTER XX.—POLICE CENTRAL OFFICE.

The Centre of a System which affords Police Protection to the City.—Headquarters of the Police Department.—Telegraph Office, Superintendent

CONTENTS

Crowley.—Third Precinct; Captain Gastlin —The Harbor Police —Superintendent's Chief Clerk Hopcroft—Bureau of Inquiry for Missing People—Commissioner French—Commissioner Fitz John Porter.—Commissioner Matthews.—Lost Children.—Chief Clerk Kipp—Property Clerk's Office—The Sanitary Company—Tenement House Squad.

CHAPTER XXI —Duties of a Policeman.

A Terror to the Wicked and Depraved, a Protector to the Upright and Virtuous—His Responsibilities and Labors.—Necessary Qualifications· Youth, Strength, Intelligence, and a Stainless Reputation—The School of Instruction.—Doing Patrol Duty.—The Laws he has to Study and Enforce—Ex-Commissioner Erhardt's Exposition of a Policeman's Life—A Keen, Wiry, Clean-cut Set—Always on Post—An Eye that Knows no Sleep—Dangers to which Policemen are Exposed—Sprains, Contusions, Incised Wounds, Fractured Limbs, Rheumatism, Pneumonia, etc—Sergeant John Delaney, a Type of a Brave Policeman

CHAPTER XXII —Sketch of the Police Pension Fund.

Created by Act of 1857—The Fund made up of the Sales of Unclaimed Property—Police Life and Health Insurance Fund.—Beneficiaries of the Act—Metropolitan Reward Fund—Police Life Insurance Fund.—The Police Commissioners a Board of Trustees—The Treasurer of the Board of Commissioners Treasurer of the Board of Trustees.—Receipts and Disbursements.—The late Commissioner Nichols—Commissioner McClave.—Bookkeeper George P Gott—Paying Pensioners—Financial Statement of the Police Pension Fund.

CHAPTER XXIII —The Way of the Transgressor.

Our Police Courts—Arraignment of Prisoners and how their Cases are Disposed of.—The Police Justices· Efficient and Discriminating.—Courts of Special Sessions, General Sessions, Oyer and Terminer, etc—District Attorney Martine and his Deputies—Fines Received from Police Courts.—Number of Prisoners Arrested, Arraigned and Convicted—The Ambulance System—Evils of Intemperance—A New Criminal Agency.—The Opium Habit—" Hitting the Pipe "—Uses and Abuses of Opium—An Opium Smoker's Outfit.—Vice Fostered by the Herding Together in Crowded Tenements.—Some Gaudy Resorts.—Criminals and Their Haunts.

LIST OF ILLUSTRATIONS.

	PAGE
Stadt Huys	4
Watchman's Rattle	8
Gov. Stuyvesant's Mansion	10
Mustering the Rattle Watch	13
A Schepen Deciding a Law Suit	15
Cornelius Steenwyck	17
New Amsterdam in 1664	18
The Pillory	20
First Seal of New York City	27
First Uniformed Policeman	28
City Hall, Wall Street	30
First Execution in New York	32
Whipping Post	33
Presentment by Grand Jury	35
First Watch House	36
First Poor House	39
Bellmen Going their Rounds	41
Jail, City Hall Park	42
Old Bridewell	44
City Hospital	45
Lock and Key of Old Bridewell	47
Early Seal of New York City	48
First House of Correction	52
Old State Prison	55
City Hall Park in 1808	60
City Hall	62
Alms House, Belleview	66
First House of Refuge	70
House of Refuge (with extensions)	71
Old Leatherhead	75
Rotunda, City Hall Park	79
Old Leatherhead and Sentry Box	82
Watchman's Hat	83
Old Sugar House and Middle Dutch Church	86
Old Brewery	87
The Tombs	90
Police Shield	91
Jacob Hays' Commission as Captain	93
Jacob Hays' Commission (High Constable)	97
Policeman's Hat	99
Chief Matsell's Shield	101
Mayor Harper	104
Police Captain's Shield	106
Eldridge Street Jail	108
Belleview Hospital, 1850	110
Washington's Residence	112
Astor Place Riot	115

	PAGE
City Arms	119
Superintendent Walling's Shield	122
Captain Walling's Star Shield	125
Police Captains, 1856	132, 134, 135
City Arms	136
Mayor Wood	141
Metropolitan Police Headquarters	145
Patrolman's Shield	150
Police Headquarters (300 Mulberry St.)	154
Old Jefferson Market	157
The Stocks	159
Process of Drafting	162
Provost Marshal's Office	165
Rioters Marching Down Second Avenue	169
Colored Orphan Asylum	172
Present Colored Orphan Asylum	173
Negro Hanged by Mob	175
Military Encampment	177
Military Firing on Rioters	178
Handcuffs	181
General Canby's Headquarters	183
Brutal Murder of Col. O'Brien	185
Cavalry Patroling Streets	187
Destruction of Weehawken Ferry	189
Escaping Rioters Surprised by Police	191
Burning of Grain Elevator	194
Nursing Wounded Policemen	196
Seth C. Hawley	206
Sixty-ninth Regiment Armory	211
First New York Colored Regiment Leaving for the Seat of War	217
Drilling a Squad of Policemen	220
Arsenal, Elm Street	222
Coat of Arms	224
Metropolitan Police Shield	227
Inspector Speight	230
Dr. Kennedy	232
Juvenile Asylum	238
Ludlow Street Jail	241
House of Refuge	242
City Seal	243
Ex-Superintendent Kelso	247
Inspector Jameson	250
Autographs	254
Flag of Honor	255
New Court House	260
Matthew T. Brennan	262
Under Arrest	264

LIST OF ILLUSTRATIONS

	PAGE
Inspector McDermott.	270
Essex Market	273
Orphan Asylum	278
St Luke's Hospital	285
The Chain Gang	286
Custom House, Wall Street.	290
Seventh Regiment Armory.	295
Post-Office	299
Broadway, South from Post-Office.	303
New First Precinct Station House	314
Floor Plan	315
Captain Caffrey.	316
Captain Webb.	317
Captain McCullagh (No 2)	319
Sixth Precinct Station House.	320
Captain Hedden	321
Captain Allaire.	323
Eleventh Precinct Station House	325
Captain Cherry (deceased).	326
Captain Petty	328
Thirteenth Precinct Station House	329
Fourteenth Precinct Station House	331
Floor Plan Station House	331
Captain Murphy	332
Captain McCullagh (No 1)	334
Captain Clinchy	336
Twenty-first Precinct Station House	337
Captain Ryan.	338
Captain Steers	340
Street Arab	341
Captain Eakins.	347
Captain McDonnell	349
Eighth Precinct Station House	350
Captain Copeland.	352
Captain Brogan	354
Fifteenth Precinct Station House	355
Captain McElwain.	358
Twentieth Precinct Station House.	359
Captain Washburn	360
Captain Garland	362
Captain Berghold	363
Captain Williams	365
Twenty-ninth Precinct Station House	366
Captain Conlin.	373
Twelfth Precinct Station House.	374
Captain Hooker.	375
Nineteenth Precinct Station House	376
Captain Mount	377
Captain Schultz	378
Captain Killilea.	379
Captain Sanders	381
Twenty-eighth Precinct Station House	382
Captain Gunner	383

	PAGE
Captain Siebert.	385
Captain Leary	386
Captain Cortright	388
Thirty-second Precinct Station House	389
Floor Plan.	390
Captain Bennett	391
Thirty-third Precinct Station House	392
Thirty-fourth Precinct Station House.	393
Captain Robbins	394
Captain Yule	395
Captain Smith.	396
Captain Kealy.	397
Captain Tynan	398
Policeman's Club	399
Examining a "Crook".	406
Rogues' Gallery and some Curiosities of Crime.	408
A Bashful Burglar	410
Inspector Byrnes in his Private Office.	412
Inspector Byrnes Receiving Reports	415
Nippers.	418
Detective Sergeants Reporting	420
A Burglar's Outfit	422
Captain's Shield	424
Sergeant's Shield.	425
Patrolman's Shield.	426
Model Cell.	428
Sergeant Bird.	430
Convict's Boat Going to the Island	433
Rescuing a Woman from Drowning	437
Police Central Office	438
Police Telegraph Office	439
Superintendent Crowley	440
Captain Gastlin.	441
Arresting Mutineers	442
Boarding a Mutinous Vessel	443
Memorial to Henry Smith	445
Superintendent Walling's Office	446
Watching for River Thieves	447
Steamboat "Patrol".	448
George Hopcroft.	449
Sergeant Brooks	450
Office of Bureau of Inquiry.	451
Architect Bush	452
Commissioner Matthews.	453
Chief Clerk's Room.	456
Property Clerk's Room	457
Commissioner Voorhis.	458
Commissioner Porter	459
Captain Kipp.	460
Matron Webb's Room for Lost Children	461
Sergeant Mullin	462
Cloth Department Room	462

LIST OF ILLUSTRATIONS.

	PAGE		PAGE
School of Instruction	467	Tombs Police Court	508
Station House Lodging Room	468	Jefferson Market Police Court	509
Station House Dormitory	469	Yorkville Police Court	510
Crossing Broadway	471	Black Maria	511
Familiar Incidents in Life of a New York Policeman	472	Conveying Prisoners from Court to Jail	511
		Woman's Prison (A Mutual Recognition)	512
Drilling a Squad of Policemen	474	Blackwell's Island and East River	512
Mounted Policemen Stopping Runaway Team	476	Roosevelt Hospital	513
		Mount Sinai Hospital	514
Part of a Policeman's Equipment	479	New York Hospital	515
Policeman's Certificate of Appointment	480	Glimpses of Chinatown	516
Sergeant John Delaney	481	A Chinese Opium Smoker	517
Police Trial Room	482	Chinese Gamblers	518
Police Monument (Cypress Hill)	490	Scale for Weighing Opium	520
Bookkeeper Gott's Office	493	Opium Tray	520
Commissioner McClave	495	Sponge, Bowl, Opium Box, Clam Shell, Pipe and Needle	521
George P Gott	500		
Policeman's Belt	502	A Chinese Teacher	522
District Attorney Martine	505	A Chinese Merchant	524
Bridge of Sighs (Tombs)	506	Harbor Police	525
Interior View of Male Prison	507	Measuring a Candidate	526
Place of Execution	507		

FULL PAGE ENGRAVINGS.

	PAGE
Frontispiece	1
Five Points in 1829	76
Jacob Hays	92
Supt. Matsell	102
Battery Park in ye olden time	110
Geo. W. Walling	120
Jno A Kennedy	152
Danl Carpenter	160
Their Brave Protector	182
Thos. C Acton	202
Jno. Jourdan	240
A Drunkard's Dream	266
William Murray	308
Thos. W Thorne	342
Geo W Dilks	370
Thos Byrnes	402
S B French	454
On Post	466
S P Nichols	499

IN THE JAWS OF DEATH

(Drawn by Thomas Nast, by permission of Messrs Harper)

OUR POLICE PROTECTORS:

HISTORY OF THE NEW YORK POLICE FROM THE EARLIEST PERIOD TO THE PRESENT DAY

CHAPTER I

PRIMITIVE POLICE REGULATIONS
1609–1664.

CHARTER ESTABLISHING THE DUTCH WEST INDIA COMPANY (1621)—DIRECTOR-GENERAL MINUET'S COUNCIL—DUTIES OF THE SCHOUT-FISCAL—FIRST TRACE OF A PENAL OR POLICE SYSTEM (1632)—THE ISLAND ASSUMING AN ASPECT OF PERMANENT SETTLEMENT (1639.)—A REASON WHY JUSTICE WAS ADMINISTERED WITH GREAT PROMPTITUDE—ERECTION OF A STADT HUYS (1642.)—REGULATIONS FOR THE BETTER OBSERVANCE OF THE SABBATH—ESTABLISHMENT OF A BURGHER GUARD (1643.)—NEW REGULATIONS CONTEMPORANEOUS WITH THE ARRIVAL OF GOVERNOR STUYVESANT—A CAREER OF REFORM.—ORDINANCE REGULATING THE SALE OF LIQUOR.—APPOINTMENT OF A RATTLE-WATCH (1651) —THE CITY INCORPORATED (1652)—THE POLICE OF THE CITY CHIEFLY CENTERED IN A SCHOUT—REGULATIONS OF THE BURGHER WATCH.—DIRK VAN SCHILLWYNE, FIRST HIGH CONSTABLE (1655)—ORGANIZATION OF A PAID RATTLE-WATCH (1658)—INSTRUCTIONS FOR THE BURGHER PROVOST.—RECORDS OF COURT CASES.—CAPTURE OF THE PROVINCE BY THE BRITISH

EVERY historical narrative relating to the City of New York must of necessity be a history of progress Whether the broad course of general events be followed, or some particular phase of the city's life be made the theme, the result is the same Growth, development, progress, underlie every change, and give a splendid vitality to every event

It is proposed in this volume to give a history of the New York Police Force—a history of that system by which the great public protects itself against its natural enemies. This narrative will, indeed, be one of progress. Starting from beginnings as humble as those of the infant city itself, it will, by an unbroken series of steps, arrive at a breadth and perfection of system commensurate with the modern glories of the American metropolis This will be the most remarkable feature of the story, that—speaking broadly—there is neither defeat, failure, nor stagnation to be chronicled. When the force stands still as respects numbers, it is becoming more perfect in organization; when development ceases for the moment in its organization, it is gaining in power and efficiency

All the world knows that in 1609, the year of Dutch independence—surely a good augury—Henry Hudson, an Englishman sailing under the colors of the Netherlands, started on a famous cruise in search of the Northwest passage to the Pacific. He did not find it, but instead discovered the noble river which immortalizes his name.

Hudson planted the flag under which he navigated on the wooded shores of the river and the bay, proclaiming the land a dependency of their Highnesses the States-General of Holland.

Manhattan Island, we are told, was named by the Indians *Man-a-hatta*, to denote not only the landing-place of the discoverer, but the effects of the "mad waters" which he gave to the natives in his first interview; the literal interpretation of the name being "the place where we all got drunk."

The Dutch very speedily began to make use of their new dominion. The trade in furs was wonderfully good, and as early as 1613 trading posts were established on Staten and Manhattan Islands.

In 1614 the States-General granted a trading charter which recognized "New Netherland" as a Dutch territory.

New Amsterdam was the title by which the Hollanders distinguished their little dorp, or village, the nucleus of which had been formed by a few huts erected as early as 1613 for sheltering their fur trade and whale fishery, on the point where it is supposed Hudson had landed. By that name it was known for more than forty years as the capital, during the administrations—1625 to 1664—of Minuet, Van Twiller, Kieft and Stuyvesant, the successive Directors or Governors-General of *Novum Belgium*, or New Netherlands, a province which embraced portions of the present States of Delaware, New Jersey, New York and Connecticut.

The charter establishing the Dutch West India Company was granted on June 3, 1621, and the supervision and government of the company were lodged in a board or assembly of nineteen delegates. The company was empowered to raise forts, to administer justice and preserve order, and with the consent of the States-General, appoint a Governor or Director-General, and all other officers, military, judicial and executive, all being bound to swear allegiance to their High Mightinesses and the Company. The Director-General and his council were then invested with all powers—judicial, legislative and executive, subject in certain cases to appeal to Holland.

In 1624 Peter Minuet, the first Director-General, arrived at New Netherland. His council consisted of Pieter Bylvelt, Jacob Elbertsen Wissinck, Jan Janssen Brouwer, Symen Dereksen Pos, and Reynert Harmenssen. This council had supreme authority, and all its proceedings, whether criminal or civil, were instituted and conducted by an officer called a "Schout Fiscal," whose duties were equivalent to those performed by a sheriff and an attorney-general. He was charged principally with enforcing and maintaining the placards, laws, ordinances, resolutions and military regulations of their High Mightinesses, the States-General, and protecting the rights, domains and jurisdiction of the company, and executing their orders, as well in as out of court, without favor or respect to individuals. He superintended all prosecutions and suits, but could not undertake any actions on behalf of the company, except by order of the council; nor arraign, nor arrest any person on a criminal charge, except on information previously received, or unless he caught him *in flagrante delictu*. In taking information he was bound to note as well those points which made for the prisoner as those which supported the charge against him, and after trial he saw to the faithful execution of the sentence pronounced by the judges, who, in indictments carrying with them loss of life and property, were not to be less than five in number. He, moreover, attended to the commissaries arriving from the Company's out-posts and to vessels arriving from or leaving for Holland, inspected their papers, and superintended the loading and discharging of their cargoes, so that smuggling might be prevented. He transmitted to the directors in Holland copies of all information taken by him, as well as of all sentences pronounced by the court, and no person was kept long in prison at the expense of the Company without special cause, but all were prosecuted as expeditiously as possible This office, perhaps the most responsible in the colony, was filled, during the administration of Director Minuet, by Jan Lampo, of Cantelberg

The nucleus of a permanent settlement was formed by the arrival of a number of emigrants in 1625. Director Minuet "took up his residence in the midst of a nation called Manhates, building a fort there, to be called Amsterdam, having four points, and faced outside with stone, as the walls of sand fall down, and are now more compact." The population consisted of two hundred and seventy, including men, women and children. Director Minuet rebuilt the fort and planned out something in the guise of a town—a very small one indeed—about it, in 1629.

Wouter van Twiller succeeded Minuet in 1632, and in his day we find the first trace of a penal or police system. It may readily be imagined that with the scant population and the simple mode of life that was, perforce, led by all, there was very little necessity indeed for any written law or display of constituted authority. Still we find that a "gibbet, or whipping post" was set up close to the water's edge. The method of punishment was curious The transgressors, it appears, were fastened to a line by their waistband, and being hoisted from the ground, were left suspended in spread-eagle fashion, "such length of time as their offences warranted." No doubt the correction was as salutary as it must have been unpleasant, and tended to intimidate such elements of disorder as existed at the time

Notwithstanding this landmark of penal legislation, however, the colony, taken as a whole, was "a good land to fall in with, and a pleasant land to see" We are informed that such was the peaceful and orderly disposition of the inhabitants at this very early day—and for some years after—that police regulations were almost entirely unknown, "not even a sentinel being kept on duty" The good folk of New Amsterdam were distinguished for their good nature, love of home, and cordial hospitality So strict were the early notions of propriety, that to be out after nine o'clock in the evening was considered a certain sign of bad morals

Though there were few laws, these few were rigidly enforced. The manners of the colonists corresponded with the simplicity of a primitive settlement.

There were also among the Dutch, individual characters whose former pursuits and vagrant modes of life little fitted them to patiently endure personal injuries or insult. Some had been freebooters among the islands in the Gulf, and been thrown by the waves of fortune upon this scene of adventure, and some, though brought hither by ordinary currents of trade and speculation, were adventurous and sanguine spirits, diverted to new pursuits from the military service

Among other improvements brought about by Van Twiller was the erection of dwellings "for the corporal, the smith, the cooper, and the midwife," persons who must have held positions of no small importance in these early days

William Kieft became Director or Governor of the New Netherlands in 1638, and in the following year considerable bodies of settlers arrived from Holland under Captain de Vries, and Jochem Pietersen Kuyter and Cornelius Melyn The island, or at least its southern part, began to lose its savage aspect fast Some thirty farms were under cultivation, and the country about the walls of the fort resembled a blooming garden Previously the population had been mainly

Stadt Huys

composed of traders in the employ of the West India Company, who, having no intention of making the place a permanent home, were content to live in any sort of huts. Now, however, many better houses were built, and an aspect of permanent settlement began to mark the place

Apropos of the primitive form in which justice was administered before Director Kieft's arrival, a good story is told, which, if it be not literally true, is at least characteristic. One of the reasons, it is said, why justice was administered with great promptness and impartiality was that there were no lawyers, and every man either pleaded his own case, or let judgment go by default. There appeared at last in the colony, however, a certain pettifogger or "Doddipol Jolterhead," as the chronicle hath it, Bobus Van Clapperclip by name In pleading a cause respecting the right of geese to swim in the pond at the head of New Street— before Alderman or Schepen Van Schlepevalkher—he made the only long speech on record at that period His eloquence was so great that he caused his clients to be incontinently non-suited, for the Alderman, losing all patience with the pleader, gave himself up to the embraces of the "balmy god," and slept out the remainder of the term

Governor Kieft was possessed of a busy, bustling temperament, and his energies found plenty of room in New Amsterdam His administration, in the main, was calculated to benefit the place in no small degree, doing much towards the establishment of a firm basis of law, and much in the way of material improvement. Most notable among the latter was the erection of a Stadt Huys—State House, or City Hall—on the corner of Pearl Street and Coenties Alley, fronting on Coenties Slip. This building was put up in 1642, and, besides containing rooms where the Governor and his Council could meet, had accommodations for the municipal authorities, a school-room, a watch-room, and dungeons in the cellar. The building saw many notable scenes in its day—the march of progress has long since swept it from the face of the island—among them the transfer of sovereignty from the Dutch to the British Government in 1664 and 1674, and the holding of the first Court of Admiralty in the province by Governor Nichols in 1665.

The Stadt Huys was taken down in the year 1700 It was built originally at the cost of the government as a city tavern, but was presented to the city in 1655 The chamber occupied for the sitting of the Magistrates was on the south-east corner of the second story, the prison chamber being in the rear—on the other side of the house—facing a yard which extended to "Hough Straat" Upon the roof was a cupola in which was hung a bell in the year 1656, which was rung for the assemblage of the Magistrates, and also on occasions of the publication of proclamations, which was done in front of the hall The Bell-ringer for a number of years was Jan Gillisen, (familiarly called "Koeck.") This ancient edifice, which was substantially built of stone, stood until the year 1699,—nearly sixty years—when it gave place to the City Hall, in Wall Street, at the head of Broad Street.

The gallows, by a barbarous anomaly, has been regarded as an evidence of civilization. In that case, New York in colonial times must have reached a high state of refinement It did not take much to send a poor wretch to the gallows, or to burn him at the stake, or to break him by torture Among the earliest institutions of the budding province were jails, prisons, a bridewell, and houses of correction Previous to the building of the Stadt Huys, there was a prison, or place of confinement for prisoners, within the old fort, but on the building of the City Hall it ceased to be used for that purpose.

The Governor issued regulations for the better observance of the Sabbath. interdicting the tapping of beer during the hours of divine service or after ten o'clock at night; brawling and all kinds of offences were to be punished by the severest penalties. In carrying out his reform measures, Governor Keift seems to have found the town bell an efficient ally. It was rung every evening at nine o'clock to warn the inhabitants that it was time to be within doors, if not in bed; and it was rung again at stated hours in the morning and afternoon, to mark the proper hours for going to labor. It was also rung as a preliminary to the reading of the Governor's proclamations That these last were not mere empty threats may be sufficiently judged from the following sentence, imposed during one of the later years of Kieft's incumbency·

"For drawing his knife upon a person, Guysbert Reygerslard is sentenced to throw himself three times from the sailyard of the yacht Hope, and to receive from each sailor three lashes at the ringing of the bell."

A Burgher Guard having been established (the first of which we find any record), an ordinance of the Director and Council of New Netherland in relation thereto was passed November 19, 1643, as follows:

"1. If any one, on the Burgher Guard, take the name of God in vain, he shall forfeit for the first offence ten stivers; for the second, twenty stivers; and for the third time, twenty stivers

"2 Whosoever on the Burgher Guard speaks ill of a comrade shall forfeit thirty stivers.

"3 Whosoever comes fuddled or intoxicated on guard, shall, for each offence, pay twenty stivers; whosoever is absent from his watch without lawful reason, shall forfeit fifty stivers.

"4. After the watch is duly performed and daylight is come, and the reveille beaten, whosoever discharges his gun or musket without orders of his Corporal shall pay one guilder."

Kieft's administration was marked by Indian wars, provoked in great part by the Director-General's imprudence. These wars almost depopulated the colony of New Amsterdam, and in the end led to his recall

Peter Stuyvesant, Kieft's successor, came out in May, 1647. New regulations were established, contemporaneous with his appointment, for the government of the province The Director, Vice-Director and Schout constituted the Council, and had supreme authority in civil and military affairs The fort was repaired and a permanent garrison of fifty-three men maintained. The colonists were counseled to provide themselves with weapons and to form a provincial militia. He began a career of reform immediately on his arrival, with all that impetuosity—not untempered by sound sense—which was displayed in his whole career Here is one of the first of his manifestoes, translated, of course, from the original Dutch:

"Whereas, we have observed and remarked the insolence of some of our inhabitants, who are in the habit of getting drunk, of quarreling, fighting, and of smiting each other on the Lord's Day of Rest (of which, on the last Sunday, we ourselves witnessed the painful scenes, and to the knowledge of which we came by report) in defiance of the magistrates, to the contempt and disregard of our person and authority, to the great annoyance of the neighborhood, and finally to the injury and dishonoring of God's holy laws and commandments, which enjoin upon us to honor and sanctify him on this, His Holy Day of Rest, and which proscribe all personal injury and murder, with the means and temptations that may lead thereunto

"Therefore, by the advice of His Excellency, the Director-General, and our ordained Council, here present, to the end that we may, so far as it is possible and practicable, take all due care and prevent the curse of God instead of His blessing from falling upon us and our good inhabitants, do, by these presents, charge, command, and enjoin upon all tapsters and innkeepers, that on the Sabbath of the Lord, commonly called Sunday, before two of the clock in the afternoon, in case there is no preaching, or otherwise before four of the clock (in the afternoon) they shall not be permitted to set, nor draw, nor bring out for any person or persons, any wines, beers, nor any strong waters of any kind whatsoever, on whatever pretext, excepting only persons traveling and the daily boarders that may from necessity be confined to their places of abode, in the penalty of being deprived of their occupations, and, over that, in the penalty of six Carolus guilders for each person that during said time may or shall have run up a score for wine or beer in their house

"And to the end that we may take all due care to prevent all rash drawing of knives, all fightings and personal injuries, and all catastrophies resulting from the same, any person or persons who shall rashly or in anger draw any knife or dagger against any other person, shall be fined the penalty of one hundred Carolus guilders, or in failure of payment of the same, they shall be put to the most menial labor, with bread and water for their subsistence; or in case any person shall have been wounded thereby, the penalty shall be three hundred Carolus guilders, or an additional half year's confinement to the most menial labor, with bread and water for their subsistence.

"We do also charge and command our Fiscal, our Lieutenant, our Sergeants, our Corporals, and every one of our citizens and inhabitants, as well as the soldiers, on all occasions to take measures that all such persons be pursued and apprehended, so that they may be proceeded against and dealt with as the law directs"

Plainly the people of the colony had grown very bad in a little while. They had a very vigorous ruler over them now The proclamation just quoted was shortly followed by a second, in which His Excellency set forth that he had learned that the former one was disregarded Many persons, he says, are diverted from their proper calling to that of tapping by the ease with which profits are realized, so much so that "almost one full fourth part of the City of New Amsterdam have become bawdy houses for the sale of ardent spirits, tobacco, and beer" The Company's servants, the Governor says, are thus led astray, and the youth are corrupted "Honest inns" too, established for travelers and strangers, and which pay their taxes and excises righteously, were seriously interfered with in their lawful business His Excellency therefore orders that from that time forth, no new tavern, inn, or other place for the sale of liquor shall be opened without his consent, and those in the business already are notified that within four years they must close and employ themselves in more "honest business"

Other ordinances were framed causing the removal of hog-pens and out-houses from the highway; prohibiting trespass upon enclosed orchards, fields, or gardens, under penalty of a hundred guilders; and ordering that all the inhabitants put their plantations in good fence so that cattle may be kept out A pound was established for trespassing cattle; greater stability in building was enjoined; and it was decreed that all grants of land should be revoked unless improvements were made within nine months.

From such simple and primitive regulations have germinated the vast system of police laws and ordinances of our day.

In 1648, Governor Stuyvesant also appointed fire wardens for the first time. Their duty was to inspect all the chimneys at stated intervals

It will be interesting at this point to take a glance at the system of administration that prevailed in the colony and in the city. The Director-General was vested with almost autocratic powers. He appointed all public officers, save such as were sent out from Holland; he made laws, imposed fines, levied taxes, inflicted penalties, incorporated towns, decided all civil and criminal causes of magnitude except capital cases, which were sent to Holland for trial—without the aid of a jury, and settled appeals from lower tribunals. The Governor was aided by a council of five of the best men of the colony. Next in importance to him were the Koopman and Schout-Fiscal, the former being the secretary of the West India Company's warehouse. The latter, as has been said, discharged the collective functions of sheriff and attorney-general, and was, besides, the executive officer of the Director and Council, and custom-house officer. The Schout-Fiscal was allowed to sit in the Council during its deliberations, but had no voice in the proceedings. He had no stated salary for his multifarious services, but was compensated by certain fees allowed him in particular cases.

The appointment of a Rattle-watch led, on October 12, 1651, to the adoption of the following rules:

Watchman's Rattle

1. Watchmen to be on duty before bell-ringing, under penalty of six stivers.

2. Whoever stays away without sending a substitute, to be fined two guilders for benefit of the regular watch.

3. One guilder fine for drunkenness.

4. Ten stivers fine for sleeping on post.

5. If any arms are stolen through negligence of the watch, the watchman to pay for the arms and be fined one guilder for the first, two guilders for the second, and the fine for the third offense to be discretionary with the court.

6. A fine of two guilders for going away from the watch, and one guilder for missing turn.

7. The Watch to call the hour at all corners from 9 A M. until reveille, for which they received an additional compensation of eighteen guilders per month.

The City was incorporated by the name of New Amsterdam in 1652, but the municipal institutions did not go into practical operation until February 2, 1653. The charter granted gave nothing but a court of municipal magistrates, with certain judicial and other functions. These officials were a Schout, to be appointed by the Company, two Burgomasters, and five Schepens—to be elected by the people. The Burgomasters were intrusted with the general regulation of city improvements. The Magistrates, together, had original jurisdiction of civil and criminal cases arising within the city limits, subject to an appeal to the Director-General. They heard and settled all disputes, tried cases for the recovery of debt, for defamation of character, for breach of promise, and for assault and theft; and even summoned parents and guardians into their presence for withholding their consent to the marriage of their children or wards without sufficient cause. They sentenced, and committed to prison like a Court of Sessions. They met once every two weeks at the Stadt Huys. The citizens of to-day will read with regretful interest that the city fathers, whose title was "My Lords" in these old times, "had a conscientious regard for equity and justice, and set themselves like flint against Sabbath-breaking, drunkenness, and all the popular vices." No grants of franchises or property, however, were made to the Magistrates, out of which a municipal fund could be constructed. The West India Company, as a commercial body, gave away nothing which it thought the stockholders might with advantage keep for themselves.

Of all the officials mentioned, the most important by far was the Schout. The police of the city was chiefly centered in him. It was his duty to personally perambulate the streets; to observe if there were any infractions of the laws and ordinances. When, either from his own observation or the information of others, he became aware of such infractions, it was his duty to present a formal complaint to the Burgomasters and Schepens. It was generally within the power of the magistrates to mitigate the penalties imposed by law, and the records show that they were, as a rule, mercifully inclined, though cases are not wanting where punishments were inflicted which to-day would seem excessive.

One of the most noted officials under the city magistrates was the bell-ringer. He seems to have been a most versatile and industrious officer. He personally discharged the duties of bell-ringer, court-messenger, grave-digger, chorister, reader, schoolmaster, waiter, messenger, and general factotum to the magistrates. He kept the room wherein the magistrates met in order, dusted the furniture, swept the floor, and presumably made the fires and placed the chairs where they belonged in time for each meeting, before he summoned it by ringing the bell.

Wall Street was then the boundary of the city.

The proceedings of the Worshipful Court of "the Schout, Burgomasters and Schepens" were all recorded by their clerk or secretary. In criminal cases the Schout prosecuted as plaintiff on behalf of the community. Bail was allowed except in cases of murder, rape, arson or treason. There were two modes of trying the prisoner; either publicly upon general evidence, which was the ordinary mode, or by examining him secretly in the presence of two Schepens, in which written interrogatories were propounded to the prisoner, to which he was obliged to return categorical answers. The Dutch laws then adhered to the general policy of extorting confessions by torture.

A war being considered imminent with the New England colonists—1653—it was ordered that the whole body of citizens should keep watch by night, that the fortress be repaired, and that money be raised.

In regard to this watch, the Director-General made the following proclamation. "That the Burghers of this city shall, in a body, keep watch by night in such places as shall be determined on by the Director and Council and Magistrates, yet in the first place at the City Tavern, now the Town Hall, to commence at this time." The Watch went into operation that night.

Another warlike resolution of the hour was that the schipper Jan Jansen should be spoken to "privately to fix his sails, to have his piece loaded, and to keep his vessel in readiness on all occasions, whether by day or by night."

The Burgher-watch had become dissatisfied, as much with the nature of their duties as with the parsimony of their employers, and they went on a "strike" in November, 1653. This excited the wrath of the choleric Director-General, who berated them roundly. The controversy thereby precipitated shook the very foundations of Dutch society in New Amsterdam. And it was all on account of the Burgher-watch not being supplied with firewood. Old Peter Stuyvesant told them contemptuously to procure the firewood themselves at their own expense; but this they refused to do. Hence the row. The difficulty was finally satisfactorily settled and peace restored.

Whether it was on account of the foregoing episode, or a desire to improve the system, it was now determined to effect a change. With that object in view, an ordinance was passed, on the 29th of April, 1654, looking towards the establishment of a "rattle-wacht," of from four to six men, to guard the city by night. "Wherefore all persons who desire to undertake the same, are warned to repair at the aforesaid time, to hear the conditions, and to act according to circumstances." But it was calling spirits from the vasty deep. The ordinance was read with official impressiveness from the steps of the City Hall, but no one responding, the formation of the proposed watch was for the time abandoned, but was renewed and put into operation in October, 1658.

Gov. Stuyvesant's Mansion.

The year of 1654 was a notable one in the city's history, for, in reply to a letter of the Director-General, urging the Magistrates to devise some means of raising money for public purposes, they replied that if the excise moneys—an institution of Governor Kieft's, by the way—were made over to them, they would engage to pay the salaries of one minister, one precentor, and one "dog-whipper"—a name then applied to sextons.

Grim old Peter Stuyvesant had little respect or sympathy for the popular pastimes or social failings of his countrymen. On the 31st of December, 1655, an ordinance interdicted the firing of guns and planting of May-poles, from which, as alleged, there had resulted much drunkenness, together with lamentable accidents. Beating of the drum, firing, pole-planting, and the sale of liquor were interdicted under a penalty of twelve guilders for the first offence, twenty-four for the second, and arbitrary correction for the third offence. The fines so imposed were equally divided among the officer, the poor, and the prosecutor.

In 1655, the Burgomasters and Schepens, finding that a better police system was necessary, appointed Dirk Van Schellywne, the notary, the first High Constable (concierge) of New Amsterdam. They furnished him with detailed instructions respecting his duty, as follows

1

He shall endeavor to levy all executions in civil matters on the order of the Burgomasters and Schepens of this City, touching the domain of this City, and that on such allowance as shall, according to circumstances, be found necessary.

2

Whenever any judgment rendered by the Burgomasters and Schepens of this City shall be placed in his hands, he shall be bound to govern himself according to the tenor thereof, and having received the same, to put it in execution according to the custom of the renowned City of Amsterdam in Holland, but with all discretion, according to the circumstances and constitution of the inhabitants here.

3

He shall not presume to receive, even through the third or fourth hand, any gifts or presents to the injury of the rights of those interested, or to delay execution on pain of deprival of his office.

4

The High Constable shall receive as salary from all judgments of a hundred guilders and upwards, rendered by the Burgomasters and Schepens, twelve stivers from the successful party on account of said judgment

5

From all other judgments below a hundred guilders, the sum of six stivers.

6

From all interlocutory judgments rendered in writing during trial, six stivers

7

From each institution, summons or renewal which the High Constable shall serve within the jurisdiction of this city, with particulars thereof, he shall receive four-and-twenty stivers, provided he keep proper register of the particulars, annotated with day and date

8

For the sale of distrained goods, six guilders per day, being reckoned from nine and eleven hours or as many hours more or less according to the circumstances.

9

For making and affixing notices on three places, each notice eight stivers

10

For all insinuations, summons, and renewals extending beyond the jusisdiction of this city to the fresh water, on the Island Manhattan, six and thirty stivers

11

For insinuations, summons, and renewals served beyond the North or East Rivers, either at Pavonia or thereabout, and on Long Island, where there is as yet no bench of justice, he shall receive sixty stivers, good money, it being understood that he shall bring in his account for boat hire and ordinary expenses, and demand the same from his employer.

12

After sale and receipt of the proceeds of the distrained goods, he shall first deduct his salary (fees) and pay over to the successful party, with all despatch, the moneys to him belonging.

13

No more of the seized property shall be sold than amounts to the sum entered in the judgment with costs thereon

14

For the better execution of his office shall the Schout, Messenger, and servants of justice assist the High Constable when necessary.

15

The Director-General reserves only unto himself to change, enlarge, or diminish these, according as circumstances hereafter may demand

The Burgomasters and Schepens who, in the preceding year, received annual salaries of $140 and $100 respectively, in 1655 ordered the "Stadt Huys" to be cleared of a quantity of salt with the storage of which it had been encumbered Various lodgers in the building, too, were ordered to put it in repair and then move out.

In 1656 a Watch, composed of a corporal's guards, was ordered to patrol the city on Sundays during divine service.

That ancient and clamorous functionary, to wit, the Town-crier, was invented, if not patented, about this time He gave notice of all public events by sounding a bell or horn at the corners, and proclaiming them aloud

In October of this year—1657—the order regulating the tapster's business on Sunday was re-proclamated, the Schouts and Marshals being urged to increased vigilance In December notice was given to surgeons that when called upon to dress wounds they should ask the patient who wounded him, and give his answer to the Schout for official action The order prohibiting fighting was re-proclamated. A fine of twenty-five guilders was imposed for one blow, and in case blood was drawn, the fine was increased to one hundred guilders, and a fine double that amount was imposed if the injury was inflicted in the presence of the officer, Burgomaster or Schepen Prisoners arrested for debt were taken to the City Hall pending judgment, if they did not wish to pay tavern expenses. The following year the first city Jailer was appointed, and the treasury being empty, the salary of the Town-drummer could not be paid

On October 4th (1658) a paid Rattle-watch of eight men, to do duty from nine o'clock at night until morning drum-beat, was established, the duty being imposed upon each of the citizens by turns, and each householder was taxed fifteen stivers for its support. The following-named persons having offered themselves for this service, were accepted and engaged Pieter Jansen, Hendrick Van Bommel, Jan Cornelisen Van Vleusburgh, Jan Pietersen, Gerrit Pietersen, Jan Jansen Van Langstraat, Hendrick Ruyter, Jacques Pyrn, Thomas Verdon The Burgomasters fixed the rate of compensation to be paid each man at "twenty-four stivers every night they watched, it being well understood four and four shall watch each night"; and they are promised "one or two beavers for candles, and two to three hundred pieces of firewood." Ludowyck Post was appointed Captain of this primitive police force.

Another incident of note recorded in this year is that the Jailer was allowed to lay in beer, free from excise, for the use of prisoners.

The Burgher Provost was also Captain of the Rattle-watch He had to see that the regular rounds were made.

The following orders were issued in connection with this Watch:

"All the Watchmen were obliged to come on the Watch at the regular hour, to wit, before the ringing of the bell, on pain of forfeiting six stivers. Whenever any one came on the Watch drunk, was insolent 'in the square of the City Hall,' or in going the rounds, should forfeit each time one guilder. Due attention

Mustering the Rattle-Watch

should be paid by each one to his Watch in going around, and whenever any one was found asleep on the street he should forfeit each time ten stivers. If, by negligence on the part of the Watch, arms were stolen, he should be bound to pay the valuation thereof, and in addition for the first offence one guilder, for the second two guilders, and for the third at the discretion of the Burgomaster

"If any one should lie still when people cried out '*val val*,' or be otherwise disobedient, he should forfeit twenty stivers A fine of ten stivers was imposed on those of the Watch who swore or blasphemed. For fighting or quarreling on the Watch, two guilders; whoever threatened another forfeited two guilders: for fighting in fact on the Watch, or even in the morning coming from the Watch, the penalty was six guilders; should any one be unwilling to go around, or in any way lose a turn, he should forfeit one guilder; for going away from his Watch on any pretence whatever, without the express consent of the others, two guilders"

Whatever any of the Watch should get from any of the prisoners, whether lock-up money or other fee which those of the Watch should receive by consent of the Burgomaster, it should be brought into the house of the Captain for the benefit of the fellow Watchmen, and preserved until it was divided around

The aforesaid fees should be brought in by each of the Watchmen under the bond of the oath they had taken to the city.

All the fines which accrued, and the profits which in anywise should be realized by insolence, fault, neglect, or otherwise, should be divided four times a year among the members of the Watch, when they, according to an old custom, should each quarter of the year receive their watch money from the city without their holding any drinking meetings thereupon, or keeping any club

They should be bound on going the rounds to call out how late it was at all the corners of the streets, from 9 P. M until the reveille beat in the morning, for which they should receive each man eighteen guilders per month The Captain was ordered to pay strict attention that these rules should be observed and obeyed

Following is the oath taken by the Watch

"We promise and swear, in the presence of the Most High, that we will fully observe the article read to us, and demean ourselves as faithful Watchmen are bound to do So truly help us, God Almighty"

The following month the Burgomasters resolved, "that the Provost shall from now, henceforth, according to and by virtue of the following commission, collect and receive from each housekeeper for the support of the rattle-watch fifteen stivers, except those whose husbands are from home, widows, preachers, also such as are in somebody's service, and according to the list thereof given him"

The following is the commission referred to·

"Ludowyck Post, Captain of the rattle-watch, is hereby authorized and qualified by the Burgomaster of the City of Amsterdam in New Netherland, to collect and receive every month fifteen stivers from every one according to the list thereof given him, for the support of the rattle-watch"

Then follow "instructions for the Burgher Provost, door-keeper of the council of war, Captain of the rattle-watch and receiver of the watch money," as follows·

"*Firstly*, The Burgher Provost shall well observe when the companies are under arms who is absent and who behaves badly in the ranks, also in marching according to the order granted them, and yet to be granted, and duly to mark down who commits a fault, to make the same known to the Captain of the company who they are and in what the fault consists

"*Secondly*, To inform the court marshal according to order, therefore summon those who are guilty of any fault

"*Thirdly*, To attend to the rattle-watch that regularly and at every hour precisely the rounds be made and the hour called from 9 o'clock in the evening to the morning at reveille, according to the instructions given

"*Fourthly*, Truly to state who are in fault and to inform on them to the Burgomaster, whereof the Captain shall receive one quarter, and also of profits from fines. He shall also go around every month to collect the money from each house according to order thereof granted and still to be granted, and place the money received in the hands of the Secretary of Burgomasters and Schepens, who shall distribute the same to spare no one, and if there are any not on the list to give in the same in writing to the Burgomasters, to speak ill to no burgher, and whosoever threatens him to complain of him to the Burgomasters, who shall order the case as circumstances of the matter direct

"Further to observe well that those of the watch impose not on any Burgher in going the rounds or on the watch, also that they steal not any firewood, nor any other timber, nor anything else"

On the 8th of July, 1660, the Heer Schout informed the Court of Burgomasters that when he goes around at night and unreasonable hours to make examination, the dogs make dangerous attacks on him, he requested therefore their honors to take some order on it

The Burgomasters at the same session resolved to draft a placard prohibiting the hallowing after Indians in Pearl Street, and the cutting of "Koeckies," "which is done by boys"

New Amsterdam has now something like a police system The Magistrates seem to have grown sterner too, for they increased the punishment for theft to whipping with a rod, instead of hoisting by the waistband Persons charged with theft were now—as had sometime been the case earlier—examined under torture

A Schepen Deciding a Law Suit
[FROM AN OLD PRINT]

The records of the court proceedings during Governor Stuyvesant's administration are the most faithful chronicles of the state of society in those days—particularly that part of society which is most brought in contact with the administration of police and penal enactments, as witness the following:

"RESOLVEERT WALDRON, *Plaintiff*, vs JAN JURRIAANZEN, *Defendant*

"Plaintiff says he went the rounds on Sunday evening, the 4th of August, with

three soldiers, and on coming to the defendant's house found three sailors there with a backgammon table and candle before them; he also found at his house on a Sunday during the sermon three sailors, who afterwards came to him and inquired if he had people's. He answered yes. Thereupon entering, he found a party of women. As his wife was in labor in the house, he thereupon reproving him, was treated by him very ill. Demanding the penalty according to the placard.

"Defendant does not deny it, but says the sailors had not any drink.

"The W. Court condemns the defendant Jan Jurriaanzen, in a fine of thirty guilders for that he entertained people after nine o'clock, and tapped during the sermon, to be paid to the officer to be applied according to law; and, for having behaved offensively to the officer, in the fine of ten guilders for the poor.

For calling the Magistrates fools and simpletons, Walewyn Vander Veen was condemned to repair the injury, "honorably and profitably honorably, by praying with uncovered head forgiveness of God and Justice; profitably, by paying as a fine the sum of twelve hundred guilders, with costs, and in case of refusal, to go into close confinement."

"THE HEER SCHOUT, PIETER TONNEMAN, *Plaintiff, vs* JAN DE WITT, *Defendant*

"The Heer, plaintiff, says that defendant insulted the Heer Schepen Tymotheus Gabry, calling him a bastard. Demanding that he shall repair the injury profitably and honorably, and pay a fine at the descretion of the court.

"Defendant acknowledges he said so, but in jest, not thinking that it should be so taken, and might well have been silent.

"The Schepen Gabry, rising, declared that one evening the clock striking nine, it was not heard by him, the defendant said, If thou can'st not hear that thou must be a bastard.

"And whereas, Jan de Witt answers, that such was spoken by him in jest and not from malice. Burgomasters and Schepens say to Jan de Witt, standing aside, that they forgive him for this turn, but he must take care not to repeat the offence, or that other provisions shall be made.

"Neeltjie Pieters and Annetje Minnens, prisoners, appear in court, against whom the Heer officer prosecutes his charge, concluding that Neeltjie Pieters shall, for her committed theft (of a few pairs of stockings) be brought to the place where justice is usually executed, and there be bound fast to a stake, severely scourged, and banished for ten years from the jurisdiction of this city, and that Annetje Minnens shall, whilst justice is administered to Neeltjie Pieters, stand by and look at her, and after justice is executed, shall be whipped severely within doors, and banished for six years out of this city's jurisdiction, as she was with those from whom the goods were stolen by the above named Neeltjie, giving them up to them.

"Mesaack Martenzen, brought forward at the request of the Heer officer, for further interrogation, examined by torture as to how many cabbages, fowls, turkies, and how much butter he had stolen, and who his abettors and co-operatives have been. Answering: he persists by his reply, as per interrogatories, that he did not steal any butter, fowls or turkies, nor had any abbettors; being again set loose, the Heer officer produces his demand against the delinquent, concluding that for his committing theft, voluntarily confessed without torture or chains, he shall be brought to the usual place of criminal justice, well fastened to a stake and severely whipped, and banished from the jurisdiction of this City of Amsterdam for the term of ten years; all with costs.

"Reyer Cornelissen, for the theft of a sack of corn, was sentenced to be 'publically set to a stake, severely scourged, branded, and banished beyond this city's jurisdiction for the term of five-and-twenty years, and further, in the costs and *mises* of justice.'"

Everything indicates that an era of great improvement and prosperity had set in, but it was destined to be short-lived, at least under Dutch rule. England, on the strength of Cabot's early visit, had always claimed the sovereignty of the New Netherlands, and she now took advantage of a war with Holland to enforce her claim. She sent a fleet to seize the country. With the hauling down of the Dutch flag from the fort the reign of the old Dutch Knickerbockers was temporarily brought to an end, and that of the Britisher began.

Cornelis Steenwyck was a native of Holland, and arrived in New Amsterdam about the year 1652. At the time of the very serious troubles between the Dutch and English, in 1653, when the city wall was built, the tax levied to raise the funds for that purpose rated Steenwyck among the wealthiest of the citizens. His public life commenced about the year 1658, and at various stages he held positions in the civil magistracy as Schepen in the years 1658 and 1660, and as Burghomaster in the year 1662. In 1663, he was requested by unanimous resolution of the General Provincial Assembly to proceed to the Fatherland as delegate from the Province of New Netherland, to lay the deplorable condition of the province before the Heeren Majores, with petitions for redress, but the pressure of business would not permit him to undertake this mission. When the province passed over to the British, Steenwyck declared that "so long as the country remained in the hands of the English he should be found a willing and obedient subject." He became a member of the Colonial Council, and occupied the position of temporary Governor of the Province during the absence of Governor Lovelace.

After the reconquest of the city by the Dutch, Steenwyck, who was justly recognized as the leading man among the citizens, was called by Benckes and Evertsen into their Councils. He, by request, called the citizens together, with the view to appoint a delegation to confer with the military officers, and he headed the list of six citizens who composed the delegation. The citizens who were called on to nominate for Burghomasters and Schepens, sent in the name of Steenwyck at the head of their nominees. He was, however, "slated" for a more important position, and, while Captain Colve was designated by the officers as Governor, citizen Steenwyck was appointed his sole Councilor. His commission read as follows:

"To all that who shall see or hear these read, greeting.

"Whereas, we have deemed it necessary for the promotion of justice and police in this conquest of New Netherland, under the superintendence and direction of the Honorable Governor-General Anthoney Colve, to appoint and commission an expert person as member of Council in this Province: We, therefore, upon the good report which we have received of the abilities of Cornelis Steenwyck, former Burgomaster of the city of New Orange, in the time of the West India Company's Government of this country, have commissioned, qualified, and appointed, as we now commission, qualify, and appoint the aforesaid Cornelis Steenwyck, Councilor of the aforesaid Province of New Netherland, to assist in the direction of all cases relative to justice and police, and further, in all such military concerns, both by water and by land, in which the Governor shall deem proper to ask his advice and assistance, to maintain good order, and to promote the welfare and prosperity of this country, for the service of the Lords Majores; to take all possible care for the security and defence of the forts in these parts, to administer justice both in criminal and in civil cases, and further, to do and execute everything relative to his office that a good Councilor is in duty bound to do, upon the oath which he shall have taken * * * *"

"Dated at Fort William Henry, on the day above (12th August, 1673)"

The following Spring (1674) the Governments of England and the Dutch States contracted a treaty of peace, by the terms of which the American provinces finally passed over to the former. The Dutch citizens yielded without opposition to the new power, but a serious misunderstanding existed between them and Governor Andros respecting the rights of the citizens under the new treaty. Governor Andros enforced obedience to his decree by imprisonment of the principal Dutch citizens, among whom was Steenwyck. The prisoners were shortly after released on bail, and no further official notice was taken of their alleged mutinous conduct. Steenwyck lived ten years subsequent to the second surrender to the English. Among other civic positions held by him during this period was that of Mayor of the City.

The cut of Steenwyck given in connection with this sketch is copied from an engraving taken from a portrait in the New York Historical Society collection

New Amsterdam (New York), 1664

CHAPTER II.

PERIOD OF BRITISH OCCUPANCY.

1664—1783.

OBF HENDRICK, FIRST CONSTABLE UNDER THE ENGLISH.—LIGHTING THE CITY BY NIGHT (1668)—WATCHMEN ORDERED TO PROVIDE THEMSELVES WITH "A LANTHERN AND A STICK OF FIREWOOD"—A STRICT POLICE ESTABLISHED THROUGHOUT THE CITY—ORDERS TO BE OBSERVED BY THE CONSTABLES' WATCH, ETC—RULES GOVERNING THE WATCH—NEW POLICE REGULATIONS (1684)—DONGAN'S CHARTER (1686)—FIRST UNIFORMED POLICEMAN—APPOINTMENT OF A CIVIL WATCH—NEW CITY HALL, WALL STREET—MODES OF PUNISHMENT INFLICTED ON CRIMINALS.—MONTGOMERIE CHARTER (1730)—FIRST MAIN WATCH-HOUSE—CITIZENS ORDERED TO WATCH OR FIND SUBSTITUTES.—FIRST POOR-HOUSE ERECTED (1734.)—"INSURRECTION AND THE PLOTS OF SLAVES."—QUAKER'S EXEMPT FROM SERVING ON THE WATCH—PETITIONING AGAINST A MILITARY WATCH.—THE OLD JAIL—BRIDEWELL—OCCUPATION OF THE CITY BY THE BRITISH.—EVACUATION.

THE first of the great political changes that New York has undergone in the course of its history was its transfer from Dutch to British rulership. It was marked, as might be expected, by a general change of system in the administration of public affairs, the police arrangements and regulations, like all the rest, undergoing radical alteration.

When, in 1664, the British first seized the Dutch possessions in America, the population of the New Netherlands had increased to "full ten thousand," and New Amsterdam contained fifteen hundred inhabitants, and "wore an appearance of great prosperity." Colonel Nicolls, who took possession of the colony in the name of the Duke of York, proceeded at the earliest possible moment to make its government conform to the English system. In 1665 he granted a charter of incorporation to the inhabitants, under the administration of a Mayor, Aldermen and Sheriff. These officials went to work promptly, for in the same year they ordered "that six burghers do every night keep the watch within the city."

At a meeting of the city fathers, November 18, 1665, we learn that the Deputy Mayor stated that the Heer-General had proposed to him to allow the burghers to watch anew, and, as the least expensive plan to the city, it was proposed "that each bring on his watch two sticks of firewood, and the two one lantern."

The Worshipful Court demurred, and thought it better still to continue the two night watch, "and therefore Resolve to agree civilly with them, together with two other Volunteers, who should then undertake the watch on the other nights."

During this year Obe Hendrick was appointed the first Constable under the English

The law required that every town was to provide a pair of stocks and a pound, and a pillory was to be erected in each place where the courts of sessions were held

The city fathers, in one of their sessions, adopted a series of resolutions, from the minutes of which the following paragraphs are extracted:

"*Further*, Class van Elsland and Pieter Schaafbank were also contd (continued) in their offices as Towne Sergeants, receivers for wages as much as they heretofore have received out of this city's revenue

"*Thirdly*, Resolved to send for the Court of Haarlem and the Constable Resolverd Waldron by letter to come hither by Saturday next"

The Pillory.

Happily a copy of this letter is still extant It is about as odd an official document, as can be found in the annals of any country Here it is

" HONORABLE AND AFFECTIONATE FRIENDS.

"These serve only that your Honors hold yourselves ready to appear here in this city on Saturday next, being 17th June, old style, with Resolverd Waldron, and to receive all such order as shall be communicated, whereunto confiding, we commend your Honors after cordial salutation unto God's protection"

The end of this little episode is no less farcical than the beginning The public record of the matter reads thus

"Resolveert Waldron, entering, is notified that he is elected Constable of N Haarlem, which undertaking he hath taken the proper oath, and the Magistrates who accompanied him are informed that they are discharged from their office; authorizing the aforesaid Constable to select three or four persons who shall have to decide any differences or dispute to the extent of five pounds sterling * * * * and no higher, and the party who shall not be contend with the decision of those elected as aforesaid shall be bound to pay to him, the Constable, the sum of six stivers, and further, to bear the costs of proceeding before his bench of Justice"

Truly this was a notable state of things, when the Constable appointed the Magistrates. However, many curious things happened in those days The oath administered to the Constables is also worthy of attention It is given in this form in the old records

"Whereas you are chosen Constable of this Cittye of New York under the jurisdiction of Mayor and Aldermen; you do sweare by the Almighty God that you will endeavour the preserving of the peace, and the discovering, and preventing all attempts against the same, and that you will faithfully and truthfully execute such warrants as you shall from time to time receive from this Court, and in case you shall absent yourself you shall make choice of some able man for your deputy, and in all things demeane yourself as a Constable ought to Soo helpe you God"

In 1668 the system of lighting the city by night was introduced. The method adopted was a very primitive one, as appears from the language of the ordinance "Every seventh house in all the streets shall, in the dark time of the moon, cause a lantern and candle to be hung out on a pole, the charge to be defrayed equally by the inhabitants of the said seven houses." Upon very dark nights every inhabitant was required to have a lighted candle in his window. At this time, too, a regular night-watch was employed, composed of men who were paid for their services by the city. The Watch was set at nine o'clock in the evening (when the city gates were shut and locked), and was kept up until daybreak. It was maintained, however, only during the winter months—that is, from the beginning of November to the end of March, that being the period when the greatest danger from fire was apprehended. Every Watchman was ordered to bring with him, when he went on duty, "his lanthern and a stick of firewood."

On a fresh outbreak of war in Europe, however, New York, as New Amsterdam was now called, received a summons to capitulate to a Dutch squadron which appeared in the port in 1673. The town surrendered and remained a dependency of Holland until February of the succeeding year. In the interim its rulers were far more concerned with military than with civil affairs, and a curious mixture of the two elements will be found in all the proceedings of the time. A calm piety, we are told, mingled with the deliberations of the Magistrates. The Schout, Burgomasters and Schepens opened their sessions daily at the City Hall with prayer. The Governor, and his Council at the fort, instituted a rigid supervision over the morals of the soldiery. A strict police was established throughout the city. The place was guarded day and night at every available point, the sentinels at the fort mounting on the ramparts, and watching by the gate. Subaltern officers made rounds during the night, visiting the walls, passing the watchword, and changing the sentinels each half hour. The Mayor or Burgomaster proceeded every morning with a guard of armed soldiers to the fort, where he received the keys of the city gates from the Governor. Then, accompanied by his guard, he opened the gates. He closed them again in the evening, and having stationed the citizens' guard, or Burgher-wacht, he returned the keys to the Governor.

The following orders regarding the policing of the city were issued in December of this year:

"Whereas the fortifications of this city, New Orange, have at great and excessive expense, trouble and labor of the burghery and inhabitants, been almost completed, and it is therefore necessary for the preservation of the same and better security of this city that some orders be made; the Honbl H'r Governor Gener'll of New Netherland doth therefore consider it necessary to enact and by publication make known the following orders to the burghery:

"*Firstly*, from now, henceforward, the burgher watch of this city shall be set and commenced at drumbeat, about half an hour before sundown, when the trainbands of this city, then on the watch, shall parade before the City Hall of this city, under the penalty previously affixed thereunto.

"*Item*, The city gate shall be closed at sundown by the Mayor and his attendant trainbands, and in like manner opened at sunrise.

"*Item*, The burghery, and inhabitants of this city, and all others of what quality soever they may be, the Watch alone excepted, are strictly interdicted and forbid to attempt coming from sunset to sunrise on the bulwarks, bastion, or batteries of this city, on pain of bodily correction.

"*Item*, It is strictly forbidden and prohibited that any person, be he who he may, presume to land within the city, or quit the same in any other manner, way or means, than through the ordinary city gate, on pain of death. And, finally, as it is found that the hogs which are kept within this city in multitudes along the public streets have from time to time committed great damage on the earthen fortifications, * * * it is therefore ordered and charged that persons take care that their hogs shall not come to, in, or on the bulwarks, bastions, gardens, or batteries, under forfeiture of said hogs, and double the value thereof to be applied, the one-half for the informer, the other half for the officer who shall put this in execution."

In December a proclamation was made, too, forbidding the exportation of provisions from the city, and charging all good citizens to lay in a supply for eight months. Evidently preparations were in progress for a siege.

The Dutch government plainly did not contemplate an easy surrender of the New Netherlands, but made laws looking towards a long stay. One of these ordered that all matters pertaining to the "police, security and peace of the inhabitants" of New Orange, or, to justice between man and man, should be finally determined by the Schout, Burgomaster, and Schepens, unless the amount involved exceeded fifty beavers, when an appeal "to the Heer Governour-General and Council" was allowed. All criminal offences committed in the city were amenable to the jurisdiction of the city officials who had power to judge, and pass even sentences of death; but no sentence of corporal punishment could be carried out until approved by the Governor or Council.

But when, on February 9, 1674, the treaty of peace between the States-General and England was signed, the New Netherlands passed definitively into the possession of the latter country. Then the old government by Burgomasters and Schepens disappeared for good, and the modern officials of Mayor and Aldermen took up a permanent position in the public system. In March of this year (1674), sixteen persons were employed to keep watch every night for one year. The compensation allowed them (£32 each) will serve as an indication of the value of money in the colony at that period. Eight men were also selected to watch every second night; they were paid £16. The following year, a committee, appointed by the Board of Aldermen to draw up orders and regulations for the City Watch, made a report. The following orders to be observed by the Constables' Watch, and the Citizens-Soldiers, were then issued, copies being delivered to the Captains of the Watch for their guidance.

"That the watch bee sett every night by eight of the clock, immediately after ringing of the bell.

"That the citty gates be locked up by the Constable or Deputy before nine of the clock, and opened in the morning presently after daylight, and at the dismissinge of the watch, and if any person goes from, or absent himself without consent, he or they shall forfeit for every such Default Tenn Guilders.

"That the Sergeant or Corporall of the Wattch shall at all times succeed the Deputy Constable upon the Wattch for the execution thereof.

"That the Constable or his Deputy (the City Gates being shut) be upon the Wattch by nine of the clock, and by his Roole, call over all the names of those who are to give their attendance there that night, and the faylers to be marked to pay their fines, which is to be as formerly, four guilders pr every default. And if anyone comes to the Wattch after the Roole is called over, he shall pay half the fine aforesaid.

"That whosoever shall come upon ye Wattch, that is overcharged with drinke, hee or they shall pay halfe the aforementioned fine; but if abusive or Quite Drunke the whole fine to be paid as if absent and secured upon the Watch all Night.

"That whosoever shall presume to make any quarrell upon the Wattch, upon the account of being different nations or any other pretense whatsoever, hee or they shall pay a whole fine and be liable to such further sensure as the meritt of the cause shall require.

"That no Centinall shall presume to come off his duty until hee bee reliefed under a severe sensure, which is to be at least twenty guilders for a fine, and three days imprisonment For the time the officer upon ye Wattch is to take care, that is to be equally proportioned, and not to exceed one hour at a time

"That frequent Rounds be made about the city, And especially towards the Bridge ; And not less than three times every night.

"Upon complaint made unto the Court It is Ordered. that no cursings or swearings shall be suffered upon the Wattch, nor any gaminge at Dice or Cards, nor any exercise of Drinkinge upon the Penalty of four guilders for every such offence

"If any disorders are committed upon the Wattch contrary to the tenure of this Order, the Constable or his Deputy shall give an account thereof the following morning to the Mayor or Deputy Mayor

"That a list of the fines be brought by the Provost to the Mayor or Deputy Mayor every month, after which there shall be power granted to levye the fines by distress ; if not otherwise satisfied

"The Sergeant belonging to every Wattch shall come with Halbert and see that every one of the Wattch bring his armes, that is to say his sword and good halfe Pike on the Penalty of four guilders for every offense

" All Citizens are hereby ordered to have in readiness in their houses for every head one good muskett or Firelock with Powder and ball, with 6 charges of Powder &c., 6 of ball at least upon the penalty of four guilders for the first offence, double for ye second, and treaple for the third offence. And the officers of each Company are required to make, or cause to be made, a due search for the same as often as they shall see cause, and at least four times every yeare

"It is also Ordered that the Citizens Soulders upon all occasions shall appear with good armes before their Captaines Coullers at the first beating of their drums on the penalty of thirty guilders for every default And for not appearing with good and sufficient armes, for every default tenn guilders "

On December 6th, 1675, the inhabitants, to protect themselves against the Indians, raised the following guard, which was divided into four Corporalships, each consisting of seven persons

"*First*—Adolph Meyer (Corporal); Meyendert L Journey; David Des Marets ; Danl Tourneur ; Nicholas DeVaux , Isaac Kip , and John Hendrikse

"*Second*—John Nagel (Corporal), Joost Van Obliuis, Jno. Hendrickse Kyckuyt , Jan de la Maistre ; Johannis Vermelie ; Jean Le Roy , and Isaac Le Maistre

"*Third:*—Simeon Courrier (Corporal), Cornelius Jansen; Daniel Demarest ; Lawrence Jansen ; William Palmer ; Isaac El Voe, and —— Rademaker

"*Fourth:*—Robert Halles (Corporal), Resolverd Waldron , Arent Harmanse; Conrad Hendrickse ; David Demarest , Cornelius Lennise ; and Isaac Cil, Jr.

The following rules, by which the Watch were to be governed, were issued in connection with the above

" 1. Either the whole or half of the corporalships, according to turns, shall at 8 o'clock in the evening, at the beating of the drum, appear at the watch-house and place their sentinels and take their necessary rounds, and not retire before the morning reveille shall be beaten, in the penalty of three guilders.

" 2. Whoever shall neglect the watch without a lawful excuse, or the corporal's permission, shall be fined for every offense six guilders.

"3 The watchmen shall come to the watch with suitable side and hand arms, with sufficient powder and lead, under the penalty of three guilders

"4 The watch is to be kept quietly without much noise or clamor, in the penalty of three guilders

"5 And the fines that occur in the premises shall be reported and collected"

In 1676, a fresh set of regulations were promulgated, by which the Watch was ordered to be set at eight o'clock in the evening "immediately after the ringing of the bell" The gates, as before, were to be locked before nine o'clock, and opened in the morning " presently after daylight, at the dismission of the watch" Should any one come upon the watch overcharged with drink the penalty imposed for such offense was two guilders The rule about quarreling among persons of different nationalities is renewed, and a fine of twenty guilders is to be imposed upon any "centinel" who leaves his post "No cursing or swearing," it is ordained, " shall be allowed upon the watch, nor any gaminges at dice or cards, nor any exercise of drinkinges upon the penalty of four guilders" A list of fines is to be submitted from time to time by the Provost to the Mayor There are other rules similar in character, and almost in the same words as those already quoted

At a meeting of the Common Council held on the tenth day of July, the Recorder acquainted them that the occasion of their meeting was to consider a way most suitable for establishing a Watch in the city, " itt being thought convenient that the military officers and troopers be excused therefrom, and proposes a rate for the same on each house" It was then ordered that the Constables in the five Wards on the South side of the Fresh Water should watch by turns successively on each night and should provide for their assistance on the Watch eight persons, " the hyre for whose service shall be paid to each twelve pence per night and out of the Citty Treasury"

The succeeding year three Constables were appointed for the city Resolverd Waldron was sworn in as Constable for Harlem, October 14, 1678

That all these regulations were not made for the mere sake of form, may be inferred from a document, still extant, bearing date of December 18, 1678 It is addressed by Peter Jacobs, "Marius" or Mayor, to the Provost "Forasmuch as I am informed," says His Honor, "that several persons do refuse or neglect to watch or to pay for ye same, and that several others do not conforme themselves according to the orders sett up in the watch-house in ye Citty Hall These are therefore to charge and command you that you forthwith levy of all and every person and persons so neglecting and offending, all and every such time and times summe and summes of Money as in and by the said Orders is mentioned and expressed (yet unpaid)" Arrearages are to be collected, and if necessary, the offenders' goods are to be sold Finally a return of all the offences and the sums collected is to be made to the Mayor as soon as possible

On February 10, 1678, Mr. Jacobs signed, in company with Jacob D. Hay and Garret Van Tricht, another characteristic document, which reads thus — "This is to certify all it may concerne that ye Elders and Deacons within this government have been excused from the Citty Watch"

In 1681, A. Brockhotts being Mayor, orders for the regulation of the military watch were drawn up The most important features of the earlier regulations are repeated, and it is enacted that "the Captain or other Commission officer doe cause frequent rounds to be made about the City through all the streets and lanes, and the Grand rounds by him or themselves" if there be need. Good order is to be kept in all "publick houses," and persons are not to be allowed to tipple in those places after "tenn of the clock." The officer of the watch was empowered to open and search any houses which he may suspect, and if he "finde any loose vagrant or disorderly persons that cannot give a good account of their lives and conversacons, and of their occasions abroad or up in the night," he may cause such persons to be secured in the watch-house, and brought before the Mayor in the morning. According to this ordinance, a list of forfeits for non-performance of duty is to be made up every third night, and turned over to the Marshal, who is to make an immediate effort to collect the fines.

Detailed orders to be observed by the military watch were issued in 1682. Each company of the militia were ordered to take their guns for the watch and guard. The city was divided into three divisions, each commissioned officer taking command of his division on the watch successively. The watch was set every night by the Captain or other commissioned officer at eight o'clock. The city gates were locked by the Captain, and opened in the morning after daylight at the dismissal of the watch, and other like rules and regulations were established.

Governor Andros was superseded by Governor Dongan, who arrived in the city on August 25, 1683. He is described as having been a man of broad and intelligent views upon all subjects of general interest, and, moreover, as being an accomplished politician. He gave the Colony its first legislative assembly, which met in New York on October 17, and consisted of the Governor himself, ten councillors appointed by him, and seventeen representatives elected by the people. He very early divided the city into six wards, and the inhabitants of each were empowered to elect an Alderman annually to represent them in the City Council. Shortly after his arrival, the municipality addressed a memorial to him on the subject of the administration of civic affairs. He and his council asked for some further information on obscure points. The result was the following document, which is valuable, not only for the light it throws on the prevailing system, but also for its quaintness as an old-time colonial official document:

"An explanation of severall heads contained in ye petition lately presented to his Honour ye Governor by ye Mayor, Aldermen and Commonalty of ye Citty of New Yorke, pursuant to ye desire of the Governor and Councill.

"Humbly presented to his Honour's ffurther consideration.

"'The Towne of Harlem is a village within and belonging to this Citty, and Corporation, and ffor ye more easy administration and despatch of justice, officers have been annually appointed by ye Mayor and Aldermen to hold courts and determine matters not exceeding 40s., both att Harlem and the Bowery, and shall do ye like ffor ye future, and is entended to be one of ye six wards.

"A marshall is an under officer assistant to ye sheriff in serving writs, summoneing jurors, looking after prisners and attending ye courts, and that office and ye Cryer hath hitherto been one person.

"Peculiar laws are laws and ordinances made by ye Mayor, Aldermen and Common Councill ffor ye well and good government of this Citty and Corporation, and to extend as far as the limits thereof.

"Court of Judicature is a court to heare and determine all causes and matters whatsoever brought before them, both civill and criminall, not extending to life or member, and had jurisdiction over all ye inhabitants within the Citty and Corporation, and over ye Harbours and all Bayes, Coves, Creeks and Inlets belonging to ye same

"The whole Island being one Corporation, ye inhabitants are all members of one body and conceive no need of distinction, the Mayor, Alderman and Common Councill having ye care and charge to make all things as easy and convenient ffor ye inhabitants as possible, and will have ye same regard thereto as fformerly.

"A Watter Bailiff is an officer belonging to a corporation, and ye Sheriff of this Citty hath usually exersed ye office by serving arrests and attachm'ts in ye harbours, bayes, coves, creeks and inletts belonging to this Citty and Corporation, by warrants ffrom ye Mayor, Sheriffe, or others his superiors to him directed as Sheriffe and Watter Bayliffe, as well in civil as criminall matters what belongeth to ye Gouvernor or prerogative think not ffit to meddle with or any ways restraine"

The City Council established by Governor Dongan issued new police regulations in 1684, including a new code for the government of the City Watch Concerning this code, it is only important to note that it contained in one digest all scattered regulations previously adjusted. The only changes are changes of spelling, but as spelling in those days was very free from rule or regulation of any sort, the variations do not call for detailed record

On February 15, however, some important rules were adopted for the general guidance of the citizens Both as illustrating the life of the period, and the sort of offences that the guardians of the peace of that day had to take account of, these ordinances will repay perusal Summarized, they were as follows —

"ORDERED, that no manner of servile work be done on the Lord's day, penalty 10s, and double for each repetition

"That no "youths, maydes, or other persons" meet together in the streets or places "for sporte or play," penalty 1s., and double for each repetition.

"That no publick house sell any liquor on that day during divine service, unless to travelers

"That no Negro or Indian slaves, above the number of four, do assemble or meet together on the Lord's day, or at any other time, at any place from their master's service, within the liberties of the city

That "noe such slave doe goe armed att any time with guns, swords, clubs, staves or any kind of weapons whatever, under the penalty of being whipped at the publique whipping-post, tenn lashes, unless the master or owner of such slave will pay 6s to excuse the same"

It was further ordered—and here we have in real earnest a foreshadowing of the modern police system—that a Constable with his staff should walk about the city during time of Divine service to see that the laws were obeyed, and further, that the Constable of each ward should keep note, and make a return of all strangers who came to reside in the ward. Penalties were established for neglect of duty Besides, the "masters of publick houses" were required under penalty of ten shillings to report the names of all who came to stop at their houses, and they were forbidden to harbor any person, male or female, who was "suspected of evil name" The Constables, too, were to see that no liquor was sold during the hours of Divine service Twenty cartmen were appointed, "and no more," under certain regulations, and a public chimney-sweep was nominated, who was to go about the streets announcing his approach by crying out He was to cleanse all chimneys at the rate of one shilling or eighteen pence according to the height of the house. There were also twenty-four bakers appointed, divided into six classes, one for each working day of the week.

At a meeting of the Common Council held at the City Hall on October 13, of the same year, it was ordered "that any persons chosen to serve in any of the offices following, and shall refuse to serve, shall pay the fine hereinafter expressed, viz:

"A Constable, - - - - - £5
"An Assessor, - - - - - - 3
"A Common Councilman, - - - - - 7 10s
"An Alderman, - - - - - - 10
"The Mayor, - - - - - - 20
"The fines to be paid to the Citty Treasurers for the publique use of the Citty."

The Common Council, on July 10, 1684, convened "to consider of a way more suitable for establishing a Watch in this Citty, it being thought convenient that the military officers and troopers be excused therefrom, and proposes a rate for the same on each house." The Constables in the five wards on the South side of the Fresh water were ordered to watch by turns successively one each night and to provide for their assistance on the Watch eight persons as they should think fit to hire, for whose service each was to receive twelve pence per night out of the City Treasury.

In 1686, a new seal was granted to the city, of which the accompaning cut is a faithful reproduction. Here are depicted millsails in saltire, a bearer in chief and base, and a flour barrel, proper, on each side, surmounted by a coronet. Supporters, two Indian chiefs proper, the one on the dexter side holds a war-club in his right hand, the one on the sinister holds in his left hand a

First Seal of New York City

bow. In the dexter corner over the Indian's head is a cross patriarchal, as emblematic of the Gospel to which he is subject. On the scroll, *Sigill Civitat: Nov· Eborac*. The whole is surrounded by a wreath of laurel.

On April 22 the Charter commonly known as Dongan's Charter was granted to the City. By this instrument—which is regarded as one of the most liberal ever decreed to a colonial city—the ancient municipal privileges of the corporation were confirmed, and other important franchises were added. This document still forms the basis of the city's rights and privileges. It provided that "for the better government of the said city, liberties and precincts thereof, there shall be forever hereafter within the said city" a Mayor and Recorder, Town Clerk and six Aldermen, and six Assistants, also one Chamberlain or Treasurer, one Sheriff, one Coroner, one Clerk of the Market, one High Constable, seven Sub-Constables, and one Marshal or Sergeant-at-Mace. The Governor retained the appointment of the Mayor, Recorder, Sheriff, Coroner, High Constable, Town

Clerk, and Clerk of the Markets, in his own hands, leaving the Aldermen, assistants, and petty Constables to be chosen by the people in annual election. The Charter contained various regulations similar to those already given.

It is interesting to note that at this time the annual cost of the City Watch was about £150, while the salaries of the Clerk, Sergeant-at-Mace, and Public Whipper aggregated about £30.

Leisler, who assumed control of the Government after the removal of Governor Dongan, issued a proclamation on the fourteenth of October, 1689, in which, among other officials, he appointed the following: Nicholas Blanck, Constable for the West Ward, Edward Brinckmaster, Constable for the Dock Ward; John Thomas, Constable for the South Ward; John Ewoirts, Constable for the North Ward; Daniel Brevoort, Constable for the East Ward; Frederick Lymouse, Constable for the Out Ward; and John Brevoort, Constable for Harlem division.

As illustrative of the penal institutions of the times, it may be mentioned that on February 4, 1691, it was ordered that there be a pillory, cage, and ducking-stool forthwith built.

First Uniformed Policeman

Perhaps the first uniformed policeman was the particular bellman mentioned in the proceedings of the Common Council of July 8, 1693, who, it was ordered by the Mayor, should be provided with "a coat of ye citty livery, with a badge of ye citty arms, shoes and stockings, and charge itt to ye account of the citty." It was also ordered "that the Treasurer pay to Mr. Smith, Thirty-six shillings to buy wood for the watch." The Captains of the Watch, too, were instructed to "disburse money for candles," and bring in their accounts quarterly to receive orders on the Treasurer. The Overseers made a report recommending that £50 be raised for furnishing the "Night Guard of the City" with fire and candles for a year. The suggestion was approved, and ordered to be carried out. But the next year the Captains had to find supplies again, for the Council ordered the Mayor to draw a warrant on the Treasurer for the payment to each Captain of the Watch seven pounds, fourteen shillings and nine pence, current money of the Province, "for supplying ye Night Guard of this City with fire and candles until the first day of August last, and that they be paid out of the Tax raised to Defray the same." Whatever fell short in the tax, the Treasurer was authorized to make good out of ordinary revenue.

For the enforcement of the law and the punishment of offenders there had already been erected (1693) a pillory, cage, whipping-post and ducking-stool, on the wharf in front of the City Hall. Hither were brought all vagrants, slanderers, pilferers, and truant children, to be exposed to the public gaze, and to receive such punishment as their offences might warrant. It may be fully understood that such punishments were meted out with no lenient hand.

Subsequently it was ordered that payment be made to Captain Brandt Schuyler, Captain Ebenezer Willson, Captain John Marrott, Captain John De Bruyer, Captain John De Royster, Captain John Kip, and Captain John Tudor, "each ye sum of nine pounds, current money, of New York, itt being money by them disbursed for fire-wood and candles for ye Night Guards," from first August, 1696, to first August, 1697.

There was a complete revolution in the system of public protection at this time. This was brought about by an order of his excellency the Governor, abolishing the city militia from duty as Night Guards, (a Military Watch) provided the officers or Magistrates appointed a bellman and other Civil Watch, to go round the city in the night time to prevent irregularities, etc. Therefore it was ordered by the board that four sober, honest men be appointed to keep watch in the City every night until the twenty-fifth of March following, and that they hourly go through the several Wards of the City during the said time, in order to prevent irregularities, fire, etc. It was further resolved that the persons so appointed Bellmen and Watchmen should give security in the sum of £500 that they would well and truly execute the said offices according to such directions and regulations as should be given them by the Mayor.

On October 17, 1698, the Mayor was again admonished to appoint four "good and honest householders," to watch from 9 P. M. to sunrise, until March 25 following. The Mayor announced his appointments on November 2 following. The four worthies were paid £60 a year each. They were supposed to make a round every hour, and to "proclaim the season of the weather and the hour of the night." If they met any disturbers of the peace, or persons lurking about other people's houses, they were to secure such persons until next morning, "that they may be examined by the Mayor or some of the Magistrates, and dealt with as the law directs." The Constables were at the same time ordered to give all the aid they could to the Watchmen. The Mayor, on November 2, appointed three bellmen at a salary of $60 a year each.

This action was repeated up to October 26, 1700, when the Mayor was ordered to appoint a Constables' Watch, to consist of a Constable and twelve able men, to be the Watch of the city, "to take care, and keep, and preserve the peace, etc., and that the Constables of each ward do take their guns, and that the High Constable take care that the said Watch be duly set and kept, and that the Mayor provide fire and wood for the same."

Two years subsequently it was ordered that all persons summoned to do duty on the Constables' Watch who should neglect or refuse to serve, for every such offence should forfeit the sum of six shillings.

The old "Stadt Huys" at Coenties Slip had become so dilapidated that the Mayor and Corporation—finding it impossible to meet there any longer—were compelled to remove to the house of George Reparreck, next door, it was therefore resolved to sell this rickety structure and to build a new Stadt Huys.

The principal event, it is averred, which settled the character of Wall Street as the centre of interest in the city, and which brought about it the leading men of business and professional life, was the erection (1699) of the City Hall, opposite Broad Street, which building became afterward the Capitol of the United

States, and the site of which is still in use for public purposes. The upper end of Broad Street was considerably elevated, and there was no continuation of the Street beyond the City wall (Wall Street), although a lane had been marked out on the present line of Nassau Street, which, being afterwards improved, was designated as "the street that runs by the pie-woman's." The design of the proposed building, by James Evetts, architect, was submitted in 1698, and the plan was approved. The foundation was laid in the fall of 1699, and the building was finished in the following year. The City Hall remained in use for the objects for which it was erected for about a century, and was demolished in 1812, when the present City Hall was built. It is thus described. "The first floor was entered by a flight of steps in front, which led into a corridor more than half the building in width, extending through to the rear. On the west side of this hall there was a room in the front appropriated to the fire engine of the City, and a dungeon in the rear for criminals. On the opposite side was a branch of the

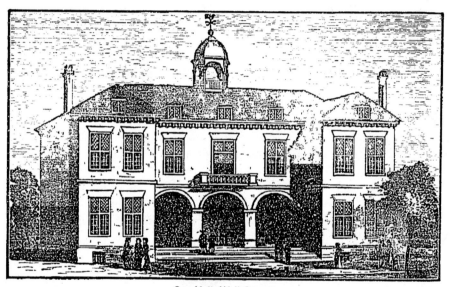

City Hall, Wall Street.

hall opening into the keeper's room in the rear, and in front into a stairway to the second story. This story was occupied in the centre above the hall by the court room, having on the east side—above the engine-house—the jury-room. The opposite side was mostly taken up by the stairway, except the Common Council room, which was in the northeast corner. The garret was used as the debtor's prison." As one of the adjuncts of the seat of justice, a cage, pillory and stocks were set up in the public thoroughfare on the opposite side of the street. After the revolutionary war this building received additional historic interest as the Capitol of the nation and the first place of meeting of the Congress of 1789.

In 1702 a proclamation was made, warning all persons to do duty on the Constables' Watch, under penalty of six shillings fine for every instance of negligence. On October 26, of this year, Aldermen Corbett and Smith and Messrs. Laroux and Cooper were appointed to agree with four or five "able cittizens to be the Watch and bellmen of this Citty to April 1, following." This committee reported on December 1, as follows:

"Pursuant to an order of the Common Council, made the 26th day of this Instant Month of October, we have agreed with Robert Drummond, Richard Yearsley, Edmund Thomas, and John Vanderbeeck, four able-bodied Cittizens of this Citty to be the Watch and Bellmen of this Citty from the 1st of November next ensuing until the 1st day of April, then next following, which service they are duly and diligently to attend by going every hour in the night through the severall streets of this Citty and publishing the time of night, and also to apprehend all disturbers of the peace, felons, &c, also to take care that no damage be done in the Citty by fire or any other casualties as much as in them lies; for which service they are to have the sum of forty-four pounds, current money of New York, six pounds whereof to be paid them in six weeks, and the remainder at the expiration of the time; and that a Lanthorn, Bell, and hour-glass be provided them att the Citty's charge."

The method of procedure in case of fire is worth recording. The Watchman who discovered it gave the alarm with his rattle, and knocked at the doors of the houses as he sped past, shouting to the occupants to throw out their buckets. The ringing of the bell at the fort spread the alarm further. It may be inferred that these methods made it lively for the resident population whenever a fire broke out after bedtime. When the buckets were thrown out they were picked up by whoever was the first to pass on the way to the fire. It was the custom for nearly every householder to render assistance to extinguish fires, whether by night or day. When they were extinguished, the buckets were taken in a wagon to the City Hall, where they were restored to their owners.

A new duty was imposed on the Constables of the several wards. This was to visit every house, and see whether the inhabitants kept the number of fire buckets required by law. Those who had not the proper number were to be warned to obtain them under pain of prosecution. It was the duty of the Aldermen to instruct the Constables in their several wards to "search for all inmates of the houses" they visited, "and to return the names thereof to the Mayor or Alderman." The Constables were required to "make a presentment of all such persons as shall neglect or refuse to clean their streets, and of all such as in any way break the Holy Sabbath, or commit other misdemeanors." The Aldermen were called upon to see that the Constables did this duty, and were to present the names of delinquents to the Mayor or Court of Quarter Sessions for punishment. A resolution was also adopted, providing for the erection of a cage, whipping-post, pillory, and stocks before the City Hall, the expense to be defrayed "out of the surplusage of the three hundred pounds raised in this City, which is not yet appropriated."

The annual expenditure in 1710 was £277 4s. Among the items of expenditures were Bellmen's salaries, £36, lanterns and hour glasses, £3; and fire and candles for Constables, £3.

The old records of this time abound in items characteristic of the manners and ideas of the time, and the condition of the city. Thus we find that in 1710 the total income of the city was £294 7s. 6d., and the annual expenditure £277 4s. Among the items making up the latter total were: Bellmen's salaries, £36, lanterns and hour-glasses, £3, and candles for the Constable's Watch, £3. The streets were still lit after the primitive fashion adopted in the end of the preceding century (1697), a lantern being set up on a pole in front of every seventh house, the inhabitants of the other six contributing to the cost of maintenance

In 1712 several fires of supposed incendiary origin took place in New York, and great alarm prevailed among the inhabitants. Many arrests were made, and nineteen negroes and one white man were executed.

The ideas which prevailed at this period regarding the treatment of criminals were neither enlightened nor humane. The modes of punishment inflicted arrest the eye with wonder. A few instances must suffice.

"Clause, Robin, Quaco and Sam, negro slaves," say the old records, "were convicted in this year of the murder of Adiran Hoghlandt, in the eleventh year of the reign of our Sovereign Lady Anne," and sentenced in the following terms.

"It is considered by the Court that the aforesaid Clause be broke Alive upon a Wheel, and so to continue languishing until he be dead; and his head and Quar-

First Execution in New York. (The Commons. City Hall Park.)

ters to be at the Queen's disposal. That the aforesaid Robin be hung up in chains alive, and so to continue without any sustenance, until he be dead. That the aforesaid Quaco be burnt with fire until he be dead and consumed. And that the aforesaid Sam be hanged by the neck until he be dead."

Mars, a negro slave was tried in 1708 "att a Court of General Sessions of the Peace at the City Hall on the first Tuesday in May, in the sixth year of the reign of our Sovereign Lady Anne." The record of the court proceedings says

"Itt is presented that a negro man, commonly called Mars, a slave of Jacob Rognier of the City of New York, with force and arms, in and upon Ephraim Pierson, then Constable of the Watch of the said City of New York, did make an assault, and did beat, wound, with evil intent, so that his life he did despair, and other harms to him did, to the grevious damage of the said Ephraim Pierson. * * * * *

Therefore it is considered by the Court that the said negro, Mars, on the 6th day of August aforesaid, in the year aforesaid, between the hours of ten and twelve in the forenoon of the same day, be stripped from the middle upwards, and tyed to the tail of a cart, at the City Hall aforesaid, and be drawn from thence to the Broadway in the said city, and from thence to the Custom House, thence to Wall Street, and from thence to the City Hall again, and that he be whipped upon the naked back ten lashes att the Corner of Every street he shall pass, and that he afterwards be discharged from his Imprisonment, pay his fees, &c."

The punishment of whipping was more generally inflicted at the whipping-post than in the manner here indicated, and that instrument of correction had been removed in 1710 from Coenties Slip to Broad Street near the City Hall

Another characteristic sentence was imposed in 1712 by "a Court held for the tryal of Negro and Indian Slaves, at the Citty Hall of the City of New York, on Tuesday the 15th of April" Tom, the slave of Nicholas Rosevelt, was the culprit in this case He was sentenced to be "carryed from hence to the place whence he came, and from thence to the place of execution; and there to be burned with a slow fire, that he may Continue in Torment for Eight or ten hours, and continue burning in the said fire until he be dead, and Consumed to ashes"

Mrs Johanna Christiana Young, and another female, her associate from Philadelphia, "being found guilty of grand larceny, at the Mayor's Court, are to be set on two chairs exalted on a cart, with their heads and faces uncovered, and to be carted from the City Hall to that part of Broadway near the old English church, from thence down Maiden Lane, then down the Fly to the White Hall, thence to the church aforesaid, and then to the whipping-post, where each of them is to receive thirty-nine lashes, to remain in jail for one week, and then to depart the city"

Whipping-Post.

Nor are these cases of an exceptional character; such sentences were common enough in those days

Something by way of explanation of the instruments and methods by which criminals were punished, may be mentioned at this part of our narrative, supplimentary to what has already been said on the same subject The early annals of New York, as we have seen, make frequent mention of these instruments of torture. They were, in fact, a part (and by no means an insignificant part) of the correctional institutions of the city Mention has been made of the cage, stocks, pillory, whipping-post and ducking-stool—all parts of the established plan "to hold the wicked and to punish guilt." They stood in front of the City Hall, and were kept in good repair That they were not there for any idle show we have evidence in abundance. The first instruments of the kind mentioned, as has been pointed out, stood in front of the old City Hall, at Coenties Slip. When the new City Hall was built at the head of Broad Street, on Wall Street, these appliances were removed thither They were, some ten years later (about 1710), removed to the upper end of Broad Street, a little below the City Hall. The law was no respecter of sex, and females were subjected to this form of punishment quite frequently, the following being by no means an exceptional case: "A woman was whipped at the whipping-post, and afforded much amusement to the spectators by her resistance." The extract is taken from a newspaper of the time. Also: "James Gain, pursuant to sentence, stood in the pillory, near the City Hall, and was most severely pelted by great numbers of the spectators, a lad was also branded in the hand." These modes of punishment (barbarous in the extreme) were derived from Holland and England, which is also true of the forms of law, the judiciary systems, and all that pertained to the administration of justice. The public whipper, in early times, was a familiar functionary. In 1713 Richard Cooper was appointed to this office, at a salary of £5. The practice of whipping and the appliances of the whipping-post were introduced into all the American colonies. In all the New England towns the whipping-post was the recognized adjunct of the courts, and flagellation was constantly resorted to for all forms of offences, whether religious, social or political. In the State of Delaware the knout survives, and the whipping-post still stands a silent but most suggestive satire upon nineteenth century civilization.

In 1730 the celebrated Montgomerie Charter was granted to the city. This is the second in the series of documents on which the municipal rights still rest. It ordained that there should forever be "one Mayor, one Recorder, seven Aldermen, seven assistants, one Sheriff, one Coroner, one Common Clerk, one Chamberlain, one High Constable, sixteen Assessors, seven Collectors, sixteen Constables, and one Marshal," to compose the City Government. The Charter appointed Edmund Peers, High Constable, John Scott, Constable for the South Ward, Christopher Nicholson, Constable for the Dock Ward, Timothy Bontecon, Constable for the North Ward; John Abrahamson, Constable for the East Ward, and Arent Bussing, Constable for the Harlem Division of the Out Ward.

The instrument also provided that within forty days after date of its publication, the freemen of the city should assemble, and by a plurality of voices, choose from the inhabitants of the several wards one additional Constable for each ward, except the Out Ward, which was to have three more, two for the Bowery Division, and one more for Harlem. It was further ordered that on the festival of St. Michael, the Archangel, every year, the freeholders of the several wards should meet, as appointed by the Aldermen, and elect for each ward, except the Out Ward, one Alderman, one Assistant, two Assessors, two Collectors, and four Constables. The Mayor, on the same day, it was arranged, should appoint a High Constable. The appointment of the Mayor himself, and of the Sheriff and Coroner, still rested with the Governor and his Council.

During the twenty years subsequent to the granting of Montgomerie's Charter, the city advanced considerably in its municipal affairs. A poor-house and watch-houses were built, fire engines were imported, and a Fire Department was permanently established.

Those who find fault with the alleged unsanitary condition of our thoroughfares, should feel comforted upon perusal of this presentment by the Grand Jury, a reduced *fac-simile* of the original.

The Jurors for our Sovereign Lord the King for the City & County of New York.

Most humbly Certifie to This Honourable Court

That in Maiden Lane there is a very large Dunghill & a Puddle of standing Water which is very Offensive.

That in the Wall Street near the City Hall is another very large Dunghill and Puddle of standing Water

That in King Street there is a Dunghill & Standing Water

That near the Corner of the Fort is a very large Dunghill, All which are very Offensive and will be more So if not Removed before the Warm Weather

To Prevent which we are humbly of Opinion that the severall Owners of those Lotts which are not Fenced in should be Obliged to Fence in their Lotts and Pave the Streets before them.

That the Street in which is the Jews Synagogue is very Offensive to the Inhabitants near the said Street by the filth and Dirt lying in it.

That there is an Old House in Queen Street next to Jacob Bratt in Danger of Falling into the Street

That Severall of the Streets in this City want paveing and are Generally very Dirty   Vera Copia

It was resolved (July 9, 1731), "to build a watch-house forthwith," on the south side of the cage in Broad Street, and a committee of Aldermen was appointed to effect the necessary preliminary arrangements. On the twenty-sixth of the following month this committee submitted their report, which was adopted. Their report set forth that the said watch-house "ought to be twenty-eight foot long and eighteen foot broad, with two rooms, one of them eighteen foot long, and the other ten foot, with a fire-place in each room, with two doors to the southeast corner thereof and to the south, and the other to the east side of the said corner, with three lights in the large room, and one small ditto in the small room."

First Main Watch-house, Wall and Broad Streets

The entire expense of which, according to computation, was to amount to about £60. This watch-house stood until 1789, when it became so dilapidated that its removal became necessary, and a new one was erected.

Robert Crannoll, Marshal of the city, was appointed Supervisor of the Watch on December 14, 1731. He was required to perform all the duties of that office, to provide fire and candle for the Watch, to keep the key of the watch-house, to keep the watch-house clean, and take care that the chimney thereof be swept and cleaned as often as there should be occasion. For which services he was allowed a salary of £20 per annum.

At a meeting of the Common Council, held on the same date, a law remodeling the system of night watching was three times read and approved. It was then ordered that "the same be forthwith printed and published, and the same, after the ringing of three bells, was published accordingly." This law opened with a long preamble, setting forth that all inhabitants of the city, "south of Fresh Water" whether "freemen of the city" or mere residents, provided they were physically able, ought by reason of their habitation to keep watch for the "preservation of the King's peace, and for the arresting and apprehending of all night-walkers, malefactors, and suspected persons, which shall be found passing, wandering and misbehaving themselves." The preamble further set forth that the functions of a Constable extended not only to the ward in which he was appointed, but also to the whole city. It was declared too, that "there is now, and of late years hath been, by reason of great numbers of people privately coming into the said city from all parts, some whereof are suspected to be convict felons, transported from Great Brittain " For this reason it was set forth that the need for a strong and efficient watch was very great.

After this formidable opening, the "Mayor, Recorder, and Aldermen assembled," went on to ordain that each one of the Constables of the six wards on the south side of Fresh Water, in turn, together with eight able-bodied Watchmen (or as many more as the Mayor and three Aldermen might from time to time direct), should keep watch every night at the public watch-house, or such other point as might be selected, from April 1 until Michaelmas Day, from nine o'clock in the evening until four o'clock in the morning; and from Michaelmas Day to April 1, from eight o'clock in the evening until six o'clock in the morning It appears that the Aldermen and assistants had lately taken "an exact survey" of the six wards, and made a list of all the inhabitants and housekeepers in them, who were able to watch or find Watchmen. From this it appeared that some of the wards were much larger than others, and ought therefore to furnish a greater number of men to the Watch In order to equalize the burden, therefore, it was ordained that all the citizens dwelling south of Fresh Water should watch according to the following arrangement·

Inhabitants of the East Ward for seventeen nights, beginning December 2.

The inhabitants of the Dock Ward next in order for twelve nights, from December 19; and when it came to their turn again, for thirteen nights

The inhabitants of the North Ward for twelve nights, from and including December 31

The inhabitants of the South Ward for ten nights, beginning January 12

The inhabitants of the West Ward for eight nights, from January 22 inclusive to the end of the month.

The inhabitants of the Montgomerie Ward for eight nights, from January 30 to February 7.

When all had performed duty in this manner, the East Ward was to begin again, and so on The Alderman and Assistant of each ward were to detail the Constables in their turn to "have the rule, care, and oversight of the Watch," and were also to choose from among the inhabitants the necessary number to watch with the Constable They were instructed to "begin at one certain place' in detailing the citizens, and "proceed and go forwards in an orderly manner," until the whole ward had watched, whereupon they were to begin again Citizens who did not choose to take their regular turns were obliged to find substitutes.

The Constable whose turn it was had to give the citizens a day's notice of their tour of duty, waiting on the Alderman or Assistant in advance to obtain the list of names The notice of watch duty was either to be personal, or else in writing, left at the house of the person to be notified. A list of these persons was then to be delivered to the Constable whose turn it was to command the Watch "And if any person," the ordinance proceeds, "appointed and warned to watch or to find an able and fit person to watch in his, her, (woman's rights seem to have been practically recognized, as she was eligible to do service on the Watch or find a substitute,) or their stead and room, as aforesaid, make default in not watching and performing the duty of a Watchman as aforesaid, or being drunk on the said Watch, leaving the Watch before the time of watching be expired, or otherwise misbehaving, (it is ordered) that then every such person so refusing, leaving the Watch, misbehaving himself, or making default as aforesaid, and not having just and reasonable cause for such his default as shall be allowed of by the Mayor of the said city or the Alderman of that ward for the time being, shall forfeit and pay for every such default the sum of eight shillings, current money, aforesaid "

The city fathers further provided for the appointment of a Supervisor of the Watch "to take care and oversee that the Watch and watches within the said city henceforth be duly kept," or else that the forfeits be paid. Boys, apprentices, or servants, were not to be permitted to serve on the Watch, but only "able and sober men of good reputation" A long paragraph is devoted to defining the duties of the Supervisor. It is a mere amplification of the phrase that he is to see the Watch "duly kept"

At the same meeting at which this enactment was made Mr. Robert Crannell was appointed Marshal of the City, and the Mayor issued his warrant to Edward Brewen, the Public Whipper, for the sum of £2 for a quarter year's salary

The system thus elaborated does not appear to have survived long, for, in 1734, an ordinance went into operation providing that twelve persons, including two Constables, should be hired to be the City Watch during the winter. One of the Constables was to be on duty with five men every alternate night, and the Watch was to be called the Constable's Watch, and was to be at the orders of the Mayor or other officials. The corporation supplied fire and light, and paid each man £5,10s. for service from December 4 to May 1 following, each of the Constables "for their encouragement," receiving 20s. additional.

In 1735 six Watchmen were appointed to serve for two months. At a meeting of the Common Council, held on October 21, 1735, Paul Richard being Mayor, it was agreed to appeal to the General Assembly to levy £300 on the real and personal estate of the city to defray the expense

In October, 1738, twelve Watchmen were appointed to serve till the first of May, "who, together with the Constables in their turns, are to be the Constable and Night-watch." The number was reduced in the next year to three. In October, 1741, the deputy clerk of the Board of Aldermen brought in a draft of a bill for a Night-watch, which was ordered to be carried to the General Assembly.

In 1740 occurred that celebrated scare known in history as the Negro Plot.

Whether any conspiracy existed against the lives and property of the colonists is a question that can never be set at rest now. There can be no doubt, however, that several unfortunates suffered death, just as if they had been actual conspirators, and that the entire community was stricken with terror at the prospect of pillage and assassination. One result of the affair was the appointment in 1741 of thirty-six night watchmen, including three overseers. They were divided into three reliefs of eleven men each, and these took regular turns in guarding the city. The hours of duty were from an hour after sunset to the beating of the reveille next morning. The expense of this Watch was defrayed from a tax of £5741 2s., which the Municipality was authorized to raise by a special Act of the General Assembly.

About the year 1714 the paupers were beginning to be both numerous and troublesome, and it was proposed, instead of maintaining them by weekly pittances, as had hitherto been done, to provide a house where they could be cared for at the public expense, and be made to contribute somewhat towards their livelihood. This scheme, however, was not carried into effect until 1734, when a commodious house was erected on the commons, in the rear of the present City Hall, and on the site of the future "old Alms House." The building was forty-six feet long, twenty-four feet wide, and two stories high, with a cellar; and was furnished with implements of labor for the use of the inmates. The Churchwardens were appointed as Overseers of the Poor, and all paupers were required to work under penalty of receiving "moderate" correction. As the building was also a house of correction it was used as a sort of calaboose for unruly slaves, their masters having permission to send them thither for punishment.

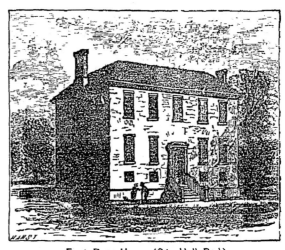

First Poor House (City Hall Park)

A number of police regulations were adopted in August, 1742. One of these ordered that twelve men, with a Constable, constantly watch every Sunday "from sunrise to sunset, and that such Watch be continued in turn as the Night-watch are." Another provided that on every Sunday morning from daylight to the time of the setting of the military guard, and from five o'clock P.M.—when the guard was dismissed—until the evening Watch came on, means be adopted "to prevent the irregularities lately so much practiced by negroes, children, and others on the Sabbath day." The method was for one Alderman, one petty Constable, and four firemen to walk around the city during the hours indicated, while on alternate Sundays the Assistant Alderman, the High Constable or Marshal, one petty Constable, and three firemen should serve.

The rules of 1741 regarding the Night-watch were in effect renewed, the ground being stated that of recent years great numbers of convicts had come into the city, and it was necessary to provide against "insurrections and the plots of slaves." Constables who failed in their duty were to be fined ten shillings; no boys or apprentices were to be allowed on the Watch; and the Constable in charge was to send out the first rounds precisely an hour after sunset, and immediately on the return of the first rounds should send out another. The rounds consisted of four Watchmen, and their duty was to walk the streets, lanes, wharves, and alleys, and they were not to return to the watch-house in less than an hour, except upon extraordinary occasions. Upon the return of the second rounds, the Constable in charge was obliged to go out himself with the remaining three Watchmen, and do just as his predecessors. The process was then repeated, and in the morning the Constable called the roll to see that all his men had done full duty. The actual expense of the Watch department was thereby increased from about £50 to £448.

In this year, Robert Bowne, a Quaker, being elected Constable for Montgomerie Ward, refused to serve, on the ground that Quakers were, by law, exempt from such duty. The case being carried to the Chief Justice it was decided in favor of the Quaker, and a new election was therefore ordered.

In 1746 the Recorder proposed to the Common Council, on the part of a joint committee of the Assembly and Council that the latter body should have a small Watch-house built near the Powder House. The committee proposed to supply Watchmen until a proper magazine could be erected within the stockades. This proposal was approved by the Common Council, and the committee charged with enlarging the Poor House was intrusted to build the Watch-house. The military watch that the troublous times rendered needful was a sore burden to the New Yorkers.

On June 3, 1747, a committee of five Aldermen were appointed to prepare a draft of an address and petition to his Excellency, the Governor, to ease the city of the burden of keeping a military watch. This committee, under instructions, reported the following day.

The petition represented that many of the inhabitants "have three or four sons and as many servants or apprentices, who are obliged to watch in their turns, the consequence of which is a loss of about forty shillings to every such inhabitant." The petition concludes by asking his Excellency to order down "one of the Independent Companies now at Albany, or one of the companies of the new levies now also there, or such part of either of them."

The Common Council, it is quite plain from the records, had an inordinate love of detail. Instances of this have been seen already; another is to be found in the minutes of December 20, 1750. The manner in which the six Watchmen were ordered to perform their rounds is as follows. Two of them were to go out first, one of them to carry a bell, and the other his staff. The bell was to be rung "in the most public places," and the time of night was to be proclaimed. The other four Watchmen were to set out soon after the first two, and take a different route, all meeting together at places appointed by the person having charge of the Watch.

These Watchmen, or Bellmen as they were sometimes called, or among the Dutch, "Kloppermannen," carried with them a kind of a bell, a lantern, and an hour-glass. At every house, with loud clattering of their "Klopper," they cried out "the time of the night, and the season of the weather." They were employed only during the winter time, or from first of November to the twenty-fifth of March, and received £15 each. They furnished their own fire and light. The expense of the Watch varied from £60 to £36, or £9 per man, during the winter season. The average expense from the year 1700 to 1740 was £44 per annum.

It is with a sigh of profound relief that one turns to consider the nocturnal habits of "The Finest" after reading the following account of the proceedings of the Watch in bygone days: "At the ringing of the bell of the Fort"—it seems as if our forefathers could do nothing without ringing a bell—"at nine o'clock, a Sergeant-Major, with his halberd, proceeded, followed by the Watch, to each of the city gates, which he locked for the night. He then stationed each man at his particular post, and to secure the vigilant discharge of his duty, each Watchman was required to go, once every hour, through that part of the city which was allotted to him, and with a bell to proclaim the time of the night and the state of the weather—a regulation which, no doubt, secured a vigilant discharge of the Watchman's duty. But it must have been disturbing to all but sound sleepers to have had their slumbers broken at regular intervals by the loud ringing of a bell, and a hoarse voice announcing such information as, "Past two o'clock, and a dark and cloudy morning."

Bellmen Going their Rounds.

The English Watchman, in no essential particular, differed from his Dutch predecessor. Both went about performing their duties in the most lugubrious fashion—carrying their bells, hour-glasses, lanterns and staffs—like some protean character of the stage who is equipped to represent Diogenes, the Man with the Scythe, a grave digger and a dustman.

The practice of the Watch calling out the time of night at regular intervals was borrowed from Germany, where, in the burghs or towns, it was at first the custom to station guardians of the night in the steeples of churches or other elevated places; and, as a security against their going to sleep, to require them every hour to proclaim the hour of the night. When this was changed to a regular patroling of the streets, the custom of calling the hour was continued probably for the same reason. The German Watchman, who, like the generality of his countrymen, was of a musical turn of mind, accompanied the calling of the time of the night by singing a verse of a religious song, inculcating some precept of

Christian doctrine, the words being so arranged or varied as to be applicable to a particular time of the night. Following is a translation of a verse of one of these Watchman's songs:

> "Hark ye, neighbors, and hear me tell
> Ten now strikes on the belfry bell,
> Ten were the holy commandments given
> To man below, by God in heaven
> Human watch from harm can't ward us,
> Yet God will watch and guide and guard us.
> May He, through his heavenly might,
> Give us all a blessed night"

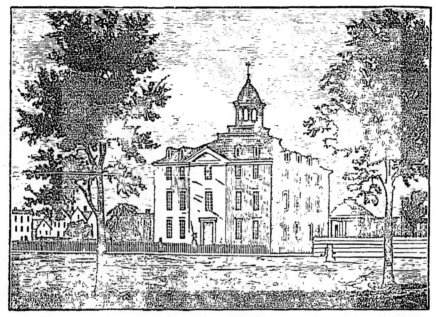

Old Jail (City Hall Park).

The old Jail was built in 1758 on what was then known as "the fields," the City Hall Park of the present day. It was a small stone building, nearly square, three stories in height, having its main entrance on the south side. The old Jail continued to be the prison of the city until 1775, when the new Bridewell was erected, and on the occupation of the city by the British they were both turned into military prisons. The Jail was then known as the "Prevost," or "Prevo," and became famous under the control of Captain William Cunningham, Provost Marshal, who, by the appointment of General Gage, was at the head of the police of the city.

In 1758 there was another change of system, back to the Citizens' Watch. Under the new rules, the inhabitants of the West Ward were to do duty for nine nights successively, those of the South Ward for five nights, of the Dock Ward for five nights; of the East Ward for ten nights; of the North Ward for eight nights; and of the Montgomerie Ward for eleven nights. When all had watched, they were to begin over again, and so on In 1761, however, we find once more a return to paid watchers, for on December 28, Mr Stoutenburgh, presumably a member of the Common Council, was authorized by that body to advertise for men to "light the lamps speedily to be erected," and to watch the city. Again, in 1762, a committee was appointed to arrange terms with persons who offered their services as Watchmen, and, later in the same year, a committee was appointed to prepare estimates of the expense of watching and lighting lamps during the ensuing year.

By act of assembly, authority was given to the corporation, in 1761, to place public lamps in the streets, which became a source of considerable expense to the city The cost after the system became established, say for the second year, 1763, was found to be about £200 per annum Four years subsequently the expense of lighting and watching the city had increased to £1,400 per annum

The year 1764 was marked in the police annals by the erection of a new pillory with a large wooden cage behind it, between the new Jail (the present Hall of Records) and the Work-house, which occupied the site of the present City Hall. The cage was for the punishment of disorderly boys who "publically" broke the Sabbath

The system showed signs of considerable progress and development about this time In 1767 the Mayor was requested by the Common Council to apply to the General Assembly for power to raise £1.400 for defraying the expenses of maintaining Watchmen, and of lighting and supplying the lamps

A similar application was made in 1772 for leave to bring in a bill for raising the sum of £1,800 to defray the expense attending the public lamps and watching the city In July, 1773, a resolution was passed, allowing the Marshals and Constables two shillings for every vagrant they arrested In 1774, sixteen men were employed to watch and to light the street lamps every night Their annual salary was fixed at £32. There were also employed eight Watchmen, to do duty on alternate nights, receiving a salary of £16 per annum each This Watch was set from March 10 to September 10 at nine o'clock P M., and remained on duty to four o'clock next morning. During the other six months the hours were from ten in the evening to six the next morning

In June, 1775, the committee appointed to draw up some necessary orders and regulations respecting the City Watch, presented the same, which were approved, and it was ordered that copies be delivered to the Captains of the Watch for their guidance These orders and regulations are not inserted in the record The Watchmen, on May 1, 1776, were reduced in number to a Captain and three men

The old Bridewell formerly stood in City Hall Park, between the City Hall and Broadway It was erected in 1775, and was demolished in 1838. The corner stone was laid with due ceremony by Mayor Hicks The building was built of dark grey stone, two stories high, besides the basement, with a pediment in the front and in the rear, which were carried up a story higher. The centre apartments were allotted to the keeper and his deputies. On the first floor on the right, there was an apartment called the Long Room, and on the left a similar apartment ; on the second floor there were two wards, the one called the Upper Hall, and the other the Chain Room. The upper hall was appropriated to the higher class of convicts

The old Bridewell derives its principal interest from its being used by the British, during the Revolution, as a place of confinement of American soldiers who were so unfortunate as to be taken prisoners Here, as in all other places used for that purpose in this city, cruelty, misery, and starvation agonized its helpless victims

The first Bridewell in New York was built as early as 1734, and it continued to be occupied for many years as a house of correction

The Old Bridewell (City Hall Park)

The City Hospital, between Duane and Anthony Streets, upon the west side of Broadway, was commenced in the year 1771, and completed before the war of Independence, when it was converted into a barrack for the reception of troops It was not until January 3, 1791, that it was opened for the admission of patients This hospital was the scene of "the Doctor's riot" The public mind had been excited over rumors that the cemeteries had been rifled of dead bodies by the students for anatomical subjects. On Sunday morning, April 13, 1788, a mischievous boy had climbed on a ladder to one of the hospital windows, and his curiosity to know what was going on inside was gratified by having an arm flourished in his face The arm aforesaid was wielded by a student, but the member was not his own—it was part of a subject on the dissecting table The boy, aghast with horror, ran home and spread the news that the students were cutting up dead bodies The hospital was soon surrounded by an infuriated mob, who burst in the doors. The doctors took refuge in the jail, where they were with difficulty protected. The mob, bent on wreaking vengeance on all the doctors in the city, started for the house of Dr. Cochrane, which they ransacked from cellar to garret in search of the doctor and anatomical subjects The house of Sir John Temple narrowly escaped destruction. Noticing the name, the mob mistook "Sir John" for surgeon, and that titled personage came near being reduced to the mutilated condition of one of the surgeons' dissecting subjects. While endeavoring to disperse the mob, Secretary Jay and Baron Steuben were severely wounded Mayor Duane and Governor Clinton then gave the order to the military to fire, and five persons were killed and seven or eight badly wounded The crowd then fled.

We have now arrived at the troublous period of the Revolution, when the military officers usurped all the functions of government, and the citizens lay at the mercy of an unscrupulous soldiery Everything was then done in compliance with orders from the

City Hospital (Scene of the Doctor's Riot).

commanders of the British troops, and the interests of the King were the foremost consideration.

The defeat of the Patriot army in the Battle of Long Island on August 27, 1776, led to the occupation of the city by the British a fortnight later Very shortly after, the whole western side of the city from Bowling Green to the present line of Vesey Street was swept by fire, Trinity Church being among the edifices destroyed. Immediately after this disaster, Major-General James Robertson, one of the British commanders, issued the proclamation of which the following is a literal copy.

"Whereas, there is ground to believe that the Rebels, not satisfied with the Destruction of Part of the City, entertain Designs of burning the Rest ; And it is thought that a Watch to inspect all Parts of the City, to apprehend Incendiaries, and to stifle Fires before they rise to a dangerous Height, might be a necessary and proper means to prevent such a calamity ; Many of the principal Inhabitants have applied to me to form such a Watch, and have all offered to watch in person

I do therefore require and direct That all Persons may take a Part in this Matter, and turn out to Watch when called for. A sense of duty and Interest will lead all good Subjects and Citizens cheerfully to give their Attendance ; And any who refuse to take Part in preserving the City will be judged unworthy to inhabit it. I have appointed Persons to summon and Superintend the Watch of each Ward, and the number of Men to be given by each is subjoined.
Signed

JAMES ROBERTSON,

Major-General, Commander in New York.

The Out Ward to furnish fourteen men each night. Montgomerie Ward to furnish fifteen men each night. North Ward to furnish fifteen men each night. These to meet at the Guard Room near Cuyler's Sugar House.

West Ward to furnish six men each night. South Ward to furnish four men each night. Dock Ward to furnish ten men each night. East Ward to furnish sixteen men each night. These to meet at the Guard House in Hanover Square.

It will be noticed that the foreign troops were more exigent than the regular City government had ever been. It is doubtful, however, if they were as well or as cheerfully served. The following year (1777), Major-General Robert Pigot commanding in the city, issued a supplementary proclamation, as follows :

Whereas, by a Proclamation issued by Major-General James Robertson, who lately commanded in New York, a City Watch was established, and all Persons, Inhabitants of said City, were thereby ordered to take their turn in Watching, when called on for that purpose

And Whereas, the Necessity of Keeping up the said Watch, and a punctual attendance thereto, must appear evident to every good Citizen ; and it having been represented unto me, that several Persons, Inhabitants of this City, altho' duly warned to take their Turn in Watching, have, notwithstanding, either neglected or refused to give their Attendance .

I have, therefore, thought fit to issue this Proclamation, hereby requiring all Persons, residing in the City of New York, to take a part in a Matter, so necessary for the Preservation of this City, hereby informing all such Persons as refuse or neglect to give their attendance, that they will be judged unworthy Inhabitants, and will be ordered to remove accordingly And I do hereby require the Persons heretofore appointed to Superintend the said Watch that they make return to me of all persons who shall hereafter refuse or neglect to watch when called upon for that purpose in order that they may be dealt with accordingly.

Given under my hand at New York on the twenty-fourth day of February, in the seventeenth year of His Majesty's reign, 1777.

R. T. PIGOT."

It was not easy work to keep the citizens up to watching in the interest of the King, and every year brought a fresh proclamation Major-General Daniel Jones, "Commanding His Majesty's Forces on the Island of New York, Long Island, Staten Island, and the Posts depending," issued one on May 4, 1778, the body of which ran as follows :

"Whereas, it is thought expedient, in order to give the necessary Assistance to the Commandant of the City, that a Superintendent-General of the Police should be appointed; I do hereby appoint Andrew Elliot, Esq., Superintendent-General of the Police of the city of New York, and its Dependencies, with Powers and Authorities to issue such orders and Regulations from Time to Time as may most effectually tend to the Suppression of Vice and Licentiousness, the Support of the Poor; the Direction of the nightly Watch; the Regulation of Markets and Ferries; and all other Matters, in which the Economy, Peace, and good Order of the City of New York and its Environs are concerned. The Superintendent-General will be assisted in the Administration of the Police by David Matthews, Esq, Mayor of this City; and I so hereby enjoin and require all Persons whatever, to pay due obedience to the Superintendent-General, the Mayor, and all others acting in authority under them, in the Execution of their Duty; and all Military Officers commanding Guards, to assist them when it shall be found necessary."

Mr Elliot used his powers for very little purpose except the annoyance of patriotically inclined persons The next document in order bears date of June 18, 1778 It is an order issued by Charles Rooke, an Aide-de-Camp, who opens by speaking of the great service which the City Watch "established soon after His Majesty's Troops took possession of New York," had done in preserving the "Safety and good Order of the City" "The Cheerfulness and Alacrity with which this duty has been performed," he says, "does Honour to the Inhabitants The General," he says, "recommends a steady Perseverance in this essential public Service That it may be the less burdensome to the good Citizens, he shall grant as few exemptions as possible" He orders that the inferior officers, artificers, and laborers employed in the King's service are to take a share in the City Watch when their duties will permit of it.

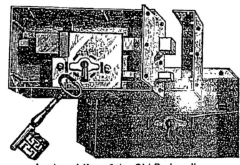

Lock and Key of the Old Bridewell

The following document is worth quoting, as developing the military use of the Police:

TO THE POLICE.

The Commandant hereby appoints Jeronymus Alstyne and John Armory, Directors of the City Watch, under the order of the Police.

The Police are to order such nightly watch and make such disposition of them as the security of the City may require.

The former regulations of the Commandant are to continue in force and the neglects of duty are to be punished according to those regulations, which the Police are to see duly executed.

The fines arising from such neglects are to be paid to Mr. Smith, Treasurer of the City Funds, and applied to pay such expenses as this establishment may incur

By order of Commandant,
          ANDREW ELLIOTT, Superintendent-General
          DAVID MATTHEWS, Mayor.
          PETER DU BOIS, Magistrate of Police

NEW YORK, May 21, 1779.

48   *OUR POLICE PROTECTORS.*

But the knell of England's power in America had already rung. Disaster had met her forces in the field. The result of the war was easily foreseen. The energies of the New York garrison were now directed mainly to persecuting the patriot residents, so many thousands of whom died in the extemporized prisons in city and harbor.

The Watchmen were allowed from 1780, one shilling a night additional to their pay for services during the months of January, February and March.

But slight progress was made in the system of policing the city under British rule. The chapter of English rule in New York closes here.

CHAPTER III.

THE CITY OUTGROWING THE SYSTEM OF WATCHING.

1783—1830.

The City divided into Seven Wards.—New York described as "A Strange Mosaic of Different Nations"—The Force and the Pay of the Men Increased—Progress of the Police System very marked—Establishing a Police Office in the City Hall—Places of Confinement State Prison, Penitentiary, Bridewell and Jail—The Watch doubled on Account of the Increase of Crime—Example of "A Good Arrest"—An Act establishing Courts of Justices of the Peace and Assistant Justices.—A Law for the Better Regulating of the City Watch—Petition for an Increase of Pay.—A perfect Police of extreme importance—Watchmen declared not eligible to act as Firemen—The Humane Society.—Result of the Watch Committee's Investigation—High Constable Hays.—His remarkable Career—How he suppressed Crime and scourged Criminals.

THE third period in the history of New York now opens. The City is a free member in a free State. She manages her institutions herself for the benefit of her people, without foreign aid or interference, and, under the changed regime, her population, wealth, and prosperity increase, and her system of government develops to keep pace with the development of her life in every other phase. In that system of government no branch of the public service has had a broader or more successful growth than the public policing of the city. It will be the province of this and following chapters to describe that growth in detail.

After the evacuation of the city by the British on November 25, 1783, no immediate change was made in the municipal system. The authority of the Dongan and Montgomerie Charters was suffered to subsist, the State of New York assuming the functions previously reserved to the English Crown or its representatives. The city remained divided into seven wards, an Alderman and an assistant being chosen from each annually by the people. The Mayor and other high officials were appointed by the state government. Half the city was still in ruins from the fire of 1776; the other half was dilapidated and impoverished by the period of war and hostile occupation. The work of rebuilding was soon begun however, and both literally and figuratively, the city speedily rose from its ashes. The early mixture of races among the population has already been alluded to. This had become so much more marked about the period of independence that the people of New York were described as "a strange mosaic of different nations." How much more true would the phrase be at this day; but is it not out of this mingling of blood that much of the energy, thrift, and keenness of the people has been derived.

It is plain, from figures which come down to us in the public records, that no time was lost in putting things in order in the city. Arrangements appear to have been made with great promptitude for a system of watching, and for lighting the streets, for the accounts of the City Treasurer show that drafts were made for this purpose from January 1, 1784, forward. These expenditures were marked by great liberality as compared with those of the Colonial days, but it must be taken into account that extensive repairs in lamps, watch-houses, and other appurtenances were necessary, before any effectual service could be obtained. Nevertheless the appropriations were extremely liberal for the period. For the first years of independence, the sums expended for watching and lighting were:

	£	s	d
Dec 31, 1783, to Aug 1, 1785	4509	18	10
Aug 1, 1785, to Oct 1, 1786	3302	4	10
Oct. 1, 1786, to Sept. 1, 1787	3284	19	11
Total	£11097	3	7

This Watch expenditure, apart from the outlay involved in lighting the streets for the year beginning May 1, 1786, and ending May 1, 1787, placed the cost of the Watch, which consisted of a Captain and twenty-eight men, at £1724 8s., of which £50 was for wood and candles, and the rest, £1674 8s., was for salaries. These were computed at the rate of £32 a week for the entire Watch, and the Captain had eight shillings a night or £2 16s. a week, while the twenty-eight Watchmen had three shillings a night, or £1 1s. per week each.

Constables' fees were fixed by law in 1789 as follows. For serving a warrant, 1s 6d mileage, for every mile going only, six pence.

For levying a fine or penalty to the amount of twenty shillings or under, one shilling; and on all sums above twenty shillings, at the rate of one shilling in the pound. Taking a defendant in custody or a witness, one shilling, conveying a prisoner to jail, one shilling, if within one mile, and for every mile more going only, sixpence.

The committee appointed to regulate the city Watch were ordered to inquire into the state of the Watchmen's caps, and report the same to the Board, and also whether an additional number of Watchmen (and how many) was necessary to fully patrol a part of the outward ward. The Common Council concluded not to enforce regulations made by the above committee, looking to the increase of the Watch, until the Legislature should have authorized the raising of a sufficient sum to defray the extra expense attendant on the augmentation of the City Watch. An allowance was made to Constables and Marshals for conveying prisoners to Bridewell, and the pay of the former was placed at four shillings per night during January, February and March, and three shillings per night for the remainder of the year.

In 1787-8 the misfortunes and sufferings of prisoners confined in the jail for debt, attracted the attention of the public. A benevolent society, which had interested itself in behalf of the unfortunate prisoners, sent a memorial to both branches of the State Legislature, "in humble confidence that the wisdom of the Legislature will provide a remedy for an evil productive of consequences dangerous, and destructive to an alarming degree." According to this memorial the poor prisoners suffered great hardships, besides their loss of liberty. It appears as if the atrocities practiced by British jailors had to some extent produced a similar disregard of human suffering in the breasts of the officials that succeeded them. The prisoners confined in the jail, we learn, were "subjected to the danger arising from putrid and contagious disorders, occasioned by crowded rooms and corrupted air, and liable to become useless, if not pernicious members of society, from the great danger they are in of acquiring habits of intemperance and debauchery, while attempting to drown the recollection of their present misfortunes and distresses by the excessive use of spirituous liquors" From the second of January, 1787, to the third of December, 1788, there had been one thousand one hundred and sixty-two commitments to the jail for debt; seven hundred and sixteen of these had been confined for sums recoverable before a justice of the peace, and many of these under twenty shillings In December, 1788, there were eighty debtors in jail, forty of whom were locked up for sums under twenty pounds

The Watch in 1788 consisted of one Captain and thirty men The former was paid eight shillings, and the latter three shillings a night, which amounted to £34, 6s per week, and £1783, 12s. per year For supplying the same with wood and candles, £50. It was proposed to add fifteen more men, which would raise the Watch to forty-five men per night, making an extra expense of £15, 15s per week, or £819 per year. There was also an additional expense for the winter (three months) of £202, 10s making a grand total of £2855, 2s. Their pay was increased in December one shilling per man per night

On December 31 of the same year, however, twenty men were added to the force, in consequence of the frequent robberies which were taking place in the city This extra protection was not of long continuance, for, on April 7, 1789, the Common Council adopted a resolution to discharge all extra men But a slow increase was soon inaugurated. On October 23, two men were added, and the number was gradually increased in this way. A new watch-house was built in the City Hall at Broad and Wall Streets, where the sub-treasury now stands, and there the Watchmen were obliged to parade at seven o'clock on winter evenings and eight in summer Toward the close of 1789, it was ordered that the Watchmen be allowed four shillings per night from the first of December to first of March ensuing, and the "Assistant Foreman" of the Watch was allowed an addition of a shilling a night to his pay above what the rank and file received

The High Constable, in 1793, was enjoined to direct that two or more of the Constables, those of the Harlem Division of the Seventh Ward excepted, on every Sunday during the time of Divine service, by turns, should walk through the several streets with their staffs and cause this law (a law for the due observance of the Lord's Day) to be duly kept and observed, and to that end the said High Constable and other Constables were authorized to enter into all or any public inns, victualers or ordinary-keepers; and if any person should be found tippling therein, or that strong liquor was sold therein contrary to law, they should make complaint thereof, that the same might be punished

Along towards 1796, the progress of the police system became very marked Four more men had been added; the pay of all was now increased On January 11, 1796, it was determined that until May 1 of each year, the Captains of the Watch should receive eleven shillings a night, the assistants, seven shillings, and the privates five shillings and sixpence. By the close of the year, too, the new watch-house at the head of Chatham Street was reported complete and ready for occupancy. A committee was then appointed to make recommendations as to the number of men to be assigned to the new house This committee made a thorough report, recommending that the Captain and one assistant be stationed at the main watch-house, Broad and Wall Street, and one assistant at the new

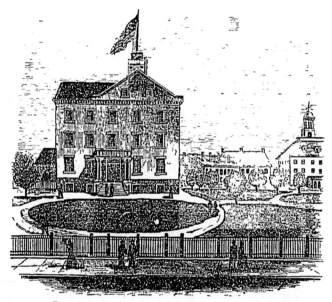

First Alms House, Chambers Street   Erected 1795

house The additional number of men to be employed was sixteen ·The committee counseled that the rounds should be performed by three bands of three men, each relieving each other; and that seven sentries should be posted as follows one at the watch-house door; one at the intersection of Pearl and Chatham Streets, two at the ship-yard, one at the "upper box" in the Bowery; one in Division Street; and one "in Mr Ivers' ropewalk"

A man could be both a policeman and a politician in those days We learn that in 1796 Alexander Lamb, one of the Captains of the City Watch, being about to depart for Albany to attend his duty as a Member of Assembly, it was ordered that Nicholas Lawrence, his assistant, take charge of the Watch until his chief's return

The Watch Department was under the immediate direction of the Corporation It was the duty of the Captains, under the direction of the Watch Committee, to fix the rounds of the Watchmen, prescribe their duties, and visit their stations. When a Watchman was guilty of misconduct, the Captain of the district might suspend him till the pleasure of the Common Council was known. He was obliged to make a return, early in the morning, to the Justices of the Police, of the number and names of Watchmen attending the preceding night, and the defaulters, if any.

The estimate for the support of the city in 1800 was as follows:

Alms House	$30,000.00
Bridewell	5,000 00
Roads	7,550 00
Streets	5,000 00
Support of prisoners	3,000 00
Contingencies	29,450.00
Watch	25,000 00
Lamps	15,000 00
Wells and pumps	2,500 00
City contingencies	7,500 00
Total	$130,000 00

An estimate of the expenses of the city for the year 1801 contained the following:

Watch, consisting of two Captains, two Deputies, and seventy-two men, 52 weeks, at $368.50 per week	$19,162 00
Extra Watch	2,000 00
Total	$21,162 00

There were four places of confinement in New York City: three for felons and one for debtors. These were 1, the State Prison, 2, Penitentiary; 3, Bridewell, 4, Jail. The State Prison, a south-east view of which is given in the accompanying cut, was "situated at Greenwich, about a mile and a half from the City Hall, and occupying one of the most healthy and pleasant spots on the banks of the Hudson." It was a strongly built structure, of the Doric order, and was constructed of free stone, the windows being grated with iron for security. It was two stories high, of fifteen feet each, besides the basement, and had a slated roof. Rising from the centre there was a neat cupola, in which a bell was hung. The centre of the principal front, towards Washington Street, was projected and surmounted by a pediment, as was also the west front. The whole front measured two hundred and four feet in length, and there were four wings, which extended backwards towards the river. The building and yards covered four acres, and the whole was inclosed by a stone wall twenty-three feet high on the river side, and fourteen feet in the front.

No convict whose sentence was below three years imprisonment was admitted into this prison.

In the beginning of the year 1796, a bill, "For making alterations in the criminal laws of the State and the erecting of a State Prison," was introduced into the Senate by General Philip Schuyler, of Revolutionary memory, and became a law on the twenty-sixth of March of the same year. By this law two State Prisons were directed to be built—one at New York and the other at Albany. The plan of the prison at Albany was afterward relinquished, and the whole of the money appropriated for both prisons was directed to be applied to the one in this city. It was begun in the summer of 1796, and so far finished that the first prisoners were received into it in the summer of 1797. The original cost of the grounds, buildings, and wharf, was two hundred and eight thousand, eight hundred and forty-six dollars. It was in later years used as a brewery—thus retaining its traditions.

On March 2, 1798, an act was passed establishing a police office in this city, the location to be selected by the Mayor, Aldermen, and Commonalty. The object was to facilitate the apprehension of criminals. The Chancellor, Mayor, Judges of the Supreme Court, Recorder and Aldermen were to act in the office as conservators of the peace. Two Justices of the Peace, at a salary of $750, were appointed, one at least to be in attendance daily at the police office. This office was located in the City Hall. A tax levy of $3,000 was also authorized for employing night watchmen and lamplighters for one year, the Mayor and Commonalty to determine the number of men required. On March 20th of the succeeding year, the Mayor, etc., were authorized to raise by tax a sum not to exceed $32,000, for purchasing oil, paying Watchmen, cleaning wells, etc. A similar law was passed for several successive years.

There was no material change, then, until September of this year, when the Common Council resolved to double the Watch on account of the increase in crime. In May, 1799, Mr. Culbertson, who had been the Captain from the time of the evacuation, died, and Mr. Van Wart was appointed in his place. In 1801, a second Captain was appointed, the number of men being then seventy-two.

The duties of the police were discharged by three Justices, appointed for the purpose by the Council of Appointment, and removable at pleasure. The Chancellor, Justices of the Supreme Court, and Members of the Common Council, as conservators of the peace, might attend and assist the Police Justices. A court was held every day, except Sunday; at which one, at least, of the Justices, and the Police Clerk, were in constant attendance at sunrise every morning to take cognizance of offences committed against the good order and peace of the city.

An act regulating the fees of the several Officers and Ministers of Justice within this State, passed April 8, 1801, regulated Constables' fees as follows:

For serving a warrant nineteen cents; serving a summons, twelve and a half cents; mileage, for every mile going only, six cents, levying a fine or penalty to the amount of two dollars and fifty cents or under, twelve and a half cents; and all sums above two dollars and fifty cents at the rate of twelve and a half cents on every two dollars and fifty cents. Taking a defendant in custody or a mittimus, twelve and a half cents; conveying a person to gaol, twelve and a half cents, if within one mile; and for every mile more going only, six cents.

In 1802 six new "Captains or Commanders of the City Watch" were appointed. Their duties were to direct the Watchmen, and visit the different stations, each in his district, once a night. The number of Watchmen was now one hundred and twenty, and the system just at this time cost an average of about $25,000 a year No person could be employed upon the Watch who was not a citizen of the United States. The Captains had to report daily to the Police Justice the names of all the men who had been on duty the night before, and they had, besides, to keep registers containing similar information It was defined as the duty of every Watchman to continue sober, orderly, and vigilant, and in every respect to obey the commands of the Captain of his district—rules of conduct not unworthy the respect of the Watchmen of the present time The old law goes on thus:

"If any watchman shall sleep while on his station, or committ any Act of violence except such as may be strictly necessary in the execution of his duty, or disobey such orders as shall from time to time be given him, it shall be the duty

Old State Prison.

of the several Captains or Commandants without delay to report the name of such offenders together with his offense to the Mayor, or, in his absence, to the Recorder, who are hereby authorized and directed immediately to supersede such offender, and to appoint some proper person in his stead " The stipend of the guardians of the peace was again increased at this time, each Watchman being allowed five shillings and six pence for every night's service, the Captains receiving eleven shillings.

In August of this year the city was divided into three police districts, as follows

First District —To begin at the ferry stairs at the lower end of Cortland Street, thence to Broadway, thence to Chatham, to the Brick meeting, down Beekman to Pearl, to the head of Peck Slip, to East River

Second District —To begin at the east side of Peck Slip, to run up East River to Bullock Street, to Bowery Lane, thence through William Street to Broadway, down to the Arch Bridge to the place of intended canal; up the line of the canal to head of same; to Cross Street, to Tryon Row, to Chatham Street, to the Brick meeting, thence down the line of the First District to the place of beginning.

Third District —To begin at the place of beginning of the First, to continue by the line of the same to the Brick meeting, to the line of the Second District, to William Street, thence in a direct line to the outlet of the meadow of Anthony Lispenard, into the North River; thence down said river to the first place of beginning

The Committee reported that the most proper place for the erection of a watch-house for the Third District "appears to be on a certain gore of ground owned by this Board at the intersection of Hudson, Barley and Duane Streets, sufficient for the same and probably of small value for any other particular purpose"

In view of the fact that the Second and Third Districts covered so large a space of ground, the Watch was ordered to patrol in lieu of having regular stands, except the Jail and Bridewell, and such other places as the Mayor for the time being should especially point out

In 1803, an ordinance was passed formally designating the Commandants "Captains of the Night Watch" The number of privates was again increased to one hundred and forty This was the year when the foundation of the present City Hall was laid It was a year of activity, and brought forth, among other things, a new set of regulations for the Watch The city was divided into three districts, fifty men being assigned to the first, fifty-four to the second, and thirty-six to the third Two Captains were appointed to each district, and they were ordered to fix the stations or rounds for the men, whom they had power to suspend for misconduct, pending the final action of the Common Council, which alone, it would appear, had power to discharge a Watchman. The Captains were required to give personal attendance to their districts every second night, and were liable to immediate removal from office in case of any neglect of duty Every Captain had to keep a roll of men who performed duty each night, and of absentees, and to furnish a transcript of the entries every morning to the Magistrates Watchmen, even though assigned to particular stations, were required to give assistance at any point where disorder might break out Intoxication or other faults on their part was to be forthwith reported by the Captains to the Mayor, or Recorder, and vacancies in their ranks by death or otherwise were to be similarly announced. Every Captain, as well as every Watchman, was placed under the orders of the Mayor, Recorder, or any of the Aldermen ; and all officers were expressly cautioned to detain prisoners until discharged by proper magistrates The pay of these guardians of the peace will strike the world of to-day as ridiculously small ; but it must be remembered that at this early period, the purchasing power of money was much greater than now, one dollar then being at least as good as two at the present time The Captains pay was set by the ordinance, which we have just been quoting, at $1 50 for every night's actual service, and each of the other Watchmen at 70 cents

The following persons were appointed Captains of the Night-Watch · Nicholas Lawrence and William Van Zandt, First District ; Magnus Beekman, Nathan H Rockwell, Second District ; Jacob Hays, Charles Van Orden, Third District.

No better illustration could be afforded of the pinching official economy practised in those days than the recorded fact that "the comptroller was directed in 1803 to let out the upper part of the Watch-House in the First District"

The High Constable, under the Dongan charter (1686), and under the Montgomerie charter (1730), was appointed by the Mayor yearly on the feast of St Michael, September 29 The time of appointment was changed by an act passed April 5, 1804, to the third Tuesday of November According to the former charter seven Constables were to be elected and chosen annually, viz one for each of the first wards respectively, and two for the out ward The number was increased to sixteen under the latter charter, two of whom were to be elected annually, for each of the first six wards respectively, and four for the out ward Should an elected Constable refuse to serve, he was liable to be fined £15, and another was elected in his place. It was his duty to attend upon the Mayor, Recorder, and on any of the Aldermen, to execute their commands; to aid and obey the Inspectors at the election for charter offices The number of Marshals was again increased to eighteen by the act of 1801 These were elected by ballot (two from each ward) on the third Tuesday and Wednesday in November, and were sworn into office on the first Monday in December. It was a part of their duty to attend fires, with their badges of authority The power of appointment and displacing Watchmen, Bellmen, etc, was conferred on the Common Council by the Montgomerie charter This charter also assigned the Mayor, Deputy Mayor, Recorder and Aldermen, by virtue of their offices, to be Justices The act of 1801 provided for the appointment of two Special Justices, as often as should be deemed necessary for the preservation of the peace One of these Special Justices and his clerk, throughout the day attended at the police office for the execution of business Each Special Justice was allowed a salary of $750 per annum, "together with such fees as are by law allowed to Justices of the Peace" The Justices examined persons detained by the Night-Watch and made such order on each case as justice might require They superintended and directed the discharge of the Night-Watch every morning upon the conclusion of the services of the night These Special Justices were invested with the powers of Aldermen in certain cases

The Montgomerie charter made the number of Aldermen six The Dongan charter increased the number to seven, and in 1803, by act, the number was increased to nine They were, under the charters named, chosen annually, one for each ward by the electors of each ward, on the feast of St Michael By the Act of 1804 they were elected by ballot, on the third Tuesday and Wednesday of November The Aldermen were invested with magisterial powers, any one of them might commit to the common jail persons guilty or suspected of crimes and misdemeanors; to the bridewell or workhouse, rogues, vagabonds and suspicious persons According to the Dongan charter, the Mayor and Recorder, "with three or more Aldermen," were assigned Justices of the Peace, to hear and determine all causes within the city Like powers were conferred upon them by the Montgomerie charter

Marshals and Constables were ordered in 1805 to go about the city during the warm season, and apprehend and bring before the Magistrates all vagrants, that they might be dealt with according to law.

By resolution of the Board, it became the duty of the Aldermen and assistants of each ward, at least once in every week, at such hour as they should deem proper, to visit the watch-houses, and, if possible, the several watch-posts, and inspect into the conduct of the Captains, Assistants, and Watchmen, and report weekly to the Common Council. The Watch Committee were also required to notify the Aldermen and Assistants in rotation, who were detailed for such duty, beginning at the First Ward.

The year 1805 gives us an early example of a "good arrest." It was rewarded by the Common Council, though not with surprising liberality. On July 8 the Watch Committee recommended the appropriation of $23 to reward the Marshals and Watchmen, who apprehended Francisco, a Portuguese, charged with murder. The allowance was made, being divided as follows: $5 to Richard Nixon, and $2 each to N. Hill, J. Lockwood, J. Williams, Stephen Hall, Robert Furlong, —— Banta, P. Paulding, Thomas Darling, and Thomas Freeburn. Francisco was afterwards committed and executed.

In 1806 the Legislaure fixed the Constable's bond at $500, and the bond of the Justices' Clerks at $2,500. The Board of Health was authorized to raise $25,000 by lottery, the money to be applied to the erection of buildings for the accommodation of persons suffering from malignant diseases, and twelve men were added to the Watch. The men returned to the charge respecting their pay. Their petition was referred to the Watch Committee. The Common Council resolved that no person should thereafter be appointed Watchman until he had been inspected and approved by the Watch Committee. This Committee was authorized to station a guard before any church during the hours of worship on the request of the congregation. The removal of the Watchmen's boxes was ordered, as being obnoxious during summer, and a preamble was adopted setting forth that several Watchmen in the Third District were reported by Captain Goodheart to be also firemen, and when fire broke out left their regular posts to aid in extinguishing it. This was followed by a resolution that no fireman should be a Watchman of the city. The City Superintendent of Repairs was instructed to furnish painted and numbered staves to Constables and Marshals.

An act for establishing Courts of Justices of the Peace and Assistant Justices, in and for the City and County of New York (April 6, 1807), empowered the Governor of the State, by and with the advice and consent of the council of appointment, to appoint and commission "one proper person" in and for each of the respective wards of the city, to be known and distinguished by the name of Assistant Justices of the City of New York.

In like manner a Justices' Court was appointed, consisting of three Justices, who held court in the City Hall.

Constables and Marshals attending the former courts were entitled to the following fees:

	Cents
For serving every Summons	.19
For serving every Warrant	.25
For returning a Summons or Warrant	. 6
For taking the defendant into custody on a mittimus, commitment or execution,	12

For serving an execution for $2 50 or under............ 25
And for every $2.50 and more, at the additional rate of 6
For traveling, if above one mile, for every mile, going only.. . ... .12¼
For summoning a Jury.. .. ..37¼
For going with the plaintiff or defendent to procure security. 25
For notifying plaintiff for trial.......... 12

The following fees were allowed to the Constables and Marshals assigned to the latter court ·

Cents
For serving every Summons......... 19
For serving every Warrant...... . . ..37¼
For taking a Bail Bond...... .. .. .25
For returning a Summons or Warrant 6
For summoning a Jury.... 50
For taking the defendant into custody.... . . . - 12¼
For conveying a person to jail 12¼
For serving an execution 25
For traveling, if above one mile, going only 12¼
For procuring security, with plaintiff or defendant.......... 25
For notifying defendant to give security 12¼
For notifying plaintiff for trial........ . ...12¼
For serving a subpoena on each witness... . . . . 12¼

On January 4, 1808, the Common Council passed a law for the better regulation of the City Watch. Six persons were appointed (citizens and householders) who were denominated Captains of the Night-Watch, and placed in command of the other Watchmen In like manner, six Assistant Captains were appointed, to take charge of the Watch and do other duties during the night when the Captain was absent from the watch-house upon his necessary duties. Such assistant, in addition to his pay as Watchman was entitled to receive the sum of eighteen cents for every night he was so employed. Other Watchmen were likewise appointed, and placed under the command and directions of the Captains of the Night-Watch; and twelve other persons were added to each of the companies of the Watch, and were denominated substitutes They possessed the same power and were subject to the same regulations, and, when employed, were entitled to the same pay as the regulars

It was the duty of the Captains to fix the stations or rounds of the Watchmen within their respective districts; to prescribe the duties of the Watchmen, and to see that such duties were faithfully executed, to visit each of the fixed stations of the Watchmen under his command at least once every night.

Each Captain was entitled to receive $1 50 for every night's actual service, and each of the other Watchmen, 75 cents.

Each Captain and every other Watchman should obey all orders given by the Mayor, Recorder or either of the Aldermen, and also of the Justices of the Police, on pain of removal from office

The above ordinance was followed by the appointment of forty-eight Watchmen

The City Hall Park at this period was a piece of enclosed ground consisting of about four acres, planted with elms, palms, willows, and catalpas, the surrounding foot-walks being encompassed with rows of poplars "This beautiful grove," in the language of a writer of the period, "in the middle of the city, combines in a high degree ornament with health and pleasure; and to enhance the enjoyment of the place, the English and French Reading-room, the Shakespeare Gallery, and the theatre, offer ready amusement to the mind, while the Mechanic's Hall, the London Hotel, and the New York Gardens present instant refreshment to the body Though the trees are but young, and of few years' growth, the Park may be pronounced an elegant and improving place" The City Hall Park apparently has not improved with age It would hardly be in accordance with the facts to describe it now as "an elegant and improving place"

By act of the legislature, passed April 8, 1808, any person convicted of petit larceny before any court of general sessions of the peace, should be punished by fine, not exceeding $200, or imprisoned in the county jail or prison any term of time not exceeding three years, or by whipping not exceeding thirty-nine lashes

School House   Engine House   Bridewell   City Hall
The Park in 1808

for one offence. This law made it the duty of any of the courts of general sessions of the peace, where any corporal punishment should be directed to be inflicted, as aforesaid, to direct any Constable or Constables attending such court to inflict said punishment, which direction such Constable or Constables were required to obey.

In 1810 it was ordered that Watchmen should be stationed nightly at the Potter's Field This is a significant order It may easily be inferred that the young doctors of those days found the same difficulty as those of to-day in obtaining a sufficient supply of dissecting material But now the salary question comes up again, and now at last something practical is done. On February 26, several petitions were received from citizens, asking an increase of pay for the Watchmen The city fathers took almost a year to think it over; but on March 25, 1811, the Police Committee reported the draft of a memorial to the legislature, and a bill to be enacted, which were approved, and ordered to be engrossed and presented by the Mayor to the legislature. The following is a copy of the memorial.

To the Honorable, the Legislature of New York, in Senate and Assembly Assembled

The Memorial of the Mayor, Aldermen, and Commonalty of the City of New York respectfully shewith.

That a perfect Police, is in the opinion of your memorialists, of extreme importance in every city, and particularly in one daily and rapidly increasing like the City of New York. In perfecting such a police, the activity of the inferior officers and agents of the police magistrates is every way important and competent. Rewards are consequently necessary to stimulate such activity. At present there are constables and marshals in the service of the city police, whose compensation arises from very trivial fees which are allowed them by law, and which are the same in all cases, whether such cases are important or unimportant. It is very apparent to your memorialists that in cases of difficulty and importance, the established fees of office can hold out very little inducement for increased exertion, and that, therefore, capital criminals may, through the want of competent remuneration to these inferior officers of justice, baffle pursuit and escape the penalties of the law.

Your memorialists are therefore anxious that some remedy be applied to this gross defect, and they beg leave to suggest the following.

Since the first establishment of a police office in the City of New York, large quantities of property of various kinds, and considerable value, seized under suspicion of being stolen, have devolved to the office by remaining unclaimed by any owner, and from the proceeds of the sale of such property, the expenses of the office have been annually paid, and a large surplus left in the hands of the magistrates, unappropriated. The proceeds of this unclaimed property, with occasional assistance from the public revenue of the State, will form a sufficient fund more effectually to encourage the vigilance and activity of the several branches of a police, confessedly of great benefit to the whole State of New York.

Your Memorialists therefore pray that provision be made by law for the disposal of the property so remaining in the said office unclaimed, at the expiration of every six months, and that the proceeds thereof may be paid into the Treasury, and an established salary, in addition to the existing fees, may be allowed out of the public Treasury to such Constables and Marshals as the Police Magistrates may select, on account of their vigilance and fidelity, to attend at the said office, and execute their commands."

This was a step in advance; yet, it will be seen, it leaves the poor Watchman unprovided for. It is not likely that the police of to-day would be content to rely on the leavings of the Property Clerk's office for their pay; neither are the owners of stolen goods, as a rule, so accommodating as to leave their property to benefit the public finances.

The legislature (April 9, 1811,) passed an act embodying the main features contained in the memorial of the corporation, as aforesaid. This act provided for the appointment of one Special Justice, and directed that all Special Justices should be, *ex-officio*, Judges of the Court of General Sessions. It empowered the Mayor, from time to time, to select as many Marshals and Constables as he should deem necessary to perform police duty, who were to report daily at the police office and execute the orders of the Justices. For these services Constables were allowed extra compensation in the discretion of the Justices and approval of the Mayor. The Special Justices were also given control of the Watchmen, insofar as their orders related to the detection of criminals. The appointment of Marshals was limited to sixty. The act also provided that two Aldermen should attend the court of General Sessions and act as Justices, and that another Special

Justice should be appointed. The Mayor was empowered to select the Constables and Marshals, who were to attend the court as policemen. Unclaimed property was directed to be sold, the proceeds to be paid to policemen for extraordinary services.

The Special Justices received from the Common Council the use of the watch-room and adjoining room of the New City Hall for the performance of their duties.

It was again re-enacted in this year that Watchmen were not eligible to accept the office of firemen, and new staves were ordered for the use of the Constables.

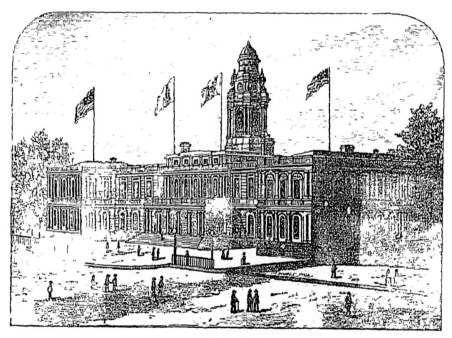

City Hall

Constables, before taking office, were obliged to give a bond with two sureties, by which such Constables agreed to pay to any person the amount he might become liable for on account of any execution he might collect. The amount of the bond is not stated, but the bond should be approved by the Supervisors, and placed in the custody of the Town Clerk. Police Justices were required to account semi-annually (January and July) to the Mayor, as to what stolen goods remained unclaimed in the police office, and to advertise the same in one daily newspaper. Constables and Bailiffs were ordered to arrest all persons who disturbed religious worship on the Sabbath, or who, on the same day, exhibited any show, promoted or aided in horse-racing, or who sold any liquor within one mile of the place of meeting, under a penalty of twenty-five dollars. Suits against a Constable were to be brought within two years after his term of office, for failure to properly perform his duty.

The foundation stone of the City Hall was laid on September 26th, 1803, during the mayoralty of Edward Livingstone. It was finished in 1812, at an expense of half a million dollars.

The building is of a square form, two stories in height, besides a basement story. It has a wing at each end, projecting from the front, and in the centre the roof is elevated to form an attic story. The whole length of the building is two hundred and sixteen feet, the breadth one hundred and five feet, and the height fifty-one feet. Including the attic story, it is sixty-five feet in height. The front and both ends, above the basement story, are built of native white marble, from Stockbridge, Massachusetts; and the rest of the building is constructed of brown freestone. The roof is covered with copper, and there is a balustrade of marble entirely around the top. Rising from the middle of the roof is a cupola, on which is placed a colossal figure of Justice, holding in her right hand, which rests on her forehead, a balance, and in her left, a sword pointing to the ground. The first story, including the portico, is of the Ionic, the second of the Corinthian, the attic of the Fancy, and the cupola of the Composite order. The first design was that the whole should be built of marble, but marble was high, the city fathers were economical, and it was desirable to make a saving. On that account, and it being maintained that the population would never, to any extent, settle above Chambers Street, and therefore, as the rear of the hall would not come into public view, it was concluded to build this portion of the edifice with red freestone. This accounts for the difference between the front and rear. What a commentary on the phenomenal growth of the city!

The committee to whom was referred the compensation to be allowed to the officers attending the police offices, on February 3, 1812, reported that they had examined the accounts of the officers, and were satisfied that these were accurate both as to the time given the public service, and the expenses incurred. The report goes on thus:

"With respect to the amount of compensation to be given to them, considering the difficulty and personal danger frequently attending a discharge of their duty, as well as the importance of it to the public, your committee respectfully recommend that the several Constables and Marshals assigned to attend the Police Office (in the watch-room in the new City Hall), be allowed the sum of $2 for every twelve hours they shall be employed in that duty on special occasions, and by direction of any one of the Special Justices in the day time, and the additional sum of $1 for every twelve hours they shall be employed in the night time, and in that proportion for any longer or shorter time; and that the accounts be presented hereafter in the name of the High Constable, and certified to by the Special Justices."

On April 6, 1812, an ordinance of the Common Council increased the number of Captains and Assistant Captains, respectively, to eight. The latter were to receive, in addition to their pay as Watchmen, fifty cents for every night they were so employed. Twelve substitutes were appointed and added to each of the companies of the Watch, who were entitled to a like pay as the regular Watchmen, whenever so employed.

The city was divided into four police districts.

Each Captain was entitled to receive one dollar and eighty-seven and a half cents for every night's actual service, and each of the other Watchmen received eighty-seven and a half cents.

An ordinance was adopted on August 3, providing for the appointment of a Standing Committee of Police, to consist of three members of the Common Council, and vested with all the usual powers for the promotion of police efficiency, the committee being authorized to act in concert with the magistrates of the city to that end

Next comes a clause ordering "that a company not exceeding one hundred active citizens should be organized in each ward, under the direction of the Committee of Police and Magistrates, as an extraordinary City Watch, to be armed with watch clubs, and to have an object placed in their hats when on duty, written 'City Watch'" This body was to have a Captain and assistant, and, on an alarm being given, it was to assemble at the City Hall to execute the behests of the Mayor and Magistrates A third section of the same ordinance placed $500 at the disposal of the Magistrates, to be used as might appear best toward the suppression of crime

The Grand Jury took a hand in police affairs, making a presentment to the effect that a Watchman should be stationed at each church, and should have ready access to the bell, so that he might be able to give an immediate alarm in case of fire The Grand Jurors also thought the Watchmen, in crying fire, should be directed to name the place where the flames were raging. This presentment was referred by the Common Council to the Watch Committee

The Captains of the Watch were charged with superintending the trimming and care of the lamps in their districts, "the people employed by the corporation having been guilty of neglect and impositions" A month later, however, the Lamp Committee expressed disapproval of the Watchmen lighting the lamps, but were in favor of their extinguishing them at a certain hour Incidents like these are eminently indicative of the state of the city during the period treated of. The reader may find unfailing food for reflection by comparing the electric fire alarm system and the electric lighting of to-day with the church bell ringing and oil lamp trimming that prevailed in the life of his grandfather.

By the act of ninth of April, 1813, the city was divided into ten wards: the electors of each ward to choose one Alderman, one Assistant Alderman, two Assessors, one Collector, and two Constables The Mayor, Recorder, and not less than five Aldermen, and five Assistant Aldermen to be a quorum of the Common Council The Mayor, Recorder, and Aldermen had the power of Police Judges, empowered to act as conservators of the peace Under this law, a police office was established and the Police Judges (otherwise called Special Justices), were authorized to exercise certain powers, which belonged to Aldermen when out of sessions.

Furthermore, it should be lawful for the Chancellor, every of the Judges of the Supreme Court, the Mayor, Recorder, and every of the Aldermen, whenever they should deem the occasion to require it, to be in the said office, "and then and there to do every act which they shall deem requisite to be done by them as conservators of the peace" This act provided also for the appointment of three Special Justices, "as often as it shall be deemed necessary," for preserving the peace in the city of New York, and likewise a clerk of the police office The salary of each Special Justice was fixed by law at the rate of $750 per annum, together with certain fees named in the statute

The Mayor of the city, from time to time, was authorized to select as many Constables and Marshals as he might deem requisite for police officers, whose duty it should be to attend daily at the police office and execute the orders and commands of the Justices. The proceeds of sales of unclaimed property were applied to compensate the said police officers for extraordinary services, and to promote the detection and apprehension of offenders. It was the duty of the Watchmen to obey such orders and directions as they should from time to time receive from the Special Justices relative to the detection and apprehension of offenders. It was the duty of the Justices, or one of them, to examine all persons apprehended and detained in custody by the Night-Watches, and to make such order thereon as the circumstances of each case and justice should require, and likewise to superintend and direct the discharge of the Watch every morning upon the conclusion of the service of the night. The act limited the number of Marshals to sixty.

One of the earliest statutes of the General Assembly in 1683 was for the relief of the poor. In 1699 a law was passed for the relief of the poor at their homes, and about 1714 the first alms house was built, on the present site of the City Hall. In 1795 a lottery of £10,000 was granted for a new alms house, and the large brick building on the Park near Chambers Street was erected. This building was destroyed by fire in 1854. In 1811, a tract on the East River, at the foot of Twenty-sixth Street, was bought; and the first stone was laid August 1, 1811. The main building at Bellevue Hospital was opened April 22, 1816, as a hospital, penitentiary, and alms house, at a cost of $421,109.

The buildings occupied by the alms house stood at Bellevue, on the banks of the East River. The principal building fronted the river. It was a plain stone structure, three stories high, with slated roof. The first stone of the alms house was laid August 1, 1811, and it was opened in the beginning of the year 1816. The inappropriateness of the location of the alms house at Chambers Street soon became manifest, and in 1810 the site at Bellevue, containing between six and seven acres, was purchased and buildings commenced, which were finished and occupied in 1812. The city authorities then agreed to devote the old building toward encouraging several enterprises of a public character then recently started, and accordingly appropriated its rooms for their occupancy, and adopted for it the name of the New York Institution.

A committee of the Common Council which was appointed to consider the subject, reported on February 12, 1816, that "an entire new modification" of the Justices' Courts was desirable. This committee recommended that the city be divided into five districts, of which the Ninth Ward was specified as one. Four Justices were to be appointed by the Council of Appointment—a body many of the functions of which are now vested in the Governor of the State—for the first four districts; the Corporation was to appoint two for the Fifth District or Ninth Ward. All these Justices were to hold court at such times and places as the Corporation might direct, and they were to make a return of all their fees, paying the amount of them monthly to the Chamberlain. Fuel, candles and stationery were to be supplied by the city. It was further proposed to extend the jurisdiction of the Justices to cases in which $50 or under was involved, the jurisdiction being concurrent with that of the Mayor's Court over $25, and the defendant having the option of removing the case to the latter tribunal on giving security. Another suggestion, which shows growth in liberality, forbids that any man who actually supported a family should be imprisoned for a debt less than $25, and finally it was proposed that the Justices should have power to grant new trials, and, except in the Ninth Ward, should be salaried officers, paid by the city. All these suggestions were approved by the Common Council, which instructed the Corporation Counsel to prepare a corresponding memorial and bill for presentation to the legislature. This was done, and an act founded on the outline here given was adopted. In 1817 the salary of Police Justices was set at $750 per annum. The Clerks of the police courts about the same time made a successful effort to have themselves, in common with Constables and Marshals, exempted from militia duty.

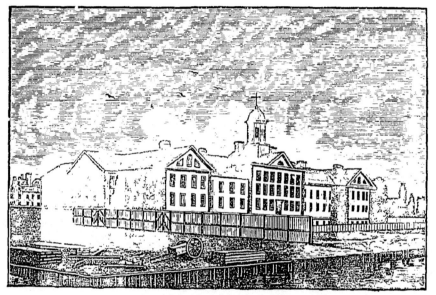

Alms House, Bellevue

The Humane Society (1817), it is to be presumed, from their printed "directions to prevent the fatal effects of drinking cold water," had but slight sympathy with the principles of St John. The remedy for which, as prescribed by this excellently humane society, was "spirits and water," or, in other words, "grog." "With the view of carrying into effect the foregoing directions," it is stated "the Society have appointed six physicians, * * * whose province it is to take charge of such persons as are contemplated in this provision, and on whom our citizens are requested to call when accidents of this nature may occur." Verily, that was a humane, not to say a philanthropic society.

The Police Committee was ordered in 1817 to report upon the propriety of allowing further compensation to peace officers for the arrest of felons. The report was made on November 17, and four propositions which it contained were agreed to These were: First, that the Police Committee be authorized to pay officers for extraordinary services in arresting criminals, such sums, not exceeding $100 in any one case, as they might deem just; Second, that sixty-two cents be allowed to every officer who should arrest on process, a prisoner who should be committed and afterwards released or convicted; Third, that every Watchman who attended court on subpoena as required by the District Attorney, in consequence of his being a Watchman, should be allowed $2 for each case of felony in which he so attended; and Fourth, that Marshals, when not attached to a court, and Constables should be allowed $1 for every attendance on subpoen

Constables and Marshals when summoned, were obliged ct March 5, 1819) to attend the sittings of the courts of Common Pleas, Oyer and Terminer, General Sessions and the jail delivery, for which services they were each paid $1.50 per day Constables were forbidden (Act April 7, 1820) to buy or become interested in any bill or promissory note, debt, etc, nor lend any money on any debt for the purpose of getting it in his hands for collection, under penalty of fine, impriso ment and forfeiture of office. Upon warrant for the non-payment of rent, Constables and Marshals were empowered to remove defaulting tenants (Act April 13, 1820) A subsequent act provided that Constables should receive reasonable compensation for services performed, and for which no specified compensation had been allowed by law

By an act of ninth February, 1788, justices of the peace were authorized to commit, for sixty days, any vagrant, disorderly person, etc, on their own views, without a trial by jury By an act of March 3, 1820, the term of commitment was extended to six months Thus the police justices had the power of taking up and imprisoning any individual at their discretion, without the form of trial by jury, although this provision was in direct collision with the Constitution of the Unit States, which declares that "the trial of all crimes, except in cases of impeachment, shall be by jury" The police at this time, it is alleged, with regard to crimes, were rather remarkable for success in detecting, than for vigilance in preventing them The police of the city were not, it would appear, over-efficient or zealous

By act of the legislature of this year, the Mayor, Recorder, five Aldermen and five Assistants, were deemed necessary to form a quorum for the tran ing of any business In the same act it was provided that the salary of Mayor might be seven thousand dollars per annum, but could not be le . than five thousand dollars, and after being fixed, it could not be lessened du t holding of the then incumbent. Formerly the salary arose chiefly fro p quisites of office.

The Mayor's Court was held in the City Hall. The Mayor, Rec . er, and Aldermen constituted this court, though the Mayor and Recorder ht meet without the Aldermen. The court held its sittings on the third Mo of every month The charter of this court is dated April 22, 1686 As a Cou of Justice the Mayor's Court stood very high in public estimation

Then there were the District Court of the United States, the Circuit Court of the United States; the Surrogate's Office, the Marine or Justices' Court—this court consisted of three Judges or Justices, who were appointed by the

Council of State, two of which should always preside. They met every lawful day at ten o'clock, and were empowered to try actions for debt to the amount of one hundred dollars; to determine as to seamen's wages to any amount, and in actions of assault, battery and false imprisonment among seamen and passengers. It was distinct from all other courts of justices; had no power to hold sessions of the peace but as to keeping the peace it had the same power as other magistrates.

Besides the Marine Court, there was a Justices' Court held in every ward, in which one person presided, who was called an Assistant Justice. He tried questions of debt and trespass to the amount of twenty-five dollars, and generally all actions competent to all other justices in the State where the amount did not exceed twenty-five dollars. The Justices of these courts were remunerated out of fees prescribed by law, on the proceedings in their respective courts.

A change was effected in the law concerning Assistant Justices, on January 4, 1820, by reducing their number, as follows: One was appointed for the first, second, and third wards, one for the fourth and sixth wards, one for the fifth and eighth wards, and one for the seventh and tenth wards; each Justice to hold a court for the trial of causes to the amount of fifty dollars and under. The salary of each was one thousand seven hundred and fifty dollars per year, and certain fees were allowed when more than twenty-five dollars was recovered. It was not lawful for more than thirty of the Marshals to serve processes issuing out of the court of any Assistant Justice, such Marshals to be commissioned by the Mayor.

The first faint movement towards uniforming the peace officers was to oblige them to wear a certain style of hat to distinguish them from the general crowd. On July 23, 1821, the order to wear these hats was abolished; a painted plate to be worn by each officer when on duty in front of his own cap, was made optional. Another and more pleasing enactment was adopted, as a sort of Christmas present, on December 24 of this year. This allowed Captains and privates of the Watch one dollar a day each for attendance at the Court of General Sessions on duty, growing out of their duties as Watchmen. The next year, this rule was made to include the Court of Oyer and Terminer. The same committee which reported this ordinance, was also ordered to consider the petition of the Watchmen for an increase of salary. The committee found that there were a great number of applications for berths as Watchmen, and that neither mechanical labor nor the cost of living was higher than it was when the pay was set at the figure that then prevailed. An increase was therefore opposed. In 1825, however, a resolution was carried allowing the Captains, assistants, and Watchmen of the different districts of the City Watch, a compensation of twelve and a half cents a night additional to their regular pay.

The Watch Committee was instructed to investigate the method of conducting the Watch which prevailed, and report thereon to the Common Council. The report was rendered April 24, 1826, and it opened with an assurance that the committee had exerted themselves to obtain that practical information necessary to form correct opinions. The result of their labors, laid before the Board, is as follows:

"Your Committee have on various occasions, and at such unexpected seasons as to render it certain that their visits were not anticipated, visited the watch-houses, have found them clean and orderly, as far as regards the Watchmen, and that in general, proper respect is paid to the commanding officers, and a wholesome subordination used in all their regulations. The Watchmen as a body are men to whom your Committee feel confident our citizens may properly confide the safety of their lives and property; they are, however, men, and it would hence be unreasonable to expect that they should be faultless, or that there should not be among them those who dishonor their station, and have been found and promptly dismissed, and your Committee believe that a rigid adherence to the present test for qualifications will rid the Watch of its improper members, and insure to the city a corps whose active exertions and integrity may be relied on."

Notwithstanding this high praise, the committee found the system in need of improvement. The whole number of Watchmen in the city at this time was two hundred for each night's service, including officers. The force was apportioned as follows:

Districts	Postmen	Roundsmen	Totals
First,	64	12	76
Second,	52	8	60
Third,	50	8	58
Three Captains and three Assistants,	-	-	6
		Grand Total,	200

The Postmen were to include those stationed at public buildings and the cupola, and doormen at the watch-houses. This left the Captains and assistants, and ninety-seven men, to protect the streets during the night. The committee believed the number wholly insufficient to guard the city. After making every effort by rearrangement of the posts to make the existing force as efficient as possible, the investigators were forced to the conclusion that twenty-four men ought to be added. They reported, however, against the addition of a new district, on the double ground of expense and the difficulty of locating the new house. They recommended, however, the addition of six Assistant Captains to the Watch, two for each district, to be on duty alternate nights. Besides, the establishment of relief watch-houses was advocated, the distance of the outposts from the main houses requiring too much time in relieving. To meet this demand it was proposed to erect a watch-room in the rear of a new engine-house, then in course of erection at Delancey and Attorney Streets, for the use of the Second District, and to use the room over the engine-house at Hudson and Christopher Streets for the Third District. Each of these relief houses was to be placed under command of an Assistant Captain, and the assignment of men to them was to be left to the Captains and the Police Committee. "If the foregoing recommendations of your Committee are carried into effect," the report says, "the number of Watchmen employed for each night will be two hundred and twenty-seven, and there will be constantly on duty three Captains, six Assistants, and one hundred and nine Watchmen, ninety-four of the latter being Postmen and fifteen Roundsmen, whose duty it is to visit the posts by divisions every two hours during the night." The estimated cost of these improvements was ten thousand dollars. From a resolution appended to the committee's report it is gathered that the boundaries of the three Watch districts were as follows:

First, commencing at the foot of North Moore Street to Chapel Street, thence through Chapel to White Street, to Orange Street, through Orange to Bayard, through Bayard to Mulberry, through Mulberry to Chatham, down James to East River, and including all that part of the City north and west of said line.

Second, commencing at the foot of James Street, to Chatham Street, through Chatham to Mulberry, through Mulberry to Bayard, through Bayard to Orange, through Orange to Grand, through Grand to Mulberry, through Mulberry to Broome, through Broome to the Bowery as far as the Lamp and Watch Districts extend, including all north and east of the said line.

Third, all the city in the Lamp and Watch Districts not included in the above.

All the recommendations of the committee just quoted were adopted by the Common Council, and were speedily put in operation.

First House of Refuge, 1806.

The Society for the Reformation of Juvenile Delinquents made an application to the City Council for a grant of land for the proposed institution. The committee to whom the request was referred recommended "that the piece of ground lying at the junction of the Bloomingdale and Old Post roads, on which the U S Arsenal was situated, which was granted on the 17th November, 1807, by the corporation to the General Government, upon the express condition and understanding that the same should be used for the purpose of an arsenal and deposit of military stores, and whenever it should cease to be used for such purposes it was to revert to the corporation, should be conveyed to the board of managers of the Society, whenever they obtained from the General Government a conveyance of the interest they had in the grounds."

In addition to this they proposed to convey to the Society the triangular plot in front, formed by the junction of the roads. The memorial to the government was granted, and the government stores were removed to Castle William, the barracks being turned over to the Society.

The site now forms part of Madison Square, lying between Twenty-third and Twenty-sixth Streets, and Madison and Fifth Avenues. Here on the first of January, 1825, in the old barracks occupied during the war of 1812-15, purified, refitted, and prepared for a limited number of inmates, the New York House of Refuge was opened. At first there was but one long building, subsequently additions were made as the number of inmates increased, as represented below. The building was burned down in the year 1835.

By act of April 15, 1826, the fees of Constables and Marshals employed in the Police office were fixed as follows: For serving a warrant or summons within one mile, thirty-seven and a half cents, and six and a quarter cents for returning if the party was arrested or served. For every mile, going only, twelve and a half cents mileage; for taking the defendant in custody on commitment, twelve

House of Refuge
[As it looked after extensions were added.]

and a half cents, for conveying the party to prison, if within a mile, twelve and a half cents; for going with a defendant to procure a security, when ordered by the Justice, fifty cents, for serving a subpoena, when within a mile, twelve and a half cents, and twelve and a half cents additional for every additional mile, going only, for serving every search warrant when goods were not found, one dollar, but if found and they should exceed fifty dollars, then any sum not over two dollars and fifty cents, which the Justice might direct.

A resolution was passed August 4 of this year, that an inquiry be made into the expediency of associating with the several Watch departments a judicial officer to admit prisoners to bail, was referred to the Watch Committee. On the eleventh of the following month a resolution was adopted providing for the sitting of Magistrates on Sundays, and during the night—the committee on applications being instructed to ask the legislature to change the law to that effect. The succeeding month a resolution was offered providing for the establishing of two branches of the Police Department, to be located at the watch-houses of the Second and Third Districts, each having Justices' clerks and Marshals to attend during the day-time, and a Justice to attend at night to dispose of the cases brought up, thereby relieving the Captains of the responsibility. In the month of December, six new posts were created, two in the First District, one in the Second, and three in the Third

The Watch Committee were directed to employ a physician to attend certain Watchmen who were injured in the riot at Anthony Street, near Elm Street, on January 1, 1827 On the fifteenth of the same month, the Watch Committee were directed to render any financial assistance necessary to the families of the wounded Watchmen The following month provision was made to fine Constables twenty-five dollars for failing to attend before a Justice when summoned to do so

Watchmen were required by ordinance (July 13, 1829) to call out fires The Captains of each Watch District were ordered to instruct the Watchmen under their direction to cause every alarm of fire to be made as general as possible, by crying aloud the name of the street or post where the fire might be

Watchmen were allowed fifty cents for attendance as witnesses at Special Sessions, by ordinance, December 27, 1830.

When on duty, Watchmen wore a fireman's old-fashioned leathern hat, bereft of its upright front plate. This hat was varnished twice a year, and soon became as hard as iron. From this they came to be called "Leatherheads" They were also dubbed "Old Charlies" They had no other badge of office than this hat, and a thirty-three inch club For many years, like their Dutch predecessors, they called out the hours of the night, but this practice ceased long before the old Charlies had run their course For over half a century the city was policed by these Watchmen The system worked well enough while the city remained in its "teens," but an ever increasing population, and a constantly expanding area, in time called for a change in the management and organization of our public guardians The jaded stevedore, teamster, or mechanic, could hardly be expected to display much enterprise or energy, when, on each alternate night, he sallied forth to patrol the streets. It is safe to assume that he performed his duty in a perfunctory manner, and that the "knights of the jimmy," and other midnight marauders, did not hold him in especial reverence or dread

The only day police during the regime of the aforesaid Leatherheads, were the Constables, generally two from each ward, and the Marshals, who were assigned to the Courts It was, then, the province of the Watchman, or "Leatherhead," to protect life and property, to preserve public order, and generally to keep the criminal classes within proper subjection He did not always succeed in doing this, it is true; but perhaps that was not entirely his fault The young bloods of those days took liberties with this official personage which no young man of our time, who valued his health and reputation, would dare take with one of "The Finest" The old "Leatherheads" had often to suffer the pranks of wild young men about town, who, like their cockney prototype, thought that a night's spree would not be appropriately ended except they had played some practical joke on the City Watch, which took the form generally of upsetting a watch-box with a snoring Leatherhead in it, or to lasso the sentry-box with a stout rope, and drag it along with its imprisoned occupant But these experiences did not seriously ruffle the temper of the Watchmen, and so nobody was much the worse off for those irregular pleasantries

Jacob Hays was then the main safeguard of the city during business hours He was accustomed to go the rounds with a few Constables, suppressing tumults and enforcing ordinances.

The Watchmen found it no easy task to cope with crime and criminals The city at this time was not remarkable for the peaceable and orderly disposition of the naturally vicious and turbulent portion of the inhabitants. Street brawls and election riots began to become numerous Gangs of rowdies not infrequently indulged in a series of serious faction fights, and, growing tired of this, they began to maltreat peaceable citizens. Robberies, burglaries and general thievery were alarmingly on the increase, and this criminal activity was not in any manner counterbalanced by a corresponding energy on the part of the city's legally constituted guardians The Watchmen of the period stood in wholesome terror of the lawbreakers they were supposed to keep within proper subjection The Constables were but a mere corporal's guard, but, under the skillful and fearless leadership of High Constable Hays, they did much towards intimidating the higher order of culprits, who organize crime and employ others to execute their plans The High Constable's duties were more in the line of detecting than preventing crime, and his services in this respect can not be over-estimated.

But those old Watchmen were, as a class, very respectable men, and many of them belonged to very good families.

The roughs and toughs of those days were in no way inferior or superior to their congeners, with whom our citizens are but too familiar. Nevertheless, the statement may be hazarded that the Watchman's lot was even a less happy one than that of the Policeman of the present day. The former was not uniformed or armed, save as to a club; he was not so well protected by the law in his warfare on criminals; the system lacked effective organization, and there was an entire absence of that *esprit du corps* which so distinguishes our own Police force.

"New York City," says Mrs Lamb, in the history of the City of New York, "by this time appeared like a youth much overgrown for his years It has shot up with a rapidity that defies calculation." Wealth was increasing faster than sobriety was inclined to measure. Swarming multitudes from every quarter of the globe were rendering the community—in a certain sense—unformed. Educational and charitable institutions were multiplying.

The rapid growth of the city, to keep pace with its constantly increasing population, may best be inferred from the following table The population in 1790 was 33,131, in 1800, 60,489, in 1810, 96,373; in 1820, 123,706; in 1830, 202,589.

On the seventh of April, 1830, an amended charter was granted to the city, which provided for separate meetings of the two boards, and excluded the Mayor and Recorder from the Common Council, giving the Mayor, however, the power of approving or disapproving the acts of this body In the course of the following year the Fifteenth Ward was added to the city.

CHAPTER IV

PROGRESS AND REPEAL OF THE OLD WATCH SYSTEM.

1831–1844.

WATCHMEN DISSATISFIED WITH THEIR PAY.—THE DUTY OF CAPTAINS AT THE BREAKING OUT OF A FIRE.—INQUIRING INTO THE EXPEDIENCY OF REORGANIZING THE POLICE DEPARTMENT.—INCREASING THE NUMBER OF POLICE JUSTICES.—"THE YEAR OF RIOTS"—ERECTION OF NEW WATCH-HOUSES.—THE FIVE POINTS.—NECESSITY OF AN INCREASE IN THE NUMBER OF THE WATCH.—FIRST ATTEMPT AT FORMING A DETECTIVE SQUAD.—THE FLOUR RIOTS.—REORGANIZATION OF THE WATCH.—POWERS OF THE MAYOR OVER THE WATCH REVOKED AND TRANSFERRED TO THE COMMON COUNCIL.—THE MAYOR REINVESTED WITH SUPREME POLICE AUTHORITY.—MAYOR MORRIS' PLAN OF FORMING THE MARSHALS INTO A DAY POLICE.—REPORT OF THE SPECIAL COMMITTEE IN RELATION TO THE REORGANIZATION OF THE WATCH.—BATTERY PARK IN FORMER TIMES.—HIGH CONSTABLE HAYS.—HIS REMARKABLE CAREER.—HOW HE SUPPRESSED CRIME AND SCOURGED CRIMINALS.

THE Night City Watchmen, in 1831, became dissatisfied with their pay, and two hundred and fifty of their number, organizing as a body, petitioned the Boards of Aldermen for an increase of wages. The question was referred to the Committee on Finance, Police, Watch and Prisons, who, after examining several of the officers and a large number of the men, advised adversely to granting the petition. Their report states that the members of the Watch were paid eighty-seven and a half cents per night, the men alternating in performing the duties, and that the majority of them were engaged in other pursuits with which their official responsibilities seldom interfered. In the summer season, the Watch was stationed at nine o'clock, and was discharged at daylight, the men having half the time to rest, the force being divided into two squads, each serving every alternate two hours. In regard to the complaint that they were obliged to attend the Police Courts in the mornings with their prisoners, the committee held that this was not very arduous, as two men in succession were assigned to that duty, and that the turn of each did not come more than once in every three months.

The same grievance was complained of in 1825, and this led to an advance from seventy-five cents to eighty-seven and a half cents per night, that continuing up to the date of the present petition for more pay.

Reporting on the complaint of the Watchmen that they were obliged to attend court as witnesses, without receiving sufficient remuneration for the time lost, the committee held that the two dollars allowed them for every case in which they were summoned was a reasonable average compensation, and should not be increased. "It may also be added," they report, "as evidence of the equity of the present wages, that there are many more applications of good,

Old Leatherhead taking his "Refreshment" on post.

suitable men for the office than are wanted." In conclusion they state. "Duly estimating the value of the services of the nightly guardians of the city, on whose vigilance and fidelity the safety and comfort of our citizens so much depend, and without taking into consideration the fact that the expenses of the city would be increased upwards of fourteen thousand dollars by assenting to the present petition, the committee are constrained to come to the conclusion that they cannot justly recommend an advance in wages to the Watchmen"

Captains were notified that it was their duty to see that the church bells should be rung at the breaking out of a fire, and that the Watchmen call out between what streets the fire was located, under penalty of dismissal, even though it should have been the first offence.

Vagrant children, of whom there appeared to have been a great number, incited the Aldermen to an effort to remedy the evil. They directed the Police Justices, through their special officers, to use all lawful means to arrest such children, particularly those loitering around junk shops in the lower part of the city. Those that were taken into custody were sent to the alms house.

It appears that the magistrates were authorized, by an ordinance of the Common Council, to employ the officers upon important business by the hour. The price, as stated by Justice Weyman, was two shillings per hour by night, and one and four pence per hour during the day. Their employment necessarily depended upon their fitness for the peculiar business to which their attention might be called, by the discretion of the magistrate. As the officers all conceived themselves equally qualified to perform any duty connected with the office, and, as the fact was otherwise, a proper exercise of this discretion in the magistrate led to complaints on the part of the men who considered themselves slighted.

A committee having been appointed to inquire into the expediency of reorganizing the Police Department, delivered their report on January 16, 1832. The report began with the general statement that in the increase of population in a city like New York, there was generally a corresponding increase of crime, and that recent experience had demonstrated that the higher and bolder grades of criminals were seeking this land to terrify the peaceful inhabitants, to set at naught the ordinary means of security, and to render dangerous the lives of prosperous citizens. Mention was made of the fact that when the population did not exceed one hundred thousand, a Police Department with three magistrates was conceived to be all that was necessary. The report pointed out that with a population of upwards of two hundred thousand, spread over an extent of land which rendered it not only hazardous, but difficult, for an officer to perform his duty at night, an extension of the Police Department was highly necessary. The committee also recommended an increase in the number of magistrates, to hold their offices in the upper part of the city. This was followed by the appointment of an additional Police Justice, and in the following year yet another, thereby increasing the number of Police Justices to five.

The pay of Captains of the Watch, in April, 1832, was fixed at one dollar and eighty-seven cents per night each, and the Assistant Captains received one dollar and fifty cents. The Watchmen in the Fifteenth Ward were increased to such a number that ten men might be on duty in that Ward at one time, and that their line of patrol should extend to Fourteenth Street. The rate of wages of Watchmen, for each and every night's service, was established at one dollar. The Captain of the Sub-watch House, at the corner of Delancey and Attorney Streets, was directed to have two more men, and to place one of them in the cupola of the said Watch-house every night to look for fires, and give the alarm by ringing the bell, and to hang out of the window a pole with a lantern

on the end, in the direction of the fire, that the firemen and citizens might know in which direction the fire was. Also, to strike the bell the different hours through the night

Another ordinance authorized the Special Justices, from time to time, to select such of the Constables or Marshals as they might deem requisite, to act as Police officers, whose duty it should be to attend daily at the Police offices and execute the commands and orders of the said Justices

The Five Points, of New York, has acquired a most notorious distinction. Originally, it was a low, swampy pond, which was gradually filled up, and as it became susceptible of occupation, it in time became the abiding place of an impoverished and desolate population, such as always exist in large cities The locality, however, by degrees, grew to be so notoriously disorderly that it was common for persons from the country to request the protection of the Police that they might visit the scenes of crime and dissipation rampant there at all times. There were, it was popularly believed, underground passages connecting blocks of houses on different streets, and the well-known names of Cow Bay and Murderer's Alley were suggestively characteristic of the place Neither education nor religion shed its softening and refining influence upon the abandoned creatures who formed this colony This is the startling picture drawn of the Five Points, at a time that religious influences were beginning to eradicate this moral plague spot:

"Certainly, as no spot of ground on this continent had the reputation of having been the witness of more crime, so no spot had such repulsive features, or where want and woe were more apparent. Every house was a brothel, the resort of persons of every age, sex, and color; every store a dram-shop, where from morning till morning the thieves and abandoned characters of the town whetted their depraved tastes, and concocted future crimes and villainies."

The Police, it may readily be believed, were not over anxious to intermeddle with the little social pleasantries that the inhabitants were so prone to indulge in Indeed, Police interference of any kind would be entirely superfluous and out of place, as the Five Points was a very active social volcano, and to attempt to stop the innumerable small eruptions would be only to intensify the death-dealing discharges from the main crater. A knowledge of these facts will serve to prepare the mind of the reader for the historical realism of the accompanying picture of the Five Points in its palmiest days.

In these years, the vicinity of the Five Points seemed to be looked upon as needing the especial care of the Police. The lawlessness of the neighborhood began to become notorious, and for the purpose of restraining the criminal disposition of its inhabitants, three additional Watchmen, besides the usual number, were assigned for that duty. Even that did not seem to satisfy the Aldermen, for they ordered that when the Watchmen went off duty at daylight, two additional Policemen should patrol the neighborhood until the Watch was again set at night But it was "love's labor lost." A regiment of soldiers, much less a handful of Police, could not have overcome the turbulence and depravity of the unregenerate denizens In this year also, the first allowance for sweeping the watch-houses was made, the average amount being four dollars per fortnight. The question of detaining prisoners arrested on Saturday until Monday morning, before arraigning them in court, seems to have attracted the attention of the Aldermen, for in August they passed a resolution directing the Police Magistrates to attend at the respective Police offices on the Sabbath day.

The Mayor in his message, June 18, 1832, expressed his gratification at the improved condition of the City Watch, "upon which the repose of our citizens, and the safety of our property so essentially depend." "The persons so engaged," said the Mayor, "had always constituted a highly respectable class, with some few exceptions, and under the judicious arrangements of their Captains, the Watch were becoming constantly more useful, and were entitled to confidence and encouragement"

The Finance Committee—to whom was referred the communication from the Comptroller on the subject of extra Police services—on July 23 reported that the thirty-fourth section of the Act to reduce the several laws relating particularly to the State of New York, into one act, together with the report of the Police Committee adopted by the Common Council, February 3, 1812, authorized the Comptroller to make such payments only under the certificate of the Special Justices. In the present case, it was claimed the Ward Magistrates, not having been aware of such regulation, employed officers without the knowledge of the Special Justices, but, as this was evidently done in good faith, the committee recommended that the Comptroller pay the sum of one hundred and thirty-two dollars and sixty-six cents to such officers. The Common Council, while adopting the report, declared it to be their opinion that the law required that the services of the Police officers in the several Wards should be obtained solely on application to the Special Police Magistrates, in order that such services might be certified to by them according to law, and that no bills should thereafter be paid that did not comply with these conditions.

Mayor Lee, in his annual message, in the succeeding year, expressed the opinion that the Watch Department required the immediate attention of the Common Council, as the number of Watchmen, however faithful and vigilant, was utterly insufficient to guard the property and persons of the citizens. There were some watch-posts, the Mayor said, which could not be carefully patroled in a less time than from one to two hours. From the best obtainable information, Mayor Lee said the Watchmen had been increased not exceeding from fifteen to twenty-five per cent., during a period of time in which the population and the property of the city had been augmented one hundred per cent.

During the year 1833 the Watch force was increased from time to time by the appointment of additional men for the different Wards. Watchmen injured in the performance of their duty were generally allowed a sum of money, varying according to the extent of their wounds.

In this year also the vices of drunkenness and pauperism led the Aldermen to incite the Police to renewed efforts to suppress the same. They passed an ordinance for the severe punishment of such as were arrested, when the testimony of the officer or the views of the Magistrate warranted a commitment. The Constables or other Police officers were directed to watch for and arrest habitual drunkards, persons refusing to support their families, lewd women, able-bodied beggars, lodgers in the watch-houses, persons sleeping in out-houses, sheds, carts, or in the open air, and to bring them before the Mayor, Recorder, or one of the Aldermen or Special Justices for examination If convicted, in the generality of cases, they were sent to the alms house, where they were kept at hard labor for a period not exceeding six months. If old offenders, they were sent to the penitentiary. For a simple case of intoxication a fine of five dollars was imposed. The Police were also directed to enforce the ordinance prohibiting driving through the streets at a greater speed than five miles an hour, the carrying of a gun or a pistol for the purpose of fowling on Sunday, or hawking and peddling through the streets, where licenses had not been obtained Able-bodied beggars were obliged to pay for their board at the alms house or in lieu thereof serve a certain number of days at any hard labor designated by the Mayor. When an officer made an arrest on a charge of assault and battery he

Rotunda, City Hall Park.

was protected if his prisoner was discharged, by the complainant being obliged to pay the costs of the proceeding or suffer imprisonment for not more than two days. Watchmen were also specially directed to arrest and bring before the Recorder all children found begging, so that they could be sent to the alms house to be educated, taken care of, and taught some useful trade in order to make them reputable citizens

The Rotunda was erected in 1818 by Vandelyn, the artist, for a studio and the exhibition of panoramic pictures. The post-office was installed in the Rotunda, immediately after the destruction of the old post-office in the great fire of 1835 When it was understood the government proposed to accept the Rotunda, the merchants got up very demonstrative indignation meetings and protests against locating a post-office so far up town. The pressure to get the post-office "down town" still continued, and advantage was taken of the fact that the Middle Dutch Church was for sale to procure it for the post-office. This was in 1845.

In the latter part of the year 1833, the building occupied by the Upper Police became inadequate for the public use and the Committee on Repairs were directed by the Aldermen to ascertain what alterations were necessary to prevent those detained for examination from suffering from the cold during the winter season. The force was still further increased by the appointment of new men and the establishment of new posts in the different Watch districts

The year 1834 may, with propriety, be called the year of riots, the civil authorities being obliged for the first time to call for military aid to assist in maintaining the peace of the city. In this year the Mayor was elected by the city for the first time. Hitherto that office had been filled by appointment by the Governor and Council The elections were then held for three successive days, and in the inefficient condition of the city Police, they were oftentimes the cause of great excitement and turbulence The Sixth Ward remained true to its title of "the bloody *ould* Sixth," party strife running even more than usually high, and giving rise to a series of brawls and riots. Three months after the National Guard had quelled the election riots they were again called upon to put down a disturbance of a much more formidable character. The abolitionists were this time the objects of the fury of the mob; their meetings were attacked and broken up, and the mob sacked the dwellings and assaulted the persons of several well-known leading abolitionists. The Twenty-seventh Regiment, N G, S N. Y, Colonel Stevens commanding, were called out to disperse the mob The latter had assembled in large numbers, and erected a barricade of carts, barrels, and ladders, chained together, in the vicinity of the Rev Mr. Ludlow's church, Spring Street, between Macdougal and Varick Streets The regiment first met the rioters in large force in Thompson Street, above Prince The Aldermen who had been deputed by Mayor Lawrence to accompany the military, and to direct, as magistrates, the action of the regiment, became greatly alarmed, and endeavored to prevail on Colonel Stevens to retreat to the City Hall. Colonel Stevens was not that kind of man For answer, he moved two companies up to the barricades under a shower of stones, broke it up, and drove the mob before him at the point of the bayonet Meeting Justice Olin M Lowndes with a force of Police, Col Stevens turned round and marched back against the mob, sending them flying before him, demoralized and beaten. The riot had been effectually put down and peace again restored without the firing of a shot.

The other riots that took place about this period were the Stone-cutter's riots, Five Points riots, O'Connell Guard riots, and Chatham Street riots

On the night of December 16, 1835, the city was visited by a terrible conflagration, the burnt district embracing thirteen acres, in which nearly seven hundred houses were leveled to the ground, with the loss of over seventeen million dollars.

During these years additional Watchmen, who merely performed Sunday duty, were appointed whenever the Board of Aldermen deemed such appointment necessary Their pay in the beginning was but seventy-five cents a day, but it was gradually increased until, in the year 1835, it was fixed at one dollar and fifty cents for each day's service. The date of payment for such service, however, was uncertain, as the Watchmen so employed, after making out their bills and having them certified to by their superior officers, had to petition the Boards to pass a resolution directing the Comptroller to draw his warrant in their favor. The Boards of Aldermen then were not different to the present Boards in the matter of expediting business. The bills were generally for a small amount. It was customary in those days to allow the High Constable from twenty to fifty dollars for the employment of Special Police officers to do duty on public holidays. Applications for these positions were numerous, as the records of both Boards show.

During the years 1835–36, the growth of the city demanded an increase of Watchmen. A number was appointed, two new watch-houses were erected, and some of the old ones were altered and repaired. Several new posts were created many of the Watch districts being extended further up town.

The doings of the Magistrates seem to have been watched with unusual interest by the Aldermen, for they decreed that the Police Courts should be kept open from the discharge of the Watch in the morning until the Watch was set in the evening, so that prisoners might be speedily granted justice. Occasionally, during these years, the Watchmen, for extra services performed, were allowed extra pay, and, on the death of a Watchman, the Board often passed a resolution directing the Comptroller to draw his warrant for a sum sufficient to defray the funeral expenses.

Mayor Lawrence, in his message, July 6, 1836, adverted to the necessity and importance of an efficient and well-regulated Police. The elements of the present system of Police, he said, he believed to be good, and that the character of the Magistrates connected with the department was a warrant for the faithful discharge of their duties. The principal point, therefore, he said, to which he desired to direct the attention of the Common Council, was the necessity of a very considerable increase in the number of the Watch. No right, he maintained, could be dearer to the citizen than to be protected in his person and property, and secured against dangerous disruptions of the public peace.

The first attempt at forming a detective squad under the name of Roundsmen was made in April of this year; at which time a law was passed directing the appointment of one hundred and ninety-two additional men to the Watch Department to be designated as Roundsmen, forty-eight to be stationed in the First District and twenty-four in each of the other districts. They were not required to wear the Watchmen's caps, nor any dress to distinguish them from other citizens. The Captains of the Watch had the arrangement of their posts, which they were obliged to patrol continuously while on duty in search of criminals, and also to discover and report any neglect of duty of any Policemen on their beat. Their pay was the same as that given to members of the Watch, and the pay of Watchmen doing duty as Sergeants was fixed at twelve shillings.

On February 12, 1837, an excited mob of four or five thousand persons assembled in the City Hall Park to be harangued by speakers, who were to inquire into the cause of the prevailing distress, the high price of flour, "and to devise a suitable remedy" for these evils. One of the speakers said: "Mr Ely Hart has fifty-three thousand barrels of flour in his store; let us go and offer him eight dollars a barrel for it, and if he will not take it"—here the speaker stopped abruptly and significantly The mob took the hint, and very soon Mr. Hart's store, in Washington Street near Dey Street, was broken into, and his flour and grain thrown into the street Other flour stores were only saved from like treatment by the interference of the Police. Forty of the mob were arrested ; but only a few were convicted.

The following places were designated as watch-houses on May 30 of the following year. "The upper part of Franklin Market in the First Ward, for the First District. The building occupied as a watch-house in Eldridge Street for the Second District. The building occupied as a watch-house at the corner of Wooster and Prince Streets for the Third District. The upper part of Jefferson Market for the Fourth District The upper part of Union Market for the Fifth District The northeasterly corner of the basement story of the Halls of Justice, or such part thereof as might be assigned by the special joint committee on buildings, for the Sixth District."

Old Leatherhead and Sentry Box

A Committee on Police, etc, of both Boards of Aldermen, to whom was referred a resolution relative to the reorganization of the Police Department, presented their report, and the draft of a law thereon, on February 12, 1838, both being laid on the table. The committee directed their principal attention to the organization of the Watch. "The welfare of the city is deeply interested in its efficiency, while the taxpayer is aware that the expenditures in this department amounted last year to about $262,-000." The committee expressed their belief that this branch of the Police required that a thorough system of subordination, and close and active inspection, should be introduced into its administration, if the protection of property and the preservation of the public peace were to be promptly and effectually secured. The adoption of the new draft of the law, accompanying the report, was recommended, which, when carried out, it was claimed, would introduce regulation and order, "where before very little of those characteristics existed;" dismissed Watchmen would no longer be able, after having neglected their duty, to find employment in another district; and the rules by which Captains of the Watch discharged their duties, would not be as diverse as the respective watch-houses they occupied. The report continues: "The Roundsmen now go out to visit the posts two at a time; this service can as well be performed by a single Watchman, and the inducement to gossip and idleness is removed."

The change proposed by the committee had, it was alleged, the additional merit of economy, by effecting a saving of twenty thousand dollars annually to the city, while the committee were confident that the Watch department would be better organized, and more effective than the system it was designed to supplant

The charter had given full power to the Mayor to appoint any number of Marshals By act of the legislature, April 8, 1813, this power was limited to the number of sixty, and subsequently to one hundred. The committee claimed that the necessity constantly arising from the increase of population and business demonstrated the propriety of the Common Council possessing the power to fix on the number of those officers, so as to be appointed by the Mayor from time to time It seemed equally just, the committee were of opinion, that the Mayor should have power to appoint Special Constables, competent to arrest offenders and preserve the public peace. It was also deemed necessary to add to the number of Special Justices for preserving the peace The Common Council, it was asserted, should have been vested with this power The Board, in view of these facts, was advised to take the necessary steps to procure the passage of an act by the legislature securing the adoption of the above suggestions

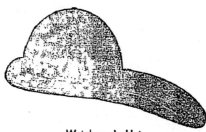

Watchman's Hat.

The draft of the bill accompanying this report, was, on May 7, 1838, approved by the Common Council and Mayor.

The leading provisions of this ordinance are as follows

There were appointed a Superintendent of the Watch, twelve Captains, twenty-four Assistant Captains, one hundred and thirty-two Sergeants, and seven hundred and eighty-four Watchmen. This force was distributed among the four Watch districts.

It was the duty of the Superintendent to constantly inspect the Watch. He had entire command of the whole force, under the direction and order of the Mayor Next to him in point of rank in the order named were the Captains, Assistant Captains, and Sergeants. Captains, in their respective districts, attended on alternate nights, and took command of the Watch; Sergeants, under the orders of their respective Captains, had charge of the inspection of the Watchmen within the beat assigned to them; they went out with the Watchmen and placed them on their posts. Sergeants visited Watchmen, and reported any neglect of duty. Their salaries were as follows: Superintendent, $1,000; Captains, $2.50 per night; Assistant Captains, $2 00; Sergeants, $1.50; and Watchmen, $1.25 per night

An ordinance of May 14, 1839, made it the duty of the Mayor to cause to be employed as many persons as he might deem sufficient, from time to time, as City Watchmen, for the purpose of preserving the peace, and protecting the city from the acts of incendiaries; and all expenses incurred thereby, were charged to the general appropriation for the Watch department.

In 1840 the Common Council made provision looking to the appointment of twelve Captains, twenty-four Assistant Captains, one hundred and twenty-eight

Roundsmen, and seven hundred and eighty-four Watchmen. These Watchmen were attached to the several districts as follows:

District	Men	Roundsmen
First District,	140 men,	of whom 20 were Roundsmen
Second "	148 "	" 16 " "
Third "	164 "	" 24 " "
Fourth "	140 "	" 20 " "
Fifth "	136 "	" 20 " "
Sixth "	188 "	" 28 " "

The Watch District then included all that portion of the city lying south of the line described as follows, commencing at the East River. One hundred feet north of Twenty-eighth Street, running thence westerly and parallel to Twenty-eighth Street, to a point one hundred feet west of the Fourth Avenue, thence southerly, and parallel to the Fourth Avenue to a point one hundred feet north of Twenty-sixth Street, and thence westerly and parallel to Twenty-sixth Street, to the Hudson River.

An act to incorporate the Watchmen's Mutual Benefit Association of the City of New York was passed April 13, 1840. The objects of this association were charitable, "and to afford relief to its members in cases of sickness and infirmity,"—a society, it appears, similar in its organization and objects to the present Police Mutual Aid Association.

In all these years physicians called in by the Police were paid only for services rendered, none being officially appointed.

The House of Detention in Harlem was, on May 6, 1841, designated as an additional Police office, to be kept open from nine o'clock in the morning until sunset.

The Justices of the Police Courts were stationed as follows:

Lower Police office (Halls of Justice), George W. Matsell, Henry W. Merritt, Ephraim Stevens, and Miln Parker.

Upper Police office (Bowery and Third Street), James Palmer, Robert Taylor.

Twenty-three officers (including High Constable Hays) were attached to the former Police office, and seven Police officers to the latter.

The Justices of the Assistant Justice's Court were:

Ambrose Kirtland, First District—First, Second and Third Wards; Nicholas C. Everett, Second District—Fourth and Sixth Wards; William Wiley, Third District—Fifth, Eighth and Fourteenth Wards; Thomas S. Brady, Fourth District—Seventh and Tenth Wards; William H. Bell, Fifth District—Ninth, Eleventh and Fifteenth Wards; James B. Theys and Isaac Daughty, Twelfth Ward.

The Watch Department was divided into six districts, as follows: First District, Franklin Market, Old Slip; Second District, Essex Market, Essex and Grand Streets; Third District, Prince and Wooster Streets; Fourth District, Jefferson Market, Greenwich Lane; Fifth District, Union Market; Sixth District, Halls of Justice, Centre and Franklin Streets.

On the tenth of May, 1843, the pay of the City Watch was increased to ten shillings per night, during the whole year. Mayor Morris, on November 21, vetoed this resolution, giving the following as his reasons for so doing:

"On the twenty-first of March, 1842, the legislature authorized that the sum of two hundred and thirty-four thousand dollars be raised by tax, for defraying the expenses of the Watch Department. This amount was arrived at by estimating the compensation of Watchmen at ten shillings per night. In September of the same year, the Common Council reduced the pay of Watchmen to one dollar per night. In December following, the Common Council established the pay of the Watch at one dollar and twenty-five cents per night, from the first of November to first of May in each year; and at one dollar per night from first of May until first of November; and, in addition, ordered that they should be paid twenty-five cents per night from first of November, so as to bring them within the rate established by the ordinance, viz. one dollar and twenty-five cents from November 1 to May 1, and one dollar from May 1 to November 1. On the seventeenth of April, 1843, the legislature authorized the raising by tax in the Watch District of the sum of two hundred and twelve thousand dollars, for the support of the Watch Department. This sum was arrived at by estimating the compensation to the Watch at one dollar per head per night, from May 1 to November 1; and one dollar and twenty-five cents per night, from November 1 to May 1. This sum was less by twenty-two thousand dollars than the amount raised for the support of the Watch Department for the preceding year, and was scarcely sufficient to pay the expenses of the Watch Department for the year, at the rate authorized by the existing ordinance."

In May following it was thought necessary to station Watchmen in the cupolas of the Halls of Justice, City Hall, Reservoir, Centre, Essex and Jefferson Markets, for the purpose of raising an alarm in case of fire, and it was ordered that the necessary number of men should be appointed, the pay being at the rate of one dollar and seventy-five cents per day. Both Boards of Aldermen in the same year became jealous of the authority possessed by the Mayor over the Police, and an ordinance revoking his powers and placing them under the control of the standing committees of each Board of Police, Watch and Prisons, was passed. The Mayor objected to the change, refusing to sign the bill. It was passed, however, over his veto. The Comptroller was also directed to pay all bills presented for the extra services of Watchmen when they were stamped as approved by the Committees of both Boards of Police, Watch and Prisons. The Aldermen became generous by voting money to supply the station houses with clocks.

There had been so much noise, confusion and quarreling among hackmen in the year 1843 at the steamboat landings that another duty was imposed upon the Police. By an ordinance passed March 27, the "Day Police Officers" of the First, Second and Third Wards, carrying their staves of office, were directed to repair to the principal steamboat landings in their respective Wards on the arrival of steamboats, to preserve the peace and assist the hack inspector in protecting travelers from the extortionate demands of the hackmen. In May of the same year both Boards, by resolution, reinvested in the Mayor the authority he had had over the Police, and which they had taken away from him the previous year.

When the British took possession of the city, on September 15, 1776, it is safe to conclude that Sir William Howe had at least five thousand prisoners to provide for, to contain whom, the ordinary places of confinement were insufficient Accordingly the Brick Church, the Middle Dutch, the North Dutch, and the French Church, were appropriated to their use. Beside these, Columbia College, the Sugar House, the New Jail, the New Bridewell, and the Old City Hall, were filled to their utmost capacity. The Old Sugar House was, *par excellence*, known as "the prison house of the Revolution."

The Middle Dutch Church was dedicated in 1732 as a house of Christian worship. Until the close of the century its services were carried on in the "Holland language," after that it was altered to the English language

The Old Sugar House (founded in 1689, and occupied as a sugar refining factory until the time of the Revolution) and the Middle Dutch Church, as seen

Old Sugar House and Middle Dutch Church.

in the accompanying illustration, stood in Liberty Street, the latter building being subsequently turned into the old General Post-office. The view was taken in 1830.

The Old Brewery, at the Five Points, has long since been removed to make room for a missionary station Its purlieus were those of wretchedness and crime; they have fitly been described as "an exhibition of poverty without a parallel—a scene of degradation too appalling to be believed, and too shocking to be disclosed, where you find crime without punishment, disgrace without shame, sin without compunction, and death without hope."

On May 15, 1843, Aldermen Tillou, Woodhull and Emmans were appointed a special committee in relation to the reorganization of the Police Department. This committee was instructed to ascertain and report the condition of the Police of the city. wherein the system was sufficient, effective or deficient; also, whether the laws of the State relative to crime, and to punishment, and to the Police of the city, were, or were not, sufficient in their scope and provisions for the due protection and good order of society, and if not, wherein they were deficient, also, whether the administration of the duties of the Magistrates or officers of Police, or of the criminal Judiciary in the city was, or was not efficient, and if not, the causes thereof. That they also ascertain and report what measures, if any, were proper or necessary to be adopted on the subjects above mentioned, and to include in their report such statements and information, and such suggestions and recommendations, as they should deem judicious.

At a meeting of the Board of Aldermen held July 3, 1843, it was resolved that so much of the message as related to the organization of Police be referred to the special committee of the Board of which Alderman Tillou was the chairman. This committee, in their report, observed that the subject of Munic-

Original View of the Old Brewery
[Site of the Five Points' Mission]

ipal Police, treated of in the message, involved the two principal departments of Criminal Police and Health Police; the object of the former being to prevent, detect, arrest and punish crime; that of the latter to preserve the public health. The outline of Criminal Police, as proposed, the report said, had for its object the diminution of a very large number of officers and persons employed in the various duties which the department—as proposed to be organized—should perform. By uniting the Fire, Watch and Constabulary force, it would, the report said, render available for other public duties, a large body of citizens employed in the services of these several departments. The report, taking its facts from the message, placed the value of the taxable property in the city limits at $227,997,090.58, and claimed that the aggregate expense of the proposed system would not equal one-quarter per cent.

"And when it is considered," the report mentions, "that the Police has for its purpose not only the protection of property, but of person, from aggression;

that besides the permanent population of the city now estimated to be about 350,000 persons thus protected, there are always, as is supposed, a floating population of about 50,000 strangers; and that at all times must be included in its limits * * * a large number of persons * * * who at no time possess home or house, and the usual proportion thereof of whom are the wicked and debased; the force, strength and expense of the proposed system will not be regarded as too great."

The evils and misfortunes, the report continues, under which the city suffered, were mainly to be attributed to the inefficiency of the police system; of the want of independence and competency of many of the most important officers, owing to political influence—and not real merit—being the great recommendation to the appointments, to the consequent paralysis of the department.

The Mayor, by the charter and laws, was the head of the Police Department. His powers included the appointment of Marshals and Watchmen. Two Constables from each Ward, making altogether thirty-four Constables, were elected annually. They were peace officers; bound to serve criminal process, assist in keeping the peace, attend the courts and assist in carrying out the sentence of law when required by the Sheriff, or the Police, or other Magistrates. Their compensation was similar to that of the Marshals.

There were one hundred Marshals (including those attached to the Police offices). Besides discharging the duties imposed upon the Constables, the Marshals were required to co-operate with the Constables at all times in keeping the peace, and attend on the various courts subject to the Sheriff.

Attached to the lower Police office for duty, were twenty-eight Marshals, and to the upper Police office twelve Marshals, who were called upon by regular turns, and in succession, to attend to the services of the office.

The city was divided into six districts, in each of which there was a watchhouse, two Captains and four Assistant Captains being assigned to each watchhouse.

The whole force employed in the Watch Department was twelve Captains at two dollars and twenty-five cents per night; twenty-four Assistant Captains at one dollar and seventy-five cents per night; nine hundred and seventy-six Watchmen at one dollar per night in summer, and one dollar and twenty-five cents in winter.

Of this force one-half only was on duty every night, each half alternately.

The Watch in summer was set at nine o'clock and in winter at eight o'clock, and varied between those two hours according to the duration of daylight, and was discharged at the break of day. They were classified as Postmen, Roundsmen and Doormen; the Roundsmen being those designated to go round each district assigned to each to see that each Postman was on his post; the Postmen being the men assigned to do post duty; the Doormen being those posted at the doors of the watch-houses. The posts varied in size, the smallest including six and the largest twenty-seven blocks. Subsequently the Watch was set at seven o'clock in the evening, the men remaining on duty until thirty minutes before sunrise in the morning.

Sixteen Day Police officers nominated by the Aldermen and Assistant Aldermen of each Ward were appointed by the Mayor, "to keep order at all times in their respective Wards" Two were assigned respectively to the Fourth, Fifth, Seventh, Eleventh, and Seventeenth Wards, and one each to the others.

Sunday officers were also appointed by the Mayor on the recommendation of the Aldermen and Assistants of each Ward There were one hundred and eight Sunday officers, each receiving one dollar and fifty cents for the day's services

There were thirteen Dock Masters, whose duty it was to direct the removal and disposition of vessels in their respective Wards, each being paid a salary of four hundred dollars per annum In all the Wards, with few exceptions, the Dock Masters and Health Wardens were united in one person.

The number of Marshals attached to the Police office at the Halls of Justice was thirty. They received no salary for their services, their fees being regulated by an act of the legislature passed in 1833; and for extra services, by an ordinance of the Common Council, they were paid one shilling per hour for every hour they were employed under the direction of a Magistrate in the day time, and eighteen pence per hour for the same services at night They were compelled to render an account of such services under oath There was no particular system of doing duty at the office, with the exception that a roll of the officers was kept, and warrants and other business given to the officers in their turn. The usual hours for business in the Police offices were from nine in the morning until the Watch was set at night; but the office was opened before daylight every morning, at which time the Magistrate, Clerk and two officers were in attendance to receive and dispose of the prisoners arrested during the night at the three lower watch-houses. The Magistrates, Clerks and officers, were not regularly on duty at night, but could be summoned whenever their services were required

The message, in pointing out the evils, defects and deficiencies of the Police system, drew attention to the following facts: The system of the criminal department was designed exclusively and only for the arrest, trial and punishment of offenders, and was not calculated sufficiently to prevent crime or to suppress the licentiousness and vices which lead to it. The incumbents were selected for political reasons and not for personal merit or competency to fulfill their duties. Their term of office was uncertain, and often very brief, depending on the change of political parties in most cases, the incumbent being liable to removal without other cause than the change in the ascendency of the party Consequently, they were not as well organized as if their office depended upon good behavior and efficiency.

The message recommended the passage of certain laws for the better government and discipline of the Police. Most of these recommendations were incorporated in an act passed by the legislature the following year, which is treated of in the succeeding chapter.

Mayor Morris conceived the idea of organizing the hundred Police Marshals, who received their appointments from the Mayor, and of dividing them into Watches The first Watch he proposed to set at sunrise. This Watch was to be relieved through the day, and the last of this Day Police was to continue on duty until sundown, when the night Watch was set. The Marshals were to be allotted among the Wards in numbers according to the requirements of the several Wards By such an arrangement, Mayor Morris hoped the services of the day and Sunday officers could be dispensed with, and the salaries paid to them; and the time allowed the Marshals would, he said, almost, if not entirely, pay the Day Police. In his message of July 24, 1843, he said he had determined to exercise the power invested in him, by putting the foregoing scheme into operation forthwith, which he hoped would meet with the approval of the Board

The Tombs building was completed in 1838. Five years previously, it was determined by the city authorities to build a prison on a plot of land that was generations ago a lake. After drainage, its site formed part of the Collect Grounds. The style of the new building was decided by the publication of a book much read in those days, "Stevens' Travels," and which contained an illus-

The Tombs (City Prison).

tration of an Egyptian tomb This grim picture was thought available in plan for the projected structure, the name of which was selected with reference to the preferred form of the building. The building as originally completed had a cupola This was burned down in November, 1842, with the apt accompaniment of the suicide of a murderer—a bridegroom of four hours—who was at the time being led out to execution

The Watch District, on September. 12, 1843, was declared to include all that portion of the city lying south of the line described as follows.

Commencing at the East River, ninety-eight feet and nine inches north of Twenty-eighth Street; running thence westerly and parallel to Twenty-eighth Street, to a point one hundred feet east of the Fourth Avenue; thence northerly, and parallel to the Fourth Avenue, to a point ninety-eight feet nine inches north of Thirtieth Street, to a point one hundred feet east of the Seventh Avenue, thence northerly, and parallel to the Seventh Avenue, to a point ninety-eight feet nine inches north of Fortieth Street; thence westerly, and parallel to Fortieth Street, to the Hudson River

By resolution of the Common Council, January 6, 1844, the Mayor was directed to create thirty new additional Watch posts, and for that purpose to appoint one hundred and twenty additional Watchmen This necessitated an alteration in the Watch posts of the city All the Watchmen were required to stay upon their posts till within thirty minutes of sunrise. Captains of the Nightwatch, in the following month, were empowered to remove and place new men on the rounds attached to their Watches, as they might think best

The pay of Watchmen in this year was as follows :

Captains, numbering twelve..........................$2.25 each.
Assistant Captains, numbering twenty-four.. ....$1.75 each.
Men, numbering one thousand and ninety-six.... .... . $1 25 each

Besides these, there was a number of Sunday officers and extra Watchmen. Even these were found to be insufficient (or inefficient), for new appointments were continually being made, and the Watch posts increased. If the Watchmen were not sufficiently numerous, there could be no such complaint made as regards criminals, as they seemed to keep on steadily increasing At this time the creation of a new station house at the Jefferson Market was ordered, the old one not affording proper accommodation for the officers or their prisoners.

HIGH CONSTABLE HAYS

The most noted official connected with the police system in his day and generation was Jacob Hays. The story of his life would read like a thrilling romance. For about forty years subsequent to the beginning of the century he was the head and front, and guiding spirit of the police of this city; in fact, Jacob Hays was a police force all by himself. He, personally, and often unaided, ran down criminals, suppressed riots, and in addition to his functions as High Constable, he originated and organized a detective department, of which he himself was the central figure and the one-man power. Nor was this all. Jacob Hays for a number of years was also Sergeant-at-Arms to the Board of Aldermen, and superintended the squad of officers detailed to preserve order in the courts. The term "eternal and universal," so often applied to our own Colonel Bliss, would be inadequate to characterize the unceasing and unflagging energy of the High Constable. But his energy was never wasted by misdirected efforts, nor did it degenerate into fussiness. He had a high appreciation of his duties, and no man worked harder or more faithfully to discharge his obligations to the public.

Jacob Hays was born on May 13, 1772, at Bedford, N. Y. His father was a prominent Whig, and was one of the soldiers serving under Washington in the expedition known as Braddock's defeat. Jacob himself was frequently of service to the Whig cause. His father's name was David Hays. He kept a country store at Bedford, Westchester County. His house was made a place of meeting by General Washington and his officers at the time that the patriot army was stationed thereabouts. Young Jacob, thus early in life, became familiar with General Washington and his officers. He was a stout, sturdy lad of eleven years, when peace was declared in 1783.

Jacob Hays was first appointed Marshal by Mayor Varick in 1798. In 1802 he was appointed High Constable by Mayor Livingston, and on March 21, 1803, ne and Charles Van Orden were appointed Captains of the Third Watch District. It is recorded in the proceedings of an old-fashioned caucus that he was removed from the latter position in the year 1804. From the time he received his first appointment to the position of High Constable up to his death, a period of nearly fifty years, he was reappointed to that office by each successive Mayor, the office of High Constable becoming extinct at his death. He was also Sergeant-at-Arms to the Board of Aldermen for a number of years, and acted as Crier of the Court of Sessions. He was, perhaps, the best-known man of his day in the city. The terror of criminals, it was his boast that there was not a rogue in the city whom he did not know. And this fact was borne out by his extraordinary success in arresting and bringing rogues of all degrees to justice. The usual popular cry being, when some bold and mysterious burglary or robbery had been perpetrated, the criminals escaping without leaving a clue as to their identity behind "Set old Hays on them."

He was the first real detective of this city. He was an honest man, of high moral and religious character, and an attendant of the Scotch Presbyterian Church, in Grand Street. In his line he was a regular autocrat, and held the monopoly of catching thieves. So successful was he as a detective that his fame

spread over the whole civilized world. He was as well known in London as in New York. It is said of him that he could track a rogue by instinct. Fifteen years after his death, letters came from the Chief of Police of London, pertaining to criminals and crime, adressed to "Jacob Hays, High Constable of New York." Following is a *fac-simile* of his commission as Captain of the Watch:

> Sir
> You are appointed a Captain of the City Watch for the Third District
> Yours &c
> J Woodman
>
> Mr Jacob Hays.
> March 22 1803.

For years after he had received his appointment of High Constable he had but a bare handful of men under his command, the number not exceeding half a dozen at the beginning. This fact rendered his achievements in keeping the criminal classes in subjection all the more wonderful. It is said, such was his zeal and activity, that, during the prolonged period of his public service, he did not, on an average, sleep more than six hours out of twenty-four. Another remarkable fact remains to be recorded: he never carried a concealed weapon; never went armed in any form; his only protection being his Constable's staff and his own indomitable fearlessness of danger. He was, besides, possessed of great physical strength, and few of the desperadoes of those days cared to cross the private or official path of the determined and sturdy High Constable. He was pre-eminently successful in quelling street brawls and dispersing rioters. Such was his success in this direction that he himself, single-handed, often put down a street fight, in which some of the worst factions were engaged, and that too, without having recourse to any violence whatever. His son, a hale and hearty gentleman, William H. Hays, who is President of the Eighth Avenue Railroad Company and a leading down-town broker, well remembers his father's exploits in this and other respects. Whenever the High Constable was made aware that a street brawl was assuming threatening proportions he at once repaired to the scene of disturbance, and, without a moment's hesitation, mingled in the throng of excited wranglers. His great strength was then exerted towards separating the combatants and in driving back the crowd. He did not crack the heads of the brawlers; he usually knocked off their hats with his staff, and while they were in the act of stooping to pick them up, he would shove them forward and throw them down, their prostrate bodies generally serving as a barrier to keep the others back. He would then deal with the principals, and by the time he was re-inforced by his men, the greater part of the trouble was generally over. The secret of his success was that he never (except in very rare and exceptional cases) used violence while dealing with a mob. He left no broken heads or bruised bodies to rankle and call for vengeance. Fearlessness, firmness, and forbearance were his predominant traits, and, as he never wantonly maltreated or injured any one, even in the face of great provocation, so, in like manner, brawlers and criminals generally—while they feared and respected the man—rarely offered him personal violence. His great presence of mind and ready tact also stood him in good stead in moments of peril and emergency. It was his habit to make little of these public outbreaks and to declare that such misdeeds were not primarily occasioned by men, but were the work of unruly boys, grown up persons being unwittingly drawn into the trouble. Then his usual method of formulating his mandates to the mob was couched in respectful language, to wit: "Now, all good citizens go home!" an advice which seldom passed unheeded. This rare mixture of forbearance and firmness triumphed over the angry passions of the mob, and rarely failed to produce the desired results. In moments of the greatest public peril he would never consent to invoking the aid of the State militia, for the reason as he grimly and quaintly put it: "If you send for the military, they may kill some one, and that will bring trouble; then there will be the trouble of burying them; and that will be the greatest trouble of all."

Only a few of the noted cases in which the High Constable distinguished himself can be referred to here. A citizen informed the High Constable that two strange men occupied a room in a certain hotel in the city; that they were much alone together in their room; that this fact excited the curiosity of the servant girl, who peered through the key-hole, and saw the men counting money.

Some time previously (1830) the City Bank of this city had been robbed of two hundred thousand dollars. The High Constable, from the nature of the robbery, suspected who the men were. Upon receiving a description of these men, he concluded that they were the men who had robbed the City Bank. Accompanied by his son, he surprised one of the robbers in the room of the hotel, and arrested him. His name was Smith, an expert bank robber. A large amount of money was found in his trunk. The money was a part of the purloined property of the City Bank.

In the meantime the High Constable was busy looking out for Smith's companion, named Murray, who had evaded arrest, and kept away from his former quarters at the hotel. A man named Parkinson, a well-known locksmith, was suspected by the High Constable as also being Smith's companion in crime. Going to Parkinson's store, the High Constable made a careful search of the place, without, however, finding anything of a criminatory character. He was about giving up the search in despair when he happened to pick up a jack-plane, one end of which, it could be seen, had been cut off and readjusted. In taking the jack-plane apart, the High Constable found in a hollow groove notes of the plundered bank amounting to twenty thousand dollars. Some forty thousand dollars was still short of the amount stolen, and the High Constable concluded that Murray must have it.

He was released, and went to Philadelphia, where the High Constable had him placed under police surveillance, and besides, had him shadowed by a former "pal," in the hopes thereby of obtaining the remainder of the money stolen from the bank.

At the High Constable's request, John McLean, High Constable of Philadelphia, arrested Murray on the second of May, 1831 Murray, when taken into custody, threw away a number of bills. These were picked up, and they proved to be bills on the Orange County Bank. He was brought to trial and convicted. While in jail, under a promise of pardon he revealed the hiding place of the stolen treasure, which was under a big tree in Independence Square, in Philadelphia. The High Constable's son, accompanied by his friend, Justice Hobson, of this city, went to Philadelphia, and after digging for the treasure, at first without success, at length found it The money so recovered completed the whole amount stolen from the City Bank.

Many years ago successful forgeries had been committed on a number of banks in this city Three men, Reed, Stephens, and Hollgate, notorious cracksmen, were suspected of the forgeries, the more so as they kept in hiding from the police. High Constable Hays arrested Reed ("Jack" Reed as he was called) in front of the old City Hotel, the site of the present Boreal Building. Reed made a desperate resistance, in which he was assisted by his confederate, Stephens. Reed drew a dirk on the High Constable, but the latter, using his great strength, pinned Reed to the wall, and held a firm grasp of the hand that held the dagger. A crowd gathered, and some of Reed's friends assisted in assaulting the High Constable, hoping thereby to rescue Reed. Fortunately, Major Noah, a well-known citizen, who happened to be passing, went to the High Constable's assistance, and Reed was disarmed. On the way to the watch-house the High Constable and his prisoner were followed by Stephens and others of the gang, who made several attempts to rescue the prisoner.

Stephens' turn came next. The High Constable, having obtained information that Stephens was one of the gang of forgers, accompanied by his son, at an early hour of the morning, went to the house where Stephens was known to live. Upon the latter refusing to open his door in response to the summons of the High Constable, the latter broke it in Stephens was ready, pistol in hand, to repulse the officers of the law As he was about firing at the head of the High Constable, young Hays knocked the pistol out of the hand of the forger, and he was secured and restrained from inflicting bodily injury on his captors.

The third man (Hollgate) remained at large. He was subsequently arrested (not by the High Constable), or at least a man who was taken for Hollgate was arrested, and in good time was arraigned for trial. This man's name was Redmond, and he kept a hotel in Pearl Street His description tallied exactly with the description given of the third forger. Redmond pleaded his innocence. He was, however, fully identified as one of the forgers by a man named Ware and a Mr Ebbitt, who was cashier and teller of the Union Bank of this city The case had been just given to the jury, all the evidence pointing to Redmond's guilt, when High Constable Hays, who had all along strenuously maintained that Redmond was not the right man, brought into court the real culprit, Hollgate Hollgate manufactured children's toys, and kept a store in Chatham Street. It was then proven that Redmond was falsely accused, and his innocence being established, he was released. He never recovered from the blow, however; his business was ruined, and he died soon after, it is said of a broken heart. The cashier who swore to Redmond's identity with the forger Hollgate, also took his trouble to heart and his health broke down, and it was long before he recovered it. Hollgate, Reed and Stephens were convicted and sent to State Prison. Hollgate was the exact counterpart of the unfortunate prisoner, Redmond.

A brutal murder, accompanied by the robbery of the victim, shocked the community about the year 1820. The man was captain of a sailing vessel. One day he was found dead in Coenties Alley, corner Water Street, with a hole in his temple. The identity of the murderer was at first wrapped in mystery. A man named Johnson, who kept a low sailor's boarding-house, and with whom the dead man boarded, was suspected as the guilty party. He was arrested by the High Constable as he (Johnson) was coming out of Trinity Church. The body of the victim was awaiting burial at the Rotunda in the City Hall Park. Thither the High Constable conveyed Johnson. The body was covered with a sheet. Johnson was brought to the side of the murdered man. Suddenly the cloth was removed, and the High Constable exclaimed in the ear of the trembling prisoner: "Look upon the body; have you ever seen that man before?" "Yes, Mr. Hays, I murdered him," was the startling reply. Johnson, who made this statement in the presence of several witnesses, subsequently denied it upon his trial, but on the scaffold he confessed his guilt. The day of his execution was a great holiday for the populace. The gallows was erected in Twenty-sixth Street, near Cedar Creek.

Mr. R. M. Blatchford, a well-known lawyer of this city, rented a cottage in Bleecker Street. At that time Bleecker Street was beyond the city limits. One morning, when Mr. Blatchford returned home after a brief absence in the country, he found the house in disorder. Thieves had broken in in the night and carried away articles of value. Mr. Blatchford's new suit of clothes had been appropriated, and an old suit (evidently the suit that had been discarded by the thief when he donned Mr. Blatchford's clothes) was left on a chair. The robbery was at once reported to High Constable Hays. Upon examining the old suit of clothes that had been left behind, the High Constable said: "I know the man these clothes belong to. He came from Baltimore to this city two weeks ago." Following up the declaration, Mr. Hays said, still addressing himself to Mr. Blatchford: "I have reason to know this man; his hair is as red as blood. If you wait here (in the High Constable's office) for half an hour I'll get him for you." To the astonishment of Mr. Blatchford, the High Constable, who had hastily departed, returned within the time mentioned, bringing with him a man whose hair was "as red as blood." The man in question was dressed in Mr. Blatchford's stolen clothes.

The interesting document on the opposite page is a *fac-simile* of Jacob Hays' commission as High Constable, which shows that there was not so much printer's ink or elaboration of detail used in the make-up of official documents in those days.

As another evidence of the intimate knowledge the High Constable possessed of criminals and their ways, and his marvelous memory of faces, the following story will not be found inappropriate.

City of New York ss. By Edward Livingston Esquire Mayor of the City of New York.

To all to whom these presents shall come, Greeting. Know Ye that I have named and appointed, and by these presents Do name and appoint Jacob Hays to be high Constable of the said city. To Hold and exercise the said Office together with all fees, perquisites, emoluments and advantages thereto lawfully belonging or appertaining unto the said Jacob Hays from the thirteenth day of October next, untill the fourteenth day of October in the year of our Lord one thousand eight hundred and three.

In Testimony whereof I have hereunto set my hand and affixed my seal this twenty ninth day of September in the twenty seventh year of the American Independence, and in the year of our Lord one thousand eight hundred and two.

One Fourth of July, upon the occasion of the usual patriotic assemblage in front of the City Hall, while the City Fathers and the Mayor were reviewing the procession, the High Constable surprised Alderman Stillwell (afterwards Lieutenant-Governor of the State), by a request to hold his (the High Constable's) staff In answer to the puzzled Alderman's inquiring look, the High Constable hastily said. "Please hurry; there's a man out there in the crowd who answers a description I have in my pocket of a man for whose arrest there is offered a reward of five hundred dollars" The High Constable then disappeared in the crowd, and in the next moment returned, holding a tight grip of the suspect, whom he marched to the Bridewell The prisoner proved to be the man for whom the reward of five hundred dollars had been offered

The late Commodore Vanderbilt used to tell a story of his relations at one time with the sturdy High Constable. Commodore Vanderbilt, in his early career, was captain of a steamboat, the boat being owned by a Mr. Gibbons. This boat was run on the North River in opposition to the regular line, which was operated by the Livingston family, who had a "patent" to run the steamboats on the North River. The Livingston's had procured an order of the Court (corresponding to an injunction), to restrain the Gibbons' boat, as operated by Commodore Vanderbilt High Constable Hays was intrusted with the service of the order of the court, and, in his usual unruffled manner, told the Commodore that discretion in the present instance, at least, was the better part of valor. "I was mad enough," the Commodore was wont to say in later years, "to defy the whole Livingston tribe, old Hays included, but when I caught a glimpse of his calm and smiling face, and a twinkle in his eye, which, singularly enough, said as plainly as words could express it 'If you don't obey the order of the court, and that damn soon, I'll make you do it, by G—,' I concluded to surrender. I didn't want to back down, however, too hurriedly, and I said that if they wanted to arrest me, they should carry me off the boat, and don't you know, old Hays took me at my word, and landed me on the dock with a suddenness that took away my breath"

To illustrate the extent to which Mr. Hays' fame had spread, the following may be related

Colonel James B. Murray while once in London witnessed quite a riot He got on an eminence, the better to see the conflict between the mob and the police. After a good deal of fighting the tumult was put down, and the ringleaders arrested. Addressing himself to an Englishman, also a spectator, Colonel Murray said "Why, I've come from a city where one man would have put down that riot" "You must have come from New York then," was the response, "as that's the only place where such a thing can be done."

The Common Council, by joint resolution, on April 31, 1836, tendered their thanks to High Constable Hays "for his persevering and efficient services in again securing those notorious and dangerous forgers, Smith and Vandergriff, who recently made their escape from the City Prison"

Mayor Lawrance, in transmitting this resolution to the High Constable, expressed his sense of appreciation of the services of Mr. Hays as follows·

"I will embrace the present opportunity to return to you my thanks for your vigilance in every case which has come under my notice, and for the readiness and alacrity with which you have discharged the duties of your office"

Mr. Hays was equally noted for his benevolence and philanthropy. While he never compromised with felons or law-breakers, he never took any illegitimate or unjust means to secure their conviction. He was firm, but moderate in all things. He was, too, possessed of a high order of intelligence, and was, besides, distinguished for his zeal and incorruptibility. His treatment of criminals was conspicuous by its entire absence of malice, or a desire to serve his own official ambition at the expense of the misfortunes of others. No man hated crime and criminals more than he; no man would go farther to bring guilt home to such criminals, and no man was more unrelenting in the discharge of such duties. On the other hand, when outraged justice had been vindicated by the conviction of a prisoner, should such a prisoner manifest a genuine desire to reform, the stern official was replaced by the humane citizen; and in every way consistent with the ends of justice and his own integrity, he was always willing to stretch forth a helping hand to the fallen, desiring that his erring brother should go in peace and sin no more. But he set his face, like flint, against professional criminals, big and small, and lashed them without pity or mercy, until they were driven from the city, or confined within the walls of a jail.

He died in the seventy-eighth year of his age, full of honors, and his funeral was attended by all the leading city dignitaries. His remains rest in Woodlawn Cemetery.

An oil painting of the High Constable, by Shegogue, which was painted in accordance with a resolution of the Common Council, hangs in the Governor's room at the City Hall.

CHAPTER V.

ORGANIZATION OF A MUNICIPAL POLICE.

1844—1853.

A Turning Point in the System of Policing the City —The Old Watch Department abolished.—Establishment of a Day and Night Police —Chief Matsell —A Man who played an important part in Police Affairs.—Harper's Police —First effort to introduce a Uniform —The New System not satisfactory —Changes in the Law.—Astor Place Riot —Battery Park —Growing Boldness of Criminals.—Citizens Alarmed —The Whole Force directed to Patrol Day and Night.—Detailment of Policemen a Growing Evil —Measures taken to suppress it —Tables of Arrests.

THE necessity for a new departure in policing the city had for a long time been forcing itself on the public mind. But, however apparent this might have been to the politicians, that body of enlightened citizens had neither the will nor inclination to change the old way of doing business. And so matters dragged along until 1840 At that time the city was in the full tide of its mercantile prosperity

George W Matsell, in the above year, became one of the Police Magistrates He was a young man of some talent and considerable energy. Born in England, he early in life came to this city, and grew up with the town. He was, in an official sense, the lineal descendant of Jacob Hays, who had grown old in the public service Mr Matsell soon became impressed with the necessity for a change in the Watch system, and he set himself to re-organize the old sleepy Leatherheads The population of the city was then about four hundred thousand souls. The city was filled with thieves and burglars, many of them of the worst kind Mr Matsell gathered some kindred spirits about him, and, with the squad of men he had at his command, he was in the habit of going about the city a great deal at night, breaking up many places of evil resort through his personal exertions Among his lieutenants were George W. Walling, afterwards Superintendent, Robert Brownsen; W. Stevens, late keeper on Randall's Island; and Joseph McGrath, afterwards a Captain, and later a Magistrate.

Mr. Matsell's efforts showed what one earnest, fearless man, could accomplish, and the public mind became impressed with the fact that what Mr Matsell was doing almost single-handed, and therefore but partially and imperfectly, was of too important a nature for individual effort, and so at last it was determined to take a decisive step in the right direction. This step was not taken, however, until James Harper was elected Mayor in 1844, but once taken there was no crying halt on the onward march of Police progress and reform

Mr Matsell was born in the year 1806, and came to this country when but six years of age. His father kept a book store on part of the site of the Metropolitan Hotel, and adjoining Niblo's Theatre. Young Matsell also learned the business from another bookseller, and in time owned a store of his own on the corner of Pearl and Chatham Streets.

The Municipal Police Act was passed in the year 1844, and William F. Havemeyer being elected Mayor the following year, he at once nominated Mr.

Chief Matsell's Shield.

Matsell Chief of Police, both Boards of Aldermen confirming the nomination. For twelve years he occupied the position, gradually improving the Police system and enforcing strict discipline. During this time he had to contend with the Astor Place riots, volunteer firemen's mobs, and election disturbances

From 1845 to 1853 the Board of Aldermen had the appointment of the Patrolmen on the force, but it being impossible to discipline the force under such circumstances, the legislature interfered, and designated the Mayor, Recorder and City Judge as a commission. In 1857 the State legislature passed what is known as the Metropolitan Police Act.

Fernando Wood was Mayor, and this legislation neither suited him nor Chief Matsell The Mayor thought it unconstitutional—as interfering with municipal prerogatives, and the Chief felt bound to obey his superior officer. A conflict with the State authorities soon resulted, a large number of the old force refusing to obey the new Commissioners.

The conflict which ensued between the State authorities and Mayor Wood as to which was entitled to appoint a Street Commissioner to fill the vacancy caused by the death of Commissioner Taylor, was bitterly waged, and was attended with the shedding of blood. Chief Matsell, who took sides with Mayor Wood, had eight hundred men stationed at the City Hall to resist any attempt to arrest the Mayor. The story of the riotous proceedings that followed between squads of the Municipal Police (Mayor Wood's partizans) and the recently created Metropolitan Police, (who enforced the Commissioners' mandates), will be narrated more fully in another place. When, at last, Mayor Wood's Police were routed by the bayonets of the military and the edicts of the courts, Chief Matsell clung to the fortunes of his chief with an unflinching devotion. Upon his failing to appear before the Police Commissioners the day following the disturbances in question, in obedience to their summons, he was tried and dismissed the force. Mayor Wood subsequently said that Mr. Matsell had acted in good faith, deeming the Mayor his superior officer.

When Wm F. Havemeyer was re-elected Mayor he re-appointed Mr Matsell Superintendent of Police *vice* James J. Kelso, on May 23, 1873. In July of the following year, when Commissioners Charlick and Gardner were removed, he was appointed a Police Commissioner, and a few days afterwards was elected President of the Board. He remained in office until December 1, 1875.

After that he practiced law in a quiet way, giving advice in criminal cases, his wide experience being found to be of great value. It was Mr. Matsell who originated the much quoted phrase, "the finest police force in the world."

Mr Matsell died at his residence, No 230 East Fifty-eighth Street, on the morning of July 25, 1877, in his seventy-first year. For two years previously he had suffered from an injury to one of his feet, and this injury, becoming aggravated by a second accident, proved fatal.

The Police system was clearly approaching a turning point in its history. Sweeping and radical changes were in contemplation, and the old order of things was fast passing away. The system of policing the city that had prevailed, with few changes and modifications, as handed down from the Dutch to the English, and by these to the government that supplanted them, was legislated out of existence on May 7, 1844. Prior to that time the Police force of the city, as we have seen, consisted of two Constables elected annually in each ward, of a small body of men appointed by the Mayor, denominated Mayor's Marshals, and of a Night-watch composed of citizens who pursued their trades or avocations during the day, and patrolled the streets at night. This act abolished the Night-watch, and established a Day and Night Police.

The act was suffered to remain for the time being inoperative, lacking the official approval of the Common Council and the Mayor. The Board of Aldermen, however, on November 27, 1844, while ignoring the Police bill passed by the legislature subject to their approval, adopted an ordinance establishing a Municipal Police, or Night and Day Watch.

This ordinance removed from office all Sunday officers, Day Police officers,

officers to attend the polls, officers to attend boats, keepers of public places, and Superintendent of junk-shops.

In lieu of these, the Mayor was empowered to select two hundred suitable men, who, with the concurrence of the Common Council, were to constitute a Municipal Police, or Night and Day Watch.

The following Police stations were appropriated to the force, and established in accordance with the above ordinance:

No. 1 Franklin Market. First Ward.
No. 2 City Hall: Second, Third and Fourth Wards
No. 3 Halls of Justice: Fifth and Sixth Wards
No. 4 Essex Market. Seventh, Tenth, and Thirteenth Wards
No. 5 Corner Prince and Wooster Streets. Eighth and Fourteenth Wards.
No. 6 Jefferson Market: Ninth, Fifteenth, and part of Sixteenth Wards
No. 7. Union Market: Eleventh, Seventeenth, and part of Sixteenth Wards.
No. 8 House of Detention, Harlem. Twelfth Ward

The officers and salaries were named as follows

Superintendent $1250
Captains 700
Assistant Captains 600
Sergeants 550
Policemen 500

The Mayor was authorized to prescribe a distinguishing badge or dress for the members of the force, and also to prescribe such rules and regulations as he might deem necessary and proper. This ordinance, it was stipulated, should not be construed to affect the Watch Department in any other way than as it rendered necessary an alteration of the Watch posts to conform to the diminution of that force by transfers into the Municipal Police.

In pursuance of the power invested in him, as aforesaid, Mayor Harper quickly went to work to uniform, or partially uniform, the corps of two hundred men which constituted the Municipal Police. This uniform consisted of a blue single-breasted cloth frock coat, buttoned to the neck, having the letters M P. on a standing collar This was the first serious attempt made to uniform the Police force, but it did not survive long. These Policemen were variously called "M. P's." and "Harper's Police"

The Police offices or courts were established by ordinance, March 12, 1845, as follows

1. Franklin Market
2. Halls of Justice.
3 Corner of Bowery and Third Street
4 Jefferson Market.

The Mayor and Special Justices were authorized to select six City Marshals, whose duty it was to attend daily at the down town Police office, and take charge of all prisoners brought to the office by Policemen, Watchmen, or private citizens. For the same purpose three Marshals were assigned to the Police office at the corner of Third Street and the Bowery, the pay of each being one dollar and fifty cents per day It having been discovered that a number of Policemen had, by direction of the Mayor and Special Justices, performed services before they had been finally appointed, and in order to compensate them for their labors, both Boards adopted a resolution granting them pay from the day on which they had assumed control of the locust

The Police of the city, by this change, consisted of three separate bodies. The Police proper, the Municipal Police, and the Watch—and the persons belonging to each of these divisions received their appointments from different sources. This was found to be a complicated and inefficient system. These separate

Mayor Harper

organizations tended to excite dissension among the individuals composing them, which was incompatible with the efficiency of a well-regulated Police

The Board of Aldermen again took counsel and reflected over the situation, the result being that they repealed the ordinance aforesaid on May 16, 1845, and removed all persons holding office or appointments under it. The Board of Aldermen at their next meeting, that is, on the twenty-third of May, adopted the Act passed May 7, 1844. In ten days thereafter the Act took effect.

The Act of 1844, as has been said, abolished the Watch and kindred departments of the City Police. In lieu of the Watch Department, Marshals, Street Inspectors, Health Wardens, Fire Wardens, Dock Masters, Lamp-lighters, Bell-ringers, Inspectors of Pawnbrokers and Junk-shops, and of the officers to attend the polls (these being sub-divisions of the then Police force), there was established a Day and Night Police, not to exceed eight hundred men, including Captains, Assistant Captains and Policemen. Each Ward was constituted a Patrol District, in each of which there was established a "District Headquarters." In addition to their other duties, the law obliged Policemen to light the lamps and ring the alarm bells. The duties of the force were more explicitly defined, but such duties in no important particular differ from those performed by Policemen at the present time. They had, for instance, to attend fires, to preserve the peace, to report to their Captains suspicious and disorderly houses, to arrest and arraign at court offenders against the law; to protect life and property, etc.

The Chief of Police, subordinate to the Mayor, was the chief executive officer. His office was located at the City Hall, in the Mayor's office. He was appointed by the Mayor, by and with the consent of the Common Council, to serve for one year, unless sooner removed.

The Aldermen, Assistant Aldermen, and Assessors of each Ward, with the concurrence of the Mayor, were empowered to appoint a Captain, one first Assistant Captain, one second Assistant Captain, and as many Policemen as the Ward was entitled to, whose term of office was also for one year.

The Common Council, in determining the salaries of the officers and men, should not, the act declared, exceed the following sums:

Chief of Police, fifteen hundred dollars; Special Justices, fifteen hundred dollars; Captains, seven hundred dollars; Assistant Captains, five hundred and fifty dollars; Policemen, five hundred dollars.

The Chief of Police was appointed on the nineteenth of June, but so much time was occupied in making necessary investigations into the character and capacity of persons nominated for places in the department, that the organization could not be judiciously advanced faster than as follows:

On the twenty-seventh of June, one hundred and seventy men were appointed, consisting of three officers and seven men for each Ward, and, on the fourteenth, fifteenth, sixteenth and seventeenth days of July, most of the six hundred and thirty men forming the complement of eight hundred officers and men were also appointed.

The City Watch was disbanded. The First District, July 15; the Sixth District on the 16th; and the Second, Third, Fourth, and Fifth Districts on July 18. The City Marshals were dismissed on the thirty-first of July, and on the first day of August the new law went into full operation, the Policemen for the various Wards being apportioned in accordance with the ordinance passed by the Common Council, June 11, 1845, as follows:

First Ward, 55; Second Ward, 40; Third Ward, 40; Fourth Ward, 55; Fifth Ward, 50; Sixth Ward, 60; Seventh Ward, 60; Eighth Ward, 50; Ninth Ward, 45; Tenth Ward, 45; Eleventh Ward, 45; Twelfth Ward, 30; Thirteenth Ward, 45; Fourteenth Ward, 50; Fifteenth Ward, 40; Sixteenth Ward, 45; Seventeenth Ward, 45; in the Police offices, 13; in the City Courts, 17; in the

Chief's office, 1; in office Commissioners of Alms House, 1; as Inspector of Stages, Hacks, Cabs and Carts, 4; as Bell-ringers, 15   Total, 851

The compensation per annum was set as follows:

Chief of Police $1500
Captains, each...$700
First and Second Assistant Captain, each $550
Policemen $500

The Mayor was authorized to prescribe rules and regulations for the government of the force, and from time to time to alter and amend the same. Two persons were appointed from each Ward by the Alderman and Assistant of such Ward, to act as Door-keepers. They were paid seven dollars per week for such service.

Mayor Havemeyer was then the Chief Magistrate of the city, and he appointed George W. Matsell Chief of Police, a position which he held for several years.

The duties of the following officers under the old system were performed by the Police Department, which offices were abolished when the new regime went into operation.

One hundred Marshals, eighteen Street Inspectors, eighteen Health Wardens, fifty-four Fire Wardens, thirteen Dock Masters, nine Day Police Officers, fifty Sunday Officers, sixteen Bell-ringers, eighteen Hydrant Inspectors, five Keepers of Public Parks, one Inspector Pawnbrokers, one Inspector Junk-shops, etc., two Inspectors of Hacks, two Inspectors of Stages, one Inspector of Carts, one Superintendent of Roads, one Superintendent of Lands and Places; also about three hundred officers to attend the polls on days of election, the whole Watch Department, consisting of eleven Captains, twenty-four Assistant Captains, and about one thousand two hundred Watchmen, making a total of one thousand eight hundred and forty-six.

Police Captain's Shield
(Star Police)

The above were supplanted by the following force, which was employed as follows: eighteen Captains on duty at all times, thirty-six Assistant Captains, one half on duty half the time; seventy-two Sergeants; seven hundred and seventy-three Policemen, of whom one hundred and two were detailed for special duty by the Mayor.

This force wore no uniform, a star-shaped badge, worn on the left breast of the outer coat, being their only insignia of office. Hence they came to be called "the Star" Police.

The City was divided into three districts, as follows: First District—First, Second, Third, Fourth, Fifth and Sixth Wards; Second District—Eighth, Ninth,

Twelfth, Fifteenth, Sixteenth and Eighteenth Wards; Third District—Seventh, Tenth, Eleventh, Thirteenth, Fourteenth and Seventeenth Wards

In each of these districts there were established a Police Court and office. The Police office for the First District continued to be held at the Halls of Justice in Centre Street; for the Second District at Jefferson Market, and for the Third District at the Essex Market.

In 1845 New York was again visited by a conflagration, second only in its ravages to the one of 1835. Three hundred and forty-five buildings were swept away, their value, with the goods, being estimated at about five millions of dollars.

The number of persons apprehended, from the first of July to the fifteenth of October, 1845, was eleven thousand four hundred and four

The list of Police Districts in 1846 was as follows.

First Ward, or A District   Franklin Market   Captain William Dill   East Station, Trinity Place.

Second Ward, or B District.   No. 60 Gold Street.   Captain John Kurtz

Third Ward, or C District   No 38 Robinson Street, now Park Place.   Captain Tobias Boudinot.

Fourth Ward, or D District.   No. 27 James Street   Captain Edward Fitzgerald.

Fifth Ward, or E District.   No. 16 Anthony Street   Captain W. C. Dusenbury

Sixth Ward, or F District   Old Watch House, Halls of Justice (the present Tombs)   Captain James McGrath   The entrance was on Franklin Street, and the prison was where the ten-day prison now is

Seventh Ward, or G District.   Corner of Pike and South Streets, up-stairs. Captain W M. Howell

Eighth Ward, or H District   The Old Watch-house, corner of Prince and Wooster Streets, where is now the Eighth Precinct Station house   Captain Benjamin P Fairchild.

Ninth Ward, or I District.   Jefferson Market, up-stairs, entrance on Greenwich Avenue   Captain James W Bush

Tenth Ward, or J District   Essex Market, up-stairs, entrance on Ludlow Street. Captain John Middleton

Eleventh Ward, or K District   Union Market, the present location.   In charge of a subordinate.

Twelfth Ward, or L District   House of Detention, or old Lock-up, Harlem, on site of present station house   In charge of a subordinate.

Thirteenth Ward, or M District   Attorney and Delancey Streets, the present station house is in part the old one   Captain John Tilley.

Fourteenth Ward, or N District   Centre Market, up-stairs   Captain David Kissner

Fifteenth Ward, or O District   No 650 Broadway, Constitution Hall.   Captain Nathaniel M. Brown

Sixteenth Ward, or P District.   Twentieth Street, between Seventh and Eighth Avenues, where is present station house   In charge of a subordinate.

Seventeenth Ward, or Q District   Third Street and the Bowery.   Captain Joseph Westerfield

The following year, under Mayor Brady, there were some changes and additions, as follows.

Fourth Ward, or D District   No. 31 Roosevelt Street, Captain Thomas Smith
Fifth Ward, or E District.   No 48 Leonard Street   Captain Ely Perry
Fifteenth Ward, or O District.   No 220 Mercer Street   Captain Brown
Eighteenth Ward   Twenty-ninth Street, between Fourth and Fifth Avenues; afterwards the Twenty-first, Twenty-ninth and Twenty-fifth precinct station house   Captain John W Brown.

Hardly had the newly-organized force become familiar with the changes that had taken place in the department, when the legislature (May 13, 1846) passed another Act "for the establishment and regulation of the Police of the City of New

The Eldridge Street Jail
(Old Debtors' Prison)

York" The changes effected thereby may be briefly enumerated as follows (the Day and Night Police remained as before) The force was not to exceed nine hundred men, and the rank of Sergeant was created. A Patrol District was established in each Ward, where a suitable room was maintained for the use of such Patrol, the name of this room being changed from District Headquarters to "Police Station House"

The Patrol of each District consisted of one Captain, a First and Second Assistant Captain, two or more Sergeants, and such number of Policemen as the Common Council should apportion to the Ward or District.

The Captains of the several Wards nominated to the Aldermen and Assistant Aldermen of their Wards suitable Policemen to perform the duties of Sergeants, not exceeding four or less than two for each Patrol District. The Chief held office for four years, unless sooner removed for cause. Policemen were appointed to office for two years. The Common Council, in determining the rate of compensation, should not, the legislature declared, exceed the following sums per annum:

Chief of Police, sixteen hundred dollars; Captains, seven hundred dollars; Assistant Captains, six hundred dollars; Sergeants and Policemen, five hundred dollars.

The **Police Department** consisted of the following:

Mayor, Chief of Police and his Clerk, Special Justices and their Clerks, Captains and Assistant Captains, Sergeants, Policemen, Constables and Doormen.

The Common Council subsequently arranged the compensation of the persons named above, as follows:

Chief of Police, sixteen hundred dollars, Special Justices, fifteen hundred dollars; Captains, seven hundred dollars, Assistant Captains, six hundred dollars, Sergeants and Policemen, five hundred dollars.

The Common Council, in May 1846, made the following re-apportionment of the force:

First Ward, 59; Second Ward, 43; Third Ward, 43, Fourth Ward, 60; Fifth Ward, 55; Sixth Ward, 66; Seventh Ward, 63; Eighth Ward, 56; Ninth Ward, 50; Tenth Ward, 48; Eleventh Ward, 45; Twelfth Ward, 33; Thirteenth Ward, 48; Fourteenth Ward, 54, Fifteenth Ward, 40, Sixteenth Ward, 43; Seventeenth Ward, 51, Eighteenth Ward, 43.

The newly created Eighteenth Ward was joined to the Second Police District.

A previous ordinance provided for the refunding to Policemen any expense necessarily incurred in bringing to the station house on a cart, any vagrant or intoxicated person. In order to meet this expense, Chief Matsell was allowed to draw one hundred dollars from the Comptroller. He was also granted a certain sum with which to meet the necessary expenses incurred by the Captains or Assistant Captains in providing prisoners with food or medicine.

All moneys paid for fines imposed by the Police Magistrates were received by one of the clerks in the respective Police offices, who entered such fines in a book, and on each Tuesday paid into the treasury all the moneys received during the week, accounting for the same under oath or affirmation to the Comptroller.

The Battery is an open space at the southwestern extremity of the city, situated between State Street and the bay. It is so called because part of its space was, in the early settlement of the city, occupied by Fort James, and much of the remainder was a battery to strengthen the fort on the water side. Military parades were frequently held here. In former days, when the Battery was a fashionable pleasure ground, on the fourth of July, and other national holidays, there was usually a martial and brilliant exhibition of the regiments of artillery, and the other uniform troops, upon the ground. The walk was open to all citizens. Here they might enjoy the fresh breezes from the bay and the shade of the trees every afternoon of the summer, and receive refreshments. In still earlier times, Battery Park was a favorite resort for the old Dutch settlers and their families.

Says Washington Irving "The old Dutch burghers would repair of an afternoon to smoke their pipes under the shade of their branches, contemplating the golden sun as he gradually sunk in the west, an emblem of that tranquil end toward which themselves were hastening; while the young men and the damsels of the town would take many a moonlight stroll among these favorite haunts, watching the chaste Cynthia tremble along the calm bosom of the bay, or light up the white sail of some gliding bark, and interchanging the honest vows of constant affection Such was the origin of the renowned walk, the Battery, which, though ostensibly devoted to the purposes of war, has ever been consecrated to the sweet delights of peace"

Nor was the enchantment of this scene confined to the time of the Knickerbockers As represented by the accompanying engraving, from a rare old print, the Battery, in comparatively modern times, drew within its precincts, by a more irresistible attraction, the young men and maidens of a by-gone generation "The favorite walk of declining age; the healthful resort of the feeble invalid; the Sunday refreshment of the dusty tradesman, the scene of many a boyish gambol, the rendezvous of many a tender assignation; the comfort of the citizen; the ornament of New York, and the pride of the lovely island of Manhattan,"—such was the encomium bestowed upon it by an enthusiastic writer. In view of the present uses of Battery Park, this is very melancholy reading. it sounds like an obituary.

Bellevue Hospital, (1850).

Mayor Brady, in his annual message, May 11, 1847, stated that the new Police system had "failed to meet the just expectations of the community," and recommended to the Common Council the propriety of memorializing the legislature to abolish the then Police force, "which affords so little protection to citizens and their property, more especially at night," and suggested the advisability of the establishment of a Night-watch to consist of one thousand two hundred men, or a virtual return to the old Watch system He estimated that, allowing to the Night-watch the sum of one dollar and twenty-five cents per night, the expense of maintaining such an establishment would be less annually by upwards of one hundred thousand dollars, while additional security at night would be insured from the increased number of men on duty, "and all the duties of Day Police would be as efficiently performed as now."

The Chief of Police reported to the Board of Aldermen that although the nominal force of the Police, under his control, comprised nine hundred men, there were but six hundred and fifty fit for ordinary duty, and that during the three months ending January 31, 1847, the actual loss of service of Policemen from sickness and suspensions amounted to six thousand one hundred and seventy-two days, being an average of sixty-seven men each day; and as there were forty-two men on day stations who did not perform duty during the night, the number actually available for night service could only be five hundred and sixty-one men, but one-half of whom were on duty at a time. This system, notwithstanding, was supported at an annual expense of four hundred and seventy-nine thousand dollars for salaries only.

The change did not seem to work well. There were still grumblings and discontent. The force at this time, it was admitted on all hands, was a long way from being "the finest in the world." An opinion prevailed that it would have been far better for the public at large to have left things as they had been. In fact there was a cry for a return to the old Watch system. Chief Matsell came to the front in vindication of his command, and by a comparison of the systems, tried to make it appear that the one of which he was at the head was by far the superior of the two. He quoted figures to prove that while the old Night-watch employed more men, they did not afford as good Police protection as the force that had succeeded it. But this did not diminish the popular discontent, and the cry continued for a change in the law.

Mayor Havemeyer, in his annual message, stated that "the defect which was most prominent in the system was the appointment of Policemen for a single year." Their term of office being the same with that of the Aldermen, Assistants and Assessors, who appointed them, there was danger, the Mayor thought, that the whole system would be involved in the incessant strifes and annual changes of parties, and its agents precluded from the experience and independence which were indispensable to their usefulness. "This evil, if it were to continue, constituted," the Mayor said, "a strong objection to the plan, but might be remedied by the legislature extending the time of appointment."

Acting upon the Mayor's suggestions, the Committee on Police, etc., recommended that application, in the usual form, be made to the legislature for the passage of an Act amending the Police Acts, passed May, 1844, and 1846.

As opposed to this attack on the new regime, a minority report of the Committee on Police, Watch and Prisons, undertook to vindicate the existing Police force, and denounced the effort that was being made to restore the old Watch Department, together with Day Policemen and Marshals. "If we adopt the Watch Department as recommended," (quoting from the minority report aforesaid) "we virtually re-establish the old system, with all its objectionable features of fees, inefficiency and corruption. We sacrifice all the advantages of experience concentrated in the Police, and which has been attained by close, constant and long continued application, we invite, again, the disorder, riot and crime, that formerly prevailed here, and which still disgrace the cities of Baltimore and Philadelphia. The influences which now restrain the young from the commission of crime, and detect the hardened offender, will be withdrawn, and scenes of personal violence and outrage, in the several Wards of the city, remain unrebuked and unpunished." For these reasons it was concluded that the unconditional repeal of the law would be "replete with danger to the best interests of society, and in violation of enlightened public opinion."

The Franklin House, one of the finest residences in the city, stood on the corner of Cherry Street and Franklin Square. It was built by Walter Franklin. This dwelling was selected as the official residence of President Washington, in 1790. The engraving represents this historic mansion as it appeared in 1850.

Provision was made, on July 16, 1847, for placing cots in station houses for the accommodation of lost children. On the seventh of September following, three rooms were set apart for the occupancy of persons not committed for a criminal offense. In November the pay of Doormen was increased from seven dollars a week to one dollar and twenty-five cents per day. On the thirteenth of

Washington's Residence—Franklin House, head of Cherry Street, in 1790, as it appeared in 1850.

January of the succeeding year the Common Council directed that two physicians be employed at a salary of one hundred dollars each per year. One of these physicians was stationed at Essex Market, and the other at Jefferson Market.

The expense of cleaning the city prison, and the employment of persons for that purpose, while prisoners were idling their time in cells, aroused the indignation of the city fathers, and they directed that the keepers of the prison should select five inmates daily, and compel them to do the chores.

The law was changed by act of the legislature (March 30, 1848) "in relation to Justices and Police Courts in the City of New York," by a division of the city into six Judicial Districts, a Justice to be elected in each district, the abolishment of the office of Assistant and Special Justices, and the election of six Police Justices to serve for four years.

The ordinance which divided the city into three districts (June 16, 1845) was amended on May 6, 1848, by the addition of a Fourth District, as follows:

First District—First, Second, Third, Fourth, Fifth, and Sixth Wards; Second District—Eighth, Ninth, Fifteenth and Sixteenth Wards; Third District—Seventh Tenth, Eleventh, Thirteenth and Fourteenth Wards; Fourth District—Twelfth Seventeenth, and Eighteenth Wards

In each of the foregoing districts there were established a Police Court and office. The business of the Police offices already established in the Halls of Justice, Centre Street, at Jefferson Market, and at Essex Market, continued to be conducted there, until otherwise directed by the Common Council. The Police office for the Fourth District, newly created, was located at the Police station house in the Eighteenth Ward.

A squad of nine Policemen was detailed at Chief Matsell's office in the basement of the City Hall, to act as Inspectors of Stages, of Carts, of Hacks, Junk-shops, and Pawnbrokers

Day stations of Policemen were designated "where citizens in the neighborhood of the stations who require the services of a Policeman, can always find one on duty, from sunrise to sunset." One such station was established in each Ward. Fourteen Policemen were detailed as Bell-ringers at the several district fire alarm bells, while others were detailed for special duty at the various Courts, namely, Courts of General and Special Sessions, Circuit Court, Common Pleas, Superior Court, and Marine Court. Others again were detailed as Street Inspectors and Dock Masters

The station houses were located at the following places:

First Ward, Franklin Market, up stairs, whole force	59
Second Ward, 60 Gold Street, whole force	43
Third Ward, 38 Robinson Street, whole force	43
Fourth Ward, 31 Roosevelt Street, whole force	60
Fifth Ward, 48 Leonard Street, whole force	55
Sixth Ward, station house (Tombs), whole force	66
Seventh Ward, Pike and South Streets, whole force	63
Eighth Ward, Prince and Wooster Streets, whole force	56
Ninth Ward, Jefferson Market, whole force	50
Tenth Ward, Essex Market, whole force	48
Eleventh Ward, Union Market, whole force	45
Twelfth Ward, House of Detention, Harlem, Bloomingdale and Yorkville, whole force	33
Thirteenth Ward, Attorney and Delancey Streets, whole force	48
Fourteenth Ward, Centre Market, whole force	54
Fifteenth Ward, 220 Mercer Street, whole force	54
Sixteenth Ward, Twentieth Street, between Seventh and Eighth Avenues, whole force	43
Seventeenth Ward, Third Street and Bowery, whole force	51
Eighteenth Ward, Twenty-ninth Street, between Fourth and Fifth Avenues, whole force	43

A squad of Police were detailed as Bell-ringers at the several district fire alarm bells, namely, City Hall Cupola, three men; Central Market Cupola, nine men; Jefferson Market Cupola, three men; Eighth District Station House Cupola, two men, Tenth District Station House Cupola, three men. Besides these there were the following details: two Scriveners at the office of Chief of Police, two Inspectors of Stages; two Inspectors of Hacks; one Inspector of Pawnbrokers; one Inspector of Junk-shops and Second-hand Dealers; one man to the office of the Commissioner of the Alms House; and one Physician, who was also appointed a Policeman There were also other details, as follows: nine Policemen to the Courts of General and Special Sessions; four to the Circuit Court; five to the Common Pleas; five to the Superior Court, one to the Marine Court. Policemen were detailed as Street Inspectors of the various Wards, and one Policeman as Dock Master, for each of the following Wards: First, Third, Fourth, Fifth, Seventh, Eighth, Ninth

The first set of printed rules and regulations issued to the force was in September, 1848. They were drafted by Chief Matsell and William McKellar, who was Matsell's chief clerk, and, generally speaking, "guide, philosopher and friend" These rules and regulations made up a handy little book of about ninety pages When issued, it was received with amazement and alarm by the men The inscription on the fly-leaf of one of these books, now in the possession of Captain Bennett, and evidently written by the particular Policeman to whom it originally belonged, is as follows: "A policeman would not live one year if he acted up to these regulations." This sentiment voices the opinion of the whole force whom the book was designed to instruct in their duty. And yet this little primer looks very simple and easy contrasted with the complicated, voluminous, and formidable digest of the laws contained in the present manual.

Mayor Havemeyer, in a preface to this book of rules and regulations, says "To this department, the most important of our city government, is intrusted the interest of the whole community—the safety of their persons, the security of their property, and the peace and good order of the city."

The instructions cannot be mentioned but quite briefly. Each member of the department was obliged to wear the emblem of his office on the outside of the outermost garment over the left breast Members of the force should, when on duty, conspicuously display their star (shield) or emblem of office The Captain of each Patrol District divided the Policemen of his district into two equal parts, to be known as the first and second platoon, which were commanded respectively by the first and second Assistant Captains The Captain also divided his district into night and day beats, and designated the Policemen who were to patrol the same, and, in like manner, established two or more day stations, in order that citizens might at all times during the day obtain the aid of Policemen when needed The beats and stations were numbered. At any alarm of fire it was the duty of Captains nearest the scene of the conflagration forthwith to proceed to the same with one half the number of their Policemen off duty, and to be diligent in preserving order and protecting property. A similar course should be adopted by the Captain in case of riot, which he should use due vigilance in suppressing.

The prevention of crime being the most important object in view, a Policeman's exertions, the rules maintained, should be constantly used to accomplish that end, and by his vigilance, to render it extremely difficult for any one to commit crime on his beat

In 1849 an amended charter was granted to the city, by which the day of the charter election was changed from the second Tuesday in April to the day of the general State election in November, the term of office to commence on the first Monday of the ensuing January. By the provisions of this charter, which was to take effect on the first of June, the Mayor and Aldermen were to hold their offices for two years, while the Assistant Aldermen were to be elected annually, as before. The city at this time consisted of eighteen Wards, an additional one having been created in 1845. Another was added in 1851, and the number was increased to twenty during the course of the following year.

The act of May 13, 1846, was amended on April 11, 1849, but the changes thereby effected were not of a radical nature. The tenure of office of the Chief of Police was made the same as that of the Mayor, and for thirty days thereafter. The tenure of office of Captains, Assistant Captains, and Policemen, was changed from two years to four years, from the date of their appointment. The section which referred to the compensation of Policemen was not affected

Astor Place Riot

by the amendment further than that their pay should not be increased or diminished during the time for which they were appointed.

The Astor Place riot, in this year, grew out of the rivalries and jealousies of two tragedians of different nationalities: Edwin Forrest an American, and James Macready, an Englishman. Each actor was filling a short engagement at different theatres in the city. To protect Mr. Macready, who was threatened with mob violence, a strong force of Police was stationed within the Astor Place Opera House, and another force of Police and military were put on guard outside. The destruction of the building was threatened, and the lives of those within were consequently endangered. The audience and Police alike were hemmed in and could not get out. The mob was growing in numbers and desperation rapidly. In this emergency the military guard delivered their first volley of shotted musketry into the mob, killing twenty-two and wounding forty.

Chief Matsell, in his quarterly report, April, 1849, gave utterance to this sentiment.

"It affords me pleasure to be able to state that the discipline of the department has been steadily improving during the past year; and it may be fairly anticipated that, under the operations of the amended law, the department will become what its original projectors intended it should be—an efficient organization for the prevention and detection of crime."

The whole number of arrests made from the first organization of the Police Department, July 15, 1845, to December 31, 1850, was as follows:

Arson	87
Assault with intent to kill	490
Assault and battery	13,896
Assault and interfering with Policemen	733
Attempt at rape	82
Attempt to steal	545
Attempt at burglary	157
Aiding and assisting to escape	212
Abandonment	336
Burglary	751
Bigamy	66
Bastardy	187
Constructive larceny	171
Disorderly conduct	20,252
Deserters	316
Driving without license	184
Embezzlement	75
Escaped convicts	303
Forgery	89
Felony	159
Fraud	101
Fighting in the street	1,987
Gambling	435
Grand larceny	2,055
Insanity	1,484
Intoxication	36,675
Intoxication and disorderly conduct	29,190
Indecent exposure	331
Insulting females in the street	138
Keeping disorderly houses	228
Miscellaneous misdemeanors and felonies	4,039
Murder	64
Obtaining goods by false pretences	240
Petit larceny	14,454
Pickpockets	215
Passing counterfeit money	425
Perjury	29
Rape	68
Robbery in first degree	169
Receiving stolen goods	183
Runaway apprentices	175
Selling spirituous liquor without license	39
Threatening life	189
Vagrancy	11,347
Violation of corporation ordinances	1,093
Grand total	144,364

The total number of persons apprehended from the first day of May, 1848, to the thirtieth day of April, 1849, inclusive, was twenty-five thousand seven hundred and sixty-nine.

The effective force on the first day of May, 1849, was eight hundred and eighty-nine, to wit: Captains, seventeen; Assistant Captains, thirty-six; Sergeants, seventy-four; and Policemen, seven hundred and sixty-two.

On the first day of January, 1851, the effective force of the Police was eight hundred and ninety-three, namely: Captains, eighteen; Assistant Captains, thirty-six; Sergeants, seventy; Policemen, seven hundred and sixty-nine.

The Police station houses were located as follows:

First Patrol District, Trinity Place, whole force	60
Second Patrol District, 70 Beekman Street, whole force	41
Third Patrol District, 35 Barclay Street, whole force	50
Fourth Patrol District, 9 Oak Street, whole force	55
Fifth Patrol District, 48 Leonard Street, whole force	56
Sixth Patrol District, the Tombs, whole force	57
Seventh Patrol District, Pike and South Streets, whole force	64
Eighth Patrol District, Prince and Wooster Streets, whole force	57
Ninth Patrol District, Jefferson Market, whole force	51
Tenth Patrol District, Essex Market, whole force	48
Eleventh Patrol District, Union Market, whole force	48
Twelfth Patrol District, One Hundred and Twenty-fifth Street, between Third and Fourth Avenues, whole force	31
Thirteenth Patrol District, Attorney and Delancey Streets, whole force	49
Fourteenth Patrol District, Centre Market, whole force	51
Fifteenth Patrol District, 220 Mercer Street, whole force	45
Sixteenth Patrol District, Twentieth Street, between Seventh and Eighth Avenues, whole force	52
Seventeenth Patrol District, Bowery and Third Streets, whole force	54
Eighteenth Patrol District, Twenty-ninth Street, between Fourth and Fifth Avenues, whole force	47
Nineteenth Patrol District, Eighth Avenue, near Forty-eighth Street, whole force	40

An ordinance (August 18, 1851) increased the salary of the officials hereinafter named, as follows: Captains, eight hundred dollars; Assistant Captains, seven hundred dollars; Sergeants and Patrolmen, six hundred dollars per annum. Ordinances of minor importance followed. One of these authorized the appointment of thirty-seven Policemen in the Nineteenth Ward, and another the appointment of two Doormen in each of the station houses of the Twelfth and Nineteenth Wards. Still another ordinance (January 15, 1852) appointed fifty-three Policemen to the Twentieth Ward, in addition to the Captain and First and Second Assistant Captains.

The legislature (July 11, 1851) amended that section of the charter of 1849 which referred to Police matters.

The amendment in question declared that should the Mayor neglect or refuse to nominate the Chief of Police for five days after the commencement of the sessions of the Common Council, held in August, 1851, it became the duty of the Board of Aldermen to appoint such officer forthwith. In like manner, in case the Mayor had made such nomination, and that it was rejected by the Common Council, that body had power to appoint such officer, provided that five days of any such session had elapsed without another nomination having been made by the Mayor

During the six months from the first day of July to the thirty-first day of December, 1852, there were arrested by the Police nineteen thousand nine hundred and ninety-one persons for various offences, being one thousand four hundred and forty-eight more than were arrested during the corresponding period of 1851 During the first part of the year 1852 offences against the person became of such frequent occurrence that peaceable citizens became alarmed, and were afraid to venture beyond their domiciles after a certain hour in the evening, while it was evident that many of the Policemen were careless, if not indolent, and rather preferred to turn away from places where they were likely to get hard usage and but little honor, than to interfere with evil disposed persons To remedy this, the Mayor had directed the whole Police force to be placed on duty during the day and night, which had, in part, the desired effect, as it was soon manifest that there was an increased watchfulness and care on the part of the force, and the order was then revoked

At the November election of 1852, Jacob A. Westervelt was elected Mayor. During the ensuing session of the legislature, the city charter was again amended in some important particulars, among which was the institution of a Board of Councilmen, composed of sixty members, to be chosen respectively from the sixty districts into which the Common Council was directed to apportion the city, in the place of the long-standing Board of Assistant Aldermen.

Of nine hundred and three Policemen, composing the entire force of the city, one hundred and seventy-eight were, on March 17, 1853, detailed to do special duty at the various civic courts, police courts, court of sessions, bell tower, etc., leaving but seven hundred and twenty-five to watch and guard the entire county of New York, being about an average of thirty-six men to each district during the night. One half of this number, say eighteen, were on duty, while the other half wer sleeping in the station-houses; so that one man had to watch from nine to fifteen blocks, according to the size of the district Should any of them be taken sick, then the size of the beat was increased; so that it was claimed it was impossible for the men to prevent crime or detect offenders as they should have done, even though they had exercised unwonted vigilance

The system of detailment, it was found, had grown to be an evil of great and increasing magnitude, alike unjust to the citizens and to the members of the Police Department. The larger part of those detailed had but light duties to perform, when compared with those on patrol duty, while on the other hand on detailed men arduous duties were imposed, keeping them employed during the day and the greater part of the night, and yet all were included under one head by the existing ordinances, and received one hundred dollars less than the Patrolmen. Under this system there had been no reward for merit, and the Policeman who could obtain the greatest number of influential friends to intercede for him could procure a berth where he might spend his time in comparative ease and idleness, while his less fortunate comrade, who had performed his duty zealously, and with a conscientious regard for the oath he had taken, received no honor, no favor, and was not advanced, simply because he had no influential friends to advocate his claim. Thus the incentive to do right and perform duty with cheerfulness was removed, and all experience has demonstrated the necessity of an incentive to induce men to push forward with active exertion in any pursuit of life which they might have undertaken; and while none existed in the Police Department, it could not be expected that the men would perform any greater amount of duties than they were absolutely compelled to perform by the vigilance of their superior officers, by which continual strife was kept up between the officers and Policemen. Ill-feelings were engendered, which soon ripened into the bitterest hatred and enmity, and which were carried out of the department into the private walks of life.

These or similar views were held and expressed by Chief Matsell, who also claimed that if promotions to posts of honor and profit were the reward of merit, it would be an incentive for each man to endeavor to surpass his peers in watchfulness and in the fidelity with which he would discharge his duty to the public. By doing so, he would be making consistent and honest efforts to advance his own interests, and thereby the public interests would be far better served, citizens would be fully protected in their persons and property, and the character of the city enhanced.

These views, it would appear, are no less sound at the present day than they were at the time in question.

CHAPTER VI.

APPOINTMENT OF A BOARD OF POLICE COMMISSIONERS.
1853-1857.

Ex-Superintendent Walling.—His Long and Honorable Connection with the Department.—Charter of 1853.—Re-organizing the Police Force—Tenure of Office to remain during Good Behavior—The Recorder, City Judge, and Mayor appointed as a Commission—A Reserve Corps Established—An Improvement in the Efficiency of the Force.—Introduction of a Police Uniform.—Hostility thereto—The "Star" Police.—Efforts made to Induce the Men to Wear the Uniform—Judgment Speedily Rendered in Trial Cases.—Beneficial Effects.—Appointment of a Drill Sergeant—Salaries Increased.—Tables of Arrests.—Sanitary Matters.

GEORGE WASHINGTON WALLING, ex-Superintendent of our New York Police, was born in Keyport, Monmouth County, N. J., a small village on Raritan Bay, about twenty-four miles from New York city, on the first of May, 1823. He attended school in his native town for a short time, but was obliged, like a large number of the Police Captains, to work very hard for his living while he was yet quite a boy. He was first employed on a farm, and then on the boats which plied between Keyport and New York. He joined the force on the twenty-second of December, 1847, and was assigned to the Third Precinct. Patrolman Walling soon had an opportunity of showing the kind of material he was made of. A party of boisterous young men were one night coming down Broadway, making night hideous with their shouting and blasphemy. They were partially intoxicated. Among their number was William Harrington, who was considered to be one of the toughest men in New York. "Gentlemen," said Patrolman Walling, "you must stop that noise, people are in bed and must not be disturbed." "Why, there are six of us here; how are you going to make us be quiet," was the answer of one of the young bloods. "Well, now, see here," said Walling, "I am here to do my duty, and I shall try and arrest some of you at least if you do not go on your way quietly." Harrington was so taken aback by the officer's coolness and determination that he separated himself from his gang and said, "By G—, I will help you." The young men, seeing that Walling was not to be trifled with, proceeded quietly on their way.

On the thirtieth of September, 1853, he was appointed Captain and assigned to the Eighteenth Ward. He retained his position of Captain when the Metropolitan Police was established. Fernando Wood, who at this time was Mayor,

George W. Walling

Resigned June 9, 1885.

refused to recognize the change from the Municipal to the Metropolitan Police, and a warrant was issued for his arrest. A detachment of the force was sent down to the City Hall to serve the warrant, but when the Police arrived they found the place in the hands of Mayor Wood's partisans. A struggle followed and some hard knocks were exchanged, but finally Wood's men beat back the Police and remained masters of the situation. Meantime the warrant had not been served on Mayor Wood. In this emergency the Commissioners asked Capt. Walling if he would serve the warrant on the Mayor. "Where is the warrant?" said Walling. "Here it is." "Well, then, I will serve it." And Captain Walling walked quietly down to the City Hall alone and unassisted, and served the warrant on Mayor Wood.

During the quarantine riots Captain Walling was sent down to Staten Island with one hundred men, where he discharged his duties in such an admirable manner that he was accorded official praise.

On his return to the city, he was placed in charge of the Fourth Precinct, where there was a good deal of crime. His administration of this district had a salutary effect on the lawbreakers. He was subsequently transferred to the Sixth Precinct, and, after serving there some time, he was placed in charge of the Detective force at headquarters, where his services were found very valuable. He was appointed Inspector on the twenty-first of November, 1866. Eight years after this Mr. Walling attained the highest position on the force; he was made Superintendent of the Metropolitan Police—a position which his ability, integrity and strict attention to duty well entitle him to hold.

One episode in particular in the official career of Superintendent Walling deserves more than passing mention, as it served to bring him into notoriety as a bright, brave, astute officer, and was, perhaps, the beginning of his success.

In 1848 he was detailed for duty at the Tombs, along with an officer named Shadbolt. About this time occurred the celebrated case known as "the Button Case." A number of burglaries had been committed for several weeks, on Saturday nights, in Maiden Lane and John Streets. John Reed, a detective, was detailed to investigate these burglaries, and, in the course of his labors, he discovered a cloth button on the floor of one of the stores that had been entered by burglars. Detective Reed, in the absence of any other clew, clutched at the button as eagerly as a drowning man would at a straw. The button was of a peculiar pattern, and was only used on certain kind of coats of not very fashionable make. The detective argued, with that refinement of reason and discernment rarely to be found except in an experienced detective, that the button in question was of great importance to him in establishing the identity of the burglars, if they were ever to be identified at all. In fact, he thought the button was a sort of a connecting link. Having settled the matter in his mind that the mysterious button had been torn from the coat, or dropped from the pocket, of one of the burglars, he next satisfied himself that none of the men employed about the store wore clothes with buttons to match the specimen in his possession; so that if any value was to be attached to his theory, the burglars were to be sought for on the outside of the establishment—a point of no mean importance to be settled in a case so critical and so mysterious. He carried the button to

Chief Matsell, who thought sufficiently well of Mr. Shadbolt's ingenious theory, to send for all the detailed men, to whom he exhibited the button, telling them to be on the alert for a man wearing a coat with that kind of button. One night thereafter, Detective Shadbolt and his side partner, Detective Walling, in the discharge of their duty, attended the old Chatham Street Theatre. Walling went up stairs and Shadbolt remained below. Shadbolt soon after joined Walling and said "There are three young fellows coming up, and one of them has buttons on his coat like the one in our possession." When the three young men passed up-stairs they seated themselves in the gallery, and our friend Walling took a vacant seat close by them, and, while pretending to scan a programme, he was paying close attention to the kind of buttons they had on their coats. This furtive scrutiny satisfied him that one of the young men had just such buttons on his coat, and, going down-stairs, he so informed Shadbolt, who was waiting at the entrance. By agreement, Shadbolt was to go to the old Bowery Theatre and stay there until he heard from Walling. Meantime, when the performance was over, Walling followed the three young men to Chatham and Duane Streets, where they entered a lodging house. Satisfied that he had followed them to their lodging, he called a citizen whom he knew and asked him to find Shadbolt in front of the old Bowery Theatre, and to send him (Shadbolt) to Walling without delay. The messenger did as he was instructed, and, when Shadbolt arrived, the two concluded to go to John Reed's house, on Tenth Street, and tell him just what they knew and what further they proposed doing. This done, they arranged to meet Reed and John Wade (another detective) at Chief Matsell's office at daybreak, whither they would bring the three young men, whom they concluded to arrest.

Ex Superintendent Walling's Shield.

When Shadbolt and Walling, after making known their business to the proprietor of the place, passed up-stairs, they knocked on the door of the room occupied by the three young men, who were in one bed. One of the three got up and opened the door. When he looked out he said to his companions, "The cops are here." The prisoners were taken to Chief Matsell's office. When searched, it was found that each wore a new pair of suspenders, of precisely the same pattern as had been stolen from one of the Maiden Lane houses. They at first denied their guilt, but soon confessed all. The stolen goods, the proceeds of eleven burglaries, were found in a receiver's house in Centre Street. The three young men were convicted, and sent to state prison each for a term of three years.

The button picked up by Detective Reed in the Maiden Lane store was thus the means of tracking the culprits. While getting away with their booty, one of the burglars had this identical button torn off his coat.

Shortly afterwards, Detective Walling, in recognition of his services, was detailed to Chief Matsell's office in the City Hall.

Patrolman Walling was on duty in Broadway the night that Tom Hyer gave Yankee Sullivan a terrible beating in a basement, at the corner of Park Place. Hyer—after the row—had a pistol in his hand, and was in the act of putting a cap on it.

"Put that pistol up," said Patrolman Walling.

"Who the h—ll are you?" he answered. "I am not going to get killed."

"You can come along with me," said Walling.

Both left the saloon by a rear door and walked together to Broadway, when Hyer crossed the Park and entered No 25 Park Row. This led to the fight between Hyer and Sullivan in 1849.

On Monday, the first day of the draft riots, Captain Walling was on duty in Third Avenue. While there he learned that the people were opposed to the draft, and that the arsenal had been burned. He went to the station house at Thirty-fifth Street, between Eighth and Ninth Avenues, and sent out a general alarm to hold men in readiness for any emergency. Soon afterwards he received an order to send a force of men to Thirty-fifth Street and Seventh Avenue to take charge of the arsenal. He and his command staid there until some soldiers came up and relieved them, when they returned to the station house. In the afternoon he received an order to report to headquarters. He and his men came down in stages. The mob was then burning buildings where the drafting was going on, at Twenty-ninth Street and Broadway. Captain Walling and his men proceeded immediately to the City Hall. There had been an attack made on the Tribune building, and they were sent down to relieve the force of Police there detailed, and protect the newspaper offices generally.

The next morning they were sent to the Twentieth and Twenty-seventh Districts to hunt for rioters who were said to be destroying property. When they arrived there a man told Captain Walling that the rioters had gone to attack the Sixth Avenue car stables, but when the Police got there, nobody was to be seen. It was then learned that the mob was attacking houses on Fifth Avenue, and thither Captain Walling went. His search for rioters was at last rewarded. He found a mob of probably two thousand persons. He had only eighty men. He ordered them to charge with drawn clubs, and, as a matter of course, they had enough to do to clear the street. Orders were given to take no prisoners. Those of the mob in front went down before the Policemen's clubs, and Captain Walling yelled out at the top of his voice, "Kill every man that has got a club," and every man that had one dropped it as quickly as he could. The crowd was dispersed in short order and driven to Forty-sixth Street.

The same afternoon, while Captain Walling was standing at the corner of Thirty-fifth Street and Eighth Avenue, he saw a big fellow in a crowd breaking in a door with a cart-rung. Captain Walling made his way through the mob, and with a scientific twirl of his locust, he laid the brawny ruffian with the cart-rung prostrate in the gutter, while those who were aiding and abetting him waited not to be clubbed, but fled. As it proved, the wielder of the cart-rung was permanently knocked out. A doctor was sent for, but as soon as he looked at the man he said "That man wants no doctor; he wants an undertaker."

After that, Captain Walling and his men went down to the colored church on Twenty-seventh Street, which was threatened by the rioters, and dispersed the crowd.

On Wednesday he remained at the station house. His was the only station house that had any communication with headquarters. The other telegraph wires were destroyed by the rioters.

During the Orange riots Superintendent Walling was put in command of the force on Eighth Avenue and Twenty-seventh Street, where they had several fights with the mob, the latter being driven back every time. The Ninth Regiment fired and killed several persons.

He received the following letter from Chief Matsell:

NEW YORK, August 13, 1850

GEORGE W. WALLING

DEAR SIR:

I take this opportunity to express to you the gratification I experienced on witnessing your noble conduct on the fifth of August inst., on the occasion of the burning of the larger part of the five story building occupied by W. & D. White, at No. 40 Spruce Street, when you toiled with your own hands, and imperiled your own life, to extricate a fellow being from a mass of rubbish in which he was buried.

Your conduct was above all praise, and not only reflects honor upon yourself as a man and an officer, but is highly creditable to the Department to which you belong.

Accompanying this note you will receive a baton, beautifully ornamented with silver, which I beg you to accept as a token of my respect and esteem, and my appreciation of your conduct on the occasion of the fire. Although the present is not intrinsically valuable, yet it will serve as a memento of the noble act that called forth the praise of all who witnessed it.

With sentiments of esteem and respect,
Yours, etc.,
GEORGE W. MATSELL,
Chief of Police.

Not only is the Superintendent of Police the chief executive of the force, not only is he the mouthpiece through whom, legitimately, all the orders of the Board must come, not only is he charged with the supreme government of the force, subject only to the written orders from the Board of Police, but he is, in addition, charged with a vast variety of other duties, which render the place one of the most onerous.

The select committee appointed by the Assembly in 1875 to investigate the cause and increase of crime in the city, while finding fault with every other Police official in high command, bears this appreciative testimony to the fidelity and worth of Superintendent Walling

"The present Superintendent is an old officer of nearly thirty years' standing on the force, of unblemished reputation, and of unquestioned Police experience."

While in command of the Eighteenth Ward station house, on the thirteenth of October, 1853, he was presented with a badge, of which the accompanying cut is an exact *fac simile*, bearing the following inscription on the reverse side:

GEORGE W. WALLING,
Eighteenth Patrol District.

Presented to George W. Walling, on his promotion to the office of Captain of the Eighteenth Ward Patrol District, by the officers attached to the office of the Chief of Police, and other friends, as a token of respect and esteem.

The law retiring " any member of the Police force who shall have reached the age of sixty years, and placing him on the roll of the Police Pension Fund " * * * took effect May 28, 1885. (Chapter 364, Sec. 307.) This led to the resignation of the veteran Superintendent on June 9, following. The Board of Police Commissioners, in accepting his resignation, unanimously approved of the following statement.

"The Board of Police cheerfully embrace this opportunity of bearing testimony to their high appreciation of the many years of valuable service rendered to the public by an honest, worthy and capable officer, appointed a Patrolman December 22, 1847, promoted in each instance through the several grades of Captain, Inspector, and Superintendent, for specially marked ability, untiring devotion to duty, and rare fidelity to trust * * * The bright character and faithful services constituting the extraordinary record of Superintendent Walling is presented to the force as an example ever worthy of emulation "

Some of the most important changes effected by the charter of 1853 consisted in abolishing the Board of Assistant Aldermen and substituting instead thereof a Board of Councilmen, consisting of sixty members, one to be elected from each of sixty districts of contiguous territory; and the appointment of the Mayor, Recorder, and City Judge as a Board of Commissioners, by whom the officers of the Police and Policemen were thereafter to be appointed

The Police Department was made to consist of the following named officers: Chief of Police, Captains, Lieutenants, Sergeants, Policemen, and Doormen It was the duty of this force to watch and guard the city day and night, and protect all general and primary elections

The title of Assistant Captains was changed to Lieutenants, the former incumbents assuming the newly-created rank until the expiration of the terms for which they were appointed such Assistant Captains

Members of the Police appointed after the passage of this Act held office during good behavior, and could be removed only for cause.

The Chief and Captains were empowered to suspend Sergeants, Policemen, and Doormen, for cause, in manner prescribed by Act of 1846

The qualifications and method of appointment were as follows The law required that a Policeman should be a citizen, a resident of the Ward; should read and write; and understand the first four rules of arithmetic; and bear a good character for honesty, morality, and sobriety. Previous to appointment he was required to present to the Mayor a certificate signed by twenty-five reputable citizens, two-thirds of whom should be residents of his own Ward, to the effect that they had known him for five years, and that his character came up to the required official standard. He was likewise obliged to present to the Mayor a surgeon's certificate that he was of sound body and robust constitution

One of the important reforms inaugurated, and by no means the least important, was the adoption of a uniform, which it was rightly believed would secure greater attention to duty, and more zealous watchfulness on the part of all A reserve corps had also been established, into which only those were admitted who had earned the privilege which membership in this corps conferred, by strict attention to duty, and by furnishing proof of fitness for the post. This was a virtual promotion, and was calculated to stimulate a laudable ambition among the men, and to encourage them to a more faithful and zealous performance of their duty The operations of the law re-organizing the department tended to place it in such a condition as to justify the expectations formed of it by the community; and the Commissioners appointed under the Act, had, it was conceded, faithfully endeavored to carry out all the provisions of the law; and the evidence of their success was to be found in the superior character of the men appointed, and the general condition and efficiency of the force

The effective force on the first day of July, 1853, was: Captains, twenty; Lieutenants, forty; Sergeants, seventy-nine; Policemen, eight hundred and sixty-four Total, 1003

The condition and efficiency of the Police Department, it was acknowledged, had materially improved since the foregoing Act of the legislature went into operation. Among the important changes thereby brought about were the tenure of office, which was limited only to the good behavior of the incumbent. The power of appointment was vested in a commission, consisting of the Recorder, City Judge, and Mayor, who had the sole power to try and punish parties violating the rules of the department, and who, in conjunction with the Chief of Police, were authorized to prescribe rules for the government of the force.

Mayor Harper, as has been pointed out, in 1844 began his reformatory measures by trying the experiment of uniforming a corps of about two hundred Policemen. The men did not take kindly to the uniform, because chiefly, the idea was borrowed from England. So averse was the public to this innovation in Police dress, that at the burning of the Old Bowery Theatre almost a riot occurred, the populace threatening to mob the Police, whom they designated as liveried lackeys. This and similar experiences served to make the uniformed Police still more unpopular, and in the succeeding year, when Havemeyer was Mayor, the uniform was abolished, and the force that wore it legislated out of office. The only insignia of office worn by the Police after that was a star-shaped copper shield, from which they received the name of "cops." The force was known as the "Star" Police from the shape of the shield. But the question of uniforming the Police continued to be agitated. Among the most strenuous advocates of the measure was James W. Gerard, father of the late Senator Gerard. He carried his zeal in this matter so far that he went to London with, it is said, the sole object of studying the Police system, for the purpose of introducing it in his native city. Upon his return home he brought with him a uniform, such as was then worn by the London Police, and made to fit himself. This suit he wore at a fancy dress ball in this city, where it attracted a good deal of favorable attention.

The next point scored by the advocates of a uniform was during the fair at the Crystal Palace. The squad of men that was there detailed for duty was placed under the command of Captain Leonard and the veteran Bob Bowyer. They were put in uniform, and were kept under strict discipline, they having for Drill Master, Officer (afterwards Inspector) Jamison, who had served through the Mexican war and seen active service in the war of the Rebellion. The men's trim and soldierly appearance made a very favorable impression, and it got to be the prevailing opinion that the uniform lent dignity to the men, and added to their official importance and self-respect. That it would produce the same beneficial results if worn by the regular Police was an inevitable conclusion. But experience and logic were alike thrown away on the men, and they universally condemned the uniform, and regarded as their mortal enemies all who counseled the wearing of it. The men carried their opposition so far as to hold an indignation meeting in front of Chief Matsell's windows, he being one of the leading champions of the measure.

The next attempt to introduce a uniform provoked at first a bitter opposition. The men urged that it conflicted with their notions of independence and self-respect. The Commissioners (Westervelt, Tillou and Beebe), as well as Chief Matsell, left no efforts untried to break down this prejudice, and after hard work, they at last succeeded. It was interesting to note how rapid was the change in public opinion just as soon as the men appeared on post clad in the new official dress which distinguished them from civilians. How this was brought about may best be told in the words of one who personally knew whereof he spoke.

"Chief Matsell," said the late Inspector Thorne, "had notified the men that they should procure uniforms to be worn while on duty. The men refused to do so, because, they said, it would give them the appearance of footmen. It was claimed also (notably by the late District Attorney, John McKeon, who was counsel for the force), that the law did not justify the Commissioners in ordering them to wear uniforms, and that they could not be compelled to do so. The men held several meetings in Military Hall, on the Bowery, where they passed resolutions that they would not wear the uniform. The Commissioners and Chief of Police were determined that they should, and matters were coming to a crisis. The men had been appointed for a certain term, which was about expiring, and the new law made the term of office during good behavior. These men were seeking for re-appointment under the life tenure, and did not know what to do. I took it upon myself," continued Inspector Thorne, "as a committee of one, to wait upon Commissioner Beebe, who was a personal friend of mine, to ascertain, if possible, if there could be any means of dispensing with the wearing of the uniform, which we all unanimously declared to be a badge of servitude. Commissioner Beebe entered into an argument with me on the subject, in which he went on to show that the wearing of a uniform would be creditable to the force, as the men—on turning out on duty—wore the poorest clothes they had, and were anything but reputable in appearance as a Police force. They had nothing to show but their star shield. The judge went on in a kindly way to express to me what the uniform consisted of, and under his advice, I had a uniform suit made, in which I appeared at the next meeting in Military Hall, and received many compliments on having such a nice new suit of clothes, they not for a moment supposing it to be the uniform. After the meeting had progressed some time, and the different speakers had ventilated their ideas for the benefit of the whole, all using strong language in opposition to the uniform scheme, and the audience being of the same mind to a man, I asked permission to say a few words relative to the resolutions passed in regard to not wearing the uniform. Receiving permission, I explained to the meeting that I had had an interview with Commissioner Beebe, that his feelings were of a kindly nature towards the men, and that he did not wish them to stand in their own light, as at that time the majority of them had to be appointed under the new Act, and that if it came to a test it would only be a matter of a little time when every man who refused to wear the uniform would be rejected. Those who had been recently appointed were under the jurisdiction of the Commissioners, and would have to come under the rules and discipline like the others. I then argued with them that the uniform was not so objectionable. I also called their attention to the suit of clothes I then had on—a coat being all the uniform then required by the Commissioners, and telling them that that was the uniform that the Commissioners had adopted, and which the men were asked to wear. The men seemed to be incredulous, and one or two ventured to say, 'Well, if that be what they call the uniform, it is a first-class thing. No' one can object to that.' Others chimed in; and then I was examined more critically, and finding them in a yielding mood, I asked them to rescind the resolution not to use the uniform, so as to relieve the men from that pledge. The men being favorably impressed, rescinded the resolution with the exception of three votes, and two of these afterwards fell into line. There were about three hundred men present at the meeting. The only exception was officer James Burnham of the Fifth Precinct, who stood aloof, and entered suit against the city for salary for the whole term of office, for four years, which suit he kept up till the day of his death, but he never received a penny. The uniform was immediately adopted by the whole force; that was the end of the old clothes and the beginning of the new."

The next innovation came when the bands and the buttons were brought on gradually. Said the late Inspector Thorne:

"On one occasion the Thirteenth Ward Police were going to a target excursion. Myself and ex-Captain Steers, father of the present Captain Steers, were appointed a committee to wait upon Chief Matsell to get permission from him to go to the excursion. The Chief consented on condition that the men would put the brass buttons on the coat furnished by the city, that was the compromise, and it was accepted.

"At that time business firms used to give from twenty-five dollars to forty dollars for the best marksman, but no matter whether the men hit the target or not, they were sure to get the reward. The early target excursions were great features with the Police, and each Ward used to turn out, and have the leading citizens as their guests.

"At this time the uniform consisted at first of a blue cloth coat with a velvet collar, and nine black buttons on the front. Afterwards an addition was made by substituting the brass buttons for the black buttons, and gray pants with a black stripe one inch in width on each side. Cloth caps were furnished by the city, and a fire cap similar to that worn by firemen to go to fires, riots, etc.

"Summer uniforms were adopted by each Ward as they thought proper, each Ward selecting uniforms of their own choice.

"Some Wards adopted white duck suits and sack coats. Other Wards adopted different colors. Uniformity did not exist in general. Some wore Panama hats, some straw, and some felt, but each Ward had a special uniform of its own.

"When the Metropolitan force was organized, the Commissioners changed the uniform, and made it a blue cloth coat with brass buttons, blue pants with white stripe, blue vest and brass buttons. In the summer the officers wore white pants, white vests, and Panama hats. That continued until they commenced wearing flannel clothes in summer."

The Commissioners, on entering upon the discharge of their duties, determined to render judgment upon cases brought before them for trial immediately after the trial came, and before interested individuals connected with the department could have an opportunity to interfere. The effect of this determination upon the department was almost magical. During the first six months but one hundred and forty-three Policemen were cited to appear before the

Commissioners for trial, being a diminution of one-fourth, as compared with the previous six months. This had resulted entirely from the certainty and not from the severity of the punishment, as but three or four trials had taken place in which judgment was not immediately rendered. The old system of detailing officers for various special duties, which was open to so many objections on account of the abuses perpetrated under it, had been abolished, and a reserve corps, as already noticed, established. The Commissioners also adopted a resolution requiring all the members of the department to wear a blue coat of uniform make, and a cap for night and day patrol duty, so that the men could be easily recognized by the citizens. The regulation had been complied with by all the members of the department, with three or four exceptions. The Policemen who had refused to comply were tried by the Commissioners of Police and dismissed the force, and the case carried up to the Supreme Court, where the action of the Commissioners was sustained.

Chief Matsell selected a competent Policeman to act as Drill Sergeant, whose duty it was to take the men appointed by the Commissioners and instruct them in the military art, and in the rules and regulations adopted for the government of the Police Department. While under instruction they were required to act as a reserve force to attend at fires, etc., and to perform patrol duty in different parts of the city, under the direction of their Sergeants. After being thus thoroughly drilled and instructed, they were directed to report themselves to their several Captains, and were ready to perform any duty he might require of them.

The greatest benefit, it was acknowledged, resulting to the community under the law of 1853, was the separation of the department from political influences. Under the former law, Policemen well understood that they had to enter the political arena, and connect themselves with the dominant clique of partisans in the separate Wards, in order to secure a re-appointment at the expiration of the term for which they were appointed. So that instead of being disinterested officers at the polls during the election, they became interested partisans, striving for the success of their favorite cliques. Policemen were found connected with clubs, committees, and other organizations of a political character, leading them to perform their duty with inattention, and sometimes to entirely neglect it, thus exercising a most baneful influence upon the efficiency and character of the department. In this way the whole force was turned into a political engine for the advancement of particular cliques or individuals. To obviate this evil, the Commissioners adopted a rule to the effect that no member would be permitted to connect himself, directly or indirectly, in any way, with a society, club, committee, or organization of any kind, the object of which was the political advancement of a party, clique or individual.

By resolution of the Common Council, passed October 21, 1853, the salaries were increased as follows: Captains, one thousand dollars; Lieutenants, eight hundred dollars, and Sergeants and Policemen, seven hundred dollars per annum. By resolution, approved the twenty-ninth of the following December, the salary of Doormen was increased to six hundred dollars per annum.

The effective force on the first day of January, 1854, was. Captains, nineteen; Lieutenants, forty; Sergeants, seventy-seven; and Policemen, eight hundred and forty-two   Total 978.

The whole number of arrests, and description of offences, from the first organization of the Police Department, July 15, 1845, to the thirty-first of December, 1853, inclusive, is as follows.

Arson	147
Assault with intent to kill	1,061
Assault and battery	27,904
Assaulting, and interfering with Police	1,321
Attempt at rape	194
Attempt to steal	1,218
Attempt at burglary	371
Aiding and assisting to escape	420
Abandonment	899
Burglary	1,308
Bigamy	112
Bastardy	644
Constructive larceny	108
Disorderly conduct	34,735
Deserters	428
Driving without license	361
Embezzlement	169
Escaped convicts	429
Forgery	195
Felony	279
Fraud	264
Fighting in the street	4,131
Gambling	735
Grand larceny	4,196
Insanity	2,873
Intoxication	63,944
Intoxication and disorderly conduct	48,217
Indecent exposure	550
Insulting females	270
Keeping disorderly houses	592
Miscellaneous misdemeanors	6,983
Murder	160
Obtaining goods under false pretences	526
Petit larceny	24,298
Pickpockets	687
Passing counterfeit money	829
Perjury	60
Rape	136
Robbing in the first degree	415
Receiving stolen goods	377
Runaway apprentices	344
Selling liquor without license	718
Threatening life	293
Vagrancy	21,155
Violation corporation ordinances	2,700
Total	257,738

From the first of January to the thirtieth of June, 1854, there were twenty-five thousand one hundred and ten persons arrested for criminal offenses, being an increase of two thousand eight hundred and seventy-four over the previous six months, and an increase of seven thousand three hundred and ninety-seven over the corresponding period of time in 1853. Of the whole number, there were

CAPT. JOHN D. MCKEE.   CAPT. MICHAEL HALPIN   CAPT EDWARD LETTS
                       CAPT. THOMAS HANNEGAN
              Police Captains, 1856

arrested by the reserve corps three thousand nine hundred and eighty-five, one thousand and thirty-five of which were for violation of the corporation ordinances. This large increase in the number of arrests resulted, as Chief Matsell claimed, from an increased activity and vigilance on the part of Policemen.

The force, without doubt, had greatly improved. The appointment of Commissioners and the introduction of a uniform had much to do with this. A stricter discipline was also enforced, and the men began to take an honest pride in their work, and to be a terror to evil-doers.

The Commissioners on Rules and Regulations promulgated a new regulation in relation to the dress to be worn by the members of the force when on duty. This regulation prescribed uniform trousers, buttons, belt for baton, and an overcoat, to be worn in winter, and lighter coats for summer use. By previous regulations, the Captains of the several districts were empowered to select the material for the summer coats to be worn by the members of their command, but this was not found to work well in practical operation, as there was no uniformity of appearance, and the force began to assume the same look of negligence in attire that existed previous to the adoption of the uniform coat and cap, and numerous complaints were made by citizens that they could scarcely distinguish a Policeman from any other citizen. This new regulation imposed upon the members of the department additional expense, which in many, if not in every instance, was found hard to be borne, and it was asked that the Common Council make an appropriation to meet the whole or a portion of these additional expenses.

Complaint having been made by Chief of Police Matsell to the Mayor, of the inadequate accommodations of the station houses, their unsanitary condition and general dilapidation, an inspection and report of the various station houses were caused to be made, from which it appears that the necessity for reform and improvement was urgent. Chief Matsell, in view of these facts, suggested that two or three eminent architects should be invited to draw plans for a model station house, and that thereafter all station houses should be required to be built according to the plan adopted.

From the first day of January to the thirtieth day of June, 1854, inclusive, two hundred and thirty-nine complaints were preferred against members of the Police Department, which were disposed of as follows:

Dismissed from office 19
Resigned, after complaint... 7
Complaints dismissed 75
Suspended from pay 138

Total 239

The effective force on the first of July, 1854, was Captains, twenty-two, Lieutenants, forty-four, Sergeants, eighty-three, Policemen, nine hundred and fifty-three. Total, 1,102.

On the first day of January, 1855, the effective force was Captains, twenty-two; Lieutenants, forty-four, Sergeants, eighty-eight, Policemen, nine hundred and sixty-two. Total, 1,116.

The sanitary condition of nearly all the station houses was defective in a marked degree, and but little attention was paid to the general health of the force. This naturally resulted in much unnecessary suffering and sickness among the members, and a consequent loss of time to the department. Under the old system station houses were rarely visited and inspected; cleanliness was not deemed a part of the discipline, and when sick at home, the men were not visited, except merely to ascertain whether the disability had been procured in the discharge of duty. This led, in 1855, to an alteration in the surgical bureau

Capt. Chas. S Turnbull Capt. John E Russell Capt. David Kissner
Capt. Abram Ackerman Capt. Peter Squires Capt. James Leonard
Capt. Jas A Hopkins

Police Captains, 1856.

Capt Galen T Porter Capt Geo W Norris Capt Daniel Witter
Capt Francis Speight Capt J Murray Ditchett. Capt Francis J Twomey
Capt J W Hartt
Police Captains, 1856

of the department. The new plan regarded the proper ventilation and cleanliness of the station houses and sleeping apartments; furnished at all times a sufficient supply of medicines, surgical instruments, tourniquets, etc., required immediate attention to be given to all invalid Policemen, whether becoming sick or disabled in the discharge of duty or not, until entirely recovered and fit for duty. In order the better to carry out this system, the city was divided into seven surgical districts, and each district was placed under the charge of a competent practicing physician, who, under the law, had to be appointed a Policeman, and detailed for this duty, with a Surgeon-General as chief of the whole, to whom reports were made by the District Surgeons once every forty-eight hours. Critical physical examinations were made of every person appointed by the Commissioners, not only by the District Surgeon in the Ward to which said person might belong, but also by the Surgeon-General stationed permanently at the office of the Chief of Police. Stephen Hasbrouck, M.D., filled the post of Surgeon-General.

During the five months succeeding the establishment of this surgical system, it appears from the records that the time lost by reason of sickness or disability of the Policemen, in all the twenty-two districts, amounted to three thousand nine hundred and forty-six and one-half days, and the time lost during a corresponding period in 1854, amounted to five thousand three hundred and seventy-nine days.

The amount thus saved was several hundred dollars over the sum necessary to pay all the surgeons, besides the advantage to the men of receiving the benefit of prompt and gratuitous attendance.

CHAPTER VII.

THE METROPOLITAN POLICE DISTRICT.

1857—1863.

THE LAW DESIGNATING THE MAYOR, RECORDER, AND CITY JUDGE, POLICE COMMISSIONERS, REPEALED —APPOINTMENT OF FIVE COMMISSIONERS —THE COUNTIES OF NEW YORK, KINGS, WESTCHESTER AND RICHMOND MADE TO COMPRISE THE NEW DISTRICT —OPPOSITION TO THE CHANGE —A YEAR OF RIOTS AND FINANCIAL FAILURES —THE METROPOLITAN POLICE DISTRICT ACT DECLARED TO BE CONSTITUTIONAL   CONFLICT BETWEEN MAYOR WOOD AND THE NEWLY-APPOINTED COMMISSIONERS.—THE MUNICIPAL POLICE AND THE METROPOLITAN POLICE ARRAYED IN OPEN BATTLE —INTERVENTION OF THE MILITARY —THE ACT AMENDED BY MAKING THE DISTRICT TO CONSIST OF THE COUNTIES OF NEW YORK, KINGS, WESTCHESTER AND RICHMOND, AND THE TOWNS OF NEWTOWN, FLUSHING AND JAMAICA —THE NUMBER OF COMMISSIONERS REDUCED TO THREE.

UP to the year 1857, with various vicissitudes, as has been set forth in the preceding pages, the city of New York had a Municipal Police force which, on the whole, was inadequate for the duties it was called upon to perform, and did not give general satisfaction   In this year the legislature established the Metropolitan Police District, and for thirteen years the City Police was merged in that body   The charter of 1870 abolished the Metropolitan Police District, and again substituted the Municipal Police, which remained in force until 1873, when the present Police Department was created

The organization of a Board of Police Commissioners (Act 1853) consisting of the Mayor, Recorder and City Judge, and the extending the tenure of office of the Police during good behavior, were instrumental in bringing about a marked change for the better in the character and efficiency of the Police   It was, however, found that the judicial duties of the Recorder and City Judge rendered them unable to discharge those duties which devolved on them as Commissioners of Police, and that the power of appointment and dismissal was virtually lodged with the Mayor   The alleged abuse of this power, and the rapid increase of population in the cities of New York and Brooklyn, conspired to make a change in the Police organization desirable

The year 1857 was a disastrous one to New York—a year of mob rule, beginning with civil strife and ending with financial ruin   In the spring of this year the State Legislature passed several bills relating to the city, and amended the charter in several important particulars.   The charter, and State elections, which had hitherto been held on the same day, were separated, the first Tuesday in December being fixed as the date of the former. The most important innovation was the transfer of the Police Department from the city to the State. By the Metropolitan Police Act, a Police District was created, comprising the counties of New York, Kings, Westchester, and Richmond; and a Board of Commissioners was instituted, to be appointed for five years by the Governor of the State, to have the sole control of the appointment, trial, and management of the Police force, which was not to outnumber two thousand, and to appoint the Chief of Police and the minor offices. The Police Commissioners were to secure the peace and protection of the city, to insure quiet at the elections, and to look after the public health.

In this instance the changes that were thereby effected were of a radical nature. The Metropolitan Police District included the Counties of New York, Kings, Westchester and Richmond. The Governor, by and with the consent of the Senate, had the appointing of five Commissioners of Police; one from the county of Richmond or Westchester, one from Kings County, and three from New York, the Mayors of New York and Brooklyn being *ex-officio* members of the Board. The officers of the Board were a president and a treasurer, the Board being empowered to appoint a chief clerk and six deputy clerks. The Police force was then made to consist of a General Superintendent, two Deputy Superintendents, five Surgeons, Inspectors and Captains not to exceed forty, Sergeants not to exceed one hundred and fifty, and as many Patrolmen as should be determined upon by the Board of Supervisors of New York, the Common Council of Brooklyn, and the Supervisors of the Counties of Kings, Richmond and Westchester.

The qualifications for appointment on the force were about the same as in the preceding Act, the term of office continuing also during good behavior.

The salaries were as follows: Treasurer of the Board, three thousand dollars per annum, the other Commissioners, eight dollars per day, for actual service performed, General Superintendent, three thousand dollars per annum; Deputy Superintendents, two thousand dollars each; Surgeons, one thousand five hundred dollars, Inspectors and Captains, one thousand two hundred dollars each, Sergeants, nine hundred dollars, Patrolmen, eight hundred dollars; and Doormen, seven hundred dollars.

The new Board possessed all the power and authority hitherto conferred by law upon the Board of Police Commissioners of the city of New York, or upon the Mayor, Recorder, and City Judge of said city, as Police Commissioners, or upon the Mayors of New York and Brooklyn, respectively, as the heads therein of the respective Police Departments of those cities, or upon the Aldermen of the city of Brooklyn.

The Chiefs of Police, in the cities of New York and Brooklyn, were designated, respectively, Deputy Superintendents of Police. From and after the passage of the Act, Captains were designated Inspectors and Captains; Lieutenants and Assistant Captains, Sergeants; and Policemen, Patrolmen.

The Police Districts were divided into precincts, without any regard to county or ward boundaries, there being assigned one Inspector, one Captain, and four Sergeants (besides such quota of Patrolmen to be thereafter determined) in each precinct. The Board was authorized to establish, from time to time, a station or sub-station in each district for the accommodation of the Police force on duty therein, to detail Police officers to the Police and Criminal Courts, to the public offices of the cities of New York and Brooklyn, the Quarantine and Emigration offices, etc., as might be deemed advisable. The Board was restrained from suspending members of the force from pay for more than thirty days. All orders and regulations of the Board were promulgated through the General Superintendent, who was the head and chief of the Police force.

The following persons were the first Commissioners appointed under this Act:

Simeon Draper, James Bowen, James W. Nye, Jacob Cholwell and James S. T. Stranahan.

Draper, Nye and Cholwell resigned, and Pelatiah Perit and S. B. Ward were appointed their successors. They in turn resigned, and Thomas B. Stillman, Michael Ulshoffer and Isaac H. Bailey were the next appointees. This resulted in the formation of the following Board of Police:

James Bowen, of Westchester County; James S. T. Stranahan, of Kings County; Thomas B. Stillman, Michael Ulshoffer and Isaac H. Bailey, of New York.

There were three terms of office: one term, for three Commissioners, expired on the first day of May, 1858; another term, for two Commissioners, expired on the first of May, 1859. It was determined by lot which Commissioners were to serve the long and which the short term. Each Commissioner appointed to fill a term succeeding an expiring one, it was provided, should be appointed thereafter for a full term of three years, such appointment to be made from the county in which the vacancy occurred. Any vacancy as Commissioner of Police should be filled by the Board of Police for the residue of the unexpired term. The Governor possessed the power of removal for cause.

The Police Commissioners successively appointed the following as General Superintendent: James R. Whitney, Joseph Keene and Welcome R. Beebe, all of whom in turn declined to serve. The Board next appointed Frederick A. Tallmadge, who accepted. He served in such capacity from the date of his appointment, May 13, 1857, to April 18, 1859, when Amos Pilsbury was appointed to succeed him, May 20, 1859. Superintendent Pilsbury did not assume the duties of the office until the first of July following, Deputy Superintendent Daniel Carpenter acting as General Superintendent, pro tem., in the interim. Pilsbury resigned as General Superintendent on March 5, 1860.

The Act declared that the Municipal or Local Police of the cities of New York and Brooklyn should be embodied in the Metropolitan force, and that the local authorities should be divested of all control over them after the first meeting of the Board of Commissioners. It had been so confidently asserted by the opponents of the Act that the courts would declare it unconstitutional that doubts were infused into the minds of members of the New York force as to the lawfulness of obeying the orders of the Commissioners. Under these circumstances, and in view of the fact that it was a question of vital importance to the

Policemen, the Board refrained from assuming the control of the force until the validity of the law was judicially determined. On the fourth of May Justice Clerke, of the Supreme Court, affirmed the constitutionality of the Act, and on the twenty-fifth of that month the Supreme Court, at general term, declared it valid and binding in all parts.

On the rendition of this decision the Commissioners assumed the direct control of the Police force. That portion on duty in the City of Brooklyn, with but few exceptions, obeyed the orders of the Board. Of the New York force, fifteen of the Captains and about eight hundred of the Patrolmen refused to recognize the authority of the Commissioners, or obey the orders of the General Superintendent. Charges of insubordination were preferred against them, and they were tried and dismissed from the service in conformity with the provisions of the law.

On the fourteenth of May, 1857, in pursuance of a requisition from the Health Officer, Deputy Superintendent Matsell was directed to detail five Patrolmen to guard the public hospitals at the Quarantine from the threatened attacks of incendiaries. He refused to obey the order, and was tried and removed from office for insubordination, and Daniel Carpenter was appointed in his place. Mr. Matsell was soon after restored to duty.

The new Metropolitan Police force, handicapped as they were by the action of the old Municipal body, and legal proceedings, found their hands full in combating public outbreaks and riotous disturbances, as well as quelling the internecine strife that kept two bodies of Policemen in open brawls, to the injury of good government and law and order.

The power exercised by the State Legislature, in respect to the Police, embodied in the Act to establish a Metropolitan Police District, was considered by Mayor Wood and his adherents in the light of a usurpation of authority, on the ground that the government of the Police was entrusted to a Board of Commissioners not appointed or selected by those who were taxed for their salaries, and who were immediately affected by the operation of those laws. The Mayor also thought it decidedly objectionable that the State Government, besides creating the Board and appointing its officers, should have also fixed their compensation to be paid out of the city treasury, without a right on the part of the people of the city to regulate or control them in any degree. The Police, the Mayor considered as an army for preserving domestic order in time of peace, just as the regular army protects us from foreign invasion in time of war. "It should be our object," he said, "to elevate the guardians of our lives and property to a position of dignity scarcely inferior to the guardians of the national honor." He therefore recommended that the Police, in the designation of its men and officers, and also in their appointment, suspension, trial and removal, should be organized and governed according to like features in our military system, the Mayor to be considered the head of the force. But his arguments proved unavailing, and the Metropolitan District went into operation, fulfilled its mission, and ran its course.

The appointment of the new Commissioners was the signal for war. Mayor Wood, who had strenuously opposed the action of the legislature, announced his determination to test the constitutionality of the law to the uttermost, and to resist its execution. He refused to surrender the Police property or to disband the old Police, and for some time the city witnessed the curious spectacle of two departments—the Metropolitan Police under the Commissioners, and the Municipal Police under the Mayor—vieing for mastery. After exhausting all the resources of the law to evade obedience to the Act, the Mayor and Municipal government finally caused it to be referred to the Court of Appeals. Before the final decision came, blood was spilled. On the sixteenth of June matters were

Mayor Wood

brought to a crisis by the forcible ejection from the City Hall of Daniel D. Conover, who had been appointed Street Commissioner by Governor King, to fill the vacancy caused by the death of the former incumbent. The Deputy Commissioner meanwhile claimed his right to hold the office, and a third competitor, Charles Devlin, had been appointed by Mayor Wood, who claimed the appointing power. Mr. Conover immediately obtained a warrant from the Recorder to arrest the Mayor on the charge of inciting a riot, and another from Judge Hoffman for the violence offered him personally, and, armed with these documents, and attended by fifty of the Metropolitan Police, returned to the City Hall. Captain Walling (later Superintendent) at first attempted in vain to gain an entrance with one warrant. Mr. Conover followed with the other, but met with no better success. The City Hall was filled with armed Policemen, who attacked the new comers. A fierce affray ensued, during which twelve of the Policemen were severely wounded. The Seventh Regiment happened to be passing down Broadway on its way to take the boat for Boston. It was summoned to the spot, and its presence almost instantly sufficed to quell the riot. Mr. Conover, accompanied by General Sanford, entered the City Hall and served the writ on the Mayor, who, seeing further resistance useless, submitted to arrest. The Metropolitan Police Act being declared constitutional by the Court of Appeals, the Mayor seemed disposed to submit, and the disturbance was supposed to be ended.

In the meantime the city had become greatly demoralized. During the civil strife of the Police, the repression of crime had been neglected. Gangs of rowdies had organized, whose purposes were disorder and plunder. These rival gangs were styled the "Dead Rabbits," and were residents of the Five Points' district, and the other was known by the name of the "Atlantic Guard" or "Bowery Boys." These two gangs of rowdies, on the fourth of July and the preceding evening, came into a conflict in Bayard Street, near the Bowery. Sticks, stones, and knives were freely used on both sides, and men, women and children were wounded in the melee. A small body of Policemen, sent to quell the disturbance, was soon repulsed, and several of their number wounded. The rioters erected barricades in the streets, and great consternation prevailed throughout the city. The Seventh Regiment was summoned back from Boston, and the city militia was called out. The riot was not quelled until late in the evening. Six men were killed and over a hundred wounded.

This riot aroused the citizens to the danger of the position, and intensified the prejudice against the Municipal Police, which was accused of abetting the rioters. Vigorous measures were at once taken to organize the Metropolitan Police and secure its efficiency. On the thirteenth and fourteenth of July another outbreak occurred in the Seventeenth Ward. The riot continued for two days, but was finally quelled by the Police.

During the month of November, the apprehension of suffering by persons thrown out of employment because of the commercial reverses, led to the assemblage of turbulent mobs, which menaced the peace of the city, but they were dispersed without resort to extreme measures.

On the seventh of November, Pelatiah Perit, of New York, was elected a Commissioner in place of Mr. Draper. Soon after, the Board was enjoined from making further appointments, on the allegation that the dismissal of the old force was illegal. The injunction was dissolved on the twenty-eighth of November, 1857, but the opinion of the Judge, delivered with the order of dismissal, in respect to questions which had not been argued before him, admonished the Commissioners of the expediency of delaying to fill the vacancies in the force until the rights and duties of the Board were finally determined by a judicial decision. Some parts of the Metropolitan Police District had been seriously disturbed by riotous assemblages, and the necessity of a vigilant Police, extending over the densely populated counties adjacent to and including the city of New York, was strikingly illustrated during the previous summer.

The opponents of the Act resorted to every artifice which their ingenuity could devise to hinder the Commissioners in the performance of their duty The members of the old force were threatened with instant dismissal by the local authorities if they recognized the orders of the Commissioners A rival Police was established, called the Day and Night Watch, which patrolled the streets and assumed the duties which devolved exclusively on the Metropolitan Police Prisoners taken by the latter in the very act of committing crime, were rescued from custody and permitted to escape from justice by the unlawful organized force of the Mayor The station houses, which by law were transferred to the Commissioners, were withheld; writs issued by the courts were resisted, and were only served when the Police were seconded by men under arms, and in order to destroy the efficiency of the law, the Corporation of New York attempted to reduce the Patrol force to five men

The station houses were located as follows.
First Precinct, Franklin Market.
Second Precinct, No 49 Beekman Street
Third Precinct, No. 79 Warren Street.
Fourth Precinct, No. 9 Oak Street.
Fifth Precinct, No 49 Leonard Street.
Sixth Precinct, No. 9 Franklin Street
Seventh Precinct, Gouverneur Market.
Eighth Precinct, No. 126 Wooster Street.
Ninth Precinct, No. 94 Charles Street.
Tenth Precinct, Grand and Ludlow Streets.
Eleventh Precinct, Union Market
Twelfth Precinct, One Hundred and Twenty-sixth Street near Fourth Avenue.
Thirteenth Precinct, Delancey and Attorney Streets
Fourteenth Precinct, No. 53 Spring Street.
Fifteenth Precinct, No. 220 Mercer Street
Sixteenth Precinct, No 156 West Twentieth Street
Seventeenth Precinct, No. 75 First Avenue
Eighteenth Precinct, Twenty-second Street near First Avenue.
Nineteenth Precinct, Fifty-ninth Street near Second Avenue.
Twentieth Precinct, No 212 West Thirty-fifth Street.
Twenty-first Precinct, No. 34 East Twenty-ninth Street.
Twenty-second Precinct, Corner Eighth Avenue and Forty-eighth Street

It was a frequent practice, with the Aldermen and Magistrates of the cities of New York and Brooklyn, to proceed to the Police station immediately upon the arrest of disorderly or riotous persons, and discharge them from custody This emboldened the dangerous classes and tended to bring the law into contempt, while it discouraged the Police in the performance of their duty.

Up to the middle of July there were not, on an average, more than five hundred men (including officers) actually doing duty, whereas, under the old law, there were upwards of one thousand two hundred. On the twenty-first of

August, an apportionment was made, giving to each Precinct its allotted number of Officers and Patrolmen. This appointment had to be made from the limited number of eight hundred and sixty regular Patrolmen, from whom had to be taken a sufficient number to be detailed at the Court of Sessions and Police District Courts, the Commissioners' office, and the General and Deputy Superintendent's offices, and for other contingent and necessary duties.

It had been a year of riots and disturbances, of financial panic and business disaster. Prior to the end of December there had been nine hundred and eighty-five failures among the merchants of the city of New York, involving liabilities exceeding one hundred and twenty millions. There were ominous mutterings of bread riots among the more impoverished part of the population. The arsenal was protected by a strong Police force, and United States troops were placed in charge of the Custom House and Assay Offices.

The Police force was inadequate to the protection of the city. With a population of eight hundred and twenty thousand, and rapidly increasing, the force numbered but one hundred and fifty-seven more than when the population was three hundred and fifty thousand. The disparity of the Police to the population, at this period, may be inferred from the following table of the force employed in the cities of Great Britain.

	Population	Miles	Area in miles	Proportion to Population
London (City),	128,851	569	1¾	1 to 226
London (Metropolitan)	2,646,278	5,813	700	1 to 455
Liverpool	423,061	906	7¼	1 to 467
Bristol	140,000	248	7	1 to 564
Dublin	291,948	775	6	1 to 376
Glasgow	400,000	684	12½	1 to 585
Manchester	337,412	552	6⅝	1 to 611

In the City of New York, the proportion of Patrolmen to the population was, in

| 1844 | as 1 to 414 |
| 1858 | as 1 to 804 |

The necessity for an increase of the Police force was demonstrated by the arrests made in a series of years. Arrests made from

May, 1846, to May, 1847	24,851
May, 1847, to May, 1848	24,081
May, 1848, to May, 1849	25,808
May, 1849, to April, 1850	24,756
April, 1850, to Jan'y, 1851	26,581
Jan'y, 1851, to Jan'y, 1852	36,224
Jan'y, 1852, to Jan'y, 1853	36,257
Jan'y, 1853, to Jan'y, 1854	40,084
Jan'y, 1854, to Jan'y, 1855	52,712
Jan'y, 1855, to Jan'y, 1856	52,815
Jan'y, 1856, to Jan'y, 1857	45,287
Jan'y, 1857, to July, 1857	18,859
July, 1857, to Nov., 1857	15,833
Nov., 1857, to Nov., 1858	61,455

The Commissioners drew the attention of the legislature and the executive to these facts, and argued that the city and its suburbs should be policed by a force adequate to patrol every street and lane by day and by night. Attention was also called to the fact that the beats of the Patrolmen at this time (1858) were in many instances two miles in length, and in several of the precincts, which contained forty thousand inhabitants, there could be detailed for regular duty during the day but eight men. The Act establishing the Metropolitan Police in-

Old Metropolitan Police Headquarters.
(413 Broome Street.)

vested the Supervisors of the several counties of the district with the power to determine the number of Patrolmen to be appointed in each. The Commissioners had urged upon the Supervisors of New York the necessity of an increase of the Police for that city without effect, and the legislature was petitioned, in view of the pressing importance to the public peace, and for the security of property, to authorize the appointment of three hundred and fifty Patrolmen in addition to the number then allowed by law.

This, in fact, was an anxious period, and a trying one, for the recently organized Police force. Its trials and troubles were many and grievous. It was the duty of the Common Councils of New York and Brooklyn to furnish the stations suitably, and to warm and light them. This, and other kindred duties, the corporations of the two cities had failed to do. Many of the station houses were so out of repair as to be unfit for habitation; others were so poorly ventilated, or so limited in size, as to engender disease. Platoons of twenty men were crowded into small and imperfectly ventilated rooms The Police surgeons designated many of the stations as pest-houses, so fruitful were they of disease. The cellars of the station houses were divided into cells, for the retention of prisoners, and into rooms for the houseless poor The stench that arose from these rooms poisoned the atmosphere of the whole building

Truly the contrast with the present commodious and well-appointed station houses is a striking one.

The Police Act required that the Comptrollers of the cities of New York and Brooklyn, the Chairman of the Boards of Supervisors of the counties of New York, Kings, Westchester, and Richmond, should meet annually as an auditing committee, and apportion the sums requisite and needful to be raised for Police purposes by each county. The Auditing Committee met for this purpose in August, 1857, and made the following apportionment:

To be raised by the County of New York for the support of the Police in that county	$868,070 00
To be raised by the City of Brooklyn for the force employed in that city	206,600 00
And for the general expenses of Police, to be raised by the City and County of New York	20,478 60
To be raised by the County of Kings	40,62 13
To be raised by the County of Westchester	1,503 95
To be raised by the County of Richmond	355 32

The Counties of Westchester and Richmond refused to pay the sums assessed on them.

The Police force of the Metropolitan Police Districts on the first of November, 1858, was as follows:

General Superintendent of Police; one Deputy Superintendent in New York; one Deputy Superintendent in Brooklyn

Captains, stationed in the City of New York	25
Captains stationed in the City of Brooklyn	6
Sergeants stationed in the City of New York	105
Sergeants stationed in the City of Brooklyn	30
Patrolmen stationed in the City of New York	1,063
Patrolmen stationed in the City of Brooklyn	198

Arrests made during the year ending October 31, 1858. In the City of New York, sixty-one thousand four hundred and fifty-five, exclusive of thirteen thousand nine hundred and eighteen in Brooklyn

Incidental duties discharged by the Policemen in the city of New York, for the year ending October 31, 1858:

    121,597 persons lodged in station houses.
    7,552 lost children restored to parents and guardians.
    58 abandoned infants taken care of.
    751 sick or disabled persons in the streets taken home.
    134 persons rescued from drowning.
    180 fires extinguished by the Police
    1,724 stores and dwellings found open at night, secured.
    584 strayed horses restored to owners.

Property stolen, as reported at station house........$165,825 47
Recovered by Police.............................. 96,065 94
Recovered by Detective Force (property stolen elsewhere than in the Police District).............. 65,025 00
Taken from lodgers and prisoners, and restored to them 55,953 00
Telegraphic messages, 78,336.

There were thirteen surgeons attached to the force, whose duty it was to examine and report to the Board of Commissioners on the physical condition of candidates for the office of Patrolmen, and to perform such professional duty as might be directed by the General or Deputy Superintendent of Police, without fee or expense to the members of the force.

New York Police Stations were located as follows:

1. Franklin Market, corner of Rector Street and Trinity Place.
2. 49 Beekman Street
3. 79 Warren Street.
4. 9 Oak Street
5. 49 Leonard Street
6. 12 Franklin Street
7. Gouverneur Market.
8. 126 Wooster Street.
9. 94 Charles Street.
10. Essex Market.
11. Houston and Second Streets
12. One Hundred and Twenty-sixth Street, near Third Avenue
13. Corner of Delancey and Attorney Streets.
14. 53 Spring Street
15. 221 Mercer Street
16. 156 West Twentieth Street.
17. 75 First Avenue
18. 163 East Twenty-second Street
19. Fifty-ninth Street, between Second and Third Avenues.
20. 212 West Thirty-fifth Street
21. 34 East Thirty-ninth Street.
22. Forty-eighth Street and Eighth Avenue.
23. Fifty-sixth Street, between Fourth and Fifth Avenues
24. Corner of State and Whitehall Streets
25. Basement of Police Headquarters, corner of Broome and Elm Streets.
26. Basement of City Hall.

During twenty-nine years ending with 1858, thirty-eight persons had been sentenced for capital crimes, of whom seventeen had been executed, fourteen had their sentences commuted to imprisonment for life, one was pardoned, one committed suicide, and to four a new trial was granted, of whom three were convicted of manslaughter, and one discharged. One was under sentence of death at the beginning of 1859.

The Metropolitan Police District was divided into precincts. The precincts were divided into beats. In the city of New York each of the several Wards constituted a precinct corresponding in number to that of the Ward; except that part of the Twelfth and part of the Nineteenth Wards which constituted Precinct No. 23; the East and Hudson Rivers, within the boundaries of New York and the Bay of New York, constituted Precinct No. 24, or Harbor Police; the Detective force constituted Precinct No 25; and the force assigned especially for the enforcement of ordinances constituted Precinct No. 26. In each of the precincts there was one or more station houses. The force was divided into companies, one company being allotted to each precinct.

The Police Commissioners, from the first, had an exalted and intelligent conception of their duties. In the latter part of 1859 they drew up and published a series of rules and regulations for the government and guidance of the force. General Superintendent Pilsbury, in his address to the Police, says "The uniform you wear should be a perpetual 'coat of mail,' to guard you against every temptation to which you may be exposed, by reminding you that no act of misconduct, or breach of discipline, can escape public observation and censure. By exemplary conduct and manly deportment, you will command the respect and cordial support of all good citizens. For the faithful performance of the important trusts committed to your care, you will be noticed approvingly, and your services will be appreciated by the community."

And again: "Every Policeman must be circumspect in his deportment, erect and manly in his carriage, and scrupulously discreet in his language and acts. He must be firm, but courteous, in the exercise of his authority. * * * He must be neat and soldierly in his appearance. * * * He must never, under any circumstances, use vulgar or profane language."

The rules and regulations were quite numerous, and space can be found but for brief mention of a few.

The General Superintendent was by law the executive head of the whole Police force of the Metropolitan Police District, and it was the duty of the members of the same to respect and obey him accordingly. It was his duty to repair in person to all serious or extensive fires in the cities of New York and Brooklyn, to all riots or tumultuous assemblages within the district, and take command of the Police present, to save and protect property, and arrest such persons as he might find disturbing the peace, or inciting others to do so. He had power to direct, temporarily, any, or all, of the Police force, to any place within the district where their services might be deemed necessary. He had the supervision of the public health of the district, and it was his duty to communicate to the Board of Police and to the Mayors of New York and Brooklyn the presence of any contagious or infectious disease, or the existence of any nuisance in the district which might be detrimental to the public health. The returns and reports of commanding officers of any patrol force stationed elsewhere than in the cities of New York and Brooklyn, were made to the General Superintendent. It was his duty to see that the laws of the State and the ordinances of the city, town, and village authorities, were duly enforced throughout the district.

Under the direction of the General Superintendent, the Deputy Superintendents had supervision of the Police force. It was their duty to see that the orders and directions of the General Superintendent in relation to the dress, discipline, deportment, and duties of members of the force were promptly obeyed, and the rules and regulations of the Police Board enforced

The Captains of Police were held strictly responsible for the preservation of the public peace in their respective precincts; and to insure good order, they were vested with the power to post the men under their command in such parts of their precincts, and to assign them such duties, as they might deem expedient.

In case of sickness, or the absence of the Captain from the Police station house, or from his precinct, the duties required of him were performed by one of the Sergeants of the precinct, selected for that purpose by the General Superintendent. The Sergeant so selected, during the absence of the Captain, possessed and exercised all the powers of a Captain, and enforced the rules and regulations established for the government of the precinct

The prevention of crime being the most important object in view, a Patrolman's exertions should be constantly used to accomplish that end, he should examine and make himself perfectly acquainted with every part of his beat, and vigilantly watch every description of person passing his way He should, to the utmost of his power, prevent the commission of assaults, breaches of the peace, and all other crimes about to be committed, and by his vigilance, render it extremely difficult for any one to commit crime on his beat (the absence of crime being considered the best proof of efficiency), and, when on any beat offences frequently occur, there is good reason to suppose that there is negligence or want of ability on the part of the person in charge of said beat.

Persons appointed to serve on the Police Force should—
First —Be able to read and write the English language
Second.—Be citizens of the United States
Third.—Have been residents of the Metropolitan Police District during a term of five years next preceding their appointment.
Fourth.—Never have been convicted of crime.
Fifth —At least five feet eight inches in height
Sixth —Not over thirty-five years of age.
Seventh —Of good health and sound body.
Eighth.—Of good moral character.

Any member of the Police force might be immediately dismissed from office, in addition to any other punishment he might be subject to by law, against whom any of the following charges should be substantiated.—

First—Intoxication.

Second—Willful disobedience of orders.

Third—Violent, coarse, or insolent language or behavior to a superior, or other person

Fourth—Receiving money, or other valuable thing, contrary to the Rules and Regulations, or the Statutes of the State.

Fifth—Willful non-compliance with the Rules and Regulations.

Sixth—Inefficiency, or gross neglect of duty.

Seventh.—Willfully maltreating or using unnecessary violence toward a prisoner or citizen.

Eighth—Any member of the Police force who was found neglecting the payment of his just debts for necessaries or rent, or was found guilty of any act of insubordination or disrespect toward his superior officers, or others, or conduct unworthy of his station, might be reprimanded, fined, or have deductions made from his pay, proportioned to his offense, or, in cases of repeated violations of the rule, might be dismissed No person should be removed from the Police force except upon written charges, preferred against him to the Board of Police, and an opportunity afforded him of being heard in his defense, as prescribed by the law

Patrolman's Shield

The mode of trial, when charges had been preferred, was by taking the testimony on oath against and for the accused officer, and reducing the substance thereof to writing The same might be taken by or before one or more of the Police Commissioners, and one of the clerks (under the direction of the Commissioner or Commissioners sitting) took down, as aforesaid, the substance of the testimony The testimony was reported to the Board of Police Commissioners, with the opinion thereon of the Commissioner or Commissioners before whom the same was taken, for the action and the decision of the Board thereon

The dress of the General Superintendent was a blue dress coat with Police buttons; the dress of the Deputy Superintendents, Captains, and Sergeants of Police, was a double-breasted frock coat, with Police buttons, and blue pantaloons Patrolmen on duty, unless specially authorized to appear in citizen's dress, on all occasions wore a black stock, a frock-coat of navy blue cloth, single-breasted, and with rolling collar, nine buttons on the breast, two buttons on the hips, also two buttons on the bottom of the skirt; blue waistcoat and blue pantaloons, on the outer seams of which there was a white cord The coat was buttoned at all times when on duty Captains, Sergeants, and Patrolmen, when on duty, wore caps, shields, badges, emblems, devices, belts and buttons, corresponding to a sample deposited in the office of the General Superintendent, and the time of wearing them was directed by him.

Deputy Superintendent Daniel Carpenter, in his quarterly report, ending January 31, 1859, mentions some of the causes of crime, namely: there were at this date seven thousand seven hundred and seventy-nine places where intoxicating liquors were sold at retail. From the reports of the Captains of nineteen precincts it appears that there were four hundred and ninety-six known houses of prostitution, and eighty-four houses of assignation These included one hundred and seventy lager beer and drinking saloons, combined with houses of ill-fame, one hundred and eighty-five low groggeries, where known thieves and fallen women daily and nightly resorted, but a strict Police surveilance was kept over them, thereby preventing them from committing depredations that they otherwise would.

The Board of Supervisors had shortly before increased the Patrol force to one thousand two hundred and fifty men

On the first of November, 1859, there were altogether (including the entire district) one thousand six hundred and ninety-nine persons belonging to the Metropolitan Police Department, namely.

General Superintendent, one ; Deputy Superintendents, two; Chief, Deputy and Property Clerks, six; Surgeons, five ; Captains, thirty-two; Sergeants, one hundred and thirty-five; Policemen on patrol duty, one thousand three hundred and twenty-seven ; Policemen on detailed duty, one hundred and eighteen ; Doormen, seventy-three.

The sick list averaged during the last quarter forty-six and two-thirds persons daily On an average, each Patrolman in New York lost two and one-half days during the quarter by sickness The aggregate lost time, by reason of sickness and disability, during this quarter, was three hundred and sixty-five and one-half days.

The Metropolitan Act was amended by the legislature on April 10, 1860. The Metropolitan Police District was then made to comprise the counties of New York, Kings, Westchester and Richmond, and the towns of Newtown, Flushing and Jamaica, in the county of Queens. The Governor appointed the following to fill vacancies:

John G. Bergen, Amos Pilsbury, and James Bowen. Pilsbury resigned, and Thomas C Acton was appointed in his place.

On May 23, 1860, the Board appointed John A. Kennedy Superintendent of Police in place of Amos Pilsbury, who was appointed Commissioner.

The designation of rank, under this chapter, was as follows· Superintendent, Inspectors, Captains, Sergeants, Patrolmen and Doormen

The office of Deputy Superintendent was abolished The following were appointed Inspectors. Daniel Carpenter, John S Folk, George W. Dilks, and James Leonard.

Salaries Treasurer, three thousand dollars per annum; other Commissioners, eight dollars for each day's actual service ; Superintendent, five thousand dollars; Inspectors, two thousand dollars; Surgeons, one thousand five hundred dollars ; Captains, one thousand two hundred dollars ; Sergeants, nine hundred dollars; Patrolmen, eight hundred dollars; Doormen, seven hundred dollars

The term of office continued to be during good behavior.

This Act essentially modified the constitution of the Board of Police, by reducing the number of its members, and by enlarging its powers, and confiding to it new and important duties. By the provisions of the Act of 1857, the Board of Police consisted of five Commissioners and the Mayors of the cities of New York and Brooklyn. The number of Commissioners was reduced to three, and the Mayors of New York and Brooklyn were relieved from the Police duties which had been imposed upon them. The change was not without its advantages. It secured, for instance, harmony of action, and the constant attention of the members of the Board to the important trusts confided to them. At the date of the passage of the amended Act, the office of Superintendent of Police was vacant. On the twenty-third of May, 1860, John A. Kennedy was appointed to fill the vacancy.

Besides the principal office in the City Hall, up to 1844, there was a branch office at the corner of Bowery and Third Street. The office hours were from nine o'clock A. M until sunset. One of the Magistrates received the Watch at daybreak every morning; which duty was performed weekly by each Magistrate alternately. In 1857, at the time of the conflict between Mayor Wood and the newly appointed Police Commissioners, the Headquarters were moved from the City Hall to No. 88 White Street, and six months later to No. 413 Broome Street, and in 1863, to the present building at No. 300 Mulberry Street. The new Headquarters, with the land and buildings, and the additions made in 1868 and 1869, cost two hundred and thirty thousand eight hundred and sixty dollars and ninety cents. The expense was defrayed from a surplus accumulated by careful economy from the annual appropriations for the maintenance of the Police in New York, and by virtue of the legal authority vested in the Board by the Police law of 1860. The title to the property is vested in the county of New York.

The area of territory embraced in the Metropolitan Police District was nine hundred and twenty square miles, and the population estimated at fourteen hundred thousand persons. Except in the cities of New York and Brooklyn, there was no Police force permanently stationed in any part of the district, and in those cities the force was quite inadequate for the population they contained.

The Police force at this time consisted of one Superintendent, four Inspectors, thirty-two Captains, one hundred and forty-six Sergeants, one thousand six hundred Patrolmen.

The cities of New York and Brooklyn were divided into precincts, to each of which there were assigned one Captain, four Sergeants, and from forty to sixty Patrolmen. There were also sub-precincts, to which two Sergeants and from ten to fifteen men were assigned. Two Doormen were attached to each station house.

In the cities of Europe, where the Police are sustained by the constant presence of a military force, there was a Policeman to about every five hundred inhabitants, while in the city of New York, the proportion which the Police bore to the population was one to six hundred and fifty, and in the city of Brooklyn as one to one thousand three hundred and eighty.

The Embassy from the Government of Japan, which visited the city of

New York in June (1860) gave to the Board for the benefit of the Metropolitan Police, the sum of thirteen thousand seven hundred and fifty dollars, with the recommendation that it should constitute a fund, and that the annual interest thereof be distributed among the force in such manner as the Board should deem expedient. The fund was called the Japanese Merit Fund, the interest of which, it was directed, should be distributed in the following manner:

To the Captain who should have best performed his duty for the preceding year, two hundred dollars.

To the two Sergeants who should have best performed their duty, each, one hundred and twenty-five dollars.

To the five Patrolmen who should have best performed their duty, each, one hundred dollars.

The whole number of arrests for the year 1860:

Offences against the person 54,820
Offences against property 10,989

Total 65,809

The drafts upon the force, for the discharge of numerous duties, reduced the active Patrol force in New York to one thousand and ten men. This number was further subject to a reduction by sickness and absence. The needful requirements for rest and refreshments prevented more than one-half of that number, except in extreme cases, from being on post at one time. Hence all the streets and piers of the city of New York were guarded by a force not exceeding four hundred and ninety-one men. In the city of New York there were, at this time, four hundred and twelve and one-eighth miles of streets, and twelve and one-eighth miles of piers, being an aggregate of four hundred and twenty-four and one-fourth miles. Should every man—whose duty it was to patrol, deducting the sick only—be on post, the average length of the beats would be eight hundred and sixty-two one-thousandths of a mile, very nearly seven-eighths of a mile for each man to guard. But as in many places, from the turbulent character of the population or other cause, the patrol was required to be doubled, and a further reduction occurring in the number of the men by occasional necessary absence, the actual force on duty would not allow the length of beats to average less than one and one-fourth miles.

The Supervisors of the County of New York had authorized the increase of the Patrol force of that county from fourteen to eighteen hundred men. The Police then consisted of a Superintendent, four Inspectors, thirty-eight Captains, one hundred and sixty Sergeants, two thousand Patrolmen, of whom thirty Captains, one hundred and twenty-nine Sergeants, and one thousand eight hundred Patrolmen were stationed in the city of New York, and the remainder in the city of Brooklyn.

It was estimated that for the proper protection of the public interests, the Police force of a city should be as one Patrolmen to every five hundred inhabitants. This proportion was maintained in the city of New York; but in Brooklyn, which contained three hundred thousand inhabitants, there were stationed but two hundred Patrolmen, or one to every one thousand five hundred inhabitants.

In the month of May, this year, the Grand Jury of New York requested the Board of Police to supervise the cleaning of streets. In accordance with this request the Board caused daily reports to be made by the Patrolmen of the streets swept and not swept, and make weekly returns thereof to the Comptroller

The Board complained to the Governor that the facility with which burglars and thieves could dispose of property through the receivers of stolen goods,

Police Headquarters, 300 Mulberry Street

formed a powerful stimulus to the commission of crime It was recommended that the Board be authorized to pay out of the Police Life and Health Fund for the conviction of every receiver of stolen goods a reward of not exceeding one hundred dollars, as a means to break up this class of lawbreakers

The total number of arrests made in New York City were:

Offences against property........................11,294
Offences against the person......................59,836

Grand Total 71,130

The value of property and money lost and recovered, for the year ending October 31, 1861, was

Lost, one hundred and thirty-three thousand six hundred and seventy-nine dollars and ninety-six cents

Recovered, seventy-nine thousand eight hundred and twenty-two dollars and eleven cents.

Exclusive of the amount, recovered as above, the Detective force, or Twenty-fifth Precinct, recovered twenty-five thousand nine hundred and ninety-seven dollars and fifteen cents

Lost time, by reason of sickness, for the year ending October 31, 1861, fourteen thousand, seven hundred and ninety-six days

The Act of April 24, 1862, provided that Constables elected or appointed after the passage of this Act, should be denominated the "Marshals of the City of New York," and they should have the same power, and perform all the duties that had hitherto appertained to the office; and each of said Marshals should be a resident of the district wherein the Court, for or to which he should be appointed, was located; such Marshal to execute a bond, with two sufficient sureties, in the penal sum of one thousand dollars

All laws relating to the election of Constables were repealed

The Board, by careful economy, had accumulated a surplus from the annual appropriations for the maintenance of the Police in New York, which, with the consent of the Supervisors of that county, they expended in the erection of a building for the Central Department of Police

The station houses in New York and Brooklyn had been condemned by the Police Surgeons as unfit for the purposes for which they were used. These evils were corrected; spacious and commodious stations having been erected in many of the precincts, while in others the houses had been enlarged and provision made for their thorough ventilation. The cells and lodging houses for the poor had been removed to separate buildings erected in the rear of the several stations

At the request of the Federal authorities, the Board, in the month of July, began to recruit for volunteers to serve in the armies of the United States. To defray the expenses of recruiting, the members of the Police and others subscribed the sum of twenty-eight thousand six hundred and sixty-nine dollars and fifteen cents, and by their efforts there was obtained from citizens the sum of seventy-seven thousand seven hundred and thirty-nine dollars and forty-six cents, which was appropriated to the families of recruits. The Board, with the means thus afforded them, was enabled to place five regiments of infantry and four companies of one hundred men each, of cavalry, in the field.

The Police force of New York, for the year 1862, consisted of one Superintendent, thirty Captains, one hundred and twenty-nine Sergeants, sixty-four Roundsmen, one thousand four hundred and twenty-eight Patrolmen, one hundred and seven Special Duty in the precinct, one hundred and seventy-four Special Duty out of the precinct, sixty-seven Doormen Total, 1,999.

Lost time by reason of sickness or disability for the same period, eighteen thousand two hundred and thirty-nine days

By the rules of the department, when sickness or disability resulted from extraordinary exertion or exposure, in discharge of Police duty, the full time lost was paid for. When it resulted from ordinary circumstances, one-half the lost time was paid for. When it was feigned, or resulted from carelessness, excess, or fault of the Policeman, no pay was allowed for the lost time

The total number of arrests were:

 For offences against property..................... 13,344
 Offences against the person...................... 68,728

  Total 82,072

Value of property and money, lost and recovered, for the year ending October 31, 1862

 Lost $202,939 76
 Recovered.. 76,912 27

  Total loss.......................................$126,027 49

The Twenty-fifth Precinct consisted of the Detective force. This force recovered large amounts of money and property which were not lost within the Police District. For this reason the figures were not carried into the foregoing table, representing the losses and recoveries within the district. The amount recovered by the Detective force, during the year ending October 31, 1862, was fifty-five thousand two hundred and eighty-five dollars and eighty-five cents.

The system of discipline established and carried out by the Board, though much criticised and opposed in the beginning, was fully vindicated to all candid persons by beneficial results. The marked fidelity, vigilance and efficiency of the Police, in ordinary as well as extraordinary occasions, was, it was claimed, the legitimate fruit of this system. Instead of fearing or despising the Policeman, the public had learned to trust him as the protector and defender of social order

On the morning of the thirteenth of July the city was startled by the lawless acts of a formidable mob, which entered on a career of robbery, arson and murder that was not completely checked until the morning of the seventeenth.

Concerning these exciting events, and the action of the Police in suppressing the rioters and restoring law and order, more will be said in another place.

The entire force for the year ending October 31, 1863, was as follows. Captains, thirty-four; Sergeants, one hundred and twenty-six; Patrolmen, (including Roundsmen and Special Duty men), one thousand seven hundred and ninety-four; Doormen, sixty-six

Lost time, by reason of sickness or disability, twenty-two thousand eight hundred and five days

This large increase of lost time over the previous year is attributable to the July riots

 Arrests

 Offences against property 8,912
 Offences against the person 52,976

  Total 61,888

The annexed cut is an accurate representation of the old Jefferson Market, showing the old fire tower, the rear of the prison, and Jefferson Assembly Rooms, which formerly was used as a watch-house by the old Leatherheads.

On the thirty-first of December, 1863, Governor Seymour appointed as Police Commissioners, Joseph S Bosworth, William McMurray, and William B Lewis, in the place of Bergen, Acton and Bowen, removed

Old Jefferson Market.

The removed Commissioners refused to obey the edict of the Governor, and held on to the office of Police Commissioners, continuing to discharge the duties thereof In this emergency the legislature stepped in, and, on March 15, 1864, by enactment, provided that "in place of the Commissioners of Metropolitan Police, appointed under and by virtue of Chapter 259, Laws of 1864, whose several terms of office are hereby vacated, there are hereby appointed, respectively, as such Commissioners, Thomas C. Acton, to hold office until March 1, 1872; Joseph S Bosworth, to hold office until March 1,

1870; John G Bergen, to hold office until March 1, 1868; and William McMurray, to hold office until March 1, 1866

Any vacancy occurring during the term of any Commissioner was filled by appointment by the remaining Commissioners, and the Commissioner so appointed continued in office until his successor had been elected by the next legislature A Commissioner whose term of office had expired continued to hold office until his successor should have qualified

Statement of convictions, acquittals, etc , had in the Courts of Oyer and Terminer and General Sessions of the Peace, in and for the city and county of New York, from 1841 to 1858, a period of seventeen years:

OFFENCES	1841	1842	1843	1844	1845	1846	1847	1848	1849	1850	1851	1852	1853	1854	1855	1856	1857
Murder	1	2			2	1	1	1	1		8	4	3	1	1		8
Arson, first degree (capital)			1						1								1
Manslaughter (various degrees)	8		3	7	2	2	1	3	6	4	8	6	17	15	9	12	13
Assault & Battery, with intent to kill or maim	2	3	4	8	4	6	4	3	6	5	9	7	10	11	12	19	12
Ass'lt & Batt'y with int. to rob			1						2	2			1	1	5	10	6
Rape, and int't to commit rape	4		1	1	5	4	5	1	4	2	1	1	4	4			4
Abandoning a child on a public highway	1							1									
Robbery (first degree)	4	5		3	2	3	11	6	4	10	3	15	10	27	5	6	22
Riot, with assault	26	6	8	17	7	2		4	13	49	6	17	45	32			
Assault and Battery	10	73	80	81	52	30	40	47	19	50	41	37	71	63	47	55	79
Procuring abortion	2			5		2	1										
Bigamy	2	1	2		3	2	5	6	1	3	1	4		2	1	5	6
Incest											1	1					
Sodomy							1		1								
Perjury, and subornation of perjury		2	2	2	2				2			2			2	1	
Arson (not capital)	1	1										1		1			8
Burglary (various degrees)	28	55	68	55	43	24	32	31	18	51	47	54	64	52	67	76	89
Attempt to commit felonies	7	2	5	6	4	6	10	6	10	10	9	14	9	19	48	64	101
Embezzlement			1		1			1	1			2		3		2	4
Grand larceny, & sec offence	90	71	84	58	73	76	61	91	87	98	105	119	155	112	62	94	89
Petit larceny, and attempt to commit petit larceny	57	48	40	42	40	88	66	54	95	101	70	51	75	91	180	100	116
Petit larceny, second offence	4			3	1	3					6	8	1		3		
Obtaining property by false pretences	4	8	5	7	8	9	10	16	10	11	8	8	12	14	11	7	8
Conspiracy		1	2	4			2	5		2							
Carrying slung shot (felony)									3	3	1	1	4	4			
Receiv'g stolen g'ds (scienter)	10	8	3	10	6	5	7	8	18	8	4	9	6	6	19	15	5
Accessory to felony				1		1					1						
Forgery (various degrees)	4	27	22	8	11	9	7	7	12	13	17	15	15	25	19	30	49
Receiv'g chall'ge to fight a duel		1															
Breaking prison				1	1			1									
Aiding prisoners to escape			1	1		1											
Keeping gambling and disorderly houses	12	16	12	24	7	86	18		16	16	15	16	14	88	7	9	3
Nuisance	13	2	2	1	4	5		3		1				2			
Selling, issuing, and advertising lottery tickets	10	4	2	3		2	2	4		1	1		6	10	2		
Libel	2	10	13	2	2	4		1			2	1					
Cruelty to animals			2									1					
Selling liquor without license	1			4	3	1	1					14	307	10	1		
Misdemeanor	3	12	7	8	1	4	8	14	1	8	7	1	6	16	10		8
Acquitted	153	103	119	103	142	72	78	107	91	102	93	106	155	108	141	77	96
Sentenced to be executed	1	2			2	1	1	1	2		8	4	3	1	1		4
" State prison	138	151	160	127	125	113	121	136	145	168	200	227	252	225	165	210	246
" County prisons	82	78	60	91	64	115	86	96	124	113	91	80	124	144	151	174	177
" House of Refuge	11	12	11	11	25	18	19	19	4	21	8	7	23	2	10	14	42
Indictments found by Gr Jury	871	909	942	807	765	767	598	631	639	788	833	945	1284	2696	997	988	1278
Compl'ts dismissed by G Jury	312	294	271	213	403	216	182	206	200	413	281	221	220	205	142	105	154

Convictions, acquittals and discharges by the Court of General Sessions from the year 1838 to 1857 inclusive.

OFFENCES.	1838	1839	1840	1841	1842	1843	1844	1845	1846	1847	1848	1849	1850	1851	1852	1853	1854	1855	1856	1857
Convictions, petit larceny	261	349	526	666	744	907	896	991	977	.	1064	1180	1419	1453	1475	1415	1411	2047	1788	2041
Acquittals	73	93	97	78	138	142	148	193	220	173	258	201	210	187	214	179	108	196	208	278
Convictions, assault & batt'y	125	163	226	296	287	305	551	615	509	834	430	558	837	662	978	1280	1152	.	936	1589
Acquittals	26	33	32	30	83	54	86	90	87	48	52	59	76	43	51	67	66	929	84	284
Discharges	429	581	488	396	375	537	838	1158	1109	697	672	933	1382	1194	1167	1120	1184	..	1454	1627
Misdemeanors																		23	25	101
Misdemeanors, acquitted																		6	4	40
Totals	914	1210	1369	1466	1577	2032	2519	3067	2922	2352	2502	2996	3933	3539	3884	3944	3921	3290	4549	5825
No of Trials in Special Sess.	434	614	839	1001	1119	1311	1495	1741	1651	1399	1635	1687	2218	2070	2403	2570	1528	1942	2803	3732
Sentenced to Co. Prisons	296	241	508	682	737	987	1058	1128	1075	981	1003	1120	1402	1179	1254	1242	1159	1528	1426	1824
Sentenced to H of Refuge	27	25	28	67	63	55	56	66	66	51	52	71	112	94	97	119	77	9	41	195

From January 1, 1830, to December 31, 1857 (twenty-eight years), thirty-seven persons had been sentenced to be executed, on convictions had in the criminal courts of the county. Of this number sixteen were executed; the sentences of thirteen were commuted to imprisonment for life; one was pardoned; one committed suicide; in four cases new trials were ordered—two were subsequently convicted of manslaughter and one discharged, and two under sentence.

CHAPTER VIII.

SKETCH OF THE DRAFT RIOTS.

JULY, 1863.

THE CITY IN THE HANDS OF A FRENZIED MOB.—AN EMERGENCY IN WHICH THE POLICE COVERED THEMSELVES WITH GLORY.—POPULAR DISCONTENT GROWING OUT OF A LATENT SYMPATHY WITH THE SOUTHERN CAUSE.—THE METHOD ADOPTED FOR THE ENFORCEMENT OF THE DRAFT NOT THE MOST JUDICIOUS ONE. SUPERINTENDENT KENNEDY'S ARRANGEMENTS IN ANTICIPATION OF TROUBLE.—GROWING DESPERATION OF THE MOB.—FIRING OF THE BUILDINGS IN WHICH THE PROVOST MARSHAL HAD HIS OFFICE.—SUPERINTENDENT KENNEDY ATTACKED AND BRUTALLY BEATEN.—HIS MIRACULOUS ESCAPE FROM DEATH.—COMMISSIONER ACTON ASSUMES COMMAND OF THE FORCE.—HIS ENERGY AND PROMPTITUDE MORE THAN A MATCH FOR THE MOB, WHO FIGHT FURIOUSLY.—THE RIOTERS BEAT BACK THE POLICE, BUT ARE IN TURN OVERCOME AND ROUTED.—CLUBS VERSUS STONES, BRICKS AND BULLETS.—"BY THE RIGHT FLANK, COMPANY FRONT, DOUBLE QUICK, CHARGE!"—MOB DESPERATION AND POLICE HEROISM.—"UP GUARDS, AND AT 'EM"—ACTION OF THE MILITARY.—END OF THE FIRST DAY'S FIGHTING.

HOWEVER admirably they may have behaved in other emergencies, there has been no occasion on which our Police Protectors covered themselves with more honor than during the terrible draft riots which convulsed the city for an entire week in the summer of 1863. At this period, too, they assumed a higher role than is generally allotted to them. They became not only the defenders of the lives and property of their fellow-citizens, but also the vindicators of the National honor. They fought for the Union in the streets of New York, just as truly as the soldiers of the Republic did upon the banks of the Potomac. Day after day they went out to combat with forces greatly their superior in numbers; day after day they imperiled life and limb; they left their own homes, their wives and children unprotected, to obey the call of duty. Nothing more honorable can be said of them, as a body, than that, in the face of every difficulty, there was no faltering. It is not recorded that any one man failed to respond to the demands of the hour, it is not on record that any man shirked duty, however dangerous or unpleasant it might be. It is on record that the utmost bravery, energy, and judgment were displayed by the entire force from the chiefs to the lowest subordinates. To their efforts, bravely seconded by a force of Federal soldiery, perhaps are due the preservation of the city from untold of horrors, and the salvation of the nation from dismemberment through the failure of the draft.

It was in July, 1863. The tide of war had turned against the Confederacy: but the fearful mortality, and the wearying effects of the long continued strife had at last compelled the Federal Government to resort to a conscription to recruit the Union armies. This proceeding was authorized by an Act of Congress passed in March, 1863. President Lincoln's proclamation, ordering the levy of three hundred thousand men, was dated April 8, but July was the time appointed for the draft

At this juncture the enemy invaded Pennsylvania, and the Governor entreated assistance from the adjoining States Governor Seymour, of New York, responded by directing General Sanford, commander of the city militia, to send every available regiment at his disposal to the seat of war for thirty days' service. While the troops were absent, the United States authorities attempted to enforce the draft, which caused a terrible insurrection The elements of disorder and crime united their forces, and were joined by thousands of frenzied workmen and idlers "For three days and three nights," says a chronicler of these events, "the rioters maintained a reign of terror. They sacked houses in great numbers, demolished the offices of the Provost Marshal, burned the colored orphan asylum, attacked the Police, and chased the negroes—women and children even—wherever they appeared on the streets, and when caught hanged them on the nearest lamp-post. They tore down and trampled under foot the National flag, and robbed stores in open day. The Secretary of War ordered home the regiments doing duty in Pennsylvania, but ere they arrived the climax of atrocities had been reached, and through the combined action of the Police and the citizens, together with the slender military force at the disposal of the authorities, the riot (one of the most formidable in the annals of riots,) had been substantially quelled The Police displayed admirable address and undaunted bravery against overwhelming numbers; they were under the command of Thomas C. Acton, President of the Police Board, who issued orders with the coolness and skill of a trained military veteran "

The drafting met with the bitterest opposition. There were many persons who conscientiously believed that as a method of raising soldiers, conscription was contrary to the spirit of American institutions—entirely forgetting that the first necessity with governments, as with individuals, is self-preservation But the principal source of discontent lay deeper. It grew out of a latent sympathy with the Southern cause, which pervaded large classes of persons in the North. If a conscription were enforced these persons saw that they might be obliged to fight in the Union armies against the side with which they sympathized, or, at best, in furtherance of a cause for which they had no love. Thus it happened that from the very day of the proclamation, symptoms of trouble were discernable An association, called the Knights of the Golden Circle, was formed, with the object, it was supposed, of rebelling against the draft, and a certain portion of the public press assumed a very inflammatory tone It must be confessed that the methods adopted by the National Government for the enforcement of the draft were not the most judicious possible Instead of making requisitions on the authorities of the various States for certain quotas of men, to be picked out from the general body of citizens by lot, the War Department sent its Provost

Marshals into the various districts to take direct charge of the selection of the conscripts. This course greatly increased the popular exasperation, and, during the preliminary work, signs and omens of coming trouble were not wanting in New York Thus, in the Ninth Conscription District, which included the lower part of the city, Captain Joel B. Erhardt, the Provost Marshal, narrowly escaped with his life while performing the necessary duty of collecting the names of those liable to being drafted He was ordered by Colonel Nugent, the Provost Marshal for the whole city, to personally collect the names of some workmen engaged on a building at the corner of Liberty Street and Broadway, who had refused to register when the regular enrolling officers approached them. Captain Erhardt

Process of Drafting in the Sixth District

was assailed, in the performance of his duty, by a man armed with an iron crowbar He drew his pistol and frustrated the attack, but after waiting a long time in vain for aid, he was compelled to retreat before an infuriated mob

More than one incident like this created anxiety among the authorities as the date for the draft drew nigh, and yet it is doubtful to this day if there was any organized design to resist. Information was given to the Police that a plan was afoot to seize the State Arsenal at Seventh Avenue and Thirty-fifth Street on Saturday, July 11, the day on which the drafting opened This was probably the case, but it is believed that the design extended no further When this was defeated by the measures of Superintendent Kennedy—as will soon be described—it is more than probable that no definite course was marked out by the lawbreakers. When the first acts of violence were committed on Monday, the 13th, it is likely that the members of the mob had no idea beyond that of breaking up the draft, and perhaps taking vengeance on some of the officials in charge of it. That afternoon and the succeeding days, an entirely new element entered into the tumult. The thirst for violence had grown furious; the craving for plunder had taken possession of the lower elements of the population. The draft became a mere pretext for lawlessness, the real object of which was the gratification of instincts of rapine and destruction. The riots were no longer draft riots, but riots for blood and booty. Their desperate character was in no way lessened, however; on the contrary, the second day's fighting was the bitterest of all.

As organized at the period under discussion, the Police force was under the management of Commissioners Thomas C. Acton and John G Bergen, Commissioner Bowen having resigned to accept a brigadier general's commission John A Kennedy was Superintendent, and Daniel Carpenter, George W Dilks and James Leonard were Inspectors.

The violent proceedings of the rioters had, as the Police Commissioners were convinced, a political origin, motive and direction, and received sympathy and encouragement from newspapers and partisans of influence and intelligence The Board of Police had long been threatened with summary removal, which was expected to occur immediately. Numbers of the force desired the removal, and a spirit of insubordination had crept in among the force, the fruit of the expected change "Under these new and extraordinary circumstances," to quote from the annual report of the Commissioners to the legislature, "there were apprehensions that the force might fail in united action, or be embarrassed by sympathy with the rioters, and be overpowered and beaten. * * The apprehension proved to be groundless. The force acted as a unit, and with an energy, courage and devotion rarely exhibited. The keenest observation failed to discover that political, religious or national feeling had any influence adverse to the efficient action of the force. The courage that arises from the aggregation of numbers, the steadiness and celerity of movement which resulted from organization and drill, and the fidelity and pride of corps which result from discipline, were exhibited in a most gratifying degree, considering the numerous and severe contests, the disparity of numbers, and the advantage enjoyed by the mob from their intrenched position in tenement houses, the small number of Policemen killed and wounded is a subject of congratulation. The number wounded was eighty, but three have died."

As bad luck would have it, the drafting began on a Saturday (July 11). There was no special disturbance, but the whole aspect of the city was uneasy. Sergeant Van Orden, with fifteen men, early took possession of the Seventh Avenue Arsenal In pursuance of the plot already mentioned, disorderly crowds gathered about the building, but the strength of the place, and the determined aspect of the little band of defenders, prevented any attack from being made. The drafting, too, passed off peaceably in the two districts—the Ninth and Eleventh—appointed for that day, and people began to hope that the danger was over—that the popular discontent would not reach the point of open outbreak.

Under more favorable circumstances this might have been so, but the day was unfavorable. All the Sunday newspapers came out with long lists of the conscript's names. These were eagerly scanned in all the tenements of the city. People found the names of relatives and friends among the number, and their rage grew in proportion. All day excited groups of unemployed men and women discussed the situation in the houses, in the streets, and, above all, in the liquor saloons, and by midnight they were ready for any madness.

Monday's sun rose hot and angry upon the seething city. The people came pouring from the tenement houses to face the fact that a fresh raid was now to be made on their households by the demon of war. Vainly confident in the strength of their numbers and their passion, they determined that this should not be.

Superintendent Kennedy, though not fully aware of the force of the coming storm, had yet the forethought to see that danger was ahead. The drafting was to proceed at two points on this day. They were No. 1190 Broadway, near Twenty-ninth Street, and a house on the corner of Third Avenue and Forty-sixth Street. Superintendent Kennedy began by collecting some force at headquarters, and sending the reserves of the Twentieth Precinct to aid in the defence of the arsenal. The drafting office at No. 1190 Broadway lay within the Twenty-ninth Precinct, and accordingly, Captain Speight took charge of it at nine o'clock in the morning. He brought with him twenty of his own men, to whom were added ten men from the Eighth Precinct under Sergeant Wade, ten from the Ninth under Sergeant Mangin, fourteen from the Fifteenth under Sergeant McCredie, and ten men from the Twenty-eighth under Sergeant Wolfe. This total force of sixty-nine men, all told, sufficed to overawe the mob. The draft proceeded peaceably until noon, when it was adjourned. The auxiliary forces were then sent to Third Avenue and Forty-sixth Street, where the state of things was very different. Captain Speight, however, with his own gallant boys, remained at the office until four o'clock in the afternoon, when he repaired to Headquarters in response to an order. During the day he dispersed many crowds, and maintained good order constantly. Ten minutes after he left, however, the mob, emboldened by its successes elsewhere, set fire to the Marshal's office, and the entire block on Broadway between Twenty-eighth and Twenty-ninth Streets was destroyed by the flames.

Far different from those on Broadway were the scenes in the Nineteenth Precinct, in which the Provost Marshal's office at Forty-sixth Street and Third Avenue was located. Captain G. T. Porter was the commanding officer at this point. He, and the brave men under his orders, had to bear the first shock of the riot, and right well they did their duty. It is no discredit to them that they were unable to resist successfully the infuriated thousands that were pitted against them. Captain Porter repaired to the Marshal's office at nine o'clock in the forenoon. He collected his entire force of sixty men about the place, stationing some in front of the building and some within it, as the crowd increased minute after minute in numbers and audacity. With Captain Porter were Captain S. Brower, of the Seventeenth Precinct, and a squad; Captain A M. Palmer, of the Twenty-first Precinct, and a squad ; Sergeant William M. Gross, of the Twenty-second Precinct, with twelve men ; and later, Sergeant Mangles, of the Twenty-eighth Precinct, with eleven men

The drafting began at a quarter past ten, A M., and went on for twenty minutes without interruption. The mob had grown to huge proportions; the excitement was intense. The Police were hooted, and curses were breathed

Provost Marshal's Office, 185 Sixth Avenue

against the negro race, the National government, the drafting authorities, and, in fact, against all public officials. Only a spark was needed to bring about the explosion.

It was supplied On a sudden some one shouted, "Stop the cars." An instantaneous rush was made Horses were uncoupled, drivers were forced from their platforms, and terrified passengers were driven from their places into the depths of the swaying, shouting mass of humanity that filled the Avenue.

But now the mob was fairly warmed to work With one awful movement it launched itself upon the band of Police drawn up before the Marshal's office. The shock was irresistible. One might as well try to dam the Hudson as oppose that mob There was a momentary struggle, and the little band gave way, taking shelter with their comrades within the building A hurricane of stones now assailed the windows and doors, which speedily gave way Then the mob dashed in, and joined in hand-to-hand encounters with the defenders. It was in vain for the Police to strike them down; as one fell beneath a blow of a club, another and another took his place. The Marshal and his clerks escaped through the rear of the building; the Police slowly followed, fighting all the way, until they emerged into Forty-sixth Street. By this time all the furniture in the office was demolished, and the mob proceeded to fire the building Then the brave Police endeavored to save the property in the adjoining houses, but were bitterly assailed at every step Sergeant Finch, of the Seventeenth Precinct, in heading the attack on the mob, had his forehead laid open with a frightful gash Officers Hill and Weill, of the same precinct, were also badly injured. Officer Cook, of the Nineteenth Precinct, was knocked down and separated from his comrades, who were themselves fully occupied keeping off the crowds that beset them At last, when it became evident that no good could be done while the men were receiving terrible punishment, Captain Porter gave the signal for retreat The force scattered into small groups forthwith, and made their way, as best they might, to their several station houses.

With their usual promptitude, the firemen were on hand almost as soon as the flames in the Marshal's office became visible. At first the mob refused to allow them to throw any water into the burning building, and two adjoining houses were speedily involved in the conflagration At length, however, Chief Engineer Decker made the rioters a speech, pointing out that the property of people with whom they had no quarrel was being destroyed To this appeal they yielded, and, the Police being driven off, the crowd began to watch with the usual interest, but unusual hilarity, the progress of the flames, and the efforts of the fire laddies to extinguish them

At this disastrous moment, by an untoward accident, Superintendent Kennedy put in an appearance on the scene Mr Kennedy's fears of riot had arisen that Monday morning, mainly from the intelligence which reached him shortly after seven o'clock, that the street contractor's men in the Nineteenth Ward had not gone to work at the usual hour. He at first deemed it sufficient to strengthen the Police forces at Provost Marshal Manierre's office on Broadway, and Marshal Jenkins' office on Third Avenue, in the manner already detailed, but as the progress of the morning brought fresh indications of trouble, he telegraphed to all the precincts to call in as reserves all the men who had gone off duty at six A M. Towards ten o'clock, all Mr Kennedy's arrangements being completed, he took his wagon, and started on a tour of personal inspection. First he called on Captain Speight, at No 1190 Broadway, and then visited the arsenal, leaving at each point directions to cover any emergency that might arise. At last he turned his horse to the eastward, and about twelve o'clock approached the quarter where, unknown to him, the first battle of the riot had been fought The Superintendent was not in uniform, and was totally unarmed. It is impossible to avoid the reflection, therefore, that his courage (or indiscretion?) ran to the point of rashness when he left his wagon at Forty-sixth Street on perceiving the fire that the rioters had kindled, and walked rapidly through the angry crowd towards it.

Everything seemed very quiet, and everybody good-natured about him, until, on a sudden, some one cried out, "There's Kennedy!"

"Where, where? Where is he?" demanded a thousand angry voices.

He was pointed out, and before he had time to realize the situation, a cowardly blow from behind sent him down an embankment six feet high into a vacant lot. In an instant the Superintendent was on his feet; a glance showed that flight was his only course, and he sped away across the lots, while the infuriate rabble pressed hard behind him. He distanced his pursuers, and succeeded in climbing the Forty-seventh Street embankment. But here a fresh crowd, as cowardly and brutal as the first, was waiting for him. They came at him with a rush, and for the second time he was hurled to the foot of the embankment. The crowd followed him. Mr. Kennedy regained his feet. A burly ruffian tried to dash his brains out with a club, and Mr. Kennedy with difficulty protected his head. By this time he must have received fully fifty blows on various parts of his body. He now turned and ran toward Lexington Avenue, where there was a pond or mud hole of considerable width and depth.

"Drown him, drown him!" shouted the rioters, and a tremendous blow sent the victim into the pond, when his face struck on some stones at the bottom and was frightfully lacerated. But even yet he was not overcome. Making his way through the mud and water through which his pursuers were unwilling to follow, he reached Lexington Avenue before they got around. As he emerged from the pond he met Mr. John Eagan, a prominent citizen, and begged for aid. Mr Eagan possessed sufficient influence with the mob to prevent them from doing any further violence, and Mr Kennedy, now fainting with pain and exhaustion, was laid on a common feed wagon, and driven to Headquarters. As the wagon drove up to the building, Commissioner Acton was standing on the steps. He noticed the bruised and bleeding man, but never guessed who it was, so far beyond recognition was the Superintendent.

When he realized the truth he had the injured man taken to the house of a friend, and surgical aid was procured. It was found that no bones were broken, and so wonderful was his constitution, and so determined his will, that the Superintendent returned to duty on the Thursday following, a fact all the more wonderful when it is remembered that he was over sixty years of age. He was shockingly disfigured for the time being, but in time the traces of his thrilling fight for life disappeared from his countenance.

The early disablement of the Superintendent placed the command of the force upon the shoulders of Commissioner Acton, at Headquarters, and of Inspector Daniel Carpenter in the field—or rather in the streets. Both proved equal to the demands upon them. To no one man was the speedy suppression of the riots due so largely as to Mr Acton. His very first step showed his consummate generalship. The moment he realized the extent of the disorder, on seeing Superintendent Kennedy's terrible condition, he telegraphed to every precinct, except the Twelfth, from which the rioters had cut off communication, ordering the entire force to concentrate at the Central Office. He also dispatched the Steamboat Squad with their vessel, under Captain Todd, to transport to the city all the Federal troops that could be spared from the forts in the harbor, and subsequently to land arms for volunteer troops. These duties, it may be remarked here, were performed with coolness and judgment

The energy displayed by Mr Acton was wonderful He did not leave the Central Office for five days, except for a couple of short periods on official business. From six o'clock on Monday morning until after two A M the following Friday, he never closed an eye in sleep During the whole period he was engaged without cessation It may serve as some index of his labors to say that he received and answered over four thousand telegrams

He was ably seconded. Hardly inferior to him in energy and executive ability was his colleague, Commissioner John G Bergen. This gentleman was constantly at Headquarters, sustaining almost equal fatigue with Mr. Acton, and sharing in all his labors Chief Clerk Seth C Hawley was also a most valuable aid. He was placed in charge of the ordinance department, serving out the arms and ammunition needed by the men as they started on their repeated expeditions He also provided for the wants of the wounded, and did all in his power to furnish accommodations for the crowds of refugees who early began to throng to Headquarters. With Chief John Young of the Detective force, assisted by Sergeant Lefferts of the Fourth District Court, and Officer Webb of the Superintendent's office, he had also to provide for the victualing of Police, military, Special Constables, and refugees, in all over five thousand persons, for an entire week. It is needless to add praise to the statement that all were well and sufficiently fed Over fifty thousand gallons of coffee, it is said, were served out while the riot lasted, and it must here be mentioned to the credit of the entire force, that coffee—during all the scenes of terror and excitement, despite all the blows and hardships—was the universal beverage Everyone took it in preference to liquor, and while the riot lasted, not one intoxicated man was seen about Headquarters

But it is time to return to the rioters who were left at the moment when they had all but beaten the Superintendent of Police to death at Lexington Avenue and Forty-sixth Street. About the same time another fierce scene was in progress only a few blocks off. A little before noon the reports of the agitation which prevailed in the Nineteenth Ward caused the sending of several contingents from various precincts, including the men relieved from duty at No 1190 Broadway, to Captain Porter's aid. Among the first of these intended reinforcements to arrive on the scene was a squad of thirteen men from the Eighth, under Sergeant Ellison. This little company first encountered the mob at Third Avenue and Forty-fourth Street A desperate hand-to-hand fight ensued The mob fought furiously; the Police were outnumbered a hundred to one, and were soon obliged to retreat Sergeant Ellison, who had been terribly beaten, remained a prisoner in the rioters hands. At this moment, Sergeant Wade arrived with his squad from Broadway. The fight was renewed, and

Ellison was extricated from his terrible captivity more dead than alive He had defended himself bravely with his revolver and a gun which he had wrested from a rioter. But he had been overwhelmed by numbers, terribly beaten, and pelted with stones until he lost consciousness. After lying as if dead for half an hour on the pavement, he was carried by two of his comrades to the Twenty-first Precinct station house. In this fight, too, Officer Van Buren had his leg broken, Sergeant Wade was struck in the breast with a stone, Officer Andre had his head badly cut, Officers Law and Hart were injured in the head and body, and Officers Crolius, Palmer, Burns, Merher and

Rioters Marching Down Second Avenue

Magersuppe were all badly cut about the head All of the officers here named distinguished themselves by their courage in attacking the mob

A platoon from the Ninth Precinct arrived at Forty-fourth Street and Third Avenue at the same time as Sergeant Wade, and participated in the fighting with equal courage. To show how well the men of this precinct played their part, it is only necessary to record that Sergeants Mangin and Smith, and ten officers were badly hurt Some members of the Tenth, under Sergeants Minor and Davenport, also had a rough encounter with the mob in the same locality

Just as these forces were defeated, Sergeant McCredie, of the Fifteenth, arrived at Forty-third Street and Third Avenue with his fourteen men. He was joined by ten men from the Twenty-eighth, under Sergeant Wolfe, and by the scattered men from the other precincts, until his force embraced altogether forty-four stout locusts. With this force, small as it was, McCredie—who was deservedly christened by his comrades "Fighting Mac"—began a furious onslaught on the rabble that filled the avenue. He met with an obstinate resistance; but discipline and courage enabled him and his gallant boys to force their way to Forty-sixth Street, where they hoped Captain Porter and his men still held their ground. Disappointed in this expectation, the little storming party found itself hemmed in on all sides by masses of infuriated men. Stones rained in on them. Their charges were fiercely resisted. Of the fourteen men from the Fifteenth station, nine were badly wounded before the force was dispersed. Officer Bennett was knocked down three times before he ceased fighting. The last time, he lay senseless. In this condition, he was stripped to his drawers, and savagely beaten. At last his seemingly dead body was taken by strangers to St. Luke's Hospital, and laid in the dead-house. His grief-stricken wife, coming to claim the supposed remains, fell on them in a transport of grief. But in a moment she sprang to her feet, almost delirious with joy. Her husband's heart still beat. Restoratives were used, and Bennett recovered, though only after three days of insensibility, and a long illness.

Officer Travis, of the same precinct, was also taken to St. Luke's. In trying to escape the crowd he was confronted by a fellow with a pistol. He captured the weapon, but before he could use it, was knocked down and beaten almost to a jelly. His jaw and right hand were broken. The mob stripped him naked before they left him. Officer Phillips had a terrible run for life. He disarmed a rioter of a musket, but had no time to use it. He was stabbed twice with a knife by a woman, and would have been killed but for the interference of some citizens who appeared to have influence with the mob. Sergeant McCredie was disabled by a blow on the wrist from a bar of iron. His life was saved by a young German woman, who hid him between two mattresses while the rioters searched her house from roof to cellar. Officer Sutherland was knocked down with a brick and beaten insensible. Officers Mingay, Broughton and Gabriel were very badly beaten, and Officer Terence Kiernan, after terrible usage, only escaped with his life through the intercession of Mrs. Eagan, whose husband had helped to save Superintendent Kennedy. The off platoon of the Fifteenth Precinct, under Roundsman Thacher, was sent to reinforce McCredie, but arrived only in time to be roughly handled. Officer Bodine was beaten insensible and stripped. Officer Gibbs was left for dead in the street. Officers Foster and Didway were shockingly mangled.

In this fight the men of the Twenty-eighth also suffered severely. Sergeant Wolfe, who was the last to retreat, was cut about the head; Officer Seibert had an arm, and Officer Holley a finger broken; Officers Dapke, Polhamus, Bryan, Bassford, Knight, and Bolman were more or less badly beaten.

These were not the only collisions between bodies of Police and the Forty-sixth Street mob. A force had been ordered to the scene from the Eighteenth Precinct, Sergeant Vosburgh in command. It was unable to effect a junction with Captain Porter, and after a brief, but courageous struggle, was forced to retreat. Officer Wynne was severely beaten and stabbed; Officers Larne and

Sanderson were beaten and had their clothes nearly torn off. The Thirteenth's boys had a similar experience. At noon, Captain Thomas Steers, with Sergeants Bird and Smith and twenty-five men, started to the aid of Captain Porter. They got as far as Thirty-fifth Street, but could penetrate no further through the turbulent crowd. They therefore retired to the Twenty-first Precinct station house, then in East Thirty-first Street, where Sergeant Forshay was in command. The rioters had been threatening to destroy the building, but decamped, afraid to encounter the increased force brought by Captain Steers.

Having thus defeated the Police in detail, the mob dispersed itself over the city, plundering and burning in all directions, and above all, committing frightful atrocities on negroes wherever they were found. Some of the cooler scoundrels among the insurrectionists saw that for any lasting success, arms were absolutely necessary. To secure these, a portion of the mob, about half-past one o'clock, gathered about the large gun factory at Twenty-first Street and Second Avenue, where a great quantity of arms was known to be in storage. This movement had been anticipated. Early in the afternoon, Sergeant Banfield, with a squad, had, by order of Captain John Cameron, of the Eighteenth Precinct, taken possession of the building. Later on they were relieved by the Broadway Squad of thirty-two men under Sergeant Burdick and Roundsmen Ferris and Sherwood. The men reached the factory singly or in pairs, escaping the notice of the rioters, who, as three o'clock approached, had swelled to thousands in number. Every Policeman was armed with a carbine, and stationed at a window.

At last the battle began. A whirlwind of stones, bricks and bullets was launched against the doors and windows. The defenders dared not show themselves. The fire of the mob was not returned. Then an effort was made to burn the building, but without success, and the attack was renewed with greater fury than ever. Presently one of the rioters assailed the office door with a sledge-hammer. His compatriots awaited the result of his efforts, and at last a panel went crashing in. The man stooped to crawl into the aperture, when the single report of a carbine was heard, and he fell back with a bullet through his skull. The rioters hesitated, but only for a moment. The attack was once again renewed, and Sergeant Burdick sent to Captain Cameron for aid. He was told that none could be afforded. "Then I cannot hold the factory," he sent word. "Draw off your men," was the response. These messages were carried by Sergeant Buckman, of the Eighteenth, in disguise, and at great risk.

The mob had now been held in check almost four hours, but longer resistance was impossible. The only means of retreat, however, which was not cut off, lay through a hole in the rear wall of the building, twelve by eighteen inches in size, and eighteen feet from the ground. Through this they squeezed their way, gaining the street through a stone yard. They had hardly got clear of the factory when the rioters gained access to it. Subsequently they had to escape from the Eighteenth Precinct station house in plain clothes. They did picket duty about the Central office all Monday night.

So far, we have found the mob victorious at every point. There is now to be a complete change, and from this time forward, the Police, aided by the military, will be found inflicting a series of crushing defeats on the disturbers of the public peace The first of these was inflicted by a force of two hundred men, under Inspector Daniel Carpenter, at the corner of Broadway and Amity Street The telegrams sent to all the precincts ordering the concentration of the entire Police force at headquarters, by three o'clock, caused a considerable number of men to muster there.

Telegrams were now pouring in announcing deeds of destruction in every quarter Buildings on Broadway and Lexington Avenue were being sacked and burned; Police stations were besieged, and, despite the efforts of Fire Chief Decker and his men, the Colored Orphan Asylum, on Fifth Avenue, was wrecked and burned, the poor little inmates narrowly escaping with their lives by a back way.

Colored Orphan Asylum
Fifth Avenue, between 43rd and 44th Streets Burned Down by the Rioters

Towards four o'clock it was announced that a vast crowd was coming down Broadway to attack Police Headquarters This was the moment for action Drill Officer T S Copeland, from the available forces, quickly organized a band of two hundred men, which he himself joined as second in-command to Inspector Carpenter There were included details from the First, Seventh, Eighth, Fourteenth, Fifteenth and Twenty-seventh Precincts Carpenter made his men a brief speech "We are going to put down a mob," he said, "take no prisoners, but strike quick and hard" Then the force marched up Broadway. The rioters were met near Amity Street. They bore a National ensign, and a standard of planks with the words "No draft" They were armed with clubs, pitchforks, crowbars, swords, guns, and pistols

In a minute the opposing bodies stood but a few feet apart.

"By the right flank, company front, double quick, charge!" shouted

Carpenter, and in a moment he and his men were upon the lawbreakers. He drew the first blood, fracturing the skull of a ringleader. His men obeyed his orders literally, striking quick and hard on all sides. The crowd wavered, broke, and in a moment fled, leaving their banners in the hands of the Police, and the pavement strewn with their wounded and dying comrades. The Police marched on to Mayor Opdyke's house on Fifth Avenue, which had been threatened, but finding all quiet, marched back to Headquarters. The Amity Street battle decided the fortunes of the city. After it, the defeat of the rioters was only a question of time and hard fighting. It was demonstrated that they could not stand up before regular discipline. Among those who won distinction in the fight were Roundsmen Connor of the First; Sergeants McConnell and Garland of the Seventh; Sergeants Wade and O'Connor of the Eighth; Sergeant Mackey of the Fourteenth; Sergeant Roe and Officer Barhebt of the Fifteenth—both

Present Colored Orphan Asylum
143rd Street   Former Building Destroyed During the Draft Riots

of whom captured ringleaders in the riot; and Sergeant Bennett and Officers Doyle, Thompson, and Rhodes of the Twenty-seventh. Doyle knocked down the rioters' standard-bearer, and Thompson captured the National flag from their hands.

Carpenter, after the Amity Street battle, took a very short rest. Shortly before eight o'clock Sergeant Copeland organized another battalion of two hundred men, including one hundred men of the Brooklyn Police—then a part of the Metropolitan force—under Inspector John S. Folk. With this body, Inspector Carpenter started to the relief of the "Tribune" building, which had been threatened all day and was finally attacked by the rioters, whose wrath was especially virulent against Horace Greeley, as an abolitionist and advocate of the war. All day a dangerous looking crowd loitered about Printing House Square. To provide against emergencies, all the newspaper offices were supplied with arms from the Islands by the Steamboat Squad, Patrolmen Blackwell seeing to the safe delivery thereof with great prudence and judgment. All day Captain Thomas W. Thorne, of the Twenty-sixth Precinct, or City Hall Police, kept five of his men in citizen's dress in the crowd to watch its intentions Captain Bryan of the Fourth, with his Sergeants, Rode and Williams, and only half his men, had had his hands full all day rescuing colored people from gangs of ruffians, and protecting their property, but towards evening he assigned Sergeant Williams, Roundsman Webb, and four Officers, to detective duty about the newspaper offices.

About seven o'clock there was a good deal of rioting in the First Ward, and the First Precinct Police and those of the Twenty-sixth, under Captain Warlow, started to quell it Sergeant Cherry and McCleary, of the First, ran ahead of the main body, and, falling in with a mob in New Street, were severely beaten. The rioting was speedily suppressed, however, when the main force came up, and the Police were leisurely returning towards the City Hall, when, in front of the the old post-office on Nassau Street, they were informed that the "Tribune" office was being sacked. They approached the scene on a run, and reached it simultaneously with a platoon under Captain Bryan from the Fourth Sergeant Snodgrass of the Second Precinct had also, by mingling in the crowd, learned of the premeditated attack in time to join the other Police parties with the reserve of the Second. He was accompanied by Sergeants Esterbrook and Cornwell, Sergeant Kelly who had been out on guard all day, remaining in charge of the station.

The several bodies of Police charged the rioters together from different points Captain Thorne, of the Twenty-sixth, was knocked down with a blow of a club. Officer Cowen brought his locust down on the skull of the man who struck the blow The rioters fell stunned and bleeding on all sides Many of the Police were hurt too, Officer Welling, of the First, receiving a bullet in the shoulder. The fight was obstinate to Frankfort Street. Then the mob took to flight in all directions. The portion of it that rushed up Centre and Chatham Streets was pursued by the officers who had dispersed it, and dreadfully punished; but by far the greater section fled across the open space in front of City Hall. Theirs was a terrible fate Just at this moment, Inspector Carpenter, with his two hundred men, were wheeling into the square. Grasping the situation at a glance, the Inspector formed his men full company front, and charging the fleeing rabble, inflicted such chastisement as they deserved, scattering and driving them in all directions, few escaping without grievous bruises, and many receiving desperate wounds.

Quiet being restored, Carpenter took up his headquarters at the City Hall A fire, which the rioters had started in the "Tribune" building, was extinguished. A handful of men from the Twenty-sixth had already cleared the building of those who had entered it to sack it, Officer McWaters having a desperate encounter with a burly ruffian at the entrance. Sergeant Devoursney, taking command about the building, prevented any crowd from re-assembling about it.

Several members of the Twenty-sixth Precinct deserve especial recognition for their conduct in this engagement Sergeant Devoursney, alone and in uniform, confronted the entire crowd, and delayed its attack on the "Tribune" building a considerable time. Officer McCord, being in plain clothes, was struck by a comrade in mistake. Officer Gardner was wounded in the leg with a brick. The wounded were all attended by Police Surgeon Kennedy, who proved eminently brave, skillful and efficient in relieving the sufferers in the cause of duty.

No sooner was quiet secured about the City Hall, than Carpenter's force was weakened by the withdrawal of Inspector Folk and his men to Brooklyn, where the aspect of affairs was considered threatening. No actual rioting, however, took place there, thanks to Mr. Folk's energetic and judicious arrangements. Carpenter and his men, however, had their hands full. First of all, a report came in that negro houses were being burned in the Sixth Precinct, and the

Negro Hanged by the Mob and Burned   32d St., bet. 6th and 7th Aves

inhabitants ill-used. Captain John Jourdan was sent with his own men to suppress this disturbance. He had been fighting the rioters all day. With Sergeants Walsh and McGiven, he dispersed a mob at No. 42 Baxter Street at three P. M. Roundsman Ryan was knocked down and badly hurt, but continued to fight vigorously. At six P. M. six hundred rioters, who attacked a house at Baxter and Leonard Streets tenanted by twenty colored families, were dispersed by the Captain and Sergeants Walsh, Quinn, and Kennedy, and the first and second platoons. The fight was very bitter. On their way to Headquarters, at six o'clock, the men had been obliged to punish another mob which assailed them. Roundsman Hopkins was here badly wounded with a stone. After the Printing House

Square affair, Captain Jourdan and his command suppressed an attempt by about a thousand men to sack Nos 104 and 105 Park Street, houses occupied by colored people

Captain Jourdan returned to City Hall in time to participate in Inspector Carpenter's tour of the Fourth Ward, in the course of which he suppressed four riotous crowds who were burning negro dwellings. Fifty men were left to protect the "Tribune" building; the rest of his force accompanied the Inspector. Captain Bryan was the guide throughout this expedition His station house had been attacked, when only Sergeant Rode and eight men were in it, by five hundred rioters The attack had been successfully resisted. Sergeants Rode and Delaney, too, had dispersed a marauding crowd in front of a negro boarding house. Inspector Carpenter was accompanied, among others, by Captain Green and Sergeants Finney, Robinson, and Webb of the Third; Captain Sebring of the Ninth; Captain Davis of the Tenth; Captain Steers of the Thirteenth; Captain Brower of the Seventeenth; Captain Slott, and Sergeants Aldis, Potter, and Murphy of the Twenty-second; Captain Dickson and Sergeant Groat of the Twenty-eighth—Sergeant O'Connor had been so badly wounded in the fight before the City Hall that he had to cease doing duty; Captain Speight of the Twenty-ninth; and Captain B G. Lord and the men of the Sanitary Corps. Captain John J. Mount and the men of the Eleventh Precinct also took part—the most active part—in this expedition They were detached to protect the persons and property of the colored residents of Roosevelt Street and New Bowery. They had much serious fighting, being stoned from the roofs, and Officer McMahon was badly injured with a brick. An incident of this tour will serve to show the ferocity of the rioters Three colored men took refuge on the roof of a house The rioters set it on fire, and the poor fellows were obliged to suspend themselves by their hands from the copings of the gable walls The Police searched in vain for ladders, and the men were at last obliged to drop to the ground, sustaining shocking injuries.

After this effective tour of the Fourth Ward, Carpenter and his men had one more exploit to perform that busy Monday. At eleven P. M. word was received that a new and great mob was marching down Broadway to raid the "Tribune" office. Carpenter at once massed his men close to the east gate of the Park, facing three companies to the west, whence the rioters were expected to come and the balance to the east The Police were concealed by the darkness, and the rioters were allowed to approach within a hundred yards, before Carpenter gave the word "Up Guards, and at them!" The Police went in with a rush Their opponents were five to one, but the shock was irresistible, and in a few minutes the Park was for the second time strewn with wounded men, while a discomfitted remnant fled up Broadway

At midnight Carpenter and his brave but wearied followers were relieved by the arrival of Inspector James Leonard with three hundred and fifty men, Capt. Thorne of the Twenty-sixth Precinct being second in command, and the battalion including details from the Fifth, Seventh, Eighth, Fourteenth, Sixteenth, Twentieth, and Twenty-ninth Precincts Inspector Leonard remained in charge at the City Hall until the following Friday, when the riots were at an end. To his energy and judgment are, in a measure, attributable the suppression of all disorder in the down-town districts of the city. He had, before taking charge at this point, headed a troop which defeated a mob about nine P. M. on Monday at Broadway and Bond Street—only a block or two distant from the scene of Carpenter's first victory.

At the City Hall the Inspector's resources were taxed to the utmost. Before daybreak on Tuesday, he sent a platoon to protect the residences of negroes at Leonard and York Streets; he dispersed a mob which was sacking a provision store on Greenwich Street near Cortlandt, he sent a squad to guard Brooks Brothers' clothing store on Catharine Street, and others to protect the hotels in

Military Encamping in Washington Square.

Fulton and Cortlandt Streets. Towards morning he learned that a mob was proceeding to Fulton Ferry to oppose the landing of marines from the Brooklyn Navy Yard, and incidentally to burn Fulton Market. He sent a large party to meet this mob; the result was a short, sharp fight, ending in the rout of the rioters. So many parties did Inspector Leonard send out in sundry directions, that by nine o'clock, A. M. he was left alone at City Hall. He went to Headquarters at once to represent in person the need for a strong force about Printing House Square. He was given two hundred men, with whom he hastened back to his post. He found an excited crowd rapidly growing in numbers. Every negro who came in sight was chased and beaten, and dire threats were heard

on all sides. By noon, the situation was such that Mr. Leonard, taking a hundred men, cleared the Park and Printing House Square, hastening the movements of the obstinate by argument with the locust. This process had to be repeated a number of times; but by far the most exciting event of the day in this vicinity occurred at eight P. M, when a mob beset a company of regular troops at Broadway and Chambers Street, and by threats and demonstrations of violence attempted to prevent the men from proceeding Seeing that an attack was imminent, Inspector Leonard, accompanied only by Sergeant Polly of the Eleventh Precinct, and one Patrolman, forced his way into the heart of the crowd, and, in order to direct attention from the soldiers, seized two of the leaders of the mob and began dragging them towards the City Hall. The officers' aim was gained; but they nearly forfeited their lives The rioters turned their full fury against the three brave men, who, each holding fast to a prisoner, faced the enemy with uplifted clubs.

Shouts of "Kill them, give them what Kennedy got!" arose on all sides; but, happily, the officers' determination rendered the ruffians rather unwilling to face them. At last, however, a rush was made Up and down went the clubs with terrific regularity, a rioter going down under every blow. The prisoners were placed in front, and were shockingly cut and bruised by the missiles aimed by their friends at the Police At last, intelligence of the fight reached the force in the City Hall Seventy-five men instantly turned out to rescue their brave commander. In a few seconds they were by his side. Then the prisoners, badly beaten men, were cast aside, and Carpenter headed a charge on the mob which sent it fleeing in all directions, while heaps of injured men marked the track along which the Police had moved This defeat seemed to break down the riot in this part of the city. Captain Mount and the men of the Eleventh Precinct guarded the Cortlandt Street Hotels all Tuesday night, but no attack was made The Sixteenth's force, under Captain Hedden, dispersed mobs during the evening at Thomas Street and West Broadway The next day some slight encounters took place, and great vigilance had to be exercised, but this was the last of Inspector Leonard's pitched battles.

He, however, remained on duty at the Hall until Friday, when, with his officers and men, he was recalled During his command there, as is recorded, he had rendered invaluable services to that section and the lower portion of the city He had immense interests to guard, and that he acted the part of a brave and zealous officer goes without saying

The Colored Orphan Asylum was burned down about four o'clock in the afternoon of Monday, July 13 A mob of some three thousand had attacked the asylum The asylum at that terrible moment held within its walls two hundred colored children, besides the officers and matrons. The main building was four stories, with wings of three stories. Superintendent William E Davis hurriedly fastened the doors, and, while the mob were breaking them in, the children were collected and taken from the building by the rear door before the mob had battered down the barricaded doors The building was first ransacked and pillaged—everything portable was carried away—and then the torch of the incendiary was applied Chief Engineer Decker, upon reaching the scene, tried by argument to draw off the miserable rabble. He forced his way into the building, was assaulted, thrice knocked down, and finally driven out. Having been joined by ten firemen, he determined upon making another effort to save the asylum. Assistant Engineers Lamb and Lewis swelled the ranks of the little band of heroic firemen, and then they pushed through the crowd and penetrated into the building. The work of demolition had progressed on all sides The furniture had been broken and piled in different parts of the house, while fires had already been kindled on the first and second floors. The firemen scattered and extinguished these incipient fires, at the imminent risk of their lives, the building being still filled with rioters Meantime, some of the latter, despite the efforts of the little band of firemen, had succeeded in setting fire to the loft. To save the structure was now an impossibility, and the firemen and the mob alike were driven forth by the rapidly-spreading flames In a little time the asylum was wrapped in flames, and within an hour or so only a small portion of the walls remained standing

After their escape from the building the poor little orphans were conducted to the Twentieth Precinct, where they were taken care of by Captain Walling, and were subsequently removed to Blackwell's Island. The loss to the society was estimated at eighty thousand dollars

There were ten precincts in Brooklyn, forming a portion of the Metropolitan Police. Its movements in this city on the first day of the riots are recorded as follows:

At half-past ten o'clock on Monday, Inspector John S. Folk received a dispatch from the New York headquarters directing him to call in his reserves, and to hold them in immediate readiness. They were on drill at Fort Green at the time, and forthwith he ordered them to their respective precincts.

At five o'clock P M., a dispatch was received from Commissioner Bergen to send his whole force to New York, if, in the Inspector's opinion, it would be safe for them to leave Brooklyn Inspector Folk lost no time in reporting himself at the Mulberry Street Headquarters with upwards of two hundred men They were retained at Headquarters for action in case of emergency About eight P. M word was received that the *Tribune* building was being threatened by the mob, and Inspector Folk, acting upon instructions, joined his force to that of Inspector Carpenter. On reaching the Park, the mob were met in their flight from Printing House Square, and received severe handling by Carpenter and Folk. The latter and his men were on the left of the wing, and he completed the rout and discomfiture of the mob. This duty over, and with parting cheers from Inspector Carpenter's men, Inspector Folk, under instructions, took up the march to Brooklyn Reaching Fulton Ferry, he learned that two negroes had just been murdered on the stocks, close by. After manœuvring his men and dispersing some evil-disposed bodies of loungers, he returned to Brooklyn, to protect his own threatened territory.

So well had Inspector Folk handled his forces, that the riotously-disposed were met whenever they showed any symptoms of disorder, and summarily dispersed before they had time to organize their forces, much less to inflict injury.

On Wednesday evening the elevators in the Basin were fired. The incendiaries, who were a gang of laborers, mingled with the crowd, and so could not be singled out by Inspector Folk and his command, who were promptly on the spot

Inspector Folk was a faithful and gallant officer, and to his constant vigilance in Brooklyn, that city owed its immunity from the horrors which had convulsed New York. He and his command lent the most valuable aid to the New York Police in their desperate and valiant battle with the mob during a week of riot

CHAPTER IX

JULY, 1863.

SUPPRESSION OF THE DRAFT RIOTS

THE CITY SAVED FROM PILLAGE AND ARSON —A DEFIANT AND UNTERRIFIED MOB —NEGROES HANGED FROM LAMP-POSTS AND THEIR BODIES BURNED —STATION HOUSES AND PRIVATE DWELLINGS FIRED AND SACKED —STONES, BRICKS, AND OTHER MISSILES SHOWERED ON THE HEADS OF POLICEMEN FROM THE HOUSETOPS —POLICE RETALIATION.—ARRIVAL OF THE MILITARY.—COL. O'BRIEN'S FRIGHTFUL DEATH —THE BATTLE ON SECOND AVENUE AND TWENTY-FIRST STREET —THE MOB TAUGHT SOME SEVERE LESSONS —ERECTING BARRICADES —FIRED UPON BY THE TROOPS —THE POLICE PLY THEIR CLUBS ON THE HEADS OF RIOTERS WITH UNBOUNDED LIBERALITY —CHILDREN FROM THE COLORED ORPHAN ASYLUM PROTECTED BY THE POLICE —HARD HAND-TO-HAND FIGHTING —BACKBONE OF THE RIOT BROKEN.—A REIGN OF MOB LAW AVERTED.—VALUABLE SERVICES PERFORMED BY THE DETECTIVE FORCE AND TELEGRAPH BUREAU —SUPPRESSION OF THE RIOT —THE BOARD OF POLICE ISSUE A CONGRATULATORY ADDRESS TO THE FORCE —GOVERNOR SEYMOUR BEARS WILLING AND APPRECIATIVE TESTIMONY TO THE GALLANT SERVICES PERFORMED BY THE POLICE —ARRAIGNMENT AND CONVICTION OF RIOTERS

TUESDAY, the second day of the Riot, was no less a busy day in other parts of the city. At two A M Drill Officer Copeland, with a hundred men of the Fourth, Ninth, Nineteenth, Twenty-third, and Twenty-eighth Precincts, marched from Headquarters to recover the body of William Jones, a negro, whom the mob beat terribly and hanged from a lamp-post in Clarkson Street. The mob lit a fire under the body, and held a saturnalia about it until Copeland and his men dispersed them, and took the corpse to Headquarters. This duty was performed amid a terrific thunder and rain storm On their way back the members of the Twenty-third received intelligence that their station house, on East Eighty-seventh Street, as well as numerous private houses in the vicinity, was pillaged and burned by rioters Doorman Ebling saved the telegraph instrument, but all other property, public and personal, was lost.

On returning from the Clarkson Street expedition, the force of the Twenty-eighth Precinct, under Captain John F. Dickson, kept guard at a fire at Houston and Washington Streets, until five o'clock, when it went to Leroy Street and rescued a colored man, named Williams, who was attacked by a crowd. One ruffian, who had fled from Williams in the most cowardly way, beat him after he was

Their Brave Protector

(Drawn by C de Grimm, by permission of Mr James Gordon Bennett)

overcome by the crowd, with a stone weighing twenty pounds Captain Dickson placed the poor fellow in a wagon, which the officers drew to Headquarters. Williams died of his injuries next day

At six o'clock in the morning our old friend Carpenter re-appears on the scene, and, as usual, his appearance brings with it a direful combat, in which he gains his customary victory. At the hour named, he started out with two hundred and fifty men, to suppress disorder along Second Avenue. He and his force entered that thoroughfare at Twenty-first Street, and found it crowded with people who hissed and cursed the Police, but suffered them to pass unmolested until the block between Thirty-second and Thirty-third Streets was reached. Here a

General Canby's Headquarters

sudden shower of bricks, paving stones, and bullets, from the windows of the houses, brought the columns to a halt Many of the men were hurt, a few were stunned Inspector Carpenter instantly ordered his men to attack the houses, go through them from cellar to roof, and render every rioter who might be encountered incapable of further mischief. The scene which ensued cannot be adequately described Barricaded doors were smashed in, and the Police began their attack with irresistible fury Their opponents' resistance was like that of so many pigmies Some fled to the roofs, only to be overtaken and terribly beaten by the officers; some leaped from upper windows and fell shockingly maimed on the flags below; men were hurled down-stairs, others were clubbed into insensibility. The few who gained the street unhurt or nearly so, fell into the hands of the reserve which Carpenter posted there, and fared no better than their fellows. The gallantry shown by individual officers was great; and some of them paid dearly for it. Captain Warlow, of the First Precinct, in heading the charge of his men had two toes crushed by a stone, but continued on duty though badly crippled. Sergeant Babcock, though on leave, returned in time to take part in this fight. Sergeant Snodgrass led the platoon of the Second Precinct. Officers Watson and Cole entered into a rivalry as to who should first reach the roof of a house from which a galling fire had been kept up on the Police. Watson won the contest, and was attacked by a scoundrel armed with an iron bar. Watson soon quieted the fellow. Cole and he won equal distinction in the melee that followed. Sergeant Robinson headed the men of the Third Precinct. He and Sergeant Finney, Roundsman Farrell, and others, forced their way into a liquor saloon, and rapidly cleared the house. The full force of the Tenth Precinct was present under Captain T. C. Davis. Four men were badly wounded, including Officers Rothschild and Sandford. Sergeant Wemyss and Roundsman Hart won especial praise. Captain Mount, of the Eleventh Precinct, led the entire storming party. He was bravely seconded by his men, among whom Sergeants Polly, Ahearn, and Reed, Roundsmen Warmsley and Donohue, and Patrolmen Warren, Beattie, Gass, Bogart, McMahon, and McCarty were singled out for commendation on account of their conspicuous courage. A portion of the contingent of the Twenty-third, under Captain Henry Hutchings, took part in the attack; the rest were stationed below to deal with fugitives from the houses, and keep the crowd in check. The Twenty-fifth's squad attacked the liquor store at Thirty-first Street, from which the rioters were firing pistols and hurling stones. One man, who had been using a gun, was flung out of a window and killed.

Captain Speight, of the Twenty-ninth Precinct, with his command, had been in the rear of the battalion as it marched up Second Avenue, and therefore sustained the first brunt of the cowardly attack. The officers instantly faced about. Captain Speight led the charge on the mob; but was brought to the ground by the blow of a brick. He sprang to his feet, and still encouraged his men by voice and example. When the crowd was driven off, the men joined in the attack on the houses with great effect. The men were nearly all more or less hurt, but they placed thirty rioters *hors du combat* in the houses they attacked. Sergeants Van Orden and Young were mentioned for bravery. A detachment from the Thirty-first Precinct was also present in this affray under Captain James Z. Bogart. Sergeant Ten Eyck, and Officers Thompson, Stevenson and Stoddard distinguished themselves for courage and energy.

While the fight was still in progress, Colonel H. J. O'Brien, of the Eleventh New York Volunteers, arrived on the scene with about fifty men and two howitzers. For a time the mob was overawed, but after the Police had marched off, an attack was begun on the soldiers, who fired a volley in reply. Several people, including a woman, were wounded, and the crowd became panic-stricken and scattered. O'Brien and his men marched away. An hour or two later the ill-starred colonel returned to the spot alone. He was recognized, and set upon by the rioters, thirsting for vengeance. Atrocities too terrible for description were committed upon his body. It was the awful plaything of a thousand maddened wretches for several hours. It is related that the wretched man lived through a long series of horrors, and only expired when subjected to the fury of some frenzied women, late in the evening. The remains, utterly unrecognizable, were recovered after nightfall.

When he had defeated the rioters at Thirty-third Street, Inspector Carpenter continued his march. He patrolled all the disturbed districts in the uptown portions of the east side of the city, only returning to Headquarters at one P. M.

Brutal Murder of Col. O'Brien

Meanwhile, stirring scenes had been in progress elsewhere. With two hundred men, including his own precinct force, Captain Petty, of the Fifth, had gone early in the morning to protect a soap factory on Sixteenth Street between Eighth and Ninth Avenues. The men were filled with contempt when the rioters fled at the mere approach of the Police. This body marched through the whole region, breaking up all gatherings, and got back to Headquarters just in time to be transferred for the most part to the command of Inspector Dilks, who, with a portion of them and other precinct details — in all two hundred men — marched at ten o'clock A. M. to the protection of a wire factory at Second Avenue and Twenty-first Street, where four thousand carbines were stored. The march to the factory was rapidly made. The building was found in possession of the rioters, thousands of whom were congregated in the avenue The arms were being passed out of the building by the marauders who had entered. The crowd hailed the Police with yells of defiance. The odds were, indeed, fearful, but the Inspector did not hesitate a moment He and his brave boys rushed on the mob. This was one of the bitterest fights of the whole riot week The mob made a stubborn resistance. The causeway was literally strewn with stunned and bleeding men At last discipline prevailed. The great crowd wavered, fled and dispersed. Then the factory was attacked. It was a repetition of the scene in the houses at Thirty-fourth Street The building was recaptured foot by foot, and the wounded covered the floors. The punishment of the rioters was fearful One doctor said that after that fight he dressed the wounds of twenty-one rioters — all in the head, and all of a fatal character When the fighting was over, the Police gathered up all the arms they could find and marched with them to Headquarters, getting there only at three o'clock in the afternoon In the fighting, Sergeant Wright and Officer Warner, of the Sixteenth Precinct, received injuries from which they were disabled Captain A. S. Wilson, of the Thirty-second, and Sergeants Huff, Whiteman and Castle took leading parts in the fray Sergeant Groat, of the Twenty-eighth, had a desperate man, who, though one-armed, proved a perfect Hercules. Groat at last put him to flight, and pursuing him, stunned him with a blow from his club.

But the mob, though checked, was not yet beaten. The Police had hardly left the neighborhood of the factory when the crowd re-assembled. The building was once more invaded, and a quantity of arms that had escaped the notice of Inspector Dilks' party was discovered But before the rioters had time to effect a distribution of the weapons, a fresh force of Police assailed them. Capt. John C. Helme, of the Twenty-seventh Precinct, had been sent out from Headquarters some time before with his own men and details from other precincts, to disperse a crowd that was besieging Mayor Opdyke's house on Fifth Avenue. This work was speedily accomplished, and some piles of building material, which might serve as ammunition for the rioters, were removed to places of safety. Then Captain Helme, hearing of the trouble at the wire factory, marched thither, arriving just as the mob re-assembled—after Inspector Dilks' departure—and had for the second time spread through the building. The Police approached from Twenty-first Street They waited for no parley, but rushed on the mob as they wheeled into the Avenue For the second time the rioters fought stubbornly, but were driven back after a short struggle. Fifty of them remained disabled on the pavement. The men of the Fourteenth, under Sergeant Hughes, were among the most active in this fight; several of them were severely wounded Sergeant Blakelock, of the Fifteenth, had a narrow escape from a bullet which grazed his cheek He had left a sick bed to take part in the fight Officer Wetmore, of the Twenty-seventh, also showed great bravery.

The mob being dispersed, Captain Petty with ten men from the Fifth, Captain Sebring with a detail of the Thirteenth, which had already given a mob a severe lesson at Spring and Crosby Streets, Sergeants Bumstead and Fulmer with a platoon of the Nineteenth, and a detachment from the Twenty-seventh under

Sergeant Wilson, entered the factory. On every floor the rioters—unconscious of the fight in the street—were ransacking the place for arms. They were taken by surprise, pursued to the very roof, and beaten in detail. It is said that not one man who was in the factory escaped punishment. Officer Follis, of the Twenty-seventh, was badly wounded in the attack with an iron bar. When all were quieted, Captain Helme despatched Sergeant Laflin and Officers Seymour and Osborn, of the Thirteenth, to seize a cart, which was laden with all the arms the Police could find. Escorting it, Captain Helme's battalion started for Headquarters; but by this time the mob was reinforced by those who had engaged in the butchery of Colonel O'Brien, and, with renewed confidence, it crowded around

Cavalry Patrolling the Streets

the Police, whose position became very critical. Not a man flinched, but it is hard to tell how the impending contest would have resulted but for the timely arrival of Inspector Dilks with a fresh force of two hundred men, with whom he had started for the scene the moment rumors of the fresh outbreak of the mob reached the Central Office. The fight which followed was very short. The mob had received two fearful lessons, and hardly waited for a third.

The united forces of Inspector Dilks and Captain Helme now made a tour of the neighborhood, engaging in several sharp fights, in which they were much aided by the military. The battalion turned down Twenty-second Street towards First Avenue, when a galling fire was opened on them from windows and roofs. The soldiers were sent to the front, and, by a well-directed fire, they soon cleared away the riotous sharpshooters. As the Police wheeled into First Avenue they were confronted by a body of rioters, who hurled a tempest of missiles upon them. The military again advanced, and silenced the rabble with several sharp volleys The rioters retreated slowly, however, and several more volleys were fired at them as the troops and Police advanced At Twenty-first Street the mob broke and fled; then the forces returned to Twenty-second Street, and through it to Second Avenue. Sergeant Devoursney, of the Twenty-sixth, remained too far behind, reconnoitering, and narrowly escaped a bullet aimed at his head from a window. At Twenty-first Street and Second Avenue the mob was again encountered, and only dispersed after several more deadly volleys During the fight Inspector Dilks and Sergeant Garland, of the Seventh, had both a happy escape from a rifle ball which cut off the branch of a tree just by the Inspector's head while the the two were speaking together Another incident of the fighting at Twenty-second Street and Second Avenue calls for special mention. A young man who had led the rioters with great courage, staggering under a blow of a club, fell upon the spike of an area railing which ran under his chin and impaled him horribly. When his corpse was taken down, it was found that he was a youth of refined appearance, and under greasy overalls he wore a suit of fashionable clothing He was not identified, and the body was secretly removed with those of the other rioters. After the battalion had withdrawn the mob re-assembled and repaired to the Eighteenth Precinct Station House in East Twenty-second Street. The place was in charge of Sergeant Burden and three men. A defence was out of the question. So the building was barricaded, and the officers retreated through a rear window. The rioters speedily broke in and burned the building

Captain George W. Walling, of the Twentieth Precinct, had a day of great excitement and danger. He began it by marching early in the morning to Pitt Street, to quell a disturbance. He arrived too late, a military detachment having already done the work. On his return he paraded through the Bowery and other streets with his men for the purpose of intimidating evil-doers Inspector Carpenter made a similar tour a little later. On the latter expedition a section from the Twelfth Precinct formed part of the patrol. A man named Patrick Carle was seen brandishing a sword and threatening general destruction Officer Banfield, of the Twelfth, seized the weapon, and dragging its possessor into the ranks, marched him off to Headquarters.

On returning from his first expedition, Captain Walling was sent with a large force into his own Precinct, the Twentieth, where the rioters were making some headway, having beaten a body of soldiers and taken away their guns at Allerton's Hotel, Eleventh Avenue, between Fortieth and Forty-first Streets. When he arrived in the neighborhood, the Captain learned that marauders were sacking the private residences on Forty-seventh Street. Thither he hastened with his men A band had just broken into Dr. Ward's house, and parties were bearing away valuables from other houses. As the Police appeared the thieves took to their heels. The Police chased in parties of three or four Every man armed with a club or other weapon was soundly beaten by the officers The only purpose of this mob had been robbery, and this whole section of the city was terrorized by similar bands

The Police next repaired to the station house on Thirty-fifth Street, and the military were telegraphed for to aid in overcoming a new movement of the rioters, who had cut down the telegraph poles all along Ninth Avenue, from Thirty-second to Forty-third Streets, and with these, and carts, and wagons, bound together with the telegraph wire, had formed barricades across the avenue at Thirty-seventh and Forty-third Streets, and across all the intervening streets. They had also set fire to and burned down the Weehawken ferry house. At six P. M. Captain Wesson, with a force of regulars, joined the Police at the station house, and both bodies sallied forth to attack the barricades.

Destruction of the Weehawken Ferry House

Captain Slott, of the Twenty-second Precinct, advanced with a body of Police to remove the barrier at Thirty-seventh Street. They were driven off by a volley of stones and bullets. The military advanced, and with a steady fusillade, cleared away the rioters. Then the Police returned and removed the obstruction. The mob rallied and attacked them a second time, but were again beaten off by the fire of the troops. The Police then advanced again, and, one by one, all the barricades were demolished. The Police at length returned to their station; but they were allowed only a brief rest. At nine o'clock a roving gang attacked a gun and hardware store on Thirty-seventh Street, between Eighth and Ninth Avenues. Captain Petty speedily appeared on the scene with a squad, and very quickly dispersed the roughs, laying many of them senseless on the pavement. At midnight there was a new alarm. A great crowd gathered in

Thirtieth Street, between Seventh and Eighth Avenues, vowing the destruction of the colored church there. Captain Walling hastened to the spot with his entire force. They charged on the mob unexpectedly, but were received with a shower of bullets from the alleys and doorways on either side. The fire was returned, then the officers rushed in, plying their clubs with unbounded liberality, so that in a few minutes only prostrate rioters were to be seen.

This practically ended the riot in this quarter of the city. The state of things had, at one time, been very bad. The children from the Colored Orphan Asylum in Fifth Avenue had been taken to this station and cared for until sent to the Island. Captain Petty, who was in charge of the station, had, at times, as many as four hundred refugees to provide for. He had, besides, to provide—by arming and barricading—for the possible event of an attack on the station house.

While the scenes just related were in progress about Thirty-fifth Street, similar ones were enacted at Twenty-ninth Street and Eighth Avenue, where a mob, which was pillaging the house of Mr. J. S. Gibbons, No. 19 Lamartine Place, was attacked by a battalion drawn from the Broadway Squad and Thirty-first Precinct, commanded by Captain James Z. Bogart. As the officers, accompanied by military, passed the house in patrolling, the crowd gathered before it retired; but when the force passed the crowd re-assembled, broke down the doors, and began the work of robbery. Meantime Sergeant Devoursney and Officer Gardner, of the Twenty-sixth, had been stoned while acting as scouts, but had learned of the attack on the house, and bore the news to Captain Bogart. The Police returned on the run, and the crowd in the street ran at the first shock. The house was full of rioters and robbers; and several officers entered to drive these out, while the main body remained outside to give them a warm reception. As they came rushing to the street, Sergeant Burdick of the Broadway Squad felled to the ground a gigantic fellow laden with booty. As he did so, a score of bullets whistled through the air, two of which struck the rioter, while one entered Officer Dipple's thigh, and breaking the bone passed up through the marrow, causing inflammation, from which this excellent officer died in a few days. It appears that the military arrived suddenly on the scene, and noticing the rush of the rioters from the house, had fired wildly, and without orders, doing more injury to friends than foes. Officer Hodgson received in this volley a ball and three buckshot in the arm; Officer Robinson was wounded in the thigh. A rioter, as he rushed out, was caught and clubbed by Officer Hill of the Twenty-sixth Precinct. He drew a pistol and shot the officer in the thigh. The next moment he fell riddled with soldiers' bullets. Officer Rice, of the Twenty-sixth, was shot in the groin and thigh; a bullet passed through Sergeant Pell's sleeve. Officer Hanifer had a desperate combat with an immense fellow, whom he drove to the street. Officer Morris, of the Broadway Squad, was the first man to enter the house; Roundsman Benson Sherwood and Jerome H. Ferris were especially noticeable for bravery. In the entire affair the women gave more trouble than the men. Many of them were in the house plundering, and it took a smart application of the locust to the fleshiest portions of their persons to make many of them relinquish their ill-gotten treasures.

OUR POLICE PROTECTORS

Tuesday night closed down town with another bloody battle, waged about Brooks Brothers' clothing store in Catharine Street. There had been a good deal of disorder all day. Sergeant Rode and a squad from the Fourth, had protected Godfrey's gun store from a mob. At dusk the crowd began to gather about

Escaping Rioters Surprised by the Police.

Brooks Brothers' establishment. Patrolmen Platt, Kennedy and Davis, mingled with the mob, in citizen's clothes, but were recognized and terribly beaten. Then the whole force of the Fourth Precinct, with twenty men from the First under Sergeant Matthew, and twenty-five from the Third under Sergeant Finney and Roundsman Farrell, repaired to the place and dispersed the mob. They had scarcely reached their station again when they heard of further rioting in Catharine Street and returned there. They cleared a boot and shoe store after a sharp fight, and halted while Captain Bryan went forward to ascertain, personally, the state of affairs about Brooks'. The store had been entered and was being pillaged. A charge was ordered, and was made in gallant style. The mob gave way, many being badly beaten; the officers entered the store, and after a fierce combat from floor to floor, cleared it, beating severely some hundreds of the rioters. In the fight, Sergeant Finney, of the Third, was shot in the face. Sergeant Delaney had his hat knocked off by the wadding of a pistol fired at him by a rioter only a few feet away. Officer Van Ranst, of the First Precinct, received a bullet in his hat, where he found it next morning. While the fight was still in progress, Inspector Carpenter arrived with a detachment from Headquarters. He rushed upon the rioters with his men, and con~~~~~d in no small measure to their punishment. A guard was kept in Brooks' all night. Sergeant Rode and Officer Irvin, of the Fourth, found some roughs trying to break into Lord & Taylor's store, and fired on them from their revolvers; the fellows ran. After this night quiet reigned in the neighborhood. The next day the officers of the First and Fourth Precincts began a search of the low rookeries, and recovered over five thousand dollars' worth of goods stolen from the Brooks' and other stores. After the dispersion of the mob on Tuesday night, Inspector Carpenter and his command made a tour of the down-town districts, meeting and scattering parties of rioters at several points. Patrolman Regan, of the Fourteenth, being separated from his comrades, was badly beaten, and narrowly escaped with his life. Later in the night, Captain C. W. Caffry, Roundsman Thacher, and six officers of the Fifteenth, patrolled Broadway, and arrested three highwaymen. During this night, Sergeant Slott, of the Seventeenth, and ten men, were ordered to duty as guides to the military. Sergeant Robinson, and fifteen men of the Third, defeated a mob which approached Printing House Square, where he was on guard, singing, "We'll Hang old Greeley on a Sour Apple Tree." After the affair in Catharine Street, the men of the Thirteenth returned to their Precinct, where their station house, though courageously defended by Sergeant Woodward, was threatened with destruction. All gatherings in the Precinct were at once broken up, the colored population were quieted, and by noon next day the men had begun the work of recovering stolen property. Among other incidents of Tuesday was an attempt by a mob to burn the Fifth Precinct Station House, No. 49 Leonard Street, in which four hundred colored persons were sheltered. Sergeant Huggins and Doorman Pallister armed the refugees, and all was ready for a desperate defence, when the arrival of Inspector Carpenter on one of his patrols, rendered the preparations needless. Officer Field, of this precinct, earned great praise by performing valuable detective work among the rioters, though he was well known to many of them. On Tuesday evening Officer Hector Moore, of the Fifteenth, saw two men garotting a returned soldier in City Hall Park. He pluckily arrested both. Sergeant Roe, of this precinct, had the tip of one of his fingers carried off by a bullet. He and Sergeant Dilks were highly praised for their energy.

The backbone of the riot was broken on Tuesday, yet there was some very lively fighting on Wednesday, the 15th. In the "wee sma' hours" of that morning, Captain S Brower, of the Seventeenth Precinct, patrolled the Eleventh, Thirteenth, and Seventeenth Precincts with a hundred and fifty men, suppressing all tendency to disorder At nine A. M. he went with a considerable force to Thirty-second Street, between Sixth and Seventh Avenues, where outrages had been perpetrated on negroes, and one had been hanged The body was recovered and taken to Headquarters. The rioters were dispersed and punished The hottest fight of the day was about Jackson's Iron Foundry at Twenty-ninth Street and Second Avenue There being a rumor abroad that the rioters meant to destroy it, a regiment of soldiers was sent to guard it, under the guidance of Officers Sutton, Riley, Dubnar, and Cannon of the Fourteenth Precinct. A mob was encountered ; the soldiers fired several volleys, and killed and wounded many men When the party was safely intrenched in the foundry, a committee approached to ask the commanding officer for the surrender of the Policemen It is needless to add that the deputation got short notice to put themselves out of rifle range.

In the morning Drill Officer Copeland, with Captain Sebring and a large squad from the Fourteenth, visited the disaffected portions of Second and Third Avenues to overawe the rioters. In the evening the Fourteenth aided in protecting a block of dwellings known as "The Arch," on Sullivan Street, and occupied by colored persons. At eleven o'clock Wednesday forenoon, Captain Jourdan, of the Sixth, with Sergeants Quinn and Kennedy, encountered and routed a mob in Centre Street near Worth, which had been ill-using colored people Sergeant Quinn, with one platoon, despite a bold resistance, beat off a mob that was endeavoring to sack a building at Mott and Centre Streets. In this fight Patrolman Charles McDonnell was knocked down and terribly cut about the face, but, nevertheless, rejoined his comrades and repaid the rioters in their own coin. Among the officers of this precinct especially commended by the Captain were Roundsmen Ryan and Hopkins. The Sixteenth Precinct men dispersed several down-town mobs during Wednesday, particularly one which attacked the bonded warehouses on Greenwich Street. Sergeant Wright and ten men were made guardians of the United States Marshal's office

In another fight, on First Avenue, the military met with a reverse on Wednesday night. They were, at the time, under guidance of Patrolmen McCort and McVay, who fought gallantly in the melee. All Wednesday and Thursday were days of terror in the Twenty-first Precinct, and on the latter day Officer Chandler was so badly beaten that he had to be taken to the hospital. Sergeant Brackett was placed in command, Captain A M. Palmer being seriously sick His admirable arrangements prevented a fresh outbreak of the riot. On Friday, Sergeant Brackett, Sergeant Hastings, and thirty-five men, visited the block bounded by First and Second Avenues, Thirty-ninth and Fortieth Streets The Seventh Regiment attended to protect them. The spot was then one of the worst in the city Every corner of every shanty was searched, and quantities of stolen goods recovered Sergeant Vaughan and Roundsman Moore, with small parties, discovered quantities of goods in other parts of the precinct

The force of the Nineteenth returned to its precinct on Thursday Sergeant Decker had taken care of the station house alone. The last service of the men in the field was the defeat of a mob at Bleecker and Thompson Streets, at noon on Wednesday. Sergeant Bumstead headed the men on this occasion Sergeants Fulmer and Holmes of this precinct did excellent service.

On Wednesday the Twenty-second closed its riot service brilliantly. Captain Slott dispersed a mob at Forty-second Street and Tenth Avenue, and Sergeant Aldis another at Twenty-seventh Street and Seventh Avenue. The latter then accompanied a party of military to Forty-Second Street and Tenth Avenue, where the crowd had re-assembled and were about to burn the residence of a

Burning of the Grain Elevator, Atlantic Dock, Brooklyn.

Mr. Campbell. General Sandford, who was in command, tried to persuade the mob to disperse. The reply was a volley and a chorus of yells Then the soldiers opened fire with deadly effect, and the rioters scattered instantly. The men of the Twenty-third Precinct returned thither just in time to put an end to a reign of mob law. No excesses were attempted after their return The arrival of the Twenty-seventh's men had the same effect They recovered a quantity of stolen goods in the following day or two. On Thursday Officers Hey, McClusker and Darrow rescued a colored man from under a North River pier, where he had taken refuge from rioters who had beaten him. The fellow was half insane from fear

During the riot week all the station houses were left inadequately guarded, and great courage and judgment were shown in their preservation. Sergeants Loudon and McConnell successively took charge of the Seventh Precinct station house, No. 247 Madison Street. Sergeant Miller was guardian of the Eighth, No. 127 Wooster, where seven hundred and fifty-one refugees were cared for during the week. The house of the Tenth Precinct, Essex Market, was attacked on Monday evening. The mob was driven off by Officers Wood and McCloud, and Officer King of the Third District Court, aided by many citizens and Surgeon Wells and Sergeant Garland of the Seventh Precinct, who was stationed at the Tenth as telegraph operator. Sergeant Upham was left in care of the Eleventh Precinct station, Union Market. Captain Relay and Sergeant Sandford were reinforced by special Constables at the Twelfth's station house, Harlem. Sergeant Wares and Officer Bertholf were very active, especially in collecting information as to riotous plots. Sergeant M. B. Wilson guarded the Twenty-seventh's station, No. 117 Cedar Street. Officer Carroll was twice knocked down while reconnoitering. Sergeant Flandreau, Patrolman Crosby and Doorman Malone, not only protected the station of the Thirty-second Precinct, but also, by their firm attitude, prevented a riot, keeping the disaffected unaware of the lack of Police protection while the main force was doing duty down town.

It may have been remarked that the Thirtieth Precinct, of Manhattanville, has not been mentioned. The force was only actively employed for a few hours; but to the excellence of the arrangements made by Captain J. Hartt, aided by Sergeant Blake and other officers, the continued peace of the district may be attributed. Captain N. R. Mills, of the Broadway Squad, was in Oneida County when the riots began. He returned to the city as soon as he heard of them, reporting for duty at Headquarters on Thursday evening.

On Sunday, the eighteenth, a large body of Police under Captain Dickson, of the Twenty-eighth, started for a tour of the small towns along the Hudson. They were accompanied by a body of troops. They remained away three days, and completely subdued all tendencies to revolt that might have existed among the rural population. The day after their return, a visit to Staten Island—where there had been rioting—was made, and on the next day Flushing, L. I., was visited.

It would be unfair to close the record of this troublous week without a word regarding the services of some other attaches of the Police system. The detective force did most valuable service in discovering the plans of rioters, and at opportune moments arresting the most dangerous ringleaders. Those who thus distinguished themselves, besides Chief Young, were Messrs. Bennett, McCord, Farley, Roach, Radford, Smith, Slowey, Dusenbury, Macdougal, Elder, Eustace, Wilson, Kelso, Lieman, and Keefe. Mr. Slowey was recognized by rioters and severely beaten.

The telegraph operators also did excellent work, above all in repairing lines broken by the rioters. In this they ran desperate risks, often having to personate rioters in order to save life and limb. They were Superintendent Crowley, and Messrs. Eldred Polhamus, Charles L. Chapin, John A. K. Duvall, and James

A. Lucas. Captain Lord and Officers Johns, Van Orden and McTaggart, of the Sanitary Police, were singled out for commendation; also Officer Wells, of the Broadway Squad, for his humanity in protecting negroes near the Astor House, on Monday. Honorable mention was also made of Clerks Daniel B. Hasbrouck, George Hopcroft, and Horace A. Bliss, and Headquarter's Messenger Alexander Stewart.

Nursing Wounded Policemen.

The number of persons known to have been killed by the rioters was eighteen, eleven of whom were colored. Officer Dibble was accidentally killed by the soldiers. It is estimated that the number of rioters killed, or who died from the effect of their wounds, was about twelve hundred. Probably seven or eight thousand persons altogether were more or less injured. Over fifty buildings were burned, including the Colored Orphan Asylum, two Police stations, and three Provost Marshal's offices. A great number of stores and dwellings were sacked. The whole history of the week was disastrous in a degree that, it is to be hoped, New York will never know again.

During the week following the riot the Board of Police Commissioners issued an address to the force, which contained the following:

"Of the Inspectors, Captains, and Sergeants of Police who led parties in the fearful contest, we are proud to say that none faltered or failed. Each was equal to the hour and the emergency. Not one failed to overcome the danger, however imminent, or to defeat the enemy, however numerous. Especial commendation is due to Drill Sergeant Copeland for his most valuable aid in commanding the movements of larger detachments of the Police. The Patrolmen who were on duty fought through the numerous and fierce conflicts with the steady courage of veteran soldiers, and have won, as they deserve, the highest commendations from the public and from this Board. In their ranks there was neither faltering nor struggling. Devotion to duty and courage in the performance of it were universal. The public and the department owe a debt of gratitude to the citizens who voluntarily became Special Patrolmen, some three thousand of whom, for several days and nights, did regular Patrolmen's duty with great effect. In the name of the public, and of the department in which they were volunteers, we thank them.

"Mr. Crowley, the Superintendent of the Police telegraph, and the attaches of his department, by untiring and sleepless vigilance in transmitting information by telegraph unceasingly through more than ten days and nights, have more than sustained the high reputation they have always possessed.

"Through all these bloody contests, through all the wearing fatigue and wasting labor, you have demeaned yourselves like worthy members of the Metropolitan Police. The public judgment will commend and reward you. A kind Providence has permitted you to escape with less casualties than could have been expected * * It is hoped that the severe but just chastisement which has been inflicted upon those guilty of riot, pillage, arson and murder will deter further attempts of that character * * Sergeant Young, of the Detective force, aided by Mr. Newcomb and other Special Patrolmen, rendered most effective service in arranging the commissary supplies for the large numbers of Police, military, Special Patrolmen, and destitute colored refugees, whose subsistence was thrown unexpectedly on the department. The duty was arduous and responsible, and was performed with vigor and fidelity. All the clerks of the department, each in his sphere, performed a manly share of the heavy duties growing out of these extraordinary circumstances."

Ex-Governor Seymour, who occupied the Gubernatorial chair at the time of the riots, and who also was in the city in his official capacity assisting in restoring order, bears this willing and appreciative testimony to the valuable services rendered by the New York Police force during the terrible days of the draft riots:

"The draft riots of 1863 were put down mainly by the energy, boldness and skill of the Police Department. In saying this I am certainly not influenced by prejudice, for the force was politically, and in some degree personally, unfriendly to myself. Indeed, in their reports they have not seen fit to make mention of any co-operation on my part with their efforts. But they did their duty bravely and efficiently. They proved that the city of New York could, by its Police alone, in the absence of its military organizations, cope with the most formidable disorders. I do not know of any instance in history where so many desperate men were shot down mainly by the Police of a city. More than a thousand of the rioters were killed or wounded to death. Yet so little justice has been done the city of New York that many think it was protected by the forces of the United States. In fact, the Navy Yard, the vast amounts of military stores of the general Government, and its money in the Sub-Treasury, were mainly protected by the civil officers. So protected while the military organizations of the

State were absent in Pennsylvania, in answer to an appeal from the Government of the United States to help it against an invasion of General Lee. Even General Grant, in one of his papers, spoke of the riots in New York as an occasion when the general Government had helped State or local authorities to maintain peace and order. I wrote to him correcting this error, and it gives me pleasure to say that he received my communication in a spirit of courtesy and fairness which ever marks the character of an honorable man. It is now time that justice should be done the city of New York in this matter, and in the hope that such justice may be done, I repeat these facts."

General Harvey Brown, in relinquishing his command, said:

Having, during the riots, been in immediate and constant co-operation with the Police Department of this city, he desires the privilege of expressing his unbounded admiration of it. Never in our civil or military life has he ever seen such untiring devotion and such efficient service. To President Acton and Commissioner Bergen he offers his thanks for their courtesy to him, and their kindness to his command. "The only merit I can claim," concludes General Brown, "in the performance of the duty which has given me the high distinction of your approbation, is that of an honest singleness of purpose in recording the very able and energetic efforts of the President of the Metropolitan Police, Mr. Acton, to whom, in my opinion, more than to any other one man, is due the credit of the early suppression of the riot."

Governor Seymour, in his annual message, in referring to the riots, says, among other things, that a dispatch was sent to him from Mayor Opdyke, informing him of the outbreak that had taken place on the thirteenth day of July, the first day of the riots. The Governor reached the city the following morning, and found it agitated with wild excitement and riotous violence. The militia were ordered to return immediately from Pennsylvania, and a proclamation was issued "To the people of the City of New York." "Riotous proceedings," the Governor's proclamation read, "must and shall be put down. The laws of the State must be enforced, its peace and order maintained, and the lives and property of all its citizens protected at any and every hazard * * * Let all citizens stand firmly by the constituted authorities, sustaining law and order in the city, and ready to answer any such demands as circumstances may render necessary for me to make upon their services, and they may rely upon a rigid enforcement of the laws of this State against all who violate them."

The city was declared in a state of insurrection. It was divided into districts, which were placed under the control of persons of influence or military experience, who were directed to organize the citizens. Three thousand stand of arms were issued to these and other organizations. The Governor likewise obtained from the Collector of the Port the service of an armed vessel to traverse the rivers and bays in the vicinity of New York, and authorized the Police Commissioners to charter another steamer, which could be used to carry policemen and soldiers to any point on the shores of the islands where disturbances were threatened. "In the sad and humiliating history of this event," to quote from Governor Seymour's annual message, "it is gratifying that the citizens of New York, without important aid from the State or Nation, were able of themselves to put down this dangerous insurrection. I do not underrate the value of the services rendered by the military or naval officers of the general

Government who were stationed in that city, or those of General Sandford ; for the public are under great obligations to them for their courage and prudent counsels But they had at their command only a handful of troops, who, alone, were entirely unequal to the duty of defending the vast amount of public property which was endangered The rioters were subdued by the exertion of the city officials, civic and military, the people, the Police, the firemen, and a small body of twelve hundred men, composed equally of the State and National forces "

In his report to Governor Seymour, General Wool said :

"The city Police force from the beginning, under the able Chief Commissioner, Superintendent, and other officers of its organization, displayed throughout the whole riot not only a willingness, but very great efficiency, in their noble exertions to quell the riot. For this and their harmonious co-operation with the troops engaged in the same cause, they deserve the warmest thanks of every lover of law and order, and my high commendations for their whole conduct on this trying occasion "

The loss in the city, in property, was not much short of three million dollars Probably fifteen hundred rioters were killed or died in consequence of injuries received

At the Court of General Sessions, twenty of the rioters were indicted, of whom nineteen were convicted The aggregate term of their imprisonment was about one hundred years From records and reliable sources, it appears that three Policemen lost their lives. A large but unknown number of citizens and officers were wounded ; twelve negroes were hanged, and many others disappeared

A week of terror and dismay, a week of horrors unparalleled in the history of New York, was drawing to a close. A great city was for a time in the grasp of robbers and cut-throats, and the very existence of the Republic imperiled. But the battle had been valiantly waged and won The Police had saved our city, the mob was vanquished and dispersed Had the rioters succeeded in overpowering the Police and military, and gained possession of the city but for one hour, there is no calculating what irreparable calamities might have, as a consequence, befallen the city and the Nation It is safe to assume that similar riotous proceedings would take place in other leading cities of the North, and thus the drafting be brought to an end, with the enemy almost within sight of the Seat of Government But happily all this was averted Had it not been so, who can say how the war would have terminated ?

The following proclamation was issued by Mayor Opdyke :

"The riotous assemblages have been dispersed. Business is running in its usual channels. The various lines of omnibuses, railway, and telegraph have resumed their ordinary operations Few symptoms of disorder remain, except in a small district in the eastern part of the city, comprising a part of the Eighteenth and Twenty-first Wards. The Police is everywhere alert A sufficient military force is now here to suppress any illegal movement, however formidable

"Let me exhort you, therefore, to pursue your ordinary business Avoid especially all crowds. Remain quietly at your homes, except when engaged in business, or assisting the authorities in some organized force When the military appear in the street, do not gather about it, being sure that it is doing its duty in obedience to orders from superior authority. Your homes and your places of business you have a right to defend, and it is your duty to defend them at all hazards Yield to no intimidation, and to no demand for money as the price of your safety If any person warns you to desist from your accustomed business, give no heed to the warning, but arrest him and bring him to the nearest station house as a conspirator. Be assured that the public authorities have the ability and the will to protect you from those who have conspired alike against your peace, against the Government of your choice, and against the laws which your representatives have enacted.

"GEORGE OPDYKE, Mayor"

Thus ends the record of the draft riots They leave a great lesson to the people as to the utter futility of mob violence; they carry a lesson to the Police and the civic authorities as to the value of a well-organized, well-disciplined band of public guardians

The Police Force was apportioned as follows

First Precinct —29 Broad Street; Captain. Jacob B Warlow; four Sergeants, sixty-three Patrolmen, two Doormen

Second Precinct —Station House, 49 Beekman Street; Captain, Nathaniel R Mills; four Sergeants, sixty Patrolmen, two Doormen

Third Precinct —Station House, No 160 Chambers Street; Captain, James Greer; three Sergeants, sixty-four Patrolmen, two Doormen

Fourth Precinct —Station House, 9 Oak Street; Captain, James Bryan, four Sergeants, seventy Patrolmen, two Doormen.

Fifth Precinct —Station House, 49 Leonard Street, Captain, Jeremiah Petty, four Sergeants, sixty-one Patrolmen, two Doormen

Sixth Precinct —Station House, 9 Franklin Street, Captain, John Jourdan; four Sergeants, sixty-three Patrolmen, two Doormen

Seventh Precinct —Station House, No 247 Madison Street, Captain, William Jamieson; four Sergeants, fifty-seven Patrolmen, two Doormen.

Eighth Precinct —Station House, No. 126 Wooster Street; Captain, Morris DeCamp; four Sergeants, fifty-two Patrolmen, two Doormen

Ninth Precinct —Station House, No 94 Charles Street; Captain, Jacob L. Sebring; four Sergeants, fifty-one Patrolmen, two Doormen

Tenth Precinct.—Station House, Essex Market, Captain, Thaddeus C. Davis, four Sergeants, sixty-two Patrolmen, Two Doormen

Eleventh Precinct —Station House, Union Market; Captain, John I Mount; four Sergeants, fifty-six Patrolmen, two Doormen.

Twelfth Precinct —Station House, One Hundred and Twenty-sixth Street, near Third Avenue, Captain, Theron R Bennett; five Sergeants, forty-one Patrolmen, two Doormen

Thirteenth Precinct — Station House, Attorney Street, corner Delancey Street, Captain, Thomas Steers, four Sergeants, fifty-three Patrolmen, two Doormen

Fourteenth Precinct —Station House, No 53 Spring Street; Captain, John J Williamson, four Sergeants, fifty-eight Patrolmen, two Doormen

Fifteenth Precinct —Station House, No. 220 Mercer Street; Captain, Charles W. Caffrey; four Sergeants, sixty-nine Patrolmen, two Doormen

Sixteenth Precinct —Station House, No 156 West Twentieth Street; Captain, Henry Hedden; four Sergeants, fifty Patrolmen, two Doormen.

Seventeenth Precinct —Station House, First Avenue, corner Fifth Street; Captain, Samuel Brower; four Sergeants, fifty-six Patrolmen, two Doormen

Eighteenth Precinct.—Station House, Twenty-second Street, near Second Avenue; Captain, John Cameron; four Sergeants, seventy-four Patrolmen, two Doormen.

Nineteenth Precinct —Station House, Fifty-ninth Street, near Third Avenue, Captain, Galen T Porter; four Sergeants, forty-nine Patrolmen, two Doormen.

Twentieth Precinct.—Station House, No. 212 West Thirty-fifth Street; Captain, George W. Walling; four Sergeants, fifty-nine Patrolmen, two Doormen

Twenty-first Precinct —Station House, 120 East Thirty-first Street; Captain, Cornelius Burdick, four Sergeants, fifty-one Patrolman, two Doormen

Twenty-second Precinct.—Station House, Forty-seventh Street, between Eighth and Ninth Avenues, Captain, Johannes C. Slott; four Sergeants, fifty-four Patrolmen, two Doormen

Twenty-third Precinct —Station House, Eighty-sixth Street, near Fourth Avenue; Captain, Henry Hutchings; four Sergeants, forty-two Patrolmen, two Doormen

Twenty-fourth Precinct —Headquarters on board of the Police Steamboat, No 1; Captain, James Todd, two Sergeants, twenty Patrolmen

Twenty-fifth Precinct (Broadway Squad) —Headquarters, 300 Mulberry Street, Captain Theron T. Copeland, one Sergeant, thirty-eight Patrolmen, two Doormen.

Twenty-sixth Precinct —Station House, City Hall; Captain, Thomas W. Thorne; four Sergeants, sixty-six Patrolmen, two Doormen

Twenty-seventh Precinct —Station House, No 117 Cedar Street, Captain, John C Helme; four Sergeants, fifty-two Patrolmen, three Doormen

Twenty-eighth Precinct —Station House, No 550 Greenwich Street, Captain, John F Dickson; four Sergeants, forty-eight Patrolmen, two Doormen

Twenty-ninth Precinct —Station House, Twenty-ninth Street, near Fourth Avenue, Captain, Francis C Speight; four Sergeants, eighty-two Patrolmen, three Doormen

Thirtieth Precinct —Station House, One Hundred and Thirty-first Street, Manhattanville; Captain, Jedediah Hart; three Sergeants, seventeen Patrolmen, two Doormen.

Thirty-first Precinct —Station House, Eighty-sixth Street and Bloomingdale Road, Captain, James Z. Bogart; two Sergeants, nineteen Patrolmen, two Doormen

Thirty-second Precinct (Mounted Police) —Station House, Tenth Avenue and One Hundred and Fifty-second Street; Captain, Alanson S. Wilson; four Sergeants, thirty-five Patrolmen, two Doormen.

CHAPTER X.

THE METROPOLITAN POLICE DISTRICT
1864–1866.

ORGANIZERS OF POLICE VICTORY—ACTON, BERGEN, HAWLEY, CARPENTER, LEONARD, ETC.—THE LAW OF 1864—ESTABLISHMENT OF THE HOUSE OF DETENTION—BOUNDARIES OF THE METROPOLITAN POLICE DISTRICT—DIVISION COMMANDS.—UNIFORM OF THE METROPOLITAN POLICE—APPROPRIATIONS FOR THE BUILDING AND REPAIRING OF STATION HOUSES.—A MARKED TENDENCY TO CRIMES OF VIOLENCE TOWARDS THE PERSON—LIST OF POLICEMEN WHO WERE KILLED OR WOUNDED AT THE HANDS OF DESPERATE RUFFIANS.—PRESIDENT ACTON FAVORS THE PASSAGE OF A LAW RENDERING IT A CRIME TO CARRY CONCEALED WEAPONS—LOST TIME—TABLES OF ARRESTS—AN ACT TO REGULATE AND INCREASE POLICE SALARIES—THE JURISDICTION OF THE BOARD EXTENDED OVER THE RURAL DISTRICTS OF YONKERS, WEST FARMS, AND RICHMOND COUNTY—AN ACT TO REGULATE THE SALE OF INTOXICATING LIQUORS—INCREASED DUTIES OF THE POLICE BOARD

IN the rapid movement of the exciting events just narrated, the achievements which make the names of Police commandants famous in the history of the department could receive but passing mention in a sketch so brief and incomplete as the one written. But the names of Acton, Carpenter, Leonard, Bergen, Walling, McCredie, Thorne, Devoursney, Dilks, Leonard, and many others spoken of in connection with the draft riots, are too well known to call for any special commendation or eulogy. Where all were brave, it is no mean praise that the deeds of the officers in command should be considered worthy of especial mention for gallant and meritorious services. Something in addition may be said of a few of the most prominent Police officials, by whose courage and sagacity the city was saved from a frenzied rabble. First among these is

THOMAS C. ACTON.—It will, it is safe to assume, excite neither envy nor jealousy in the breasts of the survivors of those notable events, to give the post of honor to Mr. Acton. He was the Commander of the Police, with his office at Police Headquarters, and he issued instructions when and where the Police were to meet the rioters. His also was the brain that conceived the plan of Police operations, and his orders which caused their execution, by which the rioters were routed and the good name of the city vindicated.

The legal organization of the Board invested the Superintendent with the command of the force, the Commissioners acting in an administrative capacity. In the absence of Superintendent Kennedy, the very first day of the draft

riots, the command was assigned to the President of the Board, and thus the duties of Mr Kennedy, who was early disabled by the rioters, were assumed by Commissioner Acton   The labor thus imposed was immense, and some estimate of it may be formed by the fact that, in the telegraph department alone, there were upward of four thousand dispatches received and orders sent, all of which, with but few exceptions, required his personal supervision.   There were upward of two thousand men under his control   To Commissioner Acton, it is generally conceded, the community is indebted to a large degree for the prompt and successful suppression of the rioters

Mr Acton was born in this city in 1823   He is of medium height, is slenderly but compactly built, and is still erect and active   He is at present Assistant United States Treasurer, having his office in the Treasury Building at Wall and Broad Streets

After receiving an academical education, Mr Acton studied law, but did not practice the profession.   Law led him naturally into city politics, and he has been a politician from his youth   When he was twenty-seven years of age, in 1850, he accepted his first office, that of Deputy Assistant County Clerk   At the close of his term he was appointed Deputy Registrar, and served six years in this capacity.   Then, in 1860, Governor Morgan appointed him Police Commissioner   Two years later he was elected President of the Board, and altogether he was in office as Commissioner for nine years, during which he was practically the ruler of New York City   The period during which Mr Acton had charge of the Police included that of our civil war, and he was, in fact, a general in command of a military force, as well as a Commissioner appointed to keep the peace

Before the war, Commissioner Acton had already shown his ability by the reorganization of the Police and the enforcement of the excise laws   During the war he was subjected to a crucial test by the sudden breaking out of the draft riots   All through the disturbances Mr. Acton had the personal direction of the entire Police force.   At first the rioters had the sympathy of the majority of our citizens in their resistance to the conscription ; but it soon became evident that thieves and ruffians had assumed command of the rioters and that the chief purpose of the mob was pillage.   Business was suspended ; the streets were comparatively deserted   Here and there, from trees and lamp-posts, hung the bodies of murdered negroes   The Colored Orphan Asylum blazed in the upper part of the city, and the houses of prominent abolitionists were sacked   Nobody knew at what moment the mob might knock at the door to demand the surrender of a negro servant and rob the house.   The principal thoroughfares were barricaded, and artillery was used during the street fights both by the rioters and the military   Portions of the city were literally in a state of seige   The people were divided against themselves

It is easy to understand how responsible was the position of President Acton during these dangerous days and nights; but he proved himself equal to the responsibility.   His vigilance and activity were wonderful   He seemed to require no sleep and to be everywhere simultaneously.   The Police, whom the rioters had hoped to demoralize, stood firm under Mr. Acton's leadership.   The force was promptly and largely recruited by men who distinguished themselves by special acts of bravery

The Police force then numbered about two thousand men, not enough to adequately protect the public offices, the banks, the telegraph lines and the ferries; but President Acton increased its efficiency by such recruits, and inspired its members with his own untiring vigilance and vigor. The station houses were made places of refuge for the poor negroes, and not one of these stations was captured by the mob. Mr. Acton held the rioters in check everywhere until the military arrived to rout them; but he sacrificed his health in the struggle. In 1869 he was compelled to resign his position as too onerous for his invalided faculties, and the general regret was the highest compliment which could have been paid him. In 1870 he was appointed by President Grant, who fully appreciated his patriotic and political services, to be Superintendent of the United States Assay Office, in which position he remained for twelve years, and was then promoted to the Assistant Treasurership

While Mr. Acton was Commissioner of Police he accomplished two municipal marvels: the reduction of the debt and taxes and the increase of the income of the city. To him is mainly due the creation of the Board of Health and the institution of the paid Fire Department

Mr Acton was one of the original founders of the Union League Club, of which he is still a prominent member. Under its auspices the first colored regiment was sent to the front; the greatest sanitary fair was held; it organized the mass meetings which encouraged the people during the darkest days of the Rebellion, and appropriately celebrated the victories of the Union. At the dinner of the original members of the Club, in 1880, Dr Bellows thus referred to Mr Acton, who was present "Our noble Police—whose honored memories have been invoked to-night, and whose welcome presence is represented here in the waving white hair of my friend Acton—dispersed the miserable mob who would have made the city of New York a battle ground; they sustained the Union League, and the Union League sustained them, in a manner which will never be forgotten" It is not forgotten, nor Mr. Acton's share in it, and the popularity thus worthily won will be as lasting as the metropolis

JOHN G. BERGEN ably and faithfully maintained his colleague of the Board During the tremor and excitement of that period he was almost constantly at Police Headquarters, and, by his prompt conclusions and steady perseverance, did much in an executive and administrative capacity in strengthening the hands of the force to suppress riotous demonstrations. The principal responsibility, however, resting upon Mr Bergen, was that of the care of Brooklyn. How well he discharged this duty is evidenced by the fact that, though there were many indications of serious disturbances there, yet the Police in that section, acting under his orders, were successful in all, except one single instance, in suppressing them.

SETH C HAWLEY, late chief clerk, also achieved an enviable prominence as a brave and zealous official. His well known integrity and devotion to duty gave him an influence in the councils of the Board such as to earn for him the title of "the fifth Commissioner."

Up to the time that he connected himself with the Police Department, Mr Hawley had been engaged as a railroad contractor The financial crash of 1857 crippled the corporation with which he was connected, and also considerably impaired his own private fortune. Abandoning that line of business, he became connected with the removal of the Quarantine.

Mr. Hawley, who had the supervision of the Clerks and Special Patrolmen, the providing and issuing of arms, the execution of orders from the Commissioners, seeing to the wounded, providing for the refugees, and disposing of the prisoners, had, it need hardly be said, his hands full But Mr. Hawley took pride in hard work of that kind, and, his energy being untiring, he acted besides as Commissary for over four thousand Police, military and special, assembled at Police Headquarters He performed an amount of work, satisfactorily and thoroughly, that well might have staggered a man of less capacity and energy

"At the reorganization of the Police Department in 1860," said Mr. Hawley, in an interview shortly before his death with the writer, "General Bowen sent for me and asked me if I'd be willing to take the place of Chief Clerk, and I consented, thinking that the appointment would be but temporary, but in that I was mistaken, for, as the result proved, I had come to stay"

Coming down to the time of the draft riots, Mr Hawley continued "I was acting in that capacity (of Chief Clerk) when the riot occurred General Bowen, who was President of the Board, had raised three regiments of volunteers to go to the war, and was appointed Brigadier-General, and went to New Orleans So that we had only two Commissioners, Bergen and Acton, but two better men for the place could not well have been found

"The authorities in Washington had ordered that the drafting should begin on a Saturday. That was a great mistake, as the dangerous element had all day Sunday to concoct their plans to foment trouble The Government didn't know at the time what a hornet's nest they were stirring up in this city There were more Secessionists in New York than in any other three Northern States The names that were drafted were published, and that helped to intensify the bad blood All day Sunday I noticed knots of excited men talking around the corners in the upper part of the city, and in the vicinity of my house Curious to know what was in the wind, I went out, and heard the talk that was going the rounds In every instance the Government was denounced for ordering the enforcement of recruits by drafting The measure was characterized as outrageous and infamous The speakers were bitter and defiant in their denunciations The stinging part of their grievance was what they called the wicked injustice of taking poor men away from their families I saw the storm approaching, and so was prepared, in a measure, for the scenes I witnessed on the following day Early in the morning a gang of rough-looking men gathered right in front of my door. They had just forced a gang of men who were building a block of houses, at Fifty-eighth Street and Sixth Avenue, to knock off work, and join the rioters The original rioters had come from the shanties on the rocks, near

Central Park. They had a leader, and he carried a bar of iron in his hand Those who refused to join his party, he threatened and commanded until he compelled compliance with his order Nearly all the workmen in the vicinity were coerced into joining his party. They marched directly to the First Provost Marshal's office to sack it, and I hurried down-town to the office

"Before I had got more than half way the Marshal's office was in flames, and that swelled the ranks of the mob By the time I had reached the office the mob was in great force, and ripe for any sort of deviltry I lost no time in informing the Commissioners of what I had seen and heard, and they were very much

startled at what I told them They ordered me to draw up an order concentrating all the Police force of this city and Brooklyn at the office of Police Headquarters in this city. That was the first Police order issued in connection with the riots I was next instructed to draft an order calling out the militia That required the concurrence of Governor Seymour, who happened to be at that very moment at the City Hall That Monday morning he had addressed the mob from the City Hall, and I went to see him by direction of the Commissioners, to tell him of the critical state of affairs I found him in the Governor's room surrounded by friends I had served in the legislature with him, and was well acquainted with him. When he saw me enter he left his friends and came to me. I told him the whole story, and said also that it was important he should be near enough to Police Headquarters to be in constant communication with the Commissioners. He told me he would go immediately to the Fifth Avenue Hotel, and that he would be glad if the Commissioners would make me the medium of communication between him and them. They did so

"Major General Sandford commanded the militia which was called out Their arsenal was on Seventh Avenue The Seventh Regiment had gone South, expecting to be at the battle of Gettysburgh, and some other city regiments had gone too, and only the remnants of other regiments were left The militia staid in their arsenal during the whole term of the riots, without lending a hand to quell disturbance or disperse the mob, or of being of the slightest service towards the security of the city and the safety of life and property On the contrary, they required to be protected, rather than to be the protectors. The Police had no aid whatever from that military force.

"The Police Commissioners then communicated with Brigadier-General Brown, of the regular army, who commanded the Federal forces in the neighborhood, and he ordered three companies—two of infantry and one of artillery—that were in the city on their way home, to be mustered out at the end of their term of service, to co-operate with the Police in dispersing the rioters. He himself took up his quarters in Superintendent Kennedy's room, where messages were being constantly received by telegraph. This was the only place in the city where official and reliable information could be obtained. These three companies were of great service. They accompanied the Police in their raids on the rioters. But they were not on hand in time to take part in the first day's great battles The Police had fought their own battles, and had practically quelled the rioters before the military took hand or part in the affray.

"The mob moved from up-town down towards the heart of the city. One of the clerks I had sent to the Fifth Avenue Hotel, on his return, told me that the mob had burned the Colored Half Orphan Asylum. The late E. D Morgan was present when this information was received, and he expressed his incredulity at the news brought by my clerk. 'It cannot be,' was the remark he made.

"Meantime the Police were gathering gradually, in response to the order they had received to report at Headquarters When the mob, which had increased to thousands, had got down to Union Square, they halted They had broken into stores and saloons on their way down town, and made themselves drunk on stolen liquor. They were preparing for a big row. There was no organization among them One big fellow carried a flag on a pole, and walked in the front.

"A messenger brought the tidings that the mob had reached Fourteenth Street. Up to this time they had met with no opposition. They had everything their own way.

"The Commissioners then concluded it was time for the Police to act

"Two hundred or two hundred and fifty Police were drawn up in line in front of Police Headquarters The greater part of them had the light, fancy stick they carry when they are on dress parade.

"The Commissioners said to me 'Now, that this force of Policemen must go out and face that mob, who shall lead them?'

"Previous to this, and after the mob had burned the Colored Half Orphan Asylum, John A Kennedy, the then Superintendent, not being posted, walked out—with his little gold-headed cane—to see what was the matter. The mob recognized him, and he barely escaped with his life. He was subsequently taken to Headquarters in a wagon, so terribly cut and bruised from the usage he had received as to be almost unrecognizable He was taken away and concealed until he recovered from his injuries, which was long after the city had become tranquil again

"So I said, in answer to the Commissioner's query as to who should lead the men against the mob, 'Carpenter is the senior Inspector, and it is his place, in the absence of the Superintendent, to take command' Commissioner Acton said, 'Will he do it?' 'He must do it: he will not refuse; he's a gallant man,' I replied 'Go to him then, and say to him that it is our wish that he assume the command' Never will I forget the words and action of Carpenter when I conveyed to him this message. Raising his clinched right hand he brought it down with a loud thump on the desk, and exclaimed, 'I'll go, and I won't come back unless I come back victorious'

"I returned to Commissioner Acton and told him what Carpenter had said Acton then saw Carpenter and told him to bring the men up Broadway and whip the mob at all hazards. He was to take no prisoners

"Carpenter went and did as he was told.

"The Police captured the colors carried by the big man, broke the big man's thick head, and littered Broadway, from Bond Street to Union Square, with disabled rioters

"It would be in vain for me to try to recall the number of Police expeditions sent out to face the mob. There was no time to make records. Up to Wednesday at midnight there was no cessation of fighting all over the town

"The Commissary Department was the great difficulty we had to contend with. We had to feed the whole Police force and military, besides seven hundred negroes who had taken refuge in the upper story of Police Headquarters. Stores were all closed, and provisions were hard to get

"But we did it"

"It was not safe for any one known to be connected with Police Headquarters to be found abroad unprotected. I had left my family alone, the only stranger in the house being a colored woman—a servant—which was anything but a comforting guarantee of their security At one o'clock Tuesday morning I started over to Sixth Avenue, and, at the junction of Carmine Street, I saw a motley crowd of men, women and children dancing around a fire in the street, in the vicinity of which a strangled negro was dangling from a tree.

"The second day some of the military made an independent movement against the rioters in Mackerelville

"We didn't know where this section of men were, or what they were doing The mob was too strong for them, and the men were chased all the way down to the Seventh Regiment's arsenal and stoned, followed by a great crowd One of the men was wounded and thrown from his horse, and left in the street.

Hearing of the affray, I was deputed to report the matter to the Governor and General Brown, both of whom were at the time at the St Nicholas Hotel. The officer, who was wounded, was a Major. A young Lieutenant, who was with the party of routed soldiers, and who escaped by making good use of his legs, had first reported the wounding of the Major and his being left disabled in the street at the mercy of the mob. General Brown heard the young Lieutenant's story to the end, and then, turning on him, said :

" 'You state here, and in my presence, that you ran away, and left the Major wounded in the hands of the mob' 'Be patient, General,' said General Wool, "and be charitable enough to reflect that the Lieutenant is a very young man'

"The result of it was that General Wool directed General Brown to send out a force, and bring in the Major. The Major was not seriously hurt, and he was found and taken to the St. Nicholas Hotel.

"If the Police hadn't acted with a vigor and earnestness that couldn't be excelled, the city would have been sacked The mob would have been in Wall Street and everywhere else where they could find plunder

"The Police took from the rioters eleven thousand stand of arms, and we have got them in the building yet We can't find any one to claim them.

"It is proper to say that the Police force was at that time at the perfection of discipline, and the *esprit du corps* was extraordinary

"One would require to think it over very carefully to realize how it would be if there was no judicial or Police authority in a city like New York During these exciting events we hadn't a Magistrate before whom to arraign a prisoner, or a box or a jail to lock a prisoner in.

"All branches of the Police service did their duty so thoroughly as to render it difficult to make any mention of special meritorious performance of duty

"Regarding the number of rioters killed it is impossible to state with any degree of accuracy. The nearest approximation that can be made to it is by comparing the mortality for that month with the corresponding month of the previous year. By this we learn that there were one thousand one hundred deaths during the month of the riots in excess of the deaths in the corresponding month of the preceding year. I should regard this as a pretty fair estimate of the number of people who lost their lives by participating in the riots

"It was an awful lesson, and one not to be forgotten

"One other lesson was learned by the Police, and that is, that in close contact with a mob there is not any weapon so effective as the club. It was then also found out that nothing would stand the strain for this kind of work like locust. In the early stages of the riot the men carried their rosewood sticks, and these splintered and broke as fast as the heads they were used on Rosewood is heavy and seems solid, but it lacks toughness and elasticity. Now, locust, besides being light, possesses these qualities. It does not split, is sonorous, and gives out a sound like a bell It is very rarely that I have seen a locust club broken. Since then locust has entirely come into use in the department."

Inspector Daniel Carpenter, under the supervision of Commissioner Acton, assumed and discharged the duties of Superintendent, after Mr Kennedy was incapacitated by reason of his injuries. The riot had quickly gained in proportions, and now assumed such a formidable shape that the entire force of the Police had to be called into requisition. Word having been received that the mob were marching to attack Mayor Opdyke's house, on Fifth Avenue, Inspector Carpenter, in person, took command of a force of two hundred men. Before starting from Police Headquarters he spoke to the men, telling them that "They had to meet and put down a mob; to take no prisoners; to strike quick and hard"—orders which were literally obeyed. It was a day of hard fighting, and Inspector Carpenter, with his command, was ever at the post of duty, which was the post of danger. That he acted gallantly and performed his whole duty goes without saying. His was a task of unceasing labor, constant peril, and great responsibility; but he did not return until he had "put down the mob," even if he had "to strike quick and strike hard" to do it.

Inspector James Leonard.—As a gallant, faithful and zealous officer, Inspector Leonard's record stands second to none in the department. It has been commented on as a remarkable fact that the officers, without a single exception, who personally led their commands against the rioters, not only displayed great bravery, but a practical knowledge of strategy and tactics that won the day against overwhelming odds. After Inspector Carpenter had left Police Headquarters with his command, shortly after Superintendent Kennedy's arrival, maimed and insensible, Inspector Leonard, under orders from Commissioner Acton, was constantly employed massing and organizing such of the force at Headquarters as was not in actual conflict with the mob. Throughout Monday Inspector Leonard had several brushes with the enemy. On Tuesday he was mainly engaged in the neighborhood of Printing House Square in repeated hand-to-hand encounters with the rioters. Wherever the fight was the hottest, there was Inspector Leonard and his intrepid force of blue-coats. Truly Superintendent Matsell's famous encomium "the finest Police force in the world," is not an overstrained estimate of the officers and men who took part in those fierce and deadly street encounters. In one of the several *emutes* that took place in the vicinity of the City Hall, the Inspector, as usual, took a leading part. Says one who had personal knowledge of the facts: "A hand-to-hand fight ensued, heads were broken, men prostrated and laid in heaps, and, in less time than it is recorded, those who a few minutes before were eager for and intent upon the lives of the three daring officers (Inspector Leonard and two of his men) were scattered like sheep before the gallant charge of the Police, or lay as slaughtered Inspector Leonard was boldly in the fray, his stalwart form being conspicuous, his rapid, earnestly-meant and muscular blows falling with telling effect"

And again "He had immense interests to guard: himself a host, his officers and men true as steel, they saved the districts committed to their care from the consummation of well-concocted plans of violence and pillage Of active intelligence and proved courage, Inspector Leonard's name shines brightly on the record of honor"

An Act passed April 25, 1864, entitled an Act to amend an Act passed April 15, 1857, and an Act passed April 10, 1860, provided that the unexplained absence, without leave, of any member of the Metropolitan Police who for five days should absent himself without leave, should be deemed and held to be a resignation by such member and be accepted as such. The Act also established the following officers. A Treasurer's Bookkeeper, a Secretary to the President, a Chief Clerk, a First Deputy Clerk, and Deputy Clerks not exceeding ten, Surgeons not exceeding ten, and a Drill Captain. The Superintendent and each Captain, the law declared, should possess powers of general Police supervision and inspection over all licensed or unlicensed pawnbrokers, venders, junk-shops, junk-boatmen, cartmen, dealers in second-hand merchandise, intelligence offices, keepers and auctioneers within the district. In like manner the following places were brought under the ban of the Police. Gaming houses, playing for wagers of money at any game of chance, selling lottery tickets or

Sixty-ninth Regiment Armory.

policies, etc. The Superintendent could authorize any member of the force to enter the same and arrest all persons found offending against the law, seize all implements and carry the person so arrested before a Magistrate; the articles so seized to be deposited with the Property Clerk. The selling of liquor on the Sabbath, or on election day, was also prohibited, under a penalty of fifty dollars for each offence. It was made a misdemeanor, punishable by imprisonment not less than one year nor exceeding two years, or a fine not less than two hundred and fifty dollars, to use personal violence upon any elector on election day. The Board of Police were empowered to appoint all Poll Clerks. The Sanitary Company, as a part of their duties, were to visit all ferry boats, manufactories, slaughter houses, tenement houses, hotels and boarding houses deemed unsafe, and report thereon; complaints to be made under oath, before any Magistrate who issued a warrant for the apprehension of the offending party. If the

Magistrate was satisfied that the charges preferred were well founded, he could, in writing, command a ferry boat to cease running, and such other nuisances complained of to cease or be closed

The Metropolitan Police District comprised the counties of New York, Kings, Westchester, and Richmond, and the towns of Newtown, Flushing, and Jamaica, in the county of Queens, as provided by Chapter 403 of the Laws of 1864

The county of New York comprised the whole of the Island of Manhattan, and is bounded on the west by the Hudson River, north by Spuyten Duyvel Creek and Harlem River, and on the east and south by the East River. Westchester County lies adjacent and to the north of New York County, and is bounded on the west by the Hudson River, east by the East River, Long Island Sound, and the State of Connecticut, and on the north by Putnam County Kings County comprises the southwest portion of Long Island, being bounded on the north-east by Queens County, and for the rest by the waters of the ocean, East River and New York Bay Richmond County embraces the whole of Staten Island The towns of Flushing, Newtown, and Jamaica, are in Queens County, Long Island, adjoining Kings County, on the north-east

That portion of the Metropolitan Police District consisting of the cities of New York and Brooklyn, were divided into two Inspection Districts, Surgeons Districts, and Precincts, the Precincts were divided into Patrolmen's beats or posts

The Police force was divided into four divisions, and an Inspector was assigned to the command of a division, and in case of riot or any other cause, when the force was called out in a body, he had command over the division to which he was assigned

The First Division was under the command of Inspector Folk, and comprised the whole force of Brooklyn, including the Sanitary Squad and Atlantic Dock Police

The Second Division was under the command of Inspector Leonard, and comprised the First, Second, Third, Fifth, Eighth, Ninth, Fifteenth, Twenty-sixth, Twenty-seventh and Twenty-eighth Precincts of New York City, and Second Police Court Squad

The Third Division was under the command of Inspector Carpenter, and comprised the Fourth, Sixth, Seventh, Tenth, Eleventh, Thirteenth, Fourteenth, Seventeenth and Twenty-fifth Precincts of New York City, the First and Third Police Court Squads, and the Sanitary Company.

The Fourth Division was under the command of Inspector Dilks, and comprised the Twelfth, Sixteenth, Eighteenth, Nineteenth, Twentieth, Twenty-first, Twenty-second, Twenty-third, Twenty-ninth, Thirtieth, Thirty-first, Thirty-second, Thirty-second (Sub), and Thirty-third Precincts of New York City, and the Fourth Police Court Squad.

The Police force was divided into companies, one company being allotted to each precinct, together with the addition of the Metropolitan Police Sanitary Company, and such squads as were ordered by the Board of Police.

The full dress of the members of the Metropolitan Police force, excepting the Surgeons, was of navy blue cloth, indigo-dyed, and all wool.

The dress for the Superintendent was a double-breasted frock coat, the waist extending to the top of the hip, and the skirt to within one inch of the bend of the knee; two rows of Police buttons on the breast, eight in each row, placed in pairs, the distance between each row being five and one-half inches at the top and three and one-half inches at the bottom; stand-up collar, to rise no higher than to permit the chin to turn freely over it, to hook in front at the bottom; cuffs three and one-half inches deep, and buttoning with three small buttons at the under seam; two buttons on the hips, one button on the bottom of each skirt-pocket welt, and two buttons intermediate, so that there would be six buttons on the back; skirt, collars, and cuffs, of dark blue velvet; lining of the coat black. The trousers plain. Black neckcloth. The vest single-breasted, with eight buttons placed at equal distances. The cap of navy blue cloth, and of the form of the pattern in the office of Superintendent, having a band of dark blue velvet, with a gold-embroidered wreath in front, encircling a a silver star.

The Patrolmen detailed as Roundsmen, in addition, had the word "Roundsman" in white metal letters, in lieu of the wreath.

The dress for Harbor Patrolmen was a sailor's jacket, rolling collar, to come down half-way between the hip-joint and the knee, five buttons on each side of the breast, two buttons on the under seam of the cuff, pockets inside, vest, single-breasted, nine buttons; trousers, plain; shirt of blue flannel; cap, same as other Patrolmen, with wreath and number the same as in the office of the Superintendent, pea jacket, overcoat three inches above the knee, five buttons on each side, side pockets with flaps.

The dress for Doormen was a double-breasted round jacket extending two inches below the hip, with five Police buttons on each breast and one on the inside seam of each cuff; pantaloons of cadet mixed cloth, plain; cap, the same as Patrolmen, without wreath, but with the word "Doorman" in white metal letters placed in front.

The dress for Inspectors the same as Superintendent, except that there were seven buttons on each row on the breast of the coat, placed at equal distances, and the gold wreath on the cap enclosed the word "Inspector," in silver.

The dress for Captains and Sergeants was the same as for the Superintendent, except that there were eight buttons in each row on the breast of the coat, placed at equal distances; the collar rolling, the collar and cuffs of the same color and material as the coat; the band of the same color and material as the coat, the band of the same color and material as the body of the cap, welted at the edges, and the wreath inclosing the word "Captain" or "Sergeant," with the number of the precinct to which the officer was attached, in gold. The Captain of the Harbor Police had a gold anchor, and the Sergeants silver anchors enclosed in the wreath in lieu of the number of the precinct.

The dress for Patrolmen was a single-breasted frock coat, with rolling collar, the waist extending to the top of the hip, and the skirt to within one inch of the bend of the knee; nine buttons on the breast, two buttons on the hips, two buttons on the bottom of each pocket, and three small buttons on the under seam of the cuffs Trousers had a white welt in the outer seam. Black neck-cloth Vest, single-breasted, with nine buttons placed at equal distances. The cap of navy blue cloth, corresponding with the sample in the office of the Superintendent, with wreath surrounding the appropriate number in white metal

The summer uniform consisted of blue flannel sack coat and blue flannel trousers The coat of Patrolmen was a single-breasted sack with short turn-over color, buttoning close up to the chin, and reaching to half-way between the articulation of the hip joint and the knee, with four buttons on the front, no pockets to show on the outside, and the trousers made same as those worn in winter.

Flannel sack coat and flannel trousers, made like the above, and Sennet hat, was the uniform of the Harbor Police

Coats for Captains were double-breasted, and buttoned close up to the chin, with short rolling collar, with two rows of buttons of five each on the front, the coat reaching to a point half way between the articulation of the hip joint and the knee; trousers without welts in the seams.

For Sergeants same as Captains, except that there were two rows of buttons of four each

The officers were permitted to wear (in the station house) while in the discharge of desk duty, an undress coat, the same as the summer uniform

The Superintendent of Police was the chief executive officer of the Metropolitan Police force, subject to the orders, rules and regulations of the Board of Metropolitan Police

An Inspector was designated by the Board of Police to perform office duty at the general office in the city of New York, and an Inspector was designated in like manner to perform office duty in the city of Brooklyn. They were called Office Inspectors

District Inspectors reported in person, daily, at the office of the Superintendent, and on the first Wednesday of every month they submitted reports, in writing, to the Superintendent, setting forth the condition of each station house in their respective districts, with such suggestions in regard to them as might conduce to the comfort of the officers and men, and insure a thorough performance of duty.

The Commissioners of the Metropolitan Police and the Comptrollers of the cities of New York and Brooklyn convened as a Board of Estimate and Apportionment, annually, on or before July 1, and made up a financial estimate of the sums required for the ensuing year

The estimate was then submitted to a committee of revision, composed of the Presidents respectively of the Board of Supervisors of the counties of New York, Kings, Westchester and Richmond, and of the Board of Aldermen of Brooklyn and the respective towns of Newtown, Flushing, and Jamaica in the county of Queens. If objection to the estimate was made, it became the duty of the Board of Estimate and Apportionment to consider and revise the same, such action being final

This Act established the House of Detention of Witnesses.

Following are the annual salaries paid to the persons named

President of the Board	$4,000
Treasurer	4,000
Other Commissioners	3,500
Superintendent	5,000
Inspectors	2,500
Surgeons	1,800
Captains	1,500
Sergeants	1,200
Patrolmen	1,000
Doormen	800

No member of the force was permitted to accept for his own benefit, or share in, any present, gift, reward, etc. The Board, however, could permit any member to accept such gift or present for any extraordinary service rendered

The sum of thirty-five thousand dollars was provided by the legislature for purchasing and fitting up a station house for the Twenty-seventh Precinct; but this amount was found to be inadequate, an addition of fifteen thousand dollars being required to secure suitable premises The sum of twenty-five thousand dollars remained in the hands of the Comptroller, applicable to rebuilding the station house of the Eighteenth Precinct, which was fired and destroyed by the mob in the draft riots It was found that there was pressing need for a station house in the Twenty-ninth Precinct, the old premises being inconvenient and insufficient The station house of the Twenty-third Precinct had also been fired and destroyed by the mob, and provisions were made for the accommodation of the precinct by fitting up suitable premises and leasing them for five years

The Thirty-second Precinct consisted of the upper portion of the city, and as the needs were great and pressing for a station house, two lots were bought on the corner of Tenth Avenue and One Hundred and Fifty-second Street, in Carmansville, each 25 x 100 feet, and a station house erected thereon, 25 x 60 feet, three stories high, and a stable for horses 20 x 50 feet, at a total cost of twelve thousand five hundred dollars There being no prison or lodging rooms for vagrants and disorderly persons, all persons arrested and requiring to be retained, were from necessity taken to the adjoining precinct

Patrolmen in the regular routine of duty, passed over every portion of the graded streets of the city each hour of the day and night, and in the thickly settled streets much more frequently It was their duty to become acquainted with every tenement on their respective beats, and to familiarize themselves with the habits, business, and characters of the permanent inhabitants

Then, as now, robbery, burglary, and larceny were pursued by a large class of remarkably acute persons The impossibility of wholly suppressing such offences against the law, did not then, no more than at present, prevent the Police from making honest and earnest efforts to make those operations neither safe nor profitable. The professional thief seems to have preserved the same traits through all ages He is not restrained by the disrepute attached to his calling, nor does the law possess sufficient terrors to exert a restraining influence, so long as detection is difficult and conviction uncertain

It was observed that during the war there was a marked tendency to crimes of violence towards persons, and other crimes of a still graver character, while petty offences had not increased in proportion. There were arrested by the Metropolitan Police, for crimes of violence of a serious character in 1863 and 1864, respectively:

	1863.	1864
Felonious assault	343	462
Assault on Policemen	19	35
Attempt at rape	23	29
Insulting females in the street	33	86
Murder	79	48
Maiming	6	6
Manslaughter	1	10
Rape	21	34
Threatening life	12	30
	537	742

A small portion of this mass of high crime received the punishment provided by the law. The fault, if any existed, was somewhere beyond the power of the Police. During the year ending the thirtieth of November, five members of the Police force had met their deaths by violence from the hands of desperate ruffians, great numbers of whom infested the city. The names of the Policemen killed were George W. Duryea, John O'Brien, Joseph Nulet, Charles Curren, and Austen Esterbrook. Thirteen had been seriously injured and wounded by collision with the same violent class. The names of the wounded were James Kiernan, William Delamater, Ellsworth F. Hoagland, James Leary, John H. Polly, Robert Thompson, John H. Arnoux, William P. Teller, Thomas Hawkins, James McGowan, James Gannon, Thomas Sweeney, and Stephen Shea; a much larger number, not reported, received injuries of a less serious character.

This, too, occurred during a year which had not been marked by any serious riot or mob. Concert and energy on the part of all good citizens and honest officials, to resist and subdue these elements of violence and crime, were urgently demanded by the Board of Police. It was claimed by President Acton that it would greatly conduce to the good order of society, and to the personal safety of the citizen, if a law were passed rendering it a crime to carry concealed deadly weapons.

The amount of time lost by sickness by Patrolmen and Doormen, New York and Brooklyn, during the year ending Nov. 1, 1863	24,672 days
For the year ending Nov. 1, 1864	24,311 "
Decrease	361 "

The amount of time lost in 1863 was increased by the unusual number wounded in the riots of that year. During the succeeding year there was no riot and no epidemic, yet the amount of sick time was not largely reduced.

The total lost time was equal to sixty-seven years, or sixty-seven men disabled so as to perform no duty.

The force for the year ending October 31, 1864, comprised the following:

Captains	33
Sergeants	126
Patrolmen	1,789
Doormen	66
Total	2,014

By Section 1 of an Act of April 13, 1865, (Laws Ch 400) all laws relating to the election of Constables in the city of New York were repealed; "and, hereafter, the Marshals of the city of New York shall be appointed by the Mayor of the city of New York, by, and with the advice and consent of the Board of Supervisors of the County of New York, and such Marshals shall not exceed thirty"

Arrests for offences of all grades, had, during the year 1865, reached the number of eighty-eight thousand three hundred and fifty-five, against sixty-nine

First New York Colored Regiment Leaving for the Seat of War.

thousand seven hundred and fifty-one for the preceding year, making an increase of eighteen thousand seven hundred and eighty-four Crimes of violence against the person had increased in even a greater ratio, as will appear from the following comparative statement·

	1864	1865
Felonious assault	462	798
Assault on Policemen	35	36
Rape	34	38
Attempt at rape	29	40
Manslaughter and murder	58	—
Homicide of all degrees	—	69
Mayhem	6	14
Total	624	995

The cost of lost time paid for during the year was forty-eight thousand three hundred and twenty-two dollars and sixty-four cents. The loss of time by sickness was more than equal to the full time of eighty-three men, or almost four per cent. of the whole force. The cost in money was more than the full pay of forty-eight men.

The force consisted of thirty-three Captains, one hundred and twenty-nine Sergeants, one thousand seven hundred and seventy-two Patrolmen, and sixty-three Doormen, making a total of one thousand nine hundred and ninety-seven.

Arrests

Offences against property	14,962
Offences against the person	53,911
Total number of arrests	68,873

The legislature, on February 28, 1866, passed an Act to amend an Act passed April 25, 1864, to amend an Act passed April 15, 1857, and an Act passed April 10, 1860, to the following effect To the County of Richmond there were apportioned one Captain, two Sergeants, and twenty-five men. Any part of any town adjoining the city of Brooklyn might be set apart by the Board of Supervisors of the county of Kings for the purpose of having a Patrol force The expenses attending this Police force were levied and collected in the annual taxes of said district

The Board of Police were authorized to appoint an Inspector of Boats, the salary not to exceed two thousand five hundred dollars. (Act April 10, 1866.)

Commissioner McMurray's term of office expired March 1, 1866, and the legislature elected Benjamin F. Manierre to fill the place

An Act to regulate and increase the salaries of certain members of the Metropolitan Police was passed April 30, 1866, with the following results

President	$5,500
Treasurer	5,500
Other Commissioners	5,000
Superintendent	7,500
Inspectors	3,500
Surgeons	2,250
Captains	2,000
Sergeants	1,600
Patrolmen	1,200
Doormen	900

The above was subject to the proviso that whenever the currency of the United States had attained a par value in gold, the foregoing salaries should be reduced twenty per cent., excepting Captains, whose salaries should be eighteen hundred dollars, and Sergeants fourteen hundred dollars.

The amount of lost time by sickness and injuries during the year exceeded the amount of the preceding year by three hundred and eleven days

This question of pay for lost time was one that was a constant source of solicitude to the Board of Commissioners Policemen are but human, and so they, like the rest of us, were subject to those physical infirmities that flesh is heir to No doubt much of those sporadic diseases were the result of natural causes and not to be avoided, while others were malingering, without a doubt But how to find a remedy for the evil was another question.

The number of arrests for offences in the cities of New York and Brooklyn from the year 1860 to 1866, both inclusive, were

```
1860 .................................................. 81,143
1861 .................................................. 87,582
1862 .................................................. 101,469
1863 .................................................. 77,212
1864 .................................................. 69,571
1865 .................................................. 88,355
1866 .................................................. 97,587
```

Aggregate in seven years................ 603,019

The average number for the seven years was eighty-six thousand one hundred and forty-five. The increase of offences which subject persons to arrest may be attributed in part to the increase of the population of the two cities, which was very great during the period under consideration, and in no small degree to the demoralizing effect of a state of war, and the disbanding of the immense armies. It might reasonably have been expected that the influences above alluded to would have exhibited themselves in an increase in the number of offences of high grade, such as are accompanied by violence to the person. In examining the records of arrests for the seven years—assault with intent to kill, felonious assaults, murder, threatening life, rape, attempt at rape, maiming, homicide, robbery in the first degree, highway robbery, burglary, and attempts at burglary—it appears that the number of arrests for offences enumerated have been

```
1860 .................................................. 1,541
1861 .................................................. 1,663
1862 .................................................. 1,310
1863 .................................................. 1,467
1864 .................................................. 1,372
1865 .................................................. 2,062
1866 .................................................. 1,917
```

Total in seven years 11,332

It thus appears that while the increase in the total number of arrests for seven years was twenty per cent, the increase during the same period in arrests for the offences of high grade was thirty per cent.

It was felt to be worthy of consideration, especially to the population of rural districts, how far the efforts of the Police of the cities to protect the people against the criminal classes tended to drive the persons composing those classes to new and more secure fields of criminal enterprise in the country adjacent to the cities. That such was the tendency in some degree, there was no question, and it here became a matter of common remark that life and property were more safe in cities under the guardianship of the Police than in the adjacent rural districts.

This was a growing opinion, and as a result of it the towns of Yonkers and West Farms, in Westchester County, proceeding under the Police Act, Chapter 403 of the Laws of 1864, had, by a vote of town meetings, respectively authorized a permanent Police, and made the required fiscal arrangements therefor.

Yonkers authorized a force of fourteen, and West Farms a force of six men In each town a portion of the Police did duty as horse patrol, which greatly increased their efficiency

The legislature, at its previous session, passed two Acts designated as Chapters 84 and 590 of the Laws of 1866 These Acts authorized the appointment, by the Board of Metropolitan Police, of a Captain, two Sergeants and twenty-five Patrolmen for the county of Richmond, and authorized and required the Supervisors of that county to make the needful fiscal provision for their maintenance

In pursuance of these proceedings in Yonkers and West Farms, and of the acts concerning Richmond County, the Board of Police appointed and organized the Police called for by proceedings and statutes above referred to.

Drilling a Squad of Policemen.

The force in West Farms entered upon their duties on the thirteenth day of January of this year; in Richmond County on the sixteenth day of June, and in Yonkers on the tenth day of August following

The town of West Farms constituted a sub-station of the Thirty-second Precinct, with a Sergeant in command. The station house at Tremont, Richmond County, was constituted a precinct designated as the Fifty-first Precinct The station house was at the village of Stapleton. The town of Yonkers was constituted a sub-station of the Thirty-second Precinct, designated as Yonkers sub-station, with a station house at the village of Yonkers The Tremont and Yonkers sub-stations were under the command of the Captain of the Thirty-second Precinct.

Thus, during the year, the jurisdiction of the Board of Metropolitan Police was potentially extended over the rural districts above named

These proceedings, as is usual and natural in the beginning, met with considerable opposition from a portion of the population

Other towns in the vicinity of the metropolis were so infested with bad characters, and so depredated upon by robberies and thieving, that they began to consider how to defend themselves and re-establish the quiet and safety which they had been accustomed to enjoy in former years

On the fourteenth of April, 1866, the legislature passed "an Act to regulate the sale of intoxicating liquors within the Metropolitan Police District," being Chapter 578 of the Laws of that session. This Act, in effect, constituted "the Metropolitan Police District, excepting and excluding the county of Westchester," into an excise district, and provided that the Commissioners of the Board of Health be a Board of Excise for such district. By the law creating a Metropolitan Sanitary District and a Board of Health therein, the Commissioners of Metropolitan Police were made members of the Board of Health, and were therefore members of the Board of Excise above referred to.

The Board of Excise, constituted in the manner above mentioned, organized in pursuance of the Act on the first day of May, and immediately entered upon their duties The duty of investigating the character and antecedents of the applicants for licenses necessarily devolved upon the Commissioners of Metropolitan Police.

At the date of entering upon their duties there were, in the cities of New York and Brooklyn, over nine thousand two hundred and fifty places where intoxicating liquors were publicly sold Of this vast number, but seven hundred and fifty-four pretended to have licenses, leaving about eight thousand five hundred open and admitted violators of the law The statutes of the State, as they had existed for many years, prohibited the sale of intoxicating liquors on the Sabbath

Prior to the enactment of this law there had existed for a number of years a Board of Excise, charged with the power and duty of granting excise licenses

Under the auspices of that Board, in 1860, the revenue contributed to the treasury of New York City by license fees amounted to fifty-four thousand five hundred and eighty thousand dollars, which was about equal to the proceeds of one thousand eight hundred and nineteen licenses at thirty dollars each, which was the maximum rate; while in 1864, the revenues had dwindled down to twelve thousand four hundred and fifty dollars, equal to the proceeds of four hundred and fifteen licenses, at the same rate What was the actual number issued and rates charged in these years is not known to the Police Department

The total number of licenses issued and delivered under the new law was five thousand six hundred and ninety-seven. Of this number, three thousand five hundred and ninety-six were of the first class, paying two hundred and fifty dollars each, two thousand and ninety-eight were of the second class, paying one hundred dollars each

The total amount of revenue arising from license fees was one million one hundred and eight thousand nine hundred and twenty-four dollars and ninety-eight cents, and was contributed as follows.

County of New York $846,275.98
County of Kings 246,150.00
County of Queens 11,850 00

The old City Armory or Arsenal is situated at the junction of Elm and White Streets, extending eighty-four feet on Elm Street, and thirty-one feet on White Street. The style of the architecture is a kind of Gothic, with castellated towers.

The population of the city had greatly increased during the past five years, and its trade and wealth had increased in greater ratio than the population. The tendency of vicious classes to resort to the metropolis, not only from our own but

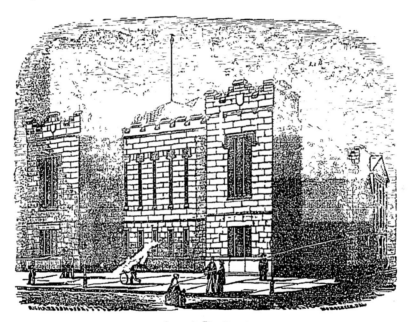

Arsenal, Elm Street

from other countries, the increase of crimes of grave character, with other considerations, indicated the propriety of a moderate increase of the force in the city of New York

Brooklyn, in this year (1866) had but three hundred and seven Patrolmen, which was less than one to one thousand two hundred of population; its territory requiring Police surveillance was equal to New York. This great extent of territory was divided into ten precincts, each of large extent. The extremes of the precinct were so remote from the respective station houses as to consume a large portion of the time of the Patrolmen in going to and returning from their tours of duty. The law, the Commissioners contended, should be amended so as to allow the division of the territory of Brooklyn into a larger number of precincts,

OUR POLICE PROTECTORS

and that the welfare of the city demanded a considerable increase in the number of Patrolmen.

The location of station houses in New York City was:

1.—54 New Street
2 —49 Beekman Street
3 — 100 Chambers Street
4 —9 Oak Street.
5 —49 Leonard Street.
6 —9 F... ..klin Street.
7 —247 Madison Street
8 —126 Wooster Street
9 —94 Charles Street.
10 —Essex Market
11 —Union Market.
12 —One Hundred and Twenty-sixth Street, near Third Avenue,
13 —Attorney Street, corner of Delancey.
14 —53 Spring Street
15 —221 Mercer Street.
16 —156 West Twentieth Street
17 —75 First Avenue, corner Fifth Street
18 —163 East Twenty-second Street
19 —118 Fifty-ninth Street, between Second and Third Avenues.
20 —352 West Thirty-fifth Street
21 —120 East Thirty-fifth Street
22 —545 and 547 West Forty-seventh Street, between Eighth and Ninth Avenues
23 —East Eighty-sixth Street, corner Fourth Avenue
24 —Police Steamboat, No. 1
25 —300 Mulberry Street.
26 —City Hall
27 —99 Liberty Street
28 —550 Greenwich Street
29 —34 East Twenty-ninth Street.
30 —Manhattanville, corner of Bloomingdale Road and Lawrence Street.
31 —Broadway, near West Eighty-sixth Street (Bloomingdale)
32 —One Hundred and Fifty-second Street, corner Tenth Avenue (Carmansville)
32 —(Sub) Tremont
33 —Central Park Arsenal.

The laws creating the Board of Health, the Board of Excise, the registry and election law, and the law for licensing boats, had greatly increased the labors, duties and responsibilities of the Police force, and especially of the officers of the force. These new and additional duties had been performed without neglecting any of the customary duties of Police

As early as the fifteenth of June, 1866, the work was begun of selecting two thousand one hundred persons, who would be recognized by all good citizens as proper men in all respects to discharge the responsible duties of inspectors of registry and election, canvassers and poll clerks; the Board taking care to divide the selections equally between the two political parties Not a few prominent citizens who were duly notified of their selection, responded in terms like the following

"I have neither time nor inclination for anything but attention to my own business"

Many gentlemen whom the Board would have taken pleasure in appointing, excused themselves, and thus the labor of making selections correspondingly increased

The amount obtained by requisition on the Comptroller for expenses of registry and elections was as follows

    For the general election and registry prior thereto. .. $52,169 00
    For the charter election and registry prior thereto. ... 39,807 00

    Total.. . .. .$92,016 00

Of this sum nearly seventy thousand dollars was required to pay the inspectors, canvassers, poll clerks and lessors of polling places, the compensation being fixed by ordinance. In the remaining expenditures a saving of nearly nine thousand dollars was effected, as shown by comparison with the report of the Department of Finance for 1865

CHAPTER XI

AN ERA OF ORGANIZATION AND DEVELOPMENT.
1866-1870.

NEW STATION HOUSES ERECTED AND OLD ONES RENOVATED.—IMPROVEMENT IN THE DISCIPLINE AND EFFICIENCY OF THE FORCE.—ESTABLISHMENT OF A CENTRAL POLICE OFFICE IN NEW YORK —DEATH OF JOHN G. BERGEN.—APPOINTMENT OF A METROPOLITAN FIRE MARSHAL AND ASSISTANT.—HOUSE OF DETENTION FOR WITNESSES.—TABLE OF ARRESTS FOR A SERIES OF YEARS.—TIME LOST BY SICKNESS.—RE-ORGANIZATION OF THE BOARD OF METROPOLITAN POLICE —RESIGNATION OF COMMISSIONER ACTON —AVERAGE LENGTH OF POSTS —AMOUNTS PAID FOR SICK TIME.—VALUE OF LOST OR STOLEN PROPERTY RECOVERED —THE SANITARY COMPANY —LOST CHILDREN —BUILDINGS FOUND OPEN AND SECURED.—TABLES OF ARRESTS.—SALARIES —LOCATION OF STATION HOUSES —AN ERA OF ORGANIZATION AND DEVELOPMENT.—"THE TWEED CHARTER"—DEATH OF SUPERINTENDENT JOURDAN

THE discipline and efficiency of the force had of recent years been fully maintained, and there was an obvious improvement in the character of the men who presented themselves as applicants for appointment

An appropriation was made in the tax levy of the sum of ten thousand dollars, to rebuild in part and repair the station house and prison of the Sixth Precinct, which had become unsafe, dilapidated and unhealthy The work was completed at a cost of about fifteen thousand dollars There was in the hands of the Comptroller the sum of twenty-five thousand dollars, applicable to the purchase of premises for a station house for the Tenth Precinct, but this sum had proved insufficient, an additional sum of twenty-five thousand dollars being required to accomplish the desired object The apartment occupied by the force in this precinct was over the Essex Market, and was unsuitable in every respect The premises devoted to the force of the Eleventh Precinct were over the Union Market, and, like those of the Tenth, were unsuitable No funds were appropriated for the building of new quarters in this precinct Provision was made in the tax levy of 1866 and former years, to the amount of thirty-five thousand dollars, to procure a permanent station house for the Twenty-first Precinct. In the tax levy of 1865 there was an appropriation of forty thousand dollars to build a station house and prison for the Twenty-ninth Precinct The place at first designed for this station house was in a triangular plot of unoccupied public ground, bounded by the lines of Sixth Avenue, Broadway, and Forty-second Street. The site named met with great opposition from the owners of property on the adjoining streets. The lease of the premises occupied by the Thirtieth Precinct having expired, the lease of the building at the corner of Bloomingdale Road and Lawrence Street was secured for a term of five years, at a rental of eight hundred dollars for the first year, and seven hundred dollars per year for the residue of the term. The house was fitted up and a prison built

During the year 1867 one thousand one hundred and twelve candidates for appointment on the force presented themselves for medical examination; of which number five hundred and three were accepted as being sound of body and limb, and possessing robust constitutions; and of which six hundred and nine were rejected

The whole number of days lost by members of the force through sickness and injuries amounted to twenty-five thousand and twenty-seven days, this being five thousand eight hundred and thirty days less than the previous year.

The whole number of cases of sickness during the year amounted to two thousand nine hundred and seventy-one, which made the average time lost by each sick man about eight days and a half

Twenty-four members of the force died during the year. It is not a little remarkable that this is the precise number of deaths each year for three years in succession. This number makes one death to one hundred and twenty-three cases of sickness The death ratio for the year was less than ten in a thousand, less than one per cent—the precise rate being 9797. When the nature of the duties, and the necessary exposure consequent thereupon are taken into consideration, this low death rate is remarkable, and vindicates the rigid method pursued in the physical examination of candidates for appointment

The Act of April 25, 1867 (Chapter 806) established a central office in the city of New York, to be known as "the Central Department of the Metropolitan Police," and in Brooklyn to be known as "the office of Inspector of Metropolitan Police" The Board of Police were likewise authorized to apply any surplus moneys which might remain from the funds contributed by the county of New York, to the Metropolitan Police Fund, towards procuring such Central Department of Metropolitan Police in the city of New York, the same course being adopted as regards Brooklyn

The quota of Policemen for the County of New York was placed at one thousand eight hundred, and such additional number as the Board of Police, from time to time, should determine, not, however, to exceed in the aggregate two thousand men, such increase to be made by unanimous vote of the Board. The Board might procure and use and employ such rowboats and steamboats as should be deemed necessary and proper. In rural districts they might employ horses and equipments The Board had official supervision over theatres and other places of amusement, keepers of boarding houses, pawnbrokers, junk dealers, venders, hawkers and peddlers, keepers of intelligence offices, auctioneers, hackney coaches, cabs, public porters, etc. All license fees, all fines imposed as above, were paid into the sinking fund of the city of New York. The Board was authorized to spend not more than one hundred thousand dollars out of excise moneys received during the year 1866, for rebuilding and repairing station houses

The Board of Police was required to keep a book of record, wherein were registered the name, number and description of all boats and vessels for which licenses were issued. The license fee to attend shipping and carrying passengers was ten dollars, and for gathering junk ten dollars. In lieu of any fee hitherto paid to the municipal authorities, for any business not specified in the Act, a license fee of three dollars was imposed The fee for boats to hire, oyster and fishing boats, pleasure boats or yachts, was one dollar each. The penalty for failing to comply with these regulations was, on conviction, one hundred dollars, or six months imprisonment, or both

JOHN G. BERGEN, one of the Commissioners of Metropolitan Police, died on the eighteenth of July, 1867. His death was a serious loss to his associates and to the public service. The sentiments of his associates, in relation to his excellent character, and his worth as a public officer and citizen, are expressed in the proceedings of the Board, on the twentieth of July, 1867, on which occasion, on the report of Commissioner Bosworth, a preamble and resolution were unanimously adopted, as follows:

Metropolitan Police Shield

Whereas, It has pleased Divine Providence to remove from the scenes of this world, on the eighteenth of July, 1867, the Hon John G. Bergen, who held, at the time of his death, the office of Police Commissioner of the Metropolitan Police District of the State of New York, and as the surviving members of the Police Board, his intimate official associates, desire to express their views of his virtues as a man, a citizen and public officer, as well as their grief for his loss; therefore they make the following brief record, and adopt the following resolutions:

The deceased was born on the fourth of December, 1814, and has passed his life and died near the place of his birth His parents were eminently worthy and respectable, and their virtues have been honored by the creditable and useful life of the deceased

The deceased was an honest man, of sound judgment and practical, discriminating intelligence He took an earnest interest in an upright, economical and efficient management of public affairs He kept these objects steadily in view in performing the duties of the various offices which he has been selected to fill, whether acting as Supervisor in his native county, or as one of its representatives in the legislature of this State, or as a member of the Board of Education of the city of Brooklyn, or as a member of the Police Board, or of the Board of Health, or of the Excise Board of this district, his efforts were alike directed to just results, and to efficiency and economy in producing them

For a little more than the last seven years of his life, he was a Police Commissioner; and during all that period was treasurer of the Police Board, except two years, when that office was worthily filled by the Hon Wm. McMurray. Whatever his confidence in the able assistants who kept the

Treasurer's books, he always had a vigilant oversight of the details of that office, and saw that everything was accurate

The deceased was one of the three Commissioners by whom the building known as the "Central Department of Metropolitan Police" was designed, erected and completed Its adaptation to the wants of the department, its materials and workmanship, and its moderate cost to the public, render it a continuing proof of the value of the public services of the deceased, and of those then officially associated with him

As a Police Commissioner the deceased endeavored to continually elevate and increase the efficiency of the Police force In appointing members of the force to office, it was his aim to reward merit, and to make this fact so apparent that it should operate at all times as an incentive to duty, upon all the members of the force.

In determining the punishment to be inflicted on Policemen who had violated the rules of the department, or had failed in some duty, he did not forget that they were men, and whenever satisfied that the error was an unintentional failure, he was lenient

In his personal and official intercourse with the other members of the Board he was frank and free, but courteous in expressing his opinions He gave to opposing views the consideration to which he thought them entitled. When, upon full reflection, and in light of all the information brought to bear upon any subject, he had formed clear convictions of what was right, he adhered to his convictions with unyielding tenacity * * *

His relations as a citizen and as a man were, in all respects, highly creditable, and he enjoyed and deserved the confidence of all classes and interests in the community

Resolved, That in the death of Hon. John G Bergen, this Board, the Police Department, and the public, have lost a valuable and efficient public officer, and the experience and tried abilities of a capable and honest man.

Resolved, That in the various public offices which he has held, as well as in those he filled at the time of his death, he has displayed uniformly a high sense of justice and regard for what was right, and a concientiousness and practical discretion in the performance of duty, well worthy of imitation, which endeared him to those who knew him most intimately, and which will command the respect and homage of all who shall hereafter become familiar with his useful though unostentatious career.

Resolved, That the surviving members of this Board sympathize with the widow, children and relatives of the deceased in their great bereavement, and with them, appreciate the many virtues of the deceased which have contributed largely to the happiness of the family circle, and the memory of which will soften the anguish of mourning hearts

Resolved, That this record and these resolutions be entered at length on the minutes of the Board, and that an engrossed copy, signed by the surviving members, be transmitted by the President of the Board, to the widow and family of the deceased.

The vacancy caused by the death of John G. Bergen was filled by the legislature, February 12, 1868, by the election of Matthew T Brennan The Board then consisted of the following members

Thomas C. Acton, Joseph S Bosworth, Benjamin F. Manierre, and Matthew T Brennan

The Act of May 4, 1868, empowered the Board of Police to appoint a Metropolitan Fire Marshal and Assistant, to inquire into the causes of fire to take testimony in such cases, and to report the same to the Board of Police. The Marshal or his Deputy could arrest persons in cases of suspected arson, and compel witnesses to appear. It was a part of the duty of the Marshal to enter and examine buildings.

Table showing the number of persons detained in the House of Detention for Witnesses, for a series of years:

Years	No. Persons	No. Days
1863	269	4,035
1864	282	4,230
1865	229	3,435
1866	410	6,150
1867	262	4,139
1868	264	3,852
Total,	1,716	25,841

Equal to seventy years, nine months, and twenty-one days.

Table of Arrests for a series of years in New York and Brooklyn:

	Year	Total	Total, both.	No. Patrolmen.	Average per officer
New York	1860	65809		1414	
Brooklyn	1860	15334	81143	198	50
New York	1861	71130		1806	
Brooklyn	1861	16552	87682	199	44
New York	1862	82072		1783	
Brooklyn	1862	19397	101469	213	51
New York	1863	61888		1711	
Brooklyn	1863	15324	77212	207	40
New York	1864	54751		1805	
Brooklyn	1864	14820	69571	227	34
New York	1865	68873		1806	
Brooklyn	1865	19482	88355	303	42
New York	1866	75630		1789	
Brooklyn	1866	21957	97587	309	40
New York	1867	80532		1848	
Brooklyn	1867	21078	101,610	336	
New York	1868	78451		1921	
Brooklyn	1868	18700	97,151	368	

The total number of arrests for nine years, from 1860 to 1868, both inclusive, is eight hundred and five thousand one hundred and forty-nine, being an average per year of eighty-nine thousand four hundred and sixty-one.

This year, 1868, the station house and prison accommodations for the use of the force were considerably improved. In the Tenth Precinct, the new station house and prison, Nos 87 and 89 Eldridge Street, were completed and occupied.

In the Eighth, Twenty-first and Thirty-second Precincts, the buildings were completed and occupied. The station house in the Fifth Precinct, Nos 19 and 21 Leonard Street, was in course of construction. A contract had been made to enlarge and repair the station house and prison of the Third Precinct. The Seventh Precinct had been renovated and made comfortable and commodious. The Twentieth Precinct Station House had contracted for the erection of a prison and lodgers' rooms in a separate building in the rear of the station house. A plot of ground 50x100 feet had been purchased on the south side of One Hundredth Street, between Ninth and Tenth Avenues, for a station house and prison for the Thirty-first Precinct. The Nineteenth Precinct had undergone extensive and thorough repairs and improvements. The First Precinct Station House consisted of two warehouses situated on New Street. The premises were leased in 1865, on a ten years' lease, at a rental of three thousand dollars per annum

The total time lost by sickness in the whole force for the year 1868, was twenty-six thousand six hundred and sixty-one days, of which fifteen thousand

Inspector Speight

four hundred and ninety-eight were paid, and eleven thousand one hundred and sixty-three unpaid, being one thousand six hundred and thirty-four days more than for the preceding year. The amount paid for lost sick time was fifty-one thousand and seventy-six dollars and thirty-five cents The time lost by sickness during the year was equivalent to the loss of one year's time for seventy-three men. The number of deaths was thirty-three, in a force numbering two thousand six hundred and sixty-eight, which is inclusive of Brooklyn, Richmond County and Westchester County.

The aggregate force of the Metropolitan Police, for the year ending November 1, 1868, was two thousand one hundred and fifty-nine, inclusive of thirty-four

Captains, one hundred and thirty-two Sergeants, and seventy-three Doormen. These were apportioned among thirty-two precincts, Court, Sanitary and Detective Squads, Special Detailed, and House of Detention.

By Act of the legislature, April 27, 1869, the term of each Commissioner of the Metropolitan Police was made to consist of eight years

By Act of May 12, 1869, the Police Commissioners of the Metropolitan District were entitled to receive a salary of three thousand dollars in addition to their regular salary.

The Board of Metropolitan Police was re-organized in 1869. Mr Thomas C. Acton, after nine years of honorable service, resigned, and on the same day, April 29th, Mr. Henry Smith was duly elected in his place. At a meeting of the Commissioners, held on the nineteenth day of May, 1869, Joseph S. Boswort'. was selected to act as President of the Board Commissioner Brennan tendered his resignation as Treasurer, which was accepted, to take effect on the fifth day of June following; whereupon Henry Smith was selected to be Treasurer of Police, on and after the date of Mr Brennan's resignation

During this year (1869) the Third Precinct Station House was put in thorough repair and enlarged; the Fifth Precinct was completed; a prison and lodging rooms had been added to the premises of the Twentieth Precinct Station House ; new first-class buildings were erected for station houses and prisons for the Twenty-ninth Precinct (Nos 137 and 139 West Thirtieth Street) and for the Thirty-first Precinct (West One Hundredth Street, between Ninth and Tenth Avenues) The new station houses of the Fifth, Twenty-ninth, and Thirty-first Precincts, in dimensions and arrangements, were a decided improvement upon those hitherto built They were designed to meet the future as well as the present wants of the precincts, and were planned with a view to afford to the Police force comfortable quarters, special regard having been paid to sanitary conditions In the Eleventh, Fourteenth, Twenty-third, and Twenty-eighth Precincts, the station house accommodations remained in the same condition as previously, notwithstanding the fact that better accommodations were much needed in those precincts Objection was made to the rooms occupied as a station house by the force of the Eleventh Precinct, that they were situated over a public market The station house of the Fourteenth was old and dilapidated and quite too small; the Twenty-third and Twenty-eighth were on leased premises The lease of the former expired on the first of May, 1870, and the latter on the first of May, 1871 None of these station houses furnished sufficient or appropriate accommodations. They were poorly ventilated, imperfectly drained, badly arranged, and insufficient for the business of the precincts. In the following precincts, the property occupied as station houses and prisons belonged to the city. The Second, Third, Fourth, Fifth, Sixth, Seventh, Eighth, Ninth, Tenth, Eleventh, Twelfth, Thirteenth, Fourteenth; Fifteenth, Sixteenth, Seventeenth, Eighteenth, Nineteenth, Twentieth, Twenty-first, Twenty-second, Twenty-sixth, Twenty-seventh; Twenty-ninth, Thirty-first and Thirty-second In the following precincts, the station houses were leased: First, Twenty-third, Twenty-fifth, Twenty-eighth, and Thirtieth

The Patrolmen numbered (in New York) two thousand, or one Patrolman to five hundred inhabitants; while in Brooklyn the number of Patrolmen was three hundred and sixty-eight, or about one Patrolman to one thousand inhabitants.

The length of open streets and piers in New York demanding patrol service was over four hundred and fifty miles, and in Brooklyn at least three hundred and fifty miles. In New York, the average length of night posts was sixty-three one-hundredths of a mile, and day tours over a mile and a quarter; while in Brooklyn the average length of night posts was two and fifty-four one-hundredth miles, and day posts five and eight one-hundredth miles. In each city there were posts of even greater length. Owing to necessary concentration of the force in the more

President of the Board of Surgeons, Metropolitan Police.

densely populated districts of both cities, where a turbulent population abounded, a portion of the night posts were of such extent that the Policeman's call could not be heard from the centre to the extremes of the posts; while in Brooklyn the Patrolmen were so far apart that they were not within supporting distance of each other.

It appears, by the report of the Board of Surgeons, that the amount of time lost by sickness and injuries in the whole force for the year was twenty-two thousand seven hundred and sixty-four days. Payment of salary was allowed for thirteen thousand one hundred and sixteen and three-quarter days; payment of salary was disallowed for nine thousand six hundred and forty-seven and one-quarter days, equal to twenty-two thousand seven hundred and sixty-four days. Though the number of the Police force was greater than in the preceding year, the amount of time lost by sickness was considerably less. In 1868, the sick time was 2 77 per cent. of the whole time. In 1869, it was 2 3 per cent. of the whole time. In 1868 the total amount paid for sick time was fifty-one thousand and seventy-six dollars and thirty-five cents. In 1869, the total amount was forty-three thousand one hundred and twenty-four dollars and forty-six cents Difference in favor of 1869 seven thousand nine hundred and fifty-one dollars and eighty-nine cents. Nevertheless, this was a serious item in the public expenditure, and represented a sum more than equal to the combined salary of thirty-five Patrolmen The reduction in the proportion of sick time was attributed by the Board in some degree, by the members who were broken down in health being induced to resign and accept pensions. The improved sanitary condition of the station houses, also, it is believed, contributed to improve the health of the force

Besides the regular force, Patrolmen were assigned to do duty in special departments or bureaus.

During the year ending October 31, 1869, the value of lost or stolen property delivered to owners at the several precincts, and by the Detective and Court Squads, was estimated and valued by the owners thereof at one million seven hundred and forty-three thousand seven hundred and six dollars and eighty-four cents The value of like property delivered to owners, for the same period, from the Property Clerk's office, was one million, two thousand one hundred and eighty-seven dollars and eighty-one cents. The total proceeds of unclaimed property, sold in pursuance of law, was three thousand two hundred and fifty-nine dollars and ninety cents; unclaimed cash, one thousand two hundred and sixty-six dollars and fifty-five cents; total value, two millions seven hundred and fifty thousand four hundred and twenty-one dollars and ten cents; returned to owners, two millions seven hundred and forty-five thousand eight hundred and ninety-four dollars and sixty-five cents; total loss to owners, four thousand five hundred and twenty-six dollars and forty-five cents.

The Sanitary Company had examined during the year three thousand five hundred and three stationary steam boilers, and tested by hydrostatic pressure three thousand and thirty-five. During the year eight hundred and thirty-five persons applied for certificates to authorize them to take charge of boilers or engines Of that number, after examination, four hundred and forty-four were granted certificates, and three hundred and ninety-one denied, as not possessing the requisite degree of skill.

In nine years, from 1861 to 1869 inclusive, the number of poor and unfortunate persons who had applied for, and been furnished lodgings at the station houses had been eight hundred and eighty thousand one hundred and sixty one, making an average of ninty-seven thousand seven hundred and ninety-six per year

During the same space of time (1861 to 1869 inclusive), the aggregate number of lost children taken charge of by the Police, and restored to parents or otherwise disposed of, was seventy-three thousand and eighty-one, to which may be added seven hundred and seventy-nine foundlings. The annual average for the nine years was eight thousand one hundred and twenty.

The total number of arrests from 1860 to 1869 inclusive was eight hundred and ninety-eight thousand four hundred and eighty-nine. The average number per year was eighty-nine thousand eight hundred and forty-eight. The largest number of arrests, one hundred and three thousand two hundred and sixty-nine, occurred in 1867. The smallest, sixty-nine thousand five hundred and seventy-one, in 1864. The difference between the highest and lowest number is thirty-three thousand six hundred and ninety-eight.

This is a noteworthy showing, for during 1864—that being the year of the smallest number of arrests, the year in which the armies of the Nation, in the field, were largest; and the largest number of arrests occurred in 1867, after the armies had been fully disbanded. Since the last-named year the number of arrests had decreased

The aggregate force of the Metropolitan Police District, on the first day of November, 1869, was. Captains, thirty-four; Sergeants, one hundred and thirty-one; Patrolmen, one thousand nine hundred and ninety-four; Doormen, seventy-three. Total, two thousand two hundred and thirty-two. This is inclusive of the following: Court Squad, forty, Sanitary Squad, sixty-three; Detective Squad, twenty; Special Detailed, twenty-two; House of Detention, four The number of precincts was thirty-two, their designation being by number The number of men authorized by law was:

New York, two thousand; Brooklyn, three hundred and sixty-eight; Richmond County, twenty-six; Yonkers, fourteen; West Farms, eight Total, two thousand four hundred and sixteen.

When the organization of the force was established with a Superintendent and four Inspectors, the number of Patrolmen was limited to one thousand six hundred men. Since then, from time to time, the force was increased more than fifty per cent, by adding eight hundred and sixteen Patrolmen, and a proportionate number of Captains, Sergeants, and Doormen

The aggregate number of buildings found open and unoccupied, secured by the Police, for a series of nine years, from 1861 to 1869, both inclusive, was forty thousand six hundred and thirty-nine.

Number of arrests for the year ending October 31, 1867: males, seventy-six thousand five hundred and forty-nine, females, twenty-six thousand seven hundred and twenty. Total, one hundred and three thousand two hundred and sixty-nine.

It has been asserted that the Metropolitan Police system was the best ever devised, and produced more satisfactory results than any of its predecessors This, after all, is not very great praise, as, properly speaking, New York previously had had no Police force worthy of the name; all being lacking in that efficiency and *esprit du corps* which spring from descipline, organization and the soldierly instinct produced by the wearing of a uniform. The force, however, was being educated in the practical school of a Policeman, and the results were beginning to be felt and appreciated In all the satisfactory characteristics named, the Metropolitan Police were undoubtedly superior to their predecessors. This, under the circumstances, was to be expected, as "progress" was the watchword, and Police reforms were being inaugurated with all the despatch commensurate with sound judgment, ripened by experience.

The number of offences against the person for the year ending on October 31, 1867, was.

Offences.	Males	Females	Total
Assault	463	86	549
Assault and battery	8,157	1,917	10,074
Assault, felonious	639	69	708
Abandonment	453	7	460
Attachment	80	5	85
Bastardy	170	—	170
Bigamy	14	5	19
Contempt of court	12	4	16
Disorderly conduct	15,018	8,153	23,161
Escaped prisoners	99	2	101
Insanity	467	183	650
Intoxication	17,969	6,143	24,112
Intoxication and disorderly conduct	7,013	3,582	10,595
Kidnapping	14	4	18
Murder	65	8	73
Suspicious persons	1,873	407	2,280
Seduction	23	—	23
Truancy	2,303	2,516	4,819
Total	55,268	23,168	78,436

The number of offences against property for the year ending on October 31, 1867, was.

	Males	Females	Total.
Arson	39	2	41
Burglary	556	12	568
Fraud	658	25	683
Forgery	132	6	138
Gambling	1,187	4	1,191
Keeping disorderly house	220	159	379
Larceny, grand	1,998	561	2,559
Larceny, petty	4,552	1,464	6,016
Mutiny	21	—	21
Malicious Mischief	1,249	160	1,409
Offences against U. S Government	189	5	194
Pickpockets	304	69	373
Perjury	12	8	20
Passing bad money	77	5	82
Receiving stolen goods	248	34	282
Robbery	171	6	177
Violation of Corporation ordinances	4,155	414	4,569
Violation of State laws	503	29	532
Violation of Health laws	1,538	417	1,955
Violation of Excise laws	3,235	166	3,401
Violation of the Election laws	138	—	138
Violation of the Boat laws	69	—	63
Witnesses	36	6	42
	21,281	3,552	24,833

Convictions, acquittals and discharges by the Court of Special Sessions, in and for the City and County of New York, from the year 1840 to 1867 inclusive.

Convictions, etc.	1840	1841	1842	1843	1844	1845	1846	1847	1848	1849	1850	1851	1852	1853
Conv. petit larc'y	526	666	744	907	896	991	977		1064	1180	1419	1453	1475	1415
Acq, "	97	78	138	142	148	193	220	173	258	261	219	187	214	179
Conv ass't & bat'y	226	296	287	395	551	615	508	334	430	558	837	662	978	1230
Acq, "	32	30	33	54	36	90	87	48	52	59	76	43	51	67
Discharges	488	396	375	537	838	1158	1109	697	672	988	1382	1194	1107	1120
Totals	1369	1466	1577	2032	1519	3047	2922	2352	2502	2966	3933	3539	3884	3944
No of trials in Spec Sessions	839	1001	1119	1311	1495	1741	1651	1309	1635	1837	2218	2079	2405	2570
Sent. to Co. pris	508	682	737	987	1058	1128	1075	981	1063	1120	1402	1179	1254	2242
Sent to H of R	28	67	63	56	55	65	56	51	52	71	112	94	97	119

Convictions, etc	1854	1855	1856	1857	1858	1859	1860	1861	1862	1863	1864	1865	1866	1867
Conv petit larc'y	1411	2047	1788	2041	1919	1953	2082	1747	1397	1512	1411	1695	2184	1824
Acq, "	108	190	208	273	317	289	365	382	256	279	263	323	345	252
Discharges					536	481	376	361	354	586	454	584	553	501
Con, ass't & bat'y	1152	929	986	1589	1697	1699	1919	1606	1475	1191	1067	1239	1110	957
Acq, "	66	84	84	284	344	349	392	285	259	168	166	186	202	185
Discharges	1184	1064	1459	1627	1784	1849	1623	1541	1330	1107	885	1051	893	811
Other misdem'rs		28	25	101	189	158	198	139	186	113	71	96	274	014
Acquittals		6	4	40	50	54	60	53	70	44	31	39	67	117
Discharges					101	125	89	75	98	60	44	27	91	78
Totals	3921	435'	4449	5825	6748	6957	7005	6189	5425	5057	4392	5508	5339	5539
No. of trials in Spec. Sessions	1528	1492	2803	3752	4476	4502	4917	4112	3639	3304	3009	3846	4182	80..
Sent to Co. pris	1159	1528	1426	1824	2061	1012	2054	2231	1720	1728	1220	1697	1678	1599
Sent to H. of R	77	69	4.	195	134	129	138	136	111	168	170	260	270	224
Tried					569	723	824	1045	1041	836	738	973	997	1046

Salaries of Department Officers and Clerks:

1	President of the Board of Police	$5,500
1	Treasurer of the Board of Police	5,500
2	Commissioners of Police, each	5,000
1	Chief Clerk	5,000
1	First Deputy Clerk	2,500
10	Deputy Clerks, each	1,500
1	Treasurer's Bookkeeper	2,500
4	President's Sec'y, Clerks of Supt. and Inspectors, each	1,500
1	Property Clerk	2,000
1	Stenographer	1,600
1	Inspector of Boats	2,000
1	Fire Marshal	5,000
1	Assistant Fire Marshal	2,500

Salaries of Officers and Members of the Force:

1	Superintendent	$7,500
4	Inspectors, each	3,500
18	Surgeons, each	2,250
45	Captains, each	2,000
181	Sergeants, each	1,600
2,321	Patrolmen, each	1,200
96	Doormen, each	900
1	Superintendent Police Telegraph	1,800
6	Telegraph Operators, each	1,500
1	Telegraph Lineman	1,200

OUR POLICE PROTECTORS.

Total Police Force, two thousand six hundred and seventy-four; Total Special Police, one hundred and fifty-eight. Grand total of all branches, two thousand eight hundred and sixty.

Location of Station Houses and names of Captains.

First Precinct, 54 New Street. Captain, Ira S Garland.
Second Precinct, 49 Beekman Street. Captain, Morris De Camp.
Third Precinct, 160 Chambers Street. Captain, Charles Ulman
Fourth Precinct, 9 Oak Street. Captain, Anthony J. Allaire.
Fifth Precinct, 49 Leonard Street. Captain, Jeremiah Petty.
Sixth Precinct, 9 Franklin Street Captain, John Jourdan.
Seventh Precinct, 247 Madison Street. Captain, Jacob B Warlow.
Eighth Precinct, 128 Prince Street Captain, Nathaniel R. Mills.
Ninth Precinct, 94 Charles Street. Captain, George Washburne
Tenth Precinct, Eldridge Street near Broome. Captain, John J. Ward.
Eleventh Precinct, Union Market. Captain, John F. Dickson.
Twelfth Precinct, One Hundred and Twenty-sixth Street, near Third Avenue Captain, James Z. Bogart
Thirteenth Precinct, Attorney Street, near Delancey. Captain, Theron R. Bennett.
Fourteenth Precinct, 53 Spring Street. Captain, Edward Walsh
Fifteenth Precinct, 221 Mercer Street Captain, Henry Hedden
Sixteenth Precinct, 230 W. Twentieth Street. Captain, John J Williamson
Seventeenth Precinct, 75 First Avenue. Captain, John J. Mount
Eighteenth Precinct, 163 E. Twenty-second Street. Captain, John Cameron.
Nineteenth Precinct, 118 E. Fifty-ninth Street. Captain, Henry Hutchings.
Twentieth Precinct, 352 W. Thirty-fifth Street. Captain, Charles W. Caffrey.
Twenty-first Precinct, 120 E. Thirty-fifth Street. Captain, Thomas Thorne.
Twenty-second Precinct, 545 W. Forty-seventh Street. Captain, Johannes C. Slott.
Twenty-third Precinct, Eighty-sixth Street, corner Fourth Avenue. Captain, Jedediah W. Hartt.
Twenty-fourth Precinct, Police Steamboat. Captain, James Todd
Twenty-fifth Precinct, 300 Mulberry Street Captain, Theron S. Copeland.
Twenty-sixth Precinct, City Hall, basement. Captain, James Greer
Twenty-seventh Precinct, 99 Liberty Street. Captain, Francis C. Speight.
Twenty-eighth Precinct, 550 Greenwich Street. Captain, Thomas Steers.
Twenty-ninth Precinct, 34 E Twenty-ninth Street. Acting Captain, Henry Burden.
Thirtieth Precinct, Manhattanville Captain, Thaddeus Davis
Thirty-first Precinct, Broadway, near W Eighty-sixth Street. Captain, John Helme
Thirty-second Precinct, One Hundred and Fifty-second Street, corner Tenth Avenue. Captain, Alanson S Wilson.
Sanitary Squad, Captain, Bowen G. Lord

Captains, thirty-four; Sergeants, one hundred and thirty-two; Patrolmen, one thousand nine hundred and twenty-one; Doormen, seventy-three. Total, 2,159

238　　　　　　*OUR POLICE PROTECTORS.*

Police and Civil Justices' Districts.
  First District—First, Second, Third and Fifth Wards
  Second District—Fourth, Sixth and Fourteenth Wards
  Third District—Eighth and Ninth Wards.
  Fourth District—Tenth, Fifteenth and Seventeenth Wards
  Fifth District—Seventh, Eleventh and Thirteenth Wards.
  Sixth District—Eighteenth and Twenty-first Wards
  Seventh District—Nineteenth and Twenty-second Wards
  Eighth District—Sixteenth and Twentieth Wards.
  Ninth District—Twelfth Ward.

The Police force for the year ending 1869 consisted of the following Captains, thirty-four, Sergeants, one hundred and thirty-one; Patrolmen, one thou-

Juvenile Asylum

sand nine hundred and ninety-five, Doormen, seventy. Total, two thousand two hundred and thirty

Amount of money lost, one million five hundred and twenty-one thousand nine hundred and forty dollars and eighty cents. Amount recovered, one million one hundred and thirty-seven thousand and twenty-eight dollars and sixty-five cents Total loss, three hundred and eighty-four thousand nine hundred and twelve dollars and three cents Amount of money taken from lodgers, and restored to them, five hundred and forty-five thousand and fifty-six dollars and eighty-seven cents.

Lost children: males, three thousand seven hundred and twenty-five; females, two thousand one hundred and ninety-eight Total, five thousand nine hundred and twenty-three

Lodgers accommodated	135,591
Buildings found open and secured	4,534
Accidents reported and persons assisted	4,855
Fires reported	1,037
Animals found astray, and restored to their owners	767

The Police Department had now entered upon another era of re-organization and development. On April 5, 1870, there was passed an Act to re-organize the local government of the city of New York. This charter is commonly known as the "Tweed Charter." By it, the Police Board was made to consist of four Commissioners, who were appointed for the respective terms of eight, seven, six, and five years. The Police Department consisted of a Superintendent, three Inspectors, Captains, Sergeants, Patrolmen, Doormen, and as many Surgeons, clerks and employees as the Board of Police, from time to time, might determine. Members were removable only upon written charges, (except the Superintendent). No person to be appointed who was not a citizen, who could not read and write understandingly the English language, and who did not reside in the State. In case of riot, etc., Special Patrolmen might be appointed to serve without pay. No member could resign without having received the consent of the Board, under penalty of forfeiting his salary. Unexplained absence for five days was deemed and held to be equivalent to a resignation. The Common Council was directed to provide office and business accommodations, station houses, etc., for the use of the Police force. The Board of Police was authorized to issue subpoenas for witnesses upon any proceedings sanctioned by its rules and regulations. All persons holding office under the department were exempt from jury duty and arrest. The Common Council was ordered to provide accommodations for the detention of witnesses; no witness to be detained longer than ten days. The Board of Police, on conviction for neglect of duty, violation of rules, disobedience of orders, incapacity, or absence without leave, might punish by reprimand, fine, withholding pay, or dismiss from the force. All such fines were paid to the Chamberlain for account of the Police Life Insurance Fund. The department was instructed to detail two Policemen to each polling place. The Board of Police annually, on or before the first of December, were called upon to make the estimates necessary for the conduct of the Board of Police for the next ensuing year. The Mayor, Comptroller, and President of the Board of Police, on or before December 15, met, and considered and revised said estimates, their action being binding. The Board of Supervisors caused the amount of such estimates to be raised by tax.

Mayor Hall, under the foregoing chapter, appointed the following as Police Commissioners: Henry Smith, Joseph S. Bosworth, Matthew T. Brennan, Benjamin F. Manierre.

The Police Department, in the name of its President and Treasurer, by Act of the legislature (April 26, 1870) was authorized to bring an action at law against the authorities of Richmond County to compel the payment of its share of the Police expenses.

The Board was empowered to increase the Patrolmen, such increase not to exceed one hundred in addition to the number hitherto allowed by law. The Treasurer was to give bonds in two sureties of twenty thousand dollars each. He was to receive fifteen hundred dollars in addition to the amount provided by law. The Board appointed a Fire Marshal and clerks. A summary of the remainder of the Act may be noted as follows. Special Patrolmen might be appointed in case of riot, etc., and military assistance might be demanded. Policemen were required to convey arrested offenders to the nearest Magistrate, the Board to prevent the undue detention of witnesses; all witnesses, in default of bail, to be committed to the House of Detention

John Jourdan, who was appointed Superintendent on April 11, 1870, died October 17 of the same year. James J. Kelso was thereupon appointed Superintendent.

Upon the death of Superintendent Jourdan, the Board of Police adopted unanimously (among others) the following resolutions.

"*Resolved*, That by the death of John Jourdan, Superintendent of Police in the Police Department of the city of New York, the department and the public have sustained a great and irreparable loss. He entered upon Police service as a Patrolman in 1855, and, excepting a brief period, has been continuously a member of the successive Police organizations until his death. He was appointed a Sergeant on the twenty-fourth of April, 1860, and a Captain on the thirty-first of January, 1863, and Superintendent on the eleventh of April, 1870.

"He was always active and vigilant in the performance of duty He felt a warm interest in the efficiency and good character of the entire Police force, and laudably exerted himself to make the men and officers in his precinct a well-instructed and well-disciplined body He felt an honest pride in a proper discharge of Police duties by his officers and men, as well as in the performance of his own He was a model Police Captain. He knew every suspicious character in his precinct, his associates, and places of resort. His capacity as a detective officer was not surpassed, and probably not equaled, by that of any other member of the force Never compromising with criminals, persistent and untiring in his efforts to secure their arrest and punishment, yet he was popular, and enjoyed unlimited general confidence He always observed good faith, and his whole official life has been characterized by a uniform purpose to be right and fearless in the performance of duty. He was as sensitive as sensible, and ever frowned upon the suggestion that anything should be done or suffered to be done which, in his judgment, would prejudice the public weal or the proper discipline of the force

"As Superintendent, he undertook more than any man of his nervous temperament can endure. Under the pressure of his arduous and varied duties, and exhausting anxieties which he could not prevent or dispel, his health soon gave way, and the result is his premature death, and the loss to the department and the public of his marked abilities and large and valuable experience.

"*Resolved*, That in his death each member of the Board and of the Police force has lost an honest and generous friend, the department an invaluable officer, and the community at large an efficient and experienced Police protector"

At the time the Act of April 5, 1870, " To re-organize the Local Government of the City of New York," went into effect, every person connected with the Metropolitan Police Department (with some few exceptions) was transferred by that Act to the Police Department created by it, and continued in the office which he held at the time of such transfer On the eleventh of April the Board was organized by the election of Joseph S Bosworth as President, Matthew T. Brennan as Treasurer, and the appointment of Seth C. Hawley as Chief Clerk. Mr Brennan resigned his office on the seventh day of October, 1870, and Henry Smith was thereupon elected Treasurer Thomas J Barr was appointed to fill the vacancy.

The Police force, in April, 1870, consisted of one Superintendent, three

John Jourdan

Inspectors, thirty-five Captains, one hundred and thirty-six Sergeants, eighty-three Roundsmen, one thousand nine hundred and ninety-two Patrolmen, and seventy-five Doormen. Total, 2,325.

Of the Patrolmen, one thousand seven hundred and thirty-nine were assigned to patrol duty, and two hundred and fifty-three to special duty. Of these, two hundred and fifty-three, twenty-nine were specially detailed on the application of corporations and individuals, who paid for their services, as provided by law, the statutory compensation.

On the eleventh of April, 1870, John A. Kennedy, who had been Superintendent of the Metropolitan Police from the twenty-third day of May, 1860, until he was transferred to the Police Department by the Act of April 5, 1870,

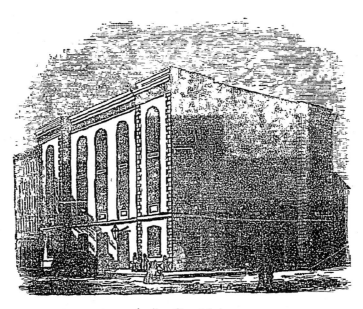

Ludlow Street Jail.

resigned his office. The vacancy created thereby was filled by appointing as Superintendent John Jourdan, then Captain of the Sixth Precinct. Superintendent Jourdan died on the tenth of October, 1870. On the seventeenth day of October, James J. Kelso, Captain of the Detective force, was appointed Superintendent of Police.

The new Superintendent, among numerous expressions of good wishes, was presented with the following set of resolutions:

We, the Detective force of the Police Department of the city of New York, while heartily joining in the general appreciation of the well-merited appointment of our former official Chief, James J. Kelso, to the more elevated and responsible office of Superintendent of Police, while approving the judiciousness of the selection, cannot refrain from expressing our sense of individual loss in the severence of ties of long association in the most delicate and arduous

branch of the public service. The duties of this service are most exacting, requiring the exercise of vigilance that knows no rest, patience to overcome obstacles, intuitive perception of character, ready and fearless action in embarrassing situations, these qualities, combined with great natural shrewdness, intensified by experience, being possessed by our late Chief in a remarkable degree, that insured success. Zealous and faithful to his trust, he enforced strict discipline, always acting in a kindly and gentle manner, impressed by the force of his own example, his high sense of honor commanded respect, and greatly added to the efficiency of the department. Although by his transfer to a higher position our late association no longer exists, it is still a source of gratification to feel that we still remain under his intelligent supervision, and that we shall be to some extent guided by his counsel. Assured that his new duties will be performed in a manner which will inspire confidence to the whole community, we wish him the enjoyment of every prosperity that should attend the faithful discharge of duty.
C. B. McDOUGAL, *Chairman.*

House of Refuge, Randall's Island.

James J. Kelso joined the force in June, 1858, and was detailed for duty as Patrolman at the then Headquarters, at the corner of Broome and Crosby Streets.

The New York County Jail (better known as Ludlow Street Jail) is situated at the corner of Ludlow Street and Essex Market Place, and was first occupied in June, 1862, taking the place of the noted Eldridge Street Jail. It is built of Philadelphia brick, ornamented with New Jersey freestone trimmings. The building is built in the form of an L, ninety feet on each street, forty feet deep, and about sixty-five feet high, leaving an angle of about fifty feet square, surrounded by a high wall, for a yard in which the prisoners are permitted to take their daily exercise. The jail contains eighty-seven cells. For light and ventilation it is probably not surpassed by any prison in the United States. The class of prisoners confined herein consists principally of all arrests and commitments upon civil process, with the few arrests made by the United States Marshal for this district.

Ludlow Street Jail has become notorious by the escape of William M Tweed from the custody of the Sheriff, while out driving in company with the Warden of the jail and one of the Keepers

The Society for the Reformation of Juvenile Delinquents (House of Refuge, Randall's Island), chartered in 1824, to care for and reform juvenile offenders, etc, was the first in the country organized for such a purpose The first House of Refuge, under the provisions of the Act of Incorporation, was opened January 1, 1825, in the building previously occupied as a United States Arsenal, located on what is now known as Madison Square. At the opening, the inmates were four boys and six girls, committed by the Police Magistrates of the city; the provisions of the law being confined to the city and county of New York Subsequent amendments extended to all parts of the State, until 1849, when the Western House of Refuge was established at Rochester In 1839 the institution was removed to the foot of Twenty-third Street, East River, and occupied the buildings formerly used as the fever hospital, it having outgrown the accommodations on Madison Square. In 1854, the constantly increasing number of inmates compelled the managers to move it to Randall's Island

The buildings are of brick, and are erected in the Italian style The two principal structures front the river, and form a facade nearly a thousand feet in length The larger of the two buildings is for the accommodation of the boys' department, the other for the girls'. Other buildings are located in the rear of these, and are inclosed by a stone wall twenty feet high.

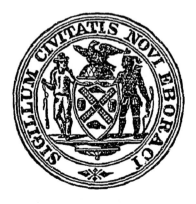

CHAPTER XII.

1871 to 1876.

CLUBS MORE TRUSTWORTHY THAN LEADEN BALLS.

ORANGE RIOTS.—POLICE AND MILITARY CALLED OUT—THE STREETS OF NEW YORK AGAIN THE SCENE OF RIOT AND BLOODSHED.—THE MILITIA, UNAUTHORIZED, FIRE UPON THE MOB.—ELEVEN KILLED AND THIRTY WOUNDED.—CLEANING OF THE STREETS CHARGED TO THE BOARD OF POLICE—COMPLETION OF THE BUILDING OF THE HOUSE OF DETENTION.—TABLES OF ARRESTS.—TIME LOST TO THE DEPARMENT BY REASON OF SICKNESS.—PROPERTY CLERK'S RETURNS—PRESENTATION OF THE FLAG OF HONOR—AN ACT TO RE-ORGANIZE THE LOCAL GOVERNMENT OF NEW YORK.—THE BOARD OF POLICE TO CONSIST OF FIVE MEMBERS—A REVISED MANUAL ISSUED TO THE FORCE—DUTIES OF THE SEVERAL HEADS OF THE DEPARTMENT AND OF THE FORCE GENERALLY.—REGULATION UNIFORMS.—QUALIFICATIONS FOR APPOINTMENT AS A PATROLMAN.—MEASURES OF ECONOMY INTRODUCED.—BOARD OF SURGEONS.—POLICE SALARIES—THE BOARD MADE TO CONSIST OF FOUR MEMBERS—CHANGES IN THE BOARD.

ONE would suppose that the terrible events narrated in the chapters devoted to a sketch of the draft riots would have so impressed themselves on the hearts and memory of the present generation that anything like their recurrence would be an impossibility. Yet eight years later the streets of New York were again alive with riotous mobs, and the Police and military were again called out to disperse them. This was on the twelfth of July, 1871. On that day the Orange societies of this and neighboring cities and towns had assembled to hold a parade. As might have been expected, scenes of great disorder followed, and, owing to the hasty action of the military, several innocent persons lost their lives by being shot down.

This time the angry passions of the mob were aroused, not by any sense of injuries inflicted, or about to be inflicted, by the general or local government, the trouble was not occasioned by any dread of hunger, persecution, or party politics. It was a revival of a quarrel of two hundred years standing, which, year by year, had increased in bitterness, the contending forces being arrayed beneath the Orange and the Green.

King James II was the reigning and lawful king of Great Britain and Ireland when driven from his throne by William of Nassau, Prince of Orange, the decisive battle having been fought on the banks of the river Boyne, in Ireland. William of Orange ascended the throne, and King James went into exile. The latter was a Catholic monarch and the former professed the Protestant faith. To commemorate this victory, Ulster Protestants in 1795 formed a religio-politico society. Both their religion and their politics were of a very pronounced type. They were, although numerically a handful, compared with the Catholic population, strong in the protection of the government, and their fanaticism and bigotry, from generation to generation, have kept ablaze in the north of Ireland, the fires of religious intolerance and political persecution. Neither has time diminished nor age decayed the intensity of these national prejudices, nor eradicated the memory of those party strifes. The Orange and the Green still maintain the irrepressible conflict, each side being tenacious of its principles and jealous of its "rights."

When, then, the Orange anniversary came round, the Orange societies turned out in great force, protected by the military and Police. Acting upon instructions recived from Mayor Hall, Superintendent Kelso, on the day before, had issued an order forbidding the parade. This, as the result proved, was but playing unintentionally into the hands of the Orangemen, as it aroused public opinion in their favor, and Governor Hoffman hastened from Albany and issued a proclamation countermanding Mayor Hall's order, and giving permission to the Orangemen to parade, promising at the same time that a Police and military escort would be furnished them. Large crowds of people congregated at several points throughout the city, who, with few exceptions, were drawn thither out of idle, but reprehensible curiosity, to see the parade and know what was to come out of it. True, it was not a sympathizing, much less a friendly mob, there being few among them who would not cheerfully lend their personal assistance in wiping the thoroughfares with the bodies of the paraders.

The line of march resolved upon was down Eighth Avenue to Twenty-third Street, and up that thoroughfare to Fifth Avenue, to Fourteenth Street, to Union Square, and down Fourth Avenue to Cooper Institute, where the procession was to break up. Eighth Avenue, in the vicinity of Lamartine Hall, where the Orange societies were forming in line, was jammed with an excited throng. The Police advanced and swept the street, from Thirtieth to Twenty-eighth Street, the Police forming several deep, and only leaving room enough for the cars to pass.

Police Headquarters, in the meantime, had assumed the air and bustle that pervaded the place during the week of the draft riots. Commissioners Manierre, Smith, and Barr were in their offices; General Shaler and staff were located in the Fire Marshal's office, while squads of soldiers and Policemen kept arriving and departing. The place presented a decidedly warlike appearance. Information was being constantly received that bands of rioters were parading certain sections of the city, making ready to join battle with the Orangemen. Inspector Jameson, with two hundred and fifty Policemen, was dispatched in stages to Forty-seventh Street and Eighth Avenue; Captain Allaire, of the Seventh Precinct, was hurried off with fifty men to protect Harper's Building in Franklin Square, which, it was rumored, was to be attacked by the rioters; five hundred Policemen were massed in Eighth Avenue; Captain Mount, with a hundred Policemen, was detailed to look after a gang of rioters who had made an attack on the Armory, at No 19 Avenue A, in the hopes of securing arms; Drill Captain Copeland was given five companies with which to seize Hibernia Hall, where he charged and dispersed the crowd

The Orange headquarters were, however, the focal point of excitement, to which converged knots of hotblooded men and women (for, as usual on such occasions, the weaker sex was well represented), and the maledictions that were breathed on the heads of the Orange societies were both loud and deep The Orangemen formed in line in Twenty-ninth Street, near Eighth Avenue A strong body of Police was massed in advance Next came the Ninth Regiment, followed at a short interval by the Sixth Regiment, while a body of Police succeeded them. Nothing of moment happened until the head of the procession reached Twenty-sixth Street, when some little disorder was occasioned by an attempt of the Police to clear the sidewalks A halt was ordered at Twenty-fourth Street. A shot was fired from a window, and in an instant the Eighty-fourth Regiment had the spot covered with their muskets, when, without waiting for orders, they discharged a volley, the Sixth and Ninth Regiments emulating the example of the Eighty-fourth. The next instant, as the smoke cleared off, eleven corpses were seen stretched on the sidewalk, with terrified men, women, and children, overturning and trampling on each other in maddened excitement to get out of the way of the slaughter. "A pause of a few minutes now followed," says Headley in his Sketches of the Great Riots, "while the troops reloaded their guns A new attack was momentarily expected, and no one moved from the ranks to succor the wounded or lift up the dead Here a dead woman lay across a dead man; there a man, streaming with blood, was creeping painfully up a doorstep, while crouching, bleeding forms appeared in every direction Women from the windows looked down on the ghastly spectacle, gesticulating wildly The Police now cleared the avenue and side streets, when the dead and wounded were attended to, and the order to move on was given. General Varian, indignant at the conduct of the Eighty-fourth in firing first without orders, sent it to the rear, and replaced it on the flank of the Orangemen with a portion of the Ninth. The procession, as it now resumed its march, and moved through Twenty-fourth Street, was a sad and mournful one * *

* * Two of the Police and military were killed, and twenty-four wounded, all, however, from the reckless discharge of the muskets of the military; while of the rioters thirty-one were killed, and sixty-seven wounded, making in all one hundred and twenty-eight victims."

The procession resumed its march and moved through Twenty-fourth Street The windows along the route of the procession were filled with spectators, and crowds lined the sidewalks, but all were silent and serious. No more trouble took place and the Cooper Intitute was reached and the procession disbanded.

Much indignation was expressed at the action of the troops for firing without waiting for orders, and firing so wildly as to wound and kill some of their own men

The scenes at Bellevue Hospital, where the dead and wounded were taken, were of a most distressing character. The ambulances kept discharging their bloody loads at the doors, and groans of distress and shrieks of pain filled the

air Long rows of cots filled with mangled forms, were stretched on every side, while the surgeons were kept constantly employed dressing the wounds of the injured. The dead lay in the morgue

Thus were the streets of New York again baptized with citizens' blood.

TABLE SHOWING LOCATION AND CONDITION OF STATION HOUSES.

Precincts	LOCATION OF STATION HOUSES	OWNER	CONDITION.	REMARKS
1	Nos 52 and 54 New Street	John J Cisco	Fair	Leased for ten years, from May 1, 1865, at $8,000 per year
2	No 49 Beekman Street	City	Good	Recently thoroughly repaired, and as well adapted as the insufficient dimensions will permit.
3	No 160 Chambers Street.	City	Good	Not sufficiently capacious
4	No 9 Oak Street	City	First class	A new and commodious station house has just been completed, and will be occupied on the tenth April inst.
5	Nos 19 and 21 Leonard Street	City	Good	New.
6	No 9 Franklin Street	City	Bad	Condemned by Superintendent of Unsafe Buildings, has been temporarily repaired, a new building in a more healthy location is imperatively needed.
7	No. 247 Madison Street	City	Good	
8	Corner Prince and Wooster Streets.	City	Good	
9	No. 94 Charles Street	City	Good	Too small for purposes required
10	Nos 87 and 89 Eldridge Street	City	Good	Building new.
11	Union Market	City		Accommodations insufficient and inappropriate, a new station house is required for the comfort and health of the force.
12	One Hundred and Twenty-fifth Street, bet. Third and Fourth Avenues.	City	First class	New.
13	Corner Attorney and Delancey Streets	City	Fair	Small and indifferent accommodations
14	No 53 Spring Street.	City		A new station house for this precinct, and a house for detention of witnesses, are now in process of erection at Nos. 201, 203, 205, and 207 Mulberry Street.
15	No 221 Mercer Street	City	Good	Building good, and in good order.
16	No 230 West Twentieth Street	City	Good	Building small, recently refitted
17	Corner First Avenue and Fifth Street.	City	Good	Indifferent accommodations for the wants of the precinct
18	No. 327 East Twenty-second Street	City	Good	Rebuilt in 1864
19	No 220 East Fifty-ninth Street	City	Bad	New house imperatively needed.
20	No 352 West Thirty-fifth Street	City	First class	New.
21	No. 120 East Thirty-fifth Street	City	Fair	An old building refitted.
22	Nos. 345 and 347 West Forty-seventh Street.	City	Good	

TABLE SHOWING LOCATION AND CONDITION OF STATION HOUSES.

Precincts	LOCATION OF STATION HOUSES	OWNER	CONDITION	REMARKS
23	Fourth Avenue and Eighty-sixth Street	Abram Wakeman.	Bad.	Leased for two years, from May 1, 1870, at $2,000 per year, accommodations unsatisfactory, premises not adapted to station house purposes, lots have been secured on East Eighty-eighth Street, with a view of erecting a new building
24	Steamer "Seneca".	City	First class	The Harbor Police are now provided with better accommodations than at any time since the institution of this branch of the service; the steamer "Seneca," bought and fitted up in 1870, is in all respects what is needed for harbor duty.
25	No. 94 East Twenty-ninth Street	Peter Golet and others	Good	Leased for fifteen years, from May 1, 1870, at $1,500 per year, premises refitted and in excellent condition.
26	City Hall (basement)	City	Fair	
27	Corner Liberty and Church Streets	City	First class	New
28	No. 550 Greenwich Street.	William A. Martin.	Bad	Leased for one year, from May 1, 1871, at $2,500 per year; accommodations entirely inadequate; a new station house is an imperatively necessity.
29	Nos 137 and 139 West Thirtieth Street	City	First class	New.
30	Corner One Hundred and Twenty eighth Street and Broadway	William H. Guion.	Bad.	Leased for one year, from May 1, 1870, at $1,500 per year, new station house indispensable.
31	One Hundredth Street, between Ninth and Tenth Avenues	City	First class	New.
32	Corner Tenth Avenue and One Hundred and Fifty-second Street	City		Arrangements have been made for a new and more commodious building to meet the requirements of the precinct.

William Jameson joined the Crystal Palace Police in 1853 as Drill Inspector for two hundred men. The uniform consisted of a blue dress coat, black buttons, military collar. After the appointment of the first Police Commissioner, Inspector Jameson was made Drill Master, and used to drill the men in the Old

Arsenal in Elm Street. When the Police were withdrawn from the Crystal Palace, they were amalgamated with the regular Police, and Inspector Jameson detailed as First Drill Instructor to the Police Department. Mr Jameson, although quite a young man, had seen active service in the Mexican War and Civil War. In 1868 he was transferred to the First Precinct, and when Inspector Leonard died, in February, 1870, he was made an Inspector, and was detailed to Police Headquarters. In April, 1872, after nineteen years honorable service, he was tried and dismissed from the department on a charge of being absent without leave for three hours from the office.

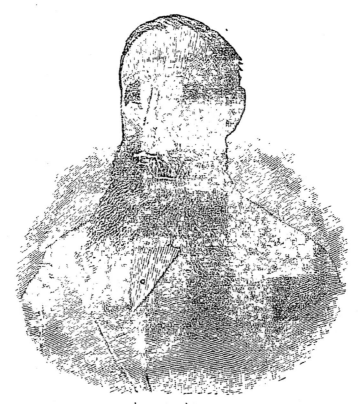

Inspector Jameson

An Act in relation to the cleaning of streets (Chapter 677, May 14, 1872), charged the Board of Police with the duty of causing all streets, avenues, lanes, etc., to be cleaned. The Board was vested with full power to supervise the execution of the agreement for cleaning the streets in the city of New York, which agreement was entered into on June 9, 1865, between the Mayor, Aldermen and commonalty of the city of New York, of the first part, and John L. Brown, William H. Devoe and Shephard F. Knapp, contractors, of the second part. Whenever said contract was canceled, the Board of Police were to forward and do the work of cleaning the streets. The Board was, furthermore, authorized to contract for the sale of street manure, dirt, sweepings, ashes, etc.; to appoint such officers, agents and employees to clean the streets; after exercising such authority for thirty days the Board was required to make an estimate of the sum of money necessary to defray the expenses during the year 1872, and, on or before the first of December, 1872, should make an estimate of the amount required for 1873 and subsequent years.

In 1872 the new building for a House of Detention of Witnesses was completed In this year, there were in the House of Detention, detained as witnesses, two hundred and eighty-two persons, who were imprisoned an aggregate of four thousand six hundred and eighty-eight days, and, strange to say, there was no fixed period to their imprisonment, and no legal process of which they could avail themselves (being unable to secure bail) to hasten or fix a day when they might claim that personal liberty which is supposed to be the constitutional right of every innocent person.

The following table shows the number of innocent persons imprisoned as witnesses in the House of Detention, since 1858 to 1872:

		No persons	No. days.
From February 9, 1858, to October 31, 1858		292	7,421
" November 1, 1858, " October 31, 1859		419	10,662
" November 1, 1859, " October 31, 1860		380	6,609
" November 1, 1860, " October 31, 1861		471	8,634
" November 1, 1861, " October 31, 1862		632	9,480
" November 1, 1862, " October 31, 1863		269	4,035
" November 1, 1863, " October 31, 1864		282	4,230
" November 1, 1864, " October 31, 1865		229	3,436
" November 1, 1865, " October 31, 1866		410	6,150
" November 1, 1866, " October 31, 1867		262	4,139
" November 1, 1867, " October 31, 1868		264	3,852
" November 1, 1868, " October 31, 1869		239	3,873
" November 1, 1869, " April 4, 1870		100	1,347
" April 5, 1870, " April 4, 1871		283	4,618
" April 5, 1871, " April 4, 1872		282	4,688
Totals		4,814	83,173

From this table it appears that the total number imprisoned was four thousand eight hundred and fourteen. The aggregate imprisonment was eighty-three thousand one hundred and seventy-three days; equaling an imprisonment of one person for a period of two hundred and twenty-seven years and three hundred and eighteen days. Of the two hundred and eighty-two persons thus imprisoned (April 5, 1871, to April 5, 1872), five were confined over one hundred days each; fifteen were confined less than one hundred and over fifty days each; ninety five were confined less than fifty and over ten days each; one hundred and sixty-seven were confined ten days and under.

There had occurred in the history of the House of Detention repeated instances of the imprisonment of innocent witnesses, while the accused person against whom they were held as witnesses were granted their liberty on bail. This, too, notwithstanding the Constitutional provision that "Witnesses shall not be unreasonably detained," and the further like provision that "No person * * shall be deprived of * * liberty * * without due process of law."

Against this oppressive system of arbitrary and unnecessary imprisonment of innocent persons, the Board protested, characterizing the system as "neither just nor necessary," and contending that it 'aught to be immediately replaced by some process of law more in accord with the common ideas of humanity and justice."

The totals of the rank and number of the force for this year are as follows: Captains, thirty-five; Sergeants, one hundred and thirty-nine; Roundsmen, one hundred and three; Patrolmen, assigned to patrol duty, one thousand six hundred and twenty; Patrolmen, assigned to special duty, two hundred and sixty-one; Doormen, seventy-four. Grand total, 2,232.

It appears that the number of arrests made by the force during the year for all causes was eighty-four thousand five hundred and fourteen. Males, sixty thousand one hundred and seventy-nine; females, twenty-four thousand three hundred and thirty-five; an excess over the number of arrests for the year last preceding of eight thousand eight hundred and twenty-two.

Table of arrests for a series of years from 1859 to April 5, 1872:

	Year.	Total	No. Patrolmen.	Average per officer.
New York City	1860	65809	1414	46
New York City	1861	71130	1806	39
New York City	1862	82072	1783	46
New York City	1863	61888	1711	36
New York City	1864	54751	1805	30
New York City	1865	68873	1806	38
New York City	1866	75630	1789	42
New York City	1867	80532	1848	44
New York City	1868	78451	1921	41
New York City	1869	72984	1922	38
New York City	From Nov 1, '69 to Apr. 5, '70.	27218	1996	14
New York City	1871	75692	2075	36
New York City	1872	84514	1984	42
Total		899544	23860	38

During the preceding year, with a total force numbering two thousand two hundred and thirty-two men, there occurred two thousand nine hundred and eighty-three cases of sickness and injury, which were treated by the Surgeons of the department. Four hundred and five of the above mentioned cases were caused by injuries, and four hundred and thirty were the result of intermittent fever, contracted from the opening and grading of so many new sreets and boulevards in the upper precincts, while the remaining two thousand one hundred and forty-six resulted from general causes.

The time lost to the department by the above named sickness and injury amounted to seventeen thousand six hundred and thirty-two days, being a decrease over the preceding year of five thousand and eighty-three and a half days.

The comparatively small number of casualties and cases of sickness resulting from the exposure of the force during the riot of July, 1871, is to be attributed to the efficient handling of the men by their officers, as well as to the superior discipline of the force under their command.

Table of lost children for a series of years, from 1860 to April 5, 1872.

	YEAR.	NUMBER LOST CHILDREN.	NUMBER FOUNDLINGS.
New York City	1861	7201	
New York City	1862	9806	
New York City	1863	7380	
New York City	1864	7204	48
New York City	1865	5723	153
New York City	1866	5912	149
New York City	1867	5979	176
New York City	1868	5748	162
New York City	1869	5923	90
New York City	From Nov. 1, 1869 to April 5, 1870	1570	28
New York City	1871	5933	161
New York City	1872	5082	37
Total		73461	1004

Average per year. 6,678

Table of lodgers for a series of years from 1861 to April 5, 1872.

	YEAR.	NUMBER OF LODGERS.
New York City	1861	119348
New York City	1862	70938
New York City	1863	68254
New York City	1864	59929
New York City	1865	64247
New York City	1866	115324
New York City	1867	105460
New York City	1868	141070
New York City	1869 (to Nov 1.)	135591
New York City	From Nov. 1, 1869, to Ap. 5, 1870.	82607
New York City	1871	141780
New York City	1872	147427
Total		1251975

Average per year.. 113,816

There was delivered by the several Precincts, Detective, and Court Squads, from April 5, 1871, to April 5, 1872, property consisting of animals, carriages, trucks, carts, and merchandise, and with money and valuables taken from prisoners as personal property, a sum aggregating one million one hundred and ninety-three thousand nine hundred and eighty-seven dollars and seventy-two cents. The Property Clerk's returns for the same period amounts to one hundred and one thousand and seventy-five dollars and ninety-three cents; making a grand total of one million two hundred and ninety-five thousand and sixty-three dollars and sixty-five cents

A committee, representing the business, professional and commercial interests of New York, desiring to pay a marked tribute to the heroism of the Police force, and their devotion to duty, sent the following communication to the Police Board:

IN COMMITTEE

NEW YORK, Oct 5, 1872

GENTLEMEN :

The commercial bodies represented by the undersigned, together with certain other corporations, and sundry private citizens of New York City, wishing to show their appreciation of the fidelity, discipline, and gallantry shown by the Police force on many occasions of public disturbance, notably during the riots of July, 1863, and 1871, have provided to be made an appropriate flag, and commissioned the undersigned to present it in their name to the Department

They wish it to be regarded and preserved by the Police Department as the "Flag of Honor," and stipulate that it shall only be carried at the annual parades, and at the funerals of members of the force who die in consequence of injuries received in the line of duty.

The undersigned feel pleasure in being selected to perform this agreeable duty on behalf of the body of their fellow-citizens, for they are satisfied that this testimony has been earned by the good behavior of the guardians of the public peace in times of great peril. They feel confident that the officers and men under your control will in the future, as in the past. be always ready to respond to the call of duty, and thus continue to deserve the approbation and respect of their fellow-citizens of the city of New York.

Requesting you to acknowledge receipt of this communication, and to designate a suitable time and place for the ceremony of presentation, we are gentlemen,

Your obedient servants,

To the Board of Police Commissioners
of the City of New York

An Act to re-organize the local government of the city of New York was passed by the legislature, April 30, 1873. The most important heads of which are as follows:

The Police Department to have for its head a Board, to consist of five persons; the Police force to consist of a Superintendent, three Inspectors, Captains, Sergeants, Patrolmen, Doormen, and as many clerks and employees as the Board might, from time to time, determine, and the funds appropriated allow; the Patrolmen not to be increased in any one year more than one hundred. The Board might appoint twenty-two Sergeants.

The qualifications for membership on the force were: Such Policeman should be a citizen of the United States, never convicted of crime, must read and write, and reside in the State one year.

A Police officer could not withdraw or resign except by permission of the Board of Police; unexplained absence for five days was to be deemed equivalent to a resignation.

The Police Department (Chapter 137, April 5, 1870) made the salaries of the Police Commissioners equal to the salary of the Recorder, namely, fifteen thousand dollars. By a subsequent Act (April 26, 1870; Chapter 383) the Treasurer of the Police Board received an additional salary of one thousand five hundred dollars. This lasted until the framing of the Charter (April 30, 1873), which designated the salaries of the Commissioners as follows: President of the Board, eight thousand dollars; other Commissioners, six thousand dollars.

The remainder of the Act simply recapitulated the leading features of preceding bills.

Mayor Havemeyer, in pursuance of the above, appointed the following Police Commissioners: Oliver Charlick, Abram Duryea, Hugh Gardner, John R. Russell, Henry Smith, the latter being President of the Board.

George W. Matsell was appointed Superintendent of Police by the Board of Police, on the twenty-third of May, 1873, vice James J. Kelso removed.

A subsequent Act (Chapter 755, June 13, 1873) provided for four Inspectors, the Board to fix the salaries of all clerks and employees.

Promotions were to be made by the Board on grounds of meritorious conduct and capacity; no person was to be appointed on the force who was over thirty years of age; the Police Department, through its Treasurer, in pursuance of orders of the Board, was to pay salaries, etc.

A revised manual was promulgated in 1873, from which the following facts are obtained. The "Department of Police" of the City of New York, consisted of a "Board of Police composed of five "Commissioners" and the "Police Force," and officers appointed by said Board. The Board of Police was the head of the Department of Police; governed and controled the Department, its business and affairs, and was invested with, and exercised all, the powers conferred by law upon the Department of Police. The government and discipline of the Department of Police were such as the Board of Police, from time to time, by rules and regulations, prescribed. The territorial jurisdiction and authority of the Board of Police, and of the Police force under their direction, were co-extensive with the territorial limits of the city of New York. For the purposes of Police government, the territory of the city of New York was divided into Inspection Districts, Surgeons' Districts, and Precincts, subject to alteration, from time to time, by the Board of Police Precincts were divided into patrol beats or posts, by the Captains, with the approval of the Superintendent, subject to alteration, from time to time by like authority.

The territory of the city of New York was divided into two Inspection Districts, which were called and known respectively as the "Eastern District" and "Western District." "The Eastern District" consisted of the following precincts, to wit First, Second, Fourth, Sixth, Seventh, Tenth, Eleventh, Twelfth, Thirteenth, Fourteenth, Seventeenth, Eighteenth, Nineteenth, Twenty-first, Twenty-third, and Twenty-sixth "The Western District" consisted of the following precincts, to wit. Third, Fifth, Eighth, Ninth, Fifteenth, Sixteenth, Twentieth, Twenty-second, Twenty-fourth, Twenty-fifth, Twenty-seventh, Twenty-eighth, Twenty-ninth, Thirtieth, Thirty-first, and Thirty-second.

The Board of Police assigned the Inspectors to office duty in the Central Department, and to district duty in the Inspection Districts

The Police force of the city of New York consisted of a Superintendent, three Inspectors, Surgeons, Captains, Sergeants, Patrolmen and Doormen, clerks and employees, to the number of each rank authorized by law.

The Police force was divided into two Divisions, known and called respectively "the Eastern Division," and "the Western Division" The members of the Police force assigned to duty in "the Eastern District" constituted "the Eastern Division" of the force. The members of the Police force assigned to duty in "the Western District," together with the members of the Court Squads, Sanitary Company, Special Service Squad, and Detective force, constituted "the Western Division" of the force. The Police force was further divided into as many Companies as there were precincts, such other Companies or Squads as the Board of Police might order, and the Sanitary Company in addition. A company consisted of the members of the force assigned to duty in a precinct, and in the Sanitary or other Company, and comprised one Captain, Sergeants, Patrolmen, and Doormen A Squad consisted of members of the force assigned to duty as such Squad

Meetings of the Board of Police were held as often as any three of the Commissioners might direct; but all meetings of the Board should be private, unless a majority of the Commissioners should otherwise determine The Chief Clerk or Deputy Clerk should be present and record its proceedings in books kept for that purpose The ayes and noes were taken on all judgments dismissing members from the force, and on such other questions as might be required by law, or by the Board of Police, and formed part of the record. The Board was empowered to enact, modify and repeal, from time to time, orders, rules and regulations of general discipline affecting the force, provided that they did not conflict with the Constitution of the United States, or with the constitution or laws of the State of New York. The Board made all appointments, assignments to duty, transfers of members, and all detailments; but the Superintendent might make detailments for any period not longer than three days Certificates of appointments to office should be signed by the President, and countersigned by the Chief Clerk or first

Deputy Clerk. The records of all judgments rendered by the Board in relation to members of the force were authenticated by the signature of the Chief Clerk Charges preferred against any member of the Police force should be in writing, and verified by the oath of the complainant, except charges by a Commissioner, the Superintendent, Inspectors, Captains, Surgeons, or Chief Clerk, who might make charges in writing without oath Charges by Sergeants and Roundsmen against members of the force, were in writing, signed by the officer making the same, and were delivered to the officer in command at the station house, who immediately entered the same in the blotter, and filed the original charge so made It was the duty of the Captains to transmit to the Superintendent a transcript of each of said charges, on the day the same were entered on the blotter When written charges were preferred against any member of the Police force, they were filed with the Chief Clerk, whereupon specifications of the charges, with a notice of the time and place of trial, were served upon the party charged two days before the day of trial, the day of such service being counted as one of the two days The judgments of the Board, upon charges proved true, were duly entered in the records of the department, and a notice thereof read to the force of the precinct to which the member belonged

The Superintendent of Police is the chief executive officer of the Police force, subject to the orders, rules, and regulations of the Board of Police

His duties, summarized, are as follows. To make quarterly reports in writing, to the Board of Police, on the state of the Department of Police, and of the Police force thereof; with such statistics and suggestions for the improvement of the Police government and discipline as he should deem advisable, to repair in person to all serious or extensive fires in the city of New York; also to all riots or tumultuous assemblages within said city, and take command of the Police force present; to enforce in the city of New York all the laws of the State and ordinances of the city of New York; and also to abate all gaming-houses, rooms and premises, and places kept or used for lewd or obscene purposes and amusements, and places kept or used for the sale of lottery tickets or policies; to communicate to the Board of Police information of the presence of any dangerous epidemic or contagious or infectious disease; and any nuisance detrimental to the public health in any part of the city of New York, to inspect, from time to time, each station house and Police prison in the city of New York, and the House of Detention of witnesses; and report to the Board in relation to their order and cleanliness; and whether the books were properly kept, and the business of the station house properly conducted

He was authorized to promulgate orders to the officers and members of the force not inconsistent with law, or the rules and regulations of the Board; and all members of the force should observe and obey them

The Superintendent, and each Captain within his precinct, possessed general Police supervision over all licensed and unlicensed pawnbrokers, venders, junk-shops, cartmen, intelligence office keepers, and auctioneers within the city Whenever, under Section 41 of Chapter 403 of the Laws of 1864, the Superintendent should come into possession of implements of gaming, he should retain the same until the prosecution against the arrested parties should be finally concluded.

The full dress of the members of the Police force, excepting the Surgeons, was of navy blue cloth, indigo dyed, and all wool

For the Superintendent —The dress was a double-breasted frock coat; the waist extending to the top of the hip, and the skirt within one inch of the bend of the knee, two rows of Police buttons on the breast, eight in each row, placed in pairs, the distance between each row, five and one half inches on the top, and three and one half inches at the bottom; stand-up collar, rising no higher than to permit the chin freely to turn over it, to hook in front at the bottom; cuffs, three and one-half inches deep, and buttoning with three small buttons at the underseam; two buttons on the hips, one button on the bottom of each skirt-pocket welt, and two buttons intermediate, so that there were six buttons on the back; collars and cuffs of dark blue velvet; lining of the coat, black. The trousers plain; black neckcloth; white gloves and collar; the vest single-breasted, with eight buttons placed at equal distances; the cap of navy blue cloth, and of the form of the pattern in the Superintendent's office, having a band of dark blue velvet, with a gold embroidered wreath in front encircling a silver star

For Inspectors —The dress the same as for Superintendent, except that there were seven buttons in each row on the breast of the coat, placed at equal distances, and the gold wreath on the cap enclosed the word "Inspector" in silver

For Captains and Sergeants —The same as for Superintendent, except that there were eight buttons in each row on the breast of the coat, placed at equal distances, the collar rolling; the collar and cuffs of the same color and material as the coat, the band of the same color and material as the body of the cap, welted at the edges, and the wreath enclosing the word "Captain" or "Sergeant," with the number of the precinct to which the officer was attached, in gold. The Captain of the Harbor Police had a gold anchor, and the Sergeants silver anchors, enclosed in a wreath in lieu of the number of the precinct

For Patrolmen.—The dress was a single-breasted frock coat with rolling collar, the waist extending to the top of the hip, and the skirt to within one inch of the bend of the knee; nine buttons on the breast, two buttons on the hips, two buttons on the bottom of each pocket, and three small buttons on the under seam of the cuffs. Trousers having a white welt in the outer seam; white shirt collar, and white gloves; black neckcloth; vest, single-breasted, with nine buttons placed at equal distances. The cap of navy blue cloth, to correspond with sample in the office of the Superintendent, with wreath surrounding the appropriate number in white metal

The Patrolmen detailed as Roundsmen, in addition had the word "Roundsman" in white metal letters, in lieu of the wreath

For Harbor Patrolmen —The dress was a sailor's jacket, rolling collar, coming down half-way between the hip-joint and knee; five buttons on each side of breast, two buttons on the under seam of the cuffs, pockets inside; vest, single-breasted, nine buttons, trousers plain; shirt of blue flannel; cap, same as other Patrolmen, with wreath and number the same as in the office of the Superintendent; pea-jacket overcoat, three inches above the knee, five buttons on each side, side pockets with flaps; in other respects, same as other Patrolmen

For Doormen —The dress was a double-breasted round jacket, extending two inches below the hip, with five Police buttons on each breast, and one on the inside seam of each cuff; trousers of Cadet-mixed cloth, plain; cap, the same as Patrolmen, without wreath, but with the word "Doorman" in white metal letters, placed in front. In other particulars, same as Patrolmen.

The officers were permitted to wear the summer uniform while in the discharge of desk duty in the station houses.

The overcoat was of navy blue beaver cloth, double-breasted, rolling collar, pocket-welts on back, outside breast pocket with flap on the right side, the waist extending to one inch below the hip, and the skirt to three inches below the

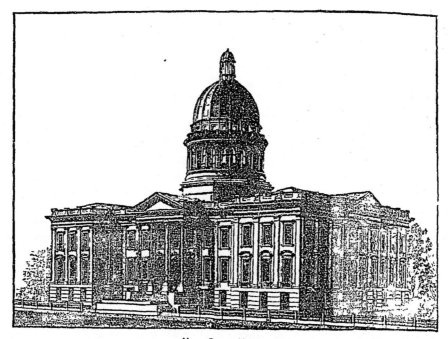

New Court House.

bend of the knee, swell edge stitched one-fourth of an inch from edge, flaps on pocket, swell edge stitched one-fourth of an inch from edge. Inspectors had seven Police buttons on each breast, and six on the back and skirt, and three on the cuffs. Captains had eight Police buttons on each breast, six on the back and skirt, and three on the cuffs. Patrolmen had nine Police buttons on each breast, four on the back and skirt, and two on the cuffs.

Captains wore the prescribed uniform at all times, unless specially authorized to wear citizen's clothes by the Board or Superintendent of Police.

Sergeants, Roundsmen, Patrolmen, and Doormen, wore the prescribed uniform at all times when their respective platoons were on patrol or reserve duty; and when the off platoon might be called on duty on extraordinary occasions.

When either of the above enumerated members of the force attended at any Court, as witness or complainant; or at the regular or special drills for exercise;

or at Headquarters, on any business whatever; or at the School of Instruction, he appeared in the prescribed uniform.

Members of the force might, for special purposes, be relieved from wearing uniform by the Board or by the Superintendent of Police; but at no time, while in citizen's dress, was any member exempted from the performance of Police duties

Special Patrolmen, during the service authorized by Chapter 383 of the Laws of 1870, wore a shield of white metal, with the Coat of Arms of the city of New York and the words "Municipal Police, Special," with serial numbers, in figures, impressed thereon, in the form to be prescribed by the Board of Police

The summer uniform consisted of blue flannel sack coat, and blue flannel trousers The coat of Patrolmen was a single-breasted sack, with short turn-over collar, buttoning close up to the chin, and reaching half-way between the articulation of the hip-joint and the knee, with four buttons on the front, no pockets showing on the outside, and the trousers made same as in winter.

For Harbor Patrolmen, flannel sack coat, and flannel trousers made like the above, and sennet hat.

Coats for Captains, double-breasted, buttoning close up to the chin, with short rolling collar, two rows of buttons of five each on the front, the coat reaching to a point half-way between the articulation of the hip-joint and the knee; trousers without welt in the seams.

For Sergeants, same as for Captains, except that there were two rows of buttons, of four each.

No person should be appointed a Patrolman unless—

He was able to read and write the English language understandingly.

He was a citizen of the United States

He had been a resident of this State during a term of one year next prior to his application for appointment, and had been a resident of the city of New York for six consecutive months immediately preceding that time.

He had never been convicted of crime.

He was at least five feet seven inches in height, measured in his bare feet; and weighed not less than one hundred and thirty-five pounds avoirdupois, without clothing

He was less than thirty years of age

He was of good health, and sound in body and mind

He was of good moral character and habits

The Police force, on the last day of December, 1873, consisted of the following

Superintendent, one; Inspectors, four; Captains, thirty-five; Sergeants, one hundred and forty-one, Patrolmen, twenty-two hundred; Doormen, seventy-two Total force, 2453.

On the twenty-third of May of this year, Messrs Oliver Charlick, Hugh Gardner, Abraham Duryea and John R Russell were appointed by the Mayor, Commissioners of Police, and, together with Henry Smith, who continued in said office, met at the Central office and organized as a Board of Police by continuing Henry Smith President, and Oliver Charlick Treasurer of the Board The Standing Committees were created and composed as follows:

Committee on Street Cleaning: Messrs Charlick, Gardner, and Duryea; Committee on Station Houses: Messrs. Gardner, Charlick and Russell, Committee on Rules and Discipline: Messrs. Duryea and Russell; Committee on Finance. Messrs Russell, Duryea and the Treasurer.

Two special committees were appointed, as follows Committee on Improvement, Efficiency and Economy, Messrs Russell and Charlick, Committee on Surgeons, Messrs Charlick, Russell and Gardner. The President was added as an *ex-officio* member of all standing committees

Matthew T. Brennan

Measures of economy were introduced on the report and recommendation of the Committee of Improvement, Efficiency and Economy, consisting in the dismissal of employees found to be in excess of the number required for the efficient dispatch of business, and in the reduction of salaries—nine clerks and four telegraph operators being dismissed. The reduction effected in the salaries amounted to eight thousand nine hundred dollars per annum.

By the provisions of Section I, Chapter 755 of the Laws of 1873, the Police force was established and limited as to number and grade of office, and their salaries, as prescribed by law, was as follows: Superintendent, seven thousand five hundred dollars; Inspectors, three thousand five hundred dollars; Captains, two thousand dollars; Sergeants, one thousand six hundred dollars, Surgeons. two thousand two hundred and fifty dollars, Patrolmen, one thousand two hundred dollars, and Doormen, nine hundred dollars

At the date of the organization of the above Board of Police, there were in office sixteen Surgeons, receiving, as above, two thousand two hundred and fifty dollars per annum each These Surgeons were dismissed, and three Surgeons appointed on salaries established by law, to examine candidates for appointment on the Police force, and to have a general supervisory care of the medical and surgical service of the department. Thirty-seven doctors residing in the various precincts of the city were designated to be sent for to attend such sick Policemen as were adjudged to require medical or surgical treatment, and to treat cases of injury or illness of citizens who might be brought to the station houses The rate of compensation for the services of this class of Surgeons was fixed at three dollars per visit to Policemen, and for calls to citizens' cases at the station houses four dollars in the day time, and five dollars for calls occurring in the night

It had become apparent to the Board of Police that the number of Patrolmen (two thousand one hundred) was inadequate to meet the increased and increasing demand for Patrol service of the city in every precinct (and especially in the uptown precincts, where the increase of population was rapid); there was a deficiency of force, and the constant calls from respectable citizens of all classes and conditions for a more complete and perfect Police protection of property and persons and human life, against the increasing menaces of ill-disposed and criminal persons.

The population of New York City was (1873) estimated at one million. The two thousand one hundred Patrolmen of the Police Department gave one Patrolman to every four hundred and sixty-seven of the population. The population of London, for the same year, was estimated at three millions. The number of Patrolmen was nine thousand two hundred and sixty, or one to every three hundred and twenty-four of the population The Board had decided to increase the force by one hundred extra Policemen, as authorized by law, but it was found that this increase could not be effected until financial means had been made to pay such an increase of the force

On April 30, 1874, the laws provided that the Board of Police should consist of four Commissioners, the Mayor to appoint without the confirmation of the Board of Aldermen, any person to fill a vacancy caused by death or resignation, or who should be removed for cause.

Abram Disbecker was appointed a Police Commissioner to fill the vacancy caused by the death of Henry Smith. Commissioner Russell's term expired May 1, 1874. Messrs Gardner and Charlick resigned in May of the same year. George W Matsell and John R. Voorhis were appointed Police Commissioners July 7, 1874. George W Walling was appointed Superintendent, July 23, 1874, in place of George W Matsell

Henry Smith, President of the Board of Police, died on the twenty-third day of February, 1874 Upon the receipt of the tidings of his death, the Board, consisting of the surviving members, unanimously adopted resolutions of regret at his untimely death, and tendered an expression of their sympathy to the grief-stricken wife and afflicted kindred of the deceased.

The death of Mr. Smith created a vacancy in the office of President of the Board of Police, which office, on the twelfth of March, 1874, was filled by the selection of Commissioner Hugh Gardner.

On the thirty-first of December, 1874, the Police force for all grades was as follows: Superintendent, one; Inspectors, four; Captains, thirty-six; Sergeants, one hundred and thirty-five; Patrolmen, two thousand two hundred and seventy-two; and Doormen, eighty; making a total of 2,521.

The total number of days lost by the whole force for the year 1874, was twenty-three thousand and twenty-six and one-half, of this, thirteen thousand nine hundred and five and three-fourth days were paid, and nine thousand one hundred and twenty and three-fourths unpaid, making the amount paid for sick time, forty-five thousand seven hundred and thirteen dollars and eighty-five cents.

The total number of arrests, males and females, for the year, was ninety-two thousand one hundred and twelve.

Mayor Wickham appointed William F Smith Police Commissioner, May 1, 1875, in place of Abram Duryea, whose term had expired.

George W. Matsell and Abram Disbecker were removed, December 31, 1875, and DeWitt C Wheeler and Joel B. Erhardt appointed in their places. Sidney P Nichols, on the expiration of the term of office of John R. Voorhis, was appointed a Police Commissioner, May 1, 1876.

CHAPTER XIII

1875-1880.

"NEW YORK SAYS, STOP!"

NEW YORK FAST BECOMING A LAW-ABIDING CITY.—PROCEEDINGS AND REPORT OF THE SELECT LEGISLATIVE COMMITTEE ON THE CAUSES AND INCREASE OF CRIME.—GOVERNMENT OF THE POLICE FORCE.—DEMORALIZATION AND INEFFICIENCY.—ALL THE BLAME FOR THESE EVILS NOT ATTRIBUTABLE TO THE POLICE —CONVICTIONS HARD TO GAIN.—LEGAL LOOP-HOLES OF RETREAT FOR CRIMINALS.—LOTTERY AND POLICY.—THE DETECTIVE POLICE NOT PROPERLY REMUNERATED FOR THEIR SERVICES —SALARY AND DUTIES OF PATROLMEN, ETC.—THE BOARD OF POLICE COMMISSIONERS.—EVIL EFFECTS OF POLITICAL INTERMEDDLING WITH THE FORCE —TOO FEW POLICEMEN.—THE GREAT RAILROAD STRIKES —SCENES OF RIOT AND BLOODSHED —THE TOMPKINS SQUARE MEETING —" NEW YORK SAYS STOP."—NEW RULES FOR THE GUIDANCE OF THE FORCE.

MUCH as has been said and written about the wickedness of "Gotham," New York, after all, is not so bad a city for a law-abiding citizen to live in. That it holds within its gates some hard citizens no one will be bold enough to gainsay; but that New York, on the whole, is worse than any other city of its size, in population and commercial importance, is an allegation which can easily be refuted, as the facts are at hand to do so Perhaps in no city in the world of its cosmopolitan character is there such protection against the criminal operations of professional robbers and the machinations of all classes of thieves and swindlers Indeed, from a Police point of view, New York, generally speaking, is at present an orderly, well-conducted city, where the higher grades of crime are remarkably few and infrequent. This change, however, has taken place within a comparatively short space of time. Up to a few years ago, the criminal classes were particularly bold and successful in their operations, but thanks to an improved Police system, and a Detective Department second to none in the world, New York has had a breathing spell; but, perhaps it would not be too much of a concession to make in deference to a pessimistic public opinion, to admit that there is still room for improvement.

The city, it would seem, was drifting into particularly bad habits about the year 1875 There was a good deal of complaining that the Police were not doing their whole duty, and that too much deference was being paid by them to the comfort and interests of criminals as a class, and too little to the peace of mind of taxpayers and citizens generally That there was some foundation for these complaints is but too conclusively proven by the proceedings and report of the

Select Committee appointed by the Assembly in 1875 "to investigate the causes of the increase of crime in the city of New York." The resolution under which their authority was conferred runs as follows.

Whereas, The steady and rapid increase of crime in the city and county of New York has created great alarm in the minds of all good citizens of that city, and,

Whereas, the proper authorities charged with its apprehension, prosecution and punishment appear to be inadequate to its speedy suppression, while the interest of good government require that all offences against the laws should be dealt with in the most summary and decisive manner, therefore,

Resolved, that the Speaker of the Assembly be and he is hereby authorized to appoint a select committee of five, which committee shall have power to send for persons and papers, and compel the attendance of witnesses, and to inquire into the causes, as far as possible, of the great increase of crime in said city and county, by making such examination and investigation of all persons and officers * * * * for the purpose of ascertaining if such increase of crime can be charged to the negligence or connivance of any of the public officers whose duty it is either to arrest, detect, prosecute or punish crime in said City and County of New York.

The duties so imposed on the committee naturally brought under their investigation the Board of Municipal Police; the Criminal Courts. from the Police Justices to the Court of Oyer and Terminer; the Coroners; the District Attorney; and all the penal institutions, public and private; and in addition to this, owing to the overwhelming evidence that intemperance was the chief cause of crime, the committee deemed it proper to inquire fully into the affairs of the Board of Excise. The testimony taken gives a condensed history of the Police Department, and throws a lurid light on the condition and management of the criminal classes in New York City, presenting a picture of moral degradation that is anything but pleasing to look upon. The report covers nearly three thousand printed pages. In condensed form, this report tells the following story.

The Police force of the city is governed by a Board of four Commissioners of Police, appointed for terms of six years, expiring at different periods, by the Mayor, with the advice and consent of the Board of Aldermen. The force, under the government of the Commissioners, consisted of one Superintendent, four Inspectors, thirty-four Captains, one hundred and twenty-six Sergeants, one hundred and forty-two Roundsmen, two thousand one hundred and seventeen Patrolmen, and seventy-three Doormen. The city was divided into thirty territorial precincts, twenty-eight of which were commanded by Captains and two by Sergeants. In addition to these, there were the Sanitary Company, commanded by a Captain; the Harbor Police, employing a steamboat and rowboats, commanded by a Captain; the Broadway Squad, designed to help people across Broadway in the daytime, commanded by a Captain, while one Captain had charge of the drilling of the Patrolmen; another was Superintendent of the Street Cleaning Department, and another one was under him in command of certain scows attached to that department. Besides these, there were the Mounted Squad, consisting of fourteen men; the Steamship Squad, of twenty-two men; the Headquarter Detectives, twelve in number; the House of Detention, commanded by a Sergeant, and employing four Policemen, and five Court Squads,

A Drunkard's Dream

(Drawn by C. DE GRIMM, by permission of MR JAMES GORDON BENNETT.)

each commanded by a Sergeant, and employing in the aggregate forty-seven Policemen.

The precincts were divided into four Inspection Districts, each of which was commanded by an Inspector, and the Superintendent had power over the whole force. All orders from the Board were issued to him alone, and the Police force should receive their orders from him alone. The committee claimed that "great abuses had sprung up in the past from individual Commissioners issuing orders to the Superintendent, and even to the Superintendent's subordinates, without consulting him."

Having gone pretty extensively into certain classes of crime that existed in the city, the committee say "In this connection it is proper to say that all the blame (for the existence of these evils) must not be laid upon the shoulders of the Police. Again and again houses of prostitution that were disorderly have been 'pulled' (a Police term, meaning arrested,) and the inmates taken before the Magistrates; again and again Magistrates have dismissed such cases, either from an honest opinion that the testimony was insufficient for a conviction, which was assuredly in most cases erroneous, or from some other less creditable motive. Hundreds of others have been held by Magistrates, have given bail to go to the General Sessions, have been indicted there, and nothing has ever been done with them After giving bail they resumed business directly, either in the same place or in an immediately adjoining one."

Referring to gambling houses, the report declares "While very great improvements in respect to the number of gambling houses has taken place, especially since the sessions of this committee began, we cannot doubt that there is room for still further amelioration in the condition of the city in this respect; and it will only come when the existence of a gambling house for any length of time in the precinct of a Captain is made adequate cause for his dismissal from the force. Several of the best officers have indicated their willingness to be subjected to a rule that shall hold their positions responsible for the continued existence of gambling houses within thirty days after power is given them to suppress it."

Very interesting information concerning lottery and policy was obtained by the committee: "The lowest, meanest, worst form, however, which gambling takes in the city of New York, is what is known as policy playing." Policy was described by one of the witnesses, who was competent to give an opinion on such a subject, as "a parasite on lottery" Policy selling appears to be a betting by individuals with policy dealers upon the result of the daily drawing of the lotteries in Kentucky It does not involve the purchase of a lottery ticket, but is merely a private wager upon the result of a lottery drawing A number of people, estimated by some at as large a figure as eleven hundred at times, were, at the time in question, engaged in the business of selling policy in the city of New York, by far the greater portion of the purchasers were found among the poorest, lowest, and the most ignorant classes of the community. One of the witnesses (himself a large policy dealer) made this remarkable statement, as coming from him '"It (policy) is a right down incorporated swindle from the word 'go,' right through; it ought to be stopped To make a long story short, it makes boys steal revenue stamps and go and sell them, and women take the bank-book of the men, and when they want to go into business, where's the money? It takes the pennies off dead men's eyes."

A curious incident is related by the committee in their report (p. 23) of the power of the "Central Organization" (a body that controled the dealers of branch offices), and the reasons why the Police were unable to suppress these criminals. A curious illustration of the intense folly, to say the least, of the way in which Courts deal with policy, will be found in the testimony of Captain Hedden (p 463) Discharging his duty efficiently and intelligently, and, indeed, in the only way in which it could be discharged, he sent an officer in plain clothes to purchase a policy slip; upon that he arrested the dealer, who was discharged by the Court on the ground that the Policeman was a party to the crime.

The detective system of the city was divided into two branches, the Headquarters Detectives and the Ward Detectives The Headquarters Detective force consisted of about twenty-five men under the command of a Captain, up to January, 1875. The Ward Detectives were about two in number in each precinct, although varying, there being sometimes only one, and sometimes three or four. The duties of the Headquarters Detectives were the investigation of crimes assigned to them for that purpose by the Superintendent. The duties of the Ward Detectives were also the investigation of crimes in the precincts, and in this respect they and their Captains at times clashed with the Headquarters Detectives.

The Headquarters Detectives had continued pretty nearly unchanged for a good many years, saving the natural changes that arose from the passage of time, "and there is no doubt whatever that in shrewdness, in experience, and in capacity, many of them were abundantly equal to the duties imposed upon them"

The pay of the detectives was precisely the same as that of the Patrolmen, one thousand two hundred dollars a year, and no increased compensation was given even to the oldest and most experienced officer among them, except when he was allowed by the grace of the Board to receive some portion of the reward paid for the recovery of stolen property. In rank and in salary the oldest detective stood merely on a par with the newest Patrolman who walked his beat

A Patrolman, on his joining the force, which he did after swearing to a considerable variety of things, and after being certified to by a number of reputable citizens who had known him for five years, and after passing medical examination as to qualifications, was put in the school of instruction, under a Drill Captain, for a month Upon receiving his appointment, and before entering the school of instruction, he became a full Patrolman, and no power existed in the Board to get rid of him except upon trial in the same manner as with any officer At the end of a month, or, if he proved an exceptionally stupid scholar, at the end of two months, he went upon the force, and from the hour that he received his appointment he drew pay at the rate of one thousand two hundred dollars per year, the same not only as the oldest and most experienced Patrolman, but as any Roundsman on the force

It was the duty of Roundsmen, who were attached to each precinct, to traverse the precinct from point to point, in order to see that the Patrolmen were discharging their duty faithfully.

Above them in grade stand the Sergeants, who received one thousand six hundred dollars per year, who were appointed by the Board at pleasure, after an examination was held, and four of whom were attached to each precinct, while a few others discharged independent duty, such as the command of Court Squads, etc. The Sergeants in turn presided at the desk in the station house, and kept the "blotter," so-called, a book in which, with great minuteness of detail, all the transactions of Police life are entered. The Sergeant, while presiding at the desk in the absence of the Captain, exercises the authority of the Captain, and their positions require grave judgment and very considerable capacity, coolness and courage

Above the Sergeants rank the Captains, who received two thousand dollars per annum. Those in command of the precincts were absolutely supreme, under the control, of course, of their superior officer and of the law

In rank above the Captains were four Inspectors, whose salary was three thousand five hundred dollars apiece, and who, up to the summer of 1875, were located as follows: one was in charge of the Street Cleaning Bureau, another acted as a sort of deputy to the Superintendent, and the other two daily inspected and reported to the Superintendent. This system was done away with, and the city was divided into four inspection districts, of which the two most important, the First and Second, included the whole of the city below Forty-second Street, and these were commanded by the two oldest and most experienced Inspectors. The Inspectors were also given authority, each in his district, over the Captains. The Captains reported daily to them, and they reported an abstract to the Superintendent. A small force, two Sergeants and a Roundsman, was allotted to each Inspector

Above the Inspectors stands the Superintendent, whose salary is six thousand dollars per annum, and who holds, perhaps, in some respects, one of the most important places in the United States. Beyond all question, more duties devolve upon the Superintendent than it is possible for any man to do well

The Board of Police Commissioners consists of four Commissioners, appointed by the Mayor, one of whom, elected by his associates as President, draws a salary of eight thousand dollars, while the other three receive six thousand dollars each. They are entrusted with the absolute government of the whole Police force of the city of New York, subject only to such restrictions as the legislature has provided in its laws. All the rules and regulations of the department emanate from them, and in addition to that, all the appointments and all the promotions are made by them. The trials of all the offenses charged against Policemen, from petty offenses against the military code, such as a disordered button, up to the very greatest charges, are held before one or all of the Commissioners, and are decided by the Board, as a Board. In addition, the legislature imposed upon the Commissioners the management of the cleaning of the streets of the city of New York, a vast labor, which employed a vast number of men and carts, and which required the almost incessant attention of one at least of the Commissioners. The Commissioners were further obliged to take charge of the Bureau of Elections, which, during a large portion of the year, consumed a great deal of their time. They appoint all the inspectors of election, something over two thousand in number, and all the poll clerks; they designate all the polling places; in fact, the whole machinery of election is under their direct and immediate control. The President of the Board of Police is, in addition, a member of the Health Board

"One of the greatest difficulties experienced in procuring an efficient Police, has been, the Committee find, the continual intermeddling of politicians with the government of the force. Patrolmen have generally been appointed through political influence, promotions have been made on the same ground, and even details for duty have frequently been regulated in the same manner * * * The present Board have announced to the force that any officer who procures

Inspector McDermott

politicians to attempt to influence the action of the Board, will receive no consideration at their hands, and it is to be hoped that the steady enforcement of this rule may lead to the abatement of this intolerable nuisance." * * *

There were not enough Policemen in New York, the committee concluded. It appears that the total number of night posts in the city at this time was eight hundred and twenty. The aggregate length of the night posts was eight hundred and twenty-five miles, three furlongs, thirty-eight rods and five yards. The average length of each night post was one mile and two rods The total force of Patrolmen in Patrol Precincts was one thousand nine hundred and forty-six. Average absent from any cause, four hundred and eight. Average effective force on each night, seven hundred and sixty-nine Average length of each actual night post, one mile, twenty-three rods and two yards. Aggregate length of day posts, eight hundred and twenty-five miles, three furlongs, thirty-eight rods, and five yards. Average effective day force, three hundred and eighty-four Average length of each actual day post, two miles and four rods. A Patrolman was required while walking his beat at night to examine the door of every house on his post and to see whether or not it was closed securely. When the average length of such a post is considered, one mile and upwards of twenty-three rods, it may be imagined easily how long a time it takes a Patrolman to get from one end of his beat to the other, and how long an interval must ensue after the time at which he leaves any given point on his beat before he returns to it again. * * * The committee concluded "that five hundred additional Policemen were absolutely essential to the safety of the lives and property of the citizens in New York."

The report of Superintendent Walling, announcing the death of Inspector Francis C Speight, March 20, 1877, was the occasion for the Board to pass resolutions of sympathy and condolence. He was appointed a Patrolman during the first term as Mayor of William F. Havemeyer, and attained the rank of Captain in 1854; in 1857 he became a member of the Metropolitan Police force, and was promoted to the rank of Inspector on the eleventh day of August, 1874 During an unusually extended term of office he discharged its difficult duties faithfully, vigorously, and, as appears by his record, to the evident satisfaction of the numerous superior officers under whom he served.

Upon the report of Inspector Thorne announcing the death of Inspector John McDermott, the nineteenth of April, 1880, the Board passed the following

Whereas, John McDermott, late an Inspector of the Police force, deceased, was appointed a Patrolman of Police of the city of New York, December 24, 1859, a Roundsman January 26, 1863, a Sergeant November 15, 1865, a Captain October 9, 1869, and an Inspector May 31, 1872, and during this extended term of office he discharged its difficult duties faithfully, vigorously, and, as appears by his record, to the evident satisfaction of the numerous superior officers under whom he served. He died on the nineteenth of April, inst., in the forty-seventh year of his age

Resolved, That in the death of Inspector McDermott the Department and the public lose a p.ompt, efficient, courteous and faithful officer, whose record of official action is commended to the force as an example worthy of study and emulation

Resolved, That the sympathy of the Board is tendered to the family, relatives, and friends of the deceased in their deep affliction

The great railroad strikes which convulsed the country in 1877, leading to desperate encounters between the rioters and the militia, were fortunately brought to a sudden stop just as an attempt had been made to organize those dangerous forces in open mass meetings in the heart of a socialistic district in this city. These railroad strikes had been unprecedented in their extent Beginning at Martinsburg, on the Baltimore and Ohio Railroad, the strikes and attendant disorders spread to all the great lines in the central and western part of the Union, in rapid succession. The hard times had pressed heavily on the hard worked masses, and the lowering of wages by railroad corporations provoked discontent and aroused a retaliatory spirit among the men It is a coincidence worthy of note, that those scenes of disorder were also enacted, like the draft and orange riots, in the month of July. So serious had grown the situation in a little time, that the President of the United States issued a proclamation in which all good citizens were admonished against countenancing, abetting, or taking part in such unlawful proceedings, and all persons engaged in or connected with said domestic violence and obstruction of laws, were warned to disperse and retire peaceably to their respective abodes on or before twelve o'clock noon, of the nineteenth of July, instant

Scenes of riot and bloodshed were witnessed in the streets of Baltimore, in which the mob was fired upon by the military In the conflict between thirty and forty of the mob were killed or wounded, and nine were killed outright

Pittsburg was the next city to experience the fury of the strikers, and a general revolt spread like a devouring flame along the line of the great railroads The country had been thoroughly aroused, and no one knew where the trouble would end Reading was the next point to feel the force of the storm, while Philadelphia and Scranton soon became the centres of similar trouble.

While the State and general Government were thus employed in grappling with those serious disturbances, it was natural that public attention should be attracted to the great State of New York, to mark what effect the revolutionary proceedings of the strikers would produce in that quarter. The hands employed at Hornellsville, on the Erie Railroad, had struck, and taken up arms in defiance of law. Governor Robinson, by proclamation, warned all persons engaged in the violation of law to desist therefrom, and offered a reward of five hundred dollars, to be paid upon the arrest and conviction of each and every striker found guilty of a breach of the law. Syracuse, Buffalo, and other cities and towns were deeply agitated by the unlawful work of the strikers

It was at this crisis that an event occurred in the city of New York, which, for weal or woe, was destined to prove of far-reaching importance This city was regarded as the pivotal point of the strike; as New York went so went the victory or defeat It caused, therefore, serious alarm throughout the State when it was announced that a mass meeting was called to take place in Tompkins Square, under the auspices of Socialistic leaders, and, of course, in sympathy with the strikers This action was regarded by the city authorities, and properly so, as being fraught with the possibilities of great danger to the peace and welfare of the State and entire country. The rioters had at this stage been checked in the several centres which they had selected as their strongholds. They had hoped to regain lost ground by making a diversion on this city, where the elements of popular disorder are but too numerous. With New York strikers and their sympathizers up in arms, an impetus would have been given to the cause, which, in the inflamed and strained condition of the temper of the masses, would have been extremely difficult to stamp out, and what untold tales of horrors and atrocities might have resulted as the natural product of such a conflict! This truly was one of those public critical emergencies where an ounce of Police prevention was better than a pound of military cure. It was a very trying and anxious moment for New York City, and it is not much of an exaggeration or an abuse of a figure of speech to say that her fate trembled in the balance.

The Police, true to their history, were not unmindful of the gravity of the situation. By their prompt and energetic measures the advancing tread of the strikers was brought to a halt before they had time to marshal their forces or fall into line. A morning paper, in three words, summed up the situation. "NEW YORK SAYS STOP!" The same paper says "The thorough and magnificent preparations made by the National Guard of the First Division and the New York Police have checked the threatened disorder in this city at the outset, and left nothing whereon to hang to-day any fear or expectation of outbreak here."

The Board of Police, by reason of disturbances and riots in other cities of the State, and the apprehensions of similar disorders taking place in this city, demanded the assistance of the Seventh, Twenty-second, Eighth and Seventy-first Regiments, which demand was approved by the Mayor. The regiments named were accordingly assembled in their respective armories, equipped for

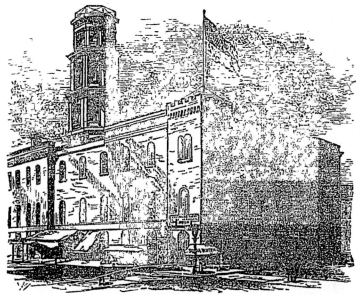

Essex Market.

service, armed with breech-loaders, and each supplied with forty rounds of ammunition per man, and directed to hold themselves in readiness to respond—until further orders—to any demand which might be made upon them by the Board of Police to aid in suppressing riot, tumult, or disturbance of the public peace.

The Police force covering Tompkins Square were distributed as follows:

Mounted Squad and mounted Patrolmen from up-town precincts, under Sergeant Revell, at the Eighteenth Ward Market, foot of East Seventeenth Street; three hundred Patrolmen at the Seventeenth Precinct Station House, Fifth Street and First Avenue, under command of Inspector Murray; two hundred Patrolmen at the Eighteenth Precinct Station House, Twenty-second Street, between First and Second Avenues, under Inspector Thorne; one hundred and sixty men at the Eleventh Precinct Station House, Sheriff and Houston Streets, under Captain Allaire; and one hundred men in reserve at Police Headquarters, under Captains Hedden and Gunner. Nearly every part of the city was covered by the Central Office Detectives, who made regular reports. Trouble being expected at the Thirtieth Street Depot of the Hudson River Railroad, Captain

Washburn, of the Twentieth Precinct, had his command strongly reinforced. The Western Steamboat Squad, under the command of Sergeant Gastlin, guarded the property of the Pennsylvania Railroad at Piers Nos 1, 2, 4, 5, 38, and 39, North River; that of the New York Central and Hudson River Railroad, Pier No 26, North River; that of the Starin Transportation Company, at Piers Nos. 14 and 15, North River, and the landings at the foot of West Twenty-second Street and Twenty-fourth Street

These preparations were too formidable for the men to cope with who had called the Tompkins Square meeting Strikers and rioters were cowed, and the meeting broke up with no public disturbance of any consequence. The turning point was safely passed and the demon of discord was crushed The public breathed more freely, and the press, voicing public opinion, gave emphatic expression to this sentiment

"The conduct both of the Police and of the citizen soldiery was simply admirable"

Mayor Ely made charges for dereliction against three Police Commissioners of this city, viz. Messrs Erhardt, Nichols, and Wheeler. The following letter to one of these Commissioners embodies the nature of these charges·

EXECUTIVE DEPARTMENT,
CITY HALL,
NEW YORK, Dec 18, 1877.

JOEL E. ERHARDT, Esq,
Police Commissioner of the City of New York·

SIR The management of the Police Department seems to call for official action on my part

The duty of cleaning the streets, which is devolved upon that Department, has been inefficiently performed. The unclean and filthy condition of the streets during the present year has not only been a public scandal and disgrace to the city, but has been recently reported by the Health Department as dangerous to the public health, although the sum of sixty thousand dollars has been taken each month from the public treasury for street cleaning purposes; an amount in my judgment amply sufficient for the proper performance of that work.

The Police Department has also assumed the right to decide when the statutes of the State should be enforced, and when they should be permitted to be ignored, and after allowing them to be disregarded for considerable periods of time, has then enforced them capriciously and by raids, in such manner as to render law odious instead of respected

For this inefficiency and maladministration of the Police Department, you, as one of the Commissioners, are in my judgment responsible.

You are hereby notified that I will give you an opportunity to be heard in answer to the above charges on the twentieth day of December instant, at twelve o'clock noon, at this office, then and there to show cause, if any exist, why you should not be removed from office as one of the Police Commissioners of the city of New York

SMITH ELY, JR, *Mayor*

To this Mr. Erhardt made an order as follows:

CITY AND COUNTY OF NEW YORK, ss.

Joel B. Erhardt, being sworn, says· That the charges herein were served upon him late in the day on Tuesday, December 18, 1877; that they are so general in their nature, that it has been impossible for him to properly prepare his defense in the time allowed in such charge; that so far as said charges relate to street cleaning, it is, as he is advised by his counsel and verily believes, necessary and important that he should present evidence to show not only that all moneys expended by the Police Department have been properly and economically expended; that the streets have been as thoroughly cleaned as the law, and the legal, and other instructions and complications permitted, and that the Police Department has not been guilty of inefficiency or maladministration. But as deponent is advised by his said counsel, it is furthermore important that he should be prepared to show that he is not responsible for any inefficiency or maladministration. That if a brief delay is allowed, deponent will be prepared with such proof. That the only reason for desiring such delay is the physical impossibility, while, by attending to the necessary duties of his office, and examining the witnesses, or procuring their statements, and preparing the necessary statistics in the brief time permitted, especially as the absence from the country of one of the members of the Board has thrown increased labors upon the remaining members. Deponent further says that the charge that the right to decide when the statutes of the State should be enforced and when they should be permitted to be ignored, has been assumed, and that the laws have been enforced capriciously and by raids, is so general in its nature, that, as he is advised by counsel and verily believes to be true, it is important and necessary to be prepared to show its falsity by evidence and statistics of the office during the two years past; and that deponent has been unable to procure the requisite statistics and proofs from the records in the brief period allowed. Deponent further says, that the said charges are each and all of them untrue, and that he has a good and substantial defence upon the merits, after a full statement of the facts, as he is advised by counsel and verily believes to be true.

JOEL B. ERHARDT.

Sworn to before me, this 20th day of December, 1877

[L S]   EDMUND C GAY,
Notary Public.

Sidney P Nichols, for nearly two years previously chairman of the Committee of the Police Department on Street Cleaning, in defending himself against this charge of dereliction, testified that the organization of the Street Cleaning Bureau was made up as follows

The person in charge was known as the Street Cleaning Inspector, and by law was required to be a Police officer. He had charge of all the operations of the Bureau, directed how and when the work should be done, and was responsible to the Commissioners of Police for the proper carrying out of the work of the Bureau. He was assisted by a person known as the Deputy Inspector, who assisted him in carrying out the orders of the Inspector, and had a general supervision of the work of the Bureau

The city was divided into Street Cleaning Districts, usually Wards, of which one or more constituted a district, which was in charge of a foreman, who had the immediate charge of the work in his district, assisted by two or more gangmen, who were in direct charge of the laborers and cartmen, of which there were employed constantly a sufficient number to perform the work in each district The gangmen reported all matters to the foreman, and the foreman made a daily report of all the men employed, the time each is entitled to, the streets cleaned, and the number of loads of ashes, garbage, and street sweepings gathered by the cartmen and delivered at the several dumping boards upon scows or barges to be taken away to places of deposit. There was one district made up of Broadway and the principal avenues and streets that need cleaning oftener and at night, which district was in charge of a foreman and gangman, the same as the other districts. The foremen directs what streets and avenues shall be cleaned each working day, unless specially ordered by the Inspector to clean certain streets or parts of streets on specified days.

There was a person employed at each dumping board known as a Dump Inspector, who had charge of all work and workmen at the dump, and kept a tally of all loads delivered by the carts, specifying each cartman by name and the number of loads each cartman delivered during the day or night. These daily returns of the foreman and Dump Inspectors were returned each day to the officer of the Street Cleaning Bureau, and there compiled and preserved

There was a person known as the Superintendent of Scows, or Boats, who had the immediate charge of all the floating property of the bureau, and directed (under orders from the Inspectors) where the materials shall be taken to to be disposed of, and has charge of the force employed in disposing of the same

There was a person known as the Superintendent of Stables, who had the immediate charge of the stables and repair shops. All horses, carts and machines owned by the bureau, except when at work in the several districts, were in charge of a foreman He had charge of and kept the time of all laborers, mechanics, etc, employed in and about the stables

The Street Cleaning Department was created by statute in 1872 The Board of Police were required to clean the streets, and to keep them clean In 1873 the amount of money expended was one million and seventy-nine thousand dollars, in 1874, it was eight hundred and twenty-nine thousand dollars, in 1875, eight hundred and one thousand dollars; in 1876 it was seven hundred and twenty-six thousand dollars, and in 1877 it was seven hundred and twenty-five thousand dollars, or five hundred and ninety-two thousand dollars to November 1, 1877, and for all four years three million four hundred and fifty-four thousand dollars The number of miles they cleaned in 1873 was eleven thousand; in 1874 twelve thousand, in 1875 it was nine thousand, and in 1876 it was eleven thousand In four years, forty-five thousand three hundred and twenty-two The loads of ashes, garbage and dirt removed were as follows: In 1873 one million one hundred and forty-seven thousand; in 1874, one million and thirty thousand; in 1875, one million and thirty-one thousand; in 1876, one million and eleven thousand, four million four hundred and twenty thousand in four years The total cost per mile in the first year was ninety-eight dollars; the second year, 1874, sixty-four dollars and eighty cents, in 1875, it was eighty dollars and fifty-six cents, in 1876, it was sixty-four dollars—making an average of seventy-six dollars and eighty-two cents per mile in each year The cost per load of material—that is the only way it can be arranged—was, for the first year, ninety-seven cents; second year, eighty cents; third, seventy-seven cents, and for the fourth year, seventy-one cents; making an average of eighty-three cents for four years; and in 1877 it has been seventy-two cents A million of loads and more was the product, two hundred and fifty miles of streets to be cleaned, and three hundred miles and over to be traversed every day for the purpose of collecting ashes, garbage and street dirt. The material so collected had the relation of about sixty-five to seventy per cent. of ashes ; of about—a large allowance—ten per cent. garbage, and the remainder street sweepings as it was collected.

The manual at present in use in the Police Department was promulgated in 1877 Amendments have been added thereto at several subsequent periods Some of the rules and regulations of the aforesaid manual are appended in a condensed form. The following was the Board of Police for 1877: William F Smith, DeWitt C Wheeler, Joel B Erhardt, Sidney P. Nichols, Commissioners. Officers William F Smith, President; DeWitt C. Wheeler, Treasurer.

COMMITTEES.—On Rules and Discipline: Commissioner Erhardt, Chairman; Commissioners Wheeler, Smith and Nichols. On Street Cleaning: Commissioners Nichols and Wheeler. On Repairs and Supplies. Commissioners Wheeler and Nichols. On Elections: Commissioners Wheeler and Nichols On Clerical Force. Commissioners Wheeler and Nichols. Seth C. Hawley, Chief Clerk; George W. Walling, Superintendent

The "Police Department" of the city of New York consists of a "Board of Police" composed of four "Commissioners" (appointed by the Mayor, by and with consent of the Board of Aldermen,) and the "Police force" and officers appointed by said Board The Board is the head of the Police Department ; governs and controls the department, its business and affairs ; is invested with and exercises all the powers conferred by law upon the Police Department The territorial jurisdiction and authority of the Board, and the Police force under their direction, are co-extensive with the territorial limits of the city of New York For the purposes of Police government, the territory of the city of New York is divided into Inspection Districts, Surgeons Districts, and Precincts, subject to alteration, from time to time, by the Board of Police. Precincts are divided into patrol beats or posts by the Captains, with the approval of the Superintendent, subject to alteration, from time to time, by like authority

The territory of the city of New York was divided into four Inspection Districts, which are respectively named the First, Second, Third, and Fourth Inspection Districts

First District consists of Precincts Nos 1, 4, 7, 10, 11, 13, 14, 17, 18, 21, 26, and First and Third District Court Squads

Second District consists of Precincts Nos 5, 8, 9, 15, 16, 20, 25, 27, 29, and Second District Court Squad

Third District consists of Precincts Nos 12, 19, 19 Sub , 23, 33, 34, and Fourth, Fifth, and Sixth District Court Squads

Fourth District consists of Precincts Nos 22, 30, 31, 32, and 35.

An Inspector of Police is assigned to each district, and has an office within the limits of his district, or at such places as the Board of Police may determine.

The Superintendent, unless otherwise ordered by the Board of Police, assigns one Inspector, in rotation, to attend to the night duty, and one to the duty pertaining to the Central Department, on Sunday.

Night duty commences at 6 P. M. and terminates at 8 A M.

Sunday duty begins at 8 A. M. and ends at 6 P M.

278   *OUR POLICE PROTECTORS.*

The Police force of the city of New York consists of a Superintendent, four Inspectors, Surgeons, Captains, Sergeants, Patrolmen and Doormen, clerks and employees, to the number of each rank, authorized by law.

The Police force is divided into as many companies as there are Precincts, and such other companies and squads as the Board of Police may order

The regulation uniform is.

For the Superintendent—The dress is a double-breasted frock coat; the waist to extend to the top of the hip, and the skirt to within one inch of the bend of the knee; two rows of Police buttons on the breast, eight in each row, placed in pairs, the distance between each row five and one-half inches at the top, and three and one-half inches at the bottom, stand-up collar, to rise no higher than to permit the chin to turn freely over it, to hook in front at the

Orphan Asylum

bottom; cuffs, three and one-half inches deep, and to button with three small buttons at the under seam; two buttons on the hips, one button on the bottom of each skirt-pocket welt, and two buttons intermediate, so that there will be six buttons on the back; collars and cuffs to be of dark blue velvet; lining of the coat, black, the pantaloons plain; black neckcloth and white collar; the waist-coat single-breasted, with eight buttons placed at equal distances

For Inspectors—The dress the same as for Superintendent, except that there are seven buttons in each row on the breast of the coat, placed at equal distances, and the gold wreath on the hat shall inclose the word "Inspector" in silver

For Captains and Sergeants—The same as for Superintendent, except that there are eight buttons in each row, on the breast of the coat, placed at equal distances, collar rolling, the collar and cuffs of the same color and material as the coat; the wreath on the hat to inclose the word "Captain" or "Sergeant," with the number of the precinct to which the officer is attached in gold. The Captain of the Harbor Police has a gold anchor, and the Sergeants silver anchors, inclosed in a wreath, in lieu of the number of the precinct.

For Patrolmen—The dress is a single-breasted frock coat with rolling collar, the waist to extend to the top of the hip, and the skirt to within one inch of the bend of the knee; nine buttons on the breast, two buttons on the hips, two buttons on the bottom of each pocket, and three small buttons on the under seam of the cuffs. Trousers have a white welt in the outer seam; white shirt collar; black neckcloth; vest, single-breasted, with nine buttons placed at equal distances. The hat, with wreath surrounding the appropriate number in white metal.

Patrolmen detailed as Roundsmen, in addition, have the word "Roundsman" in white metal letters, in lieu of the wreath.

Roundsmen wear on each arm of the overcoat, dress coat, and blouse, a United States Infantry chevron of two stripes, above the point of the elbow.

The officers of the force rank in the following order: First, Superintendent; second, Inspector; third, Captain; fourth, Sergeant; fifth, Roundsman.

Mounted Roundsmen wear, as above mentioned, the United States cavalry chevron.

For Harbor Patrolmen—The dress is a sailor's jacket, rolling collar, to come down half way between the hip joint and knee; five buttons on each side of breast, two buttons on the under seam of the cuff; pockets inside; vest, single-breasted, nine buttons; trousers, plain, shirt of blue flannel; hat, same as other Patrolmen, with wreath and number; pea-jacket overcoat, three inches above the knee, five buttons on each side, side pockets with flaps; in other respects, same as other Patrolmen.

The coat of Mounted Patrolmen and officers in charge is the same as previously described, except that the skirt of the coat extends only to a point midway between the waist and the bend of the knee; and is trimmed on collar, lappels, and cuffs with yellow cord, as per sample in the office of the "Department of Clothing and Equipment." Trousers are the same as above, except that the cord on them shall be yellow. The metallic ornaments on hat and belt are composed of yellow metal. The cord and tassel are of the style prescribed, except that they are yellow.

For Doormen—The dress is a double-breasted round jacket, extending two inches below the hip, with five Police buttons on each breast, and one on the inside seam of each cuff; trousers of Cadet-mixed cloth, plain; hat, the same as Patrolmen, without wreath, but with the word "Doorman" in white metal letters, placed in front. In other particulars, same as Patrolmen.

The summer uniform consists of blue flannel sack coat, and blue flannel trousers. The coat of Patrolmen is a single-breasted sack, with short turn-over collar, to button close up to the chin, and reach to a point four inches above the bend of the knee, with four buttons on the front; no pockets to show on the outside, and the trousers to be made same as winter trousers.

For Harbor Patrolmen—Flannel sack coat and flannel trousers made like the above.

Officers are permitted to wear the summer uniform while in the discharge of desk duty in the station house

No person will be appointed Patrolman of the Police force unless—

First.—He is able to read and write the English language understandingly.

Second.—He is a citizen of the United States

Third.—He has been a resident of this State during a term of one year next prior to his application for appointment

Fourth.—He has never been convicted of crime.

Fifth.—He is at least five feet seven and a half inches in height, measured in his bare feet, and weighs not less than one hundred and thirty-eight pounds, avoirdupois, without clothing

Sixth.—He is less than thirty years of age

Seventh.—He is of good health, and sound in body and mind.

Eighth.—He is of good moral character and habits.

SURGEON'S CERTIFICATE.

QUESTIONS, EACH OF WHICH IS TO BE ANSWERED BY THE MEDICAL EXAMINERS

N B.—It is understood that the Examiners will, of course, put such other questions bearing upon each case as they may think proper, and that the whole Examination will be thorough, exact and circumstantial

Name .. . Age. .. .Residence

Has the Applicant ever been examined by the Surgeons of the Department, and if so, state the result?		
* State the exact Weight, A, Height B, Circumference of Chest under Clothing, C, figure and general appearance, D	Wg't Height. A B. ft | In	C† D Circumference chest in in .. . Under Clothing At Forced Expiration On Full Inspiration
A Is the Respiring Murmur clear and distinct over both Lungs? B. Is the character of the Respiration Full, Easy and Regular? C Are there any indications of Disease of the Organs of Respiration or their Appendages?	A. B. C.	
A Is the Character of the Heart's Action Uniform, Free and Steady? B. Are its Sounds and Rhythm Regular and Normal? C Are there any indications of Disease of this Organ or of the Blood Vessels?	A. B. C.	

A State the Rate and Quality of Respiration? B. State the Rate and other Qualities of the Pulse. C Does it Intermit, or become Irregular or Unsteady?	A. .... B. .... C. ....
Is the Applicant subject to Cough, Expectoration, Difficulty of Breathing, or Palpitation?	....
A. Are the functions of the Brain and Nervous System in a Healthy State? B Have the Brain or Spinal Cord ever been Diseased?	A .... B ....
If the Applicant has had any serious Illness or Injury, state expressly what effect, if any, is perceptible in the heart, lungs, kidneys or other abdominal organs, or the skin, eyes, ears, limbs, etc	....
Has the Applicant any predisposition, either hereditary or acquired, to any constitutional disease, as phthisis, scrofula, rheumatism?	....
Does the Applicant display any evidence of having, or having had, syphilis?‡	....
Do the Answers to Questions in the Application, and to the Certificates thereto attached, give, in your opinion, a full and, in all respects, a satisfactory description of the Person?	....

* The Examiners are called upon to pay especial attention to the annexed schedules in determining the fitness of the applicant for the duties of a patrolman

† There should be a difference, at least, of two inches at forced expiration and on full inspiration

** Obesity must be regarded as a good cause for rejection, whenever it exists to the extent of interfering with the activity and usefulness demanded of a policeman under emergencies

‡ Syphilitic taint in the applicant must always be regarded as good cause of rejection

† Minimum Circumference of the Chest tolerable in applicants

Height ft inches	Circumference of Chest inches
5 7½	33¼
5 8	34
5 9	34½
5 10	35
5 11	35½
6 —	36
6 1	36½
6 2	37
6 3	37½
6 4	38

STATURE AND WEIGHT.—The stature shall not be below 5 ft 7½ in., nor the weight below that marked as its minimum accompaniment in the subjoined table

Height ft inches.	Min Weight lbs
5 7½	138
5 8	140
5 9	145
5 10	150
5 11	155
6 —	160
6 1	165
6 2	170
6 3	175
6 4	180
6 5	185

REMARKS ....

WE HEREBY CERTIFY, that we have this day carefully and thoroughly examined, in accordance with the above instructions... . ... and find that he is .. sound in limb and body, is ... . able-bodied..... . .... of a robust constitution, has .... good eyesight and........good hearing, and in our opinion is physically qualified to sustain the labors and exposures, and perform the duties of a Patrolman, and that the above is a truthful record of the examination

New York . . .. 187 ....: } Surgeons of Police

POLICE DEPARTMENT, 300 Mulberry Street, N. Y.

I HEREBY CERTIFY, *that I have carefully reviewed the foregoing record of examination, and find the same to be in accordance with the instructions of the Board*

.............*Ch'ef Surgeon.*

Dated........187.

No......

....

Examined ....187.

....

S. C. HAWLEY, *Chief Clerk.*

You will cause the bearer..........................*to be Examined by the Committee of Surgeons in pursuance of the Rule*

.................*Commissioner*

Signature of Applicant.....................

Preliminary examinations for appointments on the force of those reported favorably by the Surgeons are held by the chief clerk in his office, in respect to their eligibility and qualifications to be Patrolmen, except as to their physical conditions. Evidence of their naturalization and honorable discharge from the army or navy shall be then produced. To those who are found clearly competent he delivers a petition in the form, properly filled up. On such petition the candidate procures the signatures of not less than ten reputable citizens, when it is to be returned to the chief clerk, who designates which of the petitioners shall verify the petition by affidavit. The chief clerk causes the confidential inquiry into the character, habits, and associations of the candidate to be made by the Captains of the precincts in which the candidate resides, and also by the Superintendent, through officers specially detailed by him for that purpose. The chief clerk, upon the return of favorable character reports, causes the candidates to appear before the full Board, when the Board decides which of the applicants shall be placed on the roll of candidates to be appointed Patrolmen as vacancies occur.

PETITION

To the Board of Police of the Police Department of the City of New York.

The undersigned request the Board of Police to appoint .... to be................in the Police force of the city of New York, and individually, and each for himself, states and represents to the Board that he has known the said ....personally, intimately, and well, for......... year last past, and is qualified to speak intelligently in relation to his character, habits and associations, and states and represents that he is a man of good moral character, correct and orderly in his deportment, and not in any respect a violator of law or good order. That he is of sober, temperate, and industrious habits, not addicted to the habitual use of intoxicating drinks, or to other hurtful excesses— that he has never seen him drunk, or known or heard of his having been drunk; nor of his having been guilty of or arrested for, any criminal or disorderly conduct or act.

And they further represent as aforsaid, that he is a man of truth and integrity, of sound mind, good understanding, and of a temper, habits and manners fit to be a Policeman. The undersigned are willing and ready at any time to appear at the Central Department and make affidavit to the truth of the above representation.

N. B.—The names and residences of at least ten petitioners are required.

Signature of Petitioners   Residence of Petitioners

(Reverse side of Petition as follows)

AFFIDAVIT

State of New York,
City and County of New York, } ss

The undersigned, being duly sworn, doth depose and say, that he has read the foregoing petition, signed by him, knows the contents thereof, and that the same is true

Sworn before me this. . . day
of   . . 187 .

....

Chief Clerk

Notice to Petitioners —The welfare and efficiency of the Police force demands that all promotions be made on the ground of merit and ability, to be proved by thorough and faithful performance of Police duties, and that all transfers from one precinct to another, as well as detailments to special duty, be decided quite independent of political or personal considerations, or influences. It is therefore desired that all applicants and their friends understand and remember that when a man is appointed a member of the force, he must submit himself to the rules, regulations, and orders of the department, and seek to win advancement and favorable positions by a faithful and thorough discharge of Police duties ; that petitions and solicitations in his behalf for promotion, transfer, or detailment, by outside parties, are regarded by the Board as subversive of discipline and subordination, and cannot advance the interest of the member in whose behalf they are made

By order of the Board,

. .. ...

Chief Clerk

Any member of the Police force may be punished by the Board of Police, in their discretion, either by reprimand, forfeiture, and withholding pay not exceeding thirty days for any one offense, or by dismissal from the force, on conviction of either of the following offenses, to wit

Of intoxication
Of any act of insubordination or disrespect towards a superior officer.
Of any acts of oppression or tyranny
Of nelgect of duty.
Of violation of the rules.
Of neglect or disobedience of orders.
Of any legal offence.
Of absence without leave
Of immoral conduct
Of conduct unbecoming an officer.
Of conduct injurious to the public peace or welfare.
Of incapacity, mental, physical, or educational.
Of any breach of discipline.
Of neglecting or refusing to pay a debt for uniform clothing.
Of contracting a debt under false or fraudulent pretences

Before being qualified as a Patrolman, the following form of statement must be made under oath, and subscribed to by the applicant·

POLICE DEPARTMENT OF THE CITY OF NEW YORK.

No. 300 MULBERRY STREET

New York..............187

STATEMENT of............*an applicant for appointment as Patrolman of the Police Force of the City of New York, made for the purpose of testing his qualifications.*

QUESTIONS	ANSWERS.
What is your name?..................	....
In what year, day, and month were you born?......	....
Where were you born?................	....
If not born in the United States, have you been naturalized. When and where?.............	....
Can you read and write English?............	....
Have you been arrested for misdemeanor, or for any crime?.................	....
Have you been convicted of any crime or misdemeanor?	....
Have you resided in this State for one continuous year last past?.................	....
Where do you now reside?.............	....
Are you Married?................	....
What Family have you?..............	....
What has been your occupation?.........	....
Have you ever had the rheumatism?.........	....
Have you ever had a fit of any kind?.........	....
Have you ever had piles, and how long since?.....	....
If your parents, or either of them, are dead, at what age and of what disease did they die?.........	....
Have you been in any military service?........	....
Were you honorably discharged?..........	....
Have you ever been a Policeman?.........	....
Have you paid, or promised to pay, or given any money or other consideration to any person, directly or indirectly, for any aid or influence towards procuring your appointment?............	....

CITY AND COUNTY OF NEW YORK, ss ....
being duly sworn, doth depose and say, as follows· I wrote the answers and signed the within statement with my own hand, and the same is true

Sworn and subscribed before me, this ....
day of........ . 187

.... *Chief Clerk.*

NOTICE.—Applicants are required to fill the blanks on the other page of this paper in their own handwriting, without any aid, assistance, or suggestion from any other person. This must be done in the office of the Chief Clerk. Any false statement, evasion or deception in answering the within questions will be good grounds for rejection of the application, and of dismissal from the Force.

All orders to the Superintendent of Police emanates from and are issued to him only by the Board of Police, and all orders to the Police force are issued by the Superintendent to the Inspectors or Captains of Police, and by him to them communicated to the force, or any member or members thereof ; he is the chief executive officer of the Police force, subject to the orders, rules, and regulations of the Board of Police.

Each Inspector is held responsible for the general good conduct and order of his district, as the Captains of Police are held responsible for the good conduct and order of their respective precincts, and while no rule is laid down by the Board of Police for his precise government, it is expected that each Inspector will visit portions of his district, and the station houses therein, at uncertain hours of the day and night. He will diligently inquire into every complaint made by citizens of laxity or misconduct in performance of duty by members of the force, and report the same to the Superintendent

St. Luke's Hospital.

Sergeants in turn, shall patrol their precincts, and see that the Roundsmen and Patrolmen of their platoons or sections are performing their duty properly It is the duty of the Sergeant on patrol to go on patrol with his section or platoon; to remain out during the tour, in the vigilant performance of duty; and to return with the men to the station house, at the end of the tour. There are four Roundsmen for each precinct, two for each platoon; to be selected from the Patrolmen by the Board of Police, and to hold the position during the pleasure of the Board The Roundsmen shall promptly obey all orders received from their superior officers; shall set an example of sobriety, discretion, skill, industry, and promptness to the Patrolmen under their command, and, at all times, appear neatly attired, and cleanly in their persons and equipments Each Sergeant, Roundsman, or other visiting officer, should see each Patrolman under his command while on post, at least once during each tour of duty.

The prevention of crime being the most important object in view, the Patrolman's exertions must be constantly used to accomplish that end. He must examine and make himself perfectly acquainted by sight with every person living on his post, vigilantly watch every description of person passing over his post; and to the utmost of his power prevent the commission of assaults, breaches of the peace, and all other crimes about to be committed.

On charges preferred by Mayor Cooper, Governor Robinson removed Commissioners Nichols and Smith. Joel B. Erhardt's term had expired. Charles F. MacLean was appointed April 18, 1879, in place of Sidney B. Nichols. Stephen B. French was appointed May 20, 1879, in place of Joel B. Erhardt, and James E. Morrison was appointed August 5, 1879, in place of William F. Smith. Morrison resigned November 24, 1879, and John R. Voorhis was appointed in his place.

Sidney P. Nichols and William F. Smith were reinstated February 7, 1880, by the Court, which caused the removal of MacLean and Voorhis. Joel W. Mason was appointed May 25, 1880, in place of DeWitt C. Wheeler, whose term of office had expired.

Mayor Grace appointed James Matthews Police Commissioner on March 11, 1881, in place of William F. Smith, resigned. Commissioner Matthews served the unexpired term of William F. Smith, and Mayor Grace re-appointed Mr. Matthews to succeed himself. Mayor Edson re-appointed Sidney P. Nichols January 9, 1883, to succeed himself.

Mr. Nichols died on the twenty-eighth of October, 1884, and Fitz John Porter was appointed to fill the unexpired term.

CHAPTER XIV.

PROVISIONS OF THE CONSOLIDATION ACT

1880—1885.

CENTRAL OFFICE BUREAU OF DETECTIVES—GOVERNMENT AND DISCIPLINE OF THE POLICE DEPARTMENT.—POWERS INVESTED IN THE BOARD OF POLICE—BUREAU OF ELECTIONS.—BOARD OF HEALTH.—POLICE SURGEONS—SPECIAL PATROLMEN—POLICE LIFE INSURANCE FUND—POWERS OF THE POLICE FORCE—PAWNBROKERS—THE SANITARY COMPANY.—DUTIES OF CAPTAINS AND SURGEANTS, OF PHYSICIANS—THE TELEGRAPH SYSTEM.—AN ACT AMENDATORY OF THE CONSOLIDATION ACT.—ROOSEVELT COMMITTEE—LOTTERY AND POLICY.

AN Act to amend Chapter 335, Laws of 1873, known as the Public Burdens Bill, was passed May 29, 1880. This placed the salaries of the Commissioners of Police, hereafter to be appointed, at five thousand dollars a year, each The salary of the force, thereafter to be appointed, was as follows Inspectors three thousand dollars; Captains, one thousand eight hundred dollars; Surgeons, one thousand five hundred dollars, Sergeants, one thousand two hundred and fifty dollars; Patrolmen, eight hundred dollars After two years of service in the third grade, such Patrolman was advanced to the second grade and received nine hundred dollars per annum. After two years service in the second grade he was advanced—should his conduct and efficiency have been satisfactory—to the first grade, at an annual salary of one thousand dollars

An Act passed May 17, 1882, authorized the Board of Police to establish a Bureau, which should be called the Central Office Bureau of Detectives, not to exceed forty detectives, who were entitled to receive the same pay as the Sergeants of Police, namely, one thousand six hundred dollars per year.

An Act to consolidate the special and local laws affecting public interests in the city of New York (Chapter 410, Laws of 1882), thus, with slight variations from the legal phraseology of the text, defines the powers and duties of the Police Department.

The government and discipline of the Police Department should be such as the Board of Police may from time to time, by rules and regulations, prescribe The Board, from time to time, in their discretion, are empowered to enact, modify, and repeal orders, rules and regulations of general discipline of the subordinates under their control, but in strict conformity to the provisions of the chapter

The Board was invested with power to issue subpoenas, attested in the name of its President, to compel the attendance of witnesses upon any proceedings authorized by its rules and regulations. Each Commissioner of Police, the Superintendent, the Chief Clerk and Deputy, are authorized and empowered to administer affirmations and oaths to any person summoned and appearing in any matter or proceeding authorized as aforesaid, and in all matters appertaining to the department or the duties of any officer, or to take any deposition necessary to be made under the orders, rules and regulations of the Board. Any person making a complaint that a felony or misdemeanor has been committed, may be required to make affirmation or oath thereto, and, for this purpose, the Inspectors, Captains and Sergeants of Police shall have power to administer affirmations and oaths. The Board of Police shall at all times cause the ordinances of the city of New York, not in conflict with law, to be properly enforced. The Board shall provide suitable accommodations for the detention of witnesses who are unable to furnish security for their appearance in criminal proceedings, to be called the House for the Detention of Witnesses. And it shall be the duty of all Magistrates, when committing witnesses in default of bail, to commit them to such House of Detention. The Board of Police may, with the authority and approval of the Mayor and Common Council, from time to time, but with special reference to locating the same as centrally in precincts as possible, establish, provide, and furnish stations and station houses, or sub-stations, at least one to each precinct, for the accommodation of members of the Police force, and as places of temporary detention for persons arrested and property taken within the precinct. The Board of Police shall have power to erect, operate, supply and maintain, all such lines of telegraph to and between such places in the city for the purposes and business of the Police Board as they shall deem necessary, the cost of which shall be chargeable to the general expenses of the Police. The Board is permitted to use the said telegraph lines to aid them in facilitating the operations of the Department of Health, and when so used, the expense thereof shall be charged to the said Department of Health.

In the performance of Police service in any precinct or precincts comprising waters of the harbor, the Board of Police may procure and use and employ such rowboats and steamboats as shall be deemed necessary and proper. In rural or sparsely inhabited precincts they may establish a mounted patrol, and procure, and use, and employ so many horses and equipments as shall be requisite for the purpose; and they may procure and cause to be used any teams and vehicles required to transport prisoners, supplies and property, whenever it shall be proper and economical to do so; and may sell and dispose of, in accordance with law, any personal property owned or used in the department whenever it shall have become old and unfit, and not required for service; and they shall have authority to detail and employ Patrolmen in any duty or service other than patrol duty, which may be necessary and proper to enable said Board to exercise the powers and perform the duties and business imposed and required by law.

It shall be the duty of the Board of Police·

To cause some intelligent and experienced person connected with the Police force to attend at the Police courts in cases where there is need of such assistance, who shall aid in bringing the facts before the Police Justices in proceedings pending in such Police courts. It is made the duty of the Police Board to provide for the lodging of vagrant and indigent persons. The Board shall have authority to offer rewards to induce all classes of persons to give information which shall lead to the detection, arrest, and conviction of persons guilty of homicide, arson, or receiving stolen goods knowing them to be stolen; and to pay such rewards to such persons as shall give such information.

To continue the bureau in the office of the Department of Police known and designated as the Bureau of Elections The affairs of said bureau shall, under and subject to such rules, regulations and orders as may from time to time be made and adopted by said Board of Police; be managed, conducted, and carried on by a suitable and proper person, chosen and selected by the said Board, who shall be known as the Chief of the Bureau of Elections; shall hold office for the period of three years, and whose salary shall be fixed and paid by the said Board at such sum as they shall deem proper, not exceeding five thousand dollars, and shall be removable by the Board of Police for cause

To perform all the duties imposed upon them in Sections eighteen hundred and forty-five, eighteen hundred and forty-six, eighteen hundred and forty-seven, eighteen hundred and fifty, eighteen hundred and fifty-two, eighteen hundred and fifty-three, and eighteen hundred and fifty-seven.

To properly advise the Board of Health of all threatened danger to human life or health, and of all matters thought to demand its attention, and to regularly report to said Board of Health all violations of its rules and ordinances, and of the health laws and all useful sanitary information. Said Boards shall, so far as practicable and appropriate, co-operate for the promotion of the public health and the safety of human life in said city.

To faithfully (by and through its proper officers, agents and men) enforce and execute the sanitary rules and regulations, and the orders of the Board of Health, upon the same being received in writing and duly authenticated as said Board of Health may direct. To employ and use the appropriate persons and means, and to make the necessary and appropriate expenditures for the execution and enforcement of said rules, orders and regulations, and such expenditures, so far as the same may not be refunded or compensated by the means herein elsewhere provided, shall be paid as the other expenses of said Board of Health are paid. In and about the execution of any order of the Board of Health, or of the Board of Police made pursuant thereto, Police officers and Policemen shall have as ample power and authority as when obeying any order of or law applicable to the Board of Police, or as if acting under a special warrant of a Justice or Judge, duly issued , but for their conduct they shall be responsible to the Board of Police, and not to the Board of Health The Board of Health may, with the consent of the Board of Police, impose any portion of the duties of subordinates in said department upon subordinates in the Police Department.

The Police Department, through its Treasurer, and in pursuance of the orders, rules and regulations of the Board, shall pay all salaries and wages to the officers and members of the Police Department and force, as established by and in pursuance of law, and all bills, claims, and obligations lawfully incurred by, or by authority of said Board ; and the Comptroller shall pay over to the Treasurer of

Police, on the requisition of the Board of Police, the total amount annually estimated, levied, raised, and appropriated for the support and maintenance of the Police Department and force, from time to time, and in such sums as shall be required (not exceeding one-twelfth part of said total annual amount in any one month), and the Treasurer of Police, if required by the Comptroller, shall transmit to the Department of Finance, each month, duplicate vouchers for the payment of all sums of money made on account of the Police Department during each month. The Board of Police shall procure and pay for all printing, books, blanks, paper, and other articles of stationery required for the administration and business of the department and each bureau thereof. Any one of the Commissioners, or any member of the Police force, who shall, after qualifying in office,

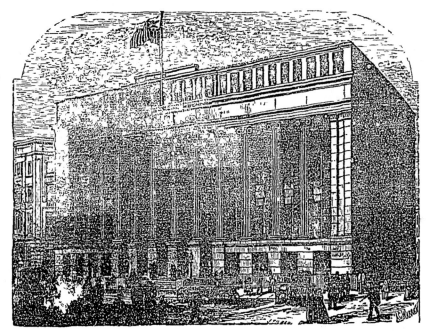

Custom House, Wall Street

accept any additional place of public trust, or civil emolument, or who shall during his term of office be publicly nominated for any office elective by the people, and shall not within ten days succeeding the same publicly decline the said nomination, shall be in either case deemed thereby to have resigned his commission, and to have vacated his office, and all votes cast at any election for any person holding the office of Police Commissioner, or within thirty days after he shall have resigned such office, shall be void.

The Commissioners of Police shall annually, or as often as a vacancy shall occur, elect one of their number to act as the President of the Board of Police. He shall preside at the meetings of the Board. They shall select one of their number to be the Treasurer of Police. He shall be the fiscal officer of the Police. He shall, on check and voucher, duly disburse, by order of the said Police

Board, all moneys belonging to the Police fund, and shall deposit the same, when paid to him, in a bank or banks designated by said Board. The Treasurer shall give a bond, with two sureties in the sum of twenty thousand dollars each, for the faithful performance of his duties; said bond to be approved by the Comptroller, and filed in his office.

The Police force shall consist of one Superintendent of Police, four Inspectors; Captains, not exceeding in number one to each fifty of the total number of Patrolmen; Sergeants, not exceeding four in number to each fifty of the total number of Patrolmen; Doormen, not exceeding two in number to each fifty of the total number of Patrolmen; not exceeding twenty-two Surgeons, one of whom shall be designated as Chief Surgeon; and Patrolmen to the number of two thousand three hundred. The Board of Police shall have power to increase the Police force by adding to the number of Patrolmen from time to time, as far as the funds appropriated allow, but such increase shall not exceed one hundred in any one year.

Whenever a vacancy shall occur in the office of Superintendent of Police, and in the absence or disability of the said Superintendent, the President shall possess all the powers and perform all the duties of that office, subject to the orders, rules and regulations of the Board of Police. But the Commissioners of Police may, by resolution, designate such other officer of the Police force as they may choose, to execute and perform the duties of the Superintendent during the period of such absence or disability.

The duties of the Police Surgeons, and the extent and bounds of their districts, shall be assigned, from time to time, by the rules and regulations of the Board of Police. The Board of Police may, if requested by the Board of Health, employ their Surgeons to aid the Sanitary Inspectors in the discharge of their duties, under such regulations and orders as the Board of Police may make and issue.

No person shall now be appointed to membership on the Police force, or continue to hold membership therein, who is not a citizen of the United States, or who has ever been convicted of crime, or who cannot read and write understandingly in the English language, or who shall not have resided within the State one year, but skilled officers of experience may be appointed for Detective duty who have not resided as herein required. No person shall be appointed Patrolman who shall be at the date of such appointment over thirty years of age, or who shall have been convicted of any crime, nor shall any person who shall have been a member of the force and resigned, or been dismissed therefrom, be re-appointed, except by the concurring vote of all of the Commissioners comprising the Board, to be taken by yeas and nays, and recorded in the minutes. The name, residence and occupation of each applicant for appointment to any position in the Police Department, as well as the name, residence, and occupation of each person appointed to any position, shall be published, and such publication shall, in every instance, be made on the Saturday next succeeding such application or appointment, in the *City Record*.

The Board may, upon an emergency or apprehension of riot, tumult, mob, insurrection, pestilence, or invasion, appoint as many Special Patrolmen, without pay, from among the citizens, as it may deem desirable. The Board of Police, with the approbation in writing of the Mayor, or, in case of their disagreement, the Governor, may, under similar circumstances, demand the assistance of the military of the First Division, and such commanding officer shall obey such order Special Patrolmen, appointed in pursuance of law, may be dismissed by resolution of the Board, and while acting as such, Special Patrolmen shall possess the powers to perform the duties, and be subject to the orders, rules, and regulations of the Board, in the same manner as regular Patrolmen. Every such Special Patrolman shall wear a badge, to be prescribed and furnished by the Board of Police

Every member of the Police force shall have issued to him by the Board of Police, a proper warrant of appointment, signed by the President of said Board and Chief Clerk or first deputy, which warrant shall contain the day of his appointment and his rank. Each member of the Police force shall, before entering upon the duties of his office, take an oath of office, and subscribe the same before any officer of the Police Department who is empowered to administer an oath

Promotions of officers or members of the Police force shall be made by the Board only on grounds of meritorious Police service and superior capacity, and shall be as follows. Sergeants of Police shall be selected from among Patrolmen assigned to duty as Roundsmen, Captains from among Sergeants, and Inspectors from among Captains.

The Board shall have power, in its discretion, on conviction of a member of the force of any legal offense or neglect of duty, or violation of rules, or neglect or disobedience of orders, or absence without leave, or any conduct injurious to the public peace or welfare, or immoral conduct, or conduct unbecoming an officer, or other breach of discipline, to punish the offending party by reprimand, forfeiting and withholding pay for a specified time, or dismissal from the force, but no more than thirty days' pay shall be forfeited for any offense. All such fines shall be paid forthwith to the Treasurer of the Department to the account of the Police Life Insurance Fund. Members of the force shall be removable only after written charges shall have been preferred against them, and after the charges have been publicly examined into, upon such reasonable notice to the person charged, and in such manner of examination as the rules and regulations of the Board of Police may prescribe

No member, under penalty of forfeiting the salary or pay which may be due to him, shall withdraw or resign, except by permission of the Board of Police Unexplained absence, without leave, of any member of the Police force, for five days, shall be deemed and held to be a resignation, and the member so absent shall, at the expiration of said period, cease to be a member of the Police force

Every person connected with the Police Department on the thirtieth day of April, eighteen hundred and seventy-three, and who remains so connected, shall continue in office, and the amount of salary or compensation then legally paid to such person, except as in this Act otherwise provided or authorized, shall be the salary and compensation fixed for his office; but the Commissioners may fix the salary and compensation of such clerks and employees other than Policemen whom they may be authorized by law to employ

No person holding office under this Department shall be liable to military or jury duty, and no officer or Patrolman, while actually on duty, shall be liable to arrest on civil process, or to service of subpoena from Civil Courts

No member of the Board of Police, under any pretense whatsoever, shall, for his own benefit, share in any present, fee, gift, or emolument for Police services, additional to his regular salary or compensation. The Board, for meritorious and extraordinary services rendered by any member of the Police force in the due discharge of his duty, may permit any member of the Police force to retain for his own benefit any reward or present tendered him therefor; and it shall be cause for removal from the Police for any member thereof to receive any such reward or present without notice thereof to the Board of Police Upon receiving said notice, the said Board may either order the said member to retain the same, or shall dispose of it for the benefit of the Police Life Insurance Fund.

The several members of the force shall have power and authority to immediately arrest, without warrant, and to take into custody, any person who shall commit, or threaten, or attempt to commit, in the presence of such member, or within his view, any breach of the peace or offense directly prohibited by Act of the legislature, or by any ordinance of the city. The members of the Police force shall possess, in the city of New York and in every part of this State, all the common law and statutory power of Constables, except for the service of civil process, and any warrant for search or arrest, issued by any Magistrate of this State, may be executed, in any part thereof, by any member of the Police force, and all the provisions of Sections seven, eight and nine of Chapter two, title two, part four, of the revised statutes, in relation to giving and taking of bail, shall apply to this chapter

Any member, as the regulations of the said Board may provide, may arrest any person who shall, in view of such member, violate or do, or be engaged in doing or committing in said city, any act or thing forbidden by Chapter twelve of this Act, or by any law or ordinance, the authority conferred by which is given to the Board of Health, or who shall, in such presence, resist, or be engaged in resisting the enforcement of any of the orders of said Board, or of the Board of Police pursuant thereto And any person so arrested shall be thereafter treated and disposed of as any other person duly arrested for a misdemeanor.

In every case of arrest by any member of the Police force, the same shall be made known immediately to the superior on duty in the precinct wherein the arrest was made, by the person making the same ; and it shall be the duty of the said superior, within twenty-four hours after such notice, to make written return thereof, according to the rules and regulations of the Board of Police, with the name of the party arrested, the alleged offense, the time and place of arrest, and the place of detention Each member of the Police force, under the penalty of ten days' fine, or dismissal from the force, at the discretion of the Board, shall, immediately upon an arrest, convey in person the offender before the nearest sitting Magistrate, that he may be dealt with according to the law. If the arrest is made during the hours that the Magistrate does not regularly hold court, or if the Magistrate is not holding court, such offender may be detained in a station house, or precinct thereof, until the next regular public sitting of the Magistrate, and no longer, and shall then be conveyed without delay before the Magistrate, to be dealt with according to law. And it shall be the duty of said Board, from time to time, to provide suitable rules and regulations to prevent the undue detention of persons arrested, which rules and regulations shall be as operative and binding as if herein specially enacted, subject, however, to the order of the court committing the person arrested.

It shall be a misdemeanor punishable by imprisonment in the penitentiary for no less than one year, nor exceeding two years, or by a fine of not less than two hundred and fifty dollars, for any person, without justifiable or excusable cause, to use, or to incite any other person to use, personal violence upon any member of the Police thereof when in the discharge of his duty, or for any member of the Police force to willfully neglect making any arrest for an offense against the law of this State, or ordinance in force in the city of New York, or for any person not a member of the Police force to falsely represent himself as being such member with a fraudulent design upon person or property, or upon any day or time to have, use, wear, or display without authority, any shield, buttons, wreaths, numbers, or other insignia or emblem such as are worn by the Police.

It shall be a misdemeanor for any person not being a regular member of the Police, established in any city of this State, or a member of the Police force of the city of New York, or a Constable of this State, or a Police Constable, or Assistant Police Constable, or a Sheriff, or one of the usual general Deputies of any Sheriff of this State, to serve any criminal process within the said city

It is hereby made the duty of the Police force, at all times of day and night, and the members of such force are hereby thereunto empowered to especially preserve the public peace, prevent crime, detect and arrest offenders, suppress riots, mobs, and insurrections, disperse unlawful or dangerous assemblages, and assemblages which obstruct the free passage of public streets, sidewalks, parks and places, protect the rights of persons and property, guard the public health; preserve order at elections and all public meetings and assemblages, prevent and regulate the movement of teams and vehicles in streets, and remove all nuisances in the public streets, parks, and highways ; arrest all street mendicants and beggars ; provide proper Police attendance at fires ; assist, advise, and protect emigrants, strangers, and travelers in public streets, at steamboat and ship landings, and at railroad stations ; carefully observe and inspect all places of public amusement, all places of business having excise or other licenses to carry on any business, all houses of ill fame or prostitution, and houses where common prostitutes resort or reside, all lottery offices, policy shops, and places where lottery tickets, or lottery policies are sold or offered for sale, all gambling houses, cock-pits, rat-pits, and public common dance houses, and to repress and restrain all unlawful or disorderly conduct or practices therein ; enforce and prevent the violation of all laws and ordinances in force in said city, and for these purposes, with or without warrant, to arrest all persons guilty of violating any law or ordinance for the suppression or punishment of crimes or offenses.

The Superintendent, and each Captain within his precinct, shall possess powers of general Police supervision and inspection over all licensed or unlicensed pawnbrokers, venders, junk-shop keepers, junk boatmen, cartmen, dealers in second-hand merchandise, intelligence office keepers and auctioneers, within the said city; and in the exercise of, and in furtherance of said supervision, may from time to time empower members of the Police force to fulfill such special duties in the aforesaid premises as may be from time to time ordained by the Board. The said Superintendent, and each Captain within his precinct, may, by authority in writing, empower any member of the force, when-

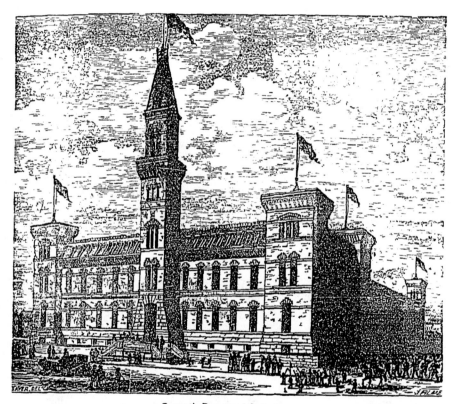

Seventh Regiment Armory.

ever such member shall be in search of property feloniously obtained, or in search of suspected offenders, or evidence to convict any person charged with crime, to examine the books of any pawnbroker, or his business premises, or the business premises of any licensed vender, or licensed junk-shop keeper, or dealer in second-hand merchandise or intelligence office keeper, or auctioneer, or boat of any junk boatmen. Any such member, when thereto authorized in writing by the said Superintendent, shall be authorized to examine property alleged to be pawned, pledged, deposited, lost or stolen, in whosesoever possession said property may be, but no such property shall be taken from the possessor thereof without due process or authority of law. Any willful interference with the said Superintendent or Captain, or with any member of the force, by any of the persons hereinbefore named in this section, whilst in official discharge of his duty, shall be punished as a misdemeanor

The Superintendent and Captains and persons acting by their, or by either of their orders, shall have power to examine the books of any pawnbroker, his clerk or clerks, if they deem it necessary, when in search of stolen property, and any person having in his possession a pawnbroker's ticket, shall, when accompanied by a Policeman, or by an order from the Superintendent or Captain, be allowed to examine the property purported to be pawned by said ticket; but no property shall be removed from the possession of any pawnbroker without the process of law required by the existing laws of this State, or the laws and ordinances of the city regulating pawnbrokers. A refusal or neglect to comply in any respect with the provisions of this section, on the part of any pawnbroker, his clerk or clerks, shall be deemed a misdemeanor, and be punishable as such.

If any member of the force, or if any two or more householders shall report in writing under his or her signature, to the Superintendent, that there are good grounds (and stating the same) for believing any house, room, or premises within the said city, to be kept or used as a common gaming house, common gaming room, or common gaming premises, for therein playing for wagers of money at any game or chance, or to be kept or used for lewd and obscene purposes or amusements, or the deposit or sale of lottery tickets or lottery policies, it shall be lawful for the Superintendent to authorize, in writing, any member or members of the Police force to enter the same, who may forthwith arrest all persons there found offending against law, but none others; and seize all implements of gaming, or lottery tickets, or lottery policies, and convey any person so arrested before a Magistrate, and bring the articles so seized to the office of the Property Clerk. It shall be the duty of the said Superintendent to cause such arrested persons to be rigorously prosecuted, and such articles seized to be destroyed, as the orders, rules, and regulations of the Board shall direct.

It shall be the duty of the Superintendent of Police to detail, on each day of election, at least two Patrolmen to each election poll. It shall be the duty of the Police force, or any member thereof, to prevent any booth, or box, or structure, for the distribution of tickets at any election, from being erected or maintained within one hundred and fifty feet of any polling place within the city, and to summarily remove any such booth, box or structure, or close and prevent the use thereof.

The annual salaries and compensation of the members of the force who became members of such force before May 29, 1880, shall be as follows: Of the Superintendent, six thousand dollars, of the Inspectors, thirty-five hundred dollars each; of Police Surgeons, twenty-two hundred and fifty dollars each; of the Captains, two thousand dollars each, and of the Sergeants, sixteen hundred dollars each; the pay of Patrolmen shall be at the yearly rate of twelve hundred dollars each; and that of Doorman at the rate of nine hundred dollars per year each. The salary attached to either of the following positions shall not exceed the sum here designated as the maximum salary of such position when held by any person appointed to the said Police force on or after May 29, 1880, to wit. For an Inspector, three thousand dollars; for a Captain, eighteen hundred dollars; for a Surgeon, fifteen hundred dollars; for a Sergeant, twelve hundred and fifty dollars. The members of the uniformed force of the Police Department, appointed to said force after May 29, 1880, shall, on their appointment, become members of what shall be known as the third grade, at a salary of eight hundred dollars per year; after two years of service in such third grade they shall, if their conduct and efficiency have been satisfactory, be advanced to what shall be known as the second grade, at a salary of nine hundred dollars per year; after two years service in such grade, they shall, on like conditions, be advanced to what shall be known as the first grade, at a salary of one thousand dollars per year But no member of such uniformed force shall be so advanced, as aforesaid, except after examination by and approval of the said Board of Police of his record, efficiency and conduct. The salaries and pay aforesaid shall be paid monthly to each person entitled thereto, in modes to be prescribed by the rules and regulations, subject to such deductions each month from the salary or pay of members of the force, as the Treasurer shall make (and which deductions he is hereby authorized to retain) to satisfy fines imposed on any member of the force by way of discipline or punishment, as prescribed by the rules and regulations of the Board

The Commissioners of Police may designate some person to take charge of all property alleged to be stolen or embezzled, and which may be brought into the Police office, and all property taken from the person of a prisoner, and all property or money alleged or supposed to have been feloniously obtained, or which shall be taken into the custody of any member of the Police force, or criminal court in the city of New York, or which shall come into the custody of any Police Justice, or officer, shall be, by such member or Justice, or by order of said court, given into the custody of and kept by the Property Clerk of the Police All such property and money shall be particularly registered by said Property Clerk in a book kept for that purpose, which shall contain the name of the owner, if ascertained, the place where found, the name of person from whom taken, with the general circumstances, the date of its receipt, the name of the the officer recovering the same, the names of all claimants thereto, and any final disposition of such property or money. The said Commissioners may prescribe regulations in regard to the duties of the Clerk so designated, and require and take security for the faithful performance of the duties imposed by this section

Whenever property or money shall be taken from persons arrested, and shall be alleged to have been feloniously obtained, or to be the proceeds of crime, and whenever so brought, with such claimant and the person arrested, before some Magistrate, for adjudication, and the Magistrate shall be then and there satisfied from evidence that the person arrested is innocent of the offense alleged, and that the property rightfully belongs to him, then said Magistrate may thereupon, in writing, order such property or money to be returned, and the Property Clerk, if he have it, to deliver such property or money to the accused person himself, and not to any attorney, agent, or clerk of said accused person.

If any claim to the ownership of such property or money shall be made on oath before the Magistrate, by or in behalf of any other person than the person arrested, and the said accused person shall be held for trial or examination, such property or money shall remain in the custody of the Property Clerk until the discharge or conviction of the person accused.

All property or money taken on suspicion of having been feloniously obtained, or of being the proceeds of crime, and for which there is no other claimant than the person from whom such property was taken, and all lost property coming into the possession of any member of the said Police force, and all property and money taken from pawnbrokers as the proceeds of crime, or by any such member from persons supposed to be insane, intoxicated, or otherwise incapable of taking care of themselves, shall be transmitted as soon as practicable to the Property Clerk, to be registered and advertised in the *City Record* for the benefit of all persons interested and for the information of the public, as to the amount and disposition of the property so taken into custody by the Police

If property stolen or embezzled be not claimed by the owner before the expiration of six months from the conviction of person for stealing or embezzling it, the officer having it in his custody must, on payment of the necessary expenses incurred in its preservation, deliver it to the Commissioners of Charities and Correction, to be applied for the benefit of the poor of this city All other property and money that shall remain in the custody of the Property Clerk for the period of six months without any lawful claimant thereto, after having been advertised in the *City Record* for the period of ten days, shall be sold at public auction in a suitable room to be designated for such purpose, and the proceeds of such sale shall be paid into the Police Life Insurance Fund.

If any property or money placed in the custody of the Property Clerk shall be desired as evidence in any Police or other criminal court, such property shall be delivered to any officer who shall present an order to that effect from such court Such property, however, shall not be retained in said court, but shall be returned to such Property Clerk, to be disposed of according to the previous provisions of this chapter.

It shall be lawful for the Police Commissioners, whenever they shall be notified in writing by the Metropolitan Association of Amateur Oarsmen that a regatta is to be given under its auspices on the Hudson River, opposite Washington Heights, New York City, to keep the course used for any such regatta free and clear of all boats and vessels of every description during the actual time of the regatta, which shall not exceed six hours in any one day; provided that there shall not be more than five regattas in any one year. 2. That the course selected for such regattas shall be above Seventy-second Street, and far enough up the river so as not to interfere with any line of ferry-boats running on their regular course, and trips. 3 That said regatta course shall not exceed in breadth more than one-fourth the width of the river from either shore, nor shall it exceed more than three miles in length.

The course selected for any such regatta shall be plainly marked out by buoys or boats, and anchored; such buoys or boats shall have a flag placed upon them so that they may be readily seen. No boat, vessel, or steamboat of any description shall be allowed on said regatta course during the actual time of any regatta, except by the consent of the officers in charge of such regatta. Any person rowing a rowboat, or pilot of a sailboat, sailing vessel or steamboat, willfully going upon such regatta course, and thereby interfering with the regatta, shall be deemed guilty of a misdemeanor, and shall be liable to a penalty of not

Post Office and United States Court Building

less than one hundred dollars, or imprisonment in the County Jail for a time not to exceed three months, or to both penalty and imprisonment The fine or penalty to go to the Police fund It shall be the duty of the Police Commissioners to furnish a sufficient number of Police to keep said regatta course clear, and they shall have power to arrest any person or persons going upon such regatta course during the time of the regatta in violation of this or the preceding section

Nothing in this or the preceding section contained shall apply to, or be so constructed as to interfere in any way with sailing vessels actually engaged in commerce while proceeding on their course.

The Board of Police, upon the requisition of the Board of Health, shall detail to the service of the said Board of Health, for the purpose of the enforcement of the provisions of the acts relating to tenements and lodging houses, not exceeding thirty suitable officers and men of experience of at least five years' service in the Police force, provided that the Board of Health shall pay monthly to the Board of Police a sum equal to the pay of all officers and men so detailed These officers and men shall belong to the Sanitary Company of Police, and shall report to the President of the Board of Health The Board of Health may report back to the Board of Police, for punishment, any member of the said Company guilty of any breach of orders or discipline, or of neglecting his duty, and thereupon the Board of Police may detail another officer or man in his place, and the discipline of the said members of the Sanitary Company shall be in the jurisdiction of the Board of Police; but at any time the Board of Health may object to the efficiency of any member of said Sanitary Company, and thereupon another officer or man may be detailed in his place. The Board of Police shall have the power, and it shall be their duty, to fill all vacancies in the Police force of the city caused by the detailing of said officers and men upon the requisition of the Board of Health.

Upon the application of any person residing within the precinct, it shall be the duty of the Captain, or other officer at the desk, to register in a book kept open for that purpose, the name or address of any person desiring or needing medical attendance, with the name or address of the person making such application, and without delay to select and notify of such application one from the list of physicians who have registered in the said precinct as thereby pledging themselves to respond to any call for medical attendance, and who have been certified by the Registrar of Vital Statistics of the Board of Health as being in good and regular standing, and it shall be the duty of the Captain or other officer at the desk, in the absence of any expressed preference by the applicant, to select and notify from the list of physicians thus registered, the name of the physician residing nearest to the residence of the said patient in whose behalf application is made.

It shall be the duty of the Captain, Sergeants, or other officer at the desk, in such Police precinct as before specified, upon registry of any application as described in the preceding section, immediately to detail an officer whose duty it shall be to call upon such physician without delay, and to conduct him to the residence of the patient, also to verify by personal inspection or inquiry, the name and address of such patient as registered by his superior officer Every officer thus detailed as messenger shall be furnished with a blank certificate, upon which the name and address of the physician responding to the call, the name and address of the patient attended, and the date and hour of the visit, shall be written by him after he has conducted the physician to the patient's residence and verified the genuineness of the application. Such certificate shall be signed by him and given to the physician, and shall specify upon its face

therein named, is entitled to the sum of three dollars from the public funds upon presentation thereof to the proper officer, and indorsement thereof in writing with the name of the Captain of the precinct. But it shall be the duty of the physician making such visit to present such certificate to the patient or his or her agent or attendant, and to request payment of the said sum specified; and in case of such payment being made, said physician shall surrender such certificate to the person or persons making it, and it shall cease to be a claim upon the public treasury. In default of the immediate payment of the said fee specified in the said certificate, by the patient or his or her attendant, it shall be the duty of the Captain of the Police Precinct in which the visit was made to indorse it with his name; and thus indorsed it shall be the duty of the Cashier of the Board of Health to pay at sight the fee aforesaid, and to enter the payment in a book provided for that purpose, and take up the certificate. And all certificates thus redeemed shall be valid debts to the amount therein named, against the patients therein named, or their guardians, which the said Board may order collected by due process of law, provided that no prosecution shall be instituted in cases where it is satisfactorily shown that the patient is without sufficient means for the payment thereof.

It shall be the duty of every physician thus called to the medical assistance of any person within the Police Precinct in which he is registered, to transmit to the Registrar of the Board of Health, within twenty-four hours after the call shall have been answered, a full and accurate statistical exhibit of the case; specifying therein the age and sex, and the employment, profession, or business of the patient, the nature of the disease, and the hour of the attack when practicable; the date, and the Police Precinct and Ward in which the case occurred; the same shall be signed with the full name and address of the physician rendering it, but the name and address of the patient shall always be omitted. And it shall be the duty of the Board of Health to provide all physicians thus registered for night medical service with appropriate blanks for the safe purpose on their application therefor.

Any Policeman who shall be detailed as messenger according to the provisions hereinbefore specified, shall, in the absence of preference expressed in the application, call the physician nearest and most convenient to the patient's residence, or, in the absence of or refusal from any cause, of the latter, the physician next nearest, and so on, and there shall be no delay or waiting for such physician to return, and any member of the force neglecting to comply with this provision shall be subject to trial and fine, or dismissal from the service by the Board of Police in the same manner as for other offenses cognizable by the said body And any physician thus registering, who shall twice refuse or neglect, without reasonable excuse, to answer a call made according to the provisions of the three preceding sections, shall be subject to have his name erased from the list, upon proper evidence thereof submitted to an executive officer who shall be appointed by the Registrar of Vital Statistics of the Board of Health, and shall be under his immediate supervision.

The Captains of the several Police Precincts shall cause the names and addresses of such physicians as have been duly certified by the Registrar of Vital

Statistics to be plainly and legibly written or printed on a bulletin provided for that purpose, which bulletin shall be placed at a convenient point near the Captain's desk, and kept open to the inspection of all persons within the precinct desiring to see the same. They may, if in their judgment it shall be necessary to the public convenience, cause the bulletins of physicians herein specified to be posted in the hotels and district telegraph offices within their respective precincts, but any applicant applying at such hotels or telegraph offices, or desiring the services of any messenger other than a member of the Police force detailed for the purpose, shall employ such messenger at his own expense, and shall be liable for any expenses incurred in communicating with the Police Precinct.

The period during which the aforesaid physicians shall be held to be subject to call shall be between the hours of ten in the evening and seven in the morning, from October 1 to March 31, inclusive, and between the hours of eleven in the evening and six in the morning from April 1 to September 30, inclusive.

Next follows an exposition of the law in relation to the Police Pension Fund, which will be treated of in a separate chapter. The Act then continues to define the duties and powers of the Police Department, as follows:

Every owner of a steam boiler or boilers in use of the city of New York shall, annually, and at such convenient times and in such manner and such form as may by rules and regulations to be made therefor by the Board of Police be provided, report to the said Board the location of such steam boiler or boilers, and thereupon, or as soon thereafter as practicable, the Sanitary Company, or such member or members thereof as may be competent for the duty herein described, and may be detailed for such duty by the Board of Police, shall proceed to inspect such steam boiler or boilers, and all apparatus and appliances connected therewith; but no person shall be detailed for such duty except he is a practical engineer, and the strength and security of each boiler shall be tested by hydrostatic pressure; and every boiler or boilers so tested shall have, under the control of such Sanitary Company, such attachments, apparatus, and appliances as may be necessary for the limitation of pressure-lock, and secured in like manner as may be from time to time adopted by the United States Inspectors of Steam Boilers, passed July 25, 1866, and they shall limit a pressure of steam to be applied to or upon such boiler, certifying each inspection and such limit of pressure to the owner of boiler inspected, and also to the engineer in charge of same, and no greater amount of steam or pressure than that certified in the case of any boiler shall be applied thereto. In limiting the amount of pressure, wherever the boiler under test will bear the same, the limit desired by the owner of boiler shall be the one certified, but all steam users, manufacturers, or corporations possessing the guaranteed certificates unrevoked in full life of any fire insurance company now incorporated or hereafter incorporated, or of any company organized or hereafter organized, for the purpose of making guaranteed steam boiler inspections, and they shall have complied with the insurance laws of the State, having duly filed a statement with the Superintendent of Insurance or other authorized officer, of its condition, and duly paid license fees and taxes, shall be exempt from such inspections.

Any company referred to in the last preceding section which has complied therewith, shall, at least once in six months, make and file returns, under oath, with the Board of Police, of all inspections made by them of steam boilers and of all certificates issued by them; and those at the time of making said return either in full force, unrevoked or canceled. Each and every company so authorized and making insurances and failing to make such returns as aforesaid, shall pay the penal sum of fifty dollars for each and every failure or

Broadway, South from Post Office

neglect to make and file said returns, the same to be recovered by suit to be brought by the Board of Police.

The Board of Police shall preserve in proper form a correct record of all inspections of steam boilers made under its direction, and of the amount of steam or pressure allowed in each case, and in cases where any steam boiler or the apparatus or appliances connected therewith shall be deemed by the Board, after inspection, to be insecure or dangerous, the Board shall prescribe such changes and alterations as may render such boilers, apparatus and appliances devoid of danger. And in the meantime and until such changes and alterations are made, and such appliances attached, such boiler, apparatus and appliances may be taken under the control of the Board of Police, and all persons prevented from using the same, and, in cases deemed necessary, the appliances, apparatus or attachments for the limitation of pressure, may be taken under the control of the said Board of Police And no owner or agent of any steam boiler shall employ any person as engineer without having a certificate as to the qualification from practical engineers, to be countersigned by the Commissioners of Police

Any person applying or causing to be applied, to any steam boiler, a higher pressure of steam than that limited for the same in accordance with the provisions of this chapter, and any person violating the provisions of the last preceding section, shall be guilty of misdemeanor In case any owner of any steam boiler in the said city shall fail or omit to have the same reported for inspection as provided by law, such boiler may be taken under control of the Board of Police, and all persons prevented from using the same until it can be satisfactorily tested as hereinbefore provided for, and the owner shall, in such case, be charged with the expense of so testing it

The Board is hereby authorized, in addition to the Police force now authorized by law, to appoint a number of persons, not exceeding two hundred, who may be designated by any company which may be operating a system or signaling by telegraph to a central office for Police assistance, to act as Special Patrolmen in connection with such telegraphic system And the person ap pointed shall in and about such service have all the powers possessed by the members of the regular force, except as may be limited by and subject to the supervision and control of the Board of Police No person shall be appointed as such Special Patrolman who does not possess the qualifications which may be required by the Board of Police for said special service, and the person so appointed shall be subject in case of emergency to the duty as part of the regular Police force. The Board of Police shall have power to revoke any such appointment or appointments at any time, and every person so appointed shall wear a badge and uniform, to be furnished by such company and approved by the Board of Police Such uniform shall be designated at the time of the first appointment under this section, and shall be the permanent uniform to be worn by the said Special Police. The pay of such Special Patrolmen and all expenses connected with their services, shall be wholly paid by such company or companies, and no ex penses or liability shall at any time be incurred, or paid by the Board of Police for, or by reason of the services of the persons so as aforesaid appointed

An Act was passed on April 21, 1884, amendatory of the Consolidation Act, the leading features of which are The Treasurer to appoint a Deputy Treasurer; in case of absence or inability to perform his duties, the Treasurer to be respon sible for the acts of the Deputy; the Board of Police to deduct and withhold pay for absence for any cause, absence without leave, sickness, or other disability, etc, not to exceed one-half, except in cases of absence without leave. No leave of absence exceeding twenty days in any one year, to be granted, except that the member waived and released not less than one-half of salary. The salaries of members appointed on and after January 1, 1885, to be as follows: Superintendent, six thousand dollars, Inspectors, three thousand five hundred dollars; Surgeons, one thousand eight hundred dollars; Captains, two thousand dollars, Patrolmen, appointed on and after January 1, 1885, known as third grade, one thousand dollars; after one year's service in such grade, if conduct and efficiency have been satisfactory, such Patrolman to be advanced to the second grade, and receive an annual salary of one thousand one hundred dollars; after one year's service in the second grade, on like conditions, to be advanced to the first grade, at one thousand two hundred dollars

Schedule of arrests made for lottery and policy violations and gambling during the years 1880, 1881, 1882, 1883 and 1884.

PRECINCT	Arrests	Discharged by Magistrate	Held by Magistrate	Tried	Convicted	Acquit'd	Pending
1	51	14	37	10	8	2	27
4	133	57	76	35	30	5	41
5	16	3	13	4	4		9
6	4	4	13	.	..	.	..
7	29	16	..	7	7		9
8	27	10	17	1	1		16
9	28	15	13	7	5	2	6
10	165	104	61	6	6	.	55
11	25	8	17	3	2	1	14
12	7	4	3	.	..	.	4
13	33	21	12	5	4	1	7
14	86	45	41	3	3		38
15	83	18	65	14	14		51
16	14	5	9	1	1	..	8
17	77	30	47	9	7	2	38
18	13	8	5	1	1	..	4
19	14	6	8	2	2	.	6
20	60	42	18	..	..	..	18
21	39	17	22	1	1	..	21
22	23	9	14	1	1	.	13
23	4	4	.	..	..		..
25	1	1	.	.	.		.
26	4	1	3	..		.	3
27	105	64	41	16	15	1	25
28	22	10	12	2	2	.	10
29	95	39	56	5	5	.	51
30	1	1	.	..	..	..	.
31	3	3	.	.	.		.
33	3	3	.	..	..		.
1st Dist office	189	30	159	69	53	16	90
2d Dist office	5		5	1	1	..	4
3d & 4th Dist office	18	6	12	.	.		12
Department bureau	210	30	180	38	38		142
	1587	628	959	241	211	30	722

An Act passed April 22, 1884, declared that "On and after the first day of January, 1885, the grade and pay or compensation of members of the Police force who are Patrolmen in all cities of this State, having, according to the last census, a population exceeding eight hundred thousand, shall be as follows. All such members who are Patrolmen on said first day of January, 1885, and who shall have served three years or upwards on said force, shall be members of the First Grade; all such members who have served on such force for less than three years, and more than one year, shall be members of the Second Grade; and all other members who are Patrolmen then on said force shall be members of the Third Grade; and all persons appointed Patrolmen after said first day of January, 1885, shall, on their appointment, become members of the Third Grade Whenever any member of the Third Grade shall have done service therein for one year, he shall be advanced to the Second Grade; and whenever any member of the Second Grade shall have done service therein for one year he shall be advanced to the First Grade; but no such Patrolman shall be advanced as aforesaid except after examination by, and approval of the Board of Police or Police Commissioners of such city, of his record, efficiency and conduct. The annual pay or compensation of the members of the Police force who are Patrolmen as aforesaid, shall be as follows. For members of the First Grade at the rate of twelve hundred dollars each; for members of the Second Grade at the rate of eleven hundred dollars each, for members of the Third Grade at the rate of one thousand dollars each The pay or compensation of aforesaid shall be paid monthly to each person entitled thereto, subject to such deductions for or on account of lost or sick time, sickness, disability, absence, fines or forfeitures, as the Board of Police may, by rules and regulations, from time to time, prescribe or adopt"

CHAPTER XV.

FIRST INSPECTION DISTRICT.

SUPERINTENDENT WILLIAM MURRAY —A BRILLIANT RECORD —WHAT A POLICEMAN MAY BECOME BY HONESTY, PERSEVERANCE AND ABILITY —A MODEL POLICE OFFICIAL.—METHODICAL, KEEN, AND DEVOTED TO HIS PROFESSION — THE FIRST PRECINCT; CAPTAIN CAFFRY —"THE IRON MAN."—THE MOST IMPORTANT POLICE DISTRICT IN THE WORLD.—FOURTH PRECINCT; CAPTAIN WEBB —SIXTH PRECINCT; CAPTAIN MCCULLAGH —SEVENTH PRECINCT; CAPTAIN HEDDEN.—TENTH PRECINCT, CAPTAIN ALLAIRE —ELEVENTH PRECINCT; CAPTAIN MEAKIM —THIRTEENTH PRECINCT; CAPTAIN PETTY.—FOURTEENTH PRECINCT, CAPTAIN MURPHY —SEVENTEENTH PRECINCT, CAPTAIN MCCULLAGH —EIGHTEENTH PRECINCT; CAPTAIN CLINCHY –TWENTY-FIRST PRECINCT; CAPTAIN RYAN —TWENTY-SIXTH PRECINCT; SERGEANT STEWART

SUPERINTENDENT WILLIAM MURRAY is an officer whose career illustrates how, by honesty, perseverance, and ability, a Patrolman may become the highest officer of the force He is a native of New York City, and was born in the year 1844 In 1861 he joined the Ellsworth Zouaves (Eleventh New York State Volunteers), and was severely wounded at the battle of Bull Run He joined the Police force in 1866, and went to the Third Precinct, which was then under the command of Captain James Greer A few days after joining the force he made some very clever arrests, one of them being a negro named Jake Joralemon, who was a notorious burglar, and who had used a revolver in one of his exploits at Newark on a woman named Mrs Ward, a clothier's wife in that place The Governor of New Jersey and the Mayor of Newark offered a reward (the former six hundred dollars and the latter two hundred and fifty dollars) for his capture Then followed the arrest of Worth, for blowing open the safe in Messrs. Steiner's tea store in Vesey Street

The routine of official duties is about as follows. He reaches his office at Police Headquarters at eight A. M. His first care is to assort the mail and next to examine the returns from the various precincts, noting any irregularities or errors that may have been made, together with the charges of serious felonies made against prisoners Visitors are admitted to his office at half-past nine A. M, when their grievances and complaints are listened to and disposed of according to the nature of each case The reports of District Inspectors are next in order These reports contain an account of the operations of the force for the previous twenty-four hours The Inspectors then are instructed in regard to Police matters in their districts. The Superintendent daily refers his reports to the Board of Police on any Police matters which may have come before him since the previous meeting of the Board. A consolidated report is next prepared and forwarded to the Board of Police Commissioners, setting forth the work done by each member of the Department for the preceding twenty-four hours. This consolidated report contains a variety of detailed information, such as giving a list of sick or absent members, those who are absent from duty without leave, those who had their night off, etc. The remainder of the day up to five P. M. is occupied in listening to citizens' complaints of all kinds, in telegraphing instructions to the precincts, and such other duties as the occasion may demand.

The Superintendent quits work at six o'clock, and goes home to dinner. As a rule he spends some portion of his time visiting the Police precincts and station houses at night, that he may see for himself if the members of the force are properly performing their duty, that the laws are being enforced, and that business pertaining to the station houses is being transacted in accordance with the prescribed rules of the Department.

After several other clever captures, Patrolman Murray was appointed Roundsman on the first of October, and one year later he was raised to the rank of Sergeant, in which capacity he served in the Eighth, Sixteenth, and Fifteenth Precincts. While in the latter station he arrested the men who had robbed Matty Dancer. Dancer always kept his money and bonds at his house, No. 50 West Eleventh Street, and the burglars, getting scent of this, one day gained admission during his absence, pretending that they were plumbers. Mrs Dancer was gagged, and the burglars carried off an enormous quantity of bonds and greenbacks, amounting at the time, it was said, to two hundred thousand dollars. Sergeant Murray recovered one hundred thousand dollars in bonds, which was part of this haul. For this burglary John Farrell and his wife were sentenced to ten years in State Prison.

Shortly after this, Sergeant Murray, in conjunction with the late Inspector McDermott, made a raid on the gambling house of The Allen, in Bleecker Street, and captured all the gambling implements.

Sergeant Murray was made Captain on the second of October, 1876, and was assigned for duty to the Fourth Precinct.

The following is a portion of the testimony elicited by the Roosevelt Committee:

"William Murray, being duly sworn, testified:

By the Chairman
  Q What is your name?
  A William Murray
  Q What position do you hold?
  A Inspector of Police in the Police Department of this city.
  Q How long have you held that position?
  A About seven years
  Q How long have you been on the Police force?
  A. Nearly eighteen years

By Mr Russell
  Q Before you became Inspector what was your position?

William Murray

Appointed Superintendent June 9, 1885

A Captain

Q How long?

A Eight months

Q. And before that you were a Sergeant?

A Yes, sir

Q How long?

A Six or seven years.

Q And before that a Roundsman how long?

A About a year, I think

Q And before that a Patrolman how long?

A Well, the remaining number of years; I think five years

Q Then you have reached your present position by the strictest application of civil service rules?

A. I have, sir, I so consider it

By Colonel Bliss

Q When you were promoted from Captain to Inspector, do you remember any particular service?

A For doing that that has never been done in the Police Department by an Inspector, by securing nearly five hundred years of convictions in the State prison—doing that that has never been done before or since by a Captain of Police

Q You were promoted on your record?

A Solely, I say to you, gentlemen, I was not a candidate or an applicant for the position of Inspector on the Police."

While he was Captain in the Fourth Precinct, in eight months he made arrests and procured convictions amounting in the aggregate to five hundred years The important services which he rendered to society in hunting down male and female abortionists will not soon be forgotten

Mary Varley, a sister of the notorious "Reddy, the blacksmith," lived at No 56 James Street. A number of burglars deposited their plunder in her house The manoeuvres of these men did not, however, escape Captain Murray's vigilance He went to Mary Varley's house one day and discovered stolen property to the amount of ten thousand dollars Mary was sent to State Prison

In the year 1875 the inhabitants of Long Island were in a state of the greatest alarm owing to the number of masked burglaries which were taking place almost every day On the night of December 22, 1875, six masked burglars entered the houses of Mr. M L Hillier, a Wall Street broker, and Mr Henry Green, at Astoria, and, holding pistols to the heads of the frightened inmates, ransacked the premises, and carried off everything portable that they could lay hands on A few days afterwards John Roberts, John James alias "Fatty" Farrell, Jerry McCarthy alias "Carrol," James Reilly alias "Juggy," and John Schmidt were arrested in New York by Capt William Murray One of the prisoners got for his share in the burglaries thirteen dollars in money and a silver pencil case, but not being of a literary turn of mind, he pawned the pencil case Half an hour afterwards the pencil case was in Capt Murray's hands With this clue the Captain went to work, and succeeded in capturing the thieves The people of Astoria, and in fact the whole community, in the vicinity of New York and Brooklyn, were so pleased at the capture of the burglars that a testimonial was presented to Captain Murray for his energetic action All the prisoners were convicted and sent to State Prison The Police Commissioners at their meeting also passed highly complimentary resolutions to Capt. Murray for these arrests.

Thomas Belton, a trusted employee of Messrs. H. B. Claflin & Company, had for years been a systematic thief. He stole about fifty thousand dollars' worth of needles and thread. Capt. Murray learned that a dealer in such articles named Hall was able to undersell other dealers at prices that made it impossible for them to make any profit. Capt Murray also ascertained that Belton left Claflin's at dinner time, and paid visits to Hall's establishment, where he was detected delivering bundles of goods. Belton was arrested, and was sent to State Prison.

Thomas Cusack murdered his wife at Rose Street on March 6, 1877. He escaped, but was captured an hour afterward by Capt. Murray. The prisoner, when placed on trial, denied all knowledge of what had occurred, but admitted that he was very drunk, therefore could not know what he was about. He was sentenced to State Prison for seven years.

On the eighteenth of September, 1877, Superintendent Walling received a telegram from Boston giving a detailed list of United States and other bonds that had been stolen on the fifteenth of the same month from the Cambridgeport, Massachusetts, Bank. The bonds, in all, amounted to sixty thousand dollars. A close watch was kept by the Police in New York, as the thieves were supposed to have gone there to dispose of their plunder. A reward of three thousand dollars was offered for the return of the United States Bonds, and one thousand five hundred dollars for the return of the Railroad Bonds. Inspector Murray had for some days noticed several suspicious-looking characters enter and come out of a house in East Twenty-ninth Street. He accordingly went there and arrested George C. Briggs, Langdon W. Moore, Rebecca Moore, and Elizabeth Hill. On searching the premises a large collection of burglars' tools were found. They consisted of sectional steel jimmies, ratchet drills, braces and bits, sledges, and several cans of powder, combination safe locks, several pairs of rubber overshoes, and a number of other instruments for blowing open bank safes. The prisoners were taken the next morning to Essex Market Police Court before Justice Smith, and remanded, to enable the Inspector to obtain the necessary evidence for their conviction. Langdon Moore alias Charley Adams, was afterwards recognized as one of the greatest bank robbers in the States, he only having been discharged a year previously for robbing a bank in New York State. George C. Briggs was identified as Thomas H. Leroy, a Boston bank burglar. Elizabeth Hill said she was Leroy's wife, and Rebecca Moore claimed to be Adams' wife. A sister of Charley Adams' wife had made a statement to the Boston Police that she saw Adams and Leroy, when they were leaving that city, packing three trunks. This clue led to their arrest in New York. The only evidence against the women was that they had been in the house in company with the male prisoners, and they were discharged. Briggs, it was proved at his trial, had exchanged baggage checks at Worcester, Mass., and by that means obtained possession of a trunk containing ten thousand dollars' worth of jewelry, which belonged to Messrs. Alling & Co., jewelers at Worcester and New York. A number of previous convictions were proved against Briggs, and he was sentenced to five years in State Prison, and Moore alias Adams, was sent to Boston to stand his trial there for stealing eight thousand dollars in bonds.

On Friday, the twenty-fifth of January, 1878, William R. Alling, of the firm of Alling Bros. & Co., jewelers, of No. 170 Broadway, and Mr. Hayes, of the firm of Wheeler, Parsons & Hayes, jewelers, of No. 2 Maiden Lane, called on the Police Commissioners at Headquarters, and presented the following letter.

"To the Board of Police.

"Gentlemen: The manufacturing jewelers and wholesale dealers in watches and jewelry of the city of New York, appreciating the service and fidelity of Inspector Murray, desire to present to him a gold watch and chain and the accompanying testimonial, and have designated the undersigned as their committee to make such presentation, and to request your permission for the Inspector to receive the same. Yours respectfully,

"W. R. ALLING,
"HENRY HAYES,
"*Committee.*"

Messrs. Alling and Hayes had taken along with them a handsomely engrossed testimonial, and a gold watch and chain valued at one thousand dollars, which they presented to Inspector Murray. The testimonial was as follows:

"The manufacturers of jewelry and wholesale dealers in watches and jewelry in the city of New York, desiring to recognize, as a trade, the valuable and skillful services rendered to them and to the whole community by Inspector of Police William Murray, in the discovery and capture of criminals, and especially the robbery of Messrs. Alling Bros. & Co., the undersigned, manufacturers of and wholesale dealers in watches and jewelry, cordially and earnestly unite in tendering to Inspector Murray this testimonial of their esteem and of their high appreciation of the fidelity, energy, and skill which he has at all times displayed in the efficient discharge of his difficult and perplexing duties."

The testimonial was signed by forty of the most prominent watchmakers and jewelers of New York.

The following is the inscription on the watch: "Presented to Inspector William Murray by manufacturers and dealers in watches and jewelry in the city of New York as a testimonial of his integrity, zeal and efficiency. January, 1878."

The Police Commissioners sanctioned the presentation of the watch and testimonial.

During the labor riots in 1877, at which time millions of dollars' worth of railway property was burned, the Socialists of New York convened a meeting to be held at Tompkins Square. They were refused permission by the Police to parade; but, nevertheless, they announced their intention to do so. They formed in line to march to Tenth Street. Inspector Murray, at the head of five hundred men, dispersed the crowd of ten thousand, and thus saved New York from the mob.

"Wash" Geary, a brother of Ed Goody, (who was recently sentenced to State Prison for a butcher cart robbery) was arrested for stealing a quantity of silk from H. B. Claflin & Co. Oakey Hall, who had just returned from Europe, defended the prisoner. Nobody being able to swear positively that they saw the silk in the bales from which they had been purloined, the prisoner was acquitted, although it was well-known that the bales were shipped as silk, and were so marked on the ship's manifest

A man named Roberts, who was also employed by Messrs Claflin & Co as superintendent in the silk department, had stolen silks which Superintendent Murray discovered were conveyed to the house of Jake Falkenberg, at No 160 Rivington Street. He followed them one evening, and when they got the box into the house he jumped in and found seven thousand dollars' worth of silk Roberts confessed to having taken fifty thousand dollars' worth of silk. He was sent to State Prison for five years

Superintendent Murray's record is a long and interesting one Suffice it to say that he has unmasked more crime, and fastened the guilt on the perpetrators thereof, than any man in the force, with the exception of Inspector Byrnes

Superintendent Murray is a methodical, keen officer, and as devoted to his profession as he is to his family, and that is saying a great deal. He lives comfortably but unostentatiously, at Seventy-eighth Street and Lexington Avenue

Superintendent Murray succeeded Superintendent Walling June 9, 1885 By act of the legislature (Chap 364, Sec. 307, Laws of 1885) the Board of Police Commissioners were empowered to retire any members of the Police force—who had reached the age of sixty years—upon a pension Under this clause Superintendent Walling could be removed from office He chose to resign For a long time previously Superintendent Murray had been looked upon as the coming man His distinguished services and conspicuous talents left him without a rival for the place The Board was not behindhand in appreciating these facts No other name was submitted, the claims of no other official considered, although the Department is not lacking in the timber out of which able superintendents are fashioned, but, with prompt unanimity, the Commissioners called Inspector William Murray to assume the chief executive control of the Police force The new Superintendent, with his accustomed energy, soon demonstrated that he was master of the situation, and he went about remodeling certain Police matters after his own ideas His first important move, three days after he assumed control, was to abolish the old system of District Inspection, and to cause the Inspectors to be aids to the Superintendent, with their offices located at Police Headquarters. The more the management was centralized, Superintendent Murray declared, the better for the efficiency of the force The change was also manifestly in the interest of economy The new system is practically a return to the old one which was abolished by General Smith. The salaries of the men detailed to Inspection District offices amounted to forty-two thousand four hundred dollars per year The men who had been so employed were sent to do duty in the several precincts, to the dismay of the six Sergeants, twelve Patrolmen, and two Doormen, who had enjoyed "soft" places under the old regime His next move was to call all the Captains and the three Inspectors before him at Police Headquarters There he laid down certain sensible and practical rules for their guidance, and issued instructions that the Captains should refrain from calling at Police Headquarters, and remain in their respective precincts, except when they were specially summoned to the Central Office He warned the Captains that they would be held accountable for order in their respective precincts, and for the efficiency of, and proper patroling by, the men under them. He also issued instructions with a view to the suppression of gambling and the parading of streets by women of immoral character. The effect of all this soon became apparent in the demeanor and efficiency of the force. Every man, from the humblest Doorman to the highest in command, was imbued with new-born energy and a more praiseworthy ambition to do his full duty by the public and the Department. The new Superintendent had imparted a portion of his own enthusiasm to the officers and men of the Police force. They worked together for the common weal with a cheerful alacrity which demonstrated the fact that they knew and felt that the transfusion of new blood at the fountain head, as was expected, would be followed by a corresponding degree of official industry throughout the subordinate branches of the Department, and, as a natural consequence, the most beneficial results were made apparent from the beginning. Superintendent Murray, it is conceded, is nothing if not thorough and practical. He is every inch a Policeman of the modern school. He is the right man in the right place.

THE POLICE PRECINCTS.

THE FIRST PRECINCT.—The First Precinct is bounded by Battery Place, Bowling Green, Broadway, Fulton Street, the east track on the East River front, and the Castle Garden and Battery fronts. The station house is in Old Slip, at Front Street. It is a model structure in every sense, and an ornament to the city. It is the most modern Police building; was finished in 1884, and the command was moved in from No. 54 New Street, which was a better station house than some which are yet erected. It cost about eighty thousand dollars. Nathaniel D. Bush was the architect, and its site is that of the old Alms House or Franklin Market, where Eighteen Hose Company "Franklin," under Foreman Hall.' Chesebrough, was stationed, the old First Precinct Station House being up-stairs. The staff of this command are Captain, Charles W. Caffrey, an officer with twenty-six years service; Sergeants, John J. Fitzgerald, Andrew McClintock, Patrick Oates and Arthur Rork. Fitzgerald was appointed in 1863, was made a Roundsman in 1869, and reached the present rank in February, 1871. McClintock became a Patrolman in 1862, Roundsman in 1865, and Sergeant in 1872. Oates was appointed in 1865, became Roundsman two years later, and was promoted in 1870. Rork's dates are Patrolman 1862, Roundsman 1865, and Sergeant 1867.

The First Precinct contains more than the usual proportion of the substantial, representative wealth of the country, and the management of the Police system of a business centre such as this brings with it a considerable amount of responsibility. In the selection of a Captain for such an important post, the Commissioners have chosen the present incumbent, who is a man of experience and sagacity, who knows every nook and corner of the precinct like a book, and is familiar with the business community of that section for a long number of years.

This precinct has twenty day posts and forty night posts, and its force of

Patrolmen should be one hundred men, but sickness and men put on detailed duties, reduce it to about eighty men. James Oates and Charles Hagan are the Precinct Detectives. The detailed men are: E. A. Burgoyne, Ordinances, Richard Ganly, Barge Office, Harvey S. Holly, Custom House, Francis Hagan, Register's Office, William Cotter, Staten Island Ferry, Daniel S. Arnold, Wall Street Ferry, Lawrence C. Daly, South Ferry, William Goodwin and Peter O'Donnell, Fulton Ferry.

CAPTAIN CHARLES W. CAFFRY was born in Provost Street, now Franklin, in the year 1822. He is the son of the principal of a school remarkable for hav-

New First Precinct Station House, Old Slip, Corner Front

ing taught the three R's to a number of well-known down town New York brokers. The Captain served his time to the carpentry business, and was very successful in his trade till the panic of 1857 brought about a change in his fortunes. While engaged in the building of a house in Abingdon Square, he, together with a number of others in the same business, failed. After this he joined the Police, not as a *dernier ressort*, but because he always had an instinctive liking for a military or semi-military life. He was detailed for duty in the first place to the Sixteenth Precinct, in the year 1858. The authorities appreciated his services so much that before the lapse of twelve months he was appointed, successively Roundsman, Sergeant, and Acting Captain in the same year. On the twenty-eighth of April, 1860, he was sent to the Broadway

Squad as a Sergeant, but wishing for a change he applied for permission to join the army. The Commissioners answered his application by again promoting him to a full Captaincy in the Fifteenth Precinct. In July, 1859, he was ordered to the Twentieth Precinct, which was one of the most notorious places in the city at that time. Speaking of Captain Caffrey, one of the Commissioners said: "It is our duty to clean out the cut-throats of that Ward (the Seventeenth), and Caffrey is the man that will do it to perfection." Captain Caffrey remained here until 1872, when he was assigned to the Second Precinct. The capture of James Buchanan, for murdering Widow Shanks in 1861, was a very clever piece of work. The bloody finger marks on the door, which had escaped the detectives' attention, were noted down by Captain Caffrey, and he immediately wrote a note for the evening papers, knowing that the news would travel as fast as the murderer. As a consequence of this the assassin was captured at Susquehanna. There was great excitement when Captain Caffrey returned to the city with his prisoner, and the men christened him the "Iron Man," for displaying such courage and determination.

This is the most important Police District in the world. No officer of Police commands men who have as many billions and vast commercial and financial interests to watch over as Captain Caffrey. Treachery on the part of

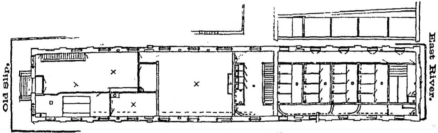

Floor Plan, New First Precinct Station House.

one of his Patrolmen for a couple of hours would enable criminals to possess themselves of booty amounting to millions. Besides the Sub-Treasury, the Assay Office, the Stock Exchange, the Custom House, and scores of money brokers and dealers in bullion, there are the following banking institutions in the First Precinct: American Exchange Bank, Bank of Commerce, Bank of New York, Bank of the Republic, Chase Bank, Chatham Bank, City Bank, Continental Bank, First National Bank, Fourth National Bank, Fulton Bank, Gallatin Bank, Hanover Bank, Leather Manufacturers' Bank, Mechanics' Bank, Merchants' Bank, Phœnix Bank, Seventh Ward Bank, the Third National Bank, the Union Bank, and the United States Bank, and National Bank, the Seamen's Savings Bank, and the following State Banks: Bank of America, Bank of North America, State of New York, Corn Exchange, German American, Manhattan Company, New York Produce Exchange, St Nicholas, and Seaboard. Brokers' offices are numbered by the hundred, and all the exchanges from the vast and magnificent Produce Exchange are here. An emigrant first lands in this precinct at Castle Garden, and within its boundaries are the Barge Office and Battery, the Chamber of Commerce, the termini of the Elevated Railroads, and the Consulates of the Argentine Republic, Bolivia, Brazil, Chili, Columbia, Corea, Costa Rica, Denmark, Ecuador, France, Germany, Great Britain, Greece, Guatemala, Hayti, Italy, Liberia, Monaco, the Netherlands, Nicaragua, Norway, Peru, Portugal, Russia, St Domingo, Salvador, Siam, Spain, Sweden, Switzerland, Turkey, Uruguay, and Venezuela. Mementoes of the great fires of half a century ago are to be found in several parts of the district. Two sensations, in the Police acceptation of the term, have occurred in this precinct, but there have been several incidents of more than ordinary moment. Many recall with a shudder the horrors of the thirty-first of July, 1871, when the boiler of the ferryboat "Westfield" blew up at the Staten Island pier, and how that calm and lovely Sunday ended in general mourning for the fate of the men, women, and

Captain Charles W Caffry.

children who were killed, maimed, or disfigured. This accident ended directly or indirectly the lives of more than eighty-five persons. Another thrilling event occurred in Burling Slip on the fifth of April, 1877. John Jewett & Son occupied the warehouse, No 182 Front Street, as manufacturers of white lead. Orville D Jewett was a member of the firm, but there was mutual dissatisfaction, and the papers for his withdrawal from it had been drafted. At a quarter past ten o'clock in the morning a hand grenade exploded in the private office on the second floor in Burling Slip, and pistol shots were fired. George W and Orville D Jewett, his nephew, were killed, and Mr Joseph A Dean was seriously injured. In spite of overwhelming evidence tending to show that Orville D Jewett threw the bomb, and shot himself with a pistol, the verdict of the Coroners's jury was vague, to say the least of it.

THE FOURTH PRECINCT.—The limits of the Fourth Precinct are Fulton Street, Broadway, Park Row, Centre Street, Chambers Street, Chatham Street,

Chatham Square, Catharine Street, and the east railroad track on the East River front. The station house is at Nos 9 and 11 Oak Street. It was built in 1870 on the site of one of the oldest station houses in New York, and is a comfortable structure; but the approaches to it are narrow, and it is weak in a strategical sense. The officers of the command are Captain, Robert O Webb, and Sergeants, Richard F Magan, Peter Ryan and John Kelly. Magan was made a Policeman in 1870, became a Roundsman in 1873, and was promoted ten years later. Ryan was appointed twenty-three years ago, was made Roundsman in 1863, and obtained rank five years later. Kelly has been on the force twelve years; he was appointed Roundsman in 1882, and the next year rose to his present rank.

Captain Robert O Webb

CAPTAIN ROBERT O WEBB was appointed on the Metropolitan Police on February 7, 1861, and assigned to the Seventh Precinct. He was promoted to be Roundsman, and sent to the Ninth Precinct on August 28, 1862, where he served during the draft riots. He was serving as Roundsman in the First Precinct when he resigned in August, 1865. Three years later (August 3, 1868) he was re-appointed on the force and assigned to the Seventh Precinct. He was promoted Roundsman on July 11, 1871, and transferred to the Twenty-eighth Precinct, made Sergeant August 21, 1873, and sent to the Tenth Precinct. He attained his present rank on May 25, 1880.

This precinct has nineteen day posts and thirty-eight night posts. It has ninety-nine Patrolmen, but details and sickness reduce the effective force to about eighty men. Edward Shalvey and Gilbert Carr are precinct detectives, Thomas Maher is detailed to Park Row, George Logan to Hunters' Point Ferry,

Mark F. Healy is at the Catharine Street Ferry, George Connor and John Grennan to Roosevelt Street Ferry, Wolf Levy to Chatham and Chambers Streets, Edward McCabe to Fulton and Nassau Streets, Edward G Walling to the Tax Office, Edmund Ryan on Corporation Ordinances, J J Nolan to the Catholic Protectory, John Kiernan to Inspector Murray's office

The Fourth Precinct takes under its wings the majority of the newspaper offices, Fulton Market, the New York terminus of the Brooklyn Bridge, the "Swamp," where the leather merchants most do congregate, and vast mercantile and commercial interests. Within its limits are much squalor, misery, and exceeding prosperity. Towards its Broadway boundary it takes in some important dry goods houses. The old Second Precinct Station House, at No 49 Beekman Street, still stands. It is now the office of the Corporation Attorney, and when the gambler Duryea was hacked by Eph. Simmons—the policy dealer in Liberty Street, his body riddled with knife thrusts by Simmons, who broke his ankle in slipping in the blood of his enemy—he was taken there. The Fourth Precinct furnishes many a newspaper story. Dating from the fatal explosion and fire in Hague Street, innumerable tales of horror have been told across its station desk. There was the fire four years ago at No. 35 Madison Street, a "rookery," by which, through the carelessness of a plumber, ten persons lost their lives in a few minutes. On the thirty-first of January, 1882, the Potter Building, at Park Row and Beekman Street, was burned down, and despite the efforts of citizens, Police and firemen, four persons lost their lives. The fatal crush on the Brooklyn Bridge shortly after it was opened is remembered with a shudder. Newspapers sometimes furnish gossip themselves, witness the slaying of Richardson by McFarland in the *Tribune* office, fifteen years ago.

THE SIXTH PRECINCT —The Sixth Precinct is bounded by Chambers Street, Chatham Street, Chatham Square, the Bowery, Hester Street, Centre Street, Howard Street, and Broadway. The station house is at Nos. 19 and 21 Elizabeth Street. It is the finest in the city except the First Precinct Station House, and is a handsome, roomy structure, admirably adopted to Police purposes. The officers are: Captain John McCullough, who signs his name McCullagh, although he says his father spelled it like the great tragedian; and Sergeants John Ryan, Robert Young, William Thompson, and Edward Colgrove. Ryan was a Policeman in 1869, a Roundsman in 1881, and a Sergeant a year later. Young joined the force in 1866, became Roundsman in 1873, and attained rank six months later. Thompson's record is: Patrolman 1866, Roundsman six months later, and Sergeant 1872. Colgrove, the senior Sergeant, put on the uniform in 1860, became Roundsman in 1862, and attained his present position in 1865

CAPT JOHN MCCULLAGH, of the Sixth Precinct, is a young man of pleasing appearance and agreeable manners. By his strict attention to duty and his innate politeness he has made a host of friends. No stronger corroboration of this fact can be adduced than that he is one of the youngest, if not the youngest, Captain on the force, as well in point of years as in point of promotion. Captain McCullagh joined the force in 1870, and was stationed in the Fifth Precinct He was appointed Roundsman in 1873 and Sergeant in 1876, and Captain in

July, 1883 He was engaged in the Orange riots in 1871, and also in the Tompkins Square riots

The precinct has nineteen day posts and thirty-four night posts, and its force of eighty men is reduced by sickness and details to seventy men David Gerrow and Thomas J Crystal are the Precinct Detectives William Looney is detailed to Corporation Ordinances

The "Bloody Sixth" no longer exists, and much that was written about its dangers and horrors was imaginary. It was mainly a slum of the city, and some parts of the present district need purging In old times its polyglot and parti-colored population huddled together in kennels, not fit for street curs, in the neighborhood of the Five Points, where are now the House of Industry, the yard of the Disinfecting Corps of the Health Department, and Paradise Park.

Captain John McCullagh

"Slumming," a cockney recreation which became fashionable last year, was fashionable in New York a quarter of a century ago. Society leaders and society dames went to "The Sixth" to sup on horrors and experience "sensations" in the gruesome squalor and naked vice they witnessed under the guidance of Police officers. Nearly all the "horrors" of those days were minor affairs, the outcome of vile rum and the most groveling passions, and in these days would hardly make an item for a decent newspaper. Italians, Chinamen and Hebrews are now, in the main, the occupants of the squalid dens in "the Bend" in Mulberry Street and the lower part of Baxter Street, and "elephant hunters," as "slummers" are termed by the Central Office Detectives—who act as cicerones now-a-days—are treated to a sight of an opium den, the "Big Flat" in Elizabeth Street, and the stale beer or "all sort" dives The Thalia Theatre and Atlantic Garden are in this precinct, as well as the White Street Depot of the Vanderbilt railroads, and the historic Tombs Prison. On the twenty-fourth of December, 1872, the same day that witnessed the destruction of the Hippotheatron and other buildings in East Fourteenth Street, fire broke out at Nos 81, 83 and 85 Centre Street, and a number of bookbindery girls were killed, and property worth one hundred and sixty-seven thousand dollars was destroyed The Sixth

Sixth Precinct Station House, 19 Elizabeth Street.

Precinct has an important Broadway boundary, and vast manufacturing and commercial interests on the Bowery, and in Canal and Centre Streets

THE SEVENTH PRECINCT—The Seventh Precinct's boundaries are. Catharine Street, Division Street, Scammel Street, Water Street, Gouverneur Slip, and the east track of the railroad on the East River front. The station house at Nos 245 and 247 Madison Street is an old structure that needs tearing down to make room for a better one. The officers are: Captain Henry Hedden; and Sergeants, Charles W. Woodward, Myron Allen, Charles O Sheldon, and Cornelius Weston Woodward was appointed in 1857; Roundsman, 1861; and ranked in 1862 Allen's dates are: Patrolman, 1866; Roundsman, 1867; Sergeant, 1868. Sheldon's dates are, Patrolman, 1873; Roundsman, 1876; Sergeant, 1885 Weston's dates are, Patrolman, 1865; Roundsman, 1867; Sergeant, 1872.

CAPTAIN HENRY HEDDEN was born in Catharine Street in this city in 1837. He joined the force June 16, 1857, and was sent to the Seventeenth Precinct. He was made Sergeant in 1859, and transferred to the Twenty-sixth Precinct On May 1, 1861, he was sent to the Fifth Precinct; and in November, 1863, he was transferred to the Sixteenth Precinct as Acting Captain, and there placed in

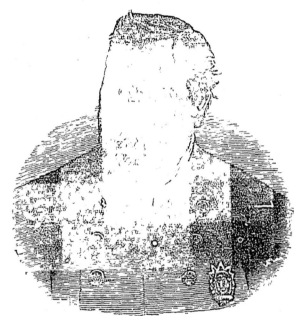

Captain Henry Hedden

command The following month he was made full Captain In the fall of 1866 he was transferred to the Twentieth Precinct In 1870 he was sent to the Fifteenth Precinct, and later he was assigned to the Twenty-first Precinct (old Twenty-eighth) in Greenwich Street, and subsequently placed in command of the Third Precinct in Beekman Street, thence alternately to the Twenty-third, Thirteenth, Thirty-third Precincts, Street Cleaning Department, Ninth and Thirty-second Precincts, to Police Headquarters, and finally to his present command Captain Hedden first distinguished himself while a Sergeant at City Hall Station by breaking up a gang of ticket swindlers who robbed emigrants While in command of the Fifteenth Precinct, he, with the assistance of Detective Sergeant Philip Reilly, worked up the evidence which convicted Ruloff, who was subsequently hanged at Binghamton, this State, for the murder of a clerk while perpetrating a burglary in a dry goods store at Binghamton. Captain Hedden also, by his energy and intelligence, helped to clear up the mystery surrounding the murder of a jew peddler in Lydig's Woods in the Thirty-Fourth Precinct. Captain Hedden was then in command of the Thirty-third Precinct. The murder had been committed by three negroes, who were arrested and convicted. Captain Hedden, besides these, has been connected with almost every case of importance that his Precinct Detectives had a hand in unearthing, but, with his characteristic modesty, he claims no merit on that score, preferring to give his detectives the entire benefit of such arrests, not seeking for notoriety himself. Captain Hedden has participated officially in the several riots that have taken place in the city since he joined the force, and carries with him honorable scars received in such hand-to-hand encounters

There are thirteen day and twenty-six night posts here. The effective force is but sixty men, although sixty-nine are on the roll. Cornelius Leary and John J Creed are the Precinct Detectives. The detailed officer is Richard J. Mullen, Corporation Ordinances

The Seventh Precinct covers territory that was formerly inhabited by New York's staid business men, and the character of its streets is the same as it was thirty years ago. Some of the houses that are now occupied by artisans were the homes of New York's business aristocracy, and were built as few builders can now afford to construct dwellings. Until recently its river front was the most important on the East Side, but the new Third Precinct cuts it off. It is what may be called a quiet precinct, peopled by citizens of the lower middle class and petty tradesmen. In some of the quiet streets which run parallel to the East River it is Sunday every day in the week. It rarely furnishes the public with material for small gossip, and the most notable events of the past few years were the burning of Hecker's Croton Mills in Cherry Street, and the mysterious burglary in a Catharine Street pawnshop which set so many detectives and "crooked" men by the ears. Catharine Market is within its boundaries, and its river front is infested with a hopelessly dishonest class, which are properly termed "dock rats" by the Police, and "river pirates" by sensational reporters

THE TENTH PRECINCT —The Tenth Precinct is included between the Bowery, Division Street, Norfolk Street, Rivington Street, Clinton Street, and Houston Street. The station house was built for station house purposes, and is yet a good one—after sixteen years of service. It has a separate prison. The officers are Captain Anthony J. Allaire; and Sergeants Gustavus Dahlgren, George W. Warner, Timothy J Creeden, and William Kass. Dahlgren's dates are Patrolman, 1866, Roundsman, 1874, Sergeant, 1866. Warner was appointed in 1868; became Roundsman 1876; and was promoted last year. Creeden joined the department in 1864; was made Roundsman in 1876, and attained his rank three years later. Kass, the Senior Sergeant, was appointed in 1859; was Roundsman in 1870; and was promoted in 1872.

CAPTAIN ANTHONY J. ALLAIRE was born in the city of Cincinnati on the seventeenth of February, 1829, and came here while he was quite young. He served his time in this city as a blacksmith, and worked for two or three years at that trade. While so employed he joined the Firemen's Brigade, and was attached to Engine Company 41. He was not long in this service when he was made foreman, as a reward for the important services he had rendered

Capt. Allaire joined the Police force on the twenty-fourth of August, 1860, and was assigned for duty to the Eighteenth Precinct

In May, 1861, he was made Roundsman, and in three months afterwards Sergeant

When the war broke out he joined the One Hundred and Thirty-third Regiment of New York Volunteers, and in August, 1862, became Captain of Company E. He was present at the battle of Port Hudson, Marksville Plains, Bisland, Cross Roads, Vermillion, and several other engagements along the Red River. On August 4, 1864, he was commissioned Major, and in December of

Captain Anthony J. Allaire.

the same year he was appointed Lieutenant Colonel. In 1865 he rose to the rank of Brigadier-General by brevet for meritorious conduct in the field.

He returned to Washington in 1864, and in a few minutes after his arrival there he was ordered to the front in defense of the Capitol, which was threatened by Jubal Early, whose advances Allaire helped to check

When peace was restored in 1865, General Allaire returned to New York, and resumed duty as a simple Roundsman. In five days later he was appointed Sergeant in the Fifteenth Precinct. On May 23, 1867, he was appointed Captain, and assigned to the Twenty-first Precinct. On July 6, 1869, he was transferred to the Fourth Precinct, which was one of the dangerous localities of New York

Captain Allaire's record is a long and interesting one. He has been engaged in so many notable cases, and his ability is so well understood and appreciated by the public that a brief summary of the more important cases in which he was engaged will suffice to explain his popularity.

He arrested Daniel McFarland for the murder, in the old *Tribune* office, of Albert D. Richardson, one of the editors of the paper. The arrest was accomplished in this wise. McFarland had a brother who kept a stationery warehouse in Broadway. Warden Finn and Captain Allaire put their heads together, and hit upon a plan which proved successful. They wrote a letter to the murderer which purported to come from his brother, asking him for an interview. They imitated the stationer's handwriting so well that his brother took the bait, and was caught in a Union Square Hotel. McFarland, in trying to get to his brother, took all sorts of precautions to avoid arrest, but Warden Finn and Captain Allaire carried out their plans successfully.

While he was in the Fourth Precinct, Captain Allaire broke up the Slaughter House Gang, whose headquarters were at a gin-mill kept by Johnny Dobbs at the corner of Water Street and James Slip. Johnny Hope, Patsy Conroy, Denny Brady, and —— Brickley were habitues of this place.

Captain Allaire also broke up the infamous dens that were located in Chatham Street.

Joe Elliot, Charley Becker, and Clem Harrison, notorious forgers, who passed a worthless check for sixty thousand dollars on the New York Safe Deposit Bank, were also arrested by Captain Allaire. Becker turned State's evidence, and amused the Court during the trial by lithographing a counterfeit sixty thousand dollar check on a piece of paper. These arrests occurred while Allaire was in the Fourth Precinct.

In 1877 Captain Allaire was transferred to the Eighteenth Precinct, and broke up the "Dutch Mob" which was composed of Johnny Irving, Sheeney Mike, Dutch Chris, Billy Porter, and Little Freddie. They carried on their depredations on Houston, Third, Fourth and Fifth Streets, east of the Bowery.

Captain Allaire was removed to Headquarters in 1877, and was appointed Instructor to the force. He was transferred to the Tenth Precinct in 1879, and has remained there since.

There are fifteen day and twenty-eight night posts in this precinct. The quota of seventy-eight men is reduced, by details and sickness, to about sixty. Etienne Bayer and Richard Sullivan are the Precinct Detectives, and the detailed officers are: Michael Harris and George S. Smock, Corporation Ordinances; Frank Wilson, Grand Street traffic, Frank Hughes, Grand Street and the Bowery traffic; Thomas E. Fitzpatrick to Inspector Murray's office; Frank J. Fuchs to the Internal Revenue office.

German Republican politics, the Grand Street dry goods trade, and lager beer, may or may not be, the chief characteristics of the Tenth Precinct. Its population is largely composed of Teutons, while the typical Hebrew quarters— the *Judenstrasse* of New York—one that smites the nose and offends the eye, is in the neighborhood of Hester and Essex Streets. "Little Germany," as the precinct is called, is thrifty, odorous, bustling and crowded. There is less crime in the tenement population of this precinct than in any other, but when a real

"Dutch" tragedy occurs, it is sure to be a ghastly one. Nothing more shocking can be imagined than some of the suicides which have occurred in this district, because of their deliberate planning and their circumstances, regardless of the carving and perforating necessary to accomplish the end decided on. Some of the crimes for gain are European in their character. Take the case of Ernest de Bagnicki or Uhling, who, to secure a life insurance policy of ten thousand dollars on the Merchants' Life Insurance Company, in April, 1874, induced Louise Germs to sham death, put her in a coffin, got her out at the time the coffin should have been closed, put in bricks, and buried the coffin. He paid

Eleventh Precinct Station House, Union Market

for his enterprise by a long term in State Prison. The most horrible tragedy that ever occurred in this city, one that furnished the bloodiest, most revolting spectacle of a murderer, who killed himself after slaying his victim, was at No. 194 Orchard Street, where, on the nineteenth of January, 1878, James Jacques or J. W. Johnson, a profligate Chicagoan, hacked Mrs. Anna Surman with a razor, pistoled her, and then shot himself. No one who saw the room and the dead persons will ever forget them. Fires are frequent in this precinct, but are generally small affairs in crowded buildings, with the result of burning the inmates out precipitately. The last great fire in this precinct was the burning, on the twenty-ninth of November, 1883, of the old Stadt Theatre and other buildings, with a loss of one hundred and twenty thousand dollars. Ludlow Street Jail and the Essex Market Police Court and Prison are in the precinct.

THE ELEVENTH PRECINCT.—The Eleventh Precinct is included between Rivington Street, Clinton Street, Avenue B, Fourteenth Street, and the East River. The station house, or quarters, are upstairs in Union Market, corner of Sheriff and Houston Streets, where they have been for the past thirty years. The rooms have just been furbished up at a cost of twenty-five thousand dollars, and enough money has been spent on this old place to build a large and commodious station house, as good as any in the city. The officers are: Captain, William Meakim; and Sergeants Michael Collins, Andrew Doyle, Judson

Captain William Meakim

Golden, and John Kelly. Collins was appointed in 1870; was Roundsman nine years, and won rank last Spring. Doyle's dates are, Patrolman, 1861; Roundsman, 1867; and Sergeant, 1868. Golden's dates are, Patrolman, 1875; Roundsman, 1883; and Sergeant, 1885. Kelly's dates are, Patrolman, 1870; Roundsman, 1882; and Sergeant, 1885.

ACTING CAPTAIN WILLIAM MEAKIM, of the Eleventh Precinct, was promoted to the rank of Captain on April 7, 1885. In 1868 he became a Patrolman in the Sixth Precinct under Captain Jourdan. He resigned two years later to go into business, but again became a member of the force in February, 1873. In 1878 he gained the rank of Sergeant, and was with Inspector Murray until after the death of Captain Cherry, when he was sent to take charge of the Eleventh Precinct. Captain Meakim's ability is unquestioned. He was associated with Inspector Murray in a number of important criminal cases, and the detective instinct is strongly marked in him.

This command has ten day and twenty night posts. Of the sixty-two men on the rolls about twelve are sick or detailed. The Precinct Detectives are John Sheridan and Patrick Brennan. The detailed officers are: James Keenan, Seventh Street Ferry; George Grassick, Tenth Street Ferry; Michael Hefferman, Houston Street Ferry; Edward Brucken, St. Francis Hospital, and William Dalton, Ordinances.

This command deals almost wholly with the poorer classes, and it has a large German and Hebrew population in the streets near Clinton Street and Avenues C and D, and an Irish and American population along the river front. Within the precinct are the mooring quarters of the Harbor Police, St Francis' Hospital, the Houston, Seventh and Tenth Street ferries, and large manufactories on the river front north of Houston Street. Besides these, there is St. Bridget's Church, on the spire of which Father Mooney, on the day of the German jubilation over the humiliation of the French nation, caused to be placed French tri-colors in testimony of the valor of the vanquished, and returned a characteristic answer when a committee from the socialistic celebrants in Tompkins Square waited on him and represented that they could not be responsible for the consequences if the flags remained. They did remain, and the priest was not molested or subjected to further bullying. Crimes of note are rare in this precinct. Now and then a newspaper affects to believe that the "Long Hairs" or "Short Hairs" or some other "gang" has the district in terror, and magnifies a squabble between some graceless idlers, but the Police, as in other precincts, have the loafing element under control. Union Market is under the station house.

THE THIRTEENTH PRECINCT.—The boundaries of the Thirteenth Precinct are Gouverneur Slip, Water Street, Scammel Street, Division Street, Norfolk Street, Rivington Street, and the East River. The station house is at No. 178 Delancey Street, and may be considered, so far as some of its walls go—it has frequently been reconstructed—as one of the oldest, if not the oldest in the city. It was a watch house long before 1848, when it is recorded as a station house; and Hose Company No. 4, the Volunteer Fire Department, occupied that portion now devoted to the desk and assembly room. The officers are: Captain, Jeremiah Petty, and Sergeants, Theron T. Thompson, Thomas Lancer, Philip M. Griffith and Wm. Strauss. Thompson's dates are: Patrolman 1862, Roundsman 1886, and Sergeant 1868. Lancer joined the force ten years ago; was Roundsman in 1882, and attained rank in January, 1884. Griffith's dates are Patrolman 1858, was shortly after made Roundsman, and was promoted in 1863. Strauss's dates are Patrolman 1873, Roundsman 1875, and Sergeant 1885.

CAPTAIN PETTY joined the Police force in 1840. He was then what was called a "chance man," that is, a man who goes to the station and waits to see if anything will turn up upon which he may be detailed. He was then put on the regular Patrol force, under Captain Fenton, at the Tombs, who occupied the quarters there that are now the offices of Warden Finn. Policemen, at that time, went on duty every alternate night at sunset, and left off at daybreak. They were paid one dollar and fifty cents a day. They slept in the Tombs the nights they were on duty, and went to their own homes the nights they were off. "The Police force, in my younger days," says Captain Petty, "was mostly composed of native Americans. Our beats did not extend above Canal Street. My beat was on Water Street, and Peck Slip to James' Slip—the very worst portion of the city. The neighborhood was then full of houses of ill-fame. The number of men on the Police was not more than twenty-five or thirty for the lower part of the city.

"One night my post was on Canal Street. I shall never forget the sight that I saw at the corner of Baxter Street (which was then called Orange Street). I heard a woman shouting 'Murder,' and I went into the house. There, in a cellar, was a woman half drunk; she said she had been beaten by her husband. He was a cripple, and was lying on some dirty straw on the cellar floor. The walls were covered with the slime of lizards. I tried to get the man up, but he

Captain Jeremiah Petty

could not stand without crutches. I examined his feet, and found that he had been frostbitten. The flesh had rotted off, and the bones were sticking out. He was half drunk. It was a sickening sight. After cautioning the man to keep quiet, I left the place for fear I should faint, and that the lizards would crawl over my body.

"I joined the Leatherheads in 1845. During that time the legislature passed a bill, one of the provisions of which was, that it was optional with the city government to adopt it. The Common Council refused to pass it, but, instead, passed an ordinance forming the Municipal Police. I was then appointed Assistant Captain, with a salary of six hundred dollars a year, and was a resident of the Fourteenth Ward. I got the position through the intercession of John J. Giles, who was then Treasurer of the Fire Department, and a real estate agent."

Captain Petty was born in the year 1814, in the city of New York, and went to what was called a "pay school," that is, the scholars paid from two-and-a-half to five dollars a quarter for tuition. There were, besides these, free schools in New York at the time.

During the Fernando Wood riot he was a clerk in the Registry office. In July, 1857, he was appointed Patrolman, and assigned to the Tenth Precinct. He was appointed Sergeant in 1858, and sent to the City Hall, and remained there until 1861. He was then transferred from the First to the Fourteenth Precinct.

Thirteenth Precinct Station House, 178 Delancey Street.

Captain Petty has been a teetotaller for the last forty-seven years.

During the draft riots he was stationed in the Fifth Precinct, and was the first to enter the Armory, which the rioters were pillaging. "We clubbed them," says Captain Petty, describing the scene, "as far as the top of the stairs, and they went headlong down to the bottom. Some of the rioters jumped from the second and third story windows. When we were in the streets we were surrounded by ten or fifteen thousand people. Bricks were thrown down on us, and I really believe if the military did not fire on the mob, the mob would have killed us."

During the Orange riots Captain Petty was on duty in plain clothes, and arrested three or four persons for carrying firearms. He went on duty on a Monday afternoon and did not have any sleep until the Friday following

In 1872 Captain Petty was presented with a gold shield by some citizens in the Fifth Ward. The inscription on the shield was as follows: "Presented to Captain Jeremiah Petty, in acknowledgment of his long services, and the faithful and impartial performance of his official duties"

Captain Petty, for his years, is one of the most vigorous and clear-headed men in the department This, perhaps, is owing to the fact that, for a long number of years, he has been a total abstainer from all sorts of stimulating or intoxicating beverages, besides being very methodical in all his habits.

This precinct has twelve day and twenty night posts. The quota of fifty-six men is reduced to about forty-five by details and sickness John McCauley and Patrick English are the Precinct Detectives. The detailed men are: Lafay Schulum, Grand Street Ferry; and Bartholomew J Owens, Ordinances.

The characteristics of the Thirteenth Precinct are those of the Tenth and Eleventh Precincts It takes in the "Hook" and its predatory loungers, the oyster trade of the East River at Grand Street, much commerce in coal and marble on the river point, the Grand Street Ferry, and some of the largest furniture and flour manufactories. The Hebrew population is large, and few crimes of note are committed. Except on Grand and Clinton Streets its mercantile interests are small

THE FOURTEENTH PRECINCT.—The limits of the Fourteenth Precinct are Broadway, Howard Street, Centre Street, Hester Street, the Bowery, and Bleecker Street. The station house is at No 205 Mulberry Street, next to the House of Detention It is a fair, modern structure, with a separate prison, but it cannot be called a healthy building, as both Captain's and Sergeants' quarters are at times unpleasant. The officers are: Captain, Michael J Murphy; and Sergeants, Thomas N. James, Marcus Horbelt, Michael Lamey and John F Maloney James, the senior Sergeant, dates back to 1858. He was Roundsman in 1859, and Sergeant in 1862. Horbelt's dates are: Patrolman 1859, Roundsman 1871, and Sergeant 1876 Lamey was appointed in 1861, made Roundsman in 1869, and got rank in 1872. Maloney joined the force in 1864, became Roundsman three years after, and has been a Sergeant since 1869.

The creation of the new Sixth Precinct cut from the Fourteenth Precinct some of the most important of the dry goods houses and manufactories in Broadway, Canal, and Centre Streets, but it has still to look after millions on millions of invested capital in the large Broadway stores, some of which carry a stock of one million dollars or over, and a multitude of shops on Grand Street and the Bowery Its resident population is mainly the working class, and it has an Italian colony of the better class in Crosby Street, and one of the worst class in Jersey Street Within its boundaries is Niblo's Garden Theatre This precinct is remarkable for the large dry goods fires that occurred almost on the same ground in 1854, 1876, and 1879 The first involved Nos 440 to 454 Broadway on the twentieth of December, 1854, and the loss was put down at only

Fourteenth Precinct Station House and House of Detention, 205 Mulberry Street.

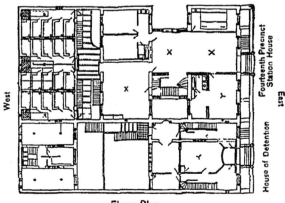

Floor Plan.

seventy thousand five hundred dollars. The next, on February 8, 1876, took in Nos. 440 to 458 Broadway, and houses in Grand, and Howard, and Crosby Streets. The loss was one million seven hundred and fifty thousand one hundred and thirty-five dollars and forty-nine cents, and several persons were injured. At the fire of January 14, 1879, a loss of one million three hundred and twenty-one thousand nine hundred and seventy-three dollars and five cents was sustained at Nos. 458 to 472 Broadway, and Nos. 134 to 136 Grand Street, and one man, a fireman, was killed. Niblo's Garden was destroyed by fire May 6, 1872, when the loss was sixty-one thousand dollars, and the Metropolitan Hotel, of which it is an annex, has been on fire several times. Within its limits are the headquarters of the Board of Education and Centre Market, and Police

Captain Michael J. Murphy

Headquarters, and the Sanitary Bureaus, and the House of Detention for Witnesses, old St. Patrick's Cathedral, the Vicar General's residence, and the Houston Street Convent. At Grand and Centre Streets is the old and historic Odd Fellows' Hall.

CAPTAIN MURPHY was born in 1844, and in his youth was a clerk. He was appointed on the force in August, 1868. His dates are: 1869, a Roundsman; 1870, a Sergeant; 1872, a Captain. Having attained the latter rank, he was placed in command of the Seventh Precinct. He held command also successively in the Eleventh, Twenty-eighth, Twenty-first, and Thirty-first Precincts. Captain Murphy is a man of superior intelligence and experience, and his record stands A No. 1.

This precinct has twelve day and twenty-four night posts. Its force of sixty-four men is on the average about fifty-five. John Brennan and James J. Hart are the Precinct Detectives. The detailed officers are James Moran, Excise; George R. Jacobs, Ordinances; Sullivan H. Bates, Centre Market; and Jacob Lay Burean, of Elections.

THE SEVENTEENTH PRECINCT.—The boundaries of the Seventeenth Precinct are Houston Street, Avenue B, Fourteenth Street, Fourth Avenue, and the Bowery. The station house is at Nos. 79 and 81 First Avenue, and dates back to 1853, when the command's headquarters were removed from Third Street and the Bowery. It is an old structure, the cells are underground, and the demand for a new station house must be met before many years have passed. Very little repairing or alteration has been done to this station house since it was erected. The officers are: Captain, John H. McCullagh; and Sergeants, Joseph Haggerty, Jacob Welsing, George Little, and John Gallagher. Haggerty joined the force in 1861, was Roundsman in two years, and was promoted the next year. Welsing's dates are: Patrolman 1870, Roundsman 1874, and Sergeant 1876. Little was a Patrolman from 1865 to 1877, and three months after he was made Roundsman he got rank. Gallagher was a Patrolman in 1868, a Roundsman in 1877, and Sergeant in 1881.

CAPTAIN JOHN H. McCULLAGH, of the Seventeenth Precinct, was born in the County Tyrone, Ireland, in January, 1842, and came to this country when he was only eleven years of age. His family went to reside at Irvington-on-the-Hudson, where the future Captain attended school. While there he was prominent in all athletic sports and games. During the draft riots, in 1863, he made the acquaintance of several members of the Police force, and resolved to join them. When McCullagh visited Headquarters with a letter of introduction, the Superintendent told him to wait until his beard grew, and that he was only yet a boy. But in a few days afterwards he received his appointment as Patrolman and was assigned to the Fifth Precinct, then in charge of Captain Jeremiah Petty. After two years' service in this district he was transferred to the Twentieth Precinct, under Captain Walling. Here McCullagh distinguished himself. The desperate ruffians known as the "Hell's Kitchen" gang, were constantly committing robberies at the Hudson River Railroad Depot, and were a terror to everybody. It is said even that Policemen were loath to interfere with them. One night, on the arrival of a train from the West, two hogsheads of hams were stolen. McCullagh, hearing of the robbery, went cautiously down towards the depot. On the way he encountered a notorious thief, nicknamed "Dutch Heinrich," and two of his companions. Heinrich, with an oath, precipitated himself on the officer. A terrific struggle ensued, but after a time the thief went under. He was afterwards tried, convicted, and sent to State Prison for five years. McCullagh was soon afterwards promoted to the rank of Roundsman and transferred to the Twelfth Precinct, but his old Captain (Walling) requested the Police Commissioners to let him have McCullagh back again, and the Commissioners acceded to the request. Soon after this there was a reckless Policeman, who, thinking he was aggrieved, swore that he would kill any Policeman who would have the temerity to report him One night, however, McCullagh, finding him off duty, did report him The Policeman was dismissed the force, and watched his opportunity to be avenged on McCullagh. One morning, while the latter was on duty at the corner of Thirty-seventh Street and Ninth Avenue, the dismissed Policeman fired at him and wounded him severely For a long time McCullagh's life trembled in the balance, but eventually he recovered His assailant was arrested and sent to Sing Sing for five years

In the Orange riots of 1871, McCullagh was shot in the leg, and was laid up for a month.

Most and Wesley Allen, two notorious characters, were arrested by McCullagh in Mercer Street for the attempted robbery of Colsatt & Company's silk store Both the prisoners were sentenced to ten years in the State Prison

Captain John H. McCullagh.

Captain McCullagh was also the principal means of breaking up the Panel House gang in the Eighth Precinct, at the head of which was "Shang" Draper

The Captain has inherited a nice house at Irvington, where he is very popular with his neighbors He is also a trustee of the school at that place

This precinct has fourteen day and twenty-six night posts Of the full complement of seventy-five men, about twenty are detailed or sick Edward Robinson and Michael Bissert are the Precinct Detectives Henry Trass and Thomas Kiernan are detailed on Ordinances; James Kiernan and George E Wood to the office of the Commissioners of Charities and Correction; Henry Schwenck and Frank Gunn to the Cooper Institute, as Day Post

No. 15; Peter Farley to Tompkins Market, as Day Post No 16; George Marsh to the Eye and Ear Infirmary and Home of the Holy Family, as Day Post No. 17.

The Seventeenth Precinct watches over a crowded tenement house population It is asserted that the most populous block in the city is here This is the home of the Bohemian colony, and there are many Germans in the district. It takes in the German part of the Bowery, and within its limits are Tompkins Market and the Sixty-ninth Regiment Armory, Cooper Institute, the Bible House, Grace Chapel, Theiss's Alhambra, the headquarters of the Commissioners of Charities and Corrections, Tompkins Square, the Eye and Ear Infirmary, Turn Halle, and other Teutonic resorts, the Marble Cemetery, and the buildings of the New York Historical Society. No occurrence ever created such a stir as the stealing of A. T. Stewart's body from the vault in the churchyard of St. Mark's Church at Ninth, Tenth, and Stuyvesant Streets and Second Avenue, on the seventh of November, 1878 One of the fiercest fires on record was at the Hippotheatron, in East Fourteenth Street, on the morning of December 24, 1872, when Nos 114 to 134 East Fourteenth Street were more or less damaged, and the loss over two hundred and seventy thousand dollars On the fifth of January, 1880, a fire at Turn Halle ended the lives of five persons, but the damage done was small. On the twenty-fifth of July, 1876, Sergeant James McGloin, of the Fifteenth Precinct, pursued Harry King, who had committed a robbery, to Second Avenue and Eighth Street, and there received his death wound. King is serving a life sentence

THE EIGHTEENTH PRECINCT.—The Eighteenth Precinct comprises the district between Fourteenth Street, Union Square, Fourth Avenue, Twenty-seventh Street, First Avenue, Twenty-sixth Street, and the East River The station house is at Nos 325 and 327 East Twenty-second Street. It is on the site of the one burned down by the mob in the draft riots of 1863. It is a third-class structure when compared with more modern station houses, but it has a separate prison. The officers are Captain, William H Clinchy; and Sergeants Thomas H Mangin, Michael Fanning, Hugh Clark, and William T Coffey. Mangin was a Patrolman in 1870, a Roundsman in 1874, a Sergeant in 1879 Fanning's dates are Patrolman 1864, Roundsman 1869, and Sergeant 1872. Hugh Clark joined the force in 1861, waited more than seventeen years to be Roundsman and got his rank last June Coffey was appointed in 1869, and ten years later was made a Roundsman In May last he was promoted.

CAPTAIN CLINCHY was born in this city in 1844, and when quite a boy he went to the far West, acting as a scout and hunter there for several years He became a Patrolman in 1865, and was assigned to the Sixth Precinct for duty. In 1867 he was promoted to be a Roundsman, and was advanced a step higher in 1869, when he was made Sergeant. The following year he reached his present rank, and was sent to the Twenty-first Precinct; thence to the Twenty-fifth Precinct, to the Broadway Squad, the Fourteenth, the Thirteenth, and finally to the Eighteenth Precinct. Captain Clinchy is a man of solid literary attainments, is a good linguist, and is self-educated.

This precinct has eighteen day and thirty-seven night posts. The full complement of men, ninety-six, is reduced by sickness and details to about ninety-seven. The Precinct Detective is J. V. B. Corey The detailed officers are. John O'Neill, Fourteenth Street; Thomas Gibbons and Thomas O'Reilly, Ordinances; George Clinchy, Stuyvesant Park; W P Leaman, Gramercy Park; Patrick Flanagan, Twenty-third Street Ferry; George F. Lewis, Inspector Murray's Office; Jacob B. Kern, Gramercy Park, and M. C Yaeger, Twenty-third Street Railroads.

The responsibilities of the Police of the Eighteenth Precinct are divided among the slums of the east side and the rich residents of such quarters as Gramercy Park, Stuyvesant Square, and the lower end of Madison Avenue This precinct takes care of Tammany Hall, the Academy of Music, Steinway Hall, Irving Hall, the headquarters of the Department of Parks, Tony Pastor's Theatre, and the East Twenty-third

Captain William H Clinchy.

Street Ferry, the Ashland House, the Hotel Dam, the Clarendon Hotel, the Westminster Hotel, the Florence Apartment House, Trinity Church, St George's Church, All Souls' Church, and the College of the City of New York. Last year the St. George's Flats, in East Seventeenth Street, near Stuyvesant Park, were destroyed by fire with a loss of seventy thousand dollars The fire was remarkable because the house was advertised as positively and absolutely fire-proof, and was barely tenanted In December, 1869, Florence Scannell, an Alderman, was wounded in an election row in a liquor saloon at Twenty-third Street and Second Avenue, and he died in Bellevue Hospital. John Scannell, his brother, made John Donohue responsible for his brother's death, and after trying to kill him in the street, deliberately slew him in the pool rooms in front of the Brower House

THE TWENTY-FIRST PRECINCT.—The Twenty-first Precinct's boundaries are Twenty-sixth Street, First Avenue, Twenty-seventh Street, Fourth Avenue, Park Avenue, Forty-second Street, and the East River. The station house is at No 160 East Thirty-fifth Street, and has been much tinkered since 1855. In 1864 a building in its rear was added to it, the cells are underground, the quarters are cramped, and it is, on the whole, a fourth-class structure The officers are: Captain, Thomas M. Ryan; and Sergeants, John Fitzgerald, Philip Cassidy, Frederick W Martens and George P Osborne Fitzgerald's dates are Patrolman 1865, Roundsman 1874, and Sergeant 1876 Cassidy was Patrolman in 1870, Roundsman in 1877, and Sergeant in 1881 Martens, in

Twenty-First Precinct Station House, 160 East Thirty Fifth Street.

1883, when he was made Roundsman, had been nine years on the force. Last April he was promoted Osborne was appointed in 1870, became Roundsman in 1876, and got his rank last January.

CAPTAIN THOMAS MEAGHER RYAN, of the Twenty-first Precinct, has done good service in his time. · Previous to his appointment to the district which he now commands, breaches of the law were numerous, and gangs of young "toughs" made themselves a terror to the peaceably disposed inhabitants; but Captain Ryan's advent struck terror into those ruffians when he assumed the Captaincy of the Twenty-first Ward. He came to this country from Ireland about twenty-eight years ago, and obtained a situation with the Adams Express Company Here his punctuality and faithful performance of duty attracted the attention of his employers, and through the President of the Company, Mr William B. Dinsmore, who took a great interest in the young man, Ryan was appointed a Policeman on November 12, 1863. He was assigned to the Eighteenth Precinct, and, after several years of steady attention to duty, he was appointed Roundsman on December 16, 1870, in the same precinct in which he served as Patrolman. He was appointed Captain on September 13, 1878, and assigned to the command of the Sixteenth Precinct. After two or three changes, he was finally located in his present precinct.

The following are some of the arrests made by him:

Peter Fenrich, arrested December 15, 1880, for the celebrated diamond robbery. Sentenced to Sing Sing for five years

Captain Thomas Meagher Ryan.

Thomas Foster, for presenting a pistol at a druggist's wife Sentenced to fifteen years imprisonment.

On the night of September 24, 1881, Thomas Kennealy, Michael McGuirk, James Nolan, Peter Henry, and Edward Gates stopped an old laboring man named Felix Smith at Fourteenth Street, near First Avenue, and forcibly took from him his hard-earned wages Each of them was sentenced to five years in State Prison

John McManus, for the killing of Michael Kerwin in a saloon, on the sixteenth of June, 1873 McManus was sentenced to imprisonment for life.

William Burke, James McKeon, Thomas Roberts, and William Walpole, for robbing a gentleman named Walter Cook, in Twenty-seventh Street, on November 25, 1882 They were arrested twelve hours afterwards from description, and sentenced to State Prison for five years.

This command has fourteen day and twenty-eight night posts. Of its seventy-one men about a dozen are sick or detailed. George Connor and Bernard Malarkey are the Precinct Detectives. The detailed men are: Richard Cahill, Ordinances, John Spencer, Bellevue Hospital; Patrick Nealis, Dock of Commissioners of Charities and Correction; Terence Gallagher, Thirty-fourth Street Ferry, Michael C. Donohue, St. John's College, Fordham.

The Twenty-first Precinct runs to aristocracy on its western border, and to squalor and petty crime as the East River is approached. The Police here have to deal with a ruffianly element east of Third Avenue, and a uniformed officer is fine game for the young thugs who infest the district. It is not exaggeration to say that on some posts a Patrolman's safety lies in his ability to handle his locust and pistol in cases of emergency, and there are endless records in the station house of minor brawls with more or less serious results to the unruly, and sometimes to the members of the force. West of Third Avenue, on Murray Hill, are aristocratic residences, and there are some of the most luxurious mansions in the city along Park Avenue. In the precinct are St Stephen's Roman Catholic Church, the Grand Union Hotel, Pottier & Stymus' furniture manufactory, and the houses in the vicinity of Prospect Place of some of the best and most worthy Hebrew families. This precinct guards the principal ferry to the Long Island Railroads, and Bellevue and the Manhattan Eye and Ear Hospitals, and the Dock of the Commissioners of Charities and Correction. An event remembered to this day was the killing of Police Officer Smedick by John Real fifteen years ago. Real, despite strenuous efforts to save him, was hung August 5, 1870. On the tenth of October, 1881, the Fourth Avenue car stable, at Thirty-third Street and Fourth Avenue, and a storage warehouse and other buildings, were destroyed by fire. The loss was eight hundred and two thousand dollars.

THE TWENTY-SIXTH PRECINCT.—The territory of the Twenty-sixth Precinct is bounded by Mail Street, Broadway, Chambers Street, Centre Street, and Park Row. This is the City Hall Squad, and its quarters are in the south-east corner of the City Hall. Formerly it was the Railroad and Steamboat Squad, until Col Joel B Erhardt, in 1876, organized the Steamboat Squad, and placed Roundsman James K Fuller in command. Before the Nineteenth Sub-Precinct was organized, a detail of officers from this precinct did duty where the Grand Central Depot now stands, and at the Harlem and New Haven Depots at Fourth Avenue and Twenty-seventh and Twenty-eighth Streets, where is now the Madison Square Garden. Nearly all the members of this command do only day duty, so that there is but one day post and two night posts to a force of fifty-six men, reduced by sickness and details to about forty-eight men. The officers of the command are: Sergeant Stewart; and Sergeants, Edward Carpenter, appointed 1869, made Roundsman 1872, and promoted 1876; George P. Kass, appointed 1862, made Roundsman 1866, and promoted 1869; and James Gaynor, appointed 1862, made Roundsman 1870, and promoted 1872.

SERGEANT JOSEPH STEWART, upon the promotion of Captain Steers to an Inspectorship, was transferred from Tremont Police Station to take command of the Twenty-sixth Precinct in the City Hall.

Inspector Henry V. Steers.

INSPECTOR HENRY V. STEERS was born in Sing Sing in 1832, and came to New York City when he was only seven years old. He served his apprenticeship to the ship building trade, and worked at this business for years. He joined the force in 1857 and went to the Thirteenth Precinct. He was promoted Roundsman in 1860, and assigned for duty to the Seventeenth; in 1865 he was made Sergeant, and in 1874 Captain of the Twenty-ninth Precinct, and was transferred to the Thirty-second in 1878 During the riots of 1863 and 1871 Captain Steers took a prominent part, and, with a few Policemen, cleared the boulevards of riotous mobs. Gangs of desperadoes, previous to Captain Steers going there, made night hideous by their depredations. Steers singled out the leader of this gang—who was a desperate bully—and thrashed him. This struck terror into the group, and peaceful citizens hailed his advent with delight. They presented him with a shield, bearing the following inscription:

"Presented to Captain Steers, in acknowledgment of his ability and zeal as an officer, by the citizens of the late town of West Farms, now the Thirty-fourth Precinct. NEW YORK CITY, December 4, 1874."

Shortly after this Captain Steers was presented with a gold watch. He was a member of the Knickerbocker Club, and was the recipient of a handsome club from the members. The club is made of black ebony, tipped at the bottom with ivory, and mounted at the top with an exquisitely worked ivory eagle, and near the handle is a wide circle of gold with this inscription:

"Presented to Captain Steers by the Knickerbocker Club of West Farms May 2, 1872"

When the change took place from the Metropolitan to the Municipal, Steers was the last Sergeant of the Metropolitan Police. While he was a Patrolman, Captain Steers saved seven persons from drowning, and on one occasion nearly lost his life

He was made Inspector on the twenty-fourth of March, 1885, in place of the late Inspector Thorne. Sergeant JOSEPH STEWART was transferred from Tremont to command the City Hall Squad.

The detailed officers are· Peter Groden and Ignatz Baumgarten, Castle Garden; John B. Wood, Comptroller's office; George Davis, City Paymaster's office; David Harvey, Police Headquarters; William Sims, Superior Court, Roundsman Charles O. Sheldon, Telegraph office, Police Headquarters, and Robert Quackenbush, Special Detective The force is on duty daily, Sundays excepted, as follows. Castle Garden, seven men; Carts, four; Hacks, two; Junkshops, two; Pawnshops, one; Runners, one; Express, one, Venders, two; Brooklyn Bridge entrance, one; Reserve Force, two; Intelligence Offices, one; License Office, two; Permit Office, one; Post-office, one; Court House, one; Vestibule, City Hall, one; Chamber of Board of Aldermen, one; Blasting, one, House Duty, two; Park Patrol, four.

CHAPTER XVI.

SECOND INSPECTION DISTRICT.

THE LATE INSPECTOR THORNE.—A VETERAN OFFICER WHOSE EXPERIENCE WAS COEVAL WITH THE EXISTENCE OF THE POLICE DEPARTMENT—INTELLIGENCE, ENERGY AND ZEAL.—A NOTABLE RECORD.—FIFTH PRECINCT; CAPTAIN EAKINS.—EIGHTH PRECINCT; CAPTAIN MCDONNELL.—NINTH PRECINCT, CAPTAIN COPELAND—FIFTEENTH PRECINCT, CAPTAIN BROGAN.—SIXTEENTH PRECINCT; CAPTAIN MCELWAIN.—TWENTIETH PRECINCT; CAPTAIN WASHBURN—TWENTY-FIFTH PRECINCT; CAPTAIN GARLAND—TWENTY-SEVENTH PRECINCT; CAPTAIN BERGHOLD—TWENTY-NINTH PRECINCT; CAPTAIN WILLIAMS.

THE Second Inspection District includes the Fifth, Eighth, Ninth, Sixteenth, Twentieth, Twenty-fifth, Twenty-seventh, and Twenty-ninth Precincts, and the Jefferson Market Police Court, known as the Second District Court. Until recently it was under the command of a veteran officer, the late Inspector Thomas W. Thorne.

THE LATE INSPECTOR THORNE was born in Ulster County, in the town of Malborough, this State, on June 20, 1823. He came to New York when he was a boy, and remained in this city until 1837, when he went to Newburgh, Orange County, this State. He there learned the trade of a carpenter, and returned to New York in 1840. He gained the position of master carpenter at the Arsenal under the late General John Stewart during the time the arsenal was being built in Central Park. He was appointed on the Police by the first Commissioners, to wit. Mayor Westervelt, Recorder Tillou, and City Judge Beebe. In 1853 he was made Sergeant, in 1857 Captain, and in 1861 Inspector. On April 20, 1872, he was admitted to the bar at General Term of the Supreme Court. He did duty in the following precincts Patrolman, Roundsman, and Sergeant in the Thirteenth; Sergeant in the Seventh and Eleventh; Captain in the Fourth, Sixteenth, Twenty-first, Twenty-sixth; Inspector in the First, Second, Third and Fourth Districts. He was made Inspector in 1872, and had charge of the Street Cleaning Department for two years and a half. During his whole time on the force he shows but two days sick time. During the Astor Place riots he had charge of the magazine used there. He was in the dead rabbit riots, the draft riots, and also had charge of the force that went to assist Superintendent Walling during the Orange riots. He commanded the force of the Fourteenth Precinct to intercept the Communists' gathering at Tompkins Square.

The identity of the murderers of the peddler in Lydeck's Woods, near West

Farms Village, in 1875, would in all probability have never been revealed but for the active services rendered by Inspector Thorne, who, at the time, was District Inspector in the Twenty-third Ward. His handling of the case led to the arrest of three negroes who were, in time, convicted of the murder, and hanged

Inspector Thorne was only two or three days on the force when his Captain detailed him on a watch stealing case. He recovered the property, and the Captain, who was highly gratified, said. "You have done enough of work for one day, and you had better go home and rest yourself."

He was made Captain just at the beginning of the war, and was stationed at the Fourth Precinct, and continued there for one year He was then sent to the Twenty-sixth Precinct (City Hall) and was there during the draft riots, and was on duty the night that the mob made a demonstration to sack the *Tribune* office He had only fifty men under his command, and with these he dispersed a mob of seven thousand who had collected on the City Hall Square. The mob was armed with hay-sticks and pistols; the Police had only their clubs

In 1853 there was a gang of thieves known as the butcher cart or hog thieves, who had their headquarters at the corner of Tompkins and Rivington streets. Their business was to steal from stores or trucks anything that could be carried by two persons—such as a tub of butter, put it into a cart and go off with it They changed from that to assaulting paymasters and clerks in banks, and robbing them. The original gang consisted of Warmsby, Ingram, Burke, Goody, Mannix, Cosgrove, Purcell and McDonnell They pretended to be butchers, and sold what is called, in butchers' parlance, small meat, around the streets Inspector Thorne had cause to arrest these thieves several times. One night, being on post in Grand Street at the corner of Columbia, and not being observed, he saw five of the gang place themselves near by, and heard them hold a conversation about twelve tubs of butter they had stolen, and how they had to dispose of them. The next morning the Inspector proceeded to the place where he suspected the butter was concealed, found it, and arrested the five thieves, who were completely surprised, as they could form no idea how their secret had leaked out. The prisoners were bailed, but after the owners of the butter were found, Judge Walsh, who was then Police Magistrate, ordered the Inspector to re-arrest the prisoners

He found them in a slaughter house in Tompkins Street, and took them to the court in their own cart, by making them believe it was for the purpose of closing the case When they got there and were arraigned, one of their number said. "Thorne, this is a shame The idea of bringing us in our own cart to the station house and charging us with robbery!" They were all sent to State Prison.

The depredations of thieves on the North River created great consternation among the inhabitants who lived on the river front Officer Smith and Inspector Thorne were detailed to look after them. The task was a most dangerous one Five men had broken open the cabin of a vessel lying at a North River pier, and stolen money and other property. When discovered, they took to a boat, followed in like manner by the Police, who chased them over to the Brooklyn side, the fugitives firing on their pursuers several times In the morning they were in the middle of the river, and the Police boat was at the side of the wharves, a circumstance not known to the thieves, who were again chased, this time to the foot of Third Street, East River, where they were captured

While Inspector Thorne was Captain in the Fourth Precinct there was there a notorious gang, all of them having done time. They were the brothers Dobbs (two), Harry Craven, —— Barclay, the man who was supposed to have killed Gefferts in Sing Sing; Sam Madden, Big Brady, Dan Kelly, Aleck Harrington, English Harry, and "Big Doyle," who were committing at that time all the burglaries in warehouses in New York.

Dan Kelly and young Jack Wright, in company with another, entered the offices of the New Haven Steamboat Company, and after breaking open the safe, succeeded in getting twenty thousand dollars They were captured, and upon examination Wright told Inspector Thorne, that on the third floor, counting off so many bales, he would find the stolen money secreted in that bale This led to the recovery of the money. Kelly was sent to State Prison for three years. Jack Wright jumped his bail Four years later the Inspector arrested Dan Kelly, Aleck Hampden, Big Harry, Pete Doyle, and others. Dan Kelly was again sent to State Prison, Aleck Hampden and Big Harry got bailed. Pete Doyle had judgment suspended, and about two years afterwards he picked pockets and got two years in State Prison.

In the year 1867 a young man named James Brown complained to Inspector Thorne that he had been robbed of his valise and some other property by a man who had got into his good graces at the ferry. The man who had robbed Brown was arrested. Brown remained at the station in the night time because he had no home. On being sent back the next night to the station house, he deposited some Government bonds with the Inspector. Brown was put in a back room to sleep About three o'clock in the morning he came out in the office and complained that he had been robbed of his pocketbook and some four hundred dollars in money The Sergeant told him that he must be mistaken. Previous to this, a seafaring man of apparently respectable appearance had come into the station house for lodging, and was given permission to remain in the sitting-room till morning On Brown's complaint that he had been robbed, the Sergeant went back, searched the seafaring man and the room, and not finding anything, the Sergeant made up his mind that Brown had made a mistake. Shortly after this the sailor came out and thanked the Sergeant for his night's lodging, and said that as it was now daylight he would go. The Sergeant jumped over the railings, searched him again, and found Brown's pocketbook, containing four hundred dollars The question then came into the Inspector's mind, "How did Brown come by so much money and property?" He, thereupon, began to look over the papers, and by this means found that two months previously a house at Saddle River had been robbed of bonds of the denomination of one hundred dollars each, giving the numbers of the bonds. On examination, it was further discovered that these numbers corresponded with the numbers on the bonds taken from Brown Without making any further bother in the affair, the two men who had robbed Brown were convicted and sent to State Prison. The following morning the Inspector took Brown along, and started, as he

(Brown) supposed, for the German steamer in Hoboken, but, in reality, to Saddle River, N. J. About three miles up the mountain they came to the house that had been robbed, and the inmates immediately recognized Brown as the thief. Brown had treated them with base ingratitude. They had taken him into the house out of pity, for he said he was destitute. During their absence at a festival the young scoundrel robbed them. The last the Inspector saw of Brown was when that worthy was tied to an ox cart, which was followed by a Constable, with a heavy club swinging in his hand.

One afternoon a young fellow came to the station house and said that the second mate of the ship Lady Bohn had stolen some three hundred dollars worth of nautical instruments from him. This was on Friday night. The vessel was to sail at one o'clock on Saturday. The boy had some one hundred and fifty pounds sterling due to him as apprentice, and as the vessel was going to sail, he had either to abandon his money or his property. The Inspector took the case before Judge Hogan, and asked him to give the prisoner an examination, and he did it right then and there. It was now nine o'clock in the morning. The case was immediately explained at the District Attorney's office. That official ordered an officer to go to the Tombs and bring down the prisoner. The indictment was drawn; the Inspector took the prisoner before the Grand Jury; he was indicted, tried and convicted, and as the clock struck twelve, was sentenced to three years in State Prison. The boy got his property, and sailed in the good ship Lady Bohn on the same day.

Inspector Thorne arrested two thieves one afternoon at the corner of Chambers and Chatham Streets, with an officer who had been wounded and was considerably under the influence of liquor, and took the two thieves to the station on suspicion that they were trying to rob the officer. On examining the prisoners at the station house there were found on one of them a watch valued at four hundred and fifty dollars, and a gold chain with Masonic emblems on it. The property was advertised very largely, but no owner could be found, and it was suspected that the man to whom the watch and chain had belonged had probably been made away with. Meantime it was ascertained that one of the emblems attached to the chain belonged to a Masonic society. There being no evidence against the prisoners, they were then discharged. The day that they were discharged a naval officer appeared in front of the Police desk, and said that the Inspector had his watch, and the man described it. He said he had been off on a China station; on the night of his return home he went to the Bowery Theatre, came out between the acts, and remembered nothing after that until he awoke the next morning, and found himself sitting in a doorway with his property and money all gone. When, on his return, he went to visit his Chapter at Philadelphia, they told him he had lost his mark and his watch, and that Inspector Thorne had the property. The man got his watch and chain, and the thieves were re-arrested, and were sent to State Prison for five years.

While Inspector Thorne was Captain in the Fourth Precinct, in the early part of 1863, a sailor came in and threw down a handkerchief containing twelve hundred dollars in gold on the desk, and said: "I want you to keep that for me." The Inspector took the money and gave the owner a receipt for it, and told him to come when he was sober and he would return it to him. The sailor left, and not returning, a search was made by the Police for the old fellow. He was found at the end of a week in a dance house, having had what he called a good time of it. When he returned to the station house he said· "I am going home; I live in Sullivan County The last time I was in New York I had seven hundred dollars, and I was cleaned out in one night. I have had all the fun I wanted now, and I will go home to my poor old mother and give her my money." The Inspector advised him to get a leather belt and put his money into it. He did so and went on his way rejoicing About a fortnight afterwards a man was brought into the station house so drunk that it was thought that he was dead. On looking at him the Inspector recognized his old friend, the sailor Upon opening his clothes the leather belt was found on him with some four hundred dollars in it. He had given all the money to his mother with the exception of that sum

When the leading agitators of the trades unions called a mass meeting to convene at the hall of the Cooper Institute shortly after the bloody Cincinnati riots, to pass resolutions of sympathy with those rioters, Inspector Thorne, who, in the absence of Superintendent Walling, was the acting Superintendent, took such prudent precautions in suppressing any riotous demonstrations, that the meeting passed over without any breach of the public peace.

Inspector Thorne's death took place unexpectedly on March 21, 1885 He had been, as usual, attending to his official duties, when he was taken suddenly ill, and, before his wife could have been summoned, he breathed his last. His funeral was largely attended by contingents from the Police force, private personal friends, and his grief-stricken family and sorrowing relatives

The vacancy caused by his death was filled the day after his interment by the appointment of Captain Steers as Inspector This appointment was made solely on the ground of merit, in recognition of the services of a brave and efficient officer Inspector Steers' appointment was made provisional, pending the decision of the question whether the Civil Service rules required that he should be subjected to an examination, which he subsequently passed.

THE FIFTH PRECINCT.—The Fifth Precinct is bounded by Warren Street, west track of the West Street Railroad, Canal Street, and Broadway The station house is at Nos. 19 and 21 Leonard Street. It is one of the oldest in the city, and was originally dwelling houses The chief officers of the command are Captain, Joseph B. Eakins; and Sergeants, Miles DeShays, Patrick H Doran, Edward R Delamater and A J Thompson. De Shays became a Policeman in 1862, a Roundsman four years later, and was made Sergeant next year Doran's dates are. Patrolman 1864, Roundsman 1869, and Sergeant 1873 Delamater came on the force in 1862, was made Roundsman in 1864, and obtained rank in 1868 Thompson is the senior Sergeant He donned the uniform in 1859, was made Roundsman in 1864, and was promoted to his present rank in 1866.

CAPTAIN JOSEPH B. EAKINS is less heard of in public or in the newspapers than any Captain on the force, notwithstanding the fact that he is in command of one of the most important precincts in the city, which includes the greater part of "the dry goods district." This is because Captain Eakins is a very modest man. He is popular, energetic, and stands high in the estimation of his official superiors. His dates are: Appointed on the force, March 1, 1866; made Roundsman, December 6, 1868; a Sergeant, March 21, 1872; and was promoted Captain October 19, 1876.

This precinct has nineteen day posts and thirty-eight night posts. Its full complement is ninety-seven men, but details and sickness reduce it to eighty men. Edward Handy and James Dunn are the Precinct Detectives. Thomas Foley

Captain Joseph B. Eakins.

is detailed to special night duty; Dermott Farley to Ordinances; Thomas Garland, Frederick Gilbert, and George A. Phillips to the Chambers Street Ferry; T. A. Moore to the Desbrosses Street Ferry; Cornelius Sullivan to West Broadway and Chambers Street, one of the worst crossings in New York; Charles S. Pike to the Laight Street Depot; Dennis McCarthy to the West Street cars, to prevent blockades and regulate the enormous stream of traffic there; Thomas Carlin to squad duty; and Antonio Perazzo to the Central Office on confidential duty as Italian interpreter and detective.

As an illustration of what a fire, getting headway in this command, can do in the way of depleting the pockets of underwriters, take the remarkable conflagration of the seventeenth of January, 1879, when business interests in Worth, Thomas, Duane, Church, and Leonard Streets suffered to the extent of one million nine hundred and seventy-six thousand seven hundred and thirty-four dollars and seventy-eight cents. Another fire, on the eleventh of April, 1875, at Nos 57 and 59 Worth Street, swept away property worth two hundred and forty-seven thousand dollars

In a mercantile sense, the Fifth Precinct is almost as important as the First Precinct It embraces nearly all the dry goods district—the quarter so dreaded by firemen—the southern terminus and depot of the Hudson River Railroad, the large grocery houses, the public stores, Chambers Street Hospital, much of the produce business, and several bonded warehouses At one time no precinct was so overrun with burglars as this, and some of the depredations were serious, but Captain Eakins has been singularly fortunate since he has been here, and a burglary is a rare occurrence. The annals of crime in this command furnish the example of the miserable, hopeless sot, thief and vagabond, Jack Reynolds, and his idle boast "Hanging is played out" Thanks to Father Duranquet, before Reynolds, on the sixth of April, 1870, met his fate for murdering the poor shoemaker in West Broadway, he saw his error and died a repentant sinner

THE EIGHTH PRECINCT.—The Eighth Precinct is bounded by Canal Street, Broadway, Houston Street, and the west track of the railroad in West Street. The station house at No. 128 Prince Street covers historical ground, and the walls enclose old structures. One was a watch-house, and the other the quarters of Engine Company No. 11, Volunteer Fire Department, of which "Jack" Wildey was foreman. The building has never been a healthy one, and a more substantial and better built house is sorely needed. The cells underground are dungeons, both damp and noisome. The officers are · Captain, Charles McDonnell; and Sergeants, Thomas H. B Carpenter, William H. Chrystie, Patrick McNally and Frank W. Robb Carpenter joined the force in 1861, was Roundsman in 1864, and was promoted next year Chrystie has been a Policeman more than twenty years; he became Roundsman in 1864, and Sergeant in 1867. McNally was appointed in 1864, waited six years to be a Roundsman, and some years later attained rank Robb's dates are· Patrolman 1866, Roundsman 1869, and Sergeant 1870.

CAPTAIN MCDONNELL—"Lightning Charley," of the Eighth Precinct, was born at No 130 Anthony (now Worth Street), and went to school in City Hall Place. At a very early age he tried to earn his own living by selling newspapers. The late sheriff, Matthew T. Brennan, Judge Dowling, and other prominent Democrats, took a great interest in the young lad when they saw that he was so industrious and bright, and he was appointed to the Police force in January, 1863 He was detailed for duty to the old Twenty-eighth Precinct (now part of the Eighth), under Captain Steers, where he remained for two years. In 1870 he was appointed Captain to the Eighth Precinct, and was shortly afterwards transferred to the Twenty-eighth Precinct. While here a man named Sheridan killed a German in a mysterious manner, at the corner of Thirty-seventh Street and Second Avenue, and within two hours he was captured by "Lightning Charley."

He also was instrumental in the arrest and conviction of the three negroes,

Thompson, Ellis and Weston, who murdered a peddler named Weisberg, in Westchester County. The three negroes were hanged.

A man named Hamilton murdered his mistress in Centre Street by inflicting several horrible stab wounds on her head and body. He was arrested the same evening by Captain McDonnell.

When he returned to the Eighth Precinct, Capt. McDonnell made a vigorous war on the several dens of infamy in that locality, and made a great clearance of them. He also arrested Hester Jane Haskins, a notorious abductor of girls for infamous purposes.

Charles Augustus Manning, Henry Williams, and George Williams, who burglarized the residence of Mr Sewell, a lawyer of West Forty-fifth Street,

Captain Charles McDonnell

were hunted down by Captain McDonnell after a four days' search. He had them arraigned the next day, and the day after they were each of them sentenced to eighteen years in State Prison.

One afternoon a poor woman, who lived in South Fifth Avenue, was discovered murdered and lying in a pool of blood in her miserable garret. The Captain put his wits to work, and that very night arrested her unnatural son, who was proved afterwards to be the murderer.

A free fight, in which razors, daggers, and pistols were used, occurred one Saturday night between rival negro clubs. After great difficulty Capt McDonnell quelled the disturbance. He made several arrests, and among others, a negro named Saunders, who was sent to State Prison. After his release he met Capt McDonnell in the street, and, with an oath, attacked that officer. Several other negroes joined in the assault on Capt McDonnell, but he managed to keep them at bay with his club until some white men came to his rescue

A few nights after the shooting of Ned O'Baldwin, the Irish giant and pugilist, a man came to the Police station, and delivered himself up to Capt. McDonnell, saying that it was no use to conceal anything from him, as he (the Captain) would be sure to find the murderer out.

A very amusing occurrence took place one evening while the Captain was sitting in his office. The door was suddenly opened, and a big black bear sauntered slowly in. He stood on his hind legs, and looked wistfully at the Captain The bear belonged to an Italian who was under arrest, and the

Eighth Precinct Station House, 128 Prince Street

animal had, by a strange coincidence, strayed in as if in search of his master The bear was locked up in the cell with his master, to the great delight of both

During a drunken quarrel at 57 Thompson Street, a negro named "Jim" Jackson killed two white women. He was arrested and convicted After his release from prison he opened a disreputable saloon in the same street Capt McDonnell made a raid on the place Jackson resisted his arrest so savagely that he had to be clubbed into submission He was subsequently convicted, and sent a second time to prison

This precinct has nineteen day posts and thirty-six night posts. The quota of men, eighty-seven, is reduced by details and average sickness to seventy-five.

Thomas Moran and John A. Savercool are the Precinct Detectives. Augustus Browning is detailed to ordinance duty, and Louis McCord to Inspector Murray's office

The Eighth Precinct takes in a most important Broadway front, necessitating unceasing vigilance to prevent burglaries; hardly less important interests in Mercer, Greene, Wooster, and Canal Streets, and South Fifth Avenue, the French colony, the bulk of the colored population, the Spring Street Market, mercantile marine interests on West Street, some squalor, less iniquity and vice than in former years, and the homes of many of the better class which are in the streets that run east from Varick Street It is not many years since that the mantle of the "Bloody Sixth" appeared to have fallen on the Eighth Precinct for mighty risks, immoral resorts which made one street a by-name for vicious negroes, and resorts for sporting men and politicians, notably Mitchell's at the corner of Broadway and Houston Street, furnished many a story that set tongues wagging Now nearly all has changed The district has been so far as is possible or can be reasonably expected, purged of the vicious classes, the resorts have moved up-town, and the colored element is under control It is rare that any event which might not occur in the best regulated precinct crops up, and the commercial and mercantile importance of the district is increasing daily. The dry goods district is spreading north from the Fifth Precinct, and at no time within the past few years have not builders been at work erecting substantial stores where once stood frame houses, which, in nine cases out of ten, were immoral resorts. One of the stirring incidents of late years was the fall of the old "rookeries" at Nos. 53 and 55 Grand Street, and the killing of eight persons On the first of February, 1883, Pier No 36, North River, used by the Inman Line, was burned, with a loss of two hundred and twenty thousand dollars. A substantial structure replaces it. Fireman's Hall, in Mercer Street, is in this precinct

THE NINTH PRECINCT.—The boundaries of the Ninth Precinct are Houston Street, Hancock Street, Bleecker Street, Carmine Street, Sixth Avenue, Fourteenth Street, and the centre line of Thirteenth Avenue and Eleventh Street, and the west track of the railroad in West Street. The station house is at No 94 Charles Street It was built for station house purposes, but it has been altered and repaired, and is cramped and unhealthy, and the cells are underground. The officers are· Captain, Theron S Copeland; and Sergeants, John A Croker, John Kellaher, William Porcher, and James B. Wilson Croker was a Policeman in 1862, a Roundsman four years later, and a Sergeant in 1872 Kellaher joined the force in 1861, became Roundsman in 1874, and attained his rank in 1876 Porcher has been in the department twenty-six years He became Roundsman in 1865, and has worn a Sergeant's uniform fourteen years Wilson is Porcher's senior, so far as Police duty goes, nine months In 1862 he became Roundsman, and three years later was promoted.

CAPTAIN THERON S. COPELAND was born in Albany, this State, in 1831, and moved to New York City in 1835. He was appointed a Patrolman in 1855, and was made Roundsman in July, 1857; was promoted to the next rank in March, 1858, and went a step higher in October, 1862. He has performed duty in the

Sixth, Seventh, Ninth, Eleventh, Thirteenth, Twenty-second and Twenty-fifth Precincts. By reason of Captain Copeland's superior knowledge of military tactics, gained by serving in the National Guard and at a military school, he was detailed by the Police Board to instruct the force in military tactics. For this purpose he was assigned to the Central Office, were he remained for a period of sixteen years, five of which he was at the head of the class of instruction, and for two years aid to the Superintendent. He succeeded so well in this branch of the service that when the draft riots occurred in July, 1863, the Police force of this city, by their knowledge of military tactics and discipline, were able to meet and overcome the rioters, who outnumbered them a hundred to one, and earned for themselves a world-wide renown. Captain Copeland has participated

Captain Thereon S. Copeland

in nearly all of the prominent Police events that have taken place since he joined the force. In recognition of his services in the draft riots the Police Board awarded him special honorable mention, a like distinction being bestowed on him by the Board for the part he took in the Orange riots of 1871. In 1862 he was sent in command of three hundred and fifty officers and men to Riker's Island, to quell a mutiny that had broken out among a large crowd of men who were quartered there. He was also sent in command of fifty men to quell a similar disturbance at Camp Washington, Staten Island, and subsequently to Tarrytown to suppress rioting while men were being drafted for the war. On the application of General Bowen, Captain Copeland was mustered into the United States military service as Adjutant, for the purpose of organizing the Second Metropolitan Regiment (One Hundred and Thirty-third New York Volunteers), a duty which was performed in thirty days. The regiment proved to be one of the best in the service, many of the ex-members of the Police force serving in its ranks. Captain Copeland has made a number of important arrests, and has been several times injured in the discharge of his duty.

There are seventeen day and thirty-four night posts in this precinct. The force is eighty-seven men, reduced to about sixty-eight by sickness and details. John Flanagan and James B. Ayers are the Precinct Detectives. The detailed men are: A. M. De Nyse, Christopher Street Ferry; Charles E. Bush, Jefferson Market, Robert B. Pitcairn, Corporation Ordinances; and Robert Kelly, Special Duty.

The Ninth Precinct was at one time the stronghold of the native Americans. To-day more people of the middle class own or occupy their own houses, despite the tendency to coalesce, or herd in flat, apartment or tenement houses, than in any other precinct. Its streets are quiet, cobble-stoned, and its iniquities, according to the Police record, few. It guards the Jefferson Market, Police Court and Prison, which are of the few architectural ornaments of the city. Gansevoort Market, which within a year will be one of the most important markets for provisions in the city, St. Vincent's Hospital, and a section of upper-tendom in West Fourteenth Street. Its West Street front embraces important interests, and within its boundaries are the walls of the old State Prison. Few events of magnitude occur here.

THE FIFTEENTH PRECINCT.—The Fifteenth Precinct's boundaries are the Bowery, Fourth Avenue, Fourteenth Street, Sixth Avenue, Carmine Street, Bleecker Street, Hancock Street, Houston Street, Broadway and Bleecker Street. The station house is at Nos. 251 and 253 Mercer Street, which were dwelling houses turned into a station house, when the station house was in Ambrose H. Kingsland's stable opposite. This stable was the quarters of Engine Company No. 4, of which Excise Commissioner John J. Morris was foreman; and it afterwards became the quarters of Engine Company No. 33, afterwards moved to Great Jones Street. The building is in fair order, and has a separate prison. The officers are: Captain, John J. Brogan; and Sergeants, Donald Grant, James J. Brophy, Joseph Douglas, and John J. Thompson. Grant's dates are: Patrolman 1876, Roundsman 1877, and Sergeant 1880. Brophy went on the force in 1871, was Roundsman in 1876, and he got his rank two years later. Douglas became Patrolman 1868, Roundsman 1870, and Sergeant the same year. Thompson, the senior Sergeant, was appointed in 1860, and waited seventeen years to be Roundsman; four years after this he was promoted.

CAPTAIN JOHN J. BROGAN, of the Fifteenth Precinct, is a New Yorker, and was born in the year 1844. While at school he generally occupied himself with drawing on the black board deeds of chivalry and heroism, for which breach of discipline he often received a flogging from his schoolmaster. He was apprenticed at an early age to the theatrical scene painting trade, but he disliked the business, his physical organization demanding a more active occupation. Accordingly, when he was twenty-one years of age, he joined the Police force, and was sent to the Second Precinct.

Captain Brogan was only a fortnight on the force when he made his first arrest, or rather arrests, for there were two burglars engaged in the robbery. As he was on his beat in Maiden Lane, he noticed the door of a fur store open. He waited and watched. Soon two desperadoes made their appearance, loaded with goods. One of them, as soon as he saw Brogan, laid down his plunder and struck at him with a jimmy Brogan put up his arm to guard the blow, but the jimmy broke one of his fingers. He, however, secured his men. They were Tom Harris and Michael Galvin They were convicted, and sent to State Prison

Soon after this, while the remains of the murdered President Lincoln were lying in City Hall, Brogan observed a well-known thief named Williams picking

Captain John J Brogan.

pockets in the crowd Brogan approached the ruffian, who fled and was followed by the officer as far as the corner of Chatham, and William Streets There Brogan shot him in the leg, and the thief, not being able to go any further, was arrested

In 1867, while Officer Brogan was doing Detective duty at Staten Island, a society called the Ancient Order of Good Fellows gave a pic-nic on a Sunday in that place, and insisted on having all the refreshments they required On some of the saloon keepers refusing to supply them, a riot ensued, but was very quickly quelled, owing to the foresight and determination of Detective Brogan.

While in the Sixth Precinct Captain Brogan made the arrest of a very tough character named "Country" Nolan, who was trying to rob an old gentleman in Donovan's Lane, behind Baxter Street A desperate encounter took place between Nolan and the officer, but the robber at last was overcome. He was sent to Sing Sing

George Smith, a negro, shot and killed his paramour, a white woman, in 1879. After the murder Smith tried to conceal himself among the colored folks in the Eighth Ward, and afterwards went on board of a vessel bound south He,

Fifteenth Precinct Station House, 251 Mercer Street.

however, could not escape Captain Brogan's vigilance. As the vessel was about to sail, that officer went quietly on board and arrested his man.

He was made Captain in September, 1878, and was placed in charge of the Fourteenth Precinct He was shortly afterwards transferred to the Fifteenth, where he is at present stationed

Towards the end of the year 1880 Captain Brogan and Detective Crowley saw four men enter the store of James McCreery & Company, at the corner of

Eleventh Street and Broadway The Captain and Detective followed them, and a regular fusilade was opened on both sides. Two of the burglars were wounded Their names were Tommy Fay, Dutch Fred, Tom Maypother, and John Brown alias Turk They were sent to State Prison for five years each

Soon after this a Sergeant of the regular army shot and killed a boy at Albany The Sergeant fled, but Capt Brogan succeeded in finding him in this city

But the most important achievement of Capt. Brogan's Police service was the capture and conviction of the notorious Mrs Johnson, a Swede, who used to induce young girls to emigrate, and when they landed at Castle Garden, she took possession of them body and soul.

This precinct has sixteen day and thirty-two night posts Eighty-one men are on the roll, but about sixty-seven do duty, sickness and details reducing the effective force The Precinct Detectives are William Warren and Thomas Reynolds The detailed men are Manuel A. White, Juvenile Asylum; Edward Gilgar, Ordinances; John J. Farley. Clinton Place and Sixth Avenue, John Fogarty Fifth Avenue and Fourteenth Street; John Cunningham, St Joseph's Home; James McAdam, Fourteenth Street and University Place; and Benjamin Tesaro, Detective and Interpreter's duty at Police Headquarters' Detective Bureau

People of every condition are under the protection or serveillance of the Fifteenth Precinct Wooster Street has its dissolute negroes, Fifth Avenue its aristocrats, Minetta Lane and Bleecker Street their negroes, Waverley Place and Clinton Place their boarding houses, Broadway, Fourteenth Street and Sixth Avenue their tradesmen There is a little of everything in this precinct, but it is principally occupied by either the respectable or the wealthy classes In this command are the Star Theatre and the Union Square Theatre, Washington Park, and Grace Church, some of the finest stores in the city, among them the Stewart Building, the University Building, the Excise Office, the Bleecker Street Savings Bank—one of the richest institutions of the kind in the world, the Astor and Mercantile Libraries, the Mission of the Immaculate Virgin, the Brevoort House, Grand Central, New York and other hotels, and Society Library. Such a precinct requires and possesses a circumspect body of Police, equal to any emergency, and it is daily mentioned in the press as having furnished at the Jefferson Market, or Police Headquarters, or the Coroner's office, some tale of interest The most stirring incidents of the past few years are the killing of James Fisk, Jr, by Edward S. Stokes at the Grand Central Hotel twelve years ago; the burglary on the twenty-seventh of October, 1878, by which the Manhattan Savings Institution lost two million seven hundred and forty-seven thousand seven hundred dollars, in money and securities, and the burning, on the sixth of March, 1877, of Jewelers Hall, Nos 1, 3 and 5 Bond Street. where six hundred thousand dollars' worth of property was destroyed. Inspectors Byrnes, Murray and Dilks were graduated from this command

THE SIXTEENTH PRECINCT —The Sixteenth Precinct is almost a parallelogram, whose sides are Fourteenth Street, Seventh Avenue, Twenty-seventh Street, and the North River The station house, at No 230 West Twentieth Street, is a very old one, constructed out of a dwelling house. It is snug and healthy, but the cells are underground, and an extra story was added to the building seventeen years ago The officers are. Captain, John McElwain; and Sergeants, Daniel Polhamus, William Blair, James Lonsdale and Oliver H Tims Polhamus was a Patrolman in 1861, a Roundsman in 1865, and a Sergeant in 1867 Blair, the senior Sergeant, joined the force in 1858, was made Roundsman in 1863, and was promoted the next year Lonsdale was appointed in 1862, became Roundsman six years later, and got rank in 1869 The dates of Tims are. Patrolman 1866, Roundsman 1870, and Sergeant 1872

CAPTAIN JOHN MCELWAIN, of the Sixteenth Precinct, was born in New York in November, 1831 His parents were well off, and he received a thoroughly good education He served his time to the jewelry business, and worked in one employment for several years He joined the force on the second of September, 1872, and was assigned to the Fifteenth Precinct During his stay here the draft riots broke out, and he took an active part in quelling the disturbance For his conduct in these riots he was promoted to the rank of Roundsman, and was transferred to the Twenty-first, and afterwards to the Seventeenth. While here he was made Sergeant, and transferred to the Eleventh He was afterwards successively stationed at the Twenty-third, Eighteenth, and Twenty-ninth. He was made Captain in September, 1872, and went to the Twenty-first He was then transferred to the Twentieth, then returned to the Twenty-first, then to the Twenty-third He went back again to the Twenty-first, then to the Seventh, and finally to the Sixteenth

Captain McElwain is an experienced, shrewd officer It is said that he can tell a thief at the first glance

He arrested Scannel for the murder of Thomas Donoghue, at Apollo Hall, November 29, 1872, for which he was presented with an elegant gold medal by the Commissioners The medal is inscribed with the names of B F. Manierre, Thomas Bosworth, Thomas J Barr, and A Oakey Hall.

During his Captaincy of the Twentieth Precinct he was instrumental in obtaining convictions which amounted in the aggregate to three hundred and twenty-three years

Minnie Davis, the notorious fire bug, was also arrested by him, as also George West alias Davis, who, four days after his capture, was amusing himself breaking stones in Sing Sing Prison

Captain McElwain was complimented by Commissioner Acton, in his annual report to the legislature, for his action in quelling a disturbance raised by the Live Oak Volunteers, who were on an excursion to Astoria The Volunteers went about that town ransacking it, and terrifying the inhabitants There were only a few men at the station house when this intelligence arrived, but Captain McElwain decided on at once going to Astoria. He concealed himself and his men in the ferryboat until its arrival at that place. He then suddenly precipitated himself on the rioters, and, after a severe struggle, arrested the ringleaders

While Captain McElwain was one day pursuing the notorious cart thief, Wilson, he was attacked by Wilson, and both fell to the ground After a fearful struggle, Wilson, however, went under, and was taken to the Police station

During his Captaincy of the Twentieth Precinct, the citizens presented Captain McElwain with a very complimentary testimonial

Galvin and McGinn, who knocked down and robbed Mr Hanks, the jeweler, were also arrested by Captain McElwain. This was considered a very clever capture, as there was no clue whatever at the time to the perpetrators of the outrage The Captain, for this, was publicly complimented by Recorder Hackett from the Bench.

"Fagan," whose proper name is Isaac Lycres, was a notorious receiver of stolen goods. He was so adroit at his work that it was very difficult for the Police to get at him. Captain McElwain worked up the case so well that he managed to secure "Fagan" and recover thousands of dollars' worth of goods.

Captain John McElwain.

This precinct has eighteen day and twenty-eight night posts Its full force is seventy-three men, but the average of them doing full duty is sixty-two Adolph Schmidt and Richard Wilson are the Precinct Detectives. The detailed officers are John Ferguson, Truancy; Richard Flynn, Ordinances, Patrick W Vallely, Twenty-third Street Ferry

The Sixteenth Precinct Police have to deal with both rich and poor, from those who inhabit the fine residences in West Fourteenth Street to those who lounge about the lumber yards of the North River front, which represents three-quarters of the lumber interest of New York. It has the Twenty-third Street Ferry, the Grand Opera House, the baths and flat houses in West Twenty-third Street, and the tradesmen of Seventh and Eighth Avenues. The most stirring event of late years within its boundaries was the

Orange riots of 1873, and the firing of the military in Eighth Avenue, near Twenty-third Street. A score of persons were killed outright, and it is estimated that as many more died afterwards. The bodies of those that fell in the streets were transported to the station house, and laid out in the basement. Old officers of the command yet remember the wails that were uttered by those who came to claim their dead. Another tragic event was the shooting, at the Vienna Flats, No. 341 West Twenty-third Street, of W. H. Haverstick by George W. Conkling, brother of Mrs. Uhler, with whom Haverstick lived in defiance of decency. This occurred March 19, 1883. Since then Conkling died out West, and Mrs. Uhler poisoned herself. Another mysterious occurrence was the killing, in the grounds of the Protestant Episcopal General Theological Seminary, at Twentieth Street and Ninth Avenue, on the morning of July 4, 1879, of John F. Seymour, of Bishop Seymour's family. He was walking in

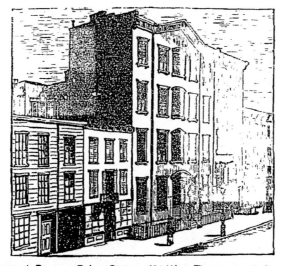

Twentieth Precinct Police Station, 434 West Thirty-seventh Street.

the grounds and was, it is supposed, killed by a small bullet discharged from a boy's toy pistol or rifle.

THE TWENTIETH PRECINCT.—The Twentieth Precinct begins at Twenty-seventh Street, goes along Seventh Avenue, and runs to Forty-second Street and the North River. The station house is at Nos. 434 and 436 West Thirty-seventh Street. When it was built, fourteen years ago, it was considered a vast improvement on any other that existed. It has a separate prison, and is so well looked after as to be always wholesome and healthy. The officers are: Captain, George Washburn, and Sergeants, Andrew J. Thomas, William F. Devery, George H. Havens and Stephen E. Brown. Thomas has been on the force twelve years. He was made Sergeant last year after doing seven months' duty as Roundsman. Devery's dates are: Patrolman 1878, Roundsman 1881, and Sergeant 1884. Havens' are: Patrolman in 1861, Roundsman in 1863, and Sergeant in 1866. Brown was appointed in 1868, was made Roundsman in 1870, and three years later obtained promotion.

CAPTAIN WASHBURN was born on the ninth of June, 1826, in the city of New York. At the age of four years his parents moved to Sing Sing, where he resided until he was fifteen years old. He traveled round the world for four years, having served alternately as sailor and soldier. In February, 1858, he was appointed on the Police, where he served until August, 1862, when he joined the Metropolitan Regiment as First Lieutenant. After one year's service he was promoted Captain, and fifteen months later he rose to the rank of Major, which position he retained until the end of the war. He served under General Banks and General Sheridan. Upon returning from the war he was re-appointed a Patrolman, and five days later he was promoted Roundsman, and within a week from that date he was made a Sergeant, that being his rank on the Police

Captain George Washburn

force when he resigned to go to the war. After serving as a Sergeant for three years he was raised to the rank of Captain. He took part in the Orange riot, and was on that day second in command, under Captain Walling.

This precinct has thirteen day and twenty-eight night posts. Its full force is seventy-eight men, from which an average of seventeen should be deducted for sickness and details. Stephen Carmick and Matthew McConnell are the Precinct Detectives. John W. King on Ordinances; and John Murphy to the Offal Dock.

In the Twentieth Precinct there are few public buildings of any note. It has a busy water front, crowded with repulsive industries, such as hog and cattle abattoirs. The offal dock, and the terminus of the Hudson River Railroad Depot make constant traffic along grimy Eleventh Avenue. Within the precinct limits are the

Institution for the Blind, Manhattan Market, the West Shore depot and ferry, large gas works, "Battle Row" and "Hell's Kitchen," the resort of the depraved adults of both sexes, and a hundred other dwelling places of the New York hoodlum, who only exists in this district. The "Tenth Avenue Gang" is what they are wrongly called. They belong to all parts of the city, but this is their stronghold, and their plunder is from the freight cars of the Hudson River Railroad. This precinct has furnished more frightful examples of juvenile depravity than all the other precincts together since 1870. One of the leaders of the gang was "Dutch" Harmon, a German freight car thief. On the sixth of February, 1874, he was planning a depredation, when he was surprised by Roundsman Stephen Carmick, and escaped after firing at the officer. On the eighteenth of that month Nicholas Schweich, a Hudson River Railroad watchman, was murdered at his post because he interfered with thieves who were robbing a freight car. The police say positively that the murder was committed by Harmon, or an associate named Dougherty. Harmon was sought for, and Officer Patrick Lahey, on the twenty-second of February, 1874, believed that he had cornered Harmon at No. 530 West Twenty-ninth Street, and fired a shot though the door, supposing Harmon had his back to it. The shot killed an innocent man named McNamara, and Harmon was not in the house. He was caught nine days later, but could not be convicted for the murder of the watchman. Since then he has served two terms in prison, and broke his leg in this city while escaping out of a hack at Fulton Street. In the hack were silks stolen from a factory at Union Hill, N. J.

THE TWENTY-FIFTH PRECINCT.—The Twenty-fifth Precinct or Broadway Squad's daily territory is Broadway from Bowling Green to Thirty-fourth Street. The station house is at No. 34 East Twenty-ninth Street, where are the quarters of the Second Inspection District. The building is private property, owned by the Goelet estate, and was not erected for Police purposes, but transformed into a station house thirty-seven years ago, when the Eighteenth Precinct had its headquarters there. It was afterwards the Twenty-first Precinct Station House and the Twenty-ninth Precinct Station House. A prison was added in 1877. The officers are: Captain, Ira S. Garland; Sergeants, Washington T. Devoe whose dates are: Patrolman 1861, Roundsman 1872, and Sergeant 1873, and William H. Lefferts, who was a Patrolman prior to 1857, and passing the grade of Roundsman, was promoted in 1858.

CAPTAIN IRA S. GARLAND, in command of the Twenty-fifth Precinct, was born in the city of Utica, N. Y., October 7, 1830. When a small boy his parents removed to Sherburne, Chenango County, N. Y., when the boy was placed in the public school. Having arrived at man's estate, he came to this city, and shipped in the Merchant Marine service. He followed the sea for eight years, and rose to the rank of mate.

On April 21, 1858, he was appointed a Patrolman of the Metropolitan Police, and was assigned to the Harbor Police on May 22, 1860. Six days afterwards he distinguished himself by an act of bravery which gained for him honorable mention by the Board of Police, "for gallant conduct in repressing a mutiny on board of the ship R. F. Starer."

Captain Garland was promoted to the grade of Roundsman in 1860, and to

Sergeant in 1862 He was then assigned to the Fifth Precinct, and was subsequently transferred to the Second Precinct (Jefferson Market Police Court), where he was placed in command, and there remained until he was promoted to the rank of Captain, on March 4, 1867, when he was assigned to the command of the Fourteenth Precinct He served alternately in the following precincts First, Seventh, Eleventh, Twelfth, Eighteenth, old Twenty-eighth, and Thirtieth. He was transferred to the Twenty-fifth Precinct on October 3, 1876, where he is at present in command

While in command of the old Twenty-eighth, Captain Garland arrested William J. Sharkey for the murder of Robert Dunn alias "Bob" Isaacs Sharkey, who was convicted, escaped from the Tombs while under sentence of death,

Captain Ira S Garland

aided by Maggie Jourdan, in whose clothes he had concealed his identity, and so eluded the vigilance of his keepers

Aided by Detective Sergeant Von Gerichten, he arrested Hugh Boran, and William and Nellie Wilsey, for the bold robbery in the day time of Mrs. Hardy, in her house at Varick and Broome Streets, whom they tortured by burning her feet with a hot iron to make her divulge the place where she had her jewelry concealed. They were convicted and sentenced to State Prison He also arrested, on December 22, 1883, at Thirty-fourth Street and Fifth Avenue, a German named Frederick A Hartman, who had shot and wounded Augustus Gardiner, a watchman at the A. T. Stewart mansion. Hartman resisted arrest, and acted like a man bereft of his reason. He committed suicide on January 8, 1884, in the Tombs Prison, by hanging himself in his cell.

This precinct has forty day posts. No night duty is done by its members, who are required to be tall and stalwart. The muster roll of the command is forty-five, but there are generally four or five men sick. The Precinct Detective is Thomas McCormack. The duty of the Patrolmen of the Broadway Squad lies along the line of Broadway. At night their posts are covered by the officers of the precincts which Broadway passes through or divides.

THE TWENTY-SEVENTH PRECINCT.—The Twenty-seventh Precinct is bounded by Warren Street, Broadway, Battery Place, Pier 1 North River, and the west track of the railroad in West Street. The station house is at No. 35 New Church Street. Formerly the building faced on Liberty Street, but the extension of Church Street cut a good lot off the station house, and, in 1870,

Captain William C. F. Berghold

Architect Bush reconstructed the station house, and made it almost a modern one. The cells for prisoners are partly underground. The officers are: Captain, William C. F. Berghold; and Sergeants, Thomas E. Willard, Richard Welch, Edward Muret, and Thomas Reilly. Willard was a Patrolman in 1866, a Roundsman in 1875, and a Sergeant in 1876. Welch's dates are: Patrolman 1858, Roundsman 1869, and Sergeant 1870. Muret joined the force in 1873, became Roundsman 1876, and was promoted in 1880. Reilly was appointed in 1866, waited five years to be a Roundsman, and won rank in 1872.

CAPTAIN WILLIAM C. F. BERGHOLD was born in the year 1838. He joined the Police force in 1864, and was made a Roundsman five years later. In 1870 he was made Sergeant, and Captain in 1878. While he served in the Eleventh Precinct he had a number of criminals arrested and sent to State Prison. He was sent to Staten Island in 1866, when a disturbance was expected in consequence of a factory having been seized and turned into an hospital In 1868, when there was some misunderstanding between the German and Irish emigrants on Ward's Island, he was sent to that place, and his coolness and determination of character won for him the respect and confidence of the two nationalities who were inclined to be mutinous

This precinct has eighteen day and thirty-six night posts. Its quota of ninety-two men is reduced about twenty by sickness and details The Precinct Detectives are Thomas Mulvey and William Flynn The detailed officers are Michael J. Hockey, Ordinances, Thomas Fay, West Street; Matthew Looram, Vesey Street; Thomas Dennin, Courtlandt Street Ferry; George Archer, Liberty Street Ferry; Frank D Weber, Barclay Street Ferry; Frederick Probst, Washington Market.

This command looks after vastly important interests. Within its limits are Trinity Church and graveyard, St Paul's Church, St. Peter's Roman Catholic Church, the Astor House, Washington Market, the Coal and Real Estate Exchanges, nearly all the west side emigrant boarding houses, several large cotton warehouses, the Western Union Telegraph Company's building, thousands of offices in Broadway, the Graphic and Frank Leslie buildings, the crockery, fireworks and glass trades, much of the produce trade, and some squalor in Greenwich and Washington Streets. In it end the surface cars of the Seventh Avenue, Sixth Avenue, Eighth Avenue and Broadway Railroads The most memorable fire in it of recent years was that on the twentieth of December, 1877, when saccharine dust exploded in Greenfield's candy factory in Barclay Street, and ten persons lost their lives. The fire did one hundred and twenty thousand dollars damage.

THE TWENTY-NINTH PRECINCT.—The Twenty-ninth Precinct is included between Seventh Avenue, Forty-second Street, Park Avenue, Fourth Avenue, Union Square, and Fourteenth Street. The station house is at Nos 137 and 139 West Thirtieth Street. It is not such a structure as the importance of the command warrants. It has a separate prison, but the office is so small that at muster the men have to form three sides of a square, and some of them are invisible to the officer at the desk It has often been planned to make two precincts out of this one, and the sooner it is done the better for the men who have the outposts at Fourteenth and Forty-second Streets The officers are. Captain, Alexander S Williams, and Sergeants, Josiah A. Westervelt, Adam A Cross, James M King, and Max F. Schmittberger. Westervelt was a Policeman in 1867, Roundsman next year, and Sergeant in 1870 Cross joined the force seven years ago, became Roundsman in 1882, and was promoted last January. King has the record of being appointed in 1874, and three years later he passed the grade of Roundsman and won rank Schmittberger's dates are Patrolman 1874, Roundsman 1880, and Sergeant 1883

CAPTAIN ALEXANDER S WILLIAMS, of the Twenty-ninth Precinct, is well known throughout the States as one of the most efficient and determined Police officers in New York. Captain Williams was born in 1839 in Nova Scotia. When he came to New York he learned the trade of a ship carpenter, and was placed in charge of a portion of the docks of the well known shipbuilders, W H Webb & Co He afterwards visited Japan, Mexico, and other countries. He was the first white man to build a ship in Japan After his return to America, he was engaged by the Government to raise a sunken vessel off the coast of Key West, Florida. He was then connected with the navy yard for a time. Having succeeded in accumulating some money, he went into partnership with a shipbuilder, but a strike occurring, Williams was obliged to dissolve partnership with his colleague. He applied for a position on the Police, and was appointed Patrolman in August, 1866, and was assigned to the Forty-seventh Precinct, Brooklyn He remained there until 1868, when he was transferred to the Broadway (New York) Squad While here he was Roundsman and Acting Sergeant,

Captain Alexander S Williams.

and was then sent to the Mounted Squad In July, 1871, he was made Sergeant, and on the twenty-fifth of September, 1871, he was promoted to the rank of Captain, and assigned for duty to the Twenty-first Precinct He was transferred from there to the Eighth Precinct, then in 1874 to the Fourth, and in 1876 to the Twenty-ninth He served four years in the Street Cleaning Department, and finally went back to his present precinct, the Twenty-ninth As a result of the energy and vigilance which he displayed while in the Eighth Precinct, he arrested no less than nine murderers

Lockwood alias Cully, a desperate burglar, was also captured by Captain Williams, and over one hundred burglars' tools were found in his possession.

The Florence Saloon, which was at the corner of Broadway and Houston Street, was the rendezvous for all classes of criminals While he was yet a

Patrolman, Captain Williams succeeded in having this notorious establishment closed.

Houses of ill-fame and the meeting places of dens of thieves have been raided and closed up by the score by this undaunted officer. He is not a favorite, by any means, with the criminal classes.

There was a place at No. 115 Broome Street which was not inaptly called "Milligan's Hell." At all hours of the night the boisterous tongues of roughs could be heard, their conversation interspersed with the most horrible oaths and blasphemy. The place was considered so dangerous that Policemen, it was said,

Twenty Ninth Police Precinct, 137 West Thirtieth Street

were loathe to enter the place. Captain Williams made a raid one night on the den and cleaned out the place. Once he has made up his mind to accomplish a thing, he will do it at any risk.

The amount of stolen property recovered by Captain Williams would foot up a fabulous sum. He returned over six thousand dollars' worth of stolen laces to Herman, Ivans & Co., of Broadway, and about five thousand dollars' worth of silks to Richards, of Broadway.

During his Captaincy in the Fourth Ward he broke up several of the low dives in Chatham, Water and Pearl Streets.

Jewelry and diamonds to the amount of seven thousand dollars were stolen in South America by two Swedes. The vessel on which they traveled had scarcely arrived at the port of New York when the two thieves were in the clutches of Captain Williams.

During his command of the Twenty-first Precinct, Captain Williams was presented with a handsome gold shield, bearing the following inscription:

"Presented to Captain Alexander S. Williams, in acknowledgment of his valuable aid in suppressing the roughs and defending his officers in the discharge of their duties. NEW YORK, September 16, 1872."

In his examination, before the Roosevelt Committee, to interrogatories, Captain Williams gave the following responses.

By the Chairman. Q. What is your name? A. Alexander S. Williams. Q. What position do you hold? A. Captain of Police. Q. How long have you been on the Police? A. Nearly eighteen years. Q. How long have you been Captain? A. Nearly thirteen—thirteen past.

By Mr. Russell. Q. You have been on the force how long, Captain? A. Nearly eighteen years. Q. And how old are you now? A. Forty-four. Q. And what was the name of the force when you went on? A. The Metropolitan. Q. And in what capacity did you first go on? A. As Patrolman. Q. Where? A. Forth-seventh Precinct, Brooklyn, now the Seventh. Q. How long did you remain a Patrolman? A. Less than five years. Q. Then what? A. Sergeant, I was made Roundsman first off. Q. How long? A. About ten minutes. I was made Sergeant and put in charge of the Thirty-third Precinct, which was the Mounted Police. Q. How long did you remain in charge of the Mounted Police? A. Eleven months. Q. Was that under the old Metropolitan system? A. Metropolitan. Q. Where was the Thirty-third Precinct? A. I had a stable fitted up in Forty-first Street and Seventh Avenue, 154 West Seventh Avenue, part of Sixth Avenue, and Fourteenth Street, and Lexington Avenue was then wooden pavement—and it was to prevent fast driving on those streets. Q. Who were the Commissioners then? A. Bosworth, Manierre, Barr, and Smith. Q. When did you become a Captain? A. May 31, 1871, I think, or 1872. Q. How long have you been in your present precinct? A. I went there the latter part of October, 1876, and remained there until the nineteenth of December, 1879, and returned there on the sixteenth of June, 1881, and have been there until now. Q. From 1879 until 1881 you were employed elsewhere? A. Superintendent of the Bureau of Street Cleaning.

This important precinct has twenty-seven day and fifty night posts. Its full force is one hundred and sixteen men, of whom about eighteen are sick or detailed. James K. Price and John Dunlap are the Precinct Detectives. The detailed officers are: John Neylan, Tax Office; John Mangam, Ordinances.

What the First Precinct is, commercially and financially, the Twenty-ninth or "Tenderloin Precinct" is socially, and—if the term may be coined—cosmopolitanly. No other command approaches it in importance as the centre of civilization and all that makes Nineteenth Century city life agreeable. It embraces nearly all the great caravansaries, parks, clubs, theatres and stores. Within it are the most frequented streets and avenues, and at night city life for the "upper ten" alone exists within its boundaries. It takes in the Union Square, Madison Square and Reservoir Parks. Its principal hotels are the St. Cloud, Rossmore, Grand, Gilsey House, Albermarle, Hoffman House, Leland, Fifth Avenue, Glenham, Brunswick, Park Avenue, Everett House, St. James, Sturtevant, and the Parker House. Its hospital, the New York, is by far the best in the city. Its clubs are the American Jockey, the American Yacht, the Blossom, the Calumet, the Carlton, the Columbia, the Coney Island Jockey, the Crescent, the German, the Grolier, the Knickerbocker, the Lotos, the Manhattan, the New York, the New York Racquet, the New York Yacht, the Owl, the Republic, the St. Nicholas, the Lamb, the Union, the Union League, and the University. Of the public buildings it has the Academy of Design, the Masonic Temple, and the Young Men's Christian Association. Its theatres and places of amusement are the Metropolitan Opera House, the Bijou Opera House, the Casino, Chickering Hall, Daly's Theatre, the Fifth Avenue Theatre, the Fourteenth Street Theatre, Madison Square Garden, the Park Theatre, the Standard, the Star, Wallack's, the Comedy, Eden Musee, Koster & Bial's, and the Metropolitan Concert Hall. The famous restaurants of Delmonico, Pinard and Clark are here. And its stores? first. Tiffany and Starr's countless attractions in jewelry, watches, gold and silverware, *bric a brac* and art objects; W. & J Sloane's carpet store, Lord & Taylor's, Arnold & Constable's, Sypher & Co.'s, the Gorham Manufacturing Co.'s, C G Gunther's Sons, Park & Tilford's, Collamore & Co.'s, and Brooks Brothers' Then there are the armories of the Twenty-second and Seventy-first Regiments of the National Guard; the Fifth, Garfield, Lincoln and Sixth National Banks, the Excelsior and Union Dime Savings Banks; the Metropolis and Madison Square State Banks; Calvary, Messiah, Tabernacle, Madison Avenue, Brick, Fourth Avenue, Twenty-third Street, St Ann's, Dr Ormiston's, St. Francis Xavier's, St Vincent de Paul, Holy Trinity, St Paul's Lutheran, St. Luke's, St Mark's, St Paul's Methodist, Covenant, Fourth Presbyterian, Madison Square, Rutger's, Scotch, Shiloh, Westminster, West Twenty-fifth Street, Annunciation, Christ, Du St. Esprit, Holy Communion, Incarnation, St. Ignatius, Trinity Chapel, Zion, Fifth Avenue Reformed, Holy Innocents, St Francis of Assisi, St Leo's, Tabernacle of Twenty-third Street and Union Tabernacle Churches, and Shearith Israel Synagogue. Its population is, mainly, the "upper ten," and those who serve them. It has a negro colony, and is infested with people who live viciously, but the law, not the Police, is at fault. The problem how to deal with this class is probably such a serious, and at the same time such a delicate one, that before it is solved we shall have to elect a special legislature to deal with it. Yet, with all its hideousness, this feature of New York is not by any means as black as the night haunts of London or the principal European cities, where vice, if not licensed, is under surveillance.

As may be expected, this command has furnished many thrilling and scandalous stories to the public. Hardly a week passes but something interesting is told over the desk in the Thirtieth Street Station House. In fires its specialty is in theatres. The Fifth Avenue Theatre went up in clouds of smoke and showers of sparks and brands January 1, 1873, with a loss of one hundred and ten thousand dollars. On the thirtieth of October, 1882, a few hours before the time that

Mrs. Langtry was to make her debut in America, there was a fatal fire that destroyed the Park Theatre, and the loss was eighty thousand dollars, and on the fourteenth of December, 1883, the Standard Theatre was destroyed, with a loss of sixty thousand dollars. On the tenth of December, 1872, a number of servant girls lost their lives by a fire which cut off escape from their quarters on the roof of the Fifth Avenue Hotel. March 8, 1877, witnessed a terrible panic in St. Francis Xavier's church, No. 36 West Sixteenth Street. Father Langcake was preaching a sermon on "Hell and the Horrors of the Damned," and his audience were worked up to a supreme degree of interest, when a boy, either through devilish inspiration or from a belief that he was doing well, cried "Fire." In the stampede that ensued six women and a boy were trampled to death at the foot of a corkscrew stairway. The murder of Benjamin Nathan, on the twenty-ninth of July, 1870, in his mansion opposite the south side of the Fifth Avenue Hotel, is one of the mysteries of the age. The true story of what occurred in that second floor room on that bright summer morning has not yet been told. The murder of Mrs. Jane L. De Forest Hull, wife of Dr. Alonzo Grandison Hull, at No. 140 West Forty-second Street, on the eleventh of June, 1879, by the negro, Chastine Cox, was the talk of all America for months. Cox was captured in Boston through a reporter named Balch, and was hanged July 16, 1880. It is almost certain he did not intend to kill Mrs. Hull, but simply to silence her. He did his work, however, so surely, that she died, and he was executed because he took life while committing a felony. A bloodier ending of a feud was probably never witnessed than that by which, in "Shang" Draper's saloon, No. 466 Sixth Avenue, on the sixteenth of October, 1883, "Johnny" Walsh alias "Johnny the Mick," and "Johnny" Irving, two noted thieves, lost their lives. An associate, William O'Brien alias "Billy" Porter, strongly suspected of shooting Walsh, who was to have been killed for Porter by Irving, was arrested, but he escaped conviction. Another celebrated case was the murder, at No. 144 West Twenty-sixth Street, on the twenty-fourth of December, 1881, of Louis Hanier, an inoffensive French saloon keeper, by Michael McGloin, whose capture, by Inspector Byrnes, was one of the finest pieces of detective work ever done in any city. McGloin, on the ninth of March, 1883, went to the gibbet. One of the saddest accidents that ever occurred in this city was the falling, on the twenty-first of April, 1880, of the west wall and part of the ball-room of the Madison Square Garden. A church fair was in progress, and a number of ladies and gentlemen were dancing in the ball-room, when the wall gave way and four persons were killed. One of the unpunished murders of this district is that of Charles P. Miller, "king of the bunko men," who, on the first of November 1881, was killed in "Dick" Darling's saloon, No. 1217 Broadway, by "Bill" Tracy, who was tried and acquitted.

CHAPTER XVII

THIRD AND FOURTH INSPECTION DISTRICTS.

INSPECTOR DILKS.—ENJOYING A RARE PRIVILEGE, NAMELY, READING HIS OWN OBITUARY —AN OFFICER WHO HAS DISTINGUISHED HIMSELF BY HIS BRAVERY AND VIGILANCE —A VETERAN WITH A HIGHLY HONORABLE RECORD.—SECOND PRECINCT, CAPTAIN CONLIN.—TWELFTH PRECINCT, CAPTAIN HOOKER.—NINETEENTH PRECINCT, CAPTAIN MOUNT —NINETEENTH SUB-PRECINCT; CAPTAIN SCHULTZ —TWENTY-SECOND PRECINCT, CAPTAIN KILLILEA —TWENTY-THIRD PRECINCT, CAPTAIN SANDERS —TWENTY-EIGHTH PRECINCT; CAPTAIN GUNNER —THIRTIETH PRECINCT; CAPTAIN SIEBERT.— THIRTY-FIRST PRECINCT, CAPTAIN LEARY —THIRTY-SECOND PRECINCT; CAPTAIN CORTRIGHT —THIRTY-THIRD PRECINCT, CAPTAIN BENNETT— THIRTY-FOURTH PRECINCT, CAPTAIN ROBBINS.—THIRTY-FIFTH PRECINCT, CAPTAIN YULE

THESE Districts cover about four times as much territory as the First and Second Inspection Districts, but they are, as a rule, sparsely settled. The commands are reached by wagon or rail, the emergencies are few and of minor importance, all things being considered, and the communication by telegraph is unsurpassed. The districts include the Nineteenth, Twenty-eighth, Twenty-third, Twelfth, Thirty-third, Thirty-fourth, Thirty-fifth, Second, Thirty-second, Thirtieth, Thirty-first, and Twenty-second Precincts, and the Yorkville, Harlem, and Morrisania Police Courts, which are known as the Fourth, Fifth, and Sixth District Courts respectively. The districts, which were consolidated, are under the command of Inspector George W. Dilks, the senior Inspector of the force.

INSPECTOR GEORGE WASHINGTON DILKS, of the Third Inspection District, was born on the twenty-sixth of December, 1816, at New Brunswick, N. J. In 1829 his parents moved to New York, and settled there for good. In 1848, Mr. Dilks was appointed on the force as Assistant Captain. In 1853 he was made Captain of the Fifteenth Ward, where he soon distinguished himself by his bravery and vigilance. While engaged in this Ward, the City Hall riot occurred, and, while he was leading a force of men against Wood's partisans, a Sergeant named Sebring was killed by a blow from a locust which had been thrown at him. There was an extraordinary likeness between Sebring and Dilks, and the rumor spread as quick as lightning that the intrepid Dilks had been killed. Dilks had the rare privilege that night, while he was at supper, of reading his own obituary notice in the *Evening Post.* Ned Davenport, an actor, and an old-time friend of Captain Dilks, who was then playing at Boston, hearing the news of

the latter's alleged death the next night, delivered speeches all over Boston on the "death" of his friend

In 1860 Captain Dilks was made Inspector, he being the first Inspector in the Department He had the whole city, Brooklyn, and a part of Westchester for a field of operation The Inspector, in his rounds, was not long in discovering that there were many evils that could be remedied and abuses that could be corrected, but his territory was too extensive and scattered for one man to attend to all Then the district was split into two, and Captain Leonard was appointed to the Second District After the organization of the present Municipal force, confined to New York City alone, the two districts continued, but in 1874, the late Superintendent and Commissioner, George W. Matsell, and Commissioner John R Voorhees, laid out the city into the present four districts

There is no doubt Matsell, who had lost his old-time snap and vigor, would have made a terrible mess of things while he was Superintendent, only Inspector Dilks was in the office with him acting as Deputy Superintendent, which position he held for about five years

Inspector Dilks has been a conspicuous figure in all the great riots that occurred in New York since 1848.

One morning during the longshoremen's strike, when these men sallied forth with everything in the shape of a weapon that they could lay their hands on, Inspector Dilks succeeded, after three days' hard struggle, in restoring peace and quiet

During one of the days of the draft riots, while the mob was howling for the arms which were stored in the armory, a bullet whizzed past the Inspector's head

"Mr Dilks," said one of the Police Commissioners on a well-known occasion, "you can have the position of Superintendent if you desire it"

"I never looked for the place of any man," replied Mr Dilks, "and never will Were the office vacant, I might consider the offer, but as there is another there I don't want it"

In 1849 there occurred the great Astor Place riot Macready, the actor, was playing at the Astor Place Opera House It seems that he became obnoxious to the friends of Mr Forest, who was playing at the old Broadway Theatre, between Pearl and Worth Streets One night Forest's friends drove Macready off the stage After this outrage a body of citizens waited on Macready and requested him to continue playing, at the same time promising him protection from the mob Macready acceded to their request, and, on the night of his re-appearance, the riot began inside and outside the theatre Assistant Captain Dilks was in charge of a posse of Police, and, with the help of the military, succeeded in at once restoring comparative quiet Several persons were arrested and confined in one of the lower rooms of the theatre, to which they attempted to set fire, but the activity of the Police saved the place from destruction. Nine persons were killed in this riot, and hundreds were severely wounded, the military having fired on the crowd.

During the longshoremen's riots, in 1857, Captain Dilks was in the Fifteenth Precinct He, in conjunction with the officers drawn from the various precincts, had a terrible fight, which lasted for four days, with the mob, who used hay-sticks, cart-rungs, clubs, etc

During the Orange riots Inspector Dilks was one of the officers who had to protect the procession down as far as Bleecker Street and the Bowery, and from thence to Astor Place.

Inspector Dilks is a thoroughly honorable, efficient and painstaking officer.

This clean-shaven, clerical-looking gentleman lives at No 34 West Ninth Street He leaves home between seven and eight o'clock in the morning, and goes through the routine of the other Inspectors at his office in Parepa Hall. The extent of this command does not permit of his making regular visits to Police Headquarters He goes there when his presence is required He visits his precincts by rail, car, or wagon, and it is almost a day's journey to go to some of the outlying districts. Generally, the Inspector lunches in his office, and starts on his visits at one P. M , to return at half-past five o'clock, when he settles what business awaits him and goes home to dinner His movements in the evening are regulated by events If a large fire occurs beyond the river he has a long journey before him Every fourth night he is booked for duty at Police Headquarters

THE SECOND PRECINCT.—The boundaries of the Second Precinct are Cromwell's Creek, Jerome or Central Avenue, the Kingsbridge Road to Farmer's Bridge, and the Harlem River The station house is at Highbridgeville It was formerly known as Mike O'Brien's Undercliff Hotel, and it was altered for the W B. Ogden estate into a station house by the Hon Andrew H Green This is known as a Mounted Police Precinct, and there are accommodations for thirty-six mounted and foot officers, and stables for horses There are five day posts and eight night posts Two of the day posts and four of the night posts are covered by horsemen. Signals can be sent to the station house from nearly every part of the precinct from signal boxes The officers of the command are Captain, Peter Conlin; and Sergeants, W. A. Revell, Edward Lucas and John McNamara Revell was appointed eighteen years ago, became Roundsman 1872, and Sergeant in 1876 He for some time commanded the First Mounted Squad Lucas was appointed in 1874, became Roundsman in 1877, and attained his rank in 1880 McNamara was appointed in 1876, was for a long time Special Detective at Police Headquarters, and was promoted late in 1883 and in May, 1884 John McGowan and Francis Smith are the Precinct Detectives John Breen, Martin Bruns, Thomas B Holland, William J Huston, William A Nevin, and William Nelson are the centaurs who do day duty on horseback, and perform feats of intrepidity almost daily on the avenues below Harlem Bridge. Their horses are trained to stop runaways, and are the pick of the stable

PETER CONLIN is a native of this city, and was born in 1841 He is a brother of William J. Florence, the actor. He graduated from Grammar School No 34, and enlisted as a private in the Twelfth New York Regiment during the war Afterwards he joined the Irish Brigade, as Lieutenant, and eventually was made Captain His dates are Joined the force July 29, 1869, Roundsman, December 6, 1872; Sergeant, July 19, 1876; and Captain, February 8, 1884 In his long years of service no charge of misconduct or breach of discipline was ever made against him.

From early spring to late in autumn the Police of the Second Precinct are nearly at all times during the day busy with the thousands who, on foot or in vehicles, come from the city to get a breath of fresh air by boats or on the railroads, and Central, High and Farmers' Bridges. For the wealthy and sporting classes are the hostelries of Judge Smith, Gus Sibberns and Gabe Case, and they are patronized all the season round. The terminus of the aqueduct has to be guarded here, and the avenues to Jerome Park and Fleetwood Park are principally through this precinct for those who go to them by vehicle. Highbridgeville, like all the desirable suburbs, is cropping out with fine villa residences,

Captain Peter Conlin

among which are the Mali estate, the residences of the Devoes, Baileys, Fitzpatricks and Fairchilds, the Ogden estate, the Lee estate, the H. B Morris estate, the Eastman estate, and the homes of Hugh N Camp, Col E. T Wood, Franklin Edson, and L G. Morris. Some day it will be an aristocratic quarter, because of its elevation. The precinct furnishes few events beyond a runaway horse, a boating accident, or a stray suicide occasionally.

THE TWELFTH PRECINCT.—The Twelfth Precinct comprises the territory bounded by One Hundred and Tenth Street, Seventh Avenue, One Hundred and Forty-fifth Street, and the Harlem River. The station house is on the site of a very ancient one, formerly a watch-house and lock-up, Nos 146 and 148 East One Hundred and Twenty-sixth Street. Although constructed fourteen years ago, it is equal in many respects to more modern ones, and has a separate prison

The officers are: Captain Henry D. Hooker; and Sergeants, De Los Reynolds, William W. Sullivan, C. C. Buddington and Matthew Tuck. Reynolds' record is Patrolman 1867, Roundsman 1870, and Sergeant 1872. Sullivan became a Policeman in 1871, was Roundsman in 1872, and got rank next year. Buddington, the senior Sergeant, joined the force in 1864, was Roundsman four years later, and was promoted in 1871. Tuck's dates are: Patrolman 1865, Roundsman 1867, and Sergeant 1870.

Twelfth Precinct Police Station, One Hundred and Twenty-sixth Street, Near Third Avenue.

HENRY D. HOOKER is a native of the United States, and was born in 1830. He was formerly a seafaring man. He joined the force in January, 1861; was promoted to be Roundsman in 1864, became a Sergeant in 1879, and when the Twenty-eighth Precinct was divided in two, he was made Captain of the Nineteenth Sub-Precinct, with the station house in the Grand Central Railroad Depot.

This precinct has fourteen day and twenty-eight night posts, all too long;

some of them cannot be faithfully covered. Of the seventy-eight men on the roll, about fifteen are detailed or incapacitated by sickness. John Irving and Bernard C. Tompson are the Precinct Detectives. The detailed men are Theophilus Holmes, Inspector Dilks' office; Henry C. Van Orden, Harlem Bridge; J. N. Morey, Ordinances; W. H. Lake and C. D. Allaire, Corporation Counsel's office; Charles R. Bliss, Randall's Island.

The Twelfth Precinct grows daily. More third and fourth-rate houses have been put up here within the past five years than in any other command. It has the most important part of the New York City proper, Harlem River front, and the monopoly almost of boating recreation. Little of its population is other than reputable and law-abiding, and at present many families occupy their own

Captain Henry D. Hooker

houses, and there are pretentious and well-appointed mansions along the river front and on some of the avenues. Within its limits are Mount Morris Park, with its cordon of aristocratic villa residences, the Harlem Police Court, the Mount Morris Theatre, the termini of the Second and Third Avenue Elevated Railroads, and the approaches to the Vanderbilt Railroad Bridge, and the Harlem River Swing Bridge. The precinct takes in Randall's and Ward's Islands, and the most memorable events of late years are the burning of the steamer Seawanhaka, off Sunken Meadow, June 28, 1880, when more than fifty persons perished; and more recently the partial destruction of the Insane Asylum on Ward's Island.

The Nineteenth Precinct.—The Nineteenth Precinct lies between Forty-second Street, Lexington Avenue, Forty-ninth Street, Fourth Avenue, Fifty-eighth Street, and the East River. The station house is at No. 163 East Fifty-first Street. It is a narrow, but deep and very comfortable building, with a separate prison The officers are. Captain, John J. Mount; and Sergeants, Henry K Woodruff, Michael M. Rooney, Walter Norris, and John Delaney Woodruff was a Policeman in 1867, a Roundsman next year, and he has been a Sergeant more than thirteen years Rooney was appointed in 1867, became a

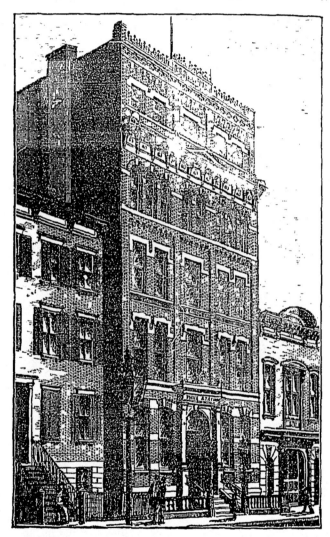

Nineteenth Precinct Police Station, 163 East Fifty-first Street.

Roundsman in 1870, and next year was promoted Norris' dates are. Patrolman 1870, Roundsman 1875, and Sergeant 1878. Delaney did his first tour of duty in 1878, was made Roundsman in 1877, and has been a Sergeant since February, 1884.

CAPTAIN JOHN J MOUNT, of the Nineteenth Precinct, joined the Municipal Police in 1850, in the Eighth Ward He was made a Roundsman in March,

1851, was detailed as Dock Master 1853, and remained in that capacity until 1857, when the Metropolitan Police was organized. He was appointed Sergeant in 1858, and Captain in April, 1861, and assigned to the Third Precinct. Captain Mount was afterwards successively transferred to the Eleventh, Seventeenth, Fourteenth, Seventh, and finally to the Nineteenth Precinct, of which he is now the respected Captain. Captain Mount, like all the old-timers, took an active part in quelling the dead rabbit, draft, and Orange riots.

This precinct has fourteen day and twenty-eight night posts. Its full force is seventy-eight, reduced to about sixty on an average. Michael Shelly and John T. Cuft are the Precinct Detectives. The detailed officers are Henry O. Corbitt, Central Office; John McDermott, Fifty-ninth Street hacks; Harrison Wilson, Ordinances, Daniel O'Conner, Orphan Asylum.

Captain John J. Mount.

This precinct deals with the extremes of society. The palaces are on the west side and north of it, and the hovels and nuisances on the east side. Beginning at Fifth Avenue and Forty-second Street, and going north, there are in succession the Temple Emanuel, the Church of the Divine Paternity, the Church of the Heavenly Rest, the Fifth Avenue Baptist Church, the Windsor Hotel, Dr. Vermilye's Church, the Buckingham Hotel, St. Patrick's Cathedral, the Vanderbilt mansions, St. Thomas' Church, St. Luke's Hospital, the Fifth Avenue Presbyterian Church, and scores of millionaires' dwellings. There are also in the precinct the Roman Catholic Orphan Asylum, Columbia College, the Women's Hospital, the Nursery and Child's Hospital, the First Reformed Church, the mansions of Madison Avenue, and the little less pretentious dwellings on Lexington Avenue and the cross streets. On the river front are collected the nuisances in the shape of slaughter-houses and rendering establishments, which, with an east wind and Hunter's Point chiming in, are a curse to the greater part of Murray Hill. The Police are not responsible for the existence of these malodorous industries

THE NINETEENTH SUB-PRECINCT —The Nineteenth Sub-Precinct, or Grand Central Depot command, has for its boundary Forty-second Street, Lexington Avenue, Forty-ninth Street, and Madison Avenue. The station house is in the basement on the west side of the depot, and the cells are underground The officers are Captain, William Schultz; and acting Sergeants, George R. Bevans and Enoch A. Goodell There are six day posts and eight night posts, covered

Captain William Schultz

by an effective force of about twenty-two men, out of the quota of twenty-four men. Zabriskie H. Mullin is the Precinct Detective

CAPTAIN WILLIAM SCHULTZ, ex-Commander of the Police Boat "Patrol," for years did active service on the North and East Rivers For a long time the depredations committed by river thieves and other criminals were a great source of annoyance to merchants and owners of vessels, but when Captain Schultz took command of the Police Boat "Patrol," things were entirely changed He is quite familiar with the ways of those river pirates who lie in wait for unsuspecting sailors, and rob them and their vessels Captain Schultz was born in this country, of German parents He joined the Police force on the twenty fourth of July, 1867, and, on September 1, 1870, was promoted to the rank of Sergeant He was appointed Captain September 13, 1878.

OUR POLICE PROTECTORS

THE TWENTY-SECOND PRECINCT—The Twenty-second Precinct is included between Forty-second Street, Sixth Avenue, Fifty-ninth Street, Eighth Avenue, Sixty-third Street and the North River. The station house is at Nos 345 and 347 West Forty-seventh Street. It is a superior, airy structure, although built nearly a quarter of a century. The officers are Captain, Thomas Killilea; and Sergeants, Charles U Combs, Patrick H Pickett, John Dunn and John T. Stephenson. Combs' dates are Patrolman 1867, Roundsman seven months later, and Sergeant 1870. Pickett was Patrolman in 1865, Roundsman in 1868, and Sergeant in 1870. Dunn joined the force in 1872, and became Roundsman in 1881, and Sergeant in 1883. Stephenson was appointed in 1877, was Roundsman in four years, and got rank last January.

Captain Thomas Killilea

THOMAS KILLILEA was born in 1838, and was appointed a Patrolman in 1866, was promoted Roundsman the following year, Sergeant in 1868, and Captain in 1870. After serving in the Central Office, the Steamboat Squad, and in other precincts, he was placed in command of the Twenty-second Precinct, where he has done good service.

This precinct has seventeen day and thirty-six night posts. It has a nominal force of ninety-four men, but the average effective force is seventy-seven. James H Riley and Charles L. Bockhorn are the Precinct Detectives. The detailed men are George W. Glass and Lotin B Hildreth, Ordinances, James Thompson and Matthias Bruen, Forty-second Street Ferry, and Thomas M Clifford, the Leake and Watts Orphan Asylum.

The character of this command has vastly improved of late, what with the march of building operations and the activity of the Police in stamping out what amounted to flat defiance on the part of the unruly and worthless inhabitants of the houses bordering on the Hudson River Railroad. Some of the most important carrying interests of this corporation lie in this district, such as the grain elevators and the shipping and cattle yards. There are also the Roosevelt Hospital, and several of the largest and best appointed apartment houses in the city; among them the Navarro Flats in Fifty-ninth Street, the quaint, old, and massive new church of the Paulist Fathers, thriving stores on Eighth Avenue, and the stables of the Eighth, Belt Line, and Seventh Avenue and Broadway Railroads, and several vast manufactories such as the Elm Flax Mills. The most remarkable event of late years was the attempted suicide of Miss Hattie J. Hull at the Fiftieth Street station of the Sixth Avenue Elevated Railroad, on the twenty-fourth of May, 1881. The young lady had been betrayed by a Custom House official, and, finding he was married, threw herself, while in his company, in front of an approaching train, and although frightfully injured, recovered, and lived to see her betrayer get his deserts.

THE TWENTY-THIRD PRECINCT.—The Twenty-third Precinct is between Seventy-ninth Street, Fifth Avenue, One Hundred and Tenth Street, and the East River. The station house is at Nos. 432 and 434 East Eighty-eighth Street. It is singularly well situated, and is a medium structure, having been built eleven years ago with the quarters of the First Mounted Squad, which no longer exists, it having been incorporated with the Second Precinct. The officers are: Captain, John Sanders; and Sergeants, William R. Haughey, Imer D. Luerssen, Michael Sheehan, and Nelson Haraden. Haughey's record is: Patrolman, 1872, Roundsman 1881, and Sergeant 1883. Luerssen joined the Department in 1876, in three years he was Roundsman, and a month later he was promoted. Sheehan was Patrolman in 1868, Roundsman in 1873, and Sergeant in 1876. Haraden was appointed in 1864, was Roundsman in 1877, and got his rank in 1880.

CAPTAIN JOHN SANDERS, of the Twenty-third Precinct, who has such a creditable record as a life-saver, was born at Poughkeepsie, N. Y., in 1844. He served with distinction in the army for four years during the late war. He was appointed on the Police force in May, 1866, and was made a Roundsman in the same year. In 1868 he was promoted to a Sergeantcy, and in 1872 was made Captain. During the last year he saved no less that seven persons from drowning. The Board of Police, at a meeting held on the twenty-third of December, 1883, passed the following resolutions:

"*Resolved*, That highly honorable mention be made in the records of this department of the gallant and courageous conduct of Captain John Sanders, of the Twenty-third Precinct, who, at the risk of his life on each occasion, fearlessly plunged into the East River and succeeded in saving the lives of five persons, two of whom were little girls, aged respectively, fourteen and seven, a lady, and two young men."

The Board further resolved that Captain Sanders "be awarded the Medal of Honor of this Department for his commendable action; and that this resolution be suitably engrossed, and with the medal, presented to Captain Sanders."

This is a precinct of long and dreary posts. There are fifteen day posts and thirty night posts. Of the quota of seventy-six men, an average of eight are sick or detailed. John J. Donovan and Samuel G Sheldon are the Precinct Detectives The detailed officers are· John Phelan, House of the Good Shepherd; and Edward O'Hara, Central Office.

This is a precinct that is being built up, and there is yet unbuilt territory on which to erect homes for thousands. Within five years one-quarter of what was bare ground has been covered with comfortable houses of superior construction. This district has an Italian colony, of which it is not very proud, House of the Good Shepherd, a shanty district, the repair shops of the Third Avenue Elevated Railroad, a neat little park opposite the Blackwell's Island lighthouse, and some elegant villas near by, the Astoria Ferry, the boat ferry to Blackwell's

Captain John Sanders.

Island, and some mansions of stately magnificence on Fifth Avenue, opposite the park There are also the Harlem Flats, with the Harlem Gas Works, and the stables of the Second Avenue Railroad Company.

THE TWENTY-EIGHTH PRECINCT.—The Twenty-eighth Precinct's limits are Fifty-eighth Street, Fifth Avenue, Seventy-ninth Street, and the East River The station house is at No. 220 East Fifty-ninth Street. Although it has a separate prison it is the unhealthiest and most antiquated structure in the city It was built by the native Americans in 1852. In a few months a magnificent station house for this command is to be built on the north side of Sixty-seventh Street, one hundred and twenty feet west of Third Avenue, by Architect Nathaniel D Bush The lot is 50 x 100·5, feet, the main building will be 50 x 68 feet, and four stories high, and the prison 50 x 23 feet, and three stories high

The cost will exceed eighty thousand dollars. The officers of the command are: Captain, John Gunner; and Sergeants, John Hamilton, William B. McMillen, Henry Roberts, and William J. Linden. Hamilton's dates are. Patrolman 1866, Roundsman, 1871, and Sergeant next year. McMillan was appointed 1869, was Roundsman 1874, and got rank last May. Roberts was appointed in 1865, became Roundsman in 1866, and six months later was promoted. Linden was Patrolman in 1861, Roundsman two years later, and Sergeant in 1872

CAPTAIN JOHN GUNNER was born in London, England, and came to this country when he was seven years old. He was apprenticed in the same shop, at

Twenty eighth Precinct Police Station, 220 East Fifty ninth Street

No. 17 John Street, in which Daniel Carpenter, who was afterwards Inspector and Superintendent under John A Kennedy, worked

Captain Gunner joined the Police on the sixth of April, 1861, and was assigned to duty in the Twenty-ninth Precinct under Captain Frank Speight. He remained there for eight years, during which time he served in the capacity of Patrolman, Roundsman, and Ward Detective. He was then transferred with Speight to the Twenty-seventh Precinct. On June 1, 1870, he was made Captain, and took charge of the Nineteenth Precinct up to 1875, when he was appointed to the Street Cleaning Bureau. At his own request he was removed from this place, and was sent to the Twenty-eighth Precinct.

In 1863, a young Russian nobleman, Eugene Count Medewitzk, came to this country and put up at the Fifth Avenue Hotel. He mixed among the best society, and insinuated himself into the good graces of everybody with whom he came in contact. A Russian war vessel happened to arrive at the port of New York during the Count's visit here. The officers belonging to the ship gave a grand ball at the Academy of Music, and Eugene Count Medewitzk was invited. He was there introduced to a young lady who resided in West Thirty-fifth Street, near Park Avenue. At the conclusion of the ball he escorted her home. The young lady was engaged to be married to a wholesale flour merchant, who had given her a diamond solitaire ring, which cost one thousand one hundred dollars. After seeing her home the Count called to see her several times. He asked her for the loan of the ring, and she acceded. A few days afterwards the lady's

Captain John Gunner.

intended asked her what she had done with the ring. She commenced crying, and said that the Russian Count admired the ring and asked to look at it. Three letters were written to the Count, but the ring was not returned. The lady's intended then made a complaint at the Twenty-ninth Street Station House, and Captain Gunner proceeded to the Fifth Avenue Hotel, where he arrested the distinguished foreigner at two A. M., on his returning from a fashionable soiree. The Count was dressed regardless of expense. He was taken to the station house, and charged with larceny. Captain Gunner discovered that the thief had abstracted the diamond from the ring, and sold it to Bishop & Ryan, jewelers, under the Fifth Avenue Hotel. When taken before Judge Kelly, at the Tombs, he admitted his guilt. He was confined for four or five months. He was not tried in consequence of some parties not wishing to have their names mixed up in the case. "During the time he was committed for trial he was placed under my charge for two days. He asked me to accompany him to a broker's for the purpose of borrowing three thousand dollars. I consented I knew the broker, and the Count went in ahead of me. He had letters of introduction to the broker, which stated that he, the Count, was a first-class, reliable and honorable gentleman. The Russian had also borrowed a ring from a lady, a resident of Syracuse, who was stopping at the Fifth Avenue Hotel. The ring was worth one thousand five hundred dollars. All the diamonds were taken out and paste put in She refused to prosecute, and he was discharged and went to Europe," said Captain Gunner.

His father, at one time, it was said, was Governor of Poland

This command has fourteen day and twenty-eight night posts. Its quota of seventy-two men is reduced by sickness and details to an effective of sixty two men. The Precinct Detectives are Samuel J Campbell and Hugh Martin. The detailed officers are Henry McCadden, Foundling Asylum; Edward O Tyler, Normal College; James Quigley, Ordinances, and James Curry, to Inspector Murray's office

The Twenty-eighth Precinct has within its wing some important charitable, social, and public institutions. There are the Mount Sinai, Hahnemann and Presbyterian Hospitals, the Foundling Asylum, the Lenox Library, the Normal College, the Seventh Regiment Armory, the Liederkranz and Arion buildings, the Third Avenue Railroad Depot, Terrace Garden, Jones' Woods, and other places of summer recreation, the repair shops of the Second Avenue Elevated Railroad, and the American Institute building. East of Third Avenue the population is mixed and troublesome, and west of it the citizens range from respectable to wealthy, and the dwellings are those of the middle class to millionaires, especially along Fifth Avenue This precinct has furnished some remarkable stories, in which the public took great interest One was the attempted abduction in April, 1881, of the daughter of Louis Strassburger, a wealthy diamond merchant, and on the seventh of April of that year Detective Campbell, in self defense, shot and killed one of her intending abductors, Edward H. J Sagert. On the twelfth of February, 1884, Jenny Avery shot Victor Andre at the downtown station of the Elevated Railroad at Third Avenue and Fifty-ninth Street, and then shot herself dead. Andre recovered and is now in Europe The disappearance of Ida Swartz, on November 22, 1882, was the talk of the city for months, and the affair has never been fully explained, although it is known that after hiding in the city for some time, friends enabled her to leave and enter an educational institution far away

THE THIRTIETH PRECINCT —The Thirtieth Precinct is bounded by One Hundred and Tenth Street, Seventh Avenue, One Hundred and Forty-fifth Street, and the North River The station house is in West One Hundred and Twenty-sixth Street, near Eighth Avenue. It was a dwelling house, belongs to the Cortlandt Otten estate, and was reconstructed by Architect Nathaniel D. Bush The prison cells are underground The officers are Captain, Jacob Siebert; and Sergeants, Charles R. Wilson, Cornelius Weston, Christopher Boehme, and Thomas L Heape. Wilson's dates are Patrolman 1866, Roundsman 1867, and Sergeant 1870. Weston was Patrolman 1865, Roundsman

1867, and Sergeant 1872   Boehme was appointed in 1862, became Roundsman in eight years, and in 1871 was promoted   Heape joined the force in 1859, was Roundsman in 1870, and next year won rank

CAPTAIN JACOB SIEBERT, of the Thirtieth Precinct, was born November 27, 1836, in Germany, and came to this country in 1853   He was appointed on the force February 4, 1861   He was made Sergeant, and was promoted Captain August 21, 1873. He has served at different times in the Thirty-second, Twenty-fourth, Seventh, Seventeenth, Thirty-first, and Thirtieth Precincts. Captain Siebert is one of the most vigilant Captains in the Department, and has on all occasions displayed good judgment, executive ability, and

Captain Jacob Siebert

has been a terror to the criminal classes in the several precincts where he has served.

There are ten day and seventeen night posts in this precinct, of magnificent but weary distances. To cover this vast territory there is an effective force of forty-five out of fifty-three men, and they need to be good travelers and inured to hardship in winter and wet weather   Matthew McSherry is the Precinct Detective. The detailed officers are· H. W Gilliland, Ordinances, Adam Meyer, Convent of the Sacre Coer; James Moody, African Asylum, Charles Miner, Fort Lee Ferry; Thomas O'Brien, Sheltering Arms

The Thirtieth Precinct covers some of the highest ground in the city, and over the ridge which runs south from One Hundred and Twenty-fifth Street, rode Aaron Burr the morning that he went to fight his duel with Hamilton The district is a growing one, and there is everything in the way of a dwelling on it, from a shanty to a mansion. Part of the best driving ground in New York runs through it, and it protects the Morningside and Riverside Parks, the Convent of the Sacred Heart, the Leake and Watts Orphan Asylum, the Association for the Benefit of Colored Orphans, Manhattan College, Bloomingdale Asylum for the Insane, and the Fort Lee Ferry.

THE THIRTY-FIRST PRECINCT.—The Thirty-first Precinct's limits are Sixty-third Street, Eighth Avenue, One Hundred and Tenth Street, and the North River. The station house, a new one of the second class, with a separate prison, is at Nos 432 and 434 West One Hundredth Street, in the rear of the Ninety-ninth Street Hospital. The officers are Captain, James M. Leary; and Sergeants, Patrick Walsh, John Fitzgerald, Richard Coffy and Frank B Randall. Walsh was a Patrolman in 1866, Roundsman 1875, and Sergeant next year. Fitz-

Captain James Madison Leary

gerald's dates are Patrolman 1862, Roundsman 1864, and Sergeant 1865 Coffy was appointed in 1873, became Roundsman in 1877, and three years later Sergeant. Randall joined the force in 1865, was Roundsman in four years, and in 1870 won rank.

CAPTAIN JAMES MADISON LEARY was born in Oswego, N Y, on the twenty-sixth of February, 1833 When quite young his father died, and the future Captain was put to work to learn the trade of printer. In those days type was cast by hand-moulds, and the apprentice boys used to be sent out to blacksmith shops to buy horse nails, which were pounded into spoons, with which the lead was lifted and cast into the moulds In those early days, young Leary and a bright lad named Conlin, worked together in the same shop, and were great "chums." The boys had never been to a theatre, and at the suggestion of young Leary, both of an evening "took in" the old Chatham Street Theatre, (afterwards known as the National Theatre). Conlin was infatuated with the play, and regularly after that he used to spend his spare dimes in patronizing the drama. Conlin, the young type-setter, became famous in after years as a histrionic star, having adopted the stage name of Billy Florence. Young Leary soon got tired of type-setting, and learned the trade of jeweler. At the breaking out of the war he enlisted in the Eleventh New York Volunteers, immediately after the first gun was fired on Fort Sumter. He was severely wounded at the first battle of Bull Run, having been shot through the thigh. He was taken prisoner and immured in Libby Prison. He, on his release, on the recommendation of his Colonel, was promoted to First Lieutenant for bravery on the battlefield. He joined the Police force in 1863, was made Roundsman in 1864, Sergeant in 1867, and Captain in August, 1871. He served as Patrolman in the Fourth Precinct, as Roundsman in the Eighteenth Precinct, as Sergeant in the Second and Eighteenth Precincts, and as Captain in the Twenty-first, Twenty-sixth, Thirtieth, Thirteenth and Thirty-first Precincts, he being in command of the latter precinct at the present time.

This precinct has thirteen day and twenty-six night posts, all long. Its quota of sixty-four men is reduced by sickness and details to fifty-two men. Herman Wagner is the Precinct Detective. The detailed officers are Lancelot J Tierney, Ordinances, and William Holmes, House of Mercy.

Territorially, and in respect of population, the Thirty-first Precinct is similar to its neighbor, the Thirtieth Precinct. The face of this district is being constantly changed by builders, and, it being high ground, it cannot fail of some day being the home of many of the better class. Its shanty population is being fast crowded out. It has within its boundaries the House of Mercy, the American Museum of Natural History, and the Dakota Flats—the largest apartment house in the city. The Riverside Drive begins here. At Seventy-ninth Street and Western Boulevard are to be found cells in which British prisoners were kept at the time of the Revolutionary War, and there is the house where Washington's officers were quartered. Elm Park, a summer pic-nic ground, was the scene, fourteen years ago, of the rough handling of a number of Orangemen.

THE THIRTY-SECOND PRECINCT.—The Thirty-second Precinct is confined between One Hundred and Forty-fifth Street, the Harlem River, Sherman's Creek, Dyckman's, Norwood Street, and the North River. The station house is at the southwest corner of One Hundred and Fifty-second Street and Tenth Avenue. Built twelve years ago, it was so well constructed, and has been so admirably kept, that it equals, in every respect, the most modern station house. It is snug in the winter, and a charming, breezy resort in summer. In spite of the arduous duty required of its Patrolmen, few are ever sick, and a sick man sent there quits it a sanitarian. The officers are: Captain, Moses W Cortright, and Sergeants Thomas F. McAvoy, William F. Kirchner, John R Groo and Eugene T Woodward. McAvoy was Patrolman in 1870, Roundsman in 1871, and Sergeant in 1877. Kirchner's dates are Patrolman 1870, Roundsman 1873, and Sergeant, 1880. Groo was appointed in 1868, became Roundsman in 1869, and two years later was promoted. Woodward joined the Department in 1862, was Roundsman in three years, and won rank in 1871.

MOSES W. CORTRIGHT is a native of this State. He was born in 1839, and joined the force as Patrolman on January 7, 1867. He was made Roundsman March 19, 1875; Sergeant, July 19, 1876; and Captain, February 8, 1884. He served with credit in the Twentieth and Twenty-second Precincts.

This is a Mounted Police Precinct, and even the horsemen are aided by boxes from which they can send necessary signals to the station house, no foot men could ever cover the posts. There are thirteen day and twenty-four night posts. Of the day posts mounted officers cover four, and of the night posts seven are covered by horsemen. The many details, and not sickness, reduce the effec-

Captain Moses W. Cortright.

tive force from seventy-one men to fifty-six. Joseph H. Thayer is the Precinct Detective. The detailed men are Roundsman H. Wagner to stable, John C. Moore, Juvenile Asylum, James Crosby, Ordinances; Charles H. Francis, Central Bridge; and Michael Kirby, Telegraph Office.

The most delightful command in the summer. A district of villa residences, a population of well-to-do citizens, who have business in New York. High in elevation, and remote from the city, it is luxurious rusticity within its walls. A zephyr down-town is found to be a breeze here. In winter it is pleasant in this neighborhood, and few of its villa residents find it necessary to move to the city. It protects the Juvenile Asylum, the Deaf and Dumb Asylum, the Trinity Cemetery, the Institution for the Blind, the High Bridge Park and Reservoir, High Bridge and its approaches, the termini of the Ninth Avenue and New

York City and Northern Railroad Audubon Park, with the magnificent residences there of George B Grinnell, Charles H. Kerner, Edward P. Griffin, Charles Shaw, Sheppard F Knapp, Andrew L. Soulard, William Forster, Jr, Eugene M. Jerome, John Dalley, Charles Miller, and Wellington Clapp, and the houses of Leopold Schipp, Nelson Chase, Richard C. Combs, J Hood Wright, Robert

Thirty second Precinct Police Station, Tenth Avenue, cor One Hundred and Fifty second Street

C Rathbone, Charles A Tatum, Louis F. Martin, Isaac P Martin, E B Whiting, Douglas Hollister, Frederick Sherman, John M. Hopkins, Mrs. Seth C. Hawley, John Haven, Hosea B. Perkins, Arthur V Briesen, Charles S Fitch, John B Hays, LL.D., George F. McCandless, James G Mitchell, William Libbey, William H Hays, James G Bennett, Warren H Ward, and hundreds of others In this villa district in summer time the scene at night is fairy-like, with the lights from brilliantly illuminated dwellings falling on cleverly mowed lawns, shrubberies, trees and flowers. Little, if any, crime is chronicled in this precinct.

THE THIRTY-THIRD PRECINCT.—The Thirty-third Precinct's limits are the Bronx River, Long Island Sound, the Bronx Hills, the Harlem River, Cromwell's Creek, Central Avenue, the Town Line of Morrisania, Horton Street, Broadway, Boston Road, Union Avenue, One Hundred and Sixty-ninth Street, an imaginary line to the West Farms Road, Lyons Street, and Westchester Avenue. The station house is the old Morrisania Town Hall, a structure of somewhat pretentious architecture, at Third and Washington Avenues, Morrisania. It stands back on an irregular plot, and the grounds are lovely in summer, rank and file taking an interest in the flower garden, pastures and lawns. The accommodations are wretched, but the place is comfortable. The cells are in the basement. The time is not far distant when two first-class modern station houses will be

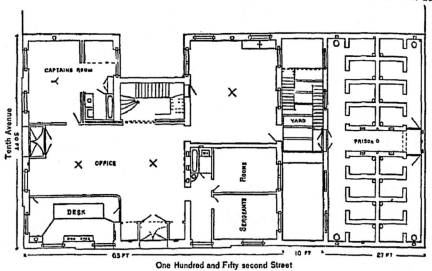

Thirty-second Precinct Police Station—Floor Plans.

required in this precinct. The officers are, the senior Captain of the force, Theron R. Bennett, and Sergeants Patrick Connor, Stephen Keating, Bernard McEveety, and Robert J. Wallace. Connor was a Westchester County Sergeant, and annexation transferred him to New York County. Keating was a Patrolman in 1868, a Roundsman in 1870, and a Sergeant in 1873. McEveety's dates are: Patrolman 1873, Roundsman 1875, and Sergeant 1880. Wallace was appointed in 1865, was made Roundsman in 1874, and got rank 1882.

CAPTAIN THERON R. BENNETT was born in Poughkeepsie, N. Y., July 8, 1813, and, while he was yet quite young, came to this city and took a position as clerk, at the corner of Greenwich and Perry Streets. He afterwards worked as a baker; was boss on the building of the Ramapo Railroad, and held the same position in the making of the Hudson River Railroad. He also served as steward and mate on a line of steamers to Boston, after which he returned to the bakery trade, and was employed at the Almshouse at the foot of Twenty-sixth Street, East River. He was appointed Assistant Police Captain by Mayor Caleb J Woodhull, in 1849, and was assigned to the Eighteenth Ward. He was made Captain of the same Ward in 1857.

Captain Bennett has had a remarkable career during his long connection with the Police force. He particularly distinguished himself during the Ward's Island riot in 1868, when he, with only six men, stood gallantly before six hundred wild rioters, and quelled the disturbance. It appears that a feeling of hatred had sprung up between the Irish and the Germans, who were then housed on Ward's Island, and on the morning of the fifth of March, 1868, the war at length opened in real earnest. While the Germans were waiting for their breakfast, they gesticulated wildly, spoke in loud tones, and it was apparent that they

Captain Theron R Bennett.

were bent on mischief. The Irishmen at this time were in the basement of the building, and as the Germans were passing through the hall on their way to breakfast they made a savage onslaught on them with clubs, stones, pitchforks, shovels, and anything they could lay their hands on. The Irishmen were taken by surprise, and beat a hasty retreat, vowing vengeance against the Germans. After a while the Irish returned, armed with bars, long poles, ice breakers, clubs and knives, and one of their number, placing a green veil on the top of a flagstaff, called out "That's your flag, boys; now rally round it" A vociferous cheer greeted these words, and a headlong rush was made towards the basement, where the Germans had taken up their quarters. Superintendent Hinck, when he saw the affair would be likely to lead to bloodshed, and being unable to quell the riot, dispatched a messenger for Captain Bennett, who was then at the Twelfth Precinct, asking for assistance. Meantime, the Irish had broken down the basement door, and were furiously attacking the Germans. When the fight was at its heighth, and as the Germans were gradually giving way, Captain Bennett, with eleven men, arrived on the scene. He ordered them to stop fighting, and on their refusal to do so, he ordered his men to draw their revolvers. This action infuriated the Irishmen, and they flung themselves on the small body of officers, who fired on them, and severely wounded four of them. This made the rioters hesitate. At this moment an additional force of men was seen hastening to the aid of Captain Bennett. The rioters immediately desisted, and went out into the grounds to await the arrival of the Police. On the arrival of reinforcements, the rioters on both sides were made to walk through a lane of Policemen with drawn clubs. They were afterwards searched, and all dangerous weapons were taken

Thirty-third Precinct Police Station, Town Hall, Morrisania

from them. The most prominent leaders in the riots were arrested, but the man who carried the green emblem could nowhere be found, and it was thought that he escaped. Neither the Germans nor the Irish ever again attempted a similar exploit on Ward's Island.

The partisans of Fernando Wood in 1857 intended to hold a meeting at the Academy of Music, but when the crowd got there the owners of the hall refused to admit them. There was a good deal of shouting, and a riot was threatened. Captain Bennett, with a force of only eight men, arrived on the scene, and, by his coolness and foresight, gradually got the crowd of seven thousand persons to quietly disperse, and thus saved the Academy of Music from destruction.

During the draft riots Captain Bennett had command of the Seventh Precinct, and on several occasions dispersed crowds of the rioters

This is a horse patrol precinct. Of the eight day posts, three are covered by horsemen, as are five of the sixteen night posts. The quota of forty-nine men has an effective force of about forty-two. There are three telegraph boxes in the precinct, from which it is possible to send communications by signal to the station house. One is at Harlem Bridge, another on the Eastern Boulevard, near Arcularius' Hotel, and the other on the Eastern Boulevard, near One Hundred and Seventy-fifth Street, the upper end of the precinct. The Precinct Detectives are William Clark and Joseph Schirmer. The detailed men are: James E Conklin, Ordinances, James A McCauley, Madison Avenue Bridge

Thirty-fourth Precinct Police Station, Tremont.

The Thirty-third Precinct takes care of the lines of the Vanderbilt railroads which trend eastward, the Portchester Railroad, Fleetwood Park, dozens of breweries, Jordan L. Mott's foundries, North and South Brothers Islands, Riker's Island, the wreck of the Hussar, the coalesced villages of North New York, Mott Haven, Melrose, Inwood, Port Morris, and Woodstock, and many manufactories. Its population is as much mixed as in any Police district It has villas of greater or less pretensions on the Sound, and negro shanties bound avenues bordered with homes for all classes, and country lanes, tenement house localities, and wastes, rocky knolls, and fetid swamps. It is a district of great promise, but sanitarians and engineers will have to do all that science can suggest before one-third of what is now bare ground can be covered with habitable houses. One of the greatest problems of the age for this district is the sewerage question and the treatment of the Bronx River banks.

THE THIRTY-FOURTH PRECINCT.—The Thirty-fourth Precinct is mapped out as follows: Central Avenue, Kingsbridge Road, Van Cortlandt Avenue, Williamsbridge Road, Bronx River, Westchester Avenue, Lyons Street, West Farms Road, an imaginary line to One Hundred and Sixty-ninth Street, Union Avenue, Boston Road, Broadway, Horton Street, and town line of Morrisania. The station house is at No. 1925 Bathgate Avenue. It was originally Tremont Town Hall, and afterwards a schoolhouse, and is among the most curious Police buildings in the country. It has one story and an attic, and is perched upon rocks which are covered with turf so that it has the appearance of a fortification.

Captain John M. Robbins

The cells are underground. It was once a sub-station under the Metropolitan Police. Plans have been prepared to have boxes at the end of remote posts to send telegraphic signals to the station house. It is a mounted Police precinct, and the stables are in the rear of the station house. The officers are: Captain, John M. Robbins; and Sergeants, Thomas Huff, James S. Mead, Joseph Stewart, and William H. Webb. Huff dates from 1858, he was Roundsman in 1860; and three years later was promoted. Mead was Patrolman in 1869, Roundsman in 1874, and Sergeant in 1876. Stewart's dates are Patrolman 1866, Roundsman 1871, and Sergeant, 1876. Webb was appointed in 1867, became Roundsman in 1871, and was promoted in 1876.

JOHN M. ROBBINS was born in this country in 1830. He joined the force during the early stages of the organization of the Municipal Police, and, at the time of the re-organization of the Police Department in 1857, he was appointed a Patrolman of the Metropolitan Police. Captain Robbins is a man of sound judgment, quick intelligence, and as a Captain he has done some very clever work in arresting criminals.

The Thirty-fourth Precinct is a more rural district than the Thirty-third Precinct, but ground is daily cleared for dwellings. It takes in the villages of Tremont, Adamsville, Belmont, Fordham, and St John's College and West Farms. Five years from now its population will be trebled. Crime is almost a curiosity in this precinct, but Lydig's woods are yet shunned because of the murder in them, on the seventeenth of December, 1875, of a poor Jew peddler by William Thompson, William Ellis and Charles Weston, negroes, who were

Captain Peter Yule

captured by Inspector Thorne and Captain McDonnell, and were executed at the Tombs.

THE THIRTY-FIFTH PRECINCT.—The Thirty-fifth Precinct's boundaries are Inwood Street, Dyckman Street, Sherman's Creek, Harlem River, Farmer's Bridge, Kingsbridge Road, Central Avenue, Van Cortlandt Avenue, Williamsbridge Road, Bronx River, northern boundary of New York and North River. The station house is at No 6 Kingsbridge Road. It is an irregular, comfortable structure, with a separate prison, and was turned into a station house by the owner, Joseph H Godwin. The precinct is a mounted one, with boxes for signals from far-off posts. The officers are Captain, Peter Yule, and Sergeants, A W. McDonald, John T Wright and William M Taylor. McDonald was Patrolman in 1876, Roundsman next year, and Sergeant in 1878. Wright's dates are: Patrolman 1858, and Sergeant 1868. Taylor was appointed in 1875, was Roundsman in 1876, and was promoted in 1884.

CAPTAIN PETER YULE was born in Edinburgh, Scotland, on March 12, 1830, and was brought to this country by his parents when he was three years old. He was appointed a Patrolman on the Metropolitan Police on February 27, 1858, and was assigned to the Fifth Precinct, and did patrol duty for ten years. On March 12, 1868, he was detailed to Commissioner Brennan's Office. He was made a Sergeant on May 4, 1870, and detailed to the Detective office. Subsequently he was transferred to take charge of the Sanitary Company, as acting Captain. In November following he attained his present rank. He remained in charge of the Sanitary Company until December, 1876, when he was sent to

Captain Elbert O. Smith

the Street Cleaning Bureau, under Captain Gunner. In July, 1877, he was placed in command of the Sixteenth Precinct, and in November following he was transferred to the Nineteenth Precinct, where he remained until the organization of the Twenty-eighth Precinct, in January, 1878. On August 4, 1879, he was given command of the Thirty-fifth Precinct, at Kingsbridge, where he has remained up to the present time.

Of the seven day posts three are mounted, and horsemen cover six of the twelve night posts. The effective force is thirty-two, out of thirty-four men. W. H. Dakin is the Precinct Detective.

This command takes in a vast stretch of promising but, in part, uninhabited territory, clean from the Hudson River to the Bronx River, which is here almost a pellucid brook. Within the boundaries of this district are Mount St. Vincent

Academy, Jerome Park, Riverdale, Spuyten Duyvil, Kingsbridge, Oloff, Mosholu, Van Cortlandt Lake, Edge Hill Park, Woodlawn Village and Cemetery, Williamsbridge, and many splendid villa residences, especially along Riverdale Avenue. The country parts of the precinct are wooded in many places, and the boom of the gun, the whirr of the quail, the whistling flight of the woodcock, the bound of the rabbit, and the scurry of the squirrel are by no means rare sounds and sights, and the irresistible temptation to cockney nimrods to wage war on the farmers here makes Sundays and holidays unbearable, in spite of ordinances and Policemen.

CAPTAIN ELBERT O. SMITH, of the Harbor Police Boat "Patrol," was made Captain on the twenty-seventh of February, 1885. He has an excellent record. He was born on Long Island in 1844, and, when a boy, enlisted in the United

Captain James Kealy (deceased)

States Navy. Afterwards he was employed by W. H. Webb as engineer on the steamship Arago, plying between New York and Bremen. Later he was a Lieutenant-Engineer in the Peruvian Navy on the Pachita and Unione. Then he returned to Mr. Webb's service, and was engineer of the Keystone State of the Bermuda Line. He became a Policeman in 1873, was made a Roundsman in a year, and was promoted to a Sergeantcy in 1876.

The late CAPTAIN JAMES KEALY was born in Massachusetts in 1841. He was only in his twenty-second year when he was appointed on the Police force, October 30, 1863. He was detailed for duty in the Eighth Precinct. On the eighth of December, 1868, he was detailed as Special Detective at the St. Nicholas Hotel on Broadway, and here it was that he was called upon to arrest

Charles J Guiteau, since then so infamous as the assassin of President Garfield Guiteau paid his bill with a bogus check, and Detective Kealy took him into custody

On the fourteenth of March, 1875, Detective Kealy was transferred from the Steamboat Squad to the Detective office, and on the twenty-fourth of March of the following year he was promoted Roundsman, and on the nineteenth of May he was made Sergeant He was placed in command of the Detective Squad On the thirteenth of September, 1878, Sergeant Kealy was raised to the rank of Captain He did much to improve the Detective force under his command, and was a most upright and zealous officer Later he was transferred to the command of the Fourteenth Precinct. His death took place on January 4, 1884.

Captain Edward Tynan (deceased).

THE LATE CAPTAIN EDWARD TYNAN was born in Hudson, N Y, November 30, 1843, where he went to school until the breaking out of the war, when he volunteered in the One Hundred and Ninth Regiment, and became a member of Company A On April 14, 1863, at the Irish Bend, near Port Hudson, he was wounded, and was confined to the hospital until February of the following year. He then returned home in order to recuperate his health He remained in Hudson until August 6, 1864, when he joined General Sheridan's command in the Shenandoah Valley Young Tynan, at the time he was wounded, had been promoted to the rank of Sergeant He was now raised to the rank of First Lieutenant, and afterwards placed on General Molineux's staff. At the termination of the war Tynan was appointed a Provost Marshal, and assigned to duty at Madison, Georgia, where he remained until November, 1865

Captain Tynan joined the Police force as Patrolman in March, 1867, and was assigned to duty in the Fifth Precinct. In one year he was promoted to the rank of Roundsman, and on August 3, 1870, he was promoted Sergeant in the Twelfth Precinct. On March 2, 1872, he was made Captain of the Tenth Precinct. While here he broke up several gangs of thieves, who, in the night time had almost complete possession of the Third Avenue Railroad. He was also instrumental in the arrest and conviction of Albert Baker and Robert Grey, noted criminals, who were sentenced to five years at Sing Sing.

After two other changes, Captain Tynan was finally located in the Fourth Precinct, which is considered to be one of the toughest in the city, and where the services of a vigorous man like Captain Edward Tynan were required. His death took place in this city. He was regretted and beloved by all.

The city of New York owns the First, Fourth, Fifth, Sixth, Seventh, Eighth, Ninth, Tenth, Eleventh, Twelfth, Thirteenth, Fourteenth, Fifteenth, Sixteenth, Seventeenth, Eighteenth, Nineteenth, Twentieth, Twenty-first, Twenty-second, Twenty-third, Twenty-fourth (the Harbor Police boat "Patrol"), Twenty-sixth (the City Hall), Twenty-seventh, Twenty-eighth, Twenty-ninth, Thirty-first, Thirty-second, Thirty-third, Thirty-fourth, and Steamboat Squad (Police Headquarters) Precinct Station Houses. The Nineteenth Sub-Precinct (Grand Central Depot) and sub-stations of the Steamboat Squad are stations owned by corporations, companies, and the United States Government, and are rent free. The Second Precinct Station House is owned by the W. B. Ogden estate, and a rental of one thousand two hundred dollars per annum is paid for it. The Goelet estate owns the Twenty-fifth Precinct Station House and office of the Second Inspection District, and receives a rental of one thousand five hundred dollars per annum. The estate of Cortlandt-Otten owns the station house of the Thirtieth Precinct, and the rent is eight hundred dollars. Joseph H. Goodwin owns the Thirty-fifth Precinct Station House, and receives one thousand seven hundred dollars per annum for it. Charles E. Quackenbush owns Parepa Hall, Eighty-sixth Street and Third Avenue, where are the offices of the Third and Fourth Inspection Districts, and the rent is four hundred and eighty dollars per annum.

CAPTAINS

NAME	Precinct	Date of Birth	Nativity	Date of Appointment	Promoted to Roundsman.	Promoted to Sergeant.	Promoted to Captain
Allaire, Anthony J.,	10	Feb. 17, 1829	Unit'd States	July 10, 1865	July 14, 1865	July 18, 1865.	May 23, 1867
Bennett, Theron R.,	33	July 8, 1815.	Unit'd States	April 23, 1857			June 10, 1858
Berghold, Wm C.,	27	July 15, 1837.	Germany	Oct 20, 1864	April 7, 1869	Sept 1, 1870	Sept 13, 1878.
Brogan, John J.,	15	Jan 21, 1843	Unit'd States	Jan 20, 1865	Oct 1, 1870	March 25, 1872.	Sept 13, 1878
Copeland, Theron S.,	9	July 28, 1831	Unit'd States	July 11, 1857		March 11, 1858	Aug 3, 1863
Cathy, Chas W.,	1	Aug 16, 1822	Unit'd States	Feb 13, 1858		June 10, 1858	May 23, 1860
Clinchy, Wm H.,	18	Oct 10, 1842	Unit'd States	May 12 1865	June 12, 1868	July 6, 1870.	Sept 15, 1870
Davis, Thaddeus C (retired)	12	Dec 14, 1817	Unit'd States	April 23, 1857			June —, 1858
Conlin, Peter,	2	April 15, 1841.	Unit'd States	July 29, 1869	Dec 6, 1872	July 19, 1876	Feb 8, 1884
Cherry, Thomas, (deceased)	11	Oct 29, 1830	Ireland	April 23, 1857		March 11, 1858	March 13, 1871
Cortright, Moses W.,	32	Dec 29, 1839	Unit'd States	Jan 17, 1867	March 19, 1875	July 19, 1876	Feb 8, 1884
Evans, Joseph B,	5	July 12, 1844	Unit'd States	March 1, 1866	Dec. 22, 1868	March 25, 1872	Oct 2, 1876
Garland, Ira S.,	25	Oct 7, 1830	Unit'd States	April 22, 1858.		March 16, 1861	March 4, 1871
Gunner, John,	28	Feb 25, 1831	England	April 6, 1861	Jan 21, 1863	Aug 23, 1865	July 1, 1870
Gastlin, Geo W.,	8 B S	April 1, 1835	Unit'd States	May 19, 1864	Feb 15, 1866	July 6, 1870.	Sept 20, 1875
Hedden, Henry,	C O	March 16, 1827	Unit'd States	June 16, 1857	Nov 16, 1864	March 11, 1858	Oct 30, 1862
Hooker, Henry,	19 Sub	Dec 19, 1830	Unit'd States	Jun 28, 1861	July 20, 1867	April 8, 1867	Aug 2, 1879
Killilea, Thomas,	22	Feb 6, 1838	Ireland	Oct 1, 1866	Sept 20, 1864	May 27, 1868	July 1, 1870
Leary, James M,	31	Feb 26, 1835	Unit'd States	Aug 15 1863	Aug 14, 1869	Feb 13, 1867	Oct 9, 1871
Murphy, Michael J,	14	July 8, 1844	Ireland	Aug 10, 1868		Nov 3, 1870	Feb 7, 1872
Mount, John J,	19	Aug 19, 1821	Unit'd States	April 23 1857		March 19, 1858	April 23, 1861
McCullagh, John,	6	Sept 29, 1843	Ireland	March 30, 1870	Feb 28, 1873	July 19, 1876	July 20, 1883
McDonnell, Charles,	8	Nov 15, 1841	Unit'd States	Jan 21, 1863	Dec 2, 1864	Nov. 11, 1867	Feb 24, 1870
McIlwain, John,	16	Nov 16, 1831	Unit'd States	Sept 28 1861	Oct 25 1863	Nov 30, 1864	Aug 31, 1872
McCullagh, John H,	17	Sept 1, 1842	Ireland	Feb 29, 1864	Oct 3, 1865	Feb 24, 1860	April 20, 1872
Petty, Jeremiah	13		Unit'd States	June 23, 1857		July 1, 1858	Jan 24, 1861
Ryan, Thomas M	21	Feb 3, 1831	Ireland	Nov 12, 1863	Dec 15, 1870	June 3, 1872	Sept 13, 1878
Robbins, John M ,	34	Jan 5, 1828	Unit'd States	Jan 1, 1874	Transferred	By annexation	Jan 1, 1874
Sanders, John,	23	Dec 13, 1844	Unit'd States	May 24, 1864	Sept 9, 1867	May 27, 1868	March 19, 1872
Schultz, Wm.,	4	March 15, 1836	Germany	July 24, 1867	Dec 22, 1868	Sept 1, 1870	Sept 13, 1878
Steers, Henry A ,	26	Jan 6, 1832	Unit'd States	Nov 19, 1857	May 1, 1860	Nov 15, 1865	April 28, 1871
Siebert, Jacob,	30	Nov 27, 1836	Germany	Feb 4, 1861	May 3, 1864	Aug 27, 1865	Aug 20, 1875

	Location		Ground & Rear	Sides	Bricks in Sunnn?	Front & Rear	Sides	Height	arate or not	Last repair'd	Built
1	Old Slip,	30 5	168 5	30 5	168 5	4 centre, 3 at ends	26 5	59 4	13 7	Not	1884	1884
2	Highbridgeville,	114 x 63 ft	86				20	7 deep		Not	1883	1883
4	Nos 9 and 11 Oak streets,	49	122 9	48 3	64 5	1	50 3	13 6	2 stories	Separate	1870	1870
5	Nos 19 and 21 Leonard street,	50 2	92 10	50 2	55	4	50 2	26 6	2 stories	Separate	1868	1868
6	Nos 19 and 21 Elizabeth street,	50	94 1	50	62 4	4	50	21 9	29 7	Separate	1881	1882
7	Nos 245 and 247 Madison street,	50 4	100 4	50 4	67 1	3	50 4	25 10	21	Separate	1863	1863
8	No 128 Prince street,	25 2	101 2	25 2	101 2	3	22	49	7	Not	1865	1865
9	No 94 Charles street	25	100	25	96	4			8 6	Not	1853	1853
10	Nos 87 and 89 Eldridge street,	50 4	100	50 4	74	1	50 4	21	2 stories	Separate	1865	1865
11	Sheriff and Houston streets,	32	195	47	114	3	36 6	20 4	87	Not	1855	1855
12	Nos 146 and 148 East 126th street,	50	99 11	50	60	4	50	25	2 stories	Separate	1870	1870
13	No 178 Delancey street,	25	100	25	100	4	22 6	26 6	87	Not	1848	1848
14	No 205 Mulberry street,	50	100	50	64	4	50	26	2 stories	Separate	1871	1871
15	Nos 251 and 253 Mercer street,	43	100	43	56 6	3	13	27 2	26 7	Separate		1860
16	No 230 West 20th street,	25	99 10	25	84 6	4	21	35	8	Not	1850	1850
17	Nos 79 and 81 First avenue	48 3	60 5	48 3	60 5	5	23	53	7	Not	1853	1853
18	No 325 East 22d street,	49 7	98 3	40	62 8	4	35 11	26	2 stories	Separate	1865	1865
19	No 163 East 51st street,	35 5	100 5	35 5	64 5	5	35 5	26	25 7	Separate	1877	1877
20	No 434 West 37th street	50	100	50	62 8	4	50	26	30	Separate	1870	1870
21	No 160 East 35th street,	44 7	100	35	100	5	21 10	51 8	6 7	Not	1855	1855
22	No 345 West 47th street,	50	100	50	66	3	50	29 5	2 stories	Separate	1860	1861
23	No 432 East 88th street,	50	101 7	50	63 3	4	50	25 10	2 stories	Separate	1873	1873
24	Steamer "Patrol,"									Not	1882	1882
25	No 34 East 29th street,	25	100	25	60	4	25	20	2 stories	Separate	1855	1855
26	City Hall,									Not		
27	No 35 New Church street,	124 4	27 6	103	22 9	5	32 8	22 9	1 story	Not	1870	1870
28	No 220 East 59th street,	25	100	25	55	4	25	28 9	2 stories	Separate	1852	1852
29	No 137 West 30th street,	50	100	50	62	4	50	25	2 stories	Separate	1869	1869
30	126th street, near 8th avenue,	25	100	25	60	3			3 stories	Not	1879	1879
31	No 432 West 100th street,	50	102 2	50	64 10	4	50	27 3	28 8	Separate	1869	1869
32	10th avenue and 152d street,	50	100	50	63 1	4	50	36 11	31	Separate	1872	1872
33	3d and Washington avenues	Irregular				2 and attic	50	64	8 6	Not	1869	1874
34	1925 Bathgate avenue,	106	100	86 6	28	1	16	24	7 8	Not	1851	1874
35	Kingsbridge,	Irregular		85	20	3	32	13		Not	1874	1874
19 Sub	Grand Central Depot,	In basement								Not		1862
3d Precinct	Steamboat Squad,	Sub Stations, Pier 39, N. R., Pier 24, E. R., and Barge Office.								Separate		
	Police Headquarters,									Prisoners to any	Organiz'd 1876	
3d and 4th Inspec Dis	Parepa Hall,	Office up stairs								station house	Re org'd 1884	

CHAPTER XVIII

DETECTIVE DEPARTMENT

ITS ORIGIN, PROGRESS AND DEVELOPMENT.—DETECTIVES CALLED "SHADOWS" IN CHIEF MATSELL'S TIME.—INSPECTOR THOMAS BYRNES.—A RECORD THAT READS LIKE A ROMANCE.—HIS REORGANIZATION OF THE DETECTIVE FORCE.—THE WALL STREET BUREAU.—DETECTIVE SERGEANTS.—INSPECTOR BYRNES' METHODS.—HOW DETECTIVES DETECT CRIMINALS.—INSPECTOR BYRNES AND "THE CROOK."—THEIR CHANCE MEETING IN THE STREET.—HOW INSPECTOR BYRNES REASONS OUT A CASE.—DECREASE OF CRIME AMONG PROFESSIONAL CRIMINALS.—CRIMINALS AND THEIR METHODS.—NEW YORK A DIFFICULT CITY TO PROTECT AGAINST THIEVES.—FORGERS, PICKPOCKETS, SNEAK THIEVES, BANK THIEVES, BUNCO STEERERS, ETC.

IN Chief Matsell's time Detectives were called "shadows." After Sergeant Lefferts, who was appointed to the command of the Detective Squad in 1857, and who served for one year, Captain George W. Walling, of the City Hall Station, was placed in charge. He alternated between the station house and the Detective office, which was in the basement of the then Headquarters, in Broome Street. He remained in command from 1858 to 1860. Next came John Young, who served from 1860 to 1867. He was succeeded by James J. Kelso, who was in charge from 1867 to 1870, and who retired to make room for James Irving. Irving's term extended from 1870 to 1875. Captain James Kealy was the next commandant, and remained as such from 1876 to 1880. Then the present incumbent, Inspector Thomas Byrnes, took charge. This really marked the first serious and successful attempt to give New York City a Detective Department worthy of the name.

In the latter part of 1857 the Board of Police adopted a resolution giving to the Deputy Superintendent the power to detail to his office twenty Policemen, to be designated "Detectives." This resolution was carried into effect by Deputy Superintendent Carpenter, by selecting those whose peculiar talents adapted them for such important service. Some of those men had for years belonged to the old force, and were attached to the office of George W. Matsell. Others were highly recommended by their respective Captains. And others, newly appointed members, but whose character for integrity and experience of life in New York, rendered them valuable acquisitions to the Detective force.

This force was divided into squads, each squad having particular cognizance of a certain class of crimes. Their instructions were to make themselves thoroughly conversant with the mode and manner by which each species of crime was committed, and the class of persons engaged in its commission.

Besides looking after these particular duties, they were directed to attend at night all large assemblies, and to arrest or drive away all known pickpockets, or others whose actions led them to suppose they were pickpockets, or thieves of any kind. Also, to arrest any known pickpockets they might see in a crowd, and carefully to watch all known shoplifters, and to take such measures as they might deem expedient to prevent their committing any depredations.

Sergeant William H. Lefferts was appointed a special aid, and placed in command of this squad.

At the suggestion of Mr. Lefferts, there was established in the Detective office an ambrotype gallery, composed of pickpockets, shoplifters, watch stuffers, etc, as well as those who were arrested for crime of a higher grade. This gallery was open to the view of the public, particularly those who had suffered by the loss of their property, or been otherwise imposed upon.

In 1859 the Detective force of New York and Brooklyn consisted of such number of Patrolmen, not exceeding forty, as the General Superintendent might detail for that service. The Detective force of Brooklyn was under the immediate command of the Deputy Superintendent, but the Detective force of New York, because of its larger number, was under the command of a Captain of the Police, and constituted a company corresponding to that of a precinct, and was subject to the general rules and regulations governing the company of a precinct. The members of the force in the different precincts assigned to Detective duties (if any) should report to the Captain of the Twenty-fifth Precinct (Detective force), as well as to the Captain of their respective precincts, at or before nine o'clock each morning.

In 1866 other rules were adopted. Each member of the Detective Squad was obliged to make daily report to the Superintendent of the business transactions submitted to his care, the progress made therein, and the disposition and results in each case, and such report was certified to by the Captain in command of said squad. The likeness of persons collected for the use of the Detective Squad should not be exhibited to any person, unless such person was accompanied by an officer of the Department.

Other rules and regulations for the government of the Detective Squad were promulgated in the years 1873 and 1877, some of which may be referred to briefly as follows

A book of records, of complaints, and applications, calling for the services or attention of the Detective Squad, was kept in the Detective Office under the supervision of the Superintendent; and the Superintendent, and in his absence, the Office Inspector, had supervision of all Detective business in general and in detail; and it was the duty of the Superintendent, or in his absence, the Office Inspector, to give special attention to the business, and see that all proper Detective cases were diligently and properly attended to and worked up. The Captain and each member of the Detective Squad should report to the Superintendent, or in his absence, to the Office Inspector, all complaints and applications requiring the services of the Detective Squad, and have a proper record made thereof, and the Superintendent or his representative were authorized to assign officers to the investigation of all Detective cases; and each member of the

Detective Squad should report to the Superintendent or Office Inspector concerning his action in each case assigned, from time to time, to his charge, and as often as required, such reports should be verified by the Captain. A record of arrests, by the Detective Squad, of all persons imprisoned at the Central Department, was kept in the Detective office, in which were entered the name of the person arrested, with a full description of such person, the time and cause of arrest, and the disposition made of each prisoner arrested. The Superintendent should, on the first of each month, make a report in writing to the Board of Police for the month preceding such report, of all arrests by the Detective Squad, and of all persons held in custody at the Central Department, setting forth the time and cause of arrest in each case, and how and when each case was disposed of.

The officer commanding the Detective force should keep a blotter and record of all the Police transactions of the "Special Service Squad," with the lost time of all the members thereof, and make a morning return to the Superintendent, under the rules and regulations applicable to precincts, and make out and attend to the settlement of the pay-roll, and pay off the members of the Squad. He possessed the same powers, and performed the same duties relating to the discipline of the Squad as were conferred and enjoined on the Captains of precincts.

On May 25, 1882, the Detective Bureau was created by an Act of the legislature. This was done at the urgent solicitation of Inspector Byrnes. Forty Detective Sergeants were then appointed, with an increased salary of one thousand six hundred dollars per annum.

On May 8, 1883, all the Ward Detectives were consolidated under one head, and placed under Inspector Byrne's jurisdiction, he believing that united action was necessary in order to cope more successfully with existing evils. Most of the Ward Detectives were sent on post duty, and their places filled by younger men from the various precincts. Subsequently, this arrangement was dispensed with, and the Ward Detectives were sent back to do service as before under the direct command of the Captain of their respective precincts.

INSPECTOR THOMAS BYRNES came to this country from Ireland when he was quite a child. In 1863 he was appointed Patrolman in the Fifteenth Precinct, and after five years of Patrol duty he was appointed Roundsman in the Third Precinct. In 1869 he was made Sergeant, and in 1870 attained the rank of Captain, when he was assigned to the Twenty-third Precinct. He was then successively transferred to the Twenty-third, Twenty-first and Fifteenth Precinct, thence to the Broadway Squad. He then returned to the Fifteenth, and remained there until he was sent to Headquarters and took charge of the Detective Bureau. He was raised to the rank of Inspector in 1880.

When interrogated by the Roosevelt Committee as to his official pedigree, Inspector Byrnes gave the following responses:

By Mr Russell. Q. How old are you? A. Forty-three, going on forty-four. Q. You are now Inspector of Police, are you? A. Yes, sir. Q. How long have you been Inspector? A. Four years. Q. Of what Bureau are you the head? A. The Detective Bureau. Q. Have you been the head of that

Bureau ever since you were appointed Inspector? A. Before that, while I was under Captain. Q. How long have you been on the Police force? A. Nearly twenty-one years. Q. What is the date of your first appointment? A. December 10, 1863. Q. As Patrolman? A. Yes, sir. Q. How long did you remain a Patrolman? A. About four years. Q. And then you became what? A. Roundsman, Sergeant and Captain. Q. When did you become a Roundsman? A. Latter part of 1868. Q. How long were you Roundsman? A. Ten or twelve months? Q. And then you were appointed Sergeant? A. Yes, sir. Q. How long a Sergeant? A. About a year. Q. And was appointed Captain when? A. I think it was in 1870, July 1, 1870. Q. And you remained a Captain until what date? A. April 23, 1880. Q. You were in what precinct as Captain? A. Twenty-third, Twenty-first, Fifteenth and Twenty-fifth. Q. What is the number of the precinct where you were when you first came here? A. The Fifteenth. Q. And it was in your precinct that the Manhattan Bank burglary occurred? A. Yes, sir. Q. And you got a good share of the burglars? A. I did; we became intimate, you were Assistant District Attorney at the time in the prosecution of those cases. Q. When you became Inspector of Police, or when you took charge of the Detective Bureau, what was done? A. The Commissioners sent for me. Q. What Commissioners? A. Mr French; he was President of the Board, and I assume he was very desirous of making a change in that Bureau; he thought it was inefficient in some respects, and wanted to have it reorganized; I was transferred there on the twelfth of March, 1880. I found there some twenty-eight or thirty men, some of whom had been there for very many years; the place was in a state of disorganization; there did not appear to be any head to it at all, and I came to the conclusion that morning, after calling the roll and looking the men over, that if there was any Detective talent in the Police Department it should be used during the daytime in the lower part of the city. On that day, the twelfth of March, I went down to Wall Street and hired an office, No. 17, and stationed ten men there, from nine and a half in the morning until four in the afternoon. A day or two after that Mr Brayton Ives had an interview with me and asked what I intended to do. I told him that I intended, if possible, to protect those gentlemen from thieves, as there had been a great deal of money for the last four or five years stolen there, amounting probably to one or two million dollars; he asked me how he could assist me in any way. I said if anything occurs in your office you would have to send to Police Headquarters, over two miles. In establishing this Bureau I intend to connect it, with telephone, to every bank and banking house in every part of New York, and you ought to have an officer from the time you ask for him by telephone, in any part of the lower section of the city, in any of those banks or banking houses, in the course of from one to five minutes. He thought it was a very good thing and called a meeting of the Committee of the Stock Exchange, and I was called before them, and made that statement to them. I said. "If I come here and do your work, and do it for nothing, and be able to do it better than anybody else (and what I do I am responsible for), you will give me your work after awhile quicker than to a man that is responsible to nobody." Q. Give us the result? A. They gave me an office in

the Stock Exchange, they connected that office by telephone with every bank and banking house in the lower part of New York, so that if any of those banking houses want an officer, in about five minutes I can have a Detective in any bank in the lower part of New York. Q. Was it the wish on the part of the Police Commissioners that you should take charge of that work? A. The Police Commissioners expressed the wish through Mr French. Q. You are at liberty to express to this committee what the result has been? A. Immediately after that—if you will pardon me and let me go back, the twelfth of March, 1880, I think it was, twenty-one men out of twenty-eight were transferred from the office—and their places substituted by new men whom I selected from various parts of the city, and educated them to do Detective duty. From the twelfth of March, 1880, until to-day, they have not lost a ten cent stamp in Wall Street by a professional thief, not a penny, not a cent. Q. Have you in your possession the statistics of the arrests made through your Bureau? A. I think I gave it to you. Q. You may state, if you will, the work of your Bureau for the last few years? A. I would like to state here that from the twelfth of March, 1876, to the twelfth of March, 1880, there were one thousand nine hundred and forty-three arrests made by the Detective force for the four years previous to my going to that office, they got five hundred and five years of conviction; for the four years that I have been there, ending on the twelfth of last month, there were three thousand three hundred and twenty-four persons arrested, and they got two thousand four hundred and eighty-eight years, two months and three days of conviction, we have recovered nearly six hundred thousand dollars' worth of property. Q. State in detail, take each of those cases that you have tabulated? A. I have them marked down here as follows. "Misdemeanors"—— Q. State them in detail? A. There were one thousand eight hundred and eighty-four felonies, eight hundred and thirty-six misdemeanors, six hundred and thirty-four suspicious persons, arrested for insanity, fifteen, truancy, forty-six, for violating poor law, twenty-nine; gambling, twenty-five, felonies, and delivered to the authorities in other cities, two hundred and eighteen, sent to the State Prison, three hundred and fifty-eight; to the Penitentiary, two hundred and ninety-one, to the City Prison, fifty-nine, to House of Refuge, twenty-seven; Elmira, ninety-four, hanged, one, arrested for murder, thirty-five."

When Inspector Byrnes accepted his present trust, and was transferred to Police Headquarters, on the twelfth of March, 1880, he found, after he had assumed control, thirty-one men classified as Detectives, a clerk who was not a member of the Police force, and who simply kept the books of the office without any responsibility being imposed on him other than that of an ordinary employee. These Detectives had been at Police Headquarters for several years, had grown old in the service, and a great many of them were unfit to perform their duties satisfactorily. There were also some young men among them who had not the slightest conception of their duty as Detective officers, who used to loll around in the morning until the roll was called. Nobody had the remotest idea where these men kept themselves from the time they left the office in the morning until roll-call on the following morning. Inspector Byrnes, from his intimate knowledge of the Police Department, having risen from the ranks, and

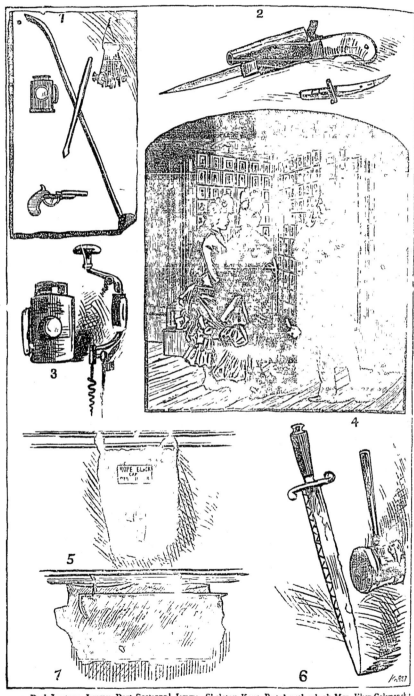

1 Dark Lantern, Jimmy, Part Sectional Jimmy, Skeleton Keys, Pistol with which Mrs Eliza Coleman shot ticket agent at Harry Miner's Theatre 2 Combination Dirk and Revolver, Dirk 3 Dark Lantern, Brace and Bit 4 Rogues' Gallery 5 Rope and Black Cap, (Christine Cox) 6 Burglar's Mallet, Dirk 7 Burglar's Bag and Broken Jimmy

The Rogues' Gallery and Some Curiosities of Crime

having had charge of a precinct adjoining Police Headquarters for a number of years, had a thorough knowledge of the ability and shortcomings of almost every man in the office.

When the Inspector took command at Headquarters, had called the roll, and had looked the men over, he came to the conclusion that there must be a radical change, and that the worthless members should be promptly weeded out. This was no easy task. The duties and responsibilities of his office were of the most trying and onerous nature, but Inspector Byrnes, with his characteristic energy, overcame them all. He soon fashioned the raw material of his office into shape, and under his manipulation the Detective Department, from being a very unpretentious and not over useful arm of the Police service, suddenly blazed into national importance, earning in an inconceivably short space of time a world wide reputation.

In the neighborhood of Wall Street, where a great portion of the financial business of the country is transacted, gangs of thieves of the better class—such as bank sneaks, forgers, and adroit pickpockets, had for years been carrying on their depredations. The disappearance of tin boxes containing money, bonds, and valuable papers, was almost of monthly occurrence, and complaints were very frequent. The Inspector thought that the men engaged in Wall Street and that neighborhood, who were doing a business of millions and millions every day, were entitled to special Police protection. About eleven o'clock on the same day that he had been appointed to take charge of the Detective Bureau, he went down town and hired a room at his own expense at No. 17 Wall Street. He returned to his office, and the next morning selected nine of his best men and sent them down to the new office to cover that section of the city bounded by Fulton Street on the north, Greenwich on the west, down to the Battery, and across to the East River. He at once gave positive orders to his men to arrest any thief that might be found within the specified district who could not give a good account of himself as being there for legitimate purposes. On the afternoon of the thirteenth of March, 1880, Brayton Ives, who was President of the Stock Exchange, sent for the Inspector, and asked him what he intended doing in that locality relative to the protection of business interests. Inspector Byrnes said that he intended to establish a special Detective bureau in Wall Street, and that he would succeed in protecting business people from the machinations of thieves. The Inspector further explained to Mr Ives that the New York Police Detectives were a responsible body, and that the private Detectives, who were often employed by financiers, were in a great many cases not over scrupulous in their official dealings. The result of the interview was, that the President of the Stock Exchange invited Inspector Byrnes to take possession of, and establish his business in, a room of the Stock Exchange. This invitation was accepted, and ten or twelve Detectives are now constantly on hand in that building. So complete is the system thus established that, on receipt of a call, a Detective can be sent to almost any place in the lower part of the city in two or three minutes. There is, in fact, no more perfect system of Detective supervision in any part of the world, and, as a consequence, thieves have given Wall Street and its vicinity a wide berth, whereas previously thousands had been stolen

While stationed in the Twenty-third Precinct, Inspector Byrnes saved a number of lives at a fire.

In the Twenty-third Precinct he broke up gangs of thieves, and sent a large number of them to prison.

In the Fifteenth he convicted the burglars who robbed Van Tine & Co., silk merchants. He also arrested Paul E. Law, son of the ex-Governor of Maryland, who was trying to escape to his native State after shooting four men in Neilson Place, and Vanderbilt Crawford after he had shot Henderson. This arrest was highly commended at the time, and reflected great credit on the force generally. Murray, the assassin of Merril, who hid himself in Brooklyn, also fell into Inspector Byrnes' hands.

But any attempt to enumerate the distinguished achievements of Inspector

A Bashful Burglar
(Taking his Picture for the Rogues' Gallery)

Byrnes within ordinary limits would be futile. Such a task would more than fill the space allotted to this entire volume. Therefore, the task cannot be attempted at all, as the subject is too vast, and is, besides, beyond the scope of this history.

Inspector Byrnes' methods are not new. But like all bright and successful men, the very common places of his profession assume the witchery of originality when manipulated by his practiced hand. Like the few really clever men who, by their astuteness and sagacity, have lifted the prosaic and plodding life of a Detective into the realms of romance, Inspector Byrnes is a consummate judge of human nature, and can "size a man for all he's worth" with an unerring judgment that is intuitive. His manners, too, are adapted to the profession which he adorns. He can be "all things to all men," as circumstances demand. However, a psychological study of Inspector Byrnes is not aimed at here. It is enough to say that in his official capacity as the head and guiding spirit of the Detective Department, he fills the bill in every particular.

In this city, criminals, as a rule, are quickly detected, but it does not follow that their punishment is equally prompt and salutary. Had criminals the same dread of the judiciary as they have of the Detective, they would give New York a very wide berth. But as matters now stand, a "crook" finds comfort in the reflection that the vigilance of the Detective Department will, in all probability, be counteracted by the lack of promptness and the absence of severity in the subsequent stages of his experience with the officers of the law; at all events he feels certain that expiation is not swift or certain.

No man has been more constantly or prominently before the public as the Nemesis of the law than Inspector Byrnes. In this respect no man in this country, or in Europe, holds so commanding a position. His name as a successful chief of Detectives will for all time be associated with Vidocq, Coco-Lacour, and M. Mace, whose fame is world-wide.

"But how do Detectives operate?" is a question frequently propounded by the uninitiated. A proper answer to this query would make a very interesting book in itself. There is no manual, no set rule, to control or guide a Detective. It is safe to say that a Detective, unlike a poet, is made, not born. If he be a man of average astuteness, alertness and physical activity, in time the experiences of his calling and the circumstances with which he has to struggle, will fully educate him up to the proper standard in his warfare on the criminal classes. Our Detectives are men who have been admirably trained, who have seen active service, who are veterans but still retain the ardor and enthusiasm of novices, directed and controlled by good judgment and a wise discretion. The corps consists of forty Detective Sergeants, who, animated by their chief, keep in check the whole criminal population of this city, a fact which speaks for itself. They follow the chase with the zest of hunters, and when they run down their quarry, their countenances flush with real delight. Such men must possess nerves of steel, and the highest courage—the true courage, that finds itself alone and in the dark in the presence of a constant danger, but a danger of an unknown kind, which may suddenly assume the least expected shape.

The devotion of these men is not always understood, even in New York, though many instances of this quality is recorded. The sagacity with which the red Indian follows the trail of his enemies, in Fenimore Cooper's works, is not greater than the eager keenness with which a New York Detective scents his prey. Sometimes he watches under the shadow of a wall a whole winter night, under heavy snow, cutting sleet, drenching rain, or piercing wind; or stands for a day before one of our many fashionable hotels, theatres, or big dry goods, or banking houses, wherever his duty calls him, waiting and watching for the favorable opportunity to lay a firm and relentless hand on the shoulder of the transgressor, who, desperado as he generally is, and armed, finds himself overmatched and overreached at the game at which he has played in his warfare on society. The perseverance born of such experiences is extraordinary, and only equals their sagacity and penetration. It happens with some mental talents as it happens with the muscles of the body: through continual exercise they become developed beyond measure. Habitual close observation, and great experience, enable them, from the most insignificant signs, to construct a complete theory, which is seldom incorrect, just as the practiced physician sees at a glance

Inspector Byrnes in His Private Office.

the nature of a patient's malady. It is related of Cauler (a celebrated French Detective) that, from four words written on a piece of paper in which some butter was wrapped up, he discovered the clue to a murder. This is characteristic of Detectives as a class. They, in time, acquire a wonderful memory, and they never fail to recognize a face they have once seen, however altered or disguised it may be. A single instance of this may be cited. One day Inspector Byrnes and the writer left the public thoroughfare of Broadway, in the vicinity of Police Headquarters, and strolled into the less frequented by-ways, while the Inspector, who was on his way home, was explaining the facts in the case of a recent arrest of some importance, the writer being then attached to the *Herald* Police Bureau as a reporter. The Inspector is an inveterate smoker. As usual, he was enjoying the weed, and in his peculiarly earnest way he was, while talking, seemingly absorbed in his subject, and apparently oblivious to all things else. Without raising his eyes, altering his tone, or changing his gait, he remarked. "See that fellow on the other side of the street; isn't he a dandy? I'll bet five dollars I know him." The reporter looked and beheld a "solitary figure," a nobby young man with a silk "tile," a silk-lined overcoat, and carrying a cane. His face was not within view, as he was walking in the same direction, but faster, and he was some yards in advance. "One of your friends, eh?" queried the reporter, languidly and mechanically, the interruption not being relished. There was a queer twinkle in the Inspector's eye. Removing his cigar, he uttered a low but penetrating sybilant sound with his half-closed lips. The man heard it, started, looked back over his shoulder, turned pale, and stood still. "I told you so," said the Inspector, with a quiet and amused smile, addressing himself to the reporter, who was now wide-awake and interested. "Sam," said the Inspector, still moving ahead in a half-abstracted manner, as before. The petrified statue again heard, and regaining animation, he slowly crossed the street diagonally and stood by the side of the Inspector and reporter, looking nervous, but remaining silent. "You are looking splendid, Sam; times must be good," said the Inspector, with a chilling sarcasm in his tone. The man's teeth were chattering now, his tongue refused to give utterance to his thoughts, and the change that had come over him in a brief moment was both radical and remarkable. From being the rakish-looking, light-hearted sport, he was metamorphosed into a cringing, frightened, abject creature, with pallid cheeks, downcast eyes, and cowering form. The three men were standing still now. The Inspector, critical and austere, the stranger cringing and frightened, and the reporter curious and observant. "It is a long time since I saw you Sam; I thought you dead or —"

"Sam" at last found his tongue. "I know what you want to add, Inspector. The latter supposition is the correct one. I have been in a tight snap; did my bit and have been out a few months. For God's sake don't run me in. I swear to you I have been keeping straight."

The man's knees shook under him, and his voice was husky with emotion.

"Sam," said the Inspector, very quietly and almost gently, only for the frigidness of the tone. "It is a long time since we've met. You did not look quite so dapper then, and there have been times since when I would have given a finger nail to have found you. How long is it since the night you shot at the officer and escaped over the house-tops?" "Six years, going on seven, Inspector," said the man thus interrogated.

"Call at my office at ten o'clock to-morrow morning, Sam," said the Inspector, moving a step forward, "I want to have a word with you privately."

The man bent his head, stood still a second, and then darted forward in a rapid walk, never once looking back.

"This is the second time I have ever met or seen that man in my life," said the Inspector, in a reminiscent way and reflectively. "The first time, he and two other men were arrested on suspicion of being concerned in a butcher wagon highway robbery case. Proof of guilt could not be brought home to Sam, and he was let go; but he was a marked man. Some months after a Broadway store was broken into, the burglars surprised, two of them captured, the third making his way to the roof, and, when pursued, emptying his pistol at the officer, none of the balls taking effect, however. I always suspected Sam of being that man, and, in his fright, now he has confessed to it." "Will he not get away out of the city?" "Not a bit of it, he is too much scared for that, besides, he is shadowed. Look there!"

At that moment Sam disappeared around the corner of a street, and a man in a long overcoat, with collar turned up (it was in winter) came into view, stood still a brief second, threw a salute in the direction of the Inspector, which was returned, accompanied by a low chuckle on the part of the Inspector, and the mysterious figure in the flowing ulster rapidly disappeared in the direction "Sam" had taken.

One more incident may be narrated.

The case of the Frenchman, Louis Hanier, who was shot dead on his own stairway, at midnight, by the young "tough" McGloin, who, with others, had broken into Hanier's liquor store for the purpose of robbery, will readily be recalled. For some time the murder remained a deep mystery. Inspector Byrnes dispatched one of his trustiest men to investigate the circumstances of the case. This man was sent on no novel or untried mission. Having made an exhaustive study of the scene of the murder, and familiarized himself with such facts in connection therewith as were obtainable, he returned to report progress to his chief. Practically he had accomplished but very little, if anything at all, theoretically he had, in his own estimation, achieved wonders. From these bewildering theories and fancies, Inspector Byrnes, by a process of inductive reasoning, sifted the very small grains of fact, and on this established his case. Three glasses had been found on the counter, each containing a small quantity of brandy. The Inspector fastened on this one central clue. His first exclamation was. "It was Hanier's rum that killed him." This remark was unintelligible to the Detective to whom it had been made. "I mean," said the Inspector, to his puzzled subordinate, "that three men (young men, most probably) were engaged in the murder. They broke into Hanier's saloon more with the expectation of finding rum than money. They drank deeply, and the brandy crazed their brain. They became noisy, and Hanier, arming himself, came to the stair-landing, when one of the half-drunken rowdies let fire at him, wounding him fatally. Terrified at their bloody work, all three escaped."

The Inspector could reason the case thus far, but there, in the absence of more specific data, he was stopped. But he had come to one highly important conclusion. He had settled it in his mind that the murderer was to be found among the young rowdy element (and there was a superabundance of the material) in the neighborhood At the autopsy the bullet was found Now, then, this was a tangible clue Calling a dozen of his best men, the Inspector instructed them singly, giving each to understand that he was the only man on the case, and pledging him to strict secrecy, to make a tour of all the gun shops, pawnbrokers shops, etc, of the city, and find out if cartridges of the calibre found in the body of the murdered man, or a revolver carrying that calibre bullet, had been sold within a reasonable period A week or ten days previous to the shooting several such sales had been made All these were investigated without arriving at tangible results A box of cartridges, it had been learned, was sold

Inspector Byrnes Receiving Reports

to a youth about a week previous to the murder They were of the calibre sought after. This clue was followed up, and this was the beginning of the solving of the mystery of the murder of Louis Hanier. Inspector Byrnes had arrived at just conclusions; his handling of the case was marked by great Detective sagacity, and the subsequent steps taken by him to fasten guilt on the beardless murderer, who had boasted of being a "tough," and gloried in having knocked out his man, were characterized by good judgment, sagacity, penetration and energy—qualities which Inspector Byrnes possesses in an eminent degree.

To unravel plots, unmask falsehoods, and extort the truth, is singularly interesting to those practiced in the arts of mental warfare The members of the Detective force are so accustomed to the study of human physiognomy that an involuntary change of countenance may reveal a weak spot, whence confession may be extracted from the criminal. Stern, harsh language, or threats, only harden the criminal, and render him more impenetrable; words of kindness are the only means of unlocking his tongue. No man understands this better than Inspector Byrnes himself. Even the greatest ruffians are amenable to the influences of a friendly address, and no man is so utterly depraved or lost as not to possess a soft chord in his heart. The question is how to strike upon it. None but a master hand can play upon this chord. Inspector Byrnes' imperturbable temper and his keenness of intellect enable him to subdue the most obstinate and tenacious prisoner; and it is possible that some of his remarkable success may have been achieved by valuable hints furnished him by grateful criminals, as no man knows better how to be just and at the same time merciful than Inspector Byrnes. Such hints, doubtless, have, on occasions, assisted him in unraveling many an entangled skein.

During the last four years crime has perceptibly decreased among professional thieves to almost nothing. The people who steal now-a-days are the rising generation of young people. All the old thieves, who have been looked upon as experts in that business, have been driven from post to pillar, and have finally disappeared altogether. The reason of that is because of the great power Detective officers have over thieves, and the intricate knowledge they possess of their ways. Another great secret of success is discipline among the men, and, as far as practicable, not to let one man know what another is doing. This, at least, has been Inspector Byrnes' experience. His control over thieves is also to be traced to the thorough knowledge he possesses of their haunts and methods. He spends a great deal of his time amongst them, and it is his belief that when thefts are perpetrated, the place to get information is among thieves. When a burglary, for instance, is committed, it is necessary to reflect, who could have done it, for every thief has his specialty and his own peculiar branch of business. Take a first-class burglar, for instance; his hobby may consist in opening a safe, and after a while he becomes a great man in the estimation of the fraternity. By studying these little details, and by keeping a record as thieves disappear and others take their place, a pretty accurate knowledge of their plans and operations can be arrived at. There is not a robbery committed throughout the State that the Inspector does not try to find out who bossed the job, and who executed it, in order that he may keep posted on what is going on about him among criminals. This is a very necessary proceeding. A good Police officer wants to find out where the thieves are, who they are, and who they are working for. The moment a Detective officer sees a thief accompanied by a stranger, it is the duty of the Detective to follow the thief and find out who his companion is, for it is fair to assume that anyone who accompanies a thief in the public street must himself be a thief. One of the best ways to find out these people is through their women. A thief has three weaknesses—women, gambling and drink.

Forgers are a very peculiar class. Some of them possess a great deal of ability. The men who lay down the counterfeit paper, as a rule, never see the forger himself, who sometimes lives luxuriously, and does his business through an agent who gets a percentage. These forgers, sometimes for months and years even, study on one series of counterfeits. They are often considered to be very reputable citizens by people who do not know their calling.

As a general thing, men who commit highway robbery do not belong to a particular class. They are men who have become desperate from various causes. This is a class of crime where every man performs his part, and it is really one of the most difficult things in the world to get at them, because the robbery is the work of a moment, and the robbers are generally disguised so that they cannot afterwards be recognized.

Pickpockets generally work in gangs of four or five. The "tool" is the one who steals, while the others do the jostling.

Sneak thieves are a numerous class. It is a low, mean, contemptible grade of crime. But bank sneaks are a different class of men. There are probably from twenty-five to thirty of them in this country. They are generally Americans, with some few exceptions. They are men of education, fine appearance, and good address, who walk up to the paying or receiving teller in the bank, and hold him in conversation on a subject that will positively interest him, while somebody else will steal stealthily in behind with rubber shoes on, and rob the safe. That has been "worked" very successfully. They have another system in country banks. A sneak thief will drive up to the bank door, alight, go inside, and tell the cashier that a certain gentleman who has hurt his leg, and is unable to get out, wishes to speak with him. The unsuspecting bank official goes out to speak to the injured gentleman, and, during his absence, the bank is robbed.

At the present time some of the most expert thieves that ever lived in this country are located in England and France.

Bunco-steerers are a class of young men who are well educated, as a general thing, and who, in the main, have come from good families. In their younger days their parents had not been able to supply them with the amount of money they were willing to spend. They had become infatuated with women or gambling, and at last were either driven from their home or had voluntarily left it. They are a class who generally live in furnished rooms in the better part of cities, and change their quarters frequently so as to disarm suspicion. What they win in gambling is generally paid by check by their victim. Then there is some convenient lawyer who positively knows the bunco-steerer's business, and who, for a consideration, will bully their victims into paying the amount of these checks. The victims are, as a rule, men who occupy prominent public positions, and would not expose themselves in a court of law as defendants in an action for the recovery of a gambling debt.

"I never met a thief in my life, provided he could benefit by peaching on his confederates, from whom I could not find out anything I was desirous to know. There is no such thing as honor among thieves," is one of Inspector Byrnes' maxims.

New York is the most difficult city in the world to protect against thieves—for this reason in the first place, thieves from abroad are constantly introducing crimes with which our Police are not familiar. The only way to find these criminals out is to hunt for them among some of their own countrymen When these foreigners come here they generally have somebody to meet them who will take them in charge, and, in spite of themselves, they are obliged to show themselves on the streets sometimes

The facilities for getting out of New York to neighboring cities make it difficult also to capture criminals

During the draft riots the duties imposed on the Detectives were of a higher role than the work ordinarily imposed upon them. They were kept employed day and night obtaining useful information concerning the plans and movements of the rioters, supplying Police Headquarters and the precinct commands with the information so obtained, and in this way doing much towards frustrating the cowardly aims of the rioters. While so occupied they ran great risks, and not a few of them had hairbreadth escapes from death at the hands of the mob. Whenever one of them was recognized, the startling cry went up, "There goes Kennedy's spies," and then the officer was lucky indeed if his self-possession and presence of mind extricated him from the dangerous dilemma. The Detective force acted throughout with great discretion, bravery and zeal.

CHAPTER XIX

INSPECTOR BYRNES' COMMAND.

The Men who Protect the City from the Depredations of Knaves of High and Low Degree —Forty Quick-witted, Wide-awake Detectives. —Their History and Record of Arrests.—How they Make the City a Safe Abiding-place for Honest People.—Interesting Tales of Some Celebrated Cases—The Romance and Reality of Crime.—Truth Stranger than Fiction —A Devoted Band of Police Officers —Their Struggles and Triumphs.—The Men who Make it Possible for Inspector Byrnes to Retain his Well-earned Laurels.

NO jealousy will be felt by any member of Inspector Byrnes' staff at prominence being given to one of the oldest officers on the force, and one of its shrewdest and most successful Detectives, Timothy Golden As far back as 1859—a quarter of a century ago—he was detailed as Detective in the Sixth Precinct, and five years later he went to Police Headquarters His career has been distinguished and useful Among his many arrests may be cited the following September, 1859, William Jones, for the murder of a stranger in an unoccupied room in Crown's Rookery at Worth and Little Water Streets The murderer got six cents for his bloody work, and left no clue Several months after Golden captured him on an oyster boat at Philadelphia, and he was sentenced for life The same year he arrested John McCue for the murder of an express driver in a grocery store at Elm and Grand Streets, and convicted him. A recommendation to mercy by the jury limited his sentence to nineteen years and six months. In May of 1860 Golden convicted eleven porters at H B Claflin & Co's, who had conspired to swindle the firm, and recovered fifteen thousand dollars' worth of goods Five months later he arrested Frederick Schacht for the murder of Thomas Kaveny at Pearl Street and City Hall Place Schacht was a grocer, and a large fund was raised for his defense, which was so ably conducted by James T Brady, who afterwards said he would never again defend a criminal, and kept his word, that Schacht escaped with a short sentence. Golden spent three years to collect evidence to justify him in arresting Peter and Mary Hefferman alias James and Ellen Johnson, expert shoplifters, who had accumulated a quarter of a million of dollars. The wife pleaded coverture and was discharged. He forfeited his bail and fled to Canada, but was arrested again in the States, and served one year. His arrest cost him, in all, fifteen thousand dollars. In August, 1864, he brought to book George F Howe, the accomplice of Smith and Stevenson the bogus bonded warehouse keepers, who, on spurious warehouse receipts, borrowed two hundred and eighty thousand dollars. The arrest was made in Rochester, after a chase through Wisconsin. All the rascals escaped, in a measure, by making restitution. Mark Shinburn, the bank burglar who became a German Baron, and who is now serving a sentence for bank burglary at Viviers, Belgium, was arrested by Golden in August, 1865, for the burglary at the Savings Bank at Walpole, New Hampshire, on the twenty-fifth of April of that year, when eighty-six thousand dollars was stolen. Shinburn escaped while serving a ten years' sentence at the Concord Prison. He also arrested George White, Shinborne's accomplice, who broke jail while awaiting a second trial, and he is now serving a fourteen years' sentence for the Barre, Vt., bank robbery. In July, 1874, he arrested a man who had hypothecated twenty-five thousand dollars in Buffalo, New York and Erie Railroad Bonds, from George Ripley, the banker, and recovered twenty thousand dollars. The same year he arrested another man for obtaining by burglary, at the office of the Commissioners of Internal Revenue at Washington, D. C., twelve thousand dollars, eleven thousand dollars of which were recovered. Then, in 1867, 1877, and 1878, came the arrests of Charles R. Beckwith, Thomas R. Lewis, and Charles H. Ketchum, who, by conspiracy, forgery, embezzlement, and falsification of accounts, stole two hundred and six

Detective Sergeant Reporting.

thousand dollars from B. T. Babbitt, the soap manufacturer and Ellen E. Peck. Beckwith was sent to prison for ten years; Lewis was followed to London by Golden and arrested, disgorged thirty thousand dollars; and Ketchum made restitution of fifteen thousand dollars. Ellen E. Peck, the alleged "confidence" woman, who, it is asserted, obtained nineteen thousand dollars from Babbitt by pretending to be able to disclose where Beckwith had put his money, is now in the Tombs awaiting trial on twelve indictments, viz.: five for grand larceny, one for perjury, and six for forgery. Then came, in 1879, the capital arrest of J. R. Robinson, who had obtained two hundred and eighty-seven thousand dollars by forgery, in Pennsylvania.

He fled to London, thence to Spain, thence to Lisbon, and had set sail for Callao when Golden started after him. He never lost trace of him; from Peru, up the west coast of South America, through Smith's Channel and the Straits of Magellan to Montevideo, Bueros Ayres, and Rio de Janeiro, where he was arrested and surrendered by Dom Pedro. His case was compromised. In December, 1879, James Tounley and Robert May fled to Washington after being foiled in an attempt to obtain one thousand five hundred dollars from the Bank of America, by forging the name of Mrs. Jones, of No. 625 Fifth Avenue. May was the lady's butler, and Golden trapped him by inserting an advertisement for a butler in a Washington paper. Tounley's arrest followed. Both were convicted. Detective Sergeant Golden is, notwithstanding his long service, still hale, and able to do first-class duty, having recovered from a serious illness which for two years threatened to invalidate him permanently.

The old side partners, Holly Lyon and Richard King, have been, and are, terrors to evil doers. Lyon became a Policeman in 1848, and eleven years later began to do duty as a Detective in the Seventh Precinct. King was a Detective in 1865, and went to the Central Office in 1873. Their arrests are numbered by the hundred. In February, 1870, they caught the notorious thieves, "Wash" and "Ed" Goodrich or Goody, for stealing seven thousand dollars' worth of silk from the truck of Dean & Albertson, and recovered the property. "Wash" was sent to prison for five years and "Ed" was discharged. In March, 1870, Daniel Ritner and Francis Degan entered the loan office No. 5 Amity Street, now Third Street, stunned the proprietor, Joseph Jackson, and stole diamonds, jewelry, and money. The Detectives caught the thieves, and recovered the property. Judge Bedford sent the prisoners to Sing Sing for nineteen years and six months. King and Lyon were the captors of the banker and brains of the Masked Burglars, George Millard alias Miller. They caught him in his saloon in West Broadway, January 5, 1874, and secured his conviction and sentence for five years by Recorder Hackett. The same year they captured "Patsey" Conroy, one of the masked burglars who robbed Judge Emott's house at New Rochelle, and obtained for him a twenty years' sentence at White Plains. "Danny" Kelly, John Reilly, "Larry" Griffin, James Campbell, "Denny" Brady, and John Burns, confederates of Conroy, were also brought to justice by these officers. They secured a twenty years' sentence for Michael Wawhee for robbery and felonious assault on George F. Feely, of Saugerties, N. Y. This, in 1874, as well as the capture and conviction of John Green, William Reed, Thomas Anguly, and "Cockney" Jones, for a one thousand five hundred dollar burglary at Edward Ridley's, at Gravesend, L. I., and the arrest and conviction of John Durkin, Louis Forside, and John Henry, who robbed Jacob Vanderbilt's house on Staten Island. In February, 1875, they arrested the lads Daniel Horey and James Sweeny, who stole an Adams Express wagon and safe, in which was thirty-one thousand dollars in bonds and twenty-five thousand three hundred and sixty dollars in currency. The money, etc., were recovered from their grave in a Nassau Street cellar, and Horey was convicted. Sweeny escaped by turning State's evidence.

Inspector Byrnes' judgment was correct when he secured the transfer from the Twenty-fifth Precinct to the Detective Squad, of Sergeant Isaac Bird, now Deputy Chief Detective, and in charge of the squad in the absence of Inspector Byrnes. Sergeant Bird was a Patrolman in February, 1859, Roundsman in 1861, and promoted to his present rank in August, 1862. He is now keen, far seeing and prompt, and, while he disclaims any title to a record, he could lay claim to much credit for his intelligent and far-sighted management of many cases which have been brought to a successful issue

FRANCIS MANGIN, JR, had his start in life in the newspaper business at Police Headquarters, and his fidelity and ability induced his employers, when he had outgrown his usefulness, and, when as a matter of justice, his services demanded fuller recognition, to obtain for him employment in the office of the late Sidney P. Nichols He was advanced to the position of confidential

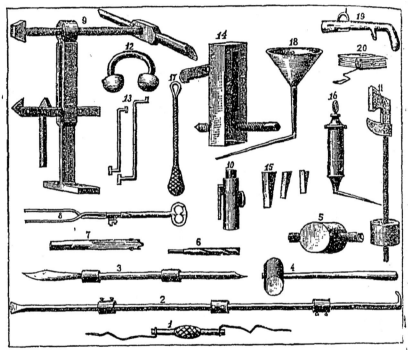

1 Gag 2 Sectional Jimmy 3 Sectional Jimmy. 4 Copper Sledge 5 Lead Sledge 6 Diamond Drill
7 Diamond Drill 8 Key Nippers 9 Improved Safe opener 10 Glim 11 Used to Obtain a Leverage. 12. Knuckles. 13 Skeleton Keys 14 Wedge 15 Wedge 16 Powder Blower 17 Slung Shot. 18. Powder Funnel 19 Dummy Pistol 20 Fuse

A Burglar's Outfit

clerk, and afterwards was made a Policeman, and in time became a Detective Sergeant. His record of arrests is a good one The following are among the best of them· May, 1883, George Gunsett, receiving stolen goods, sent to the Elmira Reformatory; August, 1883, W D. Biglow, larceny at the Grand Union Hotel, sentenced to three years; April, 1883, Edward Kelly, highway robbery on a woman, sentenced to five years; January, 1883, Ella Bonk alias Ada Forrester, shoplifting; May, 1885, F. B Tults, E J Foster, Gordon

R. Cummings, W. McKeon, Matthew Shaw and David Davis, clerks at LeBoutillier Bros., all convicted for robbing their employers, December, 1883; J. J. Wilkins, arrested at Havana for forging checks on Brown Bros. In September, 1884, he caught Charles Stepsic for stealing two thousand five hundred dollars' worth of jewelry from William Schwensen's store, No. 254 Third Avenue, where he was employed as salesman, recovered the property, and convicted the prisoner.

JACOB TOOKER, who is as brave and competent an officer as any on the force, was made a Detective in the Nineteenth Precinct, January 12, 1877. His precinct career was an exemplary one, and at Police Headquarters he has proved himself trustworthy. In January, 1877, he arrested John Ford for shooting James Burnham at the "Burnt Rag" in West Seventeenth Street, on the ninth of November, 1876, and Kate Donnelly at Seventy-second Street and Avenue A a week later. Ford received a sentence of seven years. On the fourteenth of February, 1882, Tooker came near being murdered by Thomas alias "Hump" Hennessy. He was "wanted" for robbery with violence, and when Tooker arrested him, Hennessy shot him in the head. Tooker refrained from taking the felon's life, and, though grievously injured, held on to his prisoner until aid came. Hennessy was sent to prison for eight years and a half. In July, 1883, he arrested the confidence woman, Bertha Heyman alias Schlesinger alias Edwards, at Paterson, N. J., for swindling, among others, Edward Saunders, of No. 43 Second Avenue, and was sent to prison for five years.

JOHN, OR "JACK" WADE, as he is affectionately called, was made a Detective in May, 1875, and for years did his full duty in the Tenth Precinct. In April, 1876, he arrested George Wilson, Patrick Boyle, William Roberts, and Martin McGowan, who drove to Brooklyn in a wagon, entered a jewelry store in Hicks Street, presented revolvers at the proprietor and his wife, and beat them after robbing the place. Each went to prison for twenty years. In November, 1876, Patrick Connors enticed James Colligan, a "sport," into a coach, and took a ride to Central Park, where he and a confederate robbed Colligan, Connors drawing with his teeth a diamond ring off the man's finger so that the flesh came with it. Connors went to Sing Sing for twenty years, thanks to Wade's persistent hunt for him. He was instrumental in securing the arrest, in November, 1879, of Joseph and Mary Volkmar, who poisoned Charles Blair at No. 114 Essex Street, and both were sentenced to twelve years imprisonment each. In October of this year he arrested the notorious "Billy" Porter or O'Brien, who broke jail in Raymond Street, Brooklyn, with "Johnny" Irving, afterwards killed by "Johnny, the Mick," in "Shang" Draper's Sixth Avenue saloon. In July, 1883, he captured James Quigley and James Ryan, who stole a trunk and two thousand dollars' worth of silk belonging to Rogers, Peet & Co., and four months later captured the notorious hotel thief "Gus" Gregory, who had set the Police of New York by the ears because of his persistent depredations and his evasion of arrest.

THOMAS W. MULRY, Wade's partner, was appointed a Detective in the Eighteenth Precinct in March, 1877, and he has a clean and creditable record. His chief arrests were: April, 1877, Patrick Lynch, burglary, sentenced for five years; May, 1878, James Creegan, grand larceny, sentenced to five years; October, 1879, James McCabe, robbery, sentenced to twenty years; August, 1880, Annie Riley, grand larceny, sentenced to three years and a half; March, 1881, John Fain, burglary, sentenced to five years; March, 1884, Arthur Price, forgery, sentenced to five years; and November 3, 1884, "Gus" Gregory, burglary, sentenced to ten years.

JAMES J. LANGAN, a thoroughly efficient member of the Detective Squad, was appointed a Detective Sergeant in May, 1882. In February, 1883, he arrested and convicted the tramp thief, William Barlow, who took a pocketbook from Miss Christina Sherwood on the steps of the Fourth Avenue tunnel, and left no clue to his identity. In November of that year he caught William E. Brockway and L. R. Martin, who had forged fifty-two thousand dollars in bonds of the Morris and Essex Railroad Company, and both were convicted. In August, 1882, he arrested and convicted Terence McQuade, the dog catcher, who wantonly murdered a boy named Doyle who clamored for the release of his pet dog at One Hundred and Tenth Street and Tenth Avenue. In August, 1883, he succeeded in bringing to justice Patrick Carroll and John Talbot, who blew open two safes at No. 10 Burling Slip; and in July, 1884, sent to prison William Parks and George Johnson, who knocked down and robbed William Kruskopp, of No. 112 Elizabeth Street.

Captain's Shield

JAMES McQUIRE was taken to the Central Office in 1881, and he has a record of arrests that demonstrates his aptitude for his profession. Some of his best arrests were November, 1882, Edward Farrington, grand larceny, sentenced to two years and a half; same year, Michael Dempsey alias "Slugger," and Paul Dewitt alias "Big Peter," and W. H. Livingstone, burglary, all convicted; April, 1883, Joseph H. Thompson alias "Doc," Titus C. Frank Morris alias Robert Langdon, forgery, each sentenced to five years; David C. Bliss alias "Doc," April, 1883, larceny of twenty-eight thousand dollars in bonds, sent to State Prison for two years; February, 1884, Frank Donohue, Frank Thomas, and George Raymond, burglary, sentenced to four years each; August, 1884, Leonard C. Davis, bigamy, sentenced to one year.

GEORGE RADFORD has handled more "gilt-edged" cases than any Detective ever in the Department. He came to the Detective Office in 1859, and is still doing excellent service. Some of his cases are as follows. In November, 1862, a box containing three hundred thousand dollars was stolen from Riggs & Co's deposit vault in the Bank of North America. Radford had no clue, but he arrested Charles Kingsbury and Robert Taylor, and made matters so warm for the thieves that they sent the box and its contents intact to Radford, at the Fifth Avenue Hotel. The prisoners were discharged, it being next to impossible to identify them. In January, 1877, Cyrus C. Clark was caught by Radford trying to negotiate a loan of twelve thousand dollars on twenty-one excellent forgeries of the one thousand dollar bonds of the Central Pacific Railroad, and was sent to prison for five years. In March, 1866, John P. Moore's residence, No. 110 Madison Avenue, was entered by a "second story" thief, who stole sixty-four thousand dollars in Government bonds and money. After several weeks of investigation, and with only a small steel jimmy as a clue, Radford arrested two "second story" men, "Troy" Dennis and Hugh Carr, and recovered forty-seven thousand dollars of the bonds, but the prisoners were released because the evidence against them, although positive to the officer, was insufficient for a jury. Carr afterwards committed suicide. Dennis was killed in 1876 at No. 64 West Fiftieth Street while committing a "second story" robbery, by a coping stone falling with and on him. In September, 1878, Charles Baker alias Walter Whelphy went to Morton Bliss & Co.'s banking house, No. 25 Nassau Street, with a forged bill of lading and drew a bill of exchange for two thousand one hundred and fifty-nine pounds sterling. He received a check for ten thousand four hundred and twenty-seven dollars, and when the forgeries were discovered, Radford hunted up Baker and recovered the checks. Baker was sent to prison for three years. He also arrested and sent to prison for twenty years, Joseph Murray, one of several desperados who, at the Central Park Savings Bank, on the third of April,

Sergeant's Shield.

1871, knocked the cashier down, and grabbed four hundred and forty-five dollars in a package. In June, 1879, he arrested and convicted George H. Clark alias "Philadelphia Pearsall" for stealing an envelope containing a United States one thousand dollar bond at Kountze Bros., No. 12 Wall Street, and recovered the bond.

One of the shrewdest and most trustworthy men on the staff is PHILIP REILLY, who became a Headquarters Detective in August, 1866. A full account of his arrests would, like those of many of Inspector Byrnes' staff, fill this book. The following is a summary of the most important or singularly creditable ones: December, 1866, Sam Moody and William Sewell for burglary, convicted and sentenced to twenty years' imprisonment. August, 1870, Edward Howard Ruloff, hung for murder seven months later. October, 1874, arrested Robert Murray alias "Bobby, the Milkman," for burglary; he was sentenced to ten years' imprisonment December 30, 1874, arrest of George alias "Rat" Riley for burglary, he served a term of ten years February, 1875, James G Triss, highway robbery; sent to jail for eighteen years by Judge Sutherland May 31, 1876, Jacob Schinholz, burglar; sent to prison for ten years by Judge Gildersleeve February 10, 1877, arrest of William Veltman and William H Leitch, for forgery on the Merchants' Exchange Bank; they were sent to prison each for ten years by Judge Sutherland.

PATRICK DOLAN and CHARLES HEIDELBERG, old, experienced, and successful Detectives, merit special mention as intelligent partners and useful public servants Dolan was appointed a Detective in the Sixth Precinct, in March, 1869, and Heidelberg has been a Detective fifteen years Much of their work of late years has been deterrent, or their labors have been with other Detectives, all of whom have shared with them and Inspector Byrnes the honor of the success Dolan, in May, 1874, arrested Joseph Callamon and Joseph Frechton for swindling John Riche out of a satchel of gold coin, recovered the money, and convicted the rascals Three years later, he convicted Charles F Clark and Charles Wirgasen of highway robbery, and the next year sent Amber Jourdan to Sing Sing for five years, for grand larceny at the residence of M Curtis, No 27 Washington Street. Next year he convicted Jeremiah Manley and John Keenan of a large dry goods robbery

Heidelberg, in 1881, made scores of good arrests, among which were the following. Joseph W Milne, who stole one thousand two hundred dollars from the First National Bank of Fall River; David Butler, a negro, charged with burglary at Elizabeth, N J, Henry Rodley, a negro, charged with forgery, William D Batchelder, the blackmailer Next year he sent to prison Frederick Fischer, James Mannard and Charles Peters, charged with burglary at Albany, Morris A Schwab and Henry Williams, charged with stealing five hundred dollars from Mrs. Helen M Lewis, of Charleston, S. C, and Frank Talcott and William Brown, who stole two cases of velvet from Lord & Taylor's In 1883 he convicted a private Detective who had been swindling credulous and ambitious Germans out of sums varying from ten to two hundred dollars, by pretending to appoint them Detectives, and giving them an elaborately engraved commission

A bright and highly interesting record is that of JOSEPH M DORCY, who was appointed a Detective in the Tenth Precinct in January, 1872. Barely two months later he arrested Michael De Rosa, an Italian, who, on account of jealousy, murdered Giovanni Pabricco in the rear of No. 37 Mulberry Street, with

Patrolman's Shield

a dirk De Rosa was caught under a heap of rags at No. 41 Mulberry Street, and went to prison for three years. His very brilliant arrest of John Dolan for the murder of James H Noe, the brush maker, at No. 275 Greenwich Street, on the twenty-second of August, 1875, is yet remembered. Noe was fatally injured by Dolan on a Sunday morning while he visited his store to see if everything was in order Dolan was robbing the place, and attacked when surprised. The only clues was a monkey-headed slung-shot left behind and Mr Noe's watch, which was pawned in Chatham Street The crime was brought home to Dolan, and he was executed March 15, 1876 Dorcy also arrested and secured the judicial taking away of Edward Reinhardt, who murdered his wife, Mary Ann, on Staten Island, July 19, 1878, and buried her body at Silver Lake On the twenty-second of June, 1883, at Grand Rapids, Michigan, he arrested Dirck C Horseling, who embezzled two thousand five hundred dollars while tax collector in the Netherlands, and Marshal Erhardt sent him to Holland Three weeks later on he arrested Pietro Edwardo Martiningo, charged with forgery and embezzlement to the extent of one hundred and sixty thousand dollars on the Banca Subaepina, of Turin, Italy. The culprit decided to go back without extradition proceedings The most stirring of his adventures was the arrest, on the twenty-first of June, 1882, of Canon Leon L J Bernard, who embezzled one million four hundred thousand dollars of the See of Tournai, Belgium. The chase after the reverend scoundrel began through the principal south-western cities, then to Mexico, and finally at Vera Cruz Dorcy secured Bernard's arrest at the Hotel Telegrafo, at Havana, by a telegraphic message which arrived in the nick of time Dorcy secured information which enabled the See of Tournai to recover one million two hundred thousand dollars

THOMAS HICKEY, who became a Central Office Detective in April, 1880, is one of the most unassuming, and, at the same time, one of the bravest and most trustworthy officers of the Detective Bureau He has been chiefly engaged in looking after the interests of Mammon in Wall Street, and how well he and his associates have done their duty is seen by the absence of reports of depredations in the financial centre Hickey has found time to do some excellent Detective work In November, 1880, he arrested and convicted Henry Freeman for stealing three thousand dollars from a safe at the New York Post-office In February, 1881, a tray of diamond rings was stolen from the show window of Alexander Newburger, No 531 Sixth Avenue Hickey soon had the thieves, James Murphy, John Dunn, John Leonard, and "Milky," McDonald, under arrest, and their conviction followed A month later, three thousand five hundred dollars' worth of laces were stolen from the truck of Lahey & Dubard, No 110 Grand Street, and the thieves, Henry Lissee, Henry Hart, August Hartrott and Marcus Raymond, were soon on their way to prison In September, 1882, he secured the conviction, and sentences of fifteen years each, of George Earle and Ambrose Schlag, for burglary at the residences of Percy L Pine and Colgate Hoyt, on the banks of the Hudson The same year he arrested Henry Hart and Marcus Raymond for stealing twelve thousand dollars' worth of baggage from a Dodd's express wagon. In February,

1883, he convicted David Kidney and John Carmody of robbing Adolph Goldsmith and his messenger, in Greenwich Street, of a cash box containing one thousand five hundred dollars ; and the same year he caught Albert Viloeky, who is now serving a life sentence for beating out the brains of a countryman near Pittsburg, Pa

MICHAEL CROWLEY was taken from the Fifteenth Precinct to Police Headquarters in March, 1881 He had made an enviable reputation long before, and has continued to be shrewd and energetic The record of his arrests are W C Rhinelander, of No. 243 Schermerhorn Street, Brooklyn, for attempting to kill John Drake, at No. 79 Cedar Street, Frank Frisbie, for stealing five thousand dollars from the Bank of Portland, Oregon; H F Graybill, for forgeries on Miller & Bro , Philadelphia, and the Savannah Steamship Company, Bernard Rose alias Russell, for a five thousand dollar burglary at Hammerslough Bros.', at 724 Broadway and William Meineck, for the murder of Katie Braderhoff, at Elmira

Model Cell.

RICHARD O'CONNOR, Sergeant of Detectives, was detailed as a Central Office Detective at the District Attorney's office, in October, 1873 He is accounted as not only having a complete knowledge of all criminals worth knowing, but with having a better knowledge of criminal law and proceedings than many practicing lawyers. He, in June, 1874, caught John H. Short, who was sent to prison for twenty years for robbing Jacob Vanderbilt's house, on Staten Island He convicted George Miles alias Bliss, for the Barre, Vt , bank robbery, in September, 1875 November, 9, 1875, he arrested John Green for a burglary at Oxford Furnace, N. J , and secured his conviction In August, 1876, he caught David Jones alias Peyton, who had committed a burglary at Baltimore, Md , and he was sentenced to twelve years' imprisonment Attilla Beyer, who robbed District Attorney Phelps' house, was arrested by O'Connor in August, 1876, and was sent to Sing Sing for ten years. In September of that year he arrested Daniel O'Brien, alias Captain Sparks, for stealing three thousand dollars' worth of diamonds from a Long Branch hotel, and he was sent to Trenton Prison for ten years.

OWEN HALEY, who was detailed as a Detective in May, 1873, has had an active, honorable and memorable career He began well, for in July, 1873, he received honorable mention by the Board of Police for arresting and convicting seventeen shoplifters and pickpockets in twenty-eight days His industry is proverbial, and he has made as good an average of arrests as any of his colleagues Some of the most important were in April, 1875 Charles D. Thompson, embezzlement of eleven thousand dollars at the Core Iron Works of Providence, R I , who shot himself in the head on the steamer Idaho, but was sent to Providence, June, 1876, William Leith, forger on Bryer & Smith, sentenced to ten years, March 31, 1877, Joseph Baldwin alias Peppermint Joe, Joseph F Adams alias Joe Butts, and "Bill" Vosburgh, for robbing Gracie, King & Co. of a box containing one hundred and eighty thousand dollars in bonds; May, 1877, John Price alias James Munroe, for stealing five thousand dollars in Boston; March, 1878, William Smith alias Shaw alias McGuin, and Frank Dwyer, for obtaining goods on forged orders from John Osborne & Co.; June, 1878, Vincent McGee, alias "Red" the "stage fiend," who so long collected fares and evaded arrest; August, 1878, William Howard, burglar, caught through imprisoning of his hands in the fanlight of a door. He charged W. T. Van Zandt, a millionaire, with arson; April, 1879, T. McDonald and Joseph Stern, who in three years had robbed E. C. Denning & Co., No. 177 Broadway, of twenty thousand dollars' worth of goods, McDonald being an employee, and Stern the receiver Haley was honorably mentioned for these arrests by the Board of Police, as he was the first to inform the firm that they were being robbed; June, 1881, James J Rooney, the barrel thief, who was convicted after being twenty years in the business of receiving casks and barrels stolen from brewers; October, 1881, Mark Koshofskie alias Michael, the forger of forty checks; a month later John W. Oliver, embezzler of eight thousand dollars at Americus, Ga., money recovered; March, 1882, George Hendrix, the blower up of the Andre Monument at Tappan, N Y; April, 1882, Manuel Montana alias Gonzalez, the forger of one hundred and thirty checks; September, 1882, William Rogers, George Smith, W. H. Burke, Louis Briggs, and W G Abbott, charged with the murder, at a pic-nic row at Elizabethport, N. J of Thomas McKeon; December, 1882, Charles E. Poucher, forger of one hundred checks in New York and Syracuse, December, 1882, George James Rice, president of the Elmira and Ithaca Railroad, charged with embezzling one hunded and fifty thousand dollars, January, 1883, William Harrison alias Hewitt, the blackmailer of Mrs Rich, whose husband so mysteriously disappeared; W H. McCabe, W H Hughes, Richard C. Swift, Michael O'Donnell, John Conlon, Edward O'Keefe, Horatio S Courtney, Richard O'Keefe, the "false fire alarm fiends," who had driven the Fire Department distracted with their malicious mischief, for which all paid dearly, October, 1883, John B. O'Reilly and Margaret Nash, for incarcerating their aunt in a lunatic asylum and possessing themselves of her money, five thousand dollars, February, 1884, John Britton and Thomas Feeney alias Freund, the blackmailer of A E G Oelrichs, October, 1884, Rollins M Strang, charged with embezzlement of four thousand five hundred dollars by Jones & Co of the New York Flour Mills. November, 1884, Alexander C. Branscom, for forging to the amount of fifty-two thousand two hundred and fifty-two dollars on a number of publishing houses

JOHN J DUNN, a veteran officer, first did Detective duty in the Eighth Precinct in 1869 He is so thoroughly trustworthy and possessed of such good judgment that he has had charge of the Wall Street Sub-Detective Bureau since it opened His chief arrests as a Detective are· John Avery for murder at Creskill, N J., who was hung at Hackensack, June 8, 1872; C H Madan, burglar, sentenced to twenty years by Recorder Hackett September 28, 1875; Abraham Bernstein sentenced for life for arson, and Charles Bernstein and A.

D. Freeman, sentenced for the same crime to the same punishment; and Henry D. Reno sentenced for ten years for arson.

ROBERT McNAUGHT has been a Central Office Detective since December, 1877, and he has done a vast amount of first-class duty. In September, 1878, he arrested the notorious forger, Julius Columbani, and secured his conviction. Columbani was afterwards arrested by him in February, 1884, at the instance of the swindler, Mrs. Peck, for negotiating bonds, stolen by burglars from E. McSorley, of Richmond, Staten Island. Samuel Kane alias "Slocum," and John Norton alias "the Kid" were stealing a valise in which were twenty-seven thousand dollars in bonds, from No. 29 Broadway, in September, 1878. A couple of weeks later he arrested Clinton Ainsworth alias Smith alias "Broker Dick," who had in his possession one thousand of four thousand unsigned ten dollar notes of the Consolidated Bank of Canada, which had been stolen from the bank. In March, 1881, McNaught arrested Samuel Hawthorn on a telegraphic description from Vicksburg, Mississippi, on a charge of murder. He was sentenced to ninety-nine years' imprisonment. Augustus D. Wheelock, who forged two checks for ten thousand dollars each, and stole forty-five thousand dollars, was, in November, 1881, traced to London through McNaught, and was brought back by Detective Sergeant Cosgrove.

Sergeant Isaac Bird.

ALVAN H. WILLIAMSON was made a Detective in November, 1873, and has done excellent service. In October, 1874, he arrested George alias "Rat" Riley, and Robert Murray alias "Bobby, the Milkman," for robbing the Messrs. Luther Bryant of one hundred and twenty thousand dollars and other property. Each was sentenced to ten years' imprisonment. He also convicted George Anderson of burglary at W. R. Lear's, No. 5 West Twenty-fourth Street; Thomas Hamilton for robbing L. Valentine, of No. 19 Fifth Avenue, James G. Twess for highway robbery on Ewald Bolemius, of No. 207 East Houston Street, Julius Bloom, the famous shoplifter; John Anderson alias "Jimmy, the Kid," the pickpocket, and Jacob Shenholz, who burglarized the store of Harris Philips at No. 107 Hester Street.

JOHN RULAND became the Detective of the Fifteenth Precinct in February, 1877, and he kept the command clear of felons, and rarely missed catching those who committed depredations or crimes. A very important arrest was made by him in June, 1881, in the person of the king of scoundrels in the confidence fraternity, "Plin" White, who so mercilessly fleeced poor Major W. L.

Hall. He was associated with Haley in the arrest of the "false fire-alarm fiends," and in other arrests made by that officer. Ruland has recovered from an affection of the eyes which, for several years, menaced him with blindness.

EDWARD SLEVIN, Sergeant in the Detective Bureau, was made Ward Detective in the Fifteenth Precinct in August, 1873, and came to Police Headquarters to receive later on, well merited promotion, in March, 1880. Sergeant Slevin is Inspector Byrne's right hand man, and his confidence in him is fully warranted. One of the most genial of men in private life, he is, in his profession, keen, indefatigable, and successful. It is hardly fair to give a history of his personal arrests, for some of the most successful and extraordinary cases in New York have been brought to the point when an arrest was necessary, and another officer stepped in to make it. In September, 1876, he convicted Henry Bruner, a sneak thief, for robbing Angelina Ambrogetti, of No 106 Clinton Place, of jewelry and money. The same year he convicted John Absender, for stealing a trunk from the City Hotel, and Mary Mitchell alias Busby, for robbing Mrs A. L. Roberts. Next year he disposed of "Sam" Bergen and "Jack" Conroy, for stealing three thousand dollars' worth of clothes from W D Woods, at No 667 Broadway. Passing by hundreds of arrests by him as a Ward Detective, we come to November 21, 1883, when he arrested Richard O. Davis and Edward Darlington for a forgery of one thousand four hundred dollars on the Continental National Bank of New York, and convicted both. The same year he made one of the cleverest arrests ever accomplished by an officer, that of the notorious forger "Steve" Raymond alias Marshall, for altering stolen coupons of the Union Pacific Railroad Company. Raymond was captured at the Bank of Commerce while cashing a check for some of the coupons which he had cashed at the office of the Union Pacific Railroad Company. He was sentenced to State Prison for life.

Much of the most important clerical work of the Detective Bureau is done by Sergeant WILLIAM W McLAUGHLIN, who was a Patrolman in 1868, a Roundsman in 1874, and won his rank in 1882. He has a clean record, and often finds time to do the best of Detective work. In 1883, William C Bullard alias Russell alias Maltby, was combining forgery with bigamy, and was criminally successful in each, but he tried his pen on the Fifth Avenue Bank, and fell into McLaughlin's clutches after much hunting up. He is serving a five years' sentence. In May, 1882, Henry Wood picked the pocket of a bank messenger of a wallet containing fifty thousand dollars in money, drafts, etc, and was convicted by McLaughlin. He caught the confidence operators, Maurice Schwab and Robert Rummels, who, in the Spring of 1882, after defrauding many persons, swindled the actress, Helen Morris Lewis, out of five hundred dollars. Samuel B Sinclair and W. H. Holliday were, in April, 1883, bookkeeper and salesman, respectively, with Lang & Robinson, of No 2 South Street. They, by forgery and embezzlement, obtained seventeen thousand five hundred dollars and fled to Cuba. McLaughlin was instrumental in securing their arrest at Nuevitas, and went to Cuba and brought them back to be tried and convicted. For the gigantic scheme to get a cool million from the Elevated Railroads by forging tickets, McLaughlin arrested Joseph B. Cole, the planner of the affair, W. H. Pindar, the confederate; and A. C. Speth, the lithographer; Cole was convicted, Pindar was discharged, and Speth's case is pending.

FRANK COSGROVE, who dates from the time of the Hon. De Witt Clinton Wheeler, has done some splendid Detective work. He owes much to his matchless *aplomb* and good education. He was associated, in 1881, in the arrest of the Vicksburg murderer, Samuel Hawthorne, who received a sentence of ninety-nine years' imprisonment. In September, 1880, he captured and convicted John Stanford and William Chrystie, for burglary at the residence of A. T. Albro, at White Plains. In July, 1881, he ran down Antonio Stadt, who, at the residence of Colgate Hoyt, at Yonkers, obtained by burglary three thousand dollars' worth of silverware and other property, and sent him to State Prison for fifteen years. He also arrested his confederate, George Ewell, who received a sentence of ten years. Cosgrove gets a great many delicate cases, when a man who has a nice discrimination, in apparel is an acquisition, and not a few times has he mingled with the *crème de la crème* of upper-tendom while investigating matters that disturbed the peace of high-toned families.

WILLIAM E. FRINK is another of Inspector Byrnes' suave, well-mannered, handsome and stylishly attired officers. He went to the Detective Bureau in February, 1882, and very soon had Franklin J. Moses, ex-Governor of South Carolina, and the profligate and swindling son of a scrupulously honest jurist, in jail. The fellow had swindled hundreds of persons, but the complaint in this case was made by E. W. Crowell, of No. 195 Broadway. Moses was sent to the penitentiary for six months. A short time after, Frink run down Jacob Weil, who had embezzled three thousand dollars from Withers Brothers & Owens, No. 32 Bond Street. Weil was traced by the officer to Liverpool, and he was brought here and convicted. Richard Gerner, who swindled a letter carrier, Richard O'Connor, out of three thousand dollars, was arrested by Frink in May, 1882, and the money was disgorged. In June, 1883, he arrested Harry Moore alias Howard, for robbing a freight car of the Pennsylvania Railroad Company of ten thousand dollars' worth of silks, and recovered the property. Louis Wilkins, who had swindled many through the medium of messenger boys, was caught by Frink in September, 1883. In November, 1884, he arrested Walter Cortwright alias "Big Walter," a notorious shoplifter, for a robbery of feathers at R. M. Morton & Co.'s, at Eleventh Street and University Place, and on January 2, 1885, he captured Frank King and Patrick Hughes, who stole a jeweler's trunk from the baggage room of the Westcott Express Company's office at the Grand Central Depot. Frink recovered the jewelry, which was worth three thousand dollars.

CHARLES O'CONNOR was appointed a Detective in the Eleventh Precinct in November, 1871. His record is unexcelled. In 1872 he arrested Samuel Maloney, who threw red pepper in the eyes of William Feldman and stole four thousand dollars from him at Rivington and Mangin Streets. Maloney served ten years in prison for the offense. In July, 1876, Julius Azeroff, Jonas Goldsmith and Daniel Warner entered Jacob Fieber's residence, No. 712 East Sixth Street, and Warner knocked Fieber senseless, while his confederates rifled a trunk and stole six hundred dollars. O'Connor ferreted out the criminals, and they were duly convicted. In March, 1877, O'Connor arrested John Dailey, Francis McCormack, John Doherty and James Lynch for murdering Frank Reilly at Stanton and Goerck Streets. Dailey received a life sentence, and the others went to prison for four years. The same year he convicted Peter Delaney and George Lewis for stabbing William Pulver at Rivington and Lewis Streets, so that he had fifteen wounds, and robbing him. Each received heavy but well merited punishment. He enabled justice to settle an account with John Burns, Edward Harrison and Joseph Smith, who, early in 1878, entered the jewelry store of Jacob Ling, at No. 453 East Ninth Street, awed Mrs Ling, who was alone, by pointing a pistol at her, and robbed the place. In February, 1874, he caught Edward Gearing alias Goodrich alias Morris alias Goody, the "butcher cart" thief, who, with a confederate, robbed William R Church of

Convicts' Boat Going to the Island.

two thousand dollars at the One Hundred and Eleventh Street station of the Second Avenue Elevated Railroad. Gearing was sent to prison for twenty years.

GEORGE H DILKS, son of the veteran Inspector, became a Detective in March, 1872. Next year he made a very brilliant arrest. The notorious "Jimmy" Brady alias Oscar Peterson, was negotiating the sale of forty thousand dollars in stolen bonds, when Dilks and Detective Tully surprised him, and Brady fled. Dilks pursued him through Carmine, Bedford and Leroy Streets, and here fired at him, wounding him in the hip. Brady plunged into a window, and Dilks fired through the window again, wounding him in the hip. Brady was tugging at his pistol, but the hammer had caught in the lining of his pocket, and Dilks had time to get in the window and compel a surrender under the muzzle of his weapon. The bonds were found where Brady was trying to sell them. He was sent to Sing Sing for ten years, and is now serving a sentence of seventeen years and a half for a petty robbery of silk underclothing in a Broadway store, when he was drunk from a carouse which celebrated the division of forty thousand dollars, the proceeds of several bank robberies, and for the shooting at and wounding of Officer Paddock, of the Broadway Squad, who pursued him. Dilks was associated with Detective Haley in the arrest of "Peppermint Joe" and "Joe Butts," for the Charlestown robbery in 1877. This year Dilks arrested and convicted John Price alias James Monroe, for stealing five thousand dollars in bonds from a hair store in Washington Street, Boston; and in 1876 he ran to earth the scoundrelly and ferocious Italian confidence operator, Andrea Bressant, and his confederate, Pietro Valgoe, who had robbed a compatriot in Boston of one thousand nine hundred dollars. Going to Boston, Bressant, although handcuffed, leaped from a train going at full speed. He was not seriously injured, and was recaptured and landed in Boston. He also arrested the skilled trickster and diamond thief, Claude Burroughs, who, by dodging out of a room at the Grand Central Hotel, swindled John R. Greason & Co., the jewelers, out of gems worth four thousand six hundred dollars. Burroughs was sent to the Elmira Reformatory. In 1884, he, with Detective Sergeant Cosgrove, convicted Catherine Murray, the expert English thief, who had robbed Mrs. H. B. Hatch, of No. 531 Fifth Avenue, of three thousand dollars' worth of property; and with the same officer ended temporarily the career of Ralph Newton, who had embezzled seven thousand dollars from A. H. Wheeler & Co., No. 30 New Street. They caught him by a ruse. He was a musical amateur, and when they found that he would not be "in" at his lodgings, they personated minstrels, procured a violin, and soon enticed him out of his retirement.

GEORGE LANTHIER was appointed a Detective in July, 1879. He is, perhaps, the best dressed member of Inspector Byrnes' staff, and very frequently does duty in a "swallow tail." He is generally one of the favored ones who are selected to attend grand receptions and entertainments to look out for light fingered gentry. His record of arrests is a capital one. He, in February, 1880, captured Langdon W. Moore alias Charley Adams, for the burglary at the Warren Savings Bank, Boston, who is completing a term of sixteen years in the Massachusetts State Prison. That month he caught Ernestine Smith, who stole five thousand dollars' worth of diamonds at No. 54 West Fifty-sixth Street; and the same year brought to book John Anderson alias "Little Andy," for obtaining five thousand five hundred dollars' worth of jewelry by a burglary at a Third Avenue pawnbroker's. In December, 1880, he arrested and convicted the blackmailer, Jacob Isleton; and in March, 1881, ran down, at Denver Col., James Orr, who had embezzled sixty-five thousand dollars from Jackson S. Schultz.

EDGAR S. SLAUSON, a pupil of Richard King, became a Detective in October, 1882, and he is an efficient, quiet and painstaking member of the Detective force. A few days after he went to the Central Office he arrested Archibald Adams and William Johnson, for robbing the pawnbroker, Thomas Green, of No. 171 Bowery, of three thousand five hundred dollars by "ringing the changes" on the tickets. The prisoners were sent to the Elmira Reformatory. In August, 1883, he locked up John Jenning alias "Liverpool Jack," a professional safe blower, for a burglary at No. 29 Frankfort Street, and convicted him.

In July, 1884, he convicted Michael and Thomas Callahan and Carroll F. Richards, for stealing four trunks containing property worth three thousand five hundred dollars, from the office of Dodd's Express Co.

SILAS W. ROGERS was made a Detective in the Twenty-ninth Precinct in 1874, and is *au fait* in anything that concerns his duties. His early arrests show a long list of burglars, hotel thieves, and sneaks. In April, 1882, he arrested and convicted James Lee, the bogus Custom House officer, and the next month checked the career of James J. Courtney, the forger, who passed a check for three thousand three hundred and ten dollars and fifty cents on the Marine Bank. The same year he convicted Michael Martin, the East River National Bank forger. Next May he caught and convicted Timothy J. Gilmore, who forged on C. T. Gorham, the First Street flour merchant; and in June, 1884, sequestered Michael Koshofski, who passed worthless checks on Mitchell, Vance & Co. and R. H. Macy & Co. Last December he aided in the capture of "Tom" Connors, William R. Hibone and John McKeon, the King's County Penitentiary burglars.

GEORGE W. McCLUSKY was made a Detective in October, 1883, and two months later arrested David Lowenthal alias "Sheeny Dave," for stealing a diamond bracelet at the jewelry store of Thomas Kirkpatrick & Co., Twenty-second Street and Broadway. He was put under bail, and left his bondsman in the lurch. In January, 1884, he arrested and convicted Thomas P. Ryan alias "Tim Simon," for robbing a man of a gold watch in Madison Square Garden; and next month he captured and convicted the professional bill dropper, Robert Hawthorne alias Hartshorn, James McGuire alias Jesse James, and Patrick McGrath alias "Blind Patsey," for robbing an Italian of six hundred dollars in Crosby Street.

ALBERTIS WOOD was made a Detective in 1881, and has done his full share of duty. His principal arrests are: April, 1882, John Fogarty, burglar, sentenced to two years; October 3, 1882, George Morton, burglar, one year; October 6, John McMahon, grand larceny, five years; March, 1883, Charles Raymond, grand larceny, five years, June, 1884, George Miller, grand larceny, three years and a half; and January, 1885, Charles H. Webb, forgery, one year.

THOMAS DOYLE was appointed a Detective in the First Precinct in April, 1864. His career has been an honorable and useful one. He aided, in July, 1875, in arresting John H. Short for the burglary at Jacob Vanderbilt's, on Staten Island, and in February, 1871, sent G. W. Lambert to Sing Sing for receiving stolen goods. He aided in the arrest of Edward J. Courtney for the three thousand three hundred dollar forgery on the Marine Bank in 1882, and in November of that year convicted Michael Martin for a forgery on the East River Bank. In February, 1884, he arrested and convicted the forger, Timothy Gilmore, who had done a rushing business in small checks.

DENNIS J. FOGARTY was made a Ward Detective in the Fifth Precinct in 1877, and has had an honorable and busy career. He shares his credit with his partner, Martin Handy, who was made a Detective in the Eighteenth Precinct in 1876. In August, 1877, Fogarty and Handy arrested the sneak thief, Daniel Brown alias French Louis, for breaking into Scott Brothers' store, 120

White Street, and convicted him. In November, 1878, they captured Francisco De Jeane, who murdered William Pease in York Street, and was sentenced for life. In November, 1877, they ran down Edward Edgar alias E. E. Hemingway, who, with others, cut into Patterson & Towers' bonded warehouse. They were surprised by a watchman when they had thirty thousand dollars' worth of silk prepared for removal. In January, 1885, they arrested and convicted the Italian confidence operators, Giovanni Rocco and Adolfo Pardinni, who swindled Felix Luigi out of one thousand six hundred dollars, part of which was recovered.

CHARLES KUSH went to the Central Office in June, 1881, and has done the best of quiet and thorough service. Among his many arrests are: April, 1882, "Red" Fogarty, burglary, sentenced to two years; December, 1882, John McMahon, grand larceny, sentenced to five years; March, 1883, Charles Raymond, grand larceny, sentenced to five years; February, 1884, "Fred" Herbert, blackmailing, sentenced to two years.

JAMES F VALLELY is the latest addition to the Chief Detective's staff. If he continues to do as well as he did in the Twentieth Precinct, where he was appointed Ward Detective in October, 1883, he will make his mark. His chief arrests are. November, 1883, Thomas Porter, the robber of Jessie Waldron at No 407 East Seventy-eighth Street, sent to prison for twenty years; March, 1884, William Messner, arson, sent to prison for two and a half years; October, 1883, William McKenna alias Dick Duffy, grand larceny, sentenced to five years; January, 1885, Patrick Hughes alias Frank King, for stealing a jeweler's trunk at the Grand Central Depot, sent to prison for six and a half years.

THE DETECTIVE OFFICERS.—With the Detective Sergeants are ten Patrol men, classed as Detective officers, who, under Inspector Byrnes' system, have more than a fair chance of becoming Detective Sergeants. They are James R. Kelsey, Edward H Doyle, Thomas Ferris, Charles A Hanley, John Killilea, John L. Langon, James E. Liston, Stephen O'Brien, Joseph C. Gehegan and Joseph D. Wooldridge. Kelsey was graduated in the Tenth Precinct, and has been a valuable aid in many cases. Doyle and Langon are partners, and have done work that has advanced them in the estimation of the Chief. Thomas Ferris is an old Detective, having been appointed in 1875. In 1877 he arrested Edward Dorsey, who committed a murder in Frederick County, Md, and was executed. Hanley was one of the best officers in the Fifteenth Precinct before he was promoted to the Central Office. His partner, Killilea, has an equally enviable reputation. Liston, two days after last Christmas Day, ferreted out the bogus messenger boys, John Cunningham and John Burns, who had reaped a holiday harvest out of Wall Street brokers at the expense of the legitimate messengers of the various companies. O'Brien has been under Inspector Byrnes nine months, and promises well. Gehegan, in December last, run down Francisco Damato, for murder in New Haven, who was sentenced to ten years imprisonment. Wooldridge is a chip of the old block. His father was a famous Central Office Detective.

JACOB VON GERICHTEN may be called a young veteran. He has done fifteen years of excellent service, first in the Eighth Ward, and then in the Central

Office Detective Bureau, and he is now in Europe on official business. He is side partner to Philip Reilly. Von Gerichten is a linguist, and has traveled many thousands of miles in this country and in Europe on Police business. He was associated with Detective Sergeant Reilly in the following cases February, 1882, P K. Post, Alexander Ross, forgery, sent to prison for ten years each; July, 1882, Jacob Weil, forgery, extradited from England, sent to prison for five years, Edward Kelly, straw bondsman, sent to prison for five years in October, 1882; Herman David, May, 1883, robbery, sent to State Prison for five years

JOHN HEARD and THOMAS MURRAY have not been long at Police Headquarters, but they promise to make as good a reputation as any under the Chief Detective. Heard distinguished himself in August, 1883, by arresting the notorious "Mart" Allen, John Moore, Edward Thomas and Walter Allen, "Mart's" son, for flat robberies in Harlem. "Mart" trained his offspring to be a thief, and in these robberies, which were many and important, sent him ahead to ring bells and reconnoitre "Mart" got ten years, Moore five years, and Thomas three years Young Allen was discharged

THOMAS F. ADAMS, an old and skilled officer, has been incapacitated by ill health from doing very active duty for several years He is now in New Orleans doing Special Detective duty for the management of the Exposition He invented the mechanical part of the present Rogues' Gallery, and has arranged and classified it.

CHAPTER XX.

POLICE CENTRAL OFFICE.

The Centre of a System which affords Police Protection to the City. —Headquarters of the Police Department.—Telegraph Office; Superintendent Crowley.—Third Precinct; Captain Gastlin.—The Harbor Police —Superintendent's Chief Clerk Hopcroft —Bureau of Inquiry for Missing People —Commissioner French —Commissioner Fitz John Porter —Commissioner Matthews —Lost Children —Chief Clerk Kipp —Property Clerk's Office.—The Sanitary Company —Tenement House Squad

POLICE HEADQUARTERS, at No 300 Mulberry Street, is a solid, massive structure, extending back to Mott Street. Here are centred the clerical force of the Department, the offices of the Superintendent, First Inspection District, Detective Department, Property Clerk, the headquarters of the Third Precinct (formerly Steamboat Squad), Telegraph Bureau, Matron Webb's rooms for lost children, the Election Bureau, and several other offices of minor importance. The Police Commissioners also have their offices here, and, altogether, it is the most important building of its kind in America. Police Headquarters attracts a great many visitors. Its portals open wide to receive alike the beggar and the merchant prince, the swindler and the philanthropist, the journalist and the politician; all meet and mingle here in true democratic fashion; while the great wheels of the visible machinery of the law keep revolving in their tireless course. This is the heart and centre of the elaborate system which affords Police protection to a great city. The entire Police force consists of two thousand eight hundred and eighty-nine men, sub-divided, according to rank, as follows· one Superintendent, four Inspectors, thirty-six Captains,

Police Central Office, 300 Mulberry Street.

OUR POLICE PROTECTORS.

forty Detective Sergeants, one hundred and fifty-two Sergeants, eight Acting Sergeants, one hundred and seventy-eight Roundsmen, two thousand three hundred and seventy-four Patrolmen, and eighty Doormen. There are, in addition, eighteen Surgeons

TELEGRAPH OFFICE.—In the basement, Rooms 1 and 2 are occupied by the telegraph office. The Superintendent of this Bureau is Mr. James Crowley, a most competent official, who has held his present important position for over twenty-five years. The operators are: Michael R. Brennan, George F. Stevens, Charles Wylie, Richard Battin, Robert D Ferguson William S Fraser, lineman, Francis H Haggerty, battery boy

The importance of the Police telegraph cannot be overestimated. It is acknowledged to be the right arm of the service Without it the Police would be powerless to cope with crime and criminals. What a compass and rudder are to a ship the telegraph is to the Police Department And this branch of the Police system is fortunate in having at its head a man of tried capacity and integrity The Superintendent, seated at his desk at Police Headquarters, knows almost in an instant what is taking place at the furthest Police point of the city He is in constant communication with his subordinate officers, and through him, orders are almost instantaneously transmitted to every Police commandant in the city, and through them to the two thousand eight hundred members of the force

Police Telegraph Office

This Bureau, during the riot week, materially assisted in saving the city from being sacked and burned. The staff then consisted of the present Superintendent, James Crowley; Eldred Polhamus, Deputy Superintendent; Charles L Chapin, John A K. Duvall and James A Lucas, Operators

There were then thirty-two telegraphic stations in the city, all centralizing at Police Headquarters, which were divided into five sections—the North, East, South, West and Central

The week after the riots the Police Commissioners issued an address to the force, in which reference was made to the efficient services of the telegraph corps, as follows

"Mr. Crowley, the Superintendent of the Police Telegraph, and the attaches of his Department, by untiring and sleepless vigilance in transmitting information by telegraph unceasingly through more than ten days and nights, have more than sustained the high reputation they have always possessed."

The office is connected by wire with the various station houses, the Fire Department, hospitals, Elevated Railroad stations, the river fronts and islands, the arsenals and armories, etc.

THIRD PRECINCT.—Rooms 3 and 4, in the basement, are occupied by the new Third Precinct Station (formerly the Steamboat Squad). This is in charge of Captain George W. Gastlin. The old Steamboat Squad was organized on the ninth of June, 1876, and Captain Gastlin, who was then Sergeant in the Tenth Precinct, assigned to the command. The Steamboat Squad insures very complete protection to the river front, wharves and piers, and gives more direct and

Superintendent Crowley.

efficient protection to travelers. On December 15, 1876, the command was divided into two squads, the Eastern and Western Steamboat Squads, the former doing duty in the First Inspection District, the latter in the Second Inspection District.

The Third Precinct is bounded on the west side of New York by low water mark on the North River, Fourteenth Street, the centre line of Thirteenth Avenue, the centre line of Eleventh Street, and the west car track in West Street, to Battery Place and the south side of Pier 1. On the east side of the city it is bounded by low water mark in the East River, Gouverneur Slip, and the east car track, to the Barge office. It has one central station at Police Headquarters, and two sub-stations, one in the United States Barge office and one in the building of the Albany Day Line of steamers, at Pier No. 39, North River. Its officers are. Sergeant Watson Vreedenburgh, who became a Policeman in 1865, was made Roundsman in 1867, and was promoted in September, 1870; Sergeant John J Taylor, who joined the force in May, 1864, was made Roundsman three years later, and gained rank in November 1869; and Sergeant Charles H. Reinisch, whose dates are: Patrolman, August, 1868; Roundsman, July, 1876, and Sergeant, September, 1877. This precinct is commanded by Captain George W. Gastlin

The command was organized in June, 1876, by Commissioner Joel B Erhardt, and Roundsman (now Sergeant) James K. Fuller, first commanded it Sergeant (now Captain) Gastlin, succeeded him. The force was known as the Eastern and Western Steamboat Squads at one time, then it was amalgamated into the Steamboat Squad, and in January, 1885, the precinct scheme, devised by Chief Clerk Kipp, went into force.

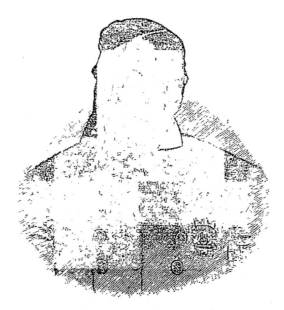

Captain George W Gastlin

CAPTAIN GEORGE W GASTLIN, of the Steamboat Squad, has done more than any other officer to free the river front from thieves and bunco men. At the time of the formation of the Squad the wharves along the river were in the charge of rowdies of all descriptions. Hundreds of confidence operators and swindlers of every description had, up to the time of his appointment, preyed on unsuspecting emigrants and people who, by the hardest kind of labor and pinching economy, had amassed a little money and wished to return to the old country

When the Squad was first organized there were two Italian swindlers who passed themselves off as priests, and in this manner won the confidence of several emigrants. One morning Captain Gastlin produced these rascals at the Tombs. Their names were Vivaldo Michele and Lorenzo Mazin. A short time before their arrest these two men had met an Italian at Bowling Green who was going to Europe. Mazin, "the priest," got into conversation with his unsophisticated countryman, whom he told that he was going to Italy, and required an interpreter, Mazin at the same time showed Mono a satchel which he said contained thousands of dollars Mono agreed to take the situation of interpreter, and gave his money to the priest for safe keeping The clerical imposter then sent Mono for some fine cigars, but when he returned with the cigars "the priest" had vanished along with his confrere Michele Both were sent to State Prison

John Goss, a well-known confidence operator, who used to lie in wait for the Troy boats and swindle the passengers, was the next victim of the Captain's vigilance.

Aleck Anderson alias W Odell, met a grey-haired old gentleman named Samuel Fraud, of Blackstone, Mass, on board the Newport boat, and told him that he (Anderson) had to pay the freight on some goods which had just come on board, and would Mr. Fraud oblige him with the loan of one hundred dollars against a gold check for eight hundred dollars on Messrs Reilly & May. Of course the check was worthless

Arresting Mutineers

Anderson was arrested by Captain Gastlin, taken before Justice Wheeler at the Tombs, convicted, and sent to State Prison

A very clever piece of Police work was the arrest of Walter Williams alias Roberts alias Slip Corcoran, and William Foster alias Fitzgerald These two sharks had operated on a poor Irishman who was returning by a White Star steamer to take out his mother from the old country They had taken every penny he had from him — one hundred and fifty pounds sterling — and decamped. Captain Gastlin just then arrived on the scene In order to avoid being recognized as an officer, he told the unfortunate victim that he would lose his passage if he did not get on board at once With the assistance of a Police man, Captain Gastlin hustled the man down on board the steamer and put him down among the steerage passengers. A short time afterwards Captain Gastlin removed the man from the steamer to Castle Garden This ruse completely threw the confidence men off their guard—of course, there would be no complainant against them, now that Henry had sailed for Ireland. Captain Gastlin, a week afterwards, captured the swindlers, and great was their surprise when Henry was produced in court as a witness against them. The prisoners were sent to State Prison.

John Leonard, a passenger by the steamship Pennsylvania from Liverpool, robbed several of his fellow-travelers of sums varying from three to eighty-five pounds sterling. One of the passengers recognized a four-penny bit which was found on Leonard's person, and this was really the only thing by which the thefts could be fastened on him. Captain Gastlin worked up the case. Leonard was arrested and sent to State Prison.

Hilza Von Zaren alias Le Marquis O'Neill de Lassantas, was employed as a waiter in the summer at Newport. In the evening he used to dress as a woman, and became the rage among the young bloods spending the season at Newport. After the Newport season closed, he came to New York, where he was employed at a house on Fifth Avenue as a waiter. He plundered the house and fled. He was afterwards employed in a West Forty-eighth Street house,

Boarding a Mutinous Vessel.

which he also plundered. His arrest in New York, by Captain Gastlin, created a great sensation and scandal. He was sent to Sing Sing.

Captain Gastlin, who is the son of a Policeman is, in a double sense, a born Policeman.

The Special Duty Officers of this precinct are: Eubo Hey, Janus Mallen, William Thomas, and R. J. Vail on the North River, and E. Grady and H. E. Van Ranst on the East River; and Nathan Sanford detailed to the Corporation Attorney's office. There are forty-one day posts on the North River, and nineteen day posts on the East River, and nine night posts on the North River, and nine night posts on the East River. The effective force is about ninty-four Patrolmen and six Roundsmen.

The day Posts on the North River are: Post 1, new Pier 1 to old Pier 1,

Post 2, Pier 2 to Pier 3; Post 3, Pier 4 to half of Pier 5; Post 4, Pier 5 to half of Pier 6, Post 5, Pier 6 to Pier 7; Post 6, half of Pier 7 to Pier 8, Post 7, Pier 9 to Pier 10; Post 8, Pier 11 to Pier 12; Post 9, Pier 12 to Pier 14; Post 10, Pier 14 to Pier 16; Post 11, Pier 18 to Pier 19; Post 12, Pier 20 to Pier 21, Post 13, Pier 22 to Pier 23, Post 14, Pier 26, Post 15, Pier 27; Post 16, Pier 28; Post 17, Pier 29, Post 18, Pier 30 to Pier 32; Post 19, Pier 33; Post 20, Pier 34 to Pier 35; Post 21, Pier 36; Post 22, Pier 37; Post 23, Pier 38 to Pier 38½; Post 24, Pier 39; Post 25, Pier 40; Post 26, Pier 41, Post 27, Pier 41½ to Pier 45; Post 28, Pier 43; Post 29, Pier 44 to half of Pier 45; Post 30, Pier 45 to Pier 46; Post 31, Pier 47; Post 32, Pier 48; Post 33, Pier 50; Post 34, Pier 50½ to Pier 51; Post 35, Pier 52; Post 36, Pier 53 to Pier 54, Post 37, West Tenth Street to Perry Street; Post 38, Perry Street to Horatio Street; Post 39, Horatio Street to West Fourteenth Street; Posts 40 and 41, West Washington Market.

Night Posts, North River: Post 1, Pier 1 to Liberty Street ferry, Post 2, Liberty Street ferry to Pier 23; Post 3, Pier 23 to Pier 29; Post 4, Pier 29 to Pier 36; Post 5, Pier 36 to Desbrosses Street ferry, Post 6, Desbrosses Street ferry to Pier 44; Post 7, Pier 44 to Pier 53, Post 8, Pier 53 to Perry Street; Post 9, Perry Street to West Fourteenth Street

Day Posts, East River Post 1, Pier 2 to Pier 6, Post 2, Pier 6 to Pier 9; Post 3, Pier 9 to Pier 15, Post 4, Pier 16 to Pier 17; Post 5, Pier 17 to Pier 19; Post 6, Pier 20 to Pier 21; Post 7, Pier 22 to Pier 23; Post 8, Pier 24, Post 9, Piers 25 and 25½; Post 10, Pier 27 to Pier 29; Post 11, Pier 33 to Pier 34; Post 12, Piers 35 and 35½, Post 13, Piers 36 and 37; Post 14, Piers 38 and 39; Post 15, Pier 40 to Pier 43, Post 16, Pier 44 to Pier 46; Post 17, Pier 46 to Pier 49; Post 18, Pier 49 to Pier 53, Post 19, Barge Office

Night Posts, East River. Post 1, Staten Island ferry to Pier 6; Post 2, Pier 6 to Pier 12, Post 3, Pier 12 to Pier 18; Post 4, Pier 18 to Pier 23, Post 5, Pier 23 to Pier 29; Post 6, Pier 29 to James Street ferry; Post 7, James Street ferry to Pier 36, Post 8, Pier 36 to Pier 45; Post 9, Pier 45 to Pier 52.

This precinct has a peculiar system. One section goes on day duty at seven A. M, and is relieved at six P. M by a section which is relieved at midnight by a section which remains on duty until seven A M The day duty men are day duty men all the time The night duty men change off every Sunday, that is to say, those who have been doing duty from midnight to seven A. M take the place of those who have been doing duty from six P. M to midnight.

Captain Gastlin has vast commercial interests and the traveling public to guard Hitherto he looked simply after the river fronts during the day time Now he takes care of nearly every pier and ferry day and night. The principal piers and ferries are

North River. Quebec Steamship Company, Anchor Line, White Star Line, Citizens' Troy Line, Delaware, Lackawanna and Western Railroad piers, Transatlantic Company, Cunard Line, National Line, Guion Line, Inman Line, Ocean Steamship Company, State Line, Pacific Mail Steamship Company, Fort Lee boats, People's Line to Albany, Norwich Line, Albany Day Line, Merchants' Line, Pennsylvania Railroad, Star, Union, and Empire Freight Lines, Old Dominion Line, Morgan Line, Hudson River boats, Stonington Line, Erie Railroad,

Desbrosses Street Ferry, Pavonia Ferry, Providence Line, Fall River Line, Clyde's Charleston Line, New York Central and Hudson River Railroad, Barclay Street Ferry, Jersey City Ferry, Mediterranean boats, New Haven Transportation Company, Pennsylvania Railroad, Philadelphia and Reading Railroad, Metropolitan Line, Cromwell Line, Long Branch boats, Baltimore Transportation Company, New York, Havana and Mexico Steamers, Lehigh Valley Railroad, Iron Steamboat Company, and Communipaw Ferry.

East River: Staten Island Ferry, North Shore Ferry, Bay Ridge route, Governor's Island Ferry, South Ferry, Hamilton Ferry, New York Central and Hudson River Railroad Freight Pier, Electro Line, Ward's Havana Line, Morgan's Bristol Line, San Francisco Packets, Mallory's Texas Line, Wall Street Ferry, Fulton Ferry, Hartford and Glen Cove boats, New Haven Line, Sag Harbor and Greenport boats, Clyde Line, Bridgeport boats, Central Vermont Railroad, Long Island Railroad, Catharine Street Ferry, Portland steamers, New Bedford propellers, Mediterranean steamers, New York, New Haven and Hartford Railroad, Hunter's Point Ferry, and Roosevelt Street Ferry.

Superintendent Murray's Room

One of the most notable members of the Steamboat Squad is Philip C. Bleil whose services as a saviour of human life have given him a world-wide reputation, and who has been the recipient of a dozen medals from different humane societies in recognition of his self-sacrifice and bravery.

Long before Bleil became a member of the Steamboat Police his coolness and courage in a desperate emergency had won him a reputation. He rescued more than a score of fellow-beings from a watery death. Many of these were cases of accident, but the majority belonged to the class of unfortunate women who seek surcease for their sorrow in the cold waters of the river

Following is a list of work done by the members of the Third Precinct Police for the month of January, 1885.

Seven persons rescued from drowning after six P. M.

Two persons found drowned.

Fourteen accidents occurring to men employed on the piers, and cared for by the Police.

Three arrests for felonious assault and battery.

Three arrests for petit larceny.

One arrest for grand larceny.

Two men, brought to this city dead, sent to Morgue.

One arrest for cruelty to animals.

One arrest for mutiny.

Twenty-six arrests for intoxication, assault and battery, and small crimes.

Two boys arrested for truancy, and restored to parents from other cities.

One large fire discovered by men from Third Precinct, and five lives saved

One fire on East River.

Property taken from prisoners, found and taken from thieves, and restored to owners, two thousand one hundred and thirty-five dollars and eighty-two cents.

Honorable mention was made by the Board of Police of the meritorious conduct of Rounds-

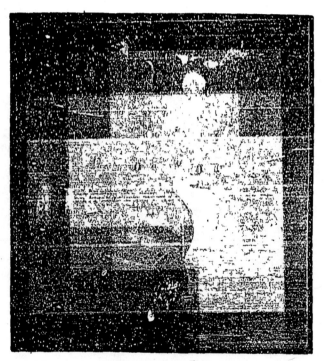
Watching for River Thieves.

man Thos Riley and Patrolman Timothy Crogan for saving five lives at the burning of the steamboat St John, January, 1885

Previous to the organization of the Steamboat Squad another body of men representing the law was in existence, and still remains an efficient co-adjutor of the Steamboat Squad in repressing crime and bringing violators of the law to justice

THE HARBOR POLICE.—At first the force consisted of but a few men, whose duty it was to patrol the river front (then much less in extent than at present) in rowboats. As the commerce of the port increased, and the wharves and piers extended northward, it was found that more rapid means of transportation were necessary, and a small steamboat, which was named the "Seneca," was built for the especial service required. This boat caught fire in some unknown manner about four years ago, and was totally destroyed. So furious and rapid was the progress of the flames that it was found impossible to save the records of the force, which extended over a period of many years, and were, consequently, of much interest and value

A new boat was built immediately, and christened the "Patrol." When not actively engaged, it lies at the foot of Third Street, East River, and serves as the Headquarters of the River Police

The duties of the Harbor Police are similar to those of the Steamboat Squad, with the exception that the services performed by the former are entirely upon the water The Police boat is called into requisition whenever a fire breaks out upon the wharves or amongst the shipping, or in any of the

Steamboat "Patrol."

streets lying adjacent to the water front The crew are also called upon to quell mutinies, to arrest quarrelsome or insubordinate sailors, and preserve order generally amongst the vessels lying in the harbor

The Harbor Police force was brought into existence on the fifteenth of February, 1858, but the service boats were not ready for use until the third of March following. the men being employed in the meantime doing patrol duty along the wharves The river was so full of ice that it was impossible to use the boats with safety until the fifteenth of March The number of arrests for actual crime was at first small, yet the services rendered the shipping interests, intercepting smuggled goods, etc , from the start proved the great utility of the scheme. The boats were directed to overhaul and examine all boats found on the rivers after night, and in numerous instances the observance of this order proved useful. The Harbor Police, in a very short time, became an indispensable auxiliary to the land force. The Harbor Police (Twenty-fourth Precinct) was then in command of Captain A. J. Gilson

The steamboat and boat's crew are under the command of the Boat Captain, who is responsible for the navigation, management, safe keeping, condition, and the perfect and complete cleaning of the steamboat, engine, boiler, fire-pump and hose, crew's quarters, tackle, apparel, and furniture, and also for the action and conduct of the boat's crew.

George Hopcroft.

The boat's crew, in addition to the Boat Captain, is made up as follows, to wit.

    1 Pilot, at a compensation at the rate of $100 per month
    1 Engineer,   "   "   "   100   "
    1 Assistant Engineer,   "   "   85   "
    2 Firemen,   "   "   "   65   "
    3 Deckmen,   "   "   "   60   "

The Boat Captain is authorized to employ the pilot, engineers, deckmen, and firemen, subject to the approval of the Board of Police

CAPTAIN E O SMITH, formerly of the Twenty-eighth Precinct, succeeded Captain Schultz in the command of the Harbor Police.

Room 4 is Superintendent Walling's office

MR. GEORGE HOPCROFT, Chief Clerk to the Superintendent, has his office in an adjoining room Mr Hopcroft became attached to Police Headquarters in 1860 On May 1 of the following year he was made a Policeman, and attached to Superintendent Kennedy's office as Chief Clerk, a position which he has worthily filled under five successive Superintendents, namely: Jourdan, Kelso, Matsell, Walling and Murray.

SERGEANT NICHOLAS BROOKS' office is in the same apartment as Mr. Hopcroft's. Sergeant Brooks is in charge of the Bureau of Inquiry for Missing People. He was appointed a Patrolman May 15, 1867, and assigned to the Thirteenth Precinct. He was in the Orange riot of 1871. On November 29, 1878, he was promoted to the rank of Sergeant. His assistant is Roundsman Joseph A Saul.

To those who are conversant with the working of this Bureau, with the tales of misery and despair that are daily reported, it becomes a matter of the greatest surprise how such things can be, and only overcome us like a summer cloud. The

Sergeant Nicholas Brooks

records of the books kept by Sergeant Brooks contain food and reflection for the moralist and the dramatist, contain material for tragedies deeper than Eschylus ever wrote But in the majority of instances, family pride, or a regard for the good name of the lost one, or a feeling prompted by hope that in the course of time he or she may "turn up" all right, seals the lips of afflicted affection. However, the present writer, not being a moralist or a dramatist, but a plain reporter of unvarnished facts, must not indulge in such speculative philosophy It is enough to say that we are dealing strictly with facts, and facts, too, that are stranger than the strangest fiction

Sergeant Brooks estimates that on an average six hundred persons are reported as missing at Police Headquarters every year Of this number it is safe to say that fully four hundred either voluntarily return to their homes, or are accounted for in some other manner. A certain percentage of the remainder, for reasons best known to themselves, bury themselves forever beyond the reach or knowledge of kith and kin, while the rest receive sepulture in unknown graves. The morgue gathers up the mutilated and unrecognizable forms of some of these. Whether they are the victims of foul play, had died by their own hand or from accidental causes, except in rare cases, there is no means of determining. Many of the bodies found floating with the tide are, from time to time, identified by some peculiar mark, the texture of the garments, or contents of the pockets, which, but for these, the bodies would be placed among the unknown and pauper dead in Potter's Field. But the clearing up of this mystery in a great many instances only serves to create another and a more inscrutable mystery, by provoking the inquiry how such a one came by such a death. But this is a secret closely guarded by lips sealed in death, and consequently never to be revealed. Various and sufficient reasons are assigned for a large class of cases of mysterious disappearances. Generally domestic troubles, mental alienation, financial difficulties, blighted affections, or dissipated habits, are at the bottom of it all. Young persons, too, of both sexes, who are dissatisfied with parental restraints, run away from home, and are numbered among the lost and missing. The following comparative statement of the ages of this shadowy six hundred has been gleaned

Bureau of Inquiry

from an official source: between fourteen and twenty years, one hundred; between twenty and thirty years, two hundred; between thirty and forty years, one hundred; between forty and fifty years, one hundred; fifty years and upwards, one hundred.

When a missing person is reported at Police Headquarters, the method or routine adopted is this

The name and general description of the missing one are telegraphed from Police Headquarters to the several Police stations, notifying members of the force to institute a search for the person named and described in the dispatch This is called a general alarm The books containing the records of arrests and accidents are scrutinized, a slip containing a history of the case is given to the press reporters stationed at Police Headquarters, and they supply their papers with the news. If the case is deemed of sufficient importance, that is, if there are suspicions of foul play, or that the missing one has absconded, the matter is placed in the hands of the Detective office

The Superintendent of Police also sends printed forms, with a list of the names of missing persons, to each of the Captains, instructing them to "ascertain whether the following named persons, reported as missing, have returned home or been heard from." This memorandum is made monthly, and is to be returned, with a report made opposite each name.

A description of the missing person is also furnished to the Superintendent of the Morgue

In Rooms 5 and 6 are located the Detective offices.

Architect NATHANIEL D. BUSH has his office in a room adjoining. He has been Architect to the Department since 1862. He built, reconstructed or repaired the north end of Police Headquarters, and the First, Fourth, Eighth, Ninth, Tenth, Eleventh, Twelfth, Fourteenth, Sixteenth, Twentieth, Twenty-first,

Architect Nathaniel D Bush

Twenty-third, Twenty-fifth ("Broadway Squad,") Twenty-seventh, Twenty ninth, Thirtieth, Thirty-first, Thirty-second, and Thirty-third Precinct Station Houses, as they now stand, and he is now engaged on plans for the new Twenty-eighth Precinct Station House   He is nothing if not thorough

At the time that Mr. Bush came into the Department as architect, in 1863, he found the Police station houses in a very crude condition   But little had been done in the line of "modern improvements," and they had been run up, so to speak, to meet pressing emergencies, and without much, if any, regard for the comfort of the men, or the sanitary or architectural advantage of the houses. Mr Bush went to work at once with characteristic energy, and in a few years our station houses began to put on very different appearances. The old ones were repaired and remodeled, and new ones designed; and thus the work went on, until to-day these station houses are models for all others over the United States. Mr. Bush, in his day, designed and built all the new station houses, and rebuilt the old ones. Some of the best specimens of his work are illustrated in this book, for instance, the First Precinct, Thirty-second Precinct, Fourteenth Precinct, Sixth Precinct, Twenty-ninth Precinct, Twelfth Precinct, etc., etc.

JAMES MATTHEWS was appointed Police Commissioner March 11, 1881, to succeed General William F. Smith, resigned.

James Matthews.

On May 1, 1882, he was re-appointed for a full term, that being the date when General Smith's term expired. General Smith's resignation gave Mayor Grace an opportunity to appoint his successor without confirmation by the Board of Aldermen. General Smith was originally appointed Police Commissioner by Mayor Wickham, May 1, 1875. He was removed by Mayor Cooper and Governor Robinson, August 5, 1879, under charges, and James E. Morrison was appointed by Mayor Cooper to succeed him. Mr. Morrison resigned November 24, 1879, and John R. Voorhis was made his successor. In the meantime General Smith appealed to the courts for reinstatement, and, o.. ,' tenth of June, 1880, his appeal was granted by the Supreme Court, thus oustı.. Mr. Voorhis Mr. Matthews was, therefore, the fourth man who had held a Police Commissionership during a single term. Resigned May 9, 1885

Commissioner STEPHEN B. FRENCH, President of the Police Board, has ni offices in Rooms 3 and 4.

The following interesting sketch of Commissioner Stephen B. French i taken from a publication, the "History of Suffolk County"

"STEPHEN B. FRENCH was born in the town of Riverhead, Suffolk County, N. Y, January 16, 1829. His father, Peter French, was born in Montreal. Ca... ada, and was of French Huguenot descent. His mother was a descendant of one of the original Dutch families who first settled in Orange County, N. Y.

"The parents of S B French removed in 1831 from Riverhead to Sag Harbor, where, until his thirteenth year, he attended school. He then entered the office of Captain John Budd, who was actively engaged in the whaling business, and with whom he remained some eighteen months Afterwards he entered the employ of Thomas Brown, a very energetic merchant, who pursued the like business

"The bewitching desire to sail on the sea impelled him to ship for a whaling voyage, which continued three years. On this voyage he visited Brazil, Chili, the Sandwich Islands, and many other islands of the South Pacific. Returning home in June, 1847, in the ship "Aeasta," of Sag Harbor, he had resolved to follow whaling as the business of his life. His father died while he was on this voyage. An elder brother was following the sea. The urgent entreaties of his mother, and his reverence for her, constrained him to remain at home and engage in mercantile pursuits

Within eighteen months came the startling news of the gold findings in California. On the eighth of February, 1849, Mr. French sailed in the ship "Sabina," in a company of ninety, from Sag Harbor, bound for San Francisco Rounding Cape Horn, they reached that port August 8, 1849. Then commenced a life full of adventure, arduous and changing fortune : working on Denisor's exchange, ascending to the mines in a whaleboat, digging for gold, returning to San Francisco and keeping a hotel there, running a vessel thence to the Sandwich Islands, projecting an express to the northern mines, starting a store in Marysville, making and losing in five years two or three moderate fortunes He sailed for the Sandwich Islands, and found there, as shipmaster, his brother, whom he had not seen for eight years; and returned home in the same ship, reaching Sag Harbor in June, 1854.

As might be anticipated, the visit home strangely lengthened out from week to week, until his marriage with a young lady, pure, beautiful, true and accomplished, whom the angel of death early summoned to the land of the blessed During these years Mr. French was engaged in mercantile life as one of the firm of H. & S. B. French

After the death of his wife, in 1865, he sought to forget his grief by interesting himself in politics and public affairs. He had been a Whig, and always afterwards a Republican. In 1868, on the resignation of Joseph H. Goldsmith,

as treasurer of Suffolk County, he was appointed to fill the position thus vacated. He was elected to this office in November, 1869, and re-elected in 1872, running hundreds ahead of his ticket. In 1874, as a candidate for Congress, he was defeated, although carrying the district outside of the vote in Long Island City In 1875, as a candidate for County Treasurer, he was carried down, in the overwhelming defeat of the Republican party, by the meagre majority of twelve votes, running nearly six hundred ahead of his ticket. In February, 1876, he was appointed Appraiser at the Port of New York by President Grant He removed to New York in March, 1877; was appointed Police Commissioner of that city in May, 1879, was elected President of the Board in the year following, and still holds the position.

Trained in the hard school of adversity, and subjected to conditions fluctuating and varied, tried in the perils of sea and land, on the shores of the Pacific and Atlantic coasts, few men have gained the large experience in a long lifetime which has been crowded into the few years of the early life of this man Mr French has great rapidity of perception, strong powers of concentration, large capacity of endurance, and almost intuitive knowledge of the material and immaterial facts of a case He has extraordinary executive capacity, is well versed in human nature, with rare tact to adapt himself to changing circumstances in human affairs He never forgets a favor or forsakes a friend. His sympathies are with the masses of mankind and their aspirations for freedom, education and mental culture, his character is positive; his convictions are decided, his action is prompt and resolute, and sometimes impulsive; his great generosity and kind heart are best known to his intimate friends.

He is short in stature, well knit in frame, athletic in physical development. The dark, luminous eyes, that gleam under a capacious forehead, tell of the thought, penetration, energy and daring he is so well known to possess There is great magnetism to his friends in his very presence, with something like unconscious defiance to foes His positiveness is as attractive to the one as repellant to the other. As an organizer, his capacity to master a multiplicity of details, to judge of men as agents to execute or obstruct, his tenacity of purpose, powers of endurance and clearness of conception, conjoin to fit him admirably for the position he now occupies as chief of the Commissioners of Police in the empire city of this continent, and as a power in any political party to which he may belong."

The term for which Mr. Henry Smith was appointed a Police Commissioner expired on the first day of May, 1877; he died before the expiration of that time, and Mr. Joel B Erhardt was appointed to fill the vacancy thus created. Had Mr. Smith lived, his term of office would have expired on the first day of May, 1877. Under the provisions of Section 25, Chapter 335, Laws of 1873, the successor of Mr Smith or of Mr. Erhardt was entitled to the office for six years from the first day of May, 1877, or until the first day of May, 1883. Mr. Stephen B. French was appointed a Police Commissioner on the twenty-sixth day of May, 1879, succeeding Mr Erhardt, who, up to this date, had continued to act under no other appointment than that by virtue of which he was to serve the unexpired term of Mr Smith Mr. Erhardt continued so to hold over until Mr. French's appointment, thereby holding into the term of his successor. On November 24, 1884, Stephen B French was appointed for the term of six years from the first day of May, 1883, to succeed himself. Mr McClave's certificate was for the balance of the unexpired term, beginning with May 1, 1884, and ending May 1, 1890. The certificates had been duly entered on the minutes A motion was made and adopted making Commissioner McClave Treasurer in place of Mr. Mason, and assigning the latter's rooms and his membership on the various committees to him

WILLIAM DELAMATER, First Deputy Clerk of the Police Department, was appointed Patrolman on the twenty-sixth day of December, 1866, and assigned to the Nineteenth Precinct for duty. After attending the School of Instruction for the required term, he was immediately detailed to clerical duty in the office of the Chief Clerk—a duty for which he was specially fitted by experience and service as Chief Clerk in the Second Army Corps during the war On the eighth of April, 1871, he was appointed a clerk, and was promoted Second Deputy Clerk on the twenty-fifth of March, 1881, the rules of the Department being on that date amended for that purpose After the death of Mr Hawley, Chief Clerk, Mr Delamater was promoted to the responsible position of First Deputy Clerk

Chief Clerk's Room.

Since April 23, 1870, Mr Delamater has kept the minutes of the Board, and devised a system of indexing the same whereby any matter of information may be found at a moment's notice. He prepares the quarterly and annual reports of the Department, and formulates the charges and specifications made against members of the Police force He is one of the most systematic of men, and manages, by reason of punctuality, regularity, rule and application, to accomplish an immense amount of work. Mr. Delamater has literary tastes and capacity, and is a contributor to several city publications. On subjects connected with Police affairs he is a cyclopedia to whom application is, and may be, constantly made. Of temperate habits, quiet and unostentatious demeanor, retiring disposition, and without egotism, he performs his every public duty, and enjoys the confidence of his superiors.

EDMUND C GAY, Clerk to Committee on Repairs and Supplies, has his office in Room 5 (Treasurer's Office). CHARLES L. GOTT, Assistant to Bookkeeper

CHARLES A GRANT is Secretary to Commissioner McClave; HUGH THOMAS is Secretary to Commissioner Porter; JOHN MATTHEWS is Secretary to

OUR POLICE PROTECTORS. 457

Commissioner Voorhis; and EMANUEL DREYFOUS is Secretary to Commissioner French. Officer HARVEY is detailed to Commissioner Porter's office. PETER MASTERSON, Records of Lost Children; WALTER E DERBY, Time Clerk.

In the Chief Clerk's office, the following corps of clerks is employed William Delamater, First Deputy, Minute Clerk; George B. Stone, Second Deputy Clerk, Force Clerk, George F Hasbrouk, Arrest Clerk; Thomas J Doran, Statistic Clerk, Thomas Feeley, Violations of the Corporation Ordinances

THE BUREAU OF RECORDS AND COMPLAINTS is located at the rear of the building, on the Mott Street side, and occupies Rooms 7 and 8. Robert S. Peterson and Seth Hawley, Jr, are in charge Colonel Parker is Supply Clerk.

JOHN F. HARRIOT, Property Clerk, occupies Room 9, first floor.

The following figures do not show the property left over or unclaimed, and sold at auction. By including which, the value of lost, stolen and unclaimed property handled by the Police, is, in round figures, a million a year The unclaimed goods are sold by auction semi-annually, and everything, from a needle to an anchor, and from a thimble to a diamond, is included in these sales Mr Harriot's collection has no equal outside of a pawnbroker's shop It is strikingly miscellaneous in character, and as interesting in its history as Mother Mandelbaum could desire

Property Clerk's Room

Value of property delivered from the office of the Property Clerk, as fixed by the several parties receiving the same, for the year ending December 31, 1884:

First quarter, March 31 ....$19,163 49
Second quarter, June 30 .... 20,114 20
Third quarter, September 30 .... 29,469 66
Fourth quarter, December 31 .... 9,643 74
                                        ——————
                                        $78,391 09

Delivered to the Property Clerk, in addition to the above, by the several Precincts, Court and Detective Squads, for the year ending December 31, 1884, the sum of.....................$831,320 67

Grand total $909,711 76

JOEL W MASON was appointed Mr. Wheeler's successor, May 25, 1880, and remained a Police Commissioner until November 24, 1884 He was born in this city about fifty-three years ago. He has been in business here as a manufacturer of chairs for nearly a quarter of a century, and has accumulated a large fortune by his extensive trade. Mr. Mason has been connected with the Republican party from its infancy At the outbreak of the rebellion he was Adjutant of the Sixth Regiment of New York Militia, of which General Joseph C Pinckney was the Colonel, and he went with the organization to the field

After three months' service they returned to this city, and Mr Mason was made Colonel of the regiment, which office he held for twelve years Mr McClave became his successor

Commissioner FITZ JOHN PORTER has his office in Rooms 4 and 5.

FITZ JOHN PORTER was appointed a Police Commissioner by Mayor Edson on October 28, 1884, to fill out the unexpired term of Sidney P. Nichols, deceased. Fitz John Porter, on March 1, 1875, was appointed Commissioner of Public Works by Mayor Wickham, and served one year. General Porter was born in New Hampshire in 1822. He was graduated from the Military Academy at West Point in 1845, and served with distinction under General Scott in the Mexican

war. During the earlier part of the Civil war he was employed in various capacities, and in the fall of 1862 enjoyed the rank of Brigadier General. After the second battle of Bull Run, charges of insubordination to his superior officer, General Pope, were preferred against him. He was court-martialed, convicted, and sentenced to be "forever disqualified from holding any office of trust or profit under the United States Government." Since the sentence was imposed General Porter has made every effort to have the case re-opened. Last winter Congress passed a bill restoring him to the rank of Colonel in the army. The President vetoed the bill. It was passed over his veto by the House in its closing days, but not by the Senate. The original sentence, therefore, stands. General Porter is a Democrat, but not a member of any of the local organizations.

John R. Voorhis was born at Pompton Plains, Morris County, N. J., on the twenty-seventh of July, 1829, and, when one year old, was brought by his parents to this city, where he has resided ever since. He attended private schools from his fourth to his thirteenth year. Upon leaving school he procured employment as messenger and clerk, and was thus occupied for three years. Upon attaining his sixteenth year, he went to learn the trade of stair-builder. When twenty years of age he was made foreman of the shop, and six years later he was admitted to partnership in the business.

In 1861, when thirty-two years old, he became the successor and sole proprietor of the business establishment in which he had been brought up. In 1873 he was nominated by Mayor W. F. Havemeyer, and confirmed by the Board of Aldermen, as Commissioner of Excise. The succeeding year he was appointed by Mayor Havemeyer as Commissioner of Police to succeed Oliver Charlick, and served in such capacity until the expiration of the term in 1876. In November, 1879, Mr. Voorhis was appointed by Mayor Edward Cooper a Police Commissioner to succeed James E. Morrison, and served until July, 1880. The following year Mr. Voorhis was appointed by Mayor William R. Grace a Commissioner of the Deparment of Docks. He served until May 11, 1885, on which date he was appointed by the Mayor a Commissioner of Police.

Successively, while a Police Commissioner, he has acted as Treasurer of the Board, Chairman of the ex-Street Cleaning Bureau, Chairman of the Committee on Rules and Discipline, Chairman on Repairs and Supplies, etc.

Notwithstanding the number of public positions that Mr. Voorhis has filled, he has never sought office in his life; he never gave a pledge to obtain office, and has always regarded a public office as a public trust.

Mr. Voorhis has always taken a deep interest in politics from a purely unselfish standpoint. He is an adherent of the County Democracy. Mr. Voorhis brings the strict business methods which obtain in the workshop—where he has spent the greater portion of his life—to bear upon his official duties.

Mr. Voorhis is the most democratic of men. His private office at Police Headquarters is always open to receive visitors who call on business matters. While urbane and polite, Mr. Voorhis has settled convictions and positive ideas of his own. He is in the habit of running himself and of conducting the affairs of his office with an eye single to the public good.

460 OUR POLICE PROTECTORS.

WILLIAM H. KIPP, Chief Clerk, occupies Room 6.

Captain WILLIAM H KIPP, the present capable and experienced Chief Clerk, succeeded the late Seth C. Hawley. Captain Kipp came into the Department in 1873. He is a member of the bar, and has been a captain in the Seventh Regiment since 1866. He joined the regiment in 1857. During the war he went three times to the front. He was appointed Chief Clerk on November 14, 1884

JOHN J O'BRIEN, Chief of the Bureau of Elections, is located at Rooms 7 and 8. His staff is composed of the following detailed Policemen: Henry Hildebrandt, William H. Plunkett, Stephen Walmsley, and Denis F. Ryan.

THIRD FLOOR—ISAAC L Mor has charge of the Police supplies, and has his office in Room 1 Room 2 is the meeting room of the Board.

Captain William H Kipp

ROBERT L WOOD, Stationery Clerk, is located in Room 5, GEORGE F MILLISH and DANIEL J CRAIG, Stenographers, have their offices in Rooms 6 and 7, and Room 8 is the Police Trial Room and School of Instruction

FOURTH FLOOR.—JANITOR WEBB's apartments take up Rooms 1, 2, 3 and 4. Room 5 is set apart for lost children, who are placed in the care of Matron WEBB Rooms 6, 7, 8 and 9 are used as storage rooms for books and records.

FIRST FLOOR—The First Inspection District (Inspector William Murray) have their offices in Rooms 1, 2 and 3

INSPECTOR MURRAY's staff are District Sergeants William Meakim and Alexander B Wartz; Roundsmen Charles Tiernan, John Harley, and Thomas O'Brien, who receive the returns in the morning from the several precincts comprising the district Two Roundsmen and one Sergeant are on duty at a time in the office; and the other two Roundsmen and Sergeant are on patrol visiting the precincts, they being on duty at all times, day and night. Their duty is to exact a strict compliance with the rules and regulations throughout the district. They make their rounds in plain clothes.

THE SANITARY COMPANY.—Room 5, in the basement, is set apart for the Sanitary Company and Steam Boiler Inspector. This branch of the Police force is divided into two squads; the Steam boiler Inspection and Engineer Bureau, and the Tenement House Squad. The former has supervision over, and annually inspects, and tests by hydrostatic pressure, all steam boilers and engines in the city, certifies to their condition, condemns those found unsafe, and prevents their further use.

There are upwards of seven thousand places where steam boilers are in use in the city, underneath buildings, sidewalks, and the streets. The lower part of the city is completely honeycombed with steam boilers, and only for the careful and constant supervision by the attaches of this bureau, boiler explosions, with great loss to life and property, would, no doubt, be frequent. They also have the supervision over all persons who take charge of and operate steam boilers and other steam apparatus in the city, and it is a misdemeanor for any person to operate such without a certificate of qualification from the officer in command of the Sanitary Company.

Matron Webb's Room for Lost Children

These examinations number eight thousand a year, and about one-third of the applicants are refused certificates for incompetency.

Sergeant WASHINGTON MULLIN has been in command of this Company for the past four years. He was appointed on the force October 6, 1864, previous to which he served his apprenticeship as a machinist and engine builder.

The force under his command are selected for their particular knowledge of the duties required in this branch of the service, and consists of the following officers: Henry Wheeler, Acting Sergeant, George E. Smith and Frederick R. Fielding, Examining Engineers; George W. Church, Thomas O'Brien, Warren

Harrington, and Owen Wheeler, Boiler Inspectors; Henry M. Quinn, Boiler Record Book; Francis B. Fabri, Engineers' Record Book; John Mi[...], George F. Woolfe, John W. McGlom, Patrick Colligan, Joseph Gilligan, and Bernard Tully, Inspectors; Wm H. Palmer, Wagon Driver; William [...], Doorman.

Sergt. Washington Mullin

The Tenement House Squad consists of thirty men, detailed to enforce the Health Ordinances, and to make inspections of all tenement and lodging houses, ascertaining the sanitary condition of such, reporting all violations of the sanitary code to the Board of Health, and abating all nuisances under the direction of that Board.

Acting Sergeant John W. Haggerty, is Superintendent of the mechanical department at Police Headquarters. He has been twenty years in the department, and has charge of fifteen men.

Thus we see that the Marble Palace, as it is sometimes called, is a veritable human kaleidoscope. Here we find the vast machinery of our municipal Police concentrated, and here are the mainsprings of Police official life and action.

Outside and beyond, at their several posts, move on their several parts the men who protect life and property, who keep in subjection the army of criminals whose energy is untiring, whose evil influences are ever living forces, and who are a constant menace to society and good government.

Cloth Department, Police Headquarters.

The Police Surgeons are: Charles Phelps, John H. Dorn, Samuel B. McLeod, Stephen G. Cook, Augustus W. Maclay, F. LeRoy Satterlee, Sigismund Waterman, George Steinert, Francis M. Purroy, William A. Varian, Samuel K. Lyon, William F. Fluhrer, David Matthews, Benjamin F. Dexter, Reese H. Voorhees, Benjamin Wood, Jr., John H. Nesbitt, Martin A. McGovern.

Names of Commissioners	By whom Appointed	Under What Law	Date of Appointment	Appointed in place of	
Simeon Draper,	Governor		April, 1857.		
James Bowen,	"				
James W. Nye,	"				
Jacob Cholwell,	"				
James S. T. Stranahan,	"	Chapter 569, Laws of 1857	Nov 5, 1857.	Simeon Draper	
Pilatiah Perit,	"		May 1, 1858	Jacob Cholwell	
Thomas B Stillman,	"		Dec. 2, 1858.	Pilatiah Perit	
S B. Ward,	"		May 1, 1859		
Michael Ulshoffer,	"		May 1, 1859		
Isaac H. Bailey,	"		April 14, 1860.		
John G Bergen,	"	Chapter 259, Laws of 1860	April 14, 1860.		
Amos Pillsbury,	"		May 15, 1860	Amos Pillsbury	
James Bowen,	"		March 15, 1864		
Thomas C Acton,	"		March 15, 1864		
Wm McMurray,	Legislature		March 15, 1864		
Joseph S Bosworth,	"	Chapter 41, Laws of 1864	March 15, 1864		Died July 15, 1867.
Thomas C. Acton,	"		March 1, 1866.	Wm McMurray	
John G. Bergen,	"		Feb 12, 1868	John G Bergen	
Benjamin F. Manierre,	"		May 1, 1869	Thos. C Acton resigned May 1, 1869	
Matthew T Brennan,	"				
Henry Smith,	"				

APRIL 5, 1870   MUNICIPAL POLICE

Names	By whom	Under What Law	Date	Appointed in place of	Notes
Joseph S Bosworth,	Mayor Hall		April, 1870.		Legislated out by Act of 1873
Matthew T Brennan,	"	Chapter 137, Laws of 1870	April, 1870		Resigned November, 1870.
Benjamin F Manierre,	"		April, 1870		Legislated out by Act of 1873
Thomas J Barr,	"		Nov 28, 1870	Matthew T Brennan	Legislated out by Act of 1873
Henry Smith,	"		April, 1870	Thomas C Acton	Henry Smith was continued in office by Act of 1873

POLICE DEPARTMENT, CITY OF NEW YORK

Names of Commissioners	By whom Appointed	Under what Law	Date of Appointment	Appointed in Place of	Expiration of Term	
Henry Smith,	Mayor Havemeyer		May 1, 1873		May 1, 1877	
Oliver Charlick,	" "		May 1, 1873		May 1, 1878	
*Hugh Gardner,	" "		May 1, 1873		May 1, 1876	
Abm Duryea,	" "		May 1, 1873		May 1, 1875	
John R Russell,	" "		May 1, 1873		May 1, 1874	
Abm Disbecker,	" "		May 1, 1874	Henry Smith	May 1, 1877	Smith died Feb. 23, 1874.
*Hugh Gardner,	" "		July 1, 1874		May 1, 1878	
Oliver Charlick,	" "		July 1, 1874		May 1, 1876	Died.
*George W Matsell,	" "		July 7, 1874	Hugh Gardner	May 1, 1878	Gardner died Sept 9, 1884
John H Voorhis,	" "		July 7, 1874	Oliver Charlick	May 1, 1876	Charlick died
*Wm F Smith,	Mayor Wickham		May 1, 1875	Abm Duryea	May 1, 1881	
Dewitt C Wheeler,	" "	Chapter 335, Laws of 1873	Dec 31, 1875	Geo W Matsell	May 1, 1878	Matsell died
Joel B Erhardt,	" "		Dec 31, 1875	Abm Disbecker	May 1, 1877	Disbecker removed by Mayor
Sidney P. Nichols,	" "		May 1, 1876	John R Voorhis	May 1, 1882	Removed by Court
Charles F MacLean,	Mayor Cooper		April 18, 1879	Sidney P Nichols	May 1, 1882	Removed by Court
*Stephen B French,	" "		May 20, 1879	Joel B Erhardt	May 1, 1877	
James E Morrison,	" "		Aug 5, 1879	Wm F Smith	May 1, 1881	
John R Voorhis,	" "		Nov 24, 1879	Jas E Morrison	May 1, 1881	Morrison resigned Nov 24, '79
Sidney P. Nichols,	" "		Feb 7, 1880	Chas F MacLean	May 1, 1882	
Wm F Smith,	" "		July 7, 1880	John R Voorhis	May 1, 1881	
Joel W Mason,	" "		May 25, 1880	Dewitt C Wheeler	May 1, 1878	Resigned March 11, 1881
James Matthews,	Mayor Grace		March 11, 1881	Wm F Smith	May 1, 1881	
James Matthews,	" "		Confirm'd Sept 14, 1881	James Matthews	May 1, 1887	
Sidney P Nichols,	Mayor Edson		Jan 9, 1883	Sidney P Nichols	May 1, 1886	Died Oct 20, 1884
Fitz John Porter,	" "		Oct 28, 1884	Sidney P Nichols	May 1, 1888	
*Stephen B French,	" "		Nov 25, 1885	Stephen B French		
John McClave,	" "		Nov 25, 1885	Joel W Mason		

* Presidents of the Board

Commissioner Nichols removed by Mayor and Governor Charles F MacLean appointed in his place

Commissioner Nichols February ... Wm F Smith and John R Voorhis

CHAPTER XXI

DUTIES OF A POLICEMAN.

A TERROR TO THE WICKED AND DEPRAVED, A PROTECTOR TO THE UPRIGHT AND VIRTUOUS — HIS RESPONSIBILITIES AND LABORS. — NECESSARY QUALIFICATIONS YOUTH, STRENGTH, INTELLIGENCE, AND A STAINLESS REPUTATION — THE SCHOOL OF INSTRUCTION — DOING PATROL DUTY. — THE LAWS HE HAS TO STUDY AND ENFORCE — EX-COMMISSIONER ERHARDT'S EXPOSITION OF A POLICEMAN'S LIFE — A KEEN, WIRY, CLEAN-CUT SET — ALWAYS ON POST. — AN EYE THAT KNOWS NO SLEEP — DANGERS TO WHICH POLICEMEN ARE EXPOSED. — SPRAINS, CONTUSIONS, INCISED WOUNDS, FRACTURED LIMBS, RHEUMATISM, PNEUMONIA, ETC — SERGEANT JOHN DELANEY, A TYPE OF A BRAVE POLICEMAN.

A WELL-INFORMED public need not be told how faithfully and bravely "Our Police Protectors" guard their interests from the depredations of criminals On that head nothing need be said, as the facts speak for themselves, and with an emphasis more convincing than words

The duties which the Police Department are called upon to perform are of vital importance to the city in its security, peace and prosperity Dishonesty, carelessness or inefficiency in the discharge of those duties are followed by such grave consequences, as to lay upon every one connected with the Department the most solemn obligations to devote all his energies to the proper protection of the city. Every one, in accepting a position in the Department, accepts voluntarily these obligations

After long years of slow development, the Police, it is safe to say, have reached that stage that their efficiency and discipline may be confidently relied upon This fact has been practically demonstrated on numerous occasions, and he must be a very young man indeed, if brought up in the city, who, by personal observation, cannot vouch for the entire accuracy of this statement

Night and day, fair weather and foul, when his tour of duty commences, the Policeman, like the trusty sentinel, must go on his post and be prepared to meet all kinds of danger, but not like the soldier in open battle, with his comrades and the noise and strife cheering him on He has to encounter the hidden, and stealthy, and desperate foe, who is about committing, or is just emerging from the commission of crime, through which, by his arrest, his life or liberty is forfeited This causes him to resist apprehension, even to the taking the life of the officer of the law Surely tragic incidents, wherein Policemen have lost their lives, been wounded and disabled, need not be cited to convince New

Yorkers of this fact, or to show that the Patrolman's duties are arduous, responsible, and dangerous

To the Police are committed the enforcement of law, the maintenance of order, and the preservation of the public peace. The protection of life and the security of property largely depend upon the zeal and fidelity with which they discharge their duties. It is essential, therefore, that they should possess discretion, integrity, activity, sobriety, fearlessness and decision. That these conditions are combined in our New York Police Protectors, few, if any, will be found so prejudiced or ill-informed as to deny.

A stranger in this city in quest of information about the Police, were he not industrious and disposed to investigate statements, would come to an opinion that is by no means that of the vicious, criminal, ignorant, or vulgar; but is held by not a few persons of education and refinement who, if they were required to say why they thought ill of the average Policeman, would have to confess that their judgment was mainly based on hearsay and newspaper gossip. Take a thousand such persons, and few will be found who have ever sought to know what a Policeman really is, and what his duties, trials, temptations, responsibilities and virtues are. Their idea of a Policeman is on a par with that of the boniface who, when asked what a gentleman was, replied, with assurance, "A gentleman's a man wot keeps a hoss and gig." The most vulgar conception is that of a bloated, drunken, brutal fellow, who depends on craft and political influence to retain his sinecure situation, and who perfunctorily does his "sixty minutes to the hour," from pay day to pay day, and from one blackmailed rumhole to another. These prejudices have been fostered by newspapers, which will one day record, as a "police outrage," an act of self defense by an officer that should be commended, and then, when fully aware of the injustice of the aspersion, refuse or omit to correct the impression that thousands of readers have formed. The same exultant shout is vented over a Policeman's backsliding, as when a minister or a citizen of good repute falls from grace, as if a Policeman were less of a man or less liable to be tempted than other people. It has been suggested, and there is some basis for the explanation, that our free institutions tend to make men who enforce the law and deprive others of their liberty, objects of contempt. In Europe it is not rare to see a Police Officer, unable to cope with one or more persons he has in custody or wishes to arrest, call on bystanders, in the name of the representatives of law and order, to aid him, and the appeal is seldom disregarded. Here such a request would be received with a guffaw, and an escaping prisoner gets more aid from a crowd than his pursuer, while in a Police Court sympathy with defendants is evinced daily. Logic is rarely applied when the question of the *morale* of the working members of the Police force is discussed, but detractors invariably refrain from meeting the issues involved in such a question as. "Take twenty-five hundred clergymen, brokers, tradesmen, lawyers, laborers, or average citizens, compare them with the Patrolmen of the force of New York, and say, conscientiously, if the officers are viler than the others, or if there is any vice that a Policeman has that the others are not guilty of." The trouble with Policemen is that they are men, and rather more of men than the rest of the community. They start in their career from the mill which

On Post.

(Drawn by C de Grimm, by permission of Mr. James Gordon Bennett.)

grinds them out at Police Headquarters with many brands, guaranteeing their manhood, both physically, intellectually and morally, on them. The uniform and badge of the force were never permitted to be worn by an idiot or a rogue, if he were known to be such when he was appointed, and no such man ever remained on the force after there was good evidence given of his being either. It should, however, be remembered that men have been dismissed for cause, and have been reinstated by the courts.

It is not every one who wills it that becomes a Policeman, and some of the best Policemen are those who have been compelled to join the force through necessity. It is safe to say that nearly every appointment is made through personal or political influence Those who cavil at this should remember that this almost invariably secures for the department men who have lived long enough in the city to know it, for politicians and friends of Police Commissioners are not disposed to interest themselves in strangers. A young man having, then, secured a sponsor, makes his first step towards appointment by going in his company to one of the Police Commissioners. Here the first weeding out system is encountered A Commissioner rarely passes a man with a grog-blossomed nose, or one so uncouth or ill-favored as to be a laughing stock If he objects to the man, he does not, however, always tell the sponsor, but the candidate has a chance of getting

School of Instruction.

very gray before he is sworn in If the Commissioner is disposed to favor the application, the candidate for appointment must be less than thirty years old, able to read and write English, a citizen of the United States, a resident of this city from a year back, of spotless character, so far as conviction of crimes is concerned, of a stature not less than five feet seven inches and-a-half, more than one hundred and thirty-eight pounds in weight, and sound in body and mind It is safe to say that in running this gauntlet of qualifications forty out of one hundred applicants find themselves ineligible The applicant is sent by the Commissioners before the Board of Surgeons, who pass on his height, weight, and sanity The examination is thorough, the candidate being stripped He may be rejected for obesity, or his stature, weight, and chest circumference may be so disproportionate as to make him unfit to be a Policeman Once passed by the Surgeons he would be an excellent risk for a life insurance company to take. If the candidate's sponsor is active, or has influence which is recognized and respected, the candidate is advanced another step He fills out a blank with his pedigree, a statement of his arrest or non-arrest, a conviction or non-conviction for crime or misdemeanor, and, among other questions, answers one which inquires if he has paid, or promised to pay, or gave money or any consideration for aid or influence towards procuring his appointment These statements he swears to He also procures the signatures of at least ten respectable citizens to a petition for his appointment, which declares that the signers know him

Station House Lodging Room.

intimately, that he is of good moral character, sober, temperate, and industrious, a man of truth and integrity, of sound mind, good understanding, and of a temper, habits and manners that fit him for the duties of a Policeman When the signatures are appended, the Chief Clerk marks them, or a few of them, and the persons thus indicated are required to visit the Central Office and make affidavit to the truth of the statements in the petition. Next, Detectives are employed to investigate the candidate's antecedents, and, on their favorable report, he may be enrolled as eligible for appointment A candidate is then only "a little lower than the angels" if all that has been sworn to in regard to him is true. What business man, in engaging an employee, would hesitate, with such a series of safeguards? The candidate is now on the anxious seat, and if his support is not of the best, he may fail at the threshold of success. The system of dealing out orders for examination by the Surgeons, application papers, and examination papers, without regard to the probable vacancies on the force, has been not too harshly criticised as pernicious. It puts a premium on political and personal influences if it does no more, encourages false hopes, and leads many young men to throw up positions, refrain from accepting employment, and to spend, not only their savings, but those of relations and friends. In one case, known to the writer, a man, who had waited two years for his appointment, spent all his cash, disposed of his wife's money and property, sold his furniture, and was such a financial wreck when he was sworn in that it took him three years to recover himself. Instances are known of men waiting more than four years for their shield. Once, certain Commissioners resolved on cancelling applications for appointment which dated back more than six months, and between seven and eight hundred were destroyed. But this was when appointment papers were given out by the ream. However, we will suppose our friend, John Brown, safely landed on the shores of official duty after running the gauntlet of the Civil Service examination. One happy day the Board has met, and he is recorded as having been voted on and appointed. He takes the official oath and receives his numbered shield. Then he busies

Station House Dormitory

himself about his uniform, buying the regulation cloth from the Police clerk, and his hat and insignia at Police Headquarters, also his baton and belt. Half uniformed, he is directed to the School of Instruction, where he passes at least a month as "citizen" Brown under the new rule, and he does one tour of night duty—six P M to midnight—with an officer of the precinct to which he is assigned. In the School of Instruction he begins to cast aside any citizen's prejudices he may have formed in regard to the little knowledge required to enable a man to twirl a locust, patrol a post, and draw pay at the end of each month. The instructor at present is Roundsman Michael Smith. His duty is to "instruct the members of the School in all the duties, discipline, and exercises of Patrolmen, including the Police law, the laws of the State of New

York, the laws and ordinances of the city of New York, and the rules, regulations and orders of the Board of Police, and their powers and privileges under the same," only this and nothing more. A matter of seven hundred and fifty rules and regulations, some two hundred and fifty general orders, many of them amending, altering, and changing the rules and regulations, gentle dalliance in "the position of the soldier," "riots," "commands," "steps," "alignments," "marching," "wheelings," "turnings," "baton exercise," etc., a little healthy mental exercise, with such questions as "When, going or returning from court or meals, there are more than two Policemen on the sidewalk, how should they conduct themselves?" "What disposition are you required to make of all prisoners you may arrest while on duty?" "In case you should arrest a person so much under the influence of liquor as to be unable to comprehend the proceedings at court, what would be required of you?" "In case you should arrest a person having stolen property in his or her possession, what disposition would you make of prisoners and property?" "In case you come in possession of lost property of a dangerous nature, what would be your duty?" "How about carrying umbrellas or walking canes when on duty?" "What is the best evidence of an officer's efficiency when on post duty?" "What information should you be prepared to give to strangers and citizens who may inquire of you?" "If any person had a long communication in regard to Police matters, what would be your duty?" "What are you to refrain from doing while on post duty?" etc. The answers to some of these questions would make a bronze statue of sorrow howl with merriment. The laws of the State and the city ordinances are other sources of innocent recreation. How much a candidate can learn about them in thirty days remains, and can well remain, a mystery. Few of the superior officers of the force claim to fairly well understand them, and some of our best lawyers are at times at fault in regard to them, especially the ordinances which include those of the Board of Health.

Then there are digressions to the Sunday Law, Excise Law, the societies for the Prevention of Cruelty to Children and the Prevention of Cruelty to Animals. No wonder if the callow "cop's" head whirls and he is *distrait* when doing his "first night tour" with his more experienced or more callous mentor. Well, at last he is discharged from the school, and, in new uniform, blossoms into a full-fledged Policeman and begins his "day," which is really one of ninety-six hours. He is now at the mercy of the public, the press, the criminal classes, his superior officers, the Roundsman, and his own weakness.

What is known as the Police day begins at six A M and ends at six P M. The Police night begins at six P M and ends at six A M. But the scheme is an extremely complicated one, and was probably devised to get all the duty out of a Patrolman that his system will stand. There is what is known as the "dog watch," from six A M to eight A M, and we will suppose John Brown to have done this trick. He goes to breakfast, to return to his station house at a quarter past nine A M, and is then "in reserve" till noon. "In reserve" does not imply that he lounges in the sitting room of the station house reading newspapers, playing checkers, or talking station house scandal. If he has not prisoners locked up the night before or during the "dog watch," he may have to go to the Courts of Special, or General Sessions, or Civil Courts, to testify against criminals or violators of ordinances. On one of a hundred excuses he may be ordered to don citizen's garb and play detective on ball players, hucksters, and others. Rain or shine, in temperate, as well as in inclement weather, he can be called away at any instant to help form fire lines in his own or another precinct; a

Crossing Broadway.

parade, unusual excitement among workmen, weddings, festivals, political gatherings, election business, quotas reduced by funerals or merrymaking in other commands, excursions, and a hundred other matters conspire against his ease "on reserve." At noon he is, in time of peace, and providing he be at the station house, allowed one hour for dinner. At one o'clock he must go on post

472 — OUR POLICE PROTECTORS.

1 Stopping a runaway team 2 Assaulted by roughs 3 A fight with rioters 4 Surprising burglars 5 Taking lost children to Headquarters 6 Rescuing a woman from the flames 7 Rescuing a woman from drowning, 8 Arraigning a prisoner at court 9 Catching a sneak thief

Familiar Incidents in the Life of a New York Policeman

again, brushed, blacked, clean-shirted, and trim. At six P. M. he goes back to the station house, has up to quarter past seven for supper, and is back "on reserve" until midnight. Sleep claims him, and he is lucky if, at a quarter to twelve, when the doorman rounds his section—a command is divided into two platoons, and each platoon into two sections—he has not been called from bed to do fire or other duty. John Brown is now a sidewalk inspector from midnight to six A. M. He has a sinecure, has he? Let us glance at some of his duties. In any precinct but the Twenty-fourth, Twenty-fifth, Twenty-sixth, Nineteenth-Sub, the Second Precinct, the five Police Courts, the Sanitary Company, the Special Service Squad, and generally the Thirty-second, Thirty-third, Thirty-fourth and Thirty-fifth Precincts, which he may not belong to unless he has seen years of service, and merits and secures a "*soft* place," or unless he be a horseman, he has to "try his doors." That is to say he should ascertain beyond peradventure that no aperture through which a thief could enter, whether it be windows, areas, area gates, door, grating, cellar flaps, or coal chutes, is open or unsecured. This he is to do "frequently" during his tour of duty, according to the rules. While doing this he may be called upon to give advice, make arrests, aid the sick and injured, quell brawls, and he should discover fires, burglaries, and property imperiled in various ways. All this time he should resist temptation. Free liquor is his at every saloon on his post, providing he return the compliment by closing his eyes to violations of the excise law.

He has, at every step, some rule to observe, and may, on the report of a Roundsman or superior officer, be tried, convicted, reprimanded, or fined from one half of a day's pay to his pay for a month, for intoxication, disrespect toward superior officers or citizens, "neglect of duty"—a comprehensive term, violation of any one of the hundreds of rules, disobedience of orders, "conduct unbecoming an officer," sitting down, conversing, not properly patroling, absence from post, or "breach of discipline." The monotony of such an existence is often varied by tussles with refractory prisoners. Some drunkards, especially females, never think a carouse satisfactory without winding it up with provoking arrest, and trying issues with a "cop," and this means for the Policeman violent walking exercise, varied with wrestles, blows, kicks, tumbles in the street and gutter, torn clothes, and general demoralization by the time the prisoner is landed at the station house. Now and then an officer has to tote a couple of drunkards each as refractory and belligerent as the other, and he is in the position of a man with two lusty shoats bent on going their own way, and "led" by a string. In the day time John Brown is not so much hampered by "trying doors," but any relief in this respect is made up by the vigilance required in the enforcement of the ordinances, the Policeman's *bete noire*. John Brown leaves the street at six A. M. If he has prisoners he conquers sleep, goes to court, and awaits the pleasure of the Magistrate. It is his "day off," that is to say, he does not go to the station house in quiet times until six P. M., but he may be robbed of his rest by dilatory court proceedings, witness duty, riots, parade duty, trials at Police Headquarters, etc. At six P. M. he goes out until midnight, and then it is his "morning home," or in other words he has no patrol duty until eight A M. Ordinary patrol duty is made all the more irksome when the command is short-handed, because of "nights off," which occur once a month per man, sickness, etc, by "doubling up" or requiring one Patrolman to cover two posts. This doubles his duties and responsibilities. After eight A M on "morning home" days, he is on patrol till one P M, when he goes to dinner till a quarter past one P M. He is again " on reserve "—this is his "short day" —till midnight, when he goes on post till six A M. Then comes another "day off;" he follows with patrol duty from six P M till midnight, is a "reserve" from midnight to six A M, and takes his "dog watch" anew from six A M to eight A M.

Drilling a Squad of Policemen

When John Brown has been a year on the force he will begin to appreciate a Patrolman's duties, and be indifferent to those who malign the force, except when he is personally attacked. By this time he will have acquired a certain practical and theoretical knowledge of surgery, and be in a small degree a diagnostician. This from cases he has had under his observation and lectures on First Aid to the Injured that he has attended. He will know much of the practice of Criminal and Police Courts, and have become careful in making arrests. He will have passed through perils and exposed life and limb often if he has done average duty in a brisk precinct. It is more than probable he will have seen the sunny side of burglar catching, and record a "night off"—the reward in any well regulated command for such an exploit. At any rate, he has shared in the capture of seventy thousand prisoners, of whom twenty thousand were drunkards and five thousand felons, each of whom, with State Prison staring him in the face, would have taken any chance, even to the life of the officers, and sacrificed even his own limbs or life to escape. Of the felons seven hundred were guilty of felonious assaults, seven hundred burglars, one hundred forgers, ninety to one hundred murderers or slayers of others in some fashion, one thousand had attained such dignity in thieving as to be charged with grand larceny, and he may have come across one or more of a score of escaped prisoners. He sent in his share of the two hundred thousand reports of violation of ordinances, and "took in" some of the seven thousand prisoners arrested for violation of the "Aldermen's" Laws, the Excise Laws, the Sanitary Code, the Lottery Law, the Pool Law, the United States Internal Revenue Law, the School Law, the Election Law, the Theatre Law, the Building Law, the Hotel Law, the Penal Code, the Railroad Law, the Gambling Laws, the Opium Laws, the Barrel Act, the Squatter's Law, and the Game Law. It is more than probable he has been tried and has contributed to one hundred and twenty thousand dollars of "sick time" and the funds derived from fines. He has shared in securing one thousand buildings, left open in various ways, has attended many of the fifteen hundred fires, taken some of the twenty-five hundred lost children to the Central Office matron, buying them dainties on the way to keep them in good humor, and may have done the "baby act," by carrying tenderly and well swathed, an abandoned foundling, to the same place, and borne the ridicule of the vulgar while exciting the admiration of the proper minded. Some of the seven hundred thousand dollars' worth of property turned over to the Property Clerk, as taken from prisoners or found in the street, has passed through his hands; and of the five thousand five hundred persons succored by the Police, he has seen men and women suffocated, sick, injured by assaults, in fits, knocked down, injured by falls, cut, scalded, shot, burned, stabbed, crushed, rescued from the water, frozen and benumbed, and otherwise helpless, and if John Brown is, as ninety-nine out of one hundred officers are, large-hearted, plucky, attentive to duty, possessed of an *esprit du corps*— which is a shield against malignant criticism and falsehood — healthy and ambitious, he will either die in harness, or linger a little while on a pension and go to Heaven, just as certainly as his foes, who are not all there, to whom apply the lines

> A rogue ne'er felt the halter draw,
> With good opinion of the law.

Joel B. Erhardt, United States Marshal and ex-Police Commissioner, at the banquet given by the Police Inspectors and Captains, at Delmonico's, on January 21, 1884, spoke to the toast of "the Police." Speaking for the Police force generally, he said:

"Now, we do not think we are a bad lot of men. Superintendent, nor Inspector, nor Captain, Sergeants, nor Patrolmen. In the first place we are *men* who do their work in uniform, under rules and regulations prescribed, and which we are bound to obey. We are charged with the enforcement of all laws, Federal, State and Municipal. We are a very hard working class; once a year, of late years, we have permission to give a dinner, and a few of us assemble as you see us; at twelve to-night we shall again be on our posts, there to remain. Almost all of us have families, and try to bring up our children so that they will not fall under the ban of the law, or in the custody of our successors; we send them to school, and we clothe them as well as we are able. We have a home, not a very large one—still it is a home; and we are not well off in the world's goods, once in a great while some kind friend gives one of us a point, and we make a few hundred dollars, but, generally, we get pricked, and attend to our

Mounted Policeman Stopping a Runaway Team.

legitimate business There is no class of citizens who fall from grace less frequently than we, and we are never better pleased than when the morals of society improve and we have no cause to make arrests.

"Please to remember that when the old world has done with her criminals they seek our shores, so that we have some of the worst of the world, which, with the aid of the best commanded and managed Detective force in the world, we keep in subjection or in jail, while we have the real population of New York, we have the floating population of the cities in close proximity, giving a population of nearly two-and-a-half millions to protect and watch

"Our hours of duty vary a little—we have a long day for patrol and a short one—but we are always on duty, subject to call at any hour of the night or day. We cannot change our residences without notice to the Board of Police, and we are obliged to change if we are transferred, if we ever expect to see our fireside; so that we have no settled habitation. We are out in all sorts of weather, often unprepared, and from exposure we have lost about seventy within the last few years. This is aside from the death rate; and we have had six killed, and any number stabbed or maimed. As we are not permitted to engage in any other business our income is always limited. We have a few days vacation annually, and at the end of five years we are fit for nothing else than to be a Policeman We thus lose many social rights, such, for instance, as assembling together, and have not even the right, as a body, to petition.

"If you will peruse recent history you will see how much crime we have detected and punished, and it requires no great stretch of imagination to realize how much we have prevented.

"We ask you, the legislature, to pay all of our men the same salary when they perform the same work. Now, this is fair And we, here assembled, must not forget the twenty-seven hundred Policemen on duty in this city, who patrol their posts as regularly and continuously as the great dipper in the sky above us which knows no setting—some of them, after deducting expenses of uniform and other necessaries, net two dollars and thirty-seven cents per day, while others only one dollar and twenty-eight cents This is not fair, it is scandalous I not be misled by the alleged price of cheap labor—ours is not cheap labor, it labor of the highest order We act instantly as a committing Magistrate and Policeman in the same breath; we are acquainted with Federal, State and city laws, and are bound to keep pace, as far as possible, with the decisions of the Courts; we are bound to learn the rules of evidence so as to be able to apply them to the case in hand, to say, therefore, that our labor, which knows no rest, can be gauged by the market value of a porter who unlocks doors and sweeps the floor, is not sound reasoning. Nor should you be misled by those who cry that the taxes are high, if they are we did not make them; on the contrary, our efforts and our labor keep them as low as they are, our eyes, which are never closed in slumber, prevent small as well as large public thefts And pertinent to this is the statement which the Comptroller told me not long since, that with the increase of the Sinking Fund, New York City will be free from debt in another eighteen years

"We ask you to provide means for those of us who are broken down in the service of the State—some have been on the force twenty-five up to forty years—and the service in which we have participated would sound like a romance

"Their associate and commander for over three years—commander by reason of power delegated to me by my colleagues—my first acquaintance ripened into a friendship, on my part, which will last as long as I shall live I found them obedient without being servile, I found them tractable and honest, courteous and uncomplaining, and I take pleasure in stating whenever an officer was sent for and asked for facts, he never told me a lie decline to answer he might, but answering, he told the truth

"I could tell you of their past, which comes down to us glorious, and, with the additional lustre of our times, will pass to posterity increasing in splendor and brilliancy Were you to ask me of the battles they had fought, their tattered flag, the undulating ground in the valley of the James and Shenandoah or Spottsylvania, would answer more eloquently Were you to ask me of the riots or incipient revolution they have prevented or overcome, let your own memory answer that from 1863 down to the threatened eruption which did not take place in 1876, when Pittsburgh and our western cities were in flames, with a larger communistic population than elsewhere in the country and every opportunity to do their work, the power and discipline of the Police force of the present prevented a second conflagration, and bloodshed which would have far exceeded the cruelties of 1863 What prevented it is the knowledge that when the Police force of the present charge, they know nothing but duty, and ties of friendship, of kindred, of religion, count as nothing to stay their progress in enforcing the law—they are irresistible.

"They are a keen, wiry, clean-cut set, with perceptive faculties sharpened by contact with the world, who wish to do right, and who will always do right if the politicians will let them alone Far be it from me to cast a slur on politicians, politics is a noble profession, and he is a poor American citizen who is not a politician, and is not proud of being one; but neither they nor their ways have place in the discipline or movements of an army which is always in line of action and always engaged For so long "As master passions in the breast, like Aaron's serpent, swallow all the rest," so long as restless, ignorant and frail humanity shall fall, so long there must be a body of men, well organized, subject to rigid discipline, doing sentry duty or sleeping on their arms, and the directors of that body have the right to say to camp-followers: You shall not tamper with our men—and if they still persist, the culprits should be held up to the execration of honest men, put in the pillory with slit ears and punctured noses.

"As Dickens' character, Tiny Tim, says 'God bless them all, every one of them'"

Those who sneer when the life of a Policeman is called a hard one would do well to read the following regulations

Rule 550 —Each member of the Police force shall devote his whole time and attention to the business of the department, and is expressly prohibited from following any other calling, or being employed in any other business Although the members of the force are, by the rules and regulations of the service, relieved at certain hours from the actual performance of duty on ordinary occasions, yet they are held to be at all times on duty, and must be prepared, while relieved as aforesaid, to act immediately on notice that their services are required.

Rule 594 —Each member of the force shall be deemed to be always on duty, subject to such relief therefrom as shall be allowed by proper authority, and the same responsibility, as to the suppression of disturbances and the arrest of offenders, rests upon them when not in uniform, as when in uniform on post duty

No better idea of the risks run by officers can be had than by a perusal of one of the monthly reports of the Police Surgeons Take for example that of a recent one, so as to illustrate how a Patrolman's life exposes him not only to wounds and broken limbs, but to sickness It appears that in one month eight men were suffering from sprains, sixty-one from rheumatism, one from malarial fever contracted from a Police station being badly drained; six from contusions received from vehicles, struggles with refractory prisoners, etc; two from bad bruises, six from pneumonia, twenty-six from bronchitis, sixteen from injuries due to falls, nineteen from severe colds, three from incised wounds, seven from fractured limbs, and fourteen from phthisis, the result of duty in all weathers and neglect of colds, because of a desire to continue to draw full pay by doing duty when unfit for it

A thousand examples of the gritty, plucky, manly stuff the "common cop" is made of, might be given Here are half a dozen taken at random On the thirty-first of May, 1879, Officer V H Marron, of the Twenty-first Precinct, encountered an ex-convict, Joseph Murphy, who "owned the street" and terrified

1 Winter Hat 2 Summer Hat 3 Day Stick 4 Shield 5 Revolver 6 Night Stick 7 Rosewood Baton for Parade 8 Belt and Frog 9 Nippers 10 New Style Handcuffs

Part of a Policeman's Equipment

law-abiding citizens. The officer could have knocked the fellow insensible, and made his task of taking him to the station house easy and devoid of danger, but he treated the felon decently, to be assaulted, shot or knocked down, and severely injured. But Murphy went to the station house, nevertheless, Marron's hand on his collar. Marron was laid up. In March, 1880, Officer Martin Finnerty, of the Twentieth Precinct, had a desperate tussle in Fortieth Street, near Eighth Avenue, with an ex-convict, Thomas Tuite, who tried to kill Finnerty with a pistol, and inflicted one wound, but Tuite was subdued, and Finnerty went to the West Thirty-seventh Street Station House to lock him up and call for a surgeon for himself.

Reduced fac-simile of a Policeman's Certificate of Appointment.

Not less heroic was the conduct of Officer J. J. Reilly, of the Eighteenth Precinct, who struggled with a desperado, John Ruddy, on the fifth of September, 1880, after he had dangerously stabbed him, and persisted in escorting him to the East Twenty-second Street Station House, when he should have been in the care of a surgeon. Officer C. S. Pike, of the Fifth Precinct, tackled a desperate burglar, William Livingstone, at dawn on the nineteenth of September, 1881, at West Broadway and Franklin Street, and immediately received what was for some time considered a fatal wound in the abdomen, but he sprang on the man, disarmed him, and took him to the Leonard Street Station House, to faint as soon as he arraigned his would-be assassin before the Sergeant on duty. Detective Sergeant Jacob Tooker will never again be the man he was on the fourteenth of February, 1882, before he confronted and commanded to halt Thomas

Hennessy, a burglar, who had laid concealed in a house that the officer had watched. Hennessy was prepared, for he had a cocked revolver in his pocket, and his first act was to fire at the officer and wound him dangerously in the head. Tooker held on to the man after disarming him, and might have killed him had he willed it, but he forbore to harm him, and two processions went to the station house, one with the prisoner and the other with the wounded officer. Tooker was laid up a year by his injury, and at times he is compelled to abstain from all duty

The best example of Police grit ever exhibited can be found in the case of Sergeant John Delaney, of the Nineteenth Precinct On the second of January, 1883, he was virtually a Patrolman of the Tombs Police Co Squad, although he had the rank of Acting Sergeant. He had been highly and honorably mentioned three years before, for risking his life to save that of George McFadden, a boy, at the foot of East Thirty-third Street, and had received the gold medal from Congress On the day above mentioned, Delaney was given a warrant for the arrest of a man who had swindled a provincial visitor at the low groggery, No 144 Hester Street, and, while seeking the rascal, encountered Patrick McGowan, a burly ruffian employed by "Billy" McGlory at Armory Hall McGowan was at that stage of drunkenness when men become brutal Delaney refused to drink with him, and was followed up-stairs by McGowan, who attacked him on the landing, and laid open his head with a pistol butt. Delaney was as nothing in the ruffian's hands, as he was very low with a pulmonary trouble contracted in the saving of the boy McFadden. But when McGowan went away, exulting, to escape in a carriage, in which sat a strumpet

Sergeant John Delaney

with whom he had caroused during the night, Delaney crawled down stairs, and, hailing McGowan as he was entering the vehicle, commanded him to halt, and advanced on him McGowan replied foully and sprang into the carriage, telling the driver, a "night hawk," to go on Delaney followed, to be shot in the eye through the rear window of the carriage and disfigured for life An instant later he fired, killing McGowan Delaney has not yet recovered from his injury, but he was rewarded by substantial promotion

On the twenty-second of last August, Officer Patrick Rabbett, of the Twenty-second Precinct, arrested a man in West Forty-seventh Street, for robbery and, while taking him to the station house, was stabbed by John Connors He would have landed both in a cell but for Connors, who beat off the officer, was arrested and "taken in"

The new Civil Service rules, in their application to the Police Department, caused no little trouble and confusion at first These regulations went into effect on August, 29, 1884

Schedule C, regulation 18, provides, first, that an applicant for a place in the Police Department must present his application to the Police Commissioners, giving full particulars of his qualifications, accompanied by testimonials that he is a man of good moral character, of sober and industrious habits, and never known to be guilty or convicted of any criminal act or disorderly conduct. Those who sign these testimonials must consent that their certificates may be made public, and they must be willing to furnish any other information respecting the applicant that they may possess. Each application must be accompanied by a full description of the applicant, a thorough description of his physical qualifications, and various particulars of his life, amounting to a considerable autobiography. The applicant must swear that he has not promised to pay for any aid or influence toward procuring his appointment. The character of the applicant must

Police Trial Room.

be inquired into by the Captain of the precinct in which he resides, and his physical qualifications must be certified to by the examining surgeons. The applicant is questioned closely as to the diseases with which he or his family may have been afflicted. He must tell whether he has had fits or injury of the head or spine, or piles or rheumatism. His stature must not be below five feet seven inches. He must have at least thirty-three inches circumference of chest, and weigh not less than one hundred and thirty-five pounds. Obesity is a good cause for rejection. "There must be a difference of at least two inches at forced expiration and on full inspiration." The examining surgeons must swear to the results of their examinations. Then there must be a test by the Examining Board of the strength, activity, and physical capacity of the applicant by suitable examination of his strength, his swiftness and endurance in running, his skill in the use of the club and firing at a mark. His general health, eyesight, and hearing are examined. He is then ready for examination as to further general qualifications, such as habits and reputation, experience, reading, writing, ciphering, rules of the Police Department, questions relating to the city government, location of streets, public buildings, and other subjects respecting which strangers in the city naturally inquire. Here is the luminous rule by which the standing of the applicant is determined.

"The general average shall be ascertained by multiplying the ascertained average standing of the applicant in each qualification by the value attached, and dividing the united products by the sum of the values by ten"

No person whose standing on any of the qualifications or obligatory subjects enumerated above is less than sixty, or whose ascertained average on all is below seventy, shall be entered on the eligible list.

At first no provision was made for the payment of the provisional or probationary corps. Not being Policemen, they could not either claim the tenure of office or receive the pay of Policemen. The law, as originally framed, deprived these men of pay for the first six months. The law was remedied, making the probationary period thirty days, and finally the Board of Estimate and Apportionment provided the necessary funds to pay the probation men regularly from the date of their appointment, the same as the regular Police

The quota of officers and men allowed by law to the Police Department is as follows One Superintendent, four Inspectors, eighteen Surgeons, thirty-six Captains, one hundred and fifty-two Sergeants, eighty Doormen, forty Detective Sergeants, eight Acting Sergeants, one hundred and seventy-eight Roundsmen, two thousand three hundred and seventy-four Patrolmen, making a grand total of two thousand eight hundred and ninety-one

The actual force varies from this in the following particulars: thirty-five Captains, one hundred and forty-seven Sergeants, seventy-nine Doormen, and two thousand three hundred and eight Patrolmen. The rest of the force is the same as allowed by law The force is apportioned as follows

District Courts	Inspector	Sergeants	Roundsmen	Men.	Doormen	Acting Sergeants.
COURT SQUADS.						
1		1	2	3	.	.
2	..	1	1	10	..	
3		1	1	8		
4		1	1	8		..
5	.	1	1	8	..	..
6		1	1	12	.	.
INSPECTION DISTRICT OFFICE.						
1	1	2	4	2	..	..
2	1	1	4		1	..
3 } 4 }	1	2	2	1	..	2
SANITARY COMPANY						
..	..	1	4	42	1	..
TENEMENT HOUSE OFFICERS						
..	..	..	..	30	..	..
SPECIAL SERVICE SQUAD						
..	.	.	..	1	..	..

Precinct	Night Posts.	Men to cover.	Captain.	Sergeants.	Rounds-men.	Total Patrolmen.	Doormen.
1	40	82	1	4	5	90	2
2	8	18	1	3	5	23	2
3	Day Posts 60 / 18	96	1	3	6	102	1
4	38	78	1	3	5	88	2
5	38	78	1	4	4	87	2
6	34	70	1	4	4	70	2
7	26	54	1	3	4	57	2
8	36	74	1	4	4	74	2
9	34	70	1	4	4	75	2
10	28	58	1	4	4	64	2
11	20	42	1	4	4	48	2
12	28	58	1	4	4	66	2
13	20	42	1	3	6	46	2
14	24	50	1	4	4	52	2
15	32	66	1	4	4	73	2
16	28	58	1	4	4	64	2
17	26	54	1	4	4	62	2
18	38	78	1	4	5	66	2
19	28	58	1	4	5	64	2
20	28	58	1	4	5	62	2
21	28	58	1	4	4	62	2
22	36	74	1	4	4	80	2
23	30	62	1	4	4	66	2
24	Steamboat Patrol			2	4	21	1
25	Broadway Squad		1	2	4	36	2
26	City Hall Squad		1	3	6	45	2
27	36	74	1	4	4	80	2
28	28	58	1	4	4	63	2
29	51	104	1	4	5	106	2
30	17	36	1	4	4	41	2
31	26	54	1	4	4	55	2
32	25	52	1	4	4	56	2
33	16	34	1	4	4	37	2
34	12	26	1	4	4	27	2
35	12	26	1	3	3	26	2

In all ages and all lands, those who risk their lives or liberties to save their fellow-beings from suffering or death, are accorded the highest praise and honor Not always, however, do such heroes receive such substantial recognition as their deeds deserve Occasionally a titled personage, or some one still higher in social rank, through personal or political considerations, dispense their favors quite liberally in requital for gallant services Such deeds as are briefly and prosaically chronicled in the annexed list are worthy of the days of chivalry Men who can make such sacrifices—who can jeopardize their health and lives to snatch from the jaws of death poor wretches, who, in a number of cases, have grown weary of life, are surely made of that sterling stuff which distinguishes heroes from common men

In their humble way, these men are more than public benefactors always on the alert, never shirking their arduous duties, they are ever prepared to protect the innocent and to alleviate suffering.

OUR POLICE PROTECTORS

ROLL OF HONOR.

HONORABLY MENTION MADE BY THE BOARD OF POLICE FOR DISTINGUISHED SERVICES RENDERED BY POLICEMEN.

Name	Rank	Precinct	Date	Nature of Service
Michael Crowley,	Patrol	28	June 12, 1870	Fearless arrest of Jno Butler, who shot at them
Chas. Burns,	"	28		
Jas. McAuley,	"	28	April 18, 1871	Rescued child from burning building
Geo J Radford,	Det Sqd		June 15, 1871	Detection and arrest of robbers Central Park Savings Bank
Philip Farley,	"			
Bernard Tully	Patrol	19	Aug 7 1871	Arrest burglar, risk of life, medal given
Wm H. McConnell,	Sergt	28	Jan 4, 1872	Prompt report of break in elevated railway
Martin F Conlon,	Patrol	6	Feb. 9, 1872	Arrest of three burglars
Jas. S Mead,	"	5	April 28, 1872	Prompt extinguishment of fire, incendiarism.
Peter Fox,	"	14	Sept. 8, 1872	Brave in presence of mob assaulting him with bricks.
John McElwain,	Capt	20	Nov 3, 1872	Arrest of Donohoe, murderer of Florence Scannell.
John J. McGinn,	Patrol	25	Nov. 23, 1872	Stop runaway team at risk of life, medal.
Thos. Bradley,	R'dsm'n	15		
Edwd. J. Buckley,	"	15		
Wm. Henderson,	Patrol	15	Nov 29, 1872	Saved ten persons from a burning building, Nos 718 and 720 Broadway.
Gilbert Carr,	"	15		
Hugh O'Reilly,	"	15		
Jno. H. McCullagh,	Capt	8		
Wm. Schultz,	Sergt	8		
Thos Riley,	R'dsm'n	8		
August Browning,	Patrol	8		
James Monell,	"	8		
Thos. Muldoon,	"	8		
Thos. Kearney,	"	8	Dec 30, 1870	Saved a number of lives at a fire, Nos 156 and 158 Mercer Street
Bernard Kiernan,	"	8		
Jas. McAdam,	"	8		
Jno. Layden,	"	8		
Philip Mohr,	"	8		
Edward Moloney,	"	8		
Isaac Ward,	"	8		
Patrick McGrath,	"	8		
Edwd H Johnson,	"	8		
Patrick Pendergast,	"	27	Jan 29, 1873	Jumped in river at risk of life and saved a man.
Geo W Gibson,	"	7	Mch 28, 1873	Grappled and held an infuriated bull—medal
Richard Jackson,	"	8	Mch 29, 1873	Arrested two notorious burglars
Edwd Maloney,	"	8		
Thos. Nugent,	"	4	April 25, 1873	Arrest of Andrew Cluff
Michael Crowle-	"	4	June 12, 1873	Rescued man from drowning
Owen Haley,	"	25	July 11, 1873	Arrest of 17 pickpockets and shoplifters, from May 30 to July 7, 1873
Patrick F Byrnes,	"	8	July 22, 1873	A brave arrest.
Michael Walsh,	"	7	July 25, 1873	Rescued a man from drowning
Jas. McCool,	"	4	Aug 20, 1873	Arrest of desperado
Jno. Morris,	R'dsm'n	22	Aug 26, 1873	Arrest of two ruffians
Chas. Hughes,	Patrol	21	Oct 21, 1873	Arrest and successfully resisting a mob.
Chas. Watson,	"	8	Dec 2, 1873	Courage in arresting a murderer.
Jas. Walstead,	"	18	Jan 6, 1874	Arrest mysterious letter box robber
Rob. J Cromie,	"	Mt'd Sqd	Jan 6, 1874	Courage when assaulted by a mob
Harrison Wilson,	"	19	Jan 17, 1874	Promptness and energy in extinguishing a fire.
John Doyle,	"	15	Feb. 4 1874	Coolness in rescuing three boys from a fire
Jas. Irving,	Capt	Det Sqd		
Thomas Sampson,	Patrol	"	April 24, 1874	Breaking up well organized conspiracies to control stock operations
Philip Farley,	"	"		

Name	Rank	Precinct	Date	Nature of Service
Wm G Elder,	Patrol	Det. Sqd		Courage, etc., in arrest and conviction of gang of masked burglars
Richd Fields,	"	"	April 24, 1874	
Richd King,	"	"		
Holly Lyons,	"	"		
Jas Irving,	Capt	"		Skill in working up case against "Steurer," for furnishing burglars' tools, clearing up mystery of Sing Sing escapes.
Thos Sampson,	Patrol	"	April 24, 1874	
Philip Farley,	"	"		
Michael Walsh,	"	7	June 19, 1874	Rescued boy from drowning
Daniel Frazier,	"	22	Sept. 8, 1874	Courage in arresting John Branstein.
James Darwin,	"	21	Dec. 23, 1874	Assistance to Health Department.
Geo. W. Skidmore,	"	5	Jan 12, 1875	Rescued two children from burning
Michael Farley,	"	18	Jan. 12, 1875	Arrest burglar, left sick bed and partly clothed at time.
Lawrence Clarson,	"	18	Jan. 12, 1875	Brave arrest of desperadoes, who shot at him
Adam Corell,	"	5	Jan. 29, 1875	For bravery
Patrick F Doyle,	"	7	Feb 16, 1875	Gallant conduct at fire
Alonzo Powell,	"	7		
Gustavus Dahlgren,	R'dsm'n	13		Courage at fire, saving lives of nine children
Abm Livingston,	Patrol	13		
Philip Reveille,	"	13	Mch 24, 1875	
John E Coombs,	"	13		
Michael Gorman,	"	13		
Wm H Thomas,	"	19	Mch 24, 1875	Courage at fire; saved nine lives No. 1106 Second Avenue
Bernard Tully,	"	19	Mch 24, 1875	Series of officer-like acts, etc.
Michael Walsh,	"	7	Mch 31, 1875	Bravery in arresting desperado
Wm Burke,	"	16	May 13, 1875	Pursuing and arresting a thief
Wm Londrigan,	"	5	May 10, 1875	Risked life to save two persons, runaway horse
George Davis,	"	26	May 29, 1875	Prompt action, assault on Deputy Comptroller Earle
Barth Gaffney,	"	18	June 8, 1875	Bravery in arrest of four burglars
James Stewart,	R'dsm'n	18		
Benj. Mallane,	Patrol	9	June 10, 1875	Rescue of man from drowning
Thos Brennan,	"	9	July 2, 1875	Rescue of boy from drowning
Wm Granger,	"	19		
John O'Brien,	"		July 20, 1875	Arresting desperado, McEveety shot at the time.
Bernard McEveety,	"	19		
Thos Burkitt,	"	9	Aug. 3, 1875	Arrest of two burglars
Manus McBride,	"	18	Aug 17, 1875	Stopping runaway horse
J W. Dychman,	"	25	Sept 3, 1875	Stopping runaway at risk of life
Thos W Thorne,	Inspect'r		Oct 1, 1875	Zeal, energy and ability in case of murder of Abm Wessbig
John McGowan,	Patrol	19	Oct. 8, 1875	Arrest of one of the murderers of Abm. Wessbig
Chas McDonnell,	Capt	8	Oct. 26, 1875	
Peter P. Lamb,	Patrol	4	Dec. 24, 1875	Jumped in river, saved a man
James Gannon,	"	Mt'd Sqd	Jan 21 1876	Stopped a runaway team
Chas. Hughes,	R'dsm'n	8		Extraordinary courage in arresting burglars
John Watson,	Patrol	8	Mch 21, 1876	
Edward Sullivan,	"	8		
Selden A Woodruff,	"	5		
Wm Darke,	"	25	April 1, 1876	Stopped runaway team at great risk.
Wm O'Conner,	"	25	April 1, 1876	" " " " "
Michael O'Ryan,	"	16	May 2, 1876	" " " " "
James Gannon,	"	Mt'd Sqd	June 20, 1876	" " " " "
James J Hart,	"	14	June 26, 1876	Arrest burglar, severe and prolonged struggle
Patrick Green,	"	21	July 21, 1876	Arrest escaped convict
John Jefferson,	"	22	Sept 19, 1876	Arrest of murderer
John Delaney,	"	29	Sept 19, 1876	Arrest of escaped convict
Michael Gorman,	"	13	Nov 29, 1876	Saving man from drowning

Name	Rank	Precinct	Date	Nature of Service
John McDowell,	Patrol	29	Jan 12, 1877	Arrest burglar in act, officer shot; medal
William Murray,	Capt	4	Jan 12, 1877	Arrest burglars
Patrick F. Byrnes,	R'dsm'n	8	Jan. 12, 1877	Rescued child from burning building.
Christopher Wall,	Patrol	8	Jan 12, 1877	Rescue of man, wife and two children from burning
John Murphy,	"	8		
Chas. McDonnell,	Capt.	8	Feb. 27, 1877	Rescue of woman and two children
Philip C Bleil,	Patrol	9	Mch 5, 1877	Jumping in river, saving a man.
John H McCullagh,	Capt	17	Mch 5, 1877	Seizure of stolen property.
Geo. E Holme,	Patrol	19	Mch 5, 1877	Rescue of man from drowning
Clemens Miller,	"	8	Mch 30, 1877	Rescued two children from burning
Joseph Johnson,	"	8		
Philip C Bleil,	"	9	April 13, 1877	Jumping in river, saving drunken man.
Lester Lewis,	R'dsm'n	25	April 13, 1877	Stopped runaway horse after being hurt by it
John Nugent,	Patrol	7	April 13, 1877	Rescued old people from burning building after great difficulty and danger, special mention of Nugent.
Thomas Regan,	"	7		
John McSweeny,	"	7		
Daniel Fitzpatrick,	"	4	May 29, 1877	Rescued man from burning
Patrick Walsh,	"	9	Sept 5, 1877	Rescued woman from burning
Geo W Paddock,	"	25	Sept 5, 1877	Arrest of bank robber
Peter O'Neil,	"	8	Dec 31, 1877	Arrest of thief after struggle, wounded
Philip C Bleil,	"	S B S	Dec. 31, 1877	Jumped in river, saved woman
Harry Green,	"	32	Mch 19, 1878	Earnest endeavors to arrest two thieves.
Francis J McCarthy,	R'dsm'n	20	April 5, 1878	Rescued lady from drowning
Gerard E. Beekman,	Patrol	S. B S	Sept 6, 1878	Rescued man from drowning.
Patrick McGloin,	"	16	Sept 6, 1878	Arrest of ex-convict.
Michael Gorman,	"	13	Oct 8, 1878	Rescued woman from drowning, risk of life (suicide)
Thomas McCormick	"	20	Oct 22, 1878	Saved life of man assaulted
James Quigley,	"	18	Oct 22, 1878	Rescued man from drowning, risk of life
Max Meiers,	"	13	Jan 30, 1879	Rescued woman from burning
Stephen O'Brien,	"	13	Jan 30, 1879	Rescued three persons from burning
Oliver Vail,	"	4	Jan 30, 1879	Rescued from drowning a woman, risk of life (suicide)
Michael Gorman,	"	13	Feb 4, 1879	Rescued woman and three children from burning
Thomas Byrnes,	Capt	15	Feb 26, 1879	Arresting highway robbers, medal
James K Price,	R'dsm'n	29	Feb 28, 1879	Arrest of thief, property recovered
John Delaney,	Patrol	21	Mch 25, 1879	Stopped runaway team, saving number of lives
Thos J Crystal,	"	10	April 25, 1879	Arrest of notorious burglar
Patrick H Marron,	"	31	June 22, 1879	Arrest of ex convict after being shot at and knocked down.
Chauncey T. Quintard	"	32	July 22, 1879	Rescued child from drowning
George A Bennett,	"	19	Aug 15, 1879	Rescued boy from drowning
Michael Fanning,	Sergt	18	Dec 27, 1879	Arrest of two desperadoes
John Delaney,	R'dsm'n	21	Dec 2, 1879	Rescued boy from drowning, risk of life
John H Genore,	Patrol	29	Jan. 25, 1880	Brave conduct at a fire
Aug. Starboro,	R'dsm'n	4	Jan. 25, 1880	Arrest of murderer of Pietro Balbo.
Gilbert Carr,	Patrol	4		
John Breen,	"	Mt'd Sqd	Mch 17, 1880	Stopped runaway team
Thomas Farley,	R'dsm'n	13	Mch 17, 1880	Rescued man from drowning, risk of life
Martin Finnerty,	Patrol	20	Mch 26, 1880	Arrest of escaped convict, shot at four times, wounded
Richard Cahill,	"	21	May 4, 1880	Rescued woman and five others from burning, risk of life
Chas A L Schier,	R'dsm'n	24	May 14, 1880	Rescued four persons from drowning, risk of their own lives
Daniel Quigley,	Patrol	24		
Miles Keon,	"	24		
Ernest Linderman,	R'dsm'n	9	June 29, 1880	Arrest of highway robber and five others, severely wounded.
James Quigley,	Patrol	8	June 29, 1880	Jumped in river and saved man, risk of life.

Name.	Rank	Precinct	Date	Nature of Service.
John McGinley,	Patrol	27	Aug 2, 1880	Rescued man from drowning.
William Gardner,	"	S B S	Jan 28, 1881	Rescued man from drowning
Thos B Holland,	"	Mt'd Sqd	Jan. 31, 1881	Stopped runaway team
Louis De Gan, .	"	S B S	Feb 15, 1881	Jumped in river, saved man, risk of life
James Gannon,	R'dsm'n	Mt'd Sqd	April 30, 1881	Stopped runaway team,
Patrick Kearney,	Patrol	S B S	May 12, 1881	Jumped in river, saved two men
John J. Reilley, .	"	18	June 15, 1881	Arrested desperado, stabbed dangerously
Thos B Holland,	"	Mt'd Sqd	June 15, 1881	Stopped runaway team
Wm J Huston,	"	"	June 30, 1881	Stopped runaway team
Chas S Pike,	"	5	Sept 29, 1881	Arrested burglar, shot dangerously.
Thomas Byrnes,	Inspect'r		Nov 15, 1881	Detection and arrest of blackmailer (medal)
Richard J Barry,	R'dsm'n	8	Nov 30, 1881	Good service at falling buildings in Grand Street
M F Schmittberger,	"	29	Dec 9. 1881	Arrest of thieves, property recovered.
Dennis O'Hara,	Patrol	27	Dec. 13, 1881	Detection and arrest of truck thieves
Thos Gleeson, .	"	17	Jan. 31, 1882	Detection and arrest of two burglars.
Jacob Tooker,	"	19	Feb. 21, 1882	Arrest of burglars after being shot at.
James Gannon, .	"	Mt'd Sqd	June 7, 1882	Stopped runaway team.
M F Schmittberger,	R'dsm'n	29	July 7, 1882	Arrest expert thief, Michael Dowdell
Wm B Deeves,	Patrol	18		Rescuing fourteen women and children from burning building, 103 Washington Street, on July 21, 1882; silver medals given.
Patrick Reynolds,	"	18	July 31, 1882	
John O'Neill, No 1,	"	18		
George Nolan, . .	"	S B S		
John Cottrell, .	"	6	Sept 1, 1882	Rescued woman and child from burning building.
George Bicknell, .	"	Mt'd Sqd	Sept 28, 1882	Stopped runaway horse, rescued child
John Delaney,	R'dsm'n	1st Court	Mch 23, 1883	After being shot, faint and bleeding, shot and killed a ruffian named McGowan
John T Clarker,	Patrol	4	May 22, 1883	In arresting an insane man who had killed Patrolman Francis Mallon
Thos. Gilbride, .	"	4		
Herman Inteman,	"	10	June 1, 1883	Arresting two burglars
John Kavanagh, .	"	12	Aug 1, 1883	Saving boy from drowning
Patrck Rabbit	"	22	Sept 11, 1883	After being stabbed, brought prisoner to station house.
John Sanders, . .	Capt	23	Sept. 22, 1883	Saving several persons from drowning
Wm. Nelson, . .	Patrol	2	Oct 27 1883	Stopping runaway horse
Chas H Francis,	"	32	Nov 5, 1883	Stopping runaway team
James K. Price,	R'dsm'n	Det. Sqd	Nov. 25, 1883	Arrest of thieves, property recovered
James J Connor,	Patrol	14	Dec 15, 1883	Saving lives from burning building
James Dougherty, .	"	14		
David H Crowley,	Sergt	7	Dec 18, 1883	Saving lives from burning building.
Thos Byrnes,	Inspect'r		Dec 21, 1883	Arrest and conviction of Edward G Raugh, for crime of arson
Edward Slevin,	Sergt			
Thos Dusenberry,	Det Sgt			
Dennis O'Hara, .	Patrol	27	Jan 21, 1884	Rescued woman and child from drowning.
Oscar Havle, . .	"	25	Jan 21, 1884	Stopping runaway team
James Taggart, .	"	15	Jan 25, 1884	Saved man from being killed by falling building.
George Walsh, .	"	5	Feb. 20, 1884	Rescue of family from burning building.
John J Meagher, .	"	5	Feb 20, 1884	
George Gick, . .	"	27	Mch 25, 1884	Rescue of woman from burning building.
Dennis Murphy,	"	18	April 11, 1884	Saved four persons from burning building
John Kelly, .	"	18	April 11, 1884	
Andrew Bradley, .	"	18	April 11, 1884	
Thomas Gilbride,	"	18	April 11, 1884	
John D Herlihy,	R'dsm'n	18	April 24, 1884	Rescued a lady from burning building
Patrick Brogan,	Patrol	27	Aug. 13, 1884	Arrest of ruffian, after being knocked down and beaten
Wm. Wright, .	"	S B. S	Oct. 21, 1884	Rescued man from drowning.

CHAPTER XXII.

SKETCH OF THE POLICE PENSION FUND

CREATED BY ACT OF 1857 —THE FUND MADE UP OF THE SALES OF UNCLAIMED PROPERTY —POLICE LIFE AND HEALTH INSURANCE FUND —BENEFICIARIES OF THE ACT —METROPOLITAN REWARD FUND —POLICE LIFE INSURANCE FUND.— THE POLICE COMMISSIONERS A BOARD OF TRUSTEES.—THE TREASURER OF THE BOARD OF COMMISSIONERS TREASURER OF THE BOARD OF TRUSTEES —RECEIPTS AND DISBURSEMENTS.— THE LATE COMMISSIONER NICHOLS — COMMISSIONER MCCLAVE —BOOKKEEPER GEORGE P. GOTT.—PAYING PENSIONERS —FINANCIAL STATEMENT OF THE POLICE PENSION FUND

THE Metropolitan Police Act, 1857, provided for the establishment of a Life and Health Insurance Fund, for the benefit of Policemen disabled by wounds received in service, or, if killed, for the support of their families. The fund was made up of the sales of unclaimed stolen property, of rewards, and of voluntary contributions, and fines collected for violation of Sunday laws. The sums, in the latter part of 1858, received from these sources amounted to two thousand six hundred and twenty-three dollars and ten cents, a portion of which was invested in New York City bonds, bearing seven per cent interest per annum.

There were then two pensioners on the fund, one, the widow of Thomas Sparks, Patrolman, who was killed by rioters on the third of July, 1857; the other, the widow of Horatio Sanger, who died from wounds received while attempting to arrest disorderly persons in November, 1857. From the insufficiency of the fund in 1858, neither had received relief. When the revenue should become adequate, it was proposed to pay them each the interest, quarter-yearly, on two thousand dollars, at six per cent per annum

The Police Life and Health Insurance Fund (Chapter 569, Laws of 1857) provided that all rewards, fees, proceeds of gifts and emoluments that might be allowed by the Board of Police, should be paid and given for account of extraordinary services of any member of the Police force, and all moneys arising from the sale of unclaimed goods should constitute a fund to be called the "Police Life and Health Insurance Fund." The persons who from time to time should fill the office of the Treasurer of the Board of Police, and that of the Comptroller of the cities of New York and Brooklyn, were declared the Trustees of said fund, and might invest the same as they should see fit, either in whole or in part. The following were entitled to the benefits of this fund.

1 Whenever any member of the Police force, in the actual performance of duty, should become bodily disabled, his necessary expenses, on the certificate

Police Monument, Cypress Hill Cemetery

of a Police Surgeon, stating the manner, cause and condition of injury, and approved by the Board, during the time his disabling as aforesaid should continue, might become a charge upon the fund, provided for in the above-mentioned chapter.

2. If such injuries were likely to continue for life, the sum of one thousand dollars might be charged upon the said fund to be paid to the person so injured.

3. If any member of the Police force should be killed in the performance of his duty, or should die from the effects of any injury received by him whilst in such performance, and that there should be any person absolutely interested, pecuniarily, in the continuance of his life, a sum of two thousand dollars might be chargeable against the said fund, to be paid to the person so interested.

This act was amended April 10, 1860, substantially as follows. All fines imposed by the Board of Police upon members of the force, by way of discipline; and all moneys remaining for the space of one year in the hands of the Property Clerk, or arising from the sale of unclaimed goods; and all proceeds of suits for penalties, should be deposited to the credit of the Police Life Insurance Fund. The Board of Metropolitan Police, and the Comptrollers of the cities of New York and Brooklyn, were declared the Trustees of the fund. Those whom the fund were designed to benefit, and the pensions they were entitled to, are as follows: (1) Any member of the force who should, in the actual discharge of his duty, become permanently disabled, so as to render his dismissal from membership necessary, or if such member became superannuated after ten years of membership, the sum of one hundred and fifty dollars as an annuity was to be paid such member. (2) should a member be killed, or die, from the immediate effects of any injury received by him whilst in the discharge of duty, should he leave a widow, or if no widow, any child or children under the age of sixteen years, a like sum by way of annuity should become chargeable upon the said fund, to be paid to such widow so long as she remained unmarried, or to such child or children under the age of sixteen years. The Board, in its discretion, might at any time order such annuity to cease.

All property and money that should remain in the custody of the Property Clerk for the period of six months without any lawful claimant thereto, after having been three times advertised in public newspapers, should be sold at public auction, and the proceeds of such sale paid into the Police Life Insurance Fund.

An amended Act (April 25, 1864) made similar provisions regarding the sources from which the revenue should be derived. Moneys and unclaimed goods remaining in the possession of the Property Clerk one year (not six months, as above) and all proceeds of suits for penalties under this amended act, should be deposited and kept as a fund to be called the "Police Life Insurance Fund." The Treasurer of the Board of Police, and the Comptroller of the cities of New York and Brooklyn, were declared the Trustees of the said fund.

The clause having reference as to who should be the beneficiaries, and the amounts they should be entitled to by way of pensions, was the same as detailed in the last paragraph of the preceding Act.

An Act to enable the Board of Supervisors of the county of New York to raise money by tax for certain county purposes, and to provide the auditing and payment of unsettled claims against said county, passed the legislature April 25, 1867. This act authorized the Board of Police to offer rewards to induce all persons to give information which should lead to the detection, arrest, and conviction of persons guilty of homicides, arson, or receiving stolen goods knowing them to be stolen, and to pay such rewards to such persons as should give such information Such rewards should be paid from "The Metropolitan Reward Fund," which fund should be formed by investing from money deducted from the pay of members of the Metropolitan Police force, on account of lost time, at a rate not exceeding fifty cents per month for each member respectively; to which should be added all sums subscribed or contributed by insurance companies and other citizens The Commissioners of Police to be the Trustees of the said fund, and to invest and manage the same.

The Act also authorized the Board of Police, in their discretion, to pay out of the Police Life Insurance Fund. (1) an amount not exceeding three hundred dollars, to the members of the force who might be disabled while in the discharge of their duties (2) In the case of death by injuries, the annuities should be continued to the widow, or children, or both, as the Board might deem best. The Board was constituted Trustees of the fund

An amendment to the above chapter, passed May 2, 1868, declared that the revenue of the Pension Fund should be derived from the following sources. All fines imposed by the Board of Police upon members of the force, by way of discipline, and collectable from pay or salary; and all rewards, fees, proceeds of gifts and emoluments that might be paid and given for account of extraordinary services of any member of the Metropolitan Police force (except when allowed to be retained by such member); and all moneys remaining for the space of one year in the hands of the Property Clerk, or arising from the sale of unclaimed goods; and all proceeds of suits for penalties under the Act thereby amended, should be deposited and paid into the bank wherein the Treasurer of the Board should keep an account The payments so made to constitute a fund to be called the "Police Life Insurance Fund" The Commissioners of Police were declared the Trustees of the said fund

The beneficiaries of the Pension Fund were in this, as in subsequent Acts, classified as follows.

1 Any member who should, whilst in the actual performance of duty, become permanently disabled, physically or mentally, so as to be unfit for duty, or any such member who, after ten years' membership, should be superannuated by age, or rendered incapable of performing Police duty by disease contracted without misconduct on his part

Each were granted and paid a pension not exceeding three hundred dollars per annum.

2 If any member of the force, while in the actual discharge of duty, should be killed, or should die from the effects of any injury received by him in like manner, or should die after ten continuous years of service (such death not being caused by misconduct on his part), leaving a widow, the name of such widow might be placed on said pension roll, and a like pension paid to her from

said fund, so long as she remained unmarried If such member, dying as aforesaid, should leave any minor child or children, but no widow (or if a widow, then after her death), the name or names of such child or children under the age of eighteen years might be placed on the pension roll, and a pension from said fund paid to such child or children, if more than one, to be divided equally between them, such pension or share of pensions to cease when the said child or the children respectively arrive at the age of eighteen years, or whenever earlier discontinued by order of the Board

Bookkeeper Gott's Office.
(Pensioners Drawing their Pay.)

The charter of 1870 (April 5) re-organizing the local government of the city of New York, made some new provisions After the Board had ascertained what portion of the Police Life Insurance Fund and Metropolitan Reward Fund, respectively, of the Metropolitan Police, belonged to, or should be set apart for, the Police of the city of New York, the amount so found was paid over to the Chamberlain of the city of New York, as trustee, for the benefit of the Police of the city of New York, as contemplated in the creation of said funds. All fines imposed by the Police Board on the members, by way of discipline, all rewards, fees, proceeds of gifts and emoluments that might be paid and given for account of extraordinary services of any members of the force, and all moneys remaining for the space of two years in the hands of the Property Clerk, or arising from the sale of unclaimed goods, and all proceeds of suits for penalties under this Act—payments so made should constitute a fund to be called the " Police Life Insurance Fund "

The City Chamberlain was made the trustee of said fund, with power to invest the same, in whole or in part, as he should deem most advantageous for the objects of the fund.

All property and money remaining in the custody of the Property Clerk for the period of six months without any lawful claimant, after having been three times advertised in public newspapers, should be sold at public auction, and the proceeds paid into the Police Life Insurance Fund.

A subsequent Act, passed April 26 of the same year (1870), made further provisions for an addition to the sources of income of the Police Life Insurance Fund, namely: there should be taken monthly out of the moneys deducted from the pay of members of the force on account of lost time, a sum calculated at the rate of fifty cents per month for each member of the force, which sum should be paid to the City Chamberlain, and invested by him as part of the Police Life Insurance Fund. Such portion of the "Metropolitan Reward Fund" as should belong to, or be awarded to the city in the division thereof, should be paid over to the City Chamberlain, as trustee of the Police Life Insurance Fund, and become a part of said last-named fund, and be invested as such. The Board of Police were empowered, in their discretion, by resolution to be adopted by a unanimous vote, to dismiss from office any Captain or Sergeant, and place the person so dismissed on the pension roll of said Police Life Insurance Fund, and allow him an annual retiring pension of (not exceeding in amount) one half the annual salary or compensation of such office In like manner, the Board might dismiss any Patrolman, and place him upon the pension roll, and allow him an annual retiring pension (not exceeding in amount) four hundred dollars per annum.

An Act concerning " The Police Life Insurance Fund," and the powers and duties of the Police Department, was passed March 17, 1871, by which the Commissioners of Police were constituted a Board of Trustees of "The Police Life Insurance Fund." They might organize as such Board by choosing one of their number to be Chairman, and appointing a Secretary. The Treasurer of the Board of Police should be the Treasurer of the Board of Trustees Such Board of Trustees should have charge of, and administer said fund, and from time to time invest the same, or any part thereof, as they should deem most beneficial to said fund. The said Board of Trustees were constituted the legal successors of the City Chamberlain, and also of the Board of the Metropolitan Police.

The Police Life Insurance Fund consisted of

First. The capital, income, interest, dividends, cash, deposits, securities and credits, then belonging to said fund, with the addition thereto from time to time of—

OUR POLICE PROTECTORS

Second   All fines imposed by the Board of Police upon members of the Police force, and

Third   All rewards, fees, gifts, testimonials and emoluments that might be presented, paid, or given to any member of the Police for account of Police service (except such as should be allowed by the Board to be retained by said member); and

Fourth   All lost or stolen moneys remaining in the hands of the Property Clerk for the space of one year, subject to the usual conditions

Fifth   One dollar per month for each member of the force, taken monthly by the Treasurer from moneys deducted from the pay of members on account of lost time

George P Gott.
(Treasurer's Bookkeeper.)

The Board was given power, in its discretion, to grant pensions of not exceeding three hundred dollars per annum, to the persons mentioned, and in the manner previously described

GEORGE P GOTT was born in the City of Albany   Having received an academical education, at the age of eighteen years he was placed in a hardware store, where he remained until the spring of the year 1853   He then came to New York, and entered the hardware house of Edward Corning & Co., 81 John Street   After a short service he was placed in a confidential position, which he continued to occupy until 1858, when he resigned   In August, 1858, he received a notice to appear at Police Headquarters, then on the corner of Broome and Elm Streets, and was offered the position of Bookkeeper of the Metropolitan Police. After some hesitation he consented to accept the situation, and was duly appointed by the Board, which office he still holds.

The law was again changed on April 30, 1873, wherein by resolution adopted by a full Board, any Inspector, Captain, Sergeant, Patrolman, or Surgeon, if disabled in the actual performance of duty, could be retired from office on an annual pension not exceeding in amount one-third their annual salary or compensation. But no such Inspector, Captain, Sergeant, Patrolman or Surgeon should be so retired from office and placed on the pension roll except at his own request in writing, unless due notice was given him of the intention so to retire him, nor unless it should be certified to the Board by two of the Police Surgeons that he was, in their opinion, permanently, mentally and physically incapacitated from duty; nor unless the Board should concur in such opinion, nor unless the nature and origin of such incapacity should be stated in the resolution so retiring him. The Board was empowered to forfeit or withhold pay for certain specified offenses from members of the force, but no more than thirty days pay should be so forfeited for any offense. All such fines to be paid by the Treasurer of the Police Department to the account of the Police Life Insurance Fund. All property and money remaining in the hands of the Property Clerk for six months without any lawful claimant, after having been advertised for ten days, should be sold at public auction, and the proceeds paid into the Police Life Insurance Fund.

A supplementary Act to the above was passed June 13, 1873. It empowered the Police Board to grant a pension to any widow of any deceased member of the Metropolitan Police force, from the time of his death, if any such member was, at the time of his death, assigned to duty in the city of New York, and his widow at the time entitled to receive a pension, provided that no such pension should have been previously granted.

The Legislature, on June 4, 1878, framed an Act to create a Police Pension Fund for disabled and retired Policemen in the city of New York, which, summarized, is as follows:

Widow $300. To terminate when remarried or at discretion of the Board	Of Member of force killed in performance of duty, or shall have died from effects of injuries received whilst in the actual discharge of such duty, or died after ten years' service, provided such death shall not have been caused by misconduct on his part
Child or Children Under 18 years, not exceeding $300. To terminate at 18 years of age, or at discretion of the Board.	Of Member of Force killed or dying as aforesaid, but leaving no widow, or if a widow, then after her death to such child or children yet under eighteen years of age
Policeman Not to exceed one half nor less than one-quarter rate of compensation. To terminate at discretion of the Board.	While in performance of police duty, and by reason of same, and without fault or misconduct, become permanently disabled, physically or mentally, so as to be unfitted to perform full police duty.
Policeman $300 To terminate at discretion of the Board	After ten years' membership, superannuated by age, or rendered incapable of performing full police duty by reason of disability or disease, contracted without misconduct on his part

POLICEMAN $400 To terminate at discretion of the Board.	After fifteen years' membership, superannuated by age, or rendered incapable of performing full police duty by reason of disability or disease, contracted without misconduct on his part
POLICEMAN Not to exceed one-half, or less than one-quarter full pay, and not to exceed $1,000 For natural life, and not to be revoked, repealed or diminished.	After twenty years or upwards, upon his own application, or upon certificate of Board of Surgeons as to permanent disability, so as to be unfit for police duty, may be retired by the unanimous vote of the full Board

NOTE.

In case any officer shall have voluntarily left the Police Department and entered into the United States service and served during the war of the rebellion, and received an honorable discharge, and afterwards shall have been reinstated in the Police Department, the time of his service in the army shall be considered as a portion of his service in the Police Department.

In determining the time of service of any member of the Force, continuous service in the late Metropolitan Force, and subsequently in the Police Department, shall be held to be Police service

Pensions on account of physical or mental disability or disease, not to be granted unless upon certificate of Board of Surgeons, setting forth cause, nature and extent of disability, disease or injury, and if same was incurred or sustained in the performance of Police duty

FUND.

First.—Capital, income, interest, dividends, cash deposits, securities and credits belonging to the Police Life Insurance Fund.

Second.—All fines imposed by the Board of Police upon members of the Police Force.

Third.—All rewards, fees, gifts, testimonials, and emoluments to members of the Force, except such as shall be allowed by the Board of Police to be retained by such member.

Fourth.—All lost or stolen money in the hands of the Property Clerk for one year unclaimed, and moneys arising from sale of unclaimed Property

Fifth.—A sum of money equal to three dollars per month for each member of the Force, to be paid monthly from moneys deducted for lost time

Section seven of the foregoing Act was amended, June 19, 1879, to read as follows:

"In determining the term of service of any member of the Police force under the provisions of this Act, service in the late Municipal and Metropolitan Police Departments, and subsequently in the Police Department of the city of New York, should be counted and held to be Police Service of the Police Department of the city of New York for all purposes of this Act."

On June 8, 1882, the legislature passed an Act to create a Police Pension Fund in the city of New York, and to provide for the equalization of pensions, of which the following is a summary:

WIDOW $300 To terminate when remarried or at discretion of the Board	Of member of force killed in performance of duty, or shall have died from effects of injuries received whilst in the actual discharge of such duty, or died after ten years' service in the Police Department or Force of the City of New York.
CHILD OR CHILDREN Under 18 years, not exceeding $200, to terminate at 18 years of age, or at discretion of the Board	Of member of force killed or dying as aforesaid, but leaving no widow, or if a widow, then after her death to such child or children yet unmarried and under eighteen years of age

Member of Police Department or Force, not to exceed $300, to terminate at discretion of the Board	While in performance of police duty, and by reason of same, and without fault or misconduct, become permanently disabled, physically or mentally, so as to be unfitted to perform full police duty
Member of Police Department or Force, not less than $300, nor exceeding $600. To terminate at discretion of the Board.	After ten years' and less than twenty years' membership, superannuated by age, or rendered incapable of performing full police duty by reason of disability or disease, contracted without misconduct on his part
Member of Police Department or Force, not less than $300, nor exceeding $500 To terminate at discretion of the Board	Permanently insane or mentally incapacitated.
Member of Police Department or Force, not less than one-half full pay, and not to exceed $1,000, except to Superintendent, for natural life, and not to be revoked, repealed or diminished.	After twenty years or upwards, upon his own application, or upon certificate of Board of Surgeons as to permanent disability, so as to be unfit for police duty, may be retired by the unanimous vote of the full Board

The First, Second, Third and Fourth Sections of the fund were the same as in the preceding Act. Section Five is as follows

A sum of money not exceeding four dollars per month for each member of the Force, to be paid monthly from moneys deducted or withheld from the pay of members of the Police Force on account of lost time

An Act to consolidate into one Act, and to declare the special and local laws affecting public interests in the city of New York, and provide a Pension Fund for the Police Department of the city, was passed July 1, 1882

An Act to amend Chapter 410 of the Laws of 1882 (Chapter 180 of the Laws of 1884, passed April 21, 1884), introduced the following changes.

The revenue of the fund is the same as in the preceding chapters, with the following exceptions. All moneys, pay, compensation, or salary, or any part thereof, forfeited, deducted or withheld from any member or members of the Police force for or on account of absence for any cause; lost or sick time, sickness or other disability, physical or mental, to be paid monthly by the Treasurer of the Board of Police Commissioners to the Treasurer of the Board of Trustees of the Police Pension Fund. Twenty-five per cent. annually of all excise moneys or license fees, derived or received by the Board of Excise, provided, however, that said twenty-five per cent. thereof shall not exceed one hundred thousand dollars in any one year, moneys derived from granting or issuing permits to carry pistols, all moneys derived or received from the granting or issuing of permits to hold or give masked balls, entertainments, or parties, moneys derived or received from the issuing or granting certificates of qualification to operate steam boilers, moneys derived or received from the suspension of Police officers, the Board being empowered for cause to suspend a Police officer without pay, for a term not exceeding thirty days.

The Board of Police, under this Act, was empowered to pension the widow of a retired Police officer.

SIDNEY P. NICHOLS

The late Sidney P. Nichols was fifty-three years old, and was born in Vermont. His father was a Presbyterian clergyman. Receiving a common school education, the boy determined to strike out a career for himself, and accordingly came to New York, where he secured employment as a clerk. After a few years, having saved some money, he embarked in the livery stable business near the site of the Ashland House, and prospered in the undertaking.

In a contest for the State Senate, Mr. Nichols was defeated by James W. Booth, but in recognition of the gallant struggle he had made, was appointed a Police Commissioner in May, 1876. Meantime he had become one of the proprietors of the Ninth Avenue line of stages, which proved a prosperous undertaking. On account of his extensive knowledge of the city, his expert judgment of horseflesh, and his experience in organizing considerable bodies of men, his colleagues insisted on making Mr Nichols Chairman of the Committee on Street Cleaning, which task was then imposed by law on the Police Board.

During Mayor Ely's term of office an attempt was unsuccessfully made to remove Mr. Nichols from the Police Board on a charge of neglect of duty. During the incumbency of Mayor Cooper the attempt was repeated (April 17, 1879), and gave rise to a notable legal contest. The Commissioner demanded to be heard through counsel and to be brought face to face with specific charges. He was summarily removed, however, with the requisite formal approval of Governor Robinson, Charles F. McLean being appointed his successor.

After protracted litigation, a decision of the Court of Appeals restored Mr Nichols to his office, February 7, 1880, thereby establishing a very important precedent. He was re-appointed by Mayor Edson January 10, 1883.

Mr. Nichols was a member of the Democratic State Committee.

Mr Nichols was of medium stature and firmly built, of fair, ruddy complexion, with bright, sparkling eyes, and pleasant mouth, and his face always wore a cheerful smile. He was the life and soul of the Police Board. It was always said that he could get through more work than any other two Commissioners who ever sat in the marble palace in Mulberry Street. His executive powers were in constant demand. He was a prime favorite throughout the force. His death, which was due to aneurism of the heart, took place at his residence, No 417 West Twenty-fifth Street, on the twenty-eighth of October, 1884. Commissioner Nichols was Treasurer of the Police Pension Fund. The interment was in Greenwood Cemetery.

COMMISSIONER JOHN MCCLAVE was appointed by Mayor Edson, November 24, 1884. He was born in this city in 1839, and is the youngest of twelve children of the late James McClave, who was—for many years prior to 1854, when he retired from business—a lumber merchant. John McClave was graduated from the College of the City of New York in 1856. Following the footsteps of his father, he entered the lumber business, and has been engaged in it ever since. He now has a large lumber yard on the North River, between Twenty-first and Twenty-second Streets, and is the owner of considerable real estate. He entered politics in 1878, when he was elected Alderman, on the Republican ticket, from the Eighth Senatorial District. He was re-elected from the same district in 1879, and, in 1880, was elected Alderman-at-Large. In 1881 he received the unanimous Republican nomination for Alderman-at-Large, but declined to run. Before the meeting of the Republican County Convention in October last his name was mentioned among the possible Republican candidates for Mayor. He is President of the Republican Association of the Seventeenth Assembly District.

Mr. McClave is Treasurer of the Board of Police, and of the Police Pension Fund. He is also a member of the Committee on Repairs and Supplies.

There is no exaggeration in the statement that Mr. McClave, whether as a business man or a public functionary, is the most active, industrious, and painstaking of men. The amount of hard work he gets rid of without seeming to be busy at all is really marvelous. In fact, it is a necessity of his nature that his mental faculties must always find occupation. The ordinary man would find more than enough to do in the management of a large business concern which gives employment to a large number of hands. Not so Mr. McClave, who, while punctually attending to his own private business affairs, bestows all the necessary time and labor to the duties he is called upon to discharge at Police Headquarters. Mr. McClave spends a large part of every week day at his office attending to Police matters. He has brought to the transaction of these duties the same comprehensive and intelligent management which has so characterized him as one of our leading business men.

None but those conversant with the inside history of Police affairs can form anything like an adequate idea of the immense amount of labor that devolves upon the Police Commissioners. Every day brings its own particular duties and responsibilities, which can neither be ignored nor relegated to subordinates. Through them the vast and complicated machinery of the Police Department is put in operation, and, if the governing body be not attentive and intelligent, demoralization is likely to ensue in the ranks—to the great and lasting detriment of the public service. No greater compliment could be paid the present Board of Police Commissioners than is to be found in the present efficient condition of the Police force. Towards this improved state of affairs no official has contributed more largely than has Commissioner McClave.

As Treasurer of the Board, and of the Police Pension Fund, for which he receives no additional compensation, Mr. McClave has a vast amount of labor and responsibility imposed upon him. But, where system and order prevail, much can be done which otherwise would be impossible of accomplishment.

Very Truly Yours
John McClave

Statement of Disbursements and Receipts of the Police Life and Health Insurance Fund, Police Life Insurance Fund, and the Police Pension Fund, from 1857 to 1885, for the subjoined years:

	Year.	Disbursements	Receipts.
Police Life and Health Insurance Fund,	1857		423 10
	1858	30 00	2,200 00
	1859	244 12	3,650 49
	1860	811 64	5,023 41
	1861	1,425 75	11,242 81
	1862	2,133 32	9,657 76
	1863	2,642 32	8,545 53
	1864	3,906 59	19,920 99
	1865	6,680 72	27,647 09
	1866	7,436 50	43,476 40
	1867	7,965 04	31,456 63
Police Life Insurance Fund,	1868	13,788 63	32,212 61
	1869	19,808 64	36,449 78
	1870	50,037 09	85,910 89
	1871	45,757 54	64,709 56
	1872	57,305 95	64,459 02
	1873	61,434 38	63,360 97
	1874	74,908 29	78,846 74
	1875	64,684 21	69,481 54
	1876	59,802 73	61,306 91
	1877	75,845 67	60,484 18
	1878	71,342 84	91,715 29
	1879	80,750 28	114,293 55
	1880	101,067 83	113,869 56
Police Pension Fund,	1881	108,358 15	117,696 90
	1882	116,593 91	87,489 21
	1883	220,609 74	96,034 92
	1884	187,855 35	184,419 42
		$1,443,227 23	$1,585,985 26

NOTE—In 1866 the donation by the Japanese Embassy was credited to the Police Life Insurance Fund

In 1870 an adjustment of the Police Life Insurance Fund and the Metropolitan Reward Fund was made in pursuance of Chapter 383, passed April 26, 1870, and the balance remaining to the credit of the Metropolitan Reward Fund was placed to the credit of the Police Life Insurance Fund, and the amount due from the Police Life Insurance Fund and charged to said fund, was as follows City of Brooklyn, $23,441 24, Yonkers, $55 76, and Richmond County, $14 76

In 1883 $77,420 29 was paid by the Trustees of the Police Pension Fund for judgments obtained against the Board for sick time deducted from members of the force, which amount was credited to the fund for the five years prior to the year 1882 This sum was paid in pursuance of a decision rendered by the Court of Appeals, in the case of John Ryan against the Board, to recover the sick time deducted from his salary.

The invested capital of the Police Pension Fund, ending December 31, 1884, is invested in bonds of the City and County of New York, and amounts to the sum of $142,000, the cash balance on said date was $758 03, making a total capital of $142,758 03, and at said date there were 540 persons beneficiaries of the fund, classified as follows 303 males, 199 females, and 38 orphans

The Board of Police during the year 1884 pensioned six sergeants, eighty-nine patrolmen and twenty-one orphans, drawing, in the aggregate, $66,925 The deaths during said year were one captain, two sergeants, twenty-five patrolmen, and six females, drawing in the aggregate $14,615, making a total added to the Pension Fund during the year of $52,310

Statement of appropriations made to the Metropolitan Police (New York Force), and the Municipal Police and the Police Department of the City of New York

1857,	$825,000 00
1858,	471,031 79
1859,	930,209 95
1860,	1,294,812 51
1861,	1,352,736 73
1862,	1,716,189 18
1863,	1,751,263 73
1864,	1,747,555 67
1865	2,061,184 18
1866,	2,222,083 60
1867,	2,174,688 54
1868,	2,654,184 85
1869,	2,815,715 54
1870,	2,885,175 55
1871,	3,263,525 66
1872,	3,349,160 17
1873,	3,168,000 00
1874,	3,890,133 33
1875,	3,391,491 14
1876,	3,376,400 00
1877,	3,352,400 00
1878,	3,292,400 00
1879,	3,286,150 00
1880,	3,346,150 00
1881,	3,270,150 00
1882,	3,423,120 00
1883	3,350,450 00
1884,	3,453,150 00
	3,641,534 61

On the first of January, 1885, there were three hundred and three males, one hundred and ninety-nine females, and thirty-eight orphans, beneficiaries of the Pension Fund, who drew in the aggregate one hundred and eighty-seven thousand and eighty-seven dollars and thirty-seven cents for the year 1884. During this year the Board pensioned six Sergeants, eighty-nine Patrolmen, thirty-five widows, and twenty-one orphans.

CHAPTER XXIII.

THE WAY OF THE TRANSGRESSOR.

OUR POLICE COURTS —ARRAIGNMENT OF PRISONERS AND HOW THEIR CASES ARE DISPOSED OF.—THE POLICE JUSTICES EFFICIENT AND DISCRIMINATING.—COURTS OF SPECIAL SESSIONS, GENERAL SESSIONS, OYER AND TERMINER, ETC. DISTRICT ATTORNEY MARTINE AND HIS DEPUTIES.—FINES RECEIVED FROM POLICE COURTS.—NUMBER OF PRISONERS ARRESTED, ARRAIGNED AND CONVICTED—THE AMBULANCE SYSTEM.—EVILS OF INTEMPERANCE—A NEW CRIMINAL AGENCY—THE OPIUM HABIT.—"HITTING THE PIPE"—USES AND ABUSES OF OPIUM—AN OPIUM SMOKER'S OUTFIT.—VICE FOSTERED BY THE HERDING TOGETHER IN CROWDED TENEMENTS.—SOME GAUDY RESORTS. —CRIMINALS AND THEIR HAUNTS.

SWIFTLY, surely, and systematically, move the wheels of justice. Turn where he will the criminal finds himself confronted with the visible forms of the law. Sooner or later justice overtakes him.

The Police Courts have to deal each day with the big haul of prisoners that are gathered within the Police nets. There the process of "sorting" these unfortunates takes place. Some, whose sins are venial, are turned loose with an admonition from the bench; others are fined; others again are sentenced to short terms of imprisonment, while a small remnant is held for trial.

Almost every offender known to the law passes daily through the hands of the Police, from the red-handed murderer down to the case of simple assault or drunk and disorderly.

The work of the Police is never done—the task allotted to Sysiphus was not more recurrent and periodical than theirs. There is no cessation to their warfare on the criminal classes.

The Police Courts are held by eleven Police Justices or Magistrates appointed by the Mayor of the city, under the provisions of the statute of 1873, and holding office for terms of varying duration. They receive salaries of eight thousand dollars per annum each, and are distributed into six courts, as follows: Tombs, two Justices; Jefferson Market, two Justices, Essex Market, two Justices; Yorkville, or Fifty-seventh Street, two Justices; Harlem, two Justices, Tremont, one Justice; the last tribunal having been created by the Act which provided for the annexation of the new Wards formerly in Westchester County.

The Police Justices that took office on the fourth of November, 1873, succeeded to a Board of Police Justices elected under the old law

The statute law of the State requires that prisoners shall be taken to the nearest Police Court, and, in the city of New York, the designation of Police

Courts to which the various Police Precincts are to send their prisoners is made by the Commissioners of Police.

Although two Justices are assigned to each of the courts, excepting the court at Tremont, but one sits at a time. For a week each assigned Justice holds court in his district, examining prisoners, receiving complaints, issuing warrants, taking bail, and discharging all the business of a Police Court. The succeeding week is an off week with him, unless he happens to sit three times during the week in the Court of Special Sessions, or unless examinations of any length are set down before him during the week

No Police Courts are held on Sunday afternoon, and persons are sometimes arrested after the close of the Police Courts on Sunday morning, who, if they cannot get bail, are locked up until Monday

The prisons attached to the Police Courts are under the control of the Commissioners of Charities and Correction, and difficulties of jurisdiction have arisen from time to time

The courts are served by squads of Police attached to each court, who serve papers, run errands, and perform other similar duties for the Police Justices

THE COURT OF SPECIAL SESSIONS OF THE PEACE, having jurisdiction over all misdemeanors and over a very few felonies, such as petty larceny, is held by three Police Justices, who sit alternately for a month at a time. They sit thrice a week for about four hours, and dispose of an average of upwards of thirty or forty cases a day. No prosecuting officer appears in this court, and in many cases the Magistrates act as prosecuting attorneys, as counsel for the prisoners, as judges and as jury, a loading of responsibility which ought not to be encouraged.

THE COURT OF GENERAL SESSIONS has for many years been held by the Recorder and the City Judge Since the first of January, 1876, an additional Justice, known as the Judge of the Court of General Sessions, has been added.

THE COURT OF OYER AND TERMINER, the highest criminal court in the city, is held four or five times a year by a Justice of the Supreme Court

SUPREME COURT.—Noah Davis, Chief Justice; John R. Brady, Geo. C. Barrett, Charles Donohue, Abram R Lawrence, Chas. H. Van Brunt, Geo. P Andrews.

GENERAL SESSIONS —Frederick Smyth, Recorder; Rufus B Cowing, City Judge, Henry A Gildersleeve.

SUPERIOR COURT.—John Sedgwick, Chief Judge; Hooper C Van Vorst, John J. Friedman, Charles H. Truax, Richard O'Gorman, Geo L Ingraham.

COMMON PLEAS —Charles P. Daly, Chief Justice; Richard L Larremore, Miles Beach, Joseph F. Daly, George M. Van Hoesen, Henry W. Allen.

CITY COURT.—David McAdam, Chief Justice; Granville P Haws, Edward Browne, Chas. J. Nehrbas, S Burdett Hyatt, Ernest Hall.

The *personnel* of the District Attorney's office comprises the following:

District Attorney, Randolph B Martine; Assistants John R Fellows, Edward L. Parris, De Lancey Nicoll, Gunning S. Bedford; Deputy Assistants. James Fitzgerald, Ambrose H Purdy, Vernon M Davis, Bernard S Douras, John M. Coman. Deputy and Chief Clerk

RANDOLPH B. MARTINE is (and the statement can be made without any approach to flattery) one of the most popular public men of this city. He is popular not because of his election to the responsible office of Prosecuting Attorney of this city and county, but for his own sterling qualities of head and heart. Suave, considerate, generous, and polite to all, Mr. Martine is every inch a true born gentleman. Mr. Martine was born in the Sixteenth Ward in 1844. He is of French-Huguenot and Irish ancestry. His father, Theodore, was an extensive grocer and real estate dealer in this city. District Attorney Martine is a graduate of Columbia College, where he also studied law, and completed his legal attainments in the office of Judge Rapallo. He was admitted to the bar in 1866. Mr. Martine is a lawyer of extensive practice and wide

District Attorney Martine.

experience. He is the Bayard of his profession, without stain, and without reproach.

JOHN R. FELLOWS has served under six administrations in the District Attorney's office, namely, Garvin, Hall, McKeon, Peckham, Olney, and Martine. He is a man of ready eloquence and solid legal attainments. His power over a jury in the handling of a case has, in innumerable instances, brought conviction home to criminals who relied upon the power of money and legal talent to save them from the consequences of their crimes. Colonel Fellows is one of the leaders of the County Democracy, and is one of their most popular campaign orators.

GUNNING S. BEDFORD has had a long experience in criminal practice. He was Assistant District Attorney from 1865 to 1869, and for several years after was City Judge. Mr Bedford discharges the duties of his office with zeal and ability.

De Lancey Nicoll has been a member of the bar for ten years, and has built up a remunerative practice at his profession. He is able and popular.

Edward L. Parris has been a practicing lawyer for twenty years in our civil courts. He is chairman of the Young Men's Democratic Club. Mr. Parris graduated from Union College, Schenectady. He is a native of Maine. He is in the prime of life, his age being forty-three years. He is a member of the law firm of Parris & Parris.

James Fitzgerald, one of the youngest, and one of the ablest as well, of Mr. Martine's staff of able assistants, is a young man of talent, who, by his own force of character, talents and industry, has forged to the front rank. He is a graduate of Columbia Law School. Mr. Fitzgerald is an able pleader, and is well versed in criminal and civil law. He served in the Assembly and Senate, and has won golden opinions for his ability, affability and incorruptibility.

The Bridge of Sighs.

Vernon M. Davis is a young lawyer of note. He is a member of the firm of Davis, Cohen & McWilliam. He has charge of the preparation of indictments.

Ambrose H. Purdy is a lawyer of wide and varied experience. He was a member of Assembly from the Twenty-fourth District, and is connected with the County Democracy. He is bright, alert, and astute.

Bernard J. Douras studied his profession in the office of Vanderpoel, Green & Cuming, former lawyers for the sheriff. He entered their office as office boy, and worked himself up to be their managing clerk. He is possessed of solid legal attainments.

John M. Coman has been a practicing lawyer for a number of years. Previous to his coming into the District Attorney's office he had been clerk in Police Justice White's Court.

William N. Penney, District Attorney Martine's private secretary, took office first under the late John McKeon. Mr. Penney is a well-known journalist, and is talented, popular, and ambitious. He is a prominent member of the Press Club.

The Police Magistracy of the city have for the past ten years been spoken of by both citizens and the press as an exemplary body of public servants, laboring for the public weal with moderation and justice. The Police Justices are: James F. Kilbreth, Henry Murray, Patrick G. Duffy, Jacob M. Patterson, Jr., Maurice J. Power, Andrew J. White, J. Harry Ford, Solon B. Smith, John J. Gorman, Daniel O'Reilly, and Charles Welde.

Fines averaging nearly forty thousand dollars per annum are collected by the Magistrates in the Police Courts, and with those collected by the Warden of the City Prison and the Clerk of the Court of Special Sessions, the yearly average amount of fines reaches about seventy-five thousand dollars

THE FIRST DISTRICT POLICE COURT, popularly known as the Tombs, comprises the district bounded by Houston Street, Broadway to Canal Street, the Bowery and Catharine Street, the East and North Rivers Seven precincts arraign their prisoners here. The Tombs Police Court tries more prisoners than any of the five other Police Courts Of late years there has been a falling away in the number of arraignments, due, largely, to the gradual disappearance of the rotten old rookeries of tenements and a corresponding increase in the number of a better class of dwellings and busi-

Interior View of "Male Prison."

ness stores and factories. Statistics show that drunkenness has decreased in this district from twenty to forty per cent This is due largely to the suppression by the Police of the low groggeries in the Fourth and Sixth Wards

The Tombs is a huge building of unique architecture—the world has no prison like it elsewhere, it receives hundreds of prisoners every day, two courts hold sessions within its gloomy walls. At all hours of the day and night officers of the law and their prisoners are passing its portals

The Tombs was erected for about two hundred prisoners. Recently, between three and four hundred a day have been received, with consequent overcrowding, notwithstanding the utmost diligence on

Place of Execution

the part of the courts in disposing of its inmates by sending them, after sentence, to the Penitentiary on Blackwell's Island, to the State Prisons at

Sing Sing or Auburn, and to reformatories, and by the liberation of the guiltless. Vehicles known as "Black Marias" are used in bringing prisoners from local places of detention in the city and taking them to the various points of departure to the jails to which they have been sentenced

The office of the "Female Prison" is as pleasant an apartment as womanly taste and skill can make it. It is light, and ornamented with flowers in the windows and pictures on the walls. Cells for inmates are twenty-two in

Interior of the Tombs Police Court.

number, and vary in appearance. Women and girls have fewer restraints than males. They take their meals together, flit about the corridors along which the cells are situated, and chat, and read, or sew. Three large cells are set apart for girls arrested for a first offense. Each contains half a dozen or more beds, covered with neat checked counterpanes, and the coarse sheeting is clean. The Tombs being simply a place of detention, no unnecessary prohibitions are imposed. Hence some of the cells are as presentable places as circumstances will admit of

The "Male Prison" is by far the largest prison structure within the architectural shell known as the Tombs. It is two hundred feet in length and forty in width, built of massive stone four stories high. The accompanying view was taken from the second tier of the four which complete the building. Murderers' Row is on the first tier, which, by the way, has the roomiest cells. Each tier is opened into through a massive gateway, where sits the officer in charge at his desk. Arrivals of prisoners, and more of visitors, keep each of these men busy inspecting papers and closing and admitting persons. The corridors on each tier front the cells, over the grated doorway of each of which is a slate giving the prisoner's name.

THE SECOND DISTRICT POLICE COURT, known as Jefferson Market, vies with the Tombs in the number of cases brought there by the Police. This is one of the handsomest public buildings in the city. Here are accommodations for a great many prisoners, criminals and vagrants. The latter are confined in one large apartment, known as "the ten day house." From thence they are conveyed in the prison van to the foot of East Twenty-sixth Street, where

Jefferson Market Police Court (Ninth Street and Sixth Avenue)

they are taken on board the "Thomas S Brennan," the "Minnahannock," or the "Bellevue," to Blackwell's Island

The district comprises the territory lying south of Forty-second Street, west of Fourth Avenue, and north of Houston Street. The precincts included in its territory are the Eighth, Ninth, Fifteenth, Sixteenth, Twentieth, and Twenty-ninth. This district embraces the territory known as Murray Hill, all the prominent hotels, and many of the theaters and other places of amusement. The best and the worst of New York's populace live within this district

THE THIRD DISTRICT, or Essex Market Police Court, has jurisdiction over "the great East Side" Catharine Street, the Bowery, Fourteenth Street, and the East River, constitute its boundaries The precincts represented in the district are the Seventh, Tenth, Eleventh, Thirteenth, and Seventeenth

THE FOURTH DISTRICT POLICE COURT, known as the Yorkville Police Court, and located in Fifty seventh Street, between Third and Lexington Avenues, is a roomy, well-lighted building The precincts that arraign their prisoners here are the Eighteenth, Nineteenth, Nineteenth Sub, Twenty-first, Twenty-second, and Twenty eighth Precincts

THE FIFTH DISTRICT POLICE COURT (Harlem) is held in the Harlem Market Building, in One Hundred and Twenty-fifth Street, near Fourth Avenue Prisoners are brought here from the Twelfth, Twenty-third, Thirtieth, Thirty-first and Thirty second Precincts

THE SIXTH DISTRICT COURT is located in Morrisania on Third Avenue, near One Hundred and Fifty-eighth Street The prisoners arraigned here come from the Second, Thirty-third, Thirty-fourth, and Thirty-fifth Precincts

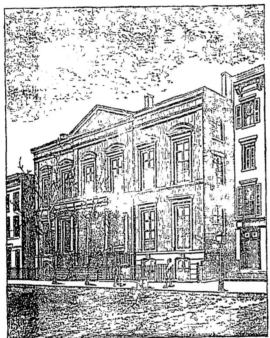

Yorkville Police Court (57th Street, near Third Avenue)

The annual report, ending November 24, 1884, of the Police Justices, shows that the number of arrests made during the year past was fifty thousand one hundred and sixty-four males, and nineteen thousand four hundred and fifty seven females, making a total of sixty-nine thousand six hundred and twenty one Those arrested on warrant process were four thousand one hundred and fifty three males and eight hundred and seventy-three females There were thirty five thousand three hundred and eight males held, while sixteen thousand five hun dred and thirty-seven females shared the same fate, making a total of fifty-one thousand eight hundred and forty-five; the number discharged being eighteen thousand seven hundred and forty-one men and three thousand seven hundred and eighty-nine women. Twenty-two cases are still pending

The fines received from the various Police Courts amounted to thirty-five thousand two hundred and fifty-eight dollars, while from the Court of Special Sessions the sum of twenty-seven thousand one hundred and fifty-six dollars was collected. Warden Finn, of the City Prison, collected thirteen thousand nine hundred and two dollars, making a total of seventy-six thousand three hundred and sixteen dollars, which is four thousand dollars short of the sum paid by malefactors the previous year

The Black Maria

There were three thousand six hundred and thirty-five persons committed in default of bail or released on bail for trial at General Sessions, and for trial at Special Sessions five thousand six hundred and fifty There were twelve thousand one hundred and three persons committed for good behavior, and seventeen thousand five hundred and fifty-four persons were committed in default of payment of fine, while five thousand seven hundred and fifty-seven were released on payment of fines The report also shows that three hundred and ninety-seven men and two hundred and eighty-four women were committed as vagrants There were sent to reformatory institutions one thousand nine hundred and thirty-two males and one thousand and ninety-two females. There were six hundred and forty-four insane persons committed —four hundred and forty-four men and two hundred and twenty women

Of persons claiming to be destitute there were

Conveying Prisoners from Court to Jail.

one thousand five hundred and eighteen men, and one thousand one hundred and fifty-three women, a total of two thousand six hundred and seventy-one persons. There were six hundred and sixty-five persons sent to the Roman Catholic Protectory; to the Mission of the Immaculate Virgin, five hundred and fifty-four, Juvenile Asylum, two hundred and eighty-three, St. Joseph's

Asylum, two hundred and thirty-seven; Institute of Mercy, two hundred; House of Refuge, one hundred and fifty; and to the Home of Good Shepherd, twenty-nine.

Woman's Prison A Mutual Recognition

The various charges were   Abduction, fourteen, abortion, eight; arson, sixteen; assault and battery, three thousand eight hundred and eighty-two; felonious assault and battery, seven hundred and fifteen; assault with intent to steal, fifty-three; attempted suicide, eighty-five; bigamy, thirteen, burglary, seven

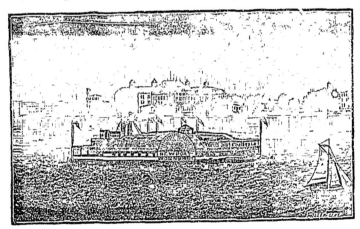

Blackwell's Island and East River.

hundred and ninety-one; cruelty to animals, two hundred and forty-two; cruelty to children, twenty-eight thousand six hundred and ninety-six, keeping a disorderly house, one hundred and fifty-nine; disorderly persons, seven hundred and eighty-five; and felonies not classified, ninety-two.

There were fifty-four forgers and thirty-nine fugitives from justice. Of these thirty-eight were discharged and only one held. The gamblers numbered fifty-five; homicides, eighty-eight; drunkards, twenty thousand four hundred and forty-five, thieves, grand larceny, one thousand four hundred and fifty-seven; petty larceny, three thousand two hundred and two; larceny from the person, six hundred and ninety; perjury, nineteen; rape, thirty-five; receivers of stolen goods, eighty-one; suspicious persons, one thousand four hundred and forty; vagrants, six thousand two hundred and seventy-five; violators of Corporation ordinances, seven hundred and seventy-one, violators of the Election law, thirty-

Roosevelt Hospital.

one, Excise law, one thousand three hundred and fifty-six; Lottery law, one hundred and eight; Sanitary Code, four hundred and twenty-one, Sunday law, twenty-nine.

There were eighty-five persons charged with attempted suicide, eighty being discharged The number of persons arrested for burglary and discharged was one hundred and fifty-one; and eight thousand three hundred and eighty persons arrested for disorderly conduct were discharged Thirty-four gamblers were discharged

The idea of disseminating among all classes of society, by means of popular lectures, general information as to the preliminary treatment of the sick and injured, originated with the St. John Ambulance Association, which was organized in London in 1877. The success achieved by this Association led the State Charities Aid Association, in January, 1882, to appoint a committee, under the chairmanship of General George B. McClellan, to establish courses of lectures on "First Aid to the Injured." So rapid was the growth of the work thus undertaken by the committee, and so general the demand for instruction, as to necessitate a more complete organization, and, accordingly, in February, 1883, the committee re-organized as "The Society for Instruction in First Aid to the Injured."

The instruction given by the Society is intended to do no more than qualify the pupil to adopt such remedial measures as may be advantageous pending the

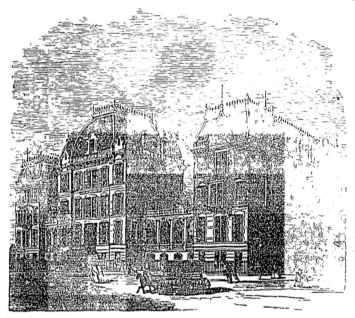

Mount Sinai Hospital, Sixty-sixth Street.

doctor's arrival, and to afford some knowledge of nursing and the laws of health. It teaches what is to be done in emergencies, when there are no proper appliances at hand.

Some of the earliest efforts of the originators of the "First Aid" movement were directed to the establishment of a course of instruction for the Police, but the large number of men on the force, the short time allowed them for recreation and other causes, rendered this a difficult matter. In the spring of 1883, however, two classes were formed, and during the ensuing fall the Society suggested to the Board of Police Commissioners the advisability of making "First Aid" a part of the training which candidates for the Police force are required to undergo before being admitted as members. The suggestion was favorably received and adopted. The Society thereupon provided the necessary lecturers

OUR POLICE PROTECTORS

and appliances, and lectures were commenced on the twelfth of February. Classes were at once organized, and, as a rule, the men have acquitted themselves creditably, two-thirds passing the examination. Many a case of accident —that, for instance, of persons run over in the streets, or injured by a fall— would probably have resulted fatally but for the knowledge so gained by the Police, who, while awaiting the arrival of the Ambulance Surgeon, are enabled to afford temporary relief to the sufferer. In some cases, owing no doubt to unavoidable or accidental causes, the ambulances are not over prompt in responding to a call, and the attendance of the Policeman on post is therefore all the more valuable.

New York Hospital (Fifteenth Street, bet Fifth and Sixth Avenues)

The Ambulance Districts are as follows:

NEW YORK HOSPITAL DISTRICT: Sixth, Sixteenth and Twenty-ninth Precincts

CHAMBERS STREET HOSPITAL DISTRICT: First, Fourth, Fifth, Seventh, Tenth, Twenty-sixth and Twenty-seventh Precincts

BELLEVUE HOSPITAL DISTRICT: Eleventh, Thirteenth, Seventeenth, Eighteenth, Nineteenth, Nineteenth Sub, Twenty-first, Twenty-fourth and Twenty-fifth Precincts, also, First, Second, Third and Fourth District Courts

ST. VINCENT'S HOSPITAL DISTRICT: Eighth, Ninth, Fourteenth and Fifteenth Precincts

NINETY-NINTH STREET HOSPITAL DISTRICT. Twelfth, Thirty-third, Thirty-fourth, Second, Thirty-first, Thirty-second, Thirty-fifth and Thirtieth Precincts.

PRESBYTERIAN HOSPITAL DISTRICT: Twenty-third and Twenty-eighth Precincts.

A comparatively new criminal agency has been at work in certain sections of the city, spreading the fruitful seeds of contamination, and throwing addi-

Glimpses of Chinatown

tional responsibilities on the already overburdened shoulders of the Police. The agency in question is what is known as "the opium habit" In a remarkably short space of time this terrible vice has taken deep root, and it is very much to be feared that, like Bancho's ghost, it will not down, but that it has come to stay The law's repressive hand has been placed upon it, but to-day it counts its victims by the thousand in this city alone Captain McCullagh, of the Elizabeth Street Station, and Detective Gerow, have quite recently made an important "raid" on one of these "joints" where opium is smoked, and arrested a number of the denizens of Chinatown, who were caught in the act of "hitting the pipe." Unfortunately, this pernicious habit is not confined to the children of the flowery kingdom; a legion of opium smokers to the manner born, and many of them people of respectability and refinement, are slaves of this habit. Accurate illustrations of some of the opium instruments found in the "joint" raided by Captain McCullagh are herewith given, for the enlightenment of the uninitiated.

The Opium Law is designated as follows: Chapter 165. An Act in relation to the sale and use of opium. Passed May 15, 1882.

A Chinese Opium Smoker ("Hitting the Pipe").

Every person who opens or maintains, to be resorted to by other persons, any place where opium, or any of its preparations, is sold or given away, to be smoked at such place; and any person who at such place sells or gives away any opium, or its said preparations, to be there smoked or otherwise used, and any person who visits or resorts to any such place for the purpose of smoking opium or its said preparations, shall be deemed guilty of a misdemeanor, and, upon conviction thereof, shall be punished by a fine not exceeding five hundred dollars, or by imprisonment in the penitentiary not exceeding three months, or by both such fine and imprisonment

The person who smokes opium always does so reclining, usually stretched across a hard wooden bunk covered with matting, a small stool or beveled board serving as a pillow. Resting upon his left side, the smoker takes up a little of the treacle-like mass upon the steel needle (or *yen hauck*) and holding it above the flame of the lamp, watches it bubble and swell to six or seven

... its original size. In doing so it loses its inky hue, and becomes of a light golden-brown color, and gives off a pleasant creamy odor, much admired by old smokers. Poor opium does not yield so pleasant an odor, is liable to drop from the needle into the flame of the lamp, and rarely gives so handsome a color, the yellow being here and there streaked with black. This process is known as "cooking" the opium. Having brought it to a proper consistence, the operator, with a rapid twirling motion of the fingers holding the long needle, rolls the mass upon the smooth surface of the bowl, submitting it occasionally to the flame, and now and then catching it upon the edge or surface of the bowl, and pulling it out into strings in order to cook it through more thoroughly. This is called *chying* the mass.

Rolling it again upon the surface of the bowl until the opium is formed into a small pea-sized mass, with the needle as a centre, the needle is thrust into the small hole in the centre of the bowl, thus leveling off the bottom of the pea. Then, grasping the stem of the pipe, near the bowl, in the left hand, the bowl is held across the flame of the lamp to warm it; the bottom of the opium mass is also warmed, and by again thrusting the needle into the small aperture in the centre of the bowl and quickly withdrawing it, the mass, with a hole in its centre communicating with the hole in the bowl, is firmly fastened upon its surface.

Inclining the body slightly forward, the smoker tips the pipe-bowl across the lamp until the opium is just above the flame, when it commences to sizz and bubble. With the lips firmly compressed against the ivory mouth button, the devotee inhales strongly and steadily, the smoke of the burning drug passing into his lungs. This smoke, which is returned through the mouth and nose, is heavy and white, and has a not unpleasant, fruity odor. Having finished this bolus, which requires but one long or a few short inspirations, the smoker cools the bowl of the pipe with a damp sponge, and repeats the operations of cooking, rolling, and smoking as often as is necessary to obtain the desired effect. Smokers are classed as "long-draw" and "short-draw" men, according as they consume the mass in one long or a few short inspirations. The "long-draw" is unquestionably the most injurious.

The habitue, after smoking his allowance, which varies from seventy-five grains to two ounces, feels a pleasant sense of exhilaration that merges into a condition of dreamy wakefulness. It is a state in which the devotee finds himself perfectly happy and contented. The squalid surroundings of the opium den, the harassing cares and trials of life, are banished, and an indescribable sense of complete satisfaction takes possession of him. This waking dream, this silken garment of the imagination, will take its shape and its coloring from the most cherished and brilliant strands that run through the web and woof of his life's story. It hides the unpleasant conditions of every-day life, and gives birth to a pleasant bubble, the brilliant play of colors and misty outline of which are born of the pipe alone. As the smoker's hopes, ambitions, aspirations are, so will be the figures and incidents of his opium *dolce far niente*.

After a time the habitue finds that the pleasant things that always came at the pipe's bidding now fail to appear, and, disgusted with the pleasureless practice, he tosses aside the pipe in disgust, only to find that at a certain hour the following day he must smoke again, not drawn to it by any fascination, but driven to it by the horrible sufferings that follow close upon the heels of any attempt to abandon it

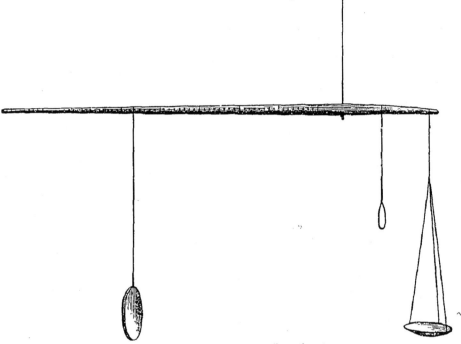

Scales for Weighing Opium (Lee thank).

Upon the habitual smoker we find the following effects resulting from a prolonged use of the drug

Loss of both desire and power for continued mental effort, tendency to lie

Opium Tray (Heen pun)

without any good reason for so doing, vacillation, deterioration of honesty and morality, decided falling off of affection for family and friends, loss of ambition, as also of all interest in business pursuits The temper, at first made more pleasant, soon becomes very irritable, and the individual very impatient He indifferently watches the approach of poverty that will soon overtake those who have been so dear to him. His every hope and desire are centered in the pipe, and nothing can draw his attention from it

Sponge (Soy pou).

Bowl.

His eyelids are bloated and darkly underlined, his eyes now bright and glistening, and again dull and apathetic Conjunctivitis is not uncommon The pupils are narrowly contracted, save when the effect of the drug is wearing off and he feels the need of opium, when they become widely dilated and water profusely

Opium Box

Financially and morally, the ruin and degradation are more complete than in any other way of using the drug An ordinary hard smoker will consume from one dollar to two dollars' worth of the drug each day, and will spend hours over the pipe to the exclusion of everything in the way of business

Clam Shell (Heen hoop)

A full outfit for smoking consists of the following a pipe, a small glass lamp, a pair of scissors (*cow ten*), a long steel needle (*yen hauck*), a saucer and sponge, a box for the ashes, two bowl cleaners, and a buffalo-horn box (*hop toy*) for holding the opium

The opium pipe, the origin and antiquity of which are unknown, though supposed to have first come from Arabia, consists of two parts, a stem and a bowl The stem is usually of bamboo, one joint and a quarter, or twenty-four inches in length and four inches in circumference When new it is of a straw color, but with long smoking becomes black and glossy The stem may be of ivory, orange, or briar wood, or sugar cane, and is occasionally made of lemon rind, cut, dried, and polished. The lemon stem gives a peculiarly pleasant taste and odor to the smoke

At about the junction of the middle and lower third, or just back of the joint, a place is hollowed out of the side of the stem and communicates with its longitudinal perforation About this hollow there fits closely a shield of metal, usually brass, that rises in a rim about the hole Into this is fitted the bowl On either side of the stem is fitted a button

Opium Pipe (Heen cheong)

Needle (Yen hauck)

OUR POLICE PROTECTORS

A Chinese Teacher.

of ivory. These stems may be plain, or ornamented with silver and gold, and variously carved. The bowl may be bell-shaped, ovate, or hexagonal. It is usually of a hard, red clay, and hollow. On its under surface is a neck or flange by which it is fitted into the stem. To make it fit tightly this is wrapped with strips of soft linen.

The upper surface of the bowl is either flat or sloping downward and outward. In its centre is an opening about sufficient to admit an ordinary darning needle. The whole pipe is called the *yen tsieng*, or opium-pistol.

The opium used for smoking is prepared in China. It is an aqueous extract, which represents fifty-four per cent of the crude or India opium from which it is made. This crude opium contains but three per cent of morphia, as against twelve per cent in the Smyrna opium used in this country.

Dr. F. N. Hammond, of Auburn, N. Y. recently read a paper before the Albany Medical Society on the opium habit. Dr. Hammond himself had formerly been an opium eater, and spoke not only as a medical, but also as a personal expert. He presented some very significant and pointed facts, showing an enormous growth in the use of opium in this country. In 1840 about twenty thousand pounds of opium were consumed in the United States; in 1880, five hundred and thirty-three thousand four hundred and fifty pounds. In 1868 there were about ninety thousand habitual opium eaters in the country, now they number over five hundred thousand. More women than men are addicted to the use of the drug. The vice is one so easily contracted, so easily practiced in private, and so difficult of detection, that it presents peculiar temptations and is very insidious. The relief from pain that it gives, and the peculiar exaltation of spirits, easily lead the victim to believe that the use of it is beneficial. Opium and chloral are to-day the most deadly foes of women. To break off from the habit, he says, the opium eater must reduce the quantity of his daily dose, using at the same time other stimulants, and gradually eliminate opium from his bill of fare.

The history of the introduction and growth of the opium habit in this city is an interesting and alarming one. The forms in which the deadly product of the poppy plant are used are manifold. It is smoked, eaten, drank in various preparations, and even injected into the circulation in the shape of morphine by the hypodermic syringe. All of these modes are equally enslaving, and all lead to the same inevitable result—death. The most debased and wretched practice of the habit is smoking, which is now engaged in in scores of "joints" in New York.

About twelve years ago, when the Chinese began to flock to this city from the Pacific coast, they brought with them their opium smoking outfits. The habit has been rife among the Celestials for generations, and those who know the New York Mongolians best say that there is not one of them but "hits the pipe" regularly every day. Chinatown is in Pell Street, the lower part of Mott Street, and the crooked old by-ways of the neighborhood. Here, packed in tall tenements and in ricketty old dwellings that were once the mansions of New York's well-to-do citizens, dwell the children of the sun, with their laundries, curio shops, and dingy grocery stores and club houses. For years the Celestials carried on their opium smoking with the utmost secrecy, and very few outsiders knew of the existence of their haunts, or what went on in them. After a while, however, the newspapers began to print highly-colored stories about scenes in the "joints," descriptions of the fashionable ladies who were alleged to be slaves to the habit, and all sorts of improbable details of gorgeously fitted up dens and wealthy patrons. Of course these stories were without foundation in fact, but the general public took kindly to them. A veteran Police Captain said to the writer recently that he had yet to hear of a wealthy or refined person who was in the habit of smoking opium in the joints; "And I think I ought to know something about the joints," he added," for I have made a study of them for years."

Still, the descriptions of the opium dens stimulated the curiosity of that large class of people who are ever on the lookout for a new sensation. Men, and in many cases, women, who had tried all other forms of dissipation and found them palling on their tastes, began to visit the resorts and to smoke the poppy juice. Those whose constitutions had been undermined by much dissipation were peculiarly susceptible to the habit, and it soon fastened firmly upon them. The lower order of theatrical people, variety actors, dancers, and many of the demi-monde found the pleasures of the poppy a new and agreeable substitute for whiskey, and they form to day by far the greater part of the white devotees of the pipe in New York. Many stories have been from time to time published about Chinamen dragging young girls into their dens and stupefying them with the drug, but they, are untrue and without foundation. "Surely they are really bad enough," said Captain McCullagh, of the Sixth Precinct, "without adding imaginary evils to the list of offenses laid at their door. The Chinamen are one of the most harmless classes of dwellers in New York. They interfere with no one, they never fight or hurt one another, and you never find them drunk or disorderly on the streets. But the opium makes sad work of them. Smokers who look reasonably stout and strong become ghastly pale, and shake like sufferers from the palsy when kept without the drug for a few days."

Chinese Merchant

In the last three years one hundred persons have been arrested by the Police of this city in their raids upon opium joints. Of these, twelve were in 1882, nineteen in 1883, and the remainder during the past year. These significant figures call for no comment as showing the spread of the vice. "Raiding the joints won't stop the smoking," said a well-known Police Captain, recently, "it only drives the Chinamen from one house to another, that's all. As long as Chinamen are Chinamen they will continue to smoke it."

The amount of vice and crime springing from and fostered by the promiscuous herding together of human beings in tenements has been a fruitful source of trouble to the Police.

In all the eastern part of New York city, notably between Houston and Fortieth Streets, there is an over-crowding of human beings in a degree far beyond anything that has ever been known in any civilized country. In the Fourth and Sixth Wards, and in portions of the Eleventh and Seventeenth, population is packed at the rate of one hundred and ninety-two thousand individuals to the square mile, and in the Fourth Ward alone at the rate of two hundred and ninety thousand inhabitants to the square mile. The most densely populated districts of London do not approach anywhere near the above figures The greatest number of persons to the square mile there is found in East London, one hundred and seventy-five thousand, while the St. James and St Luke districts follow with only one hundred and forty-four thousand and one hundred and fifty-one thousand people per square mile respectively Some five hundred thousand p   , live in the tenement houses of this city, and there is one house in New York wherein one thousand five hundred tenants dwell Twenty-four separate tenements, each occupied by four or five persons, are common in a large number of these

Harbor Police Surprising River Thieves.

houses, or an average of one hundred souls to a house of twenty-five feet front. Forty-eight families are not uncommon, and they often keep boarders, so that ten, and often fifteen persons, will be found in a single dwelling

What refining or restraining influences of family life are possible under such surroundings? Drunkenness is but too prevalent Weary and complaining wives, cross and hungry husbands, wild and ungoverned children, will inevitably jar and wrangle with each other Dr Elisha Harris, of the New York Prison Association, says. "The younger criminals seem to come almost exclusively from the worst tenement house districts, that is, when traced back to the very places where they first had homes Those very domiciles are nurseries of crime, and of the vices and disorderly courses which lead to crime At least eighty per cent of the crimes against property and against the person are perpetrated by individuals who never had any home-life, or whose homes had ceased to be sufficiently separate, decent and desirable, to afford what are regarded as ordinary wholesome influences of home and family. This statement is based upon accurate observations in the history of crimes and criminals in this State"

Whatever may be the cause or causes, whether intemperance, overcrowded tenements, ignorance, or inherited depravity, the unwelcome fact remains that crime is steadily on the increase, and outstrips in proportion the growth of population A comparison of the statistics, as taken from the census of New York City for the past ten years, and the record of arrests and convictions in Criminal Courts for the same period, show that the preponderance in the growth of crime over population is as eleven to ten. This ought to cause our lawmakers and all thoughtful men to consider quickly the best means of checking the rising tide of evil doings, by improving the public morals, and thus lighten the labors imposed upon "OUR POLICE PROTECTORS."

OUR POLICE PROTECTORS.

Following is a complete list of members of the Police force up to May 1, 1885, and the date of their appointment:

Name	Date of Appointment
A	
Abbott, N. B.	Aug. 21, 1866
Ackerson, Wm. T.	Oct 10, 1865
Adams, Geo W.	July 2, 1884
Adams, James	Feb 10, 1882
Adams, Richard	June 18, 1870
Adams, T F.	June 27, 1882
Adler, Anton	Jan 2, 1873
Agnew, Jno.	Feb 17, 1869
Ahearn, Thos.	Feb 11, 1858
Ahearn, Thos.	Feb. 16, 1881
Ahearn, W H.	Feb 11, 1873
Ahearn, Wm	Aug 5, 1882
Ahern, James	Mch. 25, 1876
Ahles, Henry	Mch 24, 1880
Ahrens, Henry	Feb 27, 1884
Ahrens, Jacob	May 20, 1870
Aiguier, Gabriel	Sep 3, 1862
Aiken, G H.	Dec 11, 1872
Aiken, Samuel	Oct. 8, 1883
Aitchison, J D.	Feb. 1, 1882
Aitkin, Henry	June 3, 1872
Albertson, C L.	Feb 7, 1879
Albin, Isaac H.	June 10, 1857
Alexander, D W	Aug. 28, 1876
Allaire, Anthony J, Capt.	July 10, 1865
Allaire, C. D	Nov 7, 1873
Allen, Christopher	Dec 7, 1863
Allen, Myron, Sergt.	Mch 9, 1866
Anderson, G J.	Dec. 13, 1866
Anderson, Geo	Nov 17, 1863
Anderson, Robert	Apr 20, 1883
Andesner, A.	Mch 20, 1875
Andrews, G J.	Feb 1, 1882
Anthes, W H.	May 7, 1874
Apple, Jno	Jan 22, 1881
Archibald, Daniel	Jan 7, 1873
Arfken, G. L.	Nov 1, 1878
Armstrong, A.	Oct 20, 1883
Armstrong, Henry, No 1	Nov 25, 1868
Armstrong, J G.	Dec. 29, 1874
Armstrong, W J.	Mch 18, 1881
Arnold, Daniel S.	June 25, 1869
Assing, Wm	Aug 15, 1884
Atkins, Lewis	July 9, 1884
Austin, E L.	Aug 18, 1869
Ayres, J B.	Apr. 27, 1883
B	
Back, Chas E.	June 21, 1884
Back, Emil	Feb 22, 1873
Back, G F.	May 14, 1872
Back, Joseph	May 8, 1882
Bailey, Sam'l	Oct 29, 1883
Baird, Alex.	Feb 7, 1873
Baker, Chas S.	Dec. 31, 1878
Baker, Frank	May 10, 1871
Baker, Jno.	May 21, 1872
Baker, Thos.	April 24, 1875
Baker, Wm.	Apr. 8, 1882
Baldwin, Sumner.	July 17, 1880
Ballester, Jno.	Apr 18, 1883
Banigan, Thos.	Oct 14, 1881
Banker, John	Mch. 25, 1865
Banks, Geo	June 17, 1881
Bannon, Francis	Feb 18, 1885
Bannon, Jno J.	July 3, 1884
Barnes, Leverett	June 3, 1873
Barnwell, Pat'k.	Oct 17, 1874
Barrett, Michael	May 25, 1863
Barrett, Peter	July 15, 1884
Barrett, Richard	Feb 27, 1875

Name	Date of Appointment	Name	Date of Appointment
Barrett, Thos	Sept. 21, 1870	Bevans, Geo. R.	Apr 8, 1867
Barron, Edward J	May 5, 1877	Bicknell, Geo.	Dec. 11, 1874
Barry, Jas. F.	Feb 1, 1884	Bingham, E. K.	Dec 22, 1877
Barry, Jas. W.	Apl. 20, 1883	Bird, Edmond	Sept 18, 1863
Barry, P J	Feb. 8, 1870	Bird, Isaac, Sergt	Feb 5, 1859
Barry, Pat'k	Sept 7, 1870	Birmingham, Bernard F.	Oct 9, 1878
Barry, R J	Feb 17, 1870	Bischoff, Henry C	Oct 9, 1883
Barth, Fred'k	Apl. 8, 1882	Bissert, Michael	Feb 18, 1868
Bartley, David	Feb 29, 1876	Black, Jas B	Aug. 26, 1868
Bates, Jno J.	Feb. 4, 1884	Blackwood, S H	July 16, 1857
Bates, S A	Oct 7, 1876	Blair, Wm., Sergt	Feb 13, 1858
Bath, D W.	Sept 8, 1875	Blanch, Thos V.	Apr 7, 1880
Baumann, Edward	May 1, 1872	Blangey, Nelson	Sept 23, 1867
Baumaster, Mich'l	Mch. 8, 1884	Blass, Philip	Oct 9, 1873
Baumgarten, Ignatz	Aug 29, 1873	Bleil, Phelp C	Sept 8, 1875
Bayer, E	Apr 15, 1878	Bliss, Chas R	Dec 3, 1867
Beagan, Owen H	June 8, 1883	Block, Henry	Apr 17, 1877
Beam, W S	Sept 1, 1863	Blonk, G W	Apr 29, 1875
Beard, Wm J.	Feb 28, 1873	Bobel, Geo	Oct 12, 1883
Beatty, Thos	June 18, 1857	Bockhorn, Chas L	Oct 31, 1881
Beatty, Wm	Aug 31, 1878	Boehme, Christopher, Sergt	Sep 3, 1862
Becker, Geo	Mch 31, 1875	Bogart, W H.	June 2, 1866
Becker, Nicholas	Feb 20, 1880	Bohan, Chas	Aug 17, 1870
Beckingham, Patrick	May 27, 1882	Bolger, Pat'k	Sept 23, 1874
Beeck, Chas.	Mch 25, 1872	Bolster, D R	Oct 13, 1869
Beesley, Theodore	Jan 4, 1882	Bon, Michael	Feb 26, 1873
Beglan, Eugene	Oct 23, 1873	Boos, Wm.	Mch 27, 1882
Behan, Jas	Mch 4, 1876	Boothney, Jno	Oct 15, 1881
Bell, James	Apr 20, 1868	Bowe, Jno J.	Aug 15, 1884
Bell, Thos	Apr. 3, 1871	Bower, Wm	Apr 12, 1865
Belton, Christopher	Sept. 9, 1874	Bowes, Thos	Feb 10, 1879
Benham, A E	Nov 14, 1879	Boylan, Henry	Nov 17, 1870
Benjamin, Chas E	Aug 28, 1876	Boyle, Chas. H	Jan 13, 1882
Benkers, H.	Dec 26, 1874	Boyle, Geo W	May 27, 1876
Bennett, J P	Apr. 23, 1857	Boyle, Jas	May 13, 1881
Bennett, Jno M	July 3, 1857	Boyle, Jno	Aug 3, 1868
Bennett, Theron R, Capt.	Apr. 23, 1857	Boyle, Thos	Jan 13, 1875
Bennett, Thos	Mch 23, 1870	Boylston, Martin	Dec 27, 1875
Berg, Frederick	Apr. 8, 1882	Bradshaw, Joseph S	Apr 26, 1882
Berghold, W C. F, Capt.	Oct 20, 1864	Bradley, Andrew	Sept 23, 1881
Berkley, Rich'd	Mch 19, 1880	Bradley, Jno J.	Oct 29, 1883
Bermholz, Louis	July 11, 1857	Bradley, Thos	June 21, 1866
Berney, H P	Jan 18, 1872	Brady, Christopher	July 13, 1870
Bernstein, Chas	May 4, 1875	Brady, Edward	May 14, 1883
Berrian, Rich'd	June 23, 1883	Brady, Jas.	Jan. 3, 1872

OUR POLICE PROTECTORS

Name	Date of Appointment
Brady, Jas T	May 20, 1881
Brady, Jno	Feb 3, 1859
Brady, Jno A	July 17, 1882
Brady, Michael	Oct 27, 1874
Brady, Thomas	July 6, 1883
Brady, Thos. F	July 28, 1869
Braisted, Geo. R	Sept 19, 1871
Brangan, Jno	Nov. 9, 1883
Brannick, Peter	Apr 17, 1882
Breakall, W H	Jan. 12, 1872
Breen, Chas R	Sept. 29, 1882
Breen, Jas	Apr. 27, 1883
Breen, Jno	Feb. 23, 1871
Breen, Jno	Apr 14, 1874
Breen, Pat'k	Oct 14, 1870
Breen, Rich'd H	Mch 14, 1876
Brennan, Edward	July 20, 1870
Brennan, Edward	Dec 27, 1875
Brennan, Denis J	June 9, 1882
Brennan, Geo	Dec 31, 1870
Brennan, Jas, No 1	Mch 18, 1874
Brennan, Jas	Sept 1, 1875
Brennan, Jas F	Aug. 14, 1878
Brennan, John	Dec 22, 1864
Brennan, Michael	Jan 6, 1870
Brennan, Pat'k	Dec 9, 1874
Brennan, Peter A	June 7, 1882
Brennan, Thos	Jan. 28, 1860
Brereton, Joseph	Apr 18, 1883
Breslin, Thos	Feb 7, 1885
Brett, Edw'd F	Sept 19, 1881
Brett, Jas F	Feb 1, 1884
Brewer, Chas E	Feb. 14, 1874
Britton, John	Dec 20, 1866
Broderick, Geo	Aug. 3, 1876
Brogan, Jno J	Nov 5, 1883
Brogan, Jno J, Capt	Jan 26, 1865
Brogan, Joseph R	June 16, 1884
Brogan, Pat'k	Apr. 24, 1874
Bromiley, Jno A	Aug 27, 1884
Brookheim, J A	Jan 17, 1872
Brooks, Daniel	Mch 1, 1872
Brooks, Jas A	July 14, 1879
Brooks, Nicholas, Sergt	Apr 15, 1867
Brophy, J J, Sergt	Sept 14, 1871
Brophy, Michael	Aug 16, 1869
Brophy, Thos	Apr. 14, 1868
Brower, Wm. T	Feb 21, 1880
Brown, Andrew	Apr. 8, 1885
Brown, H M	Jan. 22, 1872
Brown, J. M	Jan. 22, 1866
Brown, Jacob	Mch 24, 1884
Brown, Jno	June 26, 1867
Brown, Jno	Oct 21, 1878
Brown, Rich'd	Oct. 25, 1883
Brown, S. E, Sergt	Apr. 18, 1868
Brownell, Seeley J	Feb. 18, 1885
Browning, August	Sept 24, 1862
Bruen, Matthias	Jan. 7, 1881
Brundage, S F	Oct 7, 1874
Bruner, Jos C	Jan 24, 1884
Brunner, Abraham	Oct. 30, 1882
Brunner, Andrew	Feb 7, 1884
Brunner, Jacob	Mch. 3, 1875
Bruns, Martin	Aug 10, 1876
Brush, J C	Sept 19, 1871
Brush, J J	Sept 27, 1870
Buckley, E. J	Dec 15, 1864
Buckley, J F	Dec 19, 1872
Buckley, John	Apr 17, 1873
Buckley, John	Nov 3, 1877
Buckridge, Stephen	Aug 3, 1868
Buddington, C C, Sergt	June 8, 1864
Budds, Jno	Dec 18, 1872
Buhler, J J	Oct 1, 1862
Burch, Chas	Sept 13, 1880
Burden, Henry	Aug 23, 1867
Burgoyne, E. A	Nov. 2, 1877
Burke, J G	Jan 3, 1873
Burke, Jas	Sept 15, 1869
Burke, Jas	Aug 15, 1884
Burke, Lawrence	Nov 22, 1867
Burke, Mich'l J	Sept 29, 1881
Burke, Richard	May 7, 1873
Burke, Wm., No. 1	Dec 20, 1867
Burkit, Thos	Mch 10, 1869
Burleigh, Thomas	July 29, 1874
Burns, Edward	Mch 20, 1875
Burns, Jas	July 1, 1876
Burns, Jas	June 27, 1882

Name	Date of Appointment	Name	Date of Appointment
Burns, Jas F.	Apr 8, 1885	Campbell, W. J.	Oct 21, 1881
Burns, Jno	Mch 12, 1884	Canavan, Jno	Feb. 12, 1866
Burns, Wm	June 15, 1883	Cannon, Jas. E.	Apr 2, 1875
Burrill, W. H	Dec 7, 1872	Caprano, Jacob	Aug. 7, 1873
Bush, Chas E.	Mch. 22, 1862	Carey, Edmund	Dec. 16, 1874
Bush, Nath'l D, Sergt	Mch 29, 1876	Carey, Jas. F.	Jan 13, 1875
Butcher, John	Feb. 17, 1865	Carey, Jno	Apr 12, 1881
Butler, Wm	Jan. 22, 1881	Carey, Mich'l J	Oct 10, 1881
Butterly, Jno	Mch 14, 1874	Carley, Jno. E	Oct 20, 1883
Buttlinger, Edward	Dec 24, 1878	Carley, Thos F.	Apr 10, 1874
Byrne, Daniel	Sept 20, 1873	Carlin, Francis	Jan 24, 1870
Byrne, Jno	June 6, 1884	Carlin, Thos	Aug 16, 1864
Byrne, Mich'l	July 10, 1882	Carman, Thos .A	Apr 7, 1882
Byrne, Pat'k	Nov. 18, 1868	Carmick, Stephen	Apr 24, 1867
Byrne, Peter	Sept 20, 1873	Carpenter, Edward, Sergt.	Aug 16, 1869
Byrne, Wm H	Apr. 24, 1880	Carpenter, T H.B, Sergt.	Jan 21, 1861
Byrnes, Edward	Jan 20, 1868	Carpenter, W. F	Sept 11, 1868
Byrnes, James	Oct. 27, 1874	Carr, Gilbert	Oct 10, 1870
Byrnes, Jno F	Sept 15, 1882	Carr, Jno. H	Mch 8, 1870
Byrnes, P F	Jan 3, 1870	Carr, John	Nov 13, 1879
Byrnes, Thomas, Insp	Dec 10, 1863	Carroll, Chas G.	June 14, 1882
Byron, Thos	Feb 1, 1882	Carroll, H B	July 31, 1872

C

Name	Date of Appointment	Name	Date of Appointment
		Carroll, Jno. W	July 19, 1882
Caddell, Francis	Apr 19, 1860	Carroll, Martin	Nov 1, 1878
Caffrey, Chas W, Capt	Feb 13, 1858	Carroll, Mich'l	Jan 10, 1873
Cagney, David	Sept 14, 1883	Carroll, Pat'k	Mch 3, 1882
Cagney, Maurice F	Mch 21, 1884	Carroll, Wm	May 10, 1872
Cahill, Bernard	Nov 25, 1874	Carstens, Jno	Apr 1, 1878
Cahill, Denis, Sergt	June 18, 1870	Carter, Jesse	May 7, 1879
Cahill, Mich'l	Feb 28, 1884	Carter, Peter	Apr 8, 1885
Cahill, Pat'k	Sept 1, 1875	Carter, Peter D	May 4, 1884
Cahill, Rich'd	Feb 5, 1878	Carter, Thos J	Dec 14, 1874
Cahill, Wm	Feb 7, 1872	Casey, Jas	Dec 2, 1872
Cairnes, Wm	Jan 27, 1873	Casey, Jno	May 26, 1883
Callaghan, T J	Feb 7, 1881	Casey, Mich'l	Dec 17, 1883
Callahan, Dan'l J	Dec 6, 1878	Cashin, Joseph H	Feb 21, 1880
Callahan, Thos.	Oct. 11, 1873	Cashin, Pat'k	Jan 1, 1874
Campbell, Jas	Feb 26, 1873	Cashman, Edw'd	Mch 8, 1871
Campbell, Jno.	Sept 16, 1870	Cassidy, Philip, Sergt	Mch 8, 1870
Campbell, Jno J	June 12, 1880	Cassidy, Thos.	Mch 10, 1884
Campbell, Jno W	Sept 4, 1876	Castle, Geo A	May 9, 1867
Campbell, Matthew	Jan 24, 1868	Cavanagh, Jno	Jan 19, 1870
Campbell, Rob't F M	Oct 11, 1873	Chapman, Geo S	May 1, 1877
Campbell, S J	Aug. 14, 1871	Chapman, Henry	June 11, 1877
		Charlton, Rob't	Mch 6, 1884

Name	Date of Appointment	Name	Date of Appointment
Christie, Wm H., Sergt.	Feb 16, 1863	Coffy, Rich'd, Sergt	May 22, 1873
Christopher, Benj	Dec 15, 1866	Cogan, Rich'd J	Mch 7, 1885
Chrystal, Thos J	Apr 15, 1876	Cogans, Jno	May 1, 1877
Church, Geo W	June 23, 1857	Colbert, M J	May 6, 1882
Churchill, Jas	Dec 18, 1883	Colby, Wm	Apr. 20, 1883
Clary, Rob't T.	Apr 15, 1885	Cole, Ambrose H	Aug. 12, 1876
Clapp, Ira M	Oct 11, 1873	Colegrove, Edward, Sergt	July 27, 1860
Clark, Chas E	Dec 22, 1869	Coleman, Law F	Dec 16, 1881
Clark, Dan'l W	Aug 15, 1884	Coleman, N H	Jan. 11, 1865
Clark, Hugh, Sergt	Jan 14, 1861	Coleman, Wm S.	June 22, 1883
Clark, Jesse R	Nov 13, 1883	Colgan, Jas. A	June 21, 1884
Clark, John	May 1, 1866	Colgan, Maurice	Jan 24, 1884
Clark, Jno. C.	Apr 8, 1876	Collard, Edward	Nov 19, 1857
Clark, Rob't W	Apr 15, 1885	Colligan, J H	Mch 28, 1881
Clark, Thos	July 16, 1867	Collins, Denis	Oct 9, 1873
Clark, Wm, Jr.	Apr. 9, 1869	Collins, Edward A	Oct 25, 1883
Clark, Wm, Sr.	Feb. 3, 1859	Collins, Eugene D	June 9, 1882
Clark, Wm A	Mch 20, 1884	Collins, Jno	Sept 28, 1883
Clarke, Christopher	June 11, 1883	Collins, Jno	Jan 24, 1884
Clarke, Francis J	June 30, 1877	Collins, Mich'l, Sergt.	Mch 16, 1870
Clarke, Jas C	Jan 1, 1874	Collins, Wm.	Sept. 7, 1874
Clarke, Wm	July 5, 1882	Collins, Wm J	Nov 24, 1883
Clarker, Jno T	Dec 27, 1875	Colvin, Jno A.	July 6, 1880
Clarkin, Peter	Dec 9, 1876	Combs, Chas U, Jr Sergt.	Apr 24, 1867
Clarkin, Thos	June 13, 1870	Conboy, Thos	Oct 8, 1881
Clarson, Law	July 9, 1870	Concannon, Jas J	June 2, 1884
Clarson, R J	Feb 4, 1884	Condon, Jno	Mch 20, 1882
Cleary, Wm	Oct 22, 1883	Condon, Jno H	Oct 27, 1874
Clemens, Dan'l W	Dec 19, 1883	Conklin, E W	Feb 25, 1873
Clifford, Edward	Apr 18, 1883	Conklin, Jas E	Jan 23, 1867
Clifford, Rob't	Sept 2, 1881	Conklin, Taylor	Mch 4, 1873
Clifford, Thos M	Apr 8, 1876	Conkling, Rich'd C	Sept 28, 1883
Clinchy, Geo	Nov 12, 1862	Conley, Wm	Nov 24, 1883
Clinchy, Wm. H, Capt	May 12, 1865	Conlin, M F	Aug 17, 1870
Clinton, Law	July 15, 1876	Conlin, Peter, Capt	July 29, 1869
Clune, Patrick	Oct 28, 1868	Conlon, Mich'l	Dec 19, 1883
Coady, Jno J	Apr 21, 1883	Connell, Jas	Feb 21, 1872
Coakley, Thos.	Nov 11, 1879	Connolly, B.	Dec 11, 1869
Cochran, Jas. H	Jan 24, 1884	Connolly, B J	Sept 28, 1883
Cody, Dan'l	Jan 22, 1861	Connolly, Law	Nov 14, 1873
Coen, Jas	Jan. 8, 1881	Connolly, Mich'l	June 21, 1882
Coen, Thos	Feb 22, 1873	Connolly, Thos	Apr 25, 1882
Coffey, P J.	Dec 2, 1869	Connor, Dan'l T	Mch 17, 1884
Coffey, Wm T, Sergt.	Aug 18, 1869	Connor, Geo.	Jan 20, 1872
Coffy, Dan'l	Nov 2, 1864	Connor, Jas J	Mch 28, 1879

Name	Date of Appointment	Name	Date of Appointment
Connor, Jno	Jan 10, 1881	Cox, Hatfield S	Aug 16, 1866
Connor, Mich'l	May 9, 1872	Cox, Pat'k	June 14, 1882
Connor, Neil W	Jan. 4, 1881	Cox, S S	Oct 24, 1874
Connor, Pat'k, Sergt	Jan 1, 1874	Coyle, Chas J	Sept 22, 1875
Connors, Geo	Apr 1, 1872	Coyle, Jas	Feb 18, 1884
Conovan, Jno	Sept. 14, 1878	Coyle, Jno T	Apr 11, 1881
Conovan, Owen	June 23, 1884	Coyle, Thos J	May 20, 1878
Constant, Jno	Aug 27, 1874	Craig, Archibald M	Apr 21, 1884
Conway, Anthony	Feb 15, 1884	Craig, Joseph J	Mch. 13, 1884
Conway, Chas	Oct 14, 1873	Crawford, David	Sept 5, 1870
Conway, Jas	Apr 12, 1876	Creamer, Francis A	Feb 18, 1885
Conway, Jas F.	Apr 23, 1883	Crean, Jno	Aug 7, 1876
Conwell, Jas	Nov 3, 1869	Creed, Jno J	Aug 3, 1876
Coogan, Patrick	May 25, 1864	Creeden, D J	Mch 29, 1884
Cook, Geo	July 11, 1857	Creeden, T J, Sergt	Oct 5, 1864
Cook, Stephen G. Surgeon	Sep 15, 1873	Creenan, Mich'l	Mch 27, 1868
Cook, Wm. H	Nov. 22, 1876	Cregan, Mich'l F	Nov 27, 1883
Coon, S H	Aug 23, 1866	Cregier, F J	Feb 14, 1884
Cooney, Jno	Aug 11, 1870	Creighton, Jno G	Mch 24, 1874
Cooney, Mich'l J	June 2, 1883	Crinnion, Jno	Apr 8, 1885
Cooper, F C	Feb 11, 1884	Crinnion, Pat'k	Sept 7, 1870
Cooper, Jas G, Jr	Jan 26, 1876	Crittenden, Chas W	Feb 13, 1861
Copeland, Martin	Mch 14, 1876	Croker, Jno A., Sergt	Nov 12, 1862
Copeland, Theron S, Capt	J'ly 11, 1857	Croker, Walter	May 31, 1865
Corbett, Jno J	Sept 11, 1875	Cromley, Jas	Dec 6, 1866
Corbitt, Henry O, Sergt	Jan 20, 1872	Cronin, Denis	Oct 11, 1870
Corey, Jno T	Jan 7, 1884	Cronin, Jas J	June 2, 1882
Corey, Jno V B	Nov. 1, 1872	Cronin, Jno J	July 16, 1883
Corkery, Timothy	Mch 21, 1884	Cronin, Jno J	Dec 17, 1883
Cortright, M W, Capt	Jan 17, 1867	Cronin, T J	Oct 22, 1883
Corvin, P J	Feb 14, 1861	Crook, Alfred	Apr 12, 1870
Cosgrove, Jno K	Mch 14, 1882	Crook, Frank	Jan 24, 1884
Cosgrove, P H	Oct 30, 1882	Crook, Jno	Sept 25, 1873
Cosgrove, Pat'k	Apr 18, 1883	Crorken, Jas	Jan 24, 1884
Cosgrove, Wm F	Nov 15, 1876	Crosby, Jas.	Feb 13, 1858
Costa, Ed J	Feb 14, 1882	Crosby, Jas. C	Dec 5, 1872
Colton, Chas S	Mch 1, 1876	Crosby, Patrick	Mch 17, 1882
Cotter, Wm	Dec 6, 1870	Cross, Adam A, Sergt	Oct 16, 1878
Cotton, Thos W	Sept 1, 1869	Crossett, Wm	Feb 6, 1882
Cottrell, Jno	Mch 26, 1875	Crowe, Jas	Feb 5, 1868
Coughlin, Joseph	Nov 3, 1877	Crowe, Jas F.	July 6, 1882
Coughlin, Pat'k	July 24, 1872	Crowley, Daniel K	June 18, 1877
Coughlin, Thos	Jan 21, 1874	Crowley, Francis B	Jan. 26, 1876
Courtlander, F J	Aug 17, 1870	Crowley, Jas, Supt Tel	Sept 12, 1860
Cowen, Jas	Mch 30, 1878	Crowley, Jno	Mch 16, 1870

Name	Date of Appointment
Crowley, Mich'l, No 1.	Oct. 18, 1869
Crowley, Mich'l, No. 2	Feb. 25, 1870
Crowley, Mich'l, No 3.	Aug 26, 1873
Cruise, Wm..	Mch 20, 1873
Cuff, Jno T.	Apr 8, 1873
Culhane, John	Apr 26, 1882
Cullen, Jas J.	Feb. 26, 1872
Cully, Pat'k	Oct 14, 1878
Cumiskey, Jas.	Aug 7, 1878
Cummings, B.	Dec 26, 1883
Cummings, G H	Dec 11, 1865
Cummings, Pat'k.	Sept 16, 1873
Cunningham, Jno.	Nov 10, 1869
Cunningham, Thos M.	Mch 14, 1876
Cunyes, Jas D.	Feb 20, 1880
Curley, Jno. T.	Sept 13, 1867
Curran, Dan'l.	July 24, 1872
Curran, Jno J	Feb 8, 1884
Curran, Peter	Sept 30, 1868
Curry, Jas	Apr 4, 1872
Curry, Jas.	July 1, 1876
Curry, Harrison	Aug 18, 1869
Curtis, Geo W	Oct 22, 1881
Cusack, John	Aug 15, 1884

D

Name	Date of Appointment
Daab, Philip	Mch 22, 1871
Dahlgren, Gustavus, Sergt	Nov 22, 1866
Dakin, Wm H	Mch 27, 1873
Dalbeck, Joseph F	Jan 6, 1868
Dalton, Jas.	Mch 21, 1882
Dalton, Thos.	Apr 29, 1876
Dalton, Wm, No 1.	Dec. 29, 1870
Dalton, Wm, No 2	Apr 14, 1874
Daly, Law C	Apr 9, 1872
Daly, Pat'k.	Aug 6, 1884
Dapping, Chas	Aug 19, 1881
D'Arcy, Geo F	Sept 20, 1880
Darke, Nath'l	Feb 5, 1861
Darke, Wm D	Oct 2, 1865
Darmody, Jno	Sept 14, 1883
Darragh, Wm	Apr 28, 1880
Davis, Chas H	June 3, 1868
Davis, Chas O	Mch 6, 1880
Davis, David	Mch 15, 1876

Name	Date of Appointment
Davis, Geo.	Aug 3, 1861
Davis, Geo.	Oct 30, 1882
Davis, Jno L.	Feb 3, 1859
Davis, Jos L	Sept 23, 1872
Day, Denis..	Oct 22, 1883
Dean, Stephen.	Mch 24, 1884
Dean, Wm.	Oct 13, 1869
Debon, Jas..	Oct. 26, 1872
Deering, Wm F.	May 16, 1883
Deeves, Wm B	Mch 3, 1875
Deevy, Jefferson	Apr 26, 1877
De Gan, Louis.	Oct 8, 1873
Deger, Jno G	Sept. 24, 1883
Degnan, Peter J	Sept 24, 1883
De Groot, L G.	Jan 31, 1881
De Lamater, E R, Sergt	Jan 11, 1862
Delamater, Jas F	Apr. 27, 1883
Delaney, Chas.	Dec 17, 1863
Delaney, Dan'l..	Sept. 3, 1873
Delaney, Edward	June 30, 1883
Delaney, Geo.	Apr 11, 1884
Delaney, Jas	Jan 11, 1871
Delaney, Jno, Sergt	Nov. 7, 1873
Delaney, Jno..	Apr 27, 1883
Delaney, Mich'l.	May 6, 1881
Delaney, Peter.	Apr 9, 1879
Delaney, Wm.	Oct 28, 1871
Dempsey, Pat'k.	May 10, 1865
Dempsey, Rob't F.	June 6, 1884
Dempsey, Thos.	Jan 9, 1871
Deneen, Peter	June 30, 1883
Dennerlein, Geo	Sept 11, 1875
Dennerlein, Jno.	Oct 27, 1874
Dennin, Thos	July 5, 1882
De Nyse, Aug M	Apr. 15, 1876
De Shays, Miles, Sergt	Apr. 30, 1862
Devery, Jno.	Apr 8, 1875
Devery, Wm S, Sergt	June 19, 1878
Devitt, Pat'k W	Sept 26, 1874
Devoe, W T, Sergt	Mch 1, 1861
De Voursney, Chas H	Sept 26, 1875
Dexter, Benj F, Surgeon	Mch 20, 1876
Dickey, Jno	July 15, 1876
Dilks, Geo H	May 20, 1876
Dilks, Geo W, Insp	Apr 23, 1857

OUR POLICE PROTECTORS

Name	Date of Appointment
Dinsmoor, J. N.	Apr. 6, 1863
Ditmars, Montgomery	Feb. 25, 1867
Dixon, Christopher	Mch 14, 1873
Dixon, Wm.	Sept. 21, 1870
Doess, Jacob H	June 4, 1874
Doherty, Sam'l	Aug 10, 1876
Dokel, Deitrich	Jan. 29, 1873
Dolan, Mich'l	Feb 23, 1884
Dolan, Pat'k	Sept 28, 1864
Dolan, Pat'k E	Apr. 8, 1885
Dolan, Thos F.	Aug 15, 1884
Donahue, Jas.	Apr 14, 1882
Donahue, Thos	Feb 4, 1884
Donegan, David B	May 28, 1884
Donehue, Jno	June 29, 1861
Donlen, Mich'l	Feb 10, 1885
Donnelly, Ed J	Apr 28, 1884
Donnelly, Francis	Feb 8, 1870
Donnelly, Peter	Feb 13, 1873
Donnelly, Thos	May 12, 1874
Donnelly, Wm	Sept 24, 1883
Donoghue, Thos	Apr 9, 1879
Donohue, Andrew	Feb 12, 1873
Donohue, Jas	Dec 28, 1872
Donohue, Jeremiah	May 18, 1868
Donohue, Jno. J.	Aug 5, 1879
Donohue, M C	Apr. 1, 1878
Donohue, Thos J.	Mch 27, 1882
Donohue, Timothy	Nov 3, 1877
Donovan, Jas	Apr 5, 1871
Donovan, Jno	Jan. 24, 1879
Donovan, Jno J	Jan 6, 1873
Dooley, Chas O	Sept 9, 1874
Dooley, Christopher	Jan. 2, 1864
Doorley, Jas	Dec 31, 1874
Doolin, Jno J.	Apr 9, 1880
Doran, Pat'k H, Sergt	Oct 3, 1864
Dorcey, Joseph M.	Apr. 7, 1865
Dormody, Jno	Apr 3, 1884
Dorn, Jno H, Surgeon	Sept 15, 1873
Doty, Theod M	Apr 19, 1871
Dougerty, Jno	Mch 5, 1878
Dougherty, Jas	Mch 9, 1881
Dougherty, Jno.	Oct 3, 1874
Dougherty, Jno E.	Apr 11, 1873
Dougherty, Mich'l	Dec 22, 1870
Doughney, Joseph	Oct. 22, 1883
Doughty, Wm	Apr 26, 1876
Douglass, Joseph, Sergt.	June 1, 1868
Dowd, Mich'l	Apr 15, 1885
Dowling, Mich'l	Jan 29, 1870
Downey, Jos C	May 24, 1884
Downey, Thos J	Oct 27, 1882
Downing, Mortimer	Dec 1, 1864
Doyle, Andrew, Sergt	Jan 22, 1861
Doyle, Dan'l	Mch 4, 1873
Doyle, Ed H	Apr 3, 1874
Doyle, Edward H	Mch 26, 1884
Doyle, Garrett F	Jan 7, 1881
Doyle, Jas	Sept 20, 1873
Doyle, Jas	Mch 5, 1881
Doyle, Jno J	Mch. 20, 1868
Doyle, Jos. T.	May 12, 1874
Doyle, Pat'k F	Mch 23, 1871
Doyle, Thos.	Mch 19, 1870
Doyle, Wm	Feb 16, 1872
Draffin, Jas	Sept 15, 1865
Drescher, Edw'd	Oct 10, 1881
Drought, Henry	June 2, 1868
Drucker, Abram	Aug 10, 1859
Du Bois, Geo C	Apr 18, 1885
Duernberger, Jno.	Jan 29, 1881
Duffy, Jno	Aug 5, 1879
Duffy, Law	Jan 22, 1881
Duffy, Thos	Feb 3, 1875
Dugan, John	Aug 20, 1884
Dugan, Mich'l	Mch 26, 1880
Duggan, Dan'l	Jan 24, 1879
Duggan, Wm H	Nov 19, 1883
Dunbar, Wm	Mch 20, 1884
Duncan, Jas	Apr 27, 1883
Dunlap, Jno	Nov 27, 1863
Dunlap, Rob't	June 29, 1870
Dunleavy, Chas.	Aug 20, 1869
Dunleavy, Jno	Feb 7, 1885
Dunn, Bernard	Nov 16, 1864
Dunn, Jas	Mch 19, 1879
Dunn, Jno	June 5, 1872
Dunn Jno	Oct 9, 1873
Dunn, Jno, Sergt.	Sept 17, 1872

Name	Date of Appointment
Dunn, Jno	July 23, 1883
Dunn, Jno. J	May 7, 1859
Dunn, Edward	Mch 19, 1880
Dunne, Pat'k	Nov. 10, 1865
Dwyer, Jno	May 25, 1863
Dyckman, D. W	May 18, 1863
Dyer, Jas S.	Nov 30, 1861
Dyruff, Chas	Sept 5, 1870

E

Name	Date of Appointment
Eagan, Jno	Apr. 29, 1876
Eagan, Thos	June 25, 1866
Eakins, Joseph B, Capt.	Mch 1, 1866
Early, Jas	Mch 27, 1884
Eastburn, Geo W	Jan 11, 1882
Eastwood, Wm	Apr 11, 1868
Eddy, Chas D	Dec 15, 1877
Edmiston, Rob't	May 13, 1874
Edwards, Rob't L	July 22, 1867
Edwards, Wm.	Sept 24, 1883
Egan, David	Dec. 16, 1881
Egan, Jno	Apr. 8, 1876
Egan, Thos J	July 15, 1876
Egan, Wm.	July 11, 1882
Elliott, Wm J	Apr. 8, 1884
Ellis, Adna.	Dec 5, 1872
Ellis, Rob't H	Mch 13, 1873
Ellis, Sam'l.	Feb. 28, 1873
Elmore, Jno W.	Jan 24, 1884
Elting, Josiah.	Dec. 19, 1872
Eltrich, Jno	June 20, 1874
Eltrich, Rich'd.	Feb 5, 1870
Empie, Geo H	Nov 21, 1872
Engehauser, Henry.	Aug. 27, 1884
English, Pat'k	Sept. 16, 1870
English, Sam'l.	Jan. 25, 1877
Enright, Jno	Jan 8, 1884
Ennis, Rich'd	Feb 1, 1882
Ensign, Wm H., Surgeon.	Sept. 15, 1873
Ergott, Dan'l.	Feb 1, 1884
Erskine, David W	Feb. 26, 1872
Erwin, Rob't.	Dec 28, 1870
Evanhoe, Frank N.	Feb. 5, 1878
Evans, Isaac.	Aug 26, 1868
Ewald, Jno.	Apr 11, 1885
Ewing, Jno.	Mch 26, 1879

F

Name	Date of Appointment
Fabri, Francis B.	Mch. 30, 1880
Fagan, Jas J	Nov. 14, 1879
Fagan, Rob't J	Feb 12, 1885
Fahey, Jas	Sept. 29, 1876
Fanning, Edward.	July 1, 1876
Fanning, Mich'l, Sergt.	June 30, 1864
Farley, Dermott	Feb. 2, 1865
Farley, Jno	Apr. 15, 1876
Farley, Jno. J.	Apr 27, 1874
Farley, Mich'l.	Dec 16, 1876
Farley, Peter.	Mch. 9, 1868
Farley, Philip.	Apr 30, 1873
Farley, Philip	Aug 5, 1879
Farley, Thos., Sergt	Feb. 3, 1875
Farrell, Edward J	Sept. 24, 1883
Farrell, Jno., No 1	Apr. 12, 1871
Farrell, Jno., No. 2	Jan 17, 1872
Farrell, Jno. J.	Dec 6, 1876
Farrell, Pat'k	Oct. 19, 1881
Farrington, Jno.	Apr 18, 1879
Fawcett, Francis.	Jan 22, 1861
Fay, Jno.	Jan 21, 1874
Fay, Jno.	Oct. 13, 1877
Fay, Martin	Oct 24, 1877
Fay, Pat'k	May 20, 1870
Fay, Thos	Feb. 5, 1870
Faye, Jas H	May 26, 1882
Feeney, Pat'k T	Oct. 9, 1873
Feess, Jacob W	May 1, 1882
Felleman, Wm M.	Nov 1, 1881
Fellman, Philip.	Dec. 12, 1874
Fellows, Sam'l B.	Feb 3, 1874
Fenker, Henry	Apr 1, 1878
Fennell, Wm H	Apr 12, 1876
Ferdon, Jas	June 11, 1857
Ferdon, Simeon L	Jan 3, 1879
Ferguson Jas E	Apr 26, 1882
Ferguson, Jno	Feb 13, 1858
Ferguson, Sam'l T	July 5, 1876
Ferre, Solomon	Feb 12, 1858
Ferris, Arthur	Feb. 18 1878
Ferris, Thos	Mch 4, 1868

Name	Date of Appointment	Name	Date of Appointment
Feuerstein, Adam	Sept 12, 1874	Fleming, Jas	May 10, 1871
Fielding, F R	Oct 26, 1878	Fleming, Mich'l	July 7, 1863
Files, Jacob	June 23, 1857	Flemming, Jno. W	Aug 18, 1869
Finerty, Kerin	Mch 10, 1869	Fletcher, Geo	Mch 19, 1879
Finerty, Martin	May 27, 1876	Flood, Chas	Jan 29, 1877
Finken, Chas W H	Aug. 3, 1876	Flood, Edward	Aug. 3, 1876
Finn, Maurice	Sept 1, 1870	Flood, Edward F	Oct 22, 1883
Finnan, Jno. A	Mch 19, 1884	Flood, Jas. C	Oct 30, 1877
Finnegan, Bernard	Apr. 8, 1885	Floyd, Chas	Feb 8, 1871
Finnegan, Jas F	June 6, 1884	Fluhrer, Wm F, Surgeon	May 29, 1876
Finnegan, Jno B	July 24, 1883	Flynn, Dan'l	Dec 15, 1866
Finnegan, Sam'l	Feb 1, 1872	Flynn, Jas	Dec 23, 1874
Finnegan, Wm B	Dec 30, 1870	Flynn, Mich'l	July 16, 1864
Finnerty, Jno	Aug 4, 1877	Flynn, Mich'l	Jan 22, 1868
Firth, Obed, Sergt.	Sept 12, 1860	Flynn, Rich'd	Aug 19, 1881
Fischer, Max J	Feb 1, 1882	Flynn, Wm	July 1, 1872
Fisher, Isaac R	Feb 3, 1859	Fogarty, Chas	Nov. 19, 1862
Fitchen, Wm F	June 17, 1874	Fogarty, Denis J	Aug 28, 1874
Fitzgerald, Jas	Oct 21, 1881	Fogarty, Jno.	Apr 6, 1867
Fitzgerald, Jno, Sergt	Feb. 5, 1862	Fohey, Jas.	Sept 14, 1883
Fitzgerald, Jno, Sergt.	Sept 19, 1865	Foley, Cornelius	Sept 3, 1862
Fitzgerald, Jno J, Sergt	Aug 15, 1865	Foley, Hugh J.	June 5, 1882
Fitzgerald, Maurice	Jan 26, 1876	Foley, Hugh	Apr 1, 1882
Fitzgerald, Rob't.	Jan 24, 1872	Foley, Jas.	Oct 31, 1872
Fitzgibbons, Edward	May 11, 1883	Foley, Jno.	Dec 8, 1866
Fitzpatrick, Andrew	May 26, 1880	Foley, Jno	July 21, 1882
Fitzpatrick, Jas	Mch 14, 1876	Foley, Jno. F	May 14, 1884
Fitzpatrick, Jno	Aug 5, 1879	Foley, Pat'k J.	Oct 24, 1881
Fitzpatrick, Jno J	Oct 9, 1883	Foley, Thos	Mch 1, 1872
Fitzpatrick, Philip	Feb 22, 1873	Foley, Wm.	Jan 23, 1873
Fitzpatrick, Thos	Apr 8, 1885	Folk, Jno W	Jan 4, 1870
Fitzpatrick, Thos E	July 2, 1880	Follis, Pat'k	Aug 10, 1861
Fitzsimons, Philip	Feb 28, 1885	Foody, Mich'l	Mch 3, 1879
Flaherty, Thos	May 19, 1884	Ford, Denis	July 7, 1869
Flahive, Jno H	Dec 29, 1871	Fosket, Alonzo	May 10, 1871
Flanagan, Jno	Feb 1, 1866	Foster, Jas	Feb 17, 1870
Flanagan, Jno	Dec. 13, 1867	Foster, Wm J	Nov 13, 1879
Flanagan, Pat'k	Sept 3, 1862	Fox, John	Jan 3, 1881
Flanagan, Wm	Oct 10, 1870	Foy, Andrew	Apr 8, 1885
Flannery, Law	Mch 31, 1873	Francis, Chas H	May 30, 1871
Flannery, Mich'l	Dec. 1, 1869	Fraser, Alex	Oct 13, 1869
Flannery, Pat'k	Apr 9, 1879	Frayler, Chas	June 21, 1884
Flannery, Thos	Feb 3, 1866	Fredericks, Jno D	Mch. 25, 1868
Flannery, Thos J	June 23, 1869	Frers, Henry	Sept 27, 1880
Flay, Chas L	Mch 18, 1881	Frink, Wm E	Mch 20, 1875

Name	Date of Appointment	Name	Date of Appointment
Frost, Geo C.	Mch 27, 1878	Genore, Jno H.	Mch 31, 1877
Fuchs, J Frank	Mch 24, 1876	Gensheimer, Jno. M	May 1, 1882
Fuller, Jas K., Sergt	Nov. 14, 1867	Germann, Franklin P	Mch 31, 1879
Fulmer, Geo W	Mch. 18, 1864	Gerrow, David	July 1, 1876
		Gibbons, David M.	Oct 22, 1873

G

Name	Date of Appointment	Name	Date of Appointment
Gabriel, Chas	Dec. 10, 1862	Gibbons, Thos	Oct 23, 1865
Gaffney, Jas	Sept. 14, 1882	Gibson, Geo W	Jan. 22, 1866
Gaffney, Jas	July 15, 1876	Gibson, Henry C	Jan 2, 1873
Gallagher, Chas	Mch 13, 1884	Gibson, Jos H	July 15, 1876
Gallagher, Peter	Apr. 18, 1883	Gibson, Wm	Apr 26, 1882
Gallagher, Edward	Mch 16, 1870	Gick, Geo	Nov 23, 1867
Gallagher, Jno.	Oct 22, 1881	Gidley, Lewis	May 1, 1877
Gallagher, Jno, No 2	June 11, 1870	Gilbride, Thos	Mch 8, 1876
Gallagher, Jno, Sergt	Jan 17, 1868	Gilgan, Hugh	Aug 3, 1876
Gallagher, Mich'l	July 1, 1884	Gilgar, Edward	July 27, 1870
Gallagher, Owen	Nov. 16, 1881	Gill, Floyd T	Sept 29, 1876
Gallagher, Terence	Dec. 4, 1869	Gill, Geo W	Jan 5, 1874
Gallagher, Terence	Apr 2, 1880	Gillespie, Edward	Aug. 23, 1866
Gallagher, Wm. F	Feb 2, 1881	Gilligan, A. M	Sept 29, 1875
Galligan, Edward	Dec. 18, 1876	Gilligan, Jno C	Oct 16, 1873
Galligan, Patrick	May 1, 1882	Gilligan, Jno F	June 6, 1882
Gamble, Jas	Mch 26, 1880	Gilligan, Mich'l	Apr 9, 1879
Ganley, Rich'd	July 31, 1873	Gilliland, Hartshorn W	May 14, 1863
Gannon, Mich'l	Aug 27, 1869	Gillman, Fred'k	May 1, 1877
Gannon, Jas, Sergt	May 8, 1873	Gilloon, Dan'l	May 13, 1881
Gardner, Joseph, No 2	Sept 9, 1874	Gilmore, John	Oct 8, 1873
Gardner, Joseph A	July 2, 1869	Gilmore, Mich'l	Aug 19, 1870
Gardner, Wm	July 26, 1870	Gilpin, Jno	June 19, 1861
Gargan, Mich'l	Feb 18, 1884	Gilroy, Jas. A	Apr 23, 1880
Gargan, Patrick F	Apr 8, 1881	Gilroy, Mich'l	May 27, 1870
Garland, Ira S, Capt	Apr. 22, 1858	Glass, Geo W	Nov 3, 1864
Garland, T F	June 14, 1882	Glass, St. Clair	Apr. 8, 1876
Garland, Thos	Aug. 17, 1864	Gleason, Thos	May 11, 1875
Garnlein, Frank	Sept 28, 1883	Glennon, Jno F	Aug 31, 1878
Garrity, Jas	July 27, 1870	Glin, Maurice	Aug 3, 1865
Garside, John W	Oct 11, 1860	Glynn, Joseph	July 17, 1873
Gastlin, Geo W	May 19, 1864	Glynn, Pat'k	Aug 3, 1876
Gath, Rob't D	Nov. 28, 1873	Godfrey, Jno	Oct 17, 1873
Gaw, John	Apr 3, 1872	Godfrey, Geo J	May 23, 1861
Gaynor, Jas, Sergt	July 16, 1862	Goetzger, Fred'k	July 4, 1876
Geary, Mich'l	Aug 5, 1874	Gohl, Christian	Sept. 6, 1878
Geddes, Andrew	July 6, 1883	Golden, Anthony J	Apr 29, 1876
Gehegan, Joseph C	June 2, 1882	Golden, Judson, Sergt	Sept 13, 1875
Geiger, Nicholas	Jan. 19, 1868	Golden, Thos F J	Jan 20, 1877
		Golden, Timothy	Jan 2, 1873

Name	Date of Appointment	Name	Date of Appointment
Goldrick, Jas F	Dec. 28, 1871	Griffin, Mich'l	Sept 6, 1869
Golle, Julius A.	Sept 28, 1872	Griffin, Thos	Mch 26, 1875
Gonigle, Wm	Apr. 26, 1877	Griffith, Chas. W	June 11, 1866
Goodchild, Jas H	Nov 3, 1882	Griffith, Eugene	Oct 3, 1868
Goodell, Enoch A.	Sept. 22, 1864	Griffith, Philip M, Sergt	May 23, 1858
Goodenough, Theodore	Mar 17, 1873	Groden, Peter	Jan 29, 1868
Goodison, Jas	Nov 16, 1883	Grogan, Timothy	Aug 10, 1870
Goodspeed, Rich'd E	Apr 8, 1885	Groo, David D	Jan 11, 1884
Goodwin, Jno. W	June 29, 1882	Groo, Jno. R., Sergt	Oct 27, 1868
Goodwin, Wm	May 15, 1867	Grossjean, E D.	Nov 4, 1878
Gorey, Mich'l	Nov 13, 1873	Guerker, Wm	Jan. 28, 1860
Gorman, Mich'l	Feb 13, 1874	Gunn, Frank	Dec 9, 1876
Gorman, Thos	Sept 7, 1870	Gunner, Jno, Capt	Apr 6, 1861
Gough, Peter	Jan 3, 1881	Gunson, Rob't	Jan 28, 1861
Grace, Edward	Mch 10, 1866		
Grace, Geo J.	Sept 24, 1883	**H**	
Grace, Stephen	Apr 23, 1884	Haagen, August	Dec 28, 1866
Grady, Edward	July 28, 1869	Haas, Chas	Feb 20, 1885
Graf, Louis	Sept. 15, 1882	Haas, Edward	July 11, 1857
Graham, Alex	Feb 26, 1862	Haas, Geo	July 28, 1877
Graham, Jno	Sept 17, 1883	Hackett, Thos H	Jan 23, 1884
Grancher, Rudolph	Sept 16, 1882	Hackett, Wm J	Jan 24, 1884
Grainger, Chas M, Sergt.	Apr 12, 1871	Hagan, Bernard	Feb 11, 1882
Granger, Wm	Sept 30, 1867	Hagan, Chas.	June 13, 1866
Grannis, David N	July 23, 1880	Hagan, Edward	Mch 6, 1880
Grant, Donald, Sergt	June 1, 1876	Hagan, Francis	Sept 13, 1875
Grant, Jerome T	May 2, 1873	Hagan, Francis W	Mch 19, 1884
Grant, Jno H, Sergt.	Jan 12, 1866	Hagan, Jno	Aug 15, 1872
Grassick, Geo.	Aug. 6, 1862	Haggerty, J. J	Nov 29, 1867
Gray, Mich'l	Aug. 19, 1881	Haggerty, Jas	Jan 18, 1878
Gray, Wm	Oct 22, 1873	Haggerty, Jno W.	Sept 10, 1878
Gray, Wm E	Apr 29, 1880	Haggerty, Joseph, Sergt.	Jan 26, 1861
Gregg, Henry	Aug 7, 1882	Haggerty, Mark	Feb 21, 1880
Green, Harry	Nov. 7, 1873	Hahn, Henry	Apr 8, 1885
Green, Patrick	Aug 13, 1873	Hahn, Wm.	Oct 11, 1869
Green, Thos. S	May 24, 1866	Haines, Rob't	Nov 8, 1871
Green, Wm L.	Jan. 8, 1884	Haley, Owen	Feb 23, 1870
Grennon, Jno	May 23, 1868	Hall, Bradley	May 4, 1883
Grey, Thos	Oct 30, 1877	Hall, David D.	July 1, 1876
Grier, Arthur.	Apr 11, 1868	Hall, Rob't H.	Mch 29, 1883
Grier, Walter	Mch. 31, 1864	Halfpenny, Robt.	Nov 16, 1874
Griesel, Conrad H	Sept 11, 1873	Halliday, Joseph.	Jan 2, 1867
Griffin, Denis	June 30, 1870	Halloway, Rich'd	Mch 7, 1861
Griffin, J J	May 26, 1880	Halpin, Henry	Oct 28, 1871
Griffin, Jas	Aug 2, 1879	Hamilton, J P	Oct 25, 1876

OUR POLICE PROTECTORS.

Name	Date of Appointment
Hamilton, Jno, Sergt	Oct 27, 1866
Hammond, Geo	Dec 20, 1872
Hammond, Sam'l, Jr	Aug 27, 1884
Hana, Jno	July 22, 1870
Hand, Henry	Oct 15, 1872
Handy, Edward	Jan 24, 1868
Handy, Martin	Jan 30, 1867
Handy, Martin	Feb 20, 1885
Hanlan, Hugh J	May 26, 1883
Hanley, Chas. A	Apr 29, 1875
Hanley, Jas	Apr 8, 1876
Hanley, Owen	Apr 7, 1873
Hanlon, Timothy	July 2, 1873
Haradon, Nelson, Sergt	July 11, 1864
Hardgrove, Jno	Nov 23, 1867
Harding, Peter	Jan. 16, 1868
Hardiman, Pat'k	Feb 12, 1884
Harey, Philip	Apr. 29, 1876
Hargrove, Thos	Feb. 3, 1868
Harley, Jno. J	Mch 22, 1871
Harly, Philip	Apr 29, 1876
Harney, Thos	Mch 9, 1868
Harper, Thos. S	Mch 5, 1880
Harrington, Warren	Oct 22, 1873
Harris, Jno	Oct 18, 1870
Harris, Mich'l	Aug 18, 1869
Harris, Wm	Sept 19, 1871
Harrold, John	May 2, 1885
Hart, Jas. J	Feb 14, 1871
Hart, Peter	Jan 21, 1860
Hartigan, Mich'l	Sept 1, 1875
Hartling, Wm	Jan 31, 1873
Hartman, Chas	Sept. 1, 1875
Harty, Pat'k	Nov 16, 1868
Harty, Thos	Feb 13, 1858
Harty, Thos	Oct 7, 1882
Harvey, David	Apr 29, 1867
Hasslacher, A G	Dec 5, 1879
Hasson, Wm H	June 24, 1869
Hathaway, Wm N	Mch 31, 1874
Hatton, John	Dec 27, 1875
Haugh, Patrick	Feb 29, 1876
Haughey, Wm R, Sergt	Nov 1, 1872
Hauser, Geo E	Mch 3, 1884
Haussler, Chas	Apr 15, 1884
Havens, Geo. H, Sergt	July 31, 1861
Hawkey, Rich'd	Dec 11, 1861
Hawkins, Jno	Feb 17, 1875
Hawley, Ira D	Apr 14, 1877
Hays, Edward	July 10, 1869
Hays, Felix	Jan 28, 1861
Hayes, Jno	June 20, 1873
Hayes, Thos F	Apr 11, 1881
Hazelton, Abraham	Feb 28, 1884
Healy, F. J	June 7, 1867
Healy, Jno	Oct 3, 1874
Healy, Mark F	Jan 9, 1880
Heard, Jno	Feb 6, 1882
Heap, Thos. L	Feb 4, 1859
Heath, Jno W	Apr 9, 1879
Heatley, M. H	Aug. 5, 1881
Heaviside, Henry	Feb 16, 1870
Hedden, Henry, Capt	June 16, 1857
Heenan, Jas	Aug 3, 1876
Hefferman, Mich'l	Jan 18, 1867
Heffernan, Fred'k	Feb 12, 1884
Heidelberg, Chas	Sept 10, 1880
Heinz, Henry	Jan 1, 1874
Helme, Geo. E	Apr 9, 1872
Hencken, Rich'd	Jan 11, 1871
Hendricks, Jacob M	June 7, 1870
Hennessey, J J	June 21, 1878
Henry, Jas. L	June 29, 1870
Henry, Thos	Jan. 24, 1884
Henze, Wm	Feb 14, 1876
Herlihy, Jno D	Sept 1, 1877
Heron, Jno	May 5, 1869
Herrick, Jno J	Jan. 3, 1873
Herring, Wm	Feb 16, 1858
Herrlich, Henry	May 14, 1884
Herrlich, Wm	Mch 5, 1880
Hersche, Henry	June 1, 1861
Hertz, Nathan	May 1, 1884
Hess, Geo A	Oct 13, 1869
Hey, Eibo	Oct 12, 1861
Heyn, Chas. F	Apr 6, 1871
Hickey, Jno	Sept 16, 1878
Hickey, Mich'l	Feb 8, 1884
Hickey, Mich'l J	Mch 6, 1868
Hickey, Thos	Mch 27, 1872

Name	Date of Appointment	Name	Date of Appointment
Hickey, Wm	Mch 8, 1872	Horn, Peter	Sept 14, 1883
Hickey, Wm D	June 16, 1884	Horton, Hanford	Dec. 4, 1871
Hicumbothen, Rob't	July 27, 1867	Hotaling, Jno E	June 17, 1874
Higgins, Chas	Feb 12, 1884	Howard, Wm	Oct. 21, 1881
Higgins, Patrick	Mch 18, 1884	Howe, Henry Q	Dec 1, 1869
Higgins, Peter H	June 28, 1878	Howe, Jas. G	Feb 3, 1859
Hildebrandt, W	May 12, 1882	Howell, Alonzo	Jan 14, 1871
Hildenbrand, Henry	Sept. 20, 1873	Howell, Jno M	July 11, 1866
Hildreth, L B	Apr 4, 1861	Hubbard, Oscar	July 5, 1881
Hill, Thos	Feb 12, 1873	Huff, Thos, Sergt	Feb. 13, 1858
Hinton, Jno W	Oct 9, 1883	Hughes, Alex, No 1	Dec 30, 1868
Hinz, Henry	Jan 1, 1874	Hughes, Alexander, No 2	Mch 14, 1876
Hitchcock, H N	July 3, 1857	Hughes, Francis	Aug 18, 1869
Hoffman, H J	Oct 13, 1882	Hughes, Francis	June 21, 1873
Hogan, Dan'l	Nov 21, 1883	Hughes, Jno	June 14, 1882
Hogan, Dan'l J	Feb 13, 1880	Hughes, Wm H	Dec 16, 1872
Hogan, John, No 1	Nov 12, 1879	Hull, Percival	Jan. 5, 1870
Hogan, Jno	Apr. 18, 1883	Hulse, Geo B	Apr 29, 1875
Hogan, Matthew	Sept 20, 1873	Hummel, Adolph	Nov 20, 1875
Hogan, Mich'l J	May 11, 1866	Humphreys, Jas	June 6, 1870
Hogan, Patrick	July 14, 1869	Hunter, Livingston	Mch 7, 1885
Hogan, Patrick	Nov 14, 1874	Hunt, Patrick F	Apr 8, 1885
Hogan, Thos	Oct. 13, 1873	Hunter, Jas	Dec 11, 1867
Hogan, Wm	Jan 9, 1880	Hunter, Wm	Aug 26, 1882
Holahan, Jas	Sept 8, 1882	Huntress, Wm A	Apr 25, 1882
Holahan, Jno C	Apr. 8, 1885	Huntzinger, Jno B	Oct 25, 1867
Holbrow, T V, Sergt	Aug 19, 1862	Hurlbut, Henry	July 20, 1877
Holder, Wm	Feb. 27, 1884	Hurley, Jno. J	May 1, 1877
Holland, Jno H	Apr 23, 1883	Huston, Wm. J	Feb 27, 1875
Holland, Thos B	Aug 3, 1876	Hyland, Thos	Nov 13, 1879
Holmes, Geo W	Feb 12, 1885		
Holmes, Rich'd, Jr	June 17, 1884	**I**	
Holmes, Theophelus	Apr 19, 1860	Immen, Chas D	Sept 1, 1865
Holmes, Wm	Oct 25, 1872	Interman, Herrman	Feb 18, 1874
Holmes, Wm J	Jan 23, 1861	Irving, John	Dec 21, 1863
Holzman, Harry	Sept 17, 1883	Irwin, George	July 14, 1857
Homan, Chas E	June 29, 1869	Isbell, Adelbert	Mar 20, 1872
Houlihan, Edward	Jan 23, 1884	Ives, Willis D	Aug 19, 1869
Hooker, Henry D, Capt	Jan 28, 1861	Ivory, Joseph	July 15, 1876
Hopper, Henry E	Apr 29, 1880		
Horan, John	Jan 23, 1884	**J**	
Horbelt, Marcus, Sergt	Feb. 3, 1859	Jackson, David	Mch 1, 1873
Horgan, Bartholemew	Feb. 26, 1862	Jackson, David H	May 4, 1870
Horn, Herman	Mch 14, 1884	Jackson, Frank G	Apr 20, 1883
Horn, Jno T	Oct 14, 1881	Jackson, Neil A	Mch 19, 1884
		Jackson, Robert	Sept 17, 1883

OUR POLICE PROTECTORS.

Name	Date of Appointment
Jackson, Simon	Apr. 30, 1861
Jacobs, Geo R	Sept. 16, 1876
Jacoby, Henry	Nov 16, 1870
Jacoby, Henry F.	July 1, 1876
Jagels, Henry	Oct. 16, 1877
James, Peter E	June 5, 1882
James, Thos. N., Sergt.	June 27, 1858
Janvrin, Dennis A	May 8, 1874
Jefferson, John	Aug. 17, 1872
Jenkins, James M	May 16, 1884
Jenney, Chas B.	Mch 6, 1884
Jennings, John	Nov 13, 1879
Jennings, Matthias	Jan 10, 1881
Jennings, Thomas	May 29, 1884
Johnson, Chas	Apr 18, 1883
Johnson, Joseph	Sept 14, 1871
Johnston, Arthur A	Apr 8, 1883
Johnston, Michael	Sept 22, 1873
Johnston, Robert S	Jan. 28, 1885
Jones, Jas	Jan 3, 1868
Jordan, Jas W	Mch 18, 1881
Jordan, John	Jan 22, 1881
Jordan, Timothy	Aug 16, 1872
Jordan, Wm.	Apr 8, 1881
Jose, John	Apr 18, 1883
Joyce, John J	Sept 12, 1870
Joyce, Redmond J	June 19, 1878
Judge, Owen	Feb 22, 1870
Judson, Chas F	Jan 17, 1872
Junker, Max	Dec 27, 1875

K

Name	Date of Appointment
Kain, Peter	Oct 27, 1874
Kane, James	Sept 28, 1883
Kane, Lawrence	June 9, 1884
Kane, Michael	Sept 13, 1875
Kappes, Geo	Aug 19, 1881
Kass, Geo B, Sergt	Oct 1, 1862
Kass, Wm, Sergt	Feb 3, 1859
Kavanagh, James	Apr 8, 1876
Kavanagh, John	Jan 3, 1873
Kavanagh, Thos	July 5, 1872
Kavanagh, Thos J	Mch 14, 1862
Kear, Francis J	May 28, 1880
Kearney, Patrick	Jan. 28, 1861
Kearney, Thomas	Aug. 28, 1867
Keating, John A	Nov 21, 1867
Keating, Michael E	Mch. 6, 1880
Keating, Stephen, Sergt.	Apr 14, 1868
Keefe, Thomas	Oct. 29, 1883
Keeley, Thomas	Aug. 31, 1878
Keeling, John R	Sept 17, 1864
Keenan, James	Oct 12, 1870
Kehoe, Michael	Oct 3, 1881
Kehoe, Thos F	Aug 6, 1883
Kehoe, Wm	Sept. 8, 1869
Keirns, Patrick	Feb 18, 1863
Kelahan, John	Feb 2, 1866
Keliher, John J	Nov 17, 1883
Kelk, Geo S	July 17, 1873
Kellaher, John, Sergt.	Jan. 26, 1861
Kellard, Michael	Sept 25, 1863
Keller, John H	June 11, 1872
Kellerhouse, Albert	May 13, 1867
Kelly, Andrew	Jan. 30, 1873
Kelly, Bartholomew	Aug 15, 1871
Kelly, Chas F.	July 1, 1876
Kelly, Cornelius J	Dec 30, 1881
Kelly, Frank	Jan 15, 1873
Kelly, James	Oct 11, 1873
Kelly, John	Mch 30, 1866
Kelly, John, Sergt	Sept 27, 1870
Kelly, John	July 20, 1882
Kelly, John P	Mch. 8, 1871
Kelly, John P	May 1, 1882
Kelly, Joseph B	Oct 10, 1881
Kelly, Michael	Sept 3, 1859
Kelly, Patrick	June 1, 1876
Kelly, Patrick	Aug 3, 1876
Kelly, Patrick	Jan 24, 1884
Kelly, Patrick H	Jan 15, 1866
Kelly, Patrick J	Oct 21, 1881
Kelly, Peter	Jan 13, 1870
Kelly, Robert	Feb 13, 1864
Kelly, Thos. H	Apr 29, 1880
Kelly, Wm	May 2, 1873
Kelly, Wm	Apr 8, 1876
Kelsey, James R.	Jan 26, 1876
Kelz, August	July 15, 1876
Kemp, John	May 2, 1873

Name	Date of Appointment	Name	Date of Appointment
Kenna, Andrew J	Mch 27, 1884	Kiernan, John	Dec 18, 1876
Kenneally, Patrick	May 2, 1872	Kiernan, Patrick	Apr 1, 1873
Kennedy, Declan	Oct 6, 1874	Kiernan, Thomas	Nov 30, 1872
Kennedy, Edward	Feb 14, 1870	Kilkenny, James	Mch 1, 1873
Kennedy, Edward	June 27, 1878	Killalea, John	Feb 8, 1873
Kennedy, Edward J	Apr 12, 1876	Killilea, Michael	June 21, 1869
Kennedy, Henry A	Dec 30, 1872	Killilea, Thomas, Capt	Oct 1, 1866
Kennedy, Jeremiah	Apr. 30, 1878	Kilmartin, James	Oct 17, 1874
Kennedy, John	Nov 13, 1879	King, Elbert S	Jan 3, 1873
Kennedy, John	June 6, 1884	King, James M, Sergt.	Apr 6, 1866
Kennedy, John S	Mch 10, 1884	King, Jas Thorne	Oct 29, 1862
Kennedy, Matthew	Mch 19, 1880	King, John	Mch 11, 1874
Kennedy, Patrick	May 13, 1867	King, John W	Sept 29, 1882
Kennedy, Patrick	Nov 18, 1870	King, Nathan W	May 8, 1884
Kennedy, Wm	Jan 24, 1884	King, Richard	Apr 23, 1857
Kenney, James	Sept 27, 1881	Kinnaird, Samuel W	Sept 23, 1873
Kenney, Jas F	Feb 11, 1884	Kirby, Cornelius	May 27, 1876
Kenney, Jas F	Dec 1, 1865	Kirley, Michael	Jan 7, 1873
Kenney, John, No. 1	Oct 11, 1877	Kirschner, Wm. F., Sergt	Dec 1, 1870
Kenney, Peter	Apr. 7, 1880	Kirtland, Geo R	Sept 25, 1875
Kenny, James E J	Jan 2, 1873	Kirzinger, John	Apr 24, 1883
Kenny, John, No 2	Apr. 23, 1883	Kivlen, James	Mar 26, 1884
Keon, Miles	June 11, 1870	Klein, Julius J	Apr 8, 1875
Keough, Martin	Jan 26, 1876	Klein, Peter J	Feb 12, 1885
Kern, Chas	Mch. 19, 1880	Klinge, Emile	Apr 8, 1875
Kern, Herrman	Apr. 20, 1883	Klinge, Hector	Feb. 17, 1873
Kern, Jacob B	Feb 18, 1867	Knisler, Geo A	May 18, 1865
Kernan, Thomas	Dec. 3, 1872	Knoff, Philip	Feb 12, 1885
Kerns, Theodore	May 12, 1884	Knox, Wm J	Feb 10, 1879
Kerns, Thos H	Aug 9, 1866	Koellsted, John	May 7, 1883
Kerrigan, James	June 17, 1874	Kohler, John	Aug 9, 1866
Kershaw, John H	May 24, 1866	Kook, Charles	Mch 24, 1880
Ketchale, Wm	Jan 3, 1884	Kopp, Robert	July 21, 1883
Kettner, Jos A	Apr 26, 1876	Kormann, Fredrick W	Apr 26, 1877
Keyes, Timothy	June 27, 1882	Kortsteger, Barney	Oct 10, 1881
Kiebrick, Jacob J	Oct 9, 1883	Krauch, John L	Feb 4, 1884
Kieley, John	Sept 28, 1870	Kremmelbein, Fredrick	Jan 8, 1884
Kiernan, Bernard	May 1, 1872	Kroner, Fredrick	Jan 13, 1866
Kiernan, Edward	Jan 26, 1876	Krowl, Geo. W.	Feb 4, 1884
Kiernan, Francis	May 20, 1881	Kuhn, Wm H	Feb 4, 1884
Kiernan, Geo W	Mch. 5, 1880	Kulle, Albert	Sept 1, 1875
Kiernan, Hugh	Feb 7, 1873	Kunzman, Clement	Feb 29, 1876
Kiernan, James	Jan. 23, 1861	Kush, Chas.	Aug 25, 1869
Kiernan, Jas J	Nov 3, 1882		
Kiernan, John	Sept 27, 1870		

L

Lacy, Edward J . . . Sept 7, 1864

Name	Date of Appointment	Name	Date of Appointment
Lahert, Richard	June 6, 1870	Leavy, Michael	Dec 7, 1881
Lahm, George	Apr. 7, 1880	Leddy, Hugh	Nov. 3, 1871
Lahr, William	Nov 5, 1883	Leddy, John	Dec 23, 1874
Laird, Thomas J	Mar 12, 1867	Lee, Michael	Sept. 25, 1872
Lake, Franklin W	Oct. 3, 1874	Lee, Thomas J	May 1, 1882
Lake, Wm. H	July 1, 1876	Leeson, Geo T	Aug. 14, 1878
Lally, Michael	June 1, 1876	Leffert, Wm. H, Sergt.	Apr. 23, 1857
Lamb, Bernard	Jan. 5, 1865	Lehane, Daniel	Sept 14, 1883
Lamb, Thos	Jan 2, 1884	Leiber, Louis	May 26, 1882
Lambrecht, Jacob	Jan 4, 1881	Leinis, Philip	Mar 7, 1885
Lambrecht, Wm. G	May 16, 1884	Leissner, Henry	Feb 4, 1884
Lamey, Michael, Sergt.	Sept 18, 1861	Leissner, John	Sept. 14, 1883
Lancer, Thomas, Sergt	Mch 18, 1880	Lemlein, Nathan	Nov 25, 1872
Landers, John	Sept 26, 1877	Lenz, Charles	Sept 27, 1876
Lane, Patrick B.	Oct 31, 1874	Leon, Jacob	Mar 3, 1882
Lane, Patrick J.	May 7, 1872	Leonard, John	Apr 29, 1880
Lane, Patrick J	Oct. 9, 1873	Leonard, John E	Jan 29, 1884
Lang, Joseph T	Sept 28, 1883	Leonard, Patrick	Feb 26, 1872
Laegan, James J	May 14, 1878	Leonard, Patrick	Feb 15, 1884
Langan, John L	Jan 7, 1881	Leonard, Terence	Feb 15, 1884
Lankton, Henry K	June 23, 1861	Leshe, Patrick H	June 2, 1884
Lanthier, Geo	July 22, 1879	Levy, Alexander	Sept 15, 1870
Larkin, Hearn J	Apr 29, 1875	Levy, Hiram	Sept 29, 1873
Larkin, Michael	Aug 17, 1870	Levy, Wolf	Feb 10, 1873
Laughlin, George	Feb 24, 1866	Lewis, Edward	July 10, 1860
Lavender, Geo, Jr	Apr 8, 1885	Lewis, Frederick R	May 6, 1867
Lavin, Patrick	Sept 14, 1883	Lewis, George F	Apr 26, 1883
Lawler, James	July 2, 1873	Lewis, Joseph A	Apr 18, 1885
Lawler, Patrick	Aug 4, 1868	Liebers, George C	Sept 1, 1883
Lawler, Thomas F	Aug 7, 1878	Lindeman, Ernest	Nov 25, 1874
Lawler, Thomas	July 5, 1882	Linden, Wm J, Sergt.	Feb 7, 1861
Lawler, Wm	Dec 27, 1875	Link, Charles	Oct 24, 1877
Lawless, John E	May 9, 1883	Linn, Daniel	Oct. 13, 1881
Lawless, Richard H	Feb 12, 1884	Linn, Wm R	Feb 12, 1884
Lawrence, Edward H	Aug 28, 1876	Liston, James E	Aug. 20, 1881
Lawrence, Thomas C	July 23, 1874	Little, Geo, Sergt	June 14, 1865
Lay, Jacob	Sept 8, 1875	Livingston, Abraham	July 1, 1872
Layton, John H	Oct 14, 1867	Livingston, Henry A	June 5, 1875
Leacraft, Charles C	Oct. 15, 1862	Lober, Frank	Sept. 2, 1871
Leahy, David	Feb 27, 1873	Lober, Michael	Oct 22, 1883
Leahy, Michael	June 7, 1865	Logan, Geo	Sept 22, 1875
Leahy, Patrick	July 1, 1872	Londrigan, Wm	Apr 11, 1873
Leamy, Joseph	Sept 1, 1875	Long, Thomas	Jan 22, 1878
Leary, Cornelius	Aug 15, 1871	Long, William	Aug 5, 1863
Leary, James M, Capt	Aug 15, 1863	Lonsdale, James, Sergt	Sept. 21, 1862

OUR POLICE PROTECTORS

Name	Date of Appointment
Loonan, Chas	Aug. 26, 1873
Looney, Wm	Oct 2, 1873
Looram, Matthew	Nov 14, 1873
Lorch, Louis	Jan 23, 1884
Lott, Charles	Aug 3, 1876
Loub, Louis	Jan 23, 1884
Loughlin, John F	April 8, 1885
Loures, James J.	Nov 21, 1883
Lovell, Lorenzo D	Jan 29, 1881
Lucas, Edward, Sergt	June 1, 1874
Lucie, John	Mch 14, 1882
Luersson, Augustus	Mch 16, 1870
Luersson, Imer D, Sergt.	Feb 4, 1876
Luthei, Wm	July 12, 1870
Lyman, Geo	May 29, 1868
Lyman, Matthew	Aug 25, 1882
Lyna, John	Oct 6, 1882
Lynch, James	Apr 20, 1864
Lynch, James	Jan 22, 1881
Lynch, Lawrence J	Jan 28, 1884
Lynch, Michael	Sept. 27, 1873
Lynch, Patrick	July 23, 1862
Lynch, Timothy	Dec 31, 1881
Lyon, Holly C	Feb 13, 1858
Lyon, John	June 18, 1884
Lyon, Samuel K, Surgeon	Feb 3, 1876
Lyon, Thomas	Jan 29, 1884

M

Name	Date of Appointment
Macfail, Geo W.	June 3, 1882
Mackey, Jas	July 2, 1880
Mackey, Wm	Feb 13, 1873
Mackin, Thos.	Feb. 28, 1879
Maclay, Aug W, Surg.	Sept 15, 1873
Macnevin, Nelson J.	Apr 8, 1881
Madden, David	June 1, 1877
Madden, Jas F.	July 15, 1876
Madigan, Jno	Apr 3, 1873
Magan, Rich'd F., Sergt	June 10, 1870
Magee, Wm	Mch 23, 1858
Magrane, S L	Oct 6, 1882
Maguire, Jas	Sept 22, 1875
Maguire, Pat'k, No 1	Feb 27, 1873
Maher, Jas	Sept. 28, 1870
Maher, Jno.	Aug 5, 1874
Maher, Thos	Oct 8, 1881
Maher, Thos	May 7, 1883
Mahon, Thos	Aug 3, 1883
Mahoney, Eugene	May 1, 1883
Mahoney, Jas	May 16, 1884
Mahoney, Jno O	Sept 7, 1870
Mahoney, P F	Mch 30, 1880
Mahoney, Wm	Dec 12, 1881
Mains, Alex.	Apr 15, 1876
Mairs, Jas	Dec 17, 1883
Major, Jas J	June 3, 1882
Mallan, Jas	Apr 6, 1868
Malley, Jas	Apr 29, 1876
Malloy, Mich'l	Sept 23, 1878
Malone, Francis	Aug 24, 1865
Malone, Geo. P	Feb 16, 1870
Malone, Henry	May 1, 1861
Malone, Joseph A	June 1, 1861
Malone, Mich'l	Nov 22, 1872
Maloney, Jas.	Jan 27, 1873
Maloney, Jas B.	June 16, 1882
Manchester, Aaron W	May 2, 1881
Mangan, Jno	Aug 28, 1868
Mangin, Frank, Jr	June 9, 1882
Mangin, Thos	July 21, 1864
Mangin, Thos H, Sergt	Dec. 31, 1870
Manning, B. D.	June 23, 1882
Manning, Joseph	May 29, 1884
Mannion, Joseph	Jan. 23, 1884
Mannion, Thos H	July 7, 1884
Mannix, Jno.	Nov 16, 1883
Marckle, Christian	Mch 29, 1878
Markey, Andrew	Mch. 30, 1865
Markey, Jno R	Mch 30, 1866
Marlarkey, Bernard	Jan 7, 1867
Marron, Pat'k H.	Oct. 1, 1877
Martens, F W, Sergt	Sept 27, 1878
Martin, Christopher E	Apr 29, 1872
Martin, David	Jan 15, 1866
Martin, Hugh	Jan 22, 1870
Martin, Jno.	May 5, 1869
Martin, Joseph.	Apr 27, 1883
Martin, M R.	Jan 3, 1881
Martin, Mich'l.	Oct 26, 1864
Martin, Richard.	June 22, 1857

Name	Date of Appointment	Name	Date of Appointment
McAdam, James	May 25, 1868	McCormack, Th. P.	Oct 26, 1883
McAdam, James C., Jr	Mar 10, 1882	McCormack, William	Feb 16, 1876
McAleer, Patrick	Nov 25, 1870	McCormack, Wm.	May 19, 1884
McArdle, Bernard	March 31, 1875	McCormick, James	Aug 21, 1863
McAuley, Edward J	Oct 10, 1881	McCormick, John	Oct 5, 1861
McAuley, James A.	Feb 15, 1865	McCormick, John W	Dec 23, 1876
McAvoy, Th's T., Sergt	Jan 20, 1870	McCormick, Thomas	Dec 9, 1872
McBride, Manus	Mar. 16, 1870	McCormick, Thos	July 15, 1876
McBride, Thomas	Apr 9, 1873	McCormick, Wm	Jan 24, 1872
McCabe, Edward	Dec 6, 1876	McCormick, Wm J	July 28, 1882
McCabe, John	July 15, 1870	McCoy, Joseph P	Apr 20, 1883
McCabe, Thomas	Feb 4, 1884	McCoy, Matthew	Sept 8, 1868
McCadden, Henry	Nov 15, 1867	McCoy, Wm F	Oct 17, 1877
McCahill, John	Aug 17, 1869	McCrohan, Denis	May 7, 1885
McCamman, Samuel	May 11, 1877	McCue, Dennis	Feb 28, 1876
McCann, Chas	Oct 21, 1881	McCue, John	Jan 17, 1873
McCann, Dominick D.	Jan 22, 1881	McCue, Thomas	May 5, 1880
McCardle, Patrick	Feb 22, 1865	McCullagh, James	Aug 1, 1867
McCarthy, Alexander F	Apr 8, 1885	McCullagh, John, Capt.	Mch 30, 1870
McCarthy, Cornelius	June 22, 1870	McCullagh, J. H., Capt.	Feb 29, 1864
McCarthy, Dennis	Mch 1, 1866	McCullough, John	Oct 16, 1878
McCarthy, Dennis	Sept 30, 1874	McCullough, Patrick	Nov 23, 1877
McCarthy, Eugene	Jan 9, 1884	McCusker, Jas., Jr	July 28, 1882
McCarthy, James	May 2, 1873	McDaniel, James	July 2, 1880
McCarthy, John	Oct 14, 1870	McDaniels, Geo. B	May 6, 1885
McCarthy, John D	Feb 10, 1874	McDermott, Charles	Sept 23, 1864
McCarthy, John T	Sept 30, 1881	McDermott, Geo S	May 6, 1885
McCarthy, Michael	Apr. 26, 1877	McDermott, James	Feb 18, 1878
McCarthy, Thomas J	Feb 10, 1873	McDermott, John	Jan 5, 1870
McCarthy, Thomas J	Feb. 10, 1885	McDermott, John	Apr 29, 1875
McCarthy, Wm	Oct 11, 1883	McDermott, John J.	Mch 26, 1867
McCarthy, Wm	May 6, 1885	McDermott, John J	Nov. 30, 1883
McCarton, Francis	Oct 9, 1883	McDermott, Michael	Aug 15, 1872
McCarty, Daniel J.	Aug 3, 1876	McDermott, Peter	Sept 15, 1869
McCarty, Moses	Sept 20, 1873	McDermott, Stephen	Sept 22, 1875
McCauley, Hugh	Dec 14, 1870	McDermott, Thomas	July 20, 1870
McCauley, Hugh J	Oct 18, 1881	McDevitt, Wm	Sept. 22, 1877
McCauley, John	July 15, 1876	McDonald, A W, Sergt.	Nov. 22, 1876
McCauley, Matthew J	Jan 7, 1881	McDonald, Bernard	May 6, 1881
McCauley, Michael	Dec 9, 1877	McDonald, Jas B	May 9, 1881
McCauley, Neill	Mch 16, 1872	McDonald, John	Apr 29, 1874
McClintock, A, Sergt	June 17, 1862	McDonald, John	June 17, 1874
McCloskey, Wm J	Apr 18, 1883	McDonald, John	Feb 20, 1882
McCluskey, Geo W.	Apr 26, 1882	McDonald, Michael	Mch 20, 1875
McConnell, Hugh	Oct 16, 1867	McDonald, Peter	Jan. 24, 1884
McConnell, Matthew	Jan 7, 1860	McDonnell, Chas, Cap	Jan. 21, 1863
McCool, James	June 29, 1872	McDonnell, John	Apr 10, 1879
McCord, Louis	Mch 19, 1880	McDonnell, Peter	Nov 1, 1872
McCormack, Hugh	Apr 1, 1882	McDonnell, P. W, Sur	Sept 15, 1873
McCormack, John J	June 14, 1882	McDonough, Francis	Jan 1, 1874
McCormack, Thomas	Jan 25, 1861	McDowell, John	Jan. 17, 1873

Name	Date of Appointment	Name	Date of Appointment
McElroy, Daniel F	May 2, 1883	McKenna, Patrick	Jan 1, 1874
McElwain, J, Capt	Sept 28, 1861	McKenzie, Chas H	June 14, 1866
McEnroe, Bernard F	Oct 8, 1870	McKeon, Bernard	Feb 17, 1866
McEveety, B, Sergt	Aug. 1, 1873	McKeon, Wm F	Sept 22, 1873
McEvoy, Jos J	July 1, 1876	McKeown, Jos	Sept. 16, 1865
McGarry, Frank	Mch 18, 1884	McKirvey, John	Sept 24, 1883
McGee, Thomas	Mch. 5, 1880	McKnight, Jas H	Oct 9, 1883
McGeorge, A B	Aug 22, 1874	McLaughlin, Edward	June 2, 1884
McGinn, John	July 9, 1870	McLaughlin, Michael	Nov 2, 1883
McGinn, John, No 2	Jan 27, 1875	McLaughlin, Michael	Mch 7, 1885
McGinley, Francis J	Apr 14, 1883	McLaughlin, W W, Serg	Nov 26, 1868
McGinley, John	June 18, 1880	McLeavy, Charles	June 2, 1876
McGinley, Mich'l J	Oct 5, 1882	McLeod, S. B. W., Sur	Sept 15, 1873
McGinley, Patrick	Mch 30, 1870	McLoughlin, John	May 8, 1882
McGinley, Patrick	Dec 27, 1875	McLoughlin, John	Sept 24, 1883
McGinley, Robert	Aug 15, 1884	McLoughlin, John	Jan 29, 1884
McGinnis, Wm	Jan 23, 1884	McLoughlin, John B	July 14, 1865
McGill, James	Jan 21, 1869	McMahon, Denis	May 7, 1883
McGloin, John W	Nov 20, 1875	McMahon, Dennis	Feb 24, 1866
McGloin, Patrick	Apr 24, 1875	McMahon, Edward	Jan 15, 1873
McGloin, Wm	May 20, 1885	McMahon, James	Jan. 27, 1873
McGlone, James H.	Feb 8, 1884	McMahon, John	Jan 31, 1874
McGlone, Wm	Jan. 24, 1884	McMahon, John	June 30, 1882
McGowan, Daniel	Apr 28, 1880	McManus, Chas. B	Jan 23, 1884
McGowan, John	Dec. 17, 1862	McMillian, W B, Sergt	Jan 21, 1869
McGowan, John H	July 1, 1872	McNally, Felix	Feb 9, 1882
McGowan, Thomas	July 9, 1870	McNally, James	Dec 21, 1883
McGowan, Wm J	Apr 8, 1885	McNally, John	Aug 19, 1868
McGovern, Lawrence	May 8, 1880	McNally, John J	Oct 3, 1881
McGovern, Martin, Sur	July 3, 1884	McNally, Patrick, Sergt	Oct. 24, 1864
McGorry, John F	Mch 14, 1885	McNamara, Daniel J	July 15, 1876
McGreevy, Owen	May 16, 1884	McNamara, Jas. F	Sept 15, 1882
McGrade, Hugh	Aug 3, 1876	McNamara, John	Feb. 10, 1875
McGrade, Michael	Oct 26, 1861	McNamara, John, Sergt	Feb 5, 1873
McGrath, James	June 23, 1869	McNamee, Michael	Apr 14, 1868
McGrath, James	May 10, 1871	McNaught, Robert	July 15, 1876
McGrath, James	Apr. 1, 1882	McNealis, John	Jan 18, 1884
McGrath, Michael	July 29, 1874	McNeely, John	Oct 29, 1883
McGuiness, Edward	Nov 23, 1883	McNiece, Patrick	Oct 19, 1880
McGuire, James	Nov 16, 1872	McNulty, Francis	Jan 22, 1879
McGuire, John J	Sept 28, 1883	McParlan, James	Jan 26, 1884
McGuire, Patrick	Dec 1, 1865	McParlan, Thomas	Nov 3, 1859
McGuire, Patrick	Jan 3, 1882	McPartlin, Owen	Feb 7, 1874
McGuire, Thomas	Aug 3, 1876	McQuade, James, No. 1	Mch 1, 1876
McGuirken, John	Nov 22, 1870	McQuade, Thomas	Aug 5, 1879
McIlhargy, Alexander	July 15, 1874	McSherry, Matthew	March 20, 1868
McInerny, Daniel J	Jan. 24, 1872	McSweeny, John	June 9, 1873
McIntyre, Edward	Mar 23, 1881	McTaggart, Francis	Apr 26, 1877
McKenna, Felix	Oct. 3, 1874	McVay, James	Oct 10, 1881
McKenna, Francis	Aug. 3, 1876	McVay, Patrick	Mch. 12, 1860
McKenna, Patrick	Sept 9, 1873		

Name	Date of Appointment	Name	Date of Appointment
Martin, Simon	Oct 9, 1858	Miller, Theodore	May 26, 1880
Martineau, Cornelius	May 5, 1869	Miller, Wm. J	Feb 4, 1884
Masters, Jas	Mch. 4, 1884	Millmore, Jno M	Mch 21, 1884
Masterson, Jno. T	May 19, 1876	Minchin, M G	Apr 21, 1882
Masterson, Mich'l	Dec 30, 1872	Miner, Charles	June 17, 1857
Masterson, Patrick	Jan. 14, 1873	Minnerly, Abraham	Nov. 13, 1872
Mathison, Dan'l	June 2, 1868	Minnick, Jno	Apr 6, 1868
Matthews, David, Surg	Apr 16, 1877	Minnie, Jno D	Sept 16, 1867
Matthews, Jno M	Oct 22, 1873	Mints, Jno. G	Feb 15, 1868
Matthews, Michael	Jan 7, 1861	Mitchell, Anthony	Oct 13, 1873
Maxwell, J H	Apr. 26, 1882	Mitchell, Artemas W	Oct 28, 1879
Mayer, Chas	Apr 23, 1881	Mitchell, Cornelius	June 27, 1884
Mayfort, H. Geo	Sept. 9, 1874	Mitchell, Jno	July 13, 1870
Maynard, Ed D	May 1, 1877	Mitchell, Jno F	Jan. 29, 1884
Meacle, Joseph	May 1, 1876	Mitchell, Thos D	July 14, 1870
Mead, Fred'k	Apr 8, 1885	Moan, Thos F	Dec 5, 1878
Mead, Jas S, Sergt	Jan. 20, 1869	Moclare, Denis	May 7, 1878
Mead, Joseph W	Sept 29, 1869	Moffitt, Geo	Apr 15, 1878
Mead, Wm H	Aug 26, 1868	Moffitt, Thos	June 16, 1874
Meagher, Jno	June 13, 1875	Mohr, Philip	Oct 16, 1872
Meagher, Jno J	Sept 24, 1873	Molloy, Jno	Apr 2, 1875
Meakin, Wm, Capt	Feb. 10, 1873	Molloy, Jno	Oct 29, 1862
Meaney, Jno A	Nov 20, 1875	Molloy, Jno. J	May 12, 1877
Meehan, Bernard	Apr 25, 1883	Moloney, Jno F, Sergt	June 14, 1864
Meehan, Chas J	June 20, 1881	Moloney, Martin	Jan 22, 1861
Meehan, Thos	Mch 5, 1881	Moloney, Owen	Aug 5, 1873
Meehan, J F	Apr 21, 1883	Moloney, Thos F	Aug 24, 1881
Meiers, Max	Mch 23, 1867	Monahan, Jas E	Nov 1, 1878
Melly, Peter	Dec. 2, 1864	Monaghan, Jas A	July 21, 1882
Mettel, Fred'k	Mch. 5, 1881	Moncrief, Ambrose	Mch 24, 1876
Meyer, Chas	Mch. 4, 1875	Mongan, Jas	July 31, 1872
Meyer, Emanuel	Nov. 23, 1883	Mongan, Jos F	Sept 15, 1882
Meyer, Ernst H	Feb. 6, 1872	Mongan, Thos	Sept 17, 1883
Meyer, Rob't L	Mch 19, 1879	Monihan, Peter J	Oct 30, 1866
Milburn, Geo J	Feb. 11, 1884	Montgomery, Geo	Aug 5, 1879
Miley, Edward F	Dec 22, 1883	Montgomery, Jas C	Oct 27, 1874
Miller, Chas	Mch. 27, 1882	Montgomery, Rob't A	Mch 22, 1872
Miller, Eustace	May 10, 1865	Moody, James	Jan 24, 1861
Miller, Harvey P	Jan. 23, 1861	Mooney, Owen	June 7, 1873
Miller, Harvy	July 15, 1876	Moore, Jas	Jan 21, 1869
Miller, Isaac	Dec 2, 1881	Moore, Jno C	Jan. 23, 1884
Miller, Israel W	Jan 14, 1873	Moore, Jno. G	Aug 17, 1870
Miller, Jas J	Jan 8, 1884	Moore, Thos. E	June 5, 1873
Miller, Joseph	Jan 10, 1881	Moore, Wm	Nov. 20, 1875
Miller, Peter T	Mch 10, 1884	Moran, Edward	Aug 28, 1876

Name	Date of Appointment	Name	Date of Appointment
Moran, Jas	Dec 24, 1868	Murphy, Denis	Aug 2, 1883
Moran, Jas S.	Apr. 7, 1880	Murphy, Edward	Sept. 8, 1869
Moran, Jeremiah	Oct 21, 1881	Murphy, Francis	Nov 20, 1868
Moran, Jno	Feb 8, 1865	Murphy, Jas	Nov. 15, 1881
Moran, Pat'k	June 18, 1883	Murphy, Jas D	May 7, 1874
Moran, Peter	Sept 24, 1874	Murphy, Jas M	June 16, 1874
Moran, Thos	Jan 8, 1862	Murphy, Jeremiah J.	Oct 22, 1883
Morey, James N.	May 24, 1860	Murphy, John	Oct 15, 1859
Morgan, Thos	Oct 30, 1871	Murphy, Jno.	May 12, 1873
Morganweek, Wm	Oct 17, 1874	Murphy, Jno	May 3, 1878
Morrell, Jefferson	Oct. 10, 1873	Murphy, Jno C	Feb 27, 1884
Morris, Pat'k.	Apr 10, 1874	Murphy, Joseph	May 11, 1874
Morris, Thos J	Nov 27, 1883	Murphy, M R	June 29, 1863
Morton, Jas W	Apr 20, 1883	Murphy, Maurice	Oct 8, 1873
Mount, John J, Capt	Apr 23, 1857	Murphy, Mich'l J, Capt	Aug. 10, 1868
Moxley, F J	July 3, 1876	Murphy, Mich'l	Sept 27, 1870
Moyland, Jeremiah.	May 25, 1864	Murphy, Myles	June 22, 1864
Moynihan, Dan'l C	Dec 23, 1876	Murphy, Patrick.	Feb 8, 1859
Mulaney, Jas	Dec 6, 1872	Murphy, Pat'k	Feb 17, 1869
Mulcahay, Wm	Oct 15, 1873	Murphy, Pat'k	Sept 1, 1869
Mulcahy, Rich'd J	Oct 26, 1883	Murphy, Rob't.	Feb 18, 1885
Muldoon, Jno	Aug 17, 1866	Murphy, Thos	Aug 31, 1870
Muldoon, Patrick F	Oct 8, 1858	Murphy, Thos.	Nov 14, 1873
Mulholland, Jno	May 16, 1881	Murphy, Thos V	Aug 5, 1876
Mulholland, Wm	Mch 7, 1882	Murphy, Wm. H	Apr 14, 1882
Mulhern, Thos	Feb 18, 1873	Murray, Andrew	May 24, 1858
Mullane, Jas P	Oct 14, 1881	Murray, Dan'l.	Apr 17, 1875
Mullane, Patrick	Feb 4, 1859	Murray, Henry T	June 13, 1884
Mullen, Feltriskie H	Sept 16, 1861	Murray, Jas E	May 14, 1883
Muller, Geo H F	Mch 22, 1861	Murray, Jas J	Oct 24, 1881
Mulligan, Jas	Jan 19, 1870	Murray, John	Sept 3, 1859
Mulligan, Joseph	Apr 21, 1875	Murray, Mich'l	Mch 14, 1876
Mullin, R J	Feb 12, 1880	Murray, Thos	Apr 8, 1882
Mullin, Washington, Sergt	Oct 6, 1864	Murray, Timothy.	Mch 9, 1881
Mullin, Wm F	July 7, 1882	Murray, Wm, Supt	May 24, 1866
Mulry, Thos	Sept 7, 1870	Murtha, Bernard	Nov 15, 1876
Mulry, Thos W	Dec 11, 1873	Murtha, Pat'k	Dec 2, 1868
Mulrooney, Mich'l	July 1, 1872	Murtagh, Mich'l	June 7, 1873
Mulvey, Jas	July 24, 1872	Myers, Bernard.	Jan 4, 1873
Munday, Thos J, Jr	Mch 18, 1880	Myers, Thos R	Oct 14, 1881
Munier, Chas B	Aug 7, 1867		
Munn, Geo H.	Mch. 19, 1880		
Munson, Jno J	May 26, 1883	Nafew, Henry B	June 6, 1870
Murdock, Geo.	May 14, 1883	Nally, Edward F.	Apr 26, 1882
Muret, Edward, Sergt.	Feb 22, 1873	Nally, Jas F	June 1, 1877

N

OUR POLICE PROTECTORS

Name	Date of Appointment
Nann, Jas B.	Mch. 1, 1884
Nash, Wm H.	Oct 26, 1878
Naton, Peter	July 1, 1876
Naughton, Mich'l	May 5, 1877
Nealis, Dan'l	Dec 23, 1875
Nealis, Jas, No 1	Jan 10, 1872
Nealis, Jas, No 2	Sept 30, 1876
Near, Emmet	Dec 8, 1866
Neihoff, Henry	Aug 29, 1872
Neil, Rob't	Aug 19, 1872
Nelson, Augustus	Aug 14, 1871
Nelson, Wm	Sept 11, 1875
Nesbitt, Wm	June 7, 1882
Nevin, Wm A C	Nov 14, 1873
Nevins, Bernard	Mch 14, 1882
Newell, Wm J	May 19, 1875
Newman, August	Aug 19, 1881
Newman, Edw'd	Jan 20, 1869
Newman, Thos J	July 5, 1881
Newman, Adam	Feb. 10, 1882
Newton, Jno	Apr 19, 1876
Neylan, Jno	Apr 9, 1879
Nichols, Cornelius V	Apr. 8, 1884
Nicholson, Geo	Oct 27, 1874
Niggersmith, Geo F	Feb 10, 1873
Nixon, Rob't	Feb 10, 1872
Nixon, Wm. B.	Feb 13, 1858
Nolan, George	Sept. 25, 1866
Nolan, Jno J.	May 13, 1874
Nolan, Mich'l	Apr 21, 1875
Nolan, Pat'k	Apr. 13, 1882
Noll, Geo, Jr	Sept 16, 1882
Norris, Walter, Sergt	Sept 5, 1870
Northrup, Benj B	Feb. 14, 1873
Norton, Henry	May 29, 1884
Norton, Jas J	June 1, 1874
Norton, Patrick	Nov 2, 1861
Norton, Wm. J, No. 1	Apr. 29, 1880
Norton, Wm J, No 2	Apr 17, 1882
Norol, Geo, Jr	Sept. 16, 1882
Nugent, Andrew	Mch 30, 1882
Nugent, Frank J	Feb 10, 1879
Nugent, Harry	Dec 17, 1883
Nugent, Peter	Nov 4, 1878
Nugent, Thos F	Feb 12, 1884

O

Name	Date of Appointment
Oakley, Jno	June 27, 1872
Oates, Jas	Aug 12, 1870
Oates, Pat'k, Sergt	July 26, 1865
O'Brien, Bernard	Oct 9, 1878
O'Brien, Edward G	May 21, 1880
O'Brien, Jeremiah	Oct 14, 1881
O'Brien, John	Feb 8, 1884
O'Brien, Jno D	Sept. 1, 1875
O'Brien, Jno J	Oct. 22, 1883
O'Brien, Laurence T	Mch 7, 1885
O'Brien, Stephen, Jr	Nov 20, 1875
O'Brien, Thos	Nov 27, 1863
O'Brien, Thos	June 15, 1868
O'Brien, Thos J	Aug 7, 1876
O'Callahan, David	Nov 24, 1869
O'Connell, David	Jan 24, 1859
O'Connell, John	Jan. 29, 1861
O'Connell, Maurice J	Apr. 7, 1882
O'Connell, Mich'l	Sept. 16, 1870
O'Connell, Nicholas	Dec 31, 1859
O'Connell, Wm	Sept 10, 1872
O'Connor, Chas	July 22, 1870
O'Connor, Dan'l	Sept 20, 1873
O'Connor, David	May 9, 1867
O'Connor, Edward	Aug 31, 1870
O'Connor, Edward H	Feb 7, 1885
O'Connor, Jas	Sept 29, 1877
O'Connor, Jno	July 7, 1869
O'Connor, Joseph	Oct 8, 1862
O'Connor, Rich'd, Sergt	Oct 11, 1873
O'Connor, Thos	Jan 8, 1884
O'Donnell, Frank	Oct 14, 1881
O'Donnell, Jno.	Dec 19, 1883
O'Donnell, Peter	Aug 11, 1865
Ogden, Amos L	June 15, 1867
O'Hara, Denis	Apr. 26, 1880
O'Hara, Edward	May 8, 1880
Ohm, Herman P	Jan 26, 1876
O'Keefe, Jno. M	Feb 1, 1871
O'Keeffe, Dan'l	July 30, 1873
O'Leary, Denis	Oct 30, 1871
O'Leary, Jno.	May 24, 1884
O'Leary, Timothy	Apr 20, 1876
O'Loughlin, Thos P	Jan 28, 1885

Name	Date of Appointment	Name	Date of Appointment
Olson, Wm A	May 14, 1884	Parker, Jno J	Mch 8, 1876
Olvaney, Hugh	Dec 24, 1878	Parker, Seymour V	Apr 15, 1876
O'Malley, Mich'l	Feb 1, 1873	Patton, Alexander, Jr	Sept 6, 1883
O'Meara, Jas J	Jan 29, 1884	Pearsall, Jno W	May 22, 1882
O'Neil, Rob't	Apr. 5, 1871	Peary, Geo H	Mch 2, 1865
O'Neil, Thos	July 20, 1870	Pellett, Henry H	Feb 1, 1866
O'Neill, Andrew	Nov 2, 1882	Penney, Frank	Mch 16, 1881
O'Neill, Dan'l	Jan 11, 1884	Pepper, Jno	Oct 10, 1881
O'Neill, Francis	Sept 7, 1870	Perkins, Jas	Dec 22, 1875
O'Neill, Jno, No 1	Dec 11, 1861	Perkins, Jas J	Aug 27, 1884
O'Neill, Jno, No 2	June 24, 1869	Perrazzo, Antonio	July 23, 1880
O'Neill, Peter	Nov 30, 1870	Pertel, Edw'd	Mch 23, 1870
O'Neill, Phelix	Dec 17, 1883	Petrosino, Joseph	Oct 9, 1883
O'Neill, Wm F	Apr 18, 1883	Pettit, Bernard	July 12, 1870
Oppelt, Mich'l	June 21, 1883	Petty, Jeremiah, Capt	June 23, 1857
O'Raw, Rob't	June 17, 1884	Petty, Wm E	May 5, 1884
O'Reilly, Bernard	Mch 19, 1879	Pfachler, Emil L	Nov 20, 1875
O'Reilly, Mich'l	Feb 29, 1876	Pfeifer, Henry E	Mch 1, 1882
O'Reilly, Pat'k	Aug 11, 1870	Phair, Jas. H	Sept 11, 1883
O'Reilly, Thos	Oct 25, 1872	Phelan, Jno	Apr 13, 1868
O'Rielly, Hugh	Jan 20, 1861	Phelan, Mich'l	Oct 13, 1869
O'Rorke, Jno M	June 2, 1884	Phelan, Thos	Feb 10, 1875
O'Rourke, Hugh	Nov 20, 1875	Phelps, Chas., Surgeon	Sept 15, 1873
O'Rourke, Thos	July 22, 1874	Phillips, Abraham	Jan 14, 1874
Orpan, Henry M	May 14, 1874	Phillips, Chas H	Mch 20, 1875
Orr, Rob't	Nov 8, 1866	Phillips, Geo A	Mch 22, 1870
O'Ryan, Mich'l	Apr 1, 1861	Phillips, Henry W	Mch 1, 1866
Osborn, Geo P, Sergt	Sept 13, 1870	Phillips, Jno W	Sept. 10, 1872
Osborne, Sylv, Sergt	Apr 27, 1857	Phyfe, David	Apr 8, 1876
O Sullivan, Jno	Oct 21, 1878	Pickett, Pat'k H, Sergt	Oct 11, 1865
O'Sullivan, Pat'k	May 27, 1870	Pierce, Chas E	Feb 14, 1867
O'Sullivan, Wm M	Sept 22, 1873	Pierce, Edward	Apr. 16, 1872
O"Toole, Wm	Sept. 15, 1871	Piggott, C S	Apr 18, 1883
Owens, B J	May 6, 1878	Piggott, Jno	May 10, 1865
		Pike, Chas S	Nov 22, 1870

P

Name	Date of Appointment	Name	Date of Appointment
		Pinckney, Sam'l T	Apr 1, 1861
Panet, Anthony J	Sept 18, 1878	Pitcairn, Rob't B	Dec 24, 1862
Paret, Stephen, Jr	July 3, 1857	Place, Jas H	May 23, 1861
Parkerson, Chas A	Feb 23, 1878	Plant, Francis J	Feb 1, 1868
Palmer, Augustus B	Oct 24, 1877	Plath, John H	Aug 3, 1876
Palmer, Jno T	Sept. 9, 1873	Platte, Casper	Jan 11, 1884
Palmer, Wm H	Aug. 10, 1864	Pless, Chas H	Sept 22, 1873
Parker, Fred'k G	Apr 27, 1883	Plott, Francis	June 25, 1862
Parker, Geo E	Apr 15, 1885	Plunkett, Wm H	Apr 9, 1869
Parker, Jno	Jan 1, 1874	Polhamus, Dan'l, Sergt	May 20, 1861

OUR POLICE PROTECTORS.

Name	Date of Appointment
Pope, David	Jan. 14, 1874
Porcher, Wm., Sergt.	Feb 13, 1858
Porter, Wm B	Mch 1, 1882
Posthoff, Fred'k W	Jan 24, 1879
Potter, Rob't	Apr 18, 1883
Powell, Alonzo	June 14, 1865
Powers, Jno F	Jan 24, 1884
Powers, Pat'k	Oct. 6, 1870
Powers, Thos.	Oct 10, 1870
Pratt, Dan'l	June 24, 1865
Pratt, Oliver A.	Oct 15, 1872
Prendergast, Pat'k	Sept 27, 1870
Price, Alexander	Feb 12, 1873
Price, Arthur J.	Sept 4, 1883
Price, Sam'l	Mch 26, 1880
Price, Frank S	Mch. 10, 1885
Price, Geo	Apr 23, 1883
Price, Jas K	Dec 4, 1874
Protey, Fred'k	Oct 7, 1868
Protz, Fred'k	May 5, 1871
Purnhagen, Henry	June 27, 1882
Purroy, Francis M., Surg'n	Feb 16, 1875
Putnam, Nathan W	Dec 15, 1883
Pyne, Thos.	July 7, 1884

Q

Name	Date of Appointment
Quackenbush, Rob't H	Feb 16, 1858
Quick, Abraham	Feb 21, 1879
Quick, Cyrus, Jr.	May 2, 1884
Quigley, Dan'l	Jan 10, 1873
Quigley, Jas, No 1	Dec 11, 1865
Quigley, Jas., No 3	Feb. 26, 1873
Quigley, Thos	Oct 10, 1870
Quinlan, Dan'l J	Feb 14, 1876
Quinlan, Martin	Sept 14, 1861
Quinn, Henry	June 4, 1870
Quinn, Henry M.	July 3, 1857
Quinn, Jas, Doorman	May 24, 1884
Quinn, Jas, No. 1	Feb 10, 1872
Quinn, Jas, No 2	Dec 16, 1872
Quinn, Jas, No. 3	Jan. 1, 1874
Quinn, Jas P	Nov 11, 1869
Quinn, Law. R	Jan 2, 1868
Quinn, Peter	Nov 5, 1883
Quinn, Rob't	Mch 13, 1873
Quinn, Thos	June 2, 1884
Quintard, Chauncey T.	July 1, 1872
Quirk, Edw'd J	Mch 23, 1880
Quirk, Jas	Apr. 8, 1885

R

Name	Date of Appointment
Rabbeitt, Christopher	Jan 23, 1875
Rabbett, Patrick	June 1, 1876
Radford, Geo J	Feb 15, 1859
Raftery, Michael	Dec. 17, 1883
Raleigh, John	Oct. 25, 1873
Ramsey, Rob't	Jan 4, 1866
Randall, Chas B	Apr 17, 1875
Randall, Frank B, Sergt	Oct. 11, 1865
Raymond, John	Oct 23, 1872
Raynor, Laban	Apr 28, 1882
Raywood, Thos.	July 1, 1876
Reagan, James	Mar 22, 1871
Reagan, Michael	Mar. 14, 1874
Reap, Michael J.	Apr. 23, 1883
Rebholz, Peter	Apr 27, 1883
Rector, Albert	Jan 15, 1866
Redgate, Stephen F	Sept 22, 1875
Redmond, Garrett	June 27, 1884
Regan, David	Dec. 30, 1867
Regan, Edward M.	Apr 10, 1874
Regan, Patrick	Sept 8, 1882
Regan, Wm	Nov 8, 1878
Reid, Albert	Apr. 8, 1875
Reid, Cornelius	Jan 28, 1861
Reid, Cornelius	Feb 21, 1867
Reid, Geo	Aug 22, 1874
Reid, Maurice	Jan 18, 1878
Reid, Thomas H	Dec 2, 1874
Reid, Wm	Apr 23, 1857
Reid, Wm S, Sergt	Nov 18, 1866
Reigel, Geo.	Aug 6, 1880
Reilly, Bernard	Jan 13, 1875
Reilly, Edward	Oct 5, 1876
Reilly, James, No 2	Mch 17, 1873
Reilly, James	May 6, 1874
Reilly, James	Apr. 29, 1875
Reilly, John	Apr 29, 1876
Reilly, John H	Feb 17, 1882
Reilly, Peter	Sept 7, 1870

Name	Date of Appointment	Name	Date of Appointment
Reilly, Philip	Nov 27, 1863	Roberts, John, No 1	Oct. 16, 1878
Reilly, Rob't P	Apr 11, 1866	Roberts, John, No 2	Feb 1, 1882
Reilly, Terence	Feb 13, 1860	Roberts, Robert	Feb 26, 1872
Reilly, Thos, Sergt	Aug 24, 1866	Robinson, Alex J	July 9, 1870
Reilly, Wm	Mch 9, 1874	Robinson, Edwin K	Apr 23, 1857
Reilly, Wm	Dec. 2, 1878	Robinson, Jas	Feb 16, 1866
Reinhardt, John	Oct 26, 1883	Robinson, Robert	Apr 8, 1876
Reinhardt, Oscar	Sept 30, 1881	Robinson, Wm	June 15, 1867
Reinisch, Chas H, Sergt	Aug. 4, 1868	Roche, Michael	Apr. 14, 1884
Reiss, Edward F	Feb 4, 1884	Rockwell, Fred S	Mch 26, 1884
Reiss, Fredrick, Jr.	Apr 15, 1876	Roe, Cornelius W	Apr 21, 1884
Relyea, Henry	Oct 6, 1877	Roe, Thomas W.	Jan 8, 1874
Remley, Napoleon B	July 31, 1877	Rogers, Frank	Mch. 21, 1884
Renken, John	Feb 12, 1884	Rogers, Owen	Dec 29, 1870
Rennie, Geo W D	Dec 8, 1866	Rogers, Silas W	Sept. 12, 1873
Renner, Jerome L	May 2, 1885	Rohloff, Albert	Dec 27, 1875
Repper, John H	Nov 3, 1882	Rollins, Ira M	June 12, 1884
Revell, Wm A, Sergt	Jan 4, 1866	Ronk, John E	July 1, 1872
Rever, Jacob	Dec 4, 1865	Rooney, Mich'l	Oct 18, 1867
Reville, Philip E	Mch 8, 1871	Rooney, Mich'l M, Sergt	Nov 29, 1867
Reynolds, Delos, Sergt.	Feb 4, 1866	Rooney, Nicholas	Oct 1, 1867
Reynolds, Thos	Feb 3, 1868	Rork, Arthur, Sergt	Dec 12, 1862
Reynolds, Thomas	Nov 1, 1871	Ross, John	Apr 7, 1873
Reynolds, Wm	Apr. 6, 1881	Rothschild, Edward	Jan 29, 1884
Rhoades, Wm	May 7, 1874	Rott, Louis	Mch 1, 1880
Rhoades, Wm H	June 15, 1863	Roughan, Michael	Nov 30, 1870
Rice, Bernard J	Jan 13, 1875	Rourke, Wm	June 3, 1882
Richards, Geo W	Aug 7, 1876	Rourke, Wm J	June 14, 1882
Richardson, Peter	June 3, 1873	Rousby, Wm	June 4, 1883
Richert, Louis	Sept 13, 1873	Rowley, Andrew H	Dec. 20, 1873
Riley, James	Feb. 3, 1872	Ruland, Gardiner	Nov 23, 1877
Riley, James H	Apr 20, 1875	Ruland, John	Aug 7, 1872
Riley, Matthew C	Nov 25, 1868	Runge, Alexander F	Nov 4, 1873
Riley, Thomas	Nov 13, 1879	Rutledge, David	May 27, 1865
Ringler, Fredrick	Apr 17, 1875	Ryan, Chas J	May 1, 1882
Ripley, Wm F	Mar. 20, 1882	Ryan, David F	Oct 22, 1883
Roach, Jno T	May 11, 1868	Ryan, Denis F	July 26, 1869
Roach, Maurice	Aug 23, 1866	Ryan, Edmund	June 15, 1868
Roache, Wm, No 1	Apr. 25, 1875	Ryan, Francis P	Feb. 27, 1884
Roan, Patrick	July 29, 1874	Ryan, Geo. J	Apr 23, 1880
Robb, Frank W., Sergt	Aug 25, 1866	Ryan, James	Sept. 22, 1877
Robb, Matthew	Feb. 14, 1861	Ryan, James	Sept. 19, 1881
Robbins, Albert E	Apr 2, 1875	Ryan, James J	Apr 14, 1882
Robbins, John M, Capt	Jan 1, 1874	Ryan, John, Sergt	Apr. 28, 1869
Roberts, Henry, Sergt	Aug 24, 1865	Ryan, John	May 26, 1879

Name	Date of Appointment	Name	Date of Appointment
Ryan, John	. Mch 7, 1884	Schmidt, Philip . .	Jan 23, 1884
Ryan, John	June 27, 1884	Schmidt, Louis .	..Apr. 8, 1885
Ryan, Nicholas	.Dec. 6, 1883	Schmidt, Wm	. Jan 7, 1884
Ryan, Patrick	.Feb 18, 1873	Schmittberger, Max F Sergt	Jan 28,'74
Ryan, Patrick	. May 4, 1875	Schmitz, Henry	Feb. 17, 1875
Ryan, Patrick H	Apr 29, 1876	Schneider, August .	.Mch 25, 1882
Ryan, Peter, Sergt.	. Mch 2, 1861	Schneider, Reinhard..	Jan 12, 1866
Ryan, Thos M, Capt	.Nov 12, 1863	Schneider, Wm	..Apr 5, 1861
Ryan, Timothy	Mch 28, 1881	Schoell, Chas	Mch 21, 1879
Ryan, Wm A	Mch 6, 1884	Schorske, Henry	.July 3, 1872
Ryckman, Nicholas A	Dec 21, 1872	Schreiber, Louis	Aug 15, 1884
Ryder, Dermott	Mch 14, 1876	Schreiber, Wm	. May 1, 1882
		Schroff, Charles T	....Oct 27, 1874
S		Schroth, Ernest	.June 10, 1870
Sachs, John J .	.. Apr 8, 1885	Schryver, Albert B, Jr	.Apr. 8, 1885
Salmon, John	.Mch 24, 1875	Schryver, Henry B.	...Sept 6, 1883
Sanders, John, Capt	.May 24, 1866	Schultz, John	......Jan 29, 1884
Sands, Chas D	Mch 25, 1876	Schultz, Wm., Capt	...July 24, 1867
Sanford, Nathan B	Feb 13, 1858	Schulum, Lafay	... Jan 16, 1871
Sarvis, James	Sept 29, 1876	Schulze, Chas W	.Jan 22, 1881
Sasse, Ernest A	July 18, 1874	Schutt, John H	.Nov 18, 1868
Satterlee, Surgeon	Sept 15, 1873	Schwenk, Henry	Feb 10, 1875
Saul, Joseph A	Dec 16, 1876	Scofield, Francis E	Apr 26, 1876
Saul, Wm H	Sept 5, 1870	Scullion, Thomas	Aug 18, 1870
Savage, Michael	.Aug 17, 1870	Scully, Cornelius	.. Dec 10, 1873
Savercool, John O	Jan 24, 1872	Scully, James ..	Dec. 17, 1883
Sawyer, Joseph	Nov 20, 1875	Sealey, David, Sergt	Apr. 8, 1874
Sayre, Geo W	. Jan 16, 1873	Seaman, Samuel B .	June 14, 1867
Sbarbars, Augustus.	. July 1, 1872	Secore, Francis.	.Mch 14, 1876
Scallan, Patrick	Aug 18, 1869	Seery, John	Nov 2, 1866
Scalley, Thomas J	. Feb 4, 1885	Seibert, Jacob, Capt.	.Feb 4, 1861
Scanlon, Edward	.. Nov. 29, 1872	Selig, Louis . . .	Nov 22, 1872
Scanlon, Michael	.June 14, 1870	Sellick, Joseph H.	Apr. 14, 1868
Schaffer, Henry .	. .Apr 15, 1885	Setzkorn, Adolph..	. Sept 28, 1883
Schaffer, Wm E	Oct. 22, 1883	Seymour, Henry J .	.Aug 15, 1884
Schanwacker, Chas L	Apr 3, 1874	Shalvey, Edward	...Mch 7, 1861
Scheffmeyer, Timothy	May 10, 1871	Shannon, John J	... .Feb 6, 1884
Schenck, Geo. A .	. Jan 29, 1873	Sharkey, John G.	. .May 6, 1885
Schick, Carl K	June 12, 1866	Sharp, Edgar ...	. .Mch. 2, 1877
Schier, Chas A L	..May 1, 1875	Shaughnessy, Daniel...	May 9, 1883
Schirmer, Joseph.	. .Dec 5, 1879	Shaw, Edward B...	Apr 18, 1883
Schleissner, Louis.	.Mch 25, 1874	Shaw, Geo D...	. Jan 15, 1873
Schlottman, Hermann W	Apr 26,1884	Shaw, Geo. E..	. ...Oct 17, 1874
Schmidt, Adolph H	Aug. 31, 1872	Shea, James	... Mar. 6, 1876
Schmidt, Charles G	.Apr. 7, 1882	Shea, John ...	. Mch. 17, 1877

Name	Date of Appointment	Name	Date of Appointment
Shea, Patrick	Mch 5, 1861	Slawson, Edgar S	July 20, 1876
Shea, Timothy	May 4, 1883	Sloan, James A	Dec 2, 1878
Sheehan, Mich'l, Sergt	Mch 6, 1868	Slott, Cornelius J	Apr 8, 1885
Sheehan, Thomas	Sept 6, 1883	Slott, Henry C	Apr 23, 1863
Sheils, John	Feb 10, 1879	Sly, Norman C	May 8, 1882
Sheldon, Chas O, Sergt	May 17, 1873	Smith, Andrew	Aug 3, 1876
Sheldon, Samuel G	Sept 9, 1873	Smith, Anton	Nov 17, 1883
Shellard, Stephen	Sept 20, 1866	Smith, Bernard J	Apr 18, 1883
Shelly, Michael F	Feb 23, 1867	Smith, Chas W	Aug 15, 1872
Sheridan, Charles	Jan 29, 1884	Smith, Christopher	Nov 11, 1869
Sheridan, James	Jan 23, 1868	Smith, Edward F	May 6, 1885
Sheridan, John	Apr. 29, 1876	Smith, Edward J	Dec 7, 1881
Sheridan, John J	Mch 28, 1882	Smith, Elwood P	Oct 12, 1882
Sheridan, Robert	Jan 19, 1881	Smith, Elbert O, Capt.	Dec 31, 1872
Sherwood, Geo T	Apr 26, 1883	Smith, Emil F	Mch 28, 1884
Sherwood, Nathan B	Jan 2, 1868	Smith, Francis	Feb 19, 1862
Shevlin, Wm	July 30, 1884	Smith, Frederick	Oct 21, 1882
Shibles, Fred W	Nov 12, 1883	Smith, Geo	Dec. 16, 1881
Shiel, John J	May 19, 1876	Smith, Geo E	June 22, 1865
Shields, Alexander	Aug 15, 1884	Smith, Geo W	Jan 2, 1873
Shields, John	June 1, 1868	Smith, James	Apr 11, 1866
Shiels, John H	Jan 11, 1884	Smith, James	Apr 4, 1873
Shiels, Michael J	Nov 20, 1875	Smith, James	May 1, 1883
Shill, Henry H	Nov. 2, 1877	Smith, James	Apr 3, 1885
Shire, Nathaniel N	Aug 1, 1879	Smith, James T	Aug 5, 1881
Shortall, John	Aug 3, 1876	Smith, John	Sept. 19, 1877
Siebelt, Gustavus	Sept 10, 1875	Smith, John E	July 8, 1879
Siems, John	Aug 7, 1878	Smith, John H	Jan 22, 1881
Sierichs, John F	Jan 4, 1884	Smith, John W	Apr 18, 1883
Silbereis, Theodore W	Sept 21, 1870	Smith, Martin A	Apr 14, 1884
Simmons, Charles J	Jan 6, 1868	Smith, Matthew	Apr 26, 1877
Sims, Orin H	May 26, 1882	Smith, Michael	Mch 2, 1875
Sims, Wm	Apr 23, 1857	Smith, Patrick	Mch 4, 1863
Sims, Wm	Dec 11, 1874	Smith, Patrick	Dec 2, 1864
Sinclair, John	Nov 27, 1863	Smith, Philip E	Jan 20, 1868
Sinclair, Wm	Apr 30, 1860	Smith, Philip H	June 11, 1867
Sinder, John	Aug 5, 1881	Smith, Philip H	Sept 23, 1867
Sinnott, Edward F	Apr 8, 1882	Smith, Valentine	Nov 27, 1873
Sisson, Frank H	Mch. 8, 1884	Smith, Wm. A	Mch 30, 1872
Skelling, Matthew	Mch. 14, 1876	Smock, Geo. S	July 3, 1866
Skelly, Wm J	Feb. 8, 1884	Smyth, Charles	Oct 11, 1873
Skidmore, Geo. M	Nov. 18, 1868	Snyder, Geo	Jan. 27, 1873
Skuse, Thos W	Dec 8, 1869	Snyder, Leroy	Mch 21, 1884
Slattery, John	Mch 24, 1880	Somerindyke, Richard D	Feb 18, 1884
Slavin, Edward, Sergt.	Nov 28, 1866	Soule, Samuel	July 2, 1862

Name	Date of Appointment	Name	Date of Appointment
Spence, Henry	Oct 19, 1859	Sullivan, Andrew	Mch. 7, 1885
Spencer, John	Oct 19, 1881	Sullivan, Cornelius	Jan 26, 1858
Spencer, Wm	Feb. 21, 1884	Sullivan, Daniel	Mch 17, 1873
Spense, Geo.	Feb. 1, 1861	Sullivan, Daniel W	Jan 17, 1872
Spolasco, Wm	July 15, 1876	Sullivan, David	Dec 15, 1870
Sprague, Josiah H	Mch 29, 1872	Sullivan, Edward	Mch 6, 1873
Stack, Patrick J	July 20, 1870	Sullivan, Florence J	Apr 21, 1875
Stahl, John	Oct 18, 1867	Sullivan, James	June 6, 1874
Stainkamp, Henry	July 7, 1871	Sullivan, James J	Jan. 10, 1881
Stange, Henry	Apr. 14, 1884	Sullivan, John D	Jan 22, 1881
Stanton, Edward	Apr 23, 1883	Sullivan, John J	Oct 18, 1867
Stanton, Wm. B	Mch 7, 1868	Sullivan, John S	Jan. 27, 1873
Stapleton, Patrick	May 10, 1876	Sullivan, John S	Mch. 28, 1884
Stapleton, Thomas	Dec. 4, 1865	Sullivan, Joseph	Feb 6, 1873
Stebbins, Anderson	Jan. 29, 1881	Sullivan, Michael	May 17, 1871
Stebbins, Emil H	May 2, 1884	Sullivan, Michael J	Apr. 9, 1879
Steed, James W	Oct 11, 1881	Sullivan, Michael J	Jan 24, 1884
Steele, James	Apr 25, 1882	Sullivan, Jas M	Oct 12, 1883
Steers, Henry V, Inspec'r	Nov 19, 1857	Sullivan, Jeremiah	May 14, 1884
Steinert, Surgeon	Sept. 15, 1873	Sullivan, Patrick, No 1	Jan 25, 1868
Stephenson, Geo H	Apr 18, 1883	Sullivan, Patrick J	Sept 17, 1883
Stephenson, James M	Mch 6, 1884	Sullivan, Richard	Jan 8, 1875
Stephenson, John T, Sergt	May 5, 1874	Sullivan, Thomas J	Dec 11, 1876
Stephenson, Jonathan B	Feb 12, 1885	Sullivan, Thomas F	Oct 9, 1883
Stephenson, Thomas	Apr 9, 1880	Sullivan, Wm W, Sergt	Feb 14, 1871
Stepper, Martin	Jan 21, 1871	Summers, John A	Sept 13, 1880
Stetter, Emil	Mch 28, 1884	Suttie, Geo L, Sergt	June 15, 1865
Stevens, Charles W	Apr 14, 1884	Swain, Wm	Mch 3, 1875
Stevens, James G	Feb. 5, 1873	Sweeney, Bernard	May 11, 1875
Stevens, Leroy	Mch 10, 1869	Sweeney, Geo P	May 7, 1883
Stewart, Alexander	Feb 12, 1858	Sweeney, Jeremiah	Mch 20, 1875
Stewart, Joseph, Sergt	Nov 5, 1866	Sweeney, John J	May 7, 1883
Stewart, Joseph	June 29, 1882	Sweeney, Michael P	July 1, 1876
Stillings, James	Apr 8, 1885	Symes, John J. N	June 16, 1881
Stoddard, David	Aug 22, 1874		
Stoddard, Elliott M	Feb 26, 1873	**T**	
Strang, John G	Feb 18, 1885	Taggart, James	Oct 21, 1881
Strang, Wm H	Sept 29, 1882	Tallon, James	Jan. 1, 1874
Strauss, Daniel	Apr 10, 1885	Tancredi, Louis	June 5, 1882
Strauss, Wm	Feb 27, 1873	Tate, Chas H	May 12, 1882
Straussner, Antoine A	May 26, 1884	Tautphoens, Chris F	Feb 11, 1884
Strope, Ezra D	Feb 10, 1879	Taylor, David H	Jan. 2, 1873
Stuart, John	May 14, 1880	Taylor, Edward C	Jan 5, 1870
Stuart, Thomas	Mch 15, 1871	Taylor, Geo M	Mch 31, 1880
Stutt, Wm	Oct. 9, 1873	Taylor, John	Nov. 27, 1863

Name	Date of Appointment
Taylor, John	Dec. 28, 1866
Taylor, John	Oct 9, 1878
Taylor, John G	Jan 26, 1876
Taylor, John J, Sergt	May 25, 1864
Taylor, John W	Apr 17, 1884
Taylor, Wm H	Sept 20, 1873
Telley, David A	Apr 15, 1876
Ten Eyck, Henry, Sergt	July 11, 1857
Terpenning, Frank A V	June 5, 1884
Terris, Roderick M	Nov 5, 1883
Terry, Wm. D	Feb 12, 1872
Tessaro, Benjamin	June 17, 1874
Thatcher, James R, Sergt	Jan 15, 1862
Thayer, James M	July 18, 1861
Thayer, Joseph H	June 17, 1857
Thoden, John	Mch. 6, 1880
Thomas, Andrew J. Sergt	Aug 5, 1879
Thomas, Wm H	Nov 17, 1863
Thompson, Andrew J Sergt	June 11, '59
Thompson, Brainard M	Feb 16, 1870
Thompson, Frank D	Aug 19, 1881
Thompson, James	Sept 13, 1880
Thompson, John J, Sergt	Sept 11, 1860
Thompson, Theron T Sergt	Aug 20, '62
Thompson, Walter L	Apr 23, 1867
Thompson, Wm, Sergt	Apr 10, 1866
Thompson, Wm	Sept 22, 1873
Thompson, Wm J	Apr 8, 1885
Thorn, Theobald	Mch 4, 1885
Thorne, Augustus J	Apr 8, 1882
Thuman, Fredrick	Oct 11, 1869
Tieman, John C	Apr 23, 1857
Tieman, Charles	Aug 14, 1872
Tierney, John H	Aug 9, 1884
Tierney, Lancelot J	Mch 1, 1861
Tierney, Thomas	May 1, 1877
Tighe, Robert A	Mch. 27, 1878
Timoney, James	Feb 11, 1884
Tims, Oliver, Sergt.	Jan 26, 1866
Todd, Orville A	Dec 18, 1876
Toerner, August H	Aug 25, 1869
Tompkins, Herbert M	Mch. 18, 1881
Tompkins, Stephen B	May 2, 1884
Tompson, Bernard C	Oct 9, 1873
Tonry, Edward C	Mch 8, 1876
Tooker, Jacob	Mch 11, 1868
Toomey, James	Sept. 23, 1881
Torbush, Henry W	Feb 5, 1868
Torbush, John H	May 1, 1877
Totten, Samuel B, Jr	Apr. 29, 1880
Townsend, Geo A	July 6, 1870
Townsend, John	Apr 7, 1873
Townsend, John	July 3, 1884
Tracy, John	Jan 23, 1884
Trass, Henry G	Sept. 11, 1867
Traver, Joshua R.	July 3, 1857
Travers, Edward	Apr. 9, 1883
Treanor, Patrick	Mch 26, 1884
Tripp, Harrison	Jan 8, 1868
Troll, Anton	May 31, 1872
Trunk, James	Apr 14, 1884
Tuck, Matthew, Sergt	Nov 8, 1865
Tucker, James P	Feb 27, 1884
Tucker, Peter J	Feb 1, 1882
Tuite, James J	Oct 13, 1873
Tully, Bernard	Jan 4, 1866
Tully, Michael	Nov 27, 1872
Twine, Geo H	June 20, 1861
Tyler, Edward O	Nov 12, 1863
Tyrell, James	May 10, 1871
Tyrrell, John	May 14, 1883

U

Name	Date of Appointment
Uhl, Peter	Apr 3, 1874
Uhl, Morris	Jan. 23, 1861

V

Name	Date of Appointment
Vail, Oliver	Aug 1, 1872
Vail, Rob't J	Aug 9, 1873
Valiant, Jno	Dec 7, 1872
Vallean, Chas	June 4, 1883
Vallely, Jas T	Aug 12, 1876
Vallely, Pat'k W	Dec 19, 1873
Van Buskirk, Geo	Mch 22, 1865
Van Cott, Chas.	June 8, 1874
Van Cott, Henry W	Aug 5, 1879
Van Dusen, Chas H	May 30, 1873
Van Etten, Byron	Apr 14, 1884
Van Gerichton, Jacob	June 29, 1868
Van Horn, Jno	Mch 10, 1881

OUR POLICE PROTECTORS. 557

Name	Date of Appointment
Van Houten, Rich'd	Jan 24, 1884
Van Nordan, Jno	Nov. 1, 1871
Van Nosdall, Jno G	Jan. 25, 1871
Van Ordan, Henry C.	June 17, 1858
Van Ranst, Horan E.	Mch. 12, 1861
Van Ranst, Jas	Oct. 24, 1872
Van Wort, Jno L	Mch 26, 1875
Van Zant, Cornelius	May 9, 1867
Varian, Wm A, Surg	Feb 16, 1875
Vaughan, Pat'k	July 1, 1876
Veitch, Thos	June 13, 1866
Velten, Chas. E	Apr 8, 1885
Verity, Oakley K	Jan 7, 1881
Vermilye, Judson	Jan. 29, 1884
Volk, Rome	June 27, 1881
Vorhees, Edgar	Sept 29, 1883
Vosburg, Abram	Apr 8, 1876
Voss, Fredinand	Sept. 16, 1870
Vredenburg, W, Sergt	Nov. 17, 1865
Vyse, Jacob	May 1, 1861

W

Name	Date of Appointment
Wachner, Wm. H	Mch 20, 1882
Wade, Bernard	Aug 10, 1876
Wade, Chas J	May 5, 1882
Wade, John	Sept 25, 1872
Wade, Thos. F.	Apr 26, 1882
Wagner, Herman	Jan 3, 1879
Wagner, Wm	Oct 21, 1881
Wagner, Watson H	Apr 23, 1857
Walker, Chas. B.	Feb 6, 1884
Walker, Mich'l	Dec. 11, 1866
Walker, Rich'd	June 19, 1873
Walkinskaw, Jno S	May 11, 1881
Wall, Dan'l	Sept 23, 1881
Wall, George	Aug 26, 1868
Wall, Thos.	Mch 29, 1884
Wall, Thos F.	Aug 3, 1876
Wallerstein, Jacob	June 18, 1883
Wallace, Rob't J, Sergt.	Dec 4, 1865
Waller, Geo F	Aug 26, 1864
Walling, Edward S	Sept 30, 1881
Walling, Geo W, Supt.	May 27, 1857
Walling, Leonard	Nov 8, 1869
Walmsley, Stephen B	Jan 13, 1859

Name	Date of Appointment
Walsh, Edward	Mch 16, 1870
Walsh, Edward	June 11, 1875
Walsh, Edward S	Apr. 18, 1883
Walsh, Francis	Apr 10, 1874
Walsh, George	Dec 17, 1883
Walsh, Jno	Feb 4, 1868
Walsh, Matthew	Apr. 3, 1882
Walsh, Mich'l	May 13, 1867
Walsh, Pat'k, Sergt	Sept 7, 1866
Walsh, Pat'k J	June 4, 1883
Walsh, Rich'd	Feb 24, 1885
Walsh, Rob't	Dec 11, 1878
Walsh, Thos	Jan 29, 1884
Walsh, Wm	June 30, 1869
Walters, Jno W	Dec 16, 1881
Walton, Pat'k	July 26, 1870
Wandling, Chas	May 3, 1865
Ward, Mich'l	Aug 21, 1873
Warner, August's W Sergt	Oct 14, 1868
Warner, George	May 6, 1881
Warren, Lewis P	June 2, 1884
Warren, Wm	July 26, 1870
Warts, Alex B., Sergt	Nov 18, 1868
Washburn, Geo, Capt	July 10, 1865
Washburn, Jno W	Apr 14, 1882
Wassner, Jno	Aug 6, 1866
Waterman, Chas	Oct 4, 1869
Waterman, Jno. S.	Nov 27, 1867
Waterman, Sigism'd, Surg'n	Sep 15, '73
Waters, Benjamin	Aug 11, 1870
Waters, Mich'l	Feb 14, 1859
Waters, Thos	May 16, 1873
Waters, Thos. J	Mch 6, 1872
Watson, Jno	Apr 3, 1874
Waugh, Sam'l S	Oct 5, 1881
Wavle, Oscar	Oct 11, 1873
Wayland, Henry	Mch. 3, 1875
Webb, Rob't O., Capt	Aug 3, 1868
Webb, Wm H, Sergt	Apr 22, 1867
Webber, Edw'd	Feb. 17, 1869
Webber, Francis D	June 13, 1871
Webster, Dan'l	Mch 1, 1865
Webster, Joseph T	Dec 30, 1874
Weed, Frank G	Jan 24, 1872
Weeks, Jno H	Dec 30, 1868

Name	Date of Appointment	Name	Date of Appointment
Weeks, Philander S	May 4, 1875	Willard, Thos E, Sergt	Jan 25, 1866
Weigand, Jno	Sept 8, 1869	Williams, Alex T, Capt	Aug 3, 1866
Weinberg, Joseph	Mch 24, 1876	Williams, Charles F, Sergt	Feb. 13, 1858
Weinkauff, Otto	Feb 28, 1879	Williamson, Alvin H	Mch 1, 1866
Weisburger, Emanuel	Aug 3, 1863	Williamson, Chas	Oct 8, 1873
Weiss, Geo	Sept 9, 1874	Willow, Augustus	Aug 10, 1870
Weiss, Herman	Jan 26, 1876	Wilson, Chas H	Dec 15, 1883
Welch, Rich'd, Sergt	Jan 27, 1858	Wilson, Chas R, Sergt	Jan 9, 1866
Weldon, Pat'k	Nov 25, 1876	Wilson, Frank	Nov 17, 1869
Weller, Philip	Apr 23, 1884	Wilson, Harrison	Mch 4, 1862
Welling, Edw'd	Dec 2, 1869	Wilson, Jas A	Mch 21, 1872
Wells, Horace M	Nov 9, 1868	Wilson, Jas B, Sergt	July 16, 1857
Welsh, John	Apr 8, 1885	Wilson, Jas E, No 2	Jan. 8, 1884
Welsh, Pat'k	Apr 26, 1876	Wilson, Rich'd	Oct 16, 1877
Welsing, Jacob, Sergt	June 29, 1870	Wimmer, Jno J	Sept. 14, 1883
Werner, Francis	Dec 30, 1881	Winchell, Jno H.	Apr 17, 1882
West, Schuyler F	Apr 5, 1880	Wines, Wm	Mch 18, 1882
Westervelt, Joshua A, Sergt	Feb 21, '67	Winner, Geo H	Sept 1, 1870
Westervelt, Norman	Aug 8, 1879	Wiseburn, Geo D	Sept 11, 1867
Weston, Cornelius, Sergt	Apr 5, 1865	Wohlfarth, Jno	Aug 15, 1884
Westphal, Anthony	Apr 8, 1881	Wolters, Louis	Aug 2, 1867
Whalen, Edw'd	Feb 27, 1875	Wood, Alburtis	Oct 24, 1877
Whalen, Pat'k	Oct 20, 1873	Wood, Edward	Feb 13, 1873
Wheeler, Henry	Sept 10, 1880	Wood, Enos V	Nov 25, 1873
Wheeler, Owen	Mch 17, 1875	Wood, Geo W.	Sept 30, 1868
Whelan, Martin	July 23, 1883	Wood, Jno A	May 19, 1875
Whispell, Wm	May 6, 1885	Wood, Rivington W	Apr 17, 1883
White, Chas	Sept 23, 1881	Wood, Wm	Mch 19, 1880
White, Emanuel F	Apr 23, 1857	Woods, Henry, Sergt	Mch 20, 1865
White, Henry P	Apr 17, 1875	Woodruff, H K, Sergt	Nov 19, 1867
White, Jno	June 22, 1857	Woodruff, Seldan A	June 16, 1873
White, Jno H	Nov 9, 1868	Woodward, C W, Sgt	June 30, 1857
White, Mich'l	Oct 18, 1865	Woodward, E T, Sergt	Aug 20, 1862
White, Morris	Jan 3, 1872	Woodward, Frank	Mch 20, 1873
White, Patrick	Oct 7, 1876	Wooldridge, Joseph D.	Oct 22, 1883
White, Patrick	Oct 11, 1883	Woolfe, Geo F	Sept 1, 1865
White, Thos J	Sept 24, 1883	Woolsen, Benj C	Nov 15, 1867
Whittle, Wm H	Feb 12, 1885	Woran, Chas B	Jan 3, 1873
Whitney, Chas L	Mch 8, 1884	Worden, Alfred W	Jan 28, 1874
Wiehe, Jacob	Jan 28, 1879	Worden, Hector	Sept 18, 1882
Wilbur, Wm H	Nov 13, 1879	Worth, George	Oct 30, 1882
Wildey, Orlando.	May 6, 1869	Wrede, George	Apr 23, 1881
Wiley, Mich'l W	July 15, 1876	Wright, Gilbert L.	Feb 5, 1868
Wilkins, Augustus	June 1, 1873	Wright, J T, Sergt	Oct 14, 1858
Wilkinson, Jno	Sept 3, 1862	Wright, Wm	Mch 3, 1860

Y

Yeager, Mich'l C	Oct 1, 1867
Young, Lozelle,	Apr 18, 1883
Young, Robert, Sergt	Mch. 17, 1866
Yule, Peter, Capt	Feb 27, 1858

Z

Zirkel, Leopold F.	Aug 31, 1872
Zwickert, Anthony, Jr	July 14, 1877

LIST OF CAPTAINS

Captains	Precinct	Locations
Charles W Caffrey	1	Old Ship
Peter Conlin	2	High Bridge
Geo W Gastlin	3	Steamboat Squad, Police H'q'rs
Robert O Webb	4	9 and 11 Oak Street
Jos B Eakins	5	19 and 21 Leonard Street
John McCullagh	6	19 Elizabeth Street
Henry Hedden	7	245 and 247 Madison Street
Charles McDonnell	8	128 Prince Street
Theron S Copeland	9	94 Charles Street
Anthony J. Allaire	10	87 and 89 Eldridge Street
William Meakim	11	Sheriff and Houston Streets
Henry D Hooker	12	146 and 148 East 126th Street
Jeremiah Petty	13	178 Delancey Street
Michael J Murphy	14	205 Mulberry Street
John J Brogan	15	251 and 253 Mercer Street
John McElwain	16	230 West Twentieth Street
John H. McCullagh	17	79 and 81 First Avenue
Wm H Clinchy	18	325 East 22d Street
John J Mount	19	163 East 51st Street
William Schultz	19 (Sub)	Grand Central Depot
George Washburn	20	434 West 37th Street
Thos M Ryan	21	160 East 35th Street
Thos Killilea	22	345 West 47th Street
John Sanders	23	432 East 88th Street
Elbert O Smith	24	Steamer "Patrol"
Ira S Garland	25	34 East 29th Street
	26	City Hall
Wm C Berghold	27	35 New Church Street
John Gunner	28	220 East 59th Street
Alex S Williams	29	137 West 30th Street
Jacob Seibert	30	126th Street, near 8th Avenue
James M Leary	31	432 West 100th Street
Moses W Cortwright	32	Tenth Avenue and 152d Street
Theron R Bennett	33	Town Hall, Morrisania
John M Robbins	34	Tremont,
Peter Yule	35	Kingsbridge

	1874	1875	1876	1877	1878	1879	1880	1881	1882	1883	1884
No. of Members of Force including Surgeons on Dec. 31	2520	2488	2547	2541	2533	2527	2519	2639	2722	2782	2832
Time lost through Sickness, Disability etc., days	23026	29579	26730	29646	25505	26269	29262	34012	33026	36447	28265
Amount paid for Sick Time Lost	$45714	61589	49538	58593	40075	28497	35999	45004	43746	123082	67796
Total Days Time of Force	905633	916948	919411	921302	917002	916414	918178	936773	977692	987199	1038099
Per cent of Sick Time to Full Time	2.53	3.23	2.91	3.21	2.78	2.86	3.18	3.64	3.38	3.73	2.63
Deaths of Members of Force	31	49	35	25	31	29	38	42	37	40	49
Charges preferred against Members	3821	3097	2499	2578	2028	1708	1526	1557	1534	1794	1667
No. of Dismissals from Force	127	148	166	51	36	47	23	14	11	26	19
No. of Persons arrested, Males	66095	66368	68232	64955	55392	48145	52771	51057	50142	52077	51779
No. of Persons arrested, Females	26017	24995	24598	23284	21182	8555	18766	18574	17687	18047	18475
No. of Lodgings to Indigent Persons, Males	148505	145163	114591	43795	52797	59744	61653	57995	59241	51980	62276
No. of Lodgings to Indigent Persons, Females	71395	72387	72225	52575	60799	64624	62302	62778	72760	67176	61240
No. of Lost Children reported, Males	2633	3078	3316	3511	2937	2957	2944	2767	2841	2635	2610
No. of Lost Children reported, Females	1470	2035	2276	2445	2090	2036	2002	1937	1721	1650	1655
Witnesses remaining in detention, Dec. 31	32	18	15	12	20	14	13	29	18	5	17
Persons sick or injured aided by Police		2670	4990	4121	5551	5723	6714	6594	6350	6328	6859
Buildings found open and secured	4986	4103	3630	3004	2614	1943	1718	1580	1260	1146	974
Suicides reported			103	94	116	86	108	93	116	113	176
Fires reported	1059	1201	1061	1260	1512	1420	1524	1497	1535	1685	1867
Sudden deaths reported			302	493	614	607	562	938	915	854	743
Violations of Corporation Ordinances	17436	18351	107013	105616	99025	69172	84705	736657	303557	351387	299976
No. of Lots of Stolen Property recovered	1705	2060	2048	1699	1336	1225	1176	1476	1408	1433	1545
No. of Lots of Stolen Property delivered	784	1009	1951	703	673	611	577	731	561	516	640
Value of Stolen Property delivered	$117908	142144	116934	94575	91572	51575	39962	53840	59476	105657	75391
Value of Stolen Property delivered by Precincts	$111550	96548	99886	91515	215175	680731	772101	734252	872364	864677	831321
Treasurer paid on account of Department proper	$3330666	3267149	2763349	3112021	2862418	3261564	3292365	3280113	3323752	3345860	3441117
Treasurer paid Bureau of Elections		83078	9121	2751	9684	11089	11891	11904	13253	14797	13152
Pension Fund—Receipts	878447	60452	81307	60454	91915	114708	119670	117697	87489	96035	184419
Pension Fund—Disbursements	81800	71164	19298	71448	72348	60722	101968	168348	116492	220610	187649

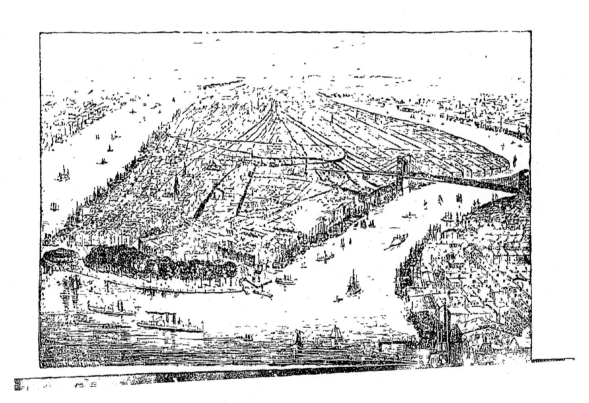

INDEX.

	PAGE		PAGE
Acquittals and discharges, 1838-1857	159	Battery Park described	110
Act of 1853 repealed	137	Battle of the Boyne	244
Acton Commr and the Draft riots	167	Beats, Divisions into	148
Acton, Commr. T C, Sketch of	151, 202	Bedford, Gunning S	505
Adams, Thos F, detective	437	Beebe, Commissioner	128
Age of applicants	291	Bell ringer, Duties of the	9
Aldermen, Assistant, abolished	126	Bell, Town, when rung	5
Aldermen or Schepens elected	8	Bellevue Almshouse	66
Aldermen release prisoners	143	Bellevue Hospital in 1850	110
Allaire Capt Anthony J	322	Bellevue Hospital opened	65
Almshouse burned in 1754	65	Belton, Thomas, the thief	310
Almshouse of Chambers St	52	Bennett, Captain, Theron R	170, 391
Almshouse on East River	65	Bennett, Officer, badly beaten	170
Amity Street battle with mob	173	Bergen, Commr John G	158
Andros, Governor	18	Bergen, Commr J G, Death of	227
Anecdotes of Jacob Hays	94	Bergen, Commr J G, Sketch of	204, 227
Apportionment of 1848	113	Berghold, Capt Wm C F	363
Apportionment of 1857	146	Biographical mention See Persons	
Appropriations, 1857-83	502	Blatchford, R M	96
Arrests for lottery and gambling	305	Bleecker St mob fight	194
Arrests for seven years, 1860-66	219	Board of Excise created	221
Arrests in N Y and Brooklyn, 1860-68	229	Board of Health regulations, 1880	289
Arrests in each year, 1847-58	144	Board of Police of 1858	139
Arrests made, 1845-50	116	Board of Police, 1877	277
Arrests made, 1845-53	131	Boat inspector appointed	218
Arrests made in 1858	146	Bogart, Capt James Z	190
Arrests made, 1860-69	234	Boiler inspection in 1869	233
Arrests of 1860	153	Boilers, Regulations of	302
Arrests of 1861	154	Bonds required of Constables	62
Arrests of 1862	156	Bosworth, Commissioner I S	157
Arrests of 1863	156	Bowen, James	139, 163
Arrests of 1865	218	Bowne, Robert, the Quaker	40
Arrests of 1867	234	Bowyer, Bob and Capt Leonard	127
Arrests, Table of, 1838-57	158, 159	Brady, Mayor, Changes under	108
Arrests without warrants	293	Brennan, Commr Matthew T	228, 239, 262
Arsenal in Elm St	222	Bridewell erected in 1775	43
Arsenal protected in 1857	144	British evacuate New York	48
Assembly report of 1875	266	British occupancy 1664	19
Assistant Justices in 1841	84	British police statistics	144
Astor Place riot, 1849	115	British seize the colony	17
Atlantic Dock elevator burned	194	Brockholts, A, made Mayor	24
Atlantic Guard or "Bowery Boys"	142	Brogan, Capt John J	353
Bailey, Isaac H.	139	Brooklyn arrests for 1860-68	229
Bailing of Prisoners	71	Brooks Bros' store threatened	191
Bands and buttons on uniforms	129	Brooks, Sergeant Nicholas	450
Bank robbery of 1830	94	Broome St headquarters	145
Bank sneak thieves	417	Brouwer, Jan J	2
Barr, I T, appointed Commr	240	Brown, Gen Harvey, resigns	198

INDEX

	PAGE
Buildings burned in Draft riots	196
Buildings found open, 1861-69	234
Bunco steerers and victims	417
Burdick, Sergeant, defends gun-factory	171
Burgher Guard established	6
Burgher Provost of the Rattle watch	12
Burgher-watch, Regulations of the	10, 13
Burglar's outfit	422
Bu.gomaster, Office of	8
Burnham, James, Suit of	129
Bush, Architect, Nath'l D	452
"Button Case," The	121
Bylvelt, Pieter	2
Byrnes, Inspector Thomas	404
Caffrey, Capt. Chas W	314
Cage for disorderly boys	43
Cambridgeport Bank robbery	310
Cameron, Capt John	171
Canby, Gen., Headquarters of	183
Capital crimes up to 1858	148
Captains, Names of, in 1846	107
Captains, Names of, in 1867	237
Captains of the Night-watch	56
Captains, Police, Table of	400
Captain's shield	424
Captains tried and dismissed	140
Captain's uniform of 1864	213
Carpenter, Daniel, appointed Inspector	151
Carpenter, Daniel, Deputy Supt	139
Carpenter, Inspector Daniel, Sketch of	210
Carpenter leads first attack	208
Carrying of concealed weapons	215
Cavalry patrolling the streets	187
Census of city, 1790-1830	73
Central Department created	226
Central Office	438
Certificate, Form of Surgeon's	280
Certificate of Appointment	480
Charity and Correction building	241
Charter amendment of 1851	117
Charter amendment in 1857	137
Charter, Montgomerie	34
Charter of 1849	114
Charter (Tweed) of 1870	239
Charter of April, 1830	73
Charter of Dutch West India Co	2
Chatham Street riots	80
Cherry, Capt Thos	326
Children lost, 1861-69	233
Chinatown glimpses	516
Chinese teacher	522
Citizenship of Applicants	291
City Bank robbery, 1830	94

	PAGE
City divided into seven wards	49
City divided into ten wards	64
City Hall of Wall Street	29
City Hall Park in 1808	60
City Hall, the First	5
City Hall, View of	62
City Hospital built	44
City watch disbanded	105
Civil watch appointed	29
Clarkson St, Negro hanged in	182
Clinchy, Capt Wm H	336
Colve, Governor, Anthony	18
Clubs the best weapons	209, 244
Cochrane, Dr, attacked	45
Colored Orphan Asylum burned	161, 172
Colored Reg't leaving for the war	217
Coman, John M	506
Commissioners address the force	197
Commissioners of 1858	139
Commissioners reduced to three	152
Commissioners term made eight years	231
Committees in 1877	277
Complaints against Officers	133
Concealed weapons, Carrying of	215
Conlin, Captain Peter	372
Conner, Roundsman	173
Conover, Daniel D	141
Consolidation act, 1880	287
Constables and marshals, Fees of	59
Constables made marshals	155
Constables watch of 1702	30
Constitutionality of Metropolitan act	140
Convictions, Table of, 1841-58	158
Convictions, Table of, 1840-67	236
Cooper, Richard, public whipper	34
Copeland, Capt Theron S	193, 197, 351
"Cops," origin of the term	127
Corporalships, the Four	23
Cortwright, Capt M W	388
Cosgrove, Frank, detective	432
Cosmopolitan character of the city	49
Councilmen, Board of, created	126
Court cases, Records of	15
Courts of Justices established	58, 504
Crannoll, Robt, supervisor	36
Crime greatly increases	73
Crime increasing in 1875	266
Crimes against the person, Table of	217
Crimes of violence during the war	215
Crimes punished, Table of 1841-58	158
Criminal arrests, 1845-50	116
Criminals captured by Hays	94
Criminals from tenements	526

INDEX.

	PAGE
Crowley, James, Supt	439
Crowley, Michael, detective	428
Cunningham, Capt Wm	42
Cusack, Thomas, the murderer	310
Cypress Hill monument	490
Davis, Minnie, the fire bug	357
Davis, Vernon M	506
Day posts on North River	443
Dead Rabbits of Five Points	142
Debtors in jail, in 1788	51
Debtor's prison in Eldridge St.	108
Decker, Engineer, Speech of	166
Delamater, William	456
Delaney, Sergt John	481
Deputy Supt abolished	151
Deputy Treasurer appointed	304
Detailment system a mistake	118
Detective Department	402
Detective Jacob Hays	73, 92
Detective officers	436
Detectives, Bureau of, 1880	287
Devlin, Charles	141
Devoursney, Serg defends Tribune bldg	174
Dickson, Capt John F	182
Dilks, Geo H, detective	433
Dilks, Geo W, appointed Inspector	151, 370
Dipple, Officer, Death of	190
Disbecker, Abram, appointed Commr	263
Discharges, Table of, 1840-67	236
Dismissals under new act	140
Districts and their captains, 1846	107
District divisions of 1845	106
Divisions defined in 1864	212
Dock masters	89
Doctor's riot of 1788	44
Dolan, Patrick, detective	426
Dongan, Governor	25
Dongan's charter granted	27
Donohue, John, murdered	336
Dorcy, Joseph M, detective	426
Doyle, Thos, detective	435
Draft riots and Capt Walling	123
Draft riots, July, 1863	156, 160
Drafting in Sixth district	162
Draper, Commissioner	139, 142
Dress See uniform	
Drill sergeant appointed	130
Drilling a squad of men	220
Ducking stool introduced	28
Dunn, John J, detective	429
Dutch West India Co	2
Duties discharged, Statistics of	147
Duties of policemen	465

	PAGE
Eakins, Capt Joseph B	347
East River day and night posts	444
East side crowding	525
Eighteenth Precinct described	335
Eighteenth ward created	109
Eighth Precinct described	348
Eldridge St Jail	108
Election Bureau continued	289
Election work provided for, 1866	223
Eleventh Precinct described	326
Elliot, Andrew, appointed	47
Ellison, Sergeant, attacks the mob	168
Ely, Smith, Jr, Letter of, 1877	274
English See British.	
Equipment of policemen	479
Era of organization and development	225
Erhardt, Capt Joel B	162
Erhardt, Joel B, Order of, 1877	275
Essex Market	273
Estimate of expenses in 1800	53
Examining a "Crook"	406
Excise law of 1866	221
Excise powers of the police	211
Execution, the first	32
Executions up to 1858	148, 159
Facsimile of Jury document	35
Fees for serving papers	58
Field, Officer, as detective	192
Fifteenth Precinct described	353
Fifth Precinct described	346
Finch, Sergeant, wounded	166
Fire Department established	34
Fire of 1776	45
Fire of Dec, 1835	80
Fire of 1845	107
Fire towers, Watchmen of	85
Fires, Captains' duties at	75
Fires put out by buckets	31
First Inspection district	307
First Precinct described	313
Fitzgerald, James	506
Five Points described	77, 86
Flag of Honor, Nov, 1872	255
Flour riot	81
Fogarty, Dennis J, detective	435
Folk, John S, appointed Inspector	151
Force and pay increased, 1784	50
Force as constituted, July, 1853	126
Force as constituted, in Jan, 1854	131
Force, 1862	155
Force as constituted in 1863	200
Force as constituted in 1864	217
Force as constituted in 1868	230

	PAGE		PAGE
Force as constituted in 1869	234, 238	Heidelburg, Chas, detective.	426
Force as constituted in 1870	240	Helme, Capt John C	186
Force as constituted Dec 31, 1873	257	Hendrick, Obe, made constable	20
Force divided into companies	212	Hickey Thos, detective	427
Forrest, Edwin, the actor	115	High Constable, Duties of the	11
Fourteenth Precinct described	330	Hoffman, Judge, Warrant of	141
Fourth District created	113	Hollgate captured by Jacob Hays	95
Fourth Inspection District	370	Honor roll	485
Fourth Precinct described	316	Honorable mention of officers	196
Francisco, Execution of	58	Hooker, Capt. Henry D	374
Franklin House, View of the	112	Hopcroft, George	449
French, Commr Stephen B	454	Hospital service	513
French, Stephen B, appointed Commr	286	House of Detention, 1863–68.	229
Frink, Wm E, detective	432	House of Detention created	214
Gallows, Early use of the	5	House of Detention, View of	331
Gambling houses in 1875	267	House of Refuge, First, 1806	70
Gambling of Chinamen	518	Hudson, Henry	1
Gambling placed in hands of police	211	Hull, Mrs., Murder of	369
Gaming houses and lotteries	296	Humane Society of 1817	66
Gardner, Hugh, appointed Commr	264	Hyer, Tom, and Yankee Sullivan	123
Garland, Capt Ira S	361	Impalement of a mob leader	188
Gastlin, Capt George W	441	Incorporation of the city	8
Gay, Edmund C	456	Increase of force in 1866	222
Geraid, James W	127	Indian wars under Kieft	6
Gibbons, J S, his house sacked	190	Injunction dissolved in 1857	142
Gilliscn, Jan	5	Inspection Districts See First, Second etc	
Good arrest, Example of	58	Inspector Byrnes' command	419
Gott, George P	500	Inspector of Boats appointed	218
Grades established	306	Inspectors of divisions named	212
Grant, Charles E	456	Instructions of 1848 summarized	114
Gun factory attacked by rioters	171	Insubordination and dismissal	140
Gunner, Capt John	382	Insurance Fund, Statement	501
Hackmen at steamboats	85	Irving, Washington, cited	110
Haley, Owen, detective	428	Italian and the bear	350
Hamer murder case	414	Jacobs, Peter, mayor	24
Harbor police patrol	448	Jack-plane containing notes	94
Harbor police, Rules for	178	Jackson's Foundry, Fight at	193
Harbor police uniform	213	Jail in Eldridge St	108
Harmensen, Reynert	2	Jail of 1758	42
Harper, James, mayor in 1844	101, 104	Jailer of the city appointed	12
Harrington, William	120	Jameson, William, inspector	127, 245, 250
Hart's store attacked	82	Japanese embassy of 1860	152
Hasbrouck, Stephen, surgeon-general	136	Jefferson Market, View of	157
Havemeyer, Wm F, mayor	101	Johnson, Mrs, the Swede	356
Haverstick murder case	359	Johnson confesses a murder	96
Hawley, Seth C	168	Jones, Maj gen Daniel	46
Hawley, Seth C, Sketch of.	204	Jones, William, negro, hanged	182
Hays carries Vanderbilt ashore	98	Jourdan, Capt., attacks rioters	176
Hays, Jacob, High constable	73, 92	Jourdan, John, appointed Supt	240
Hays, William H	93	Judgments speedily rendered	129
Headquarters in Mulberry St	154, 438	Justice under Gov Kieft	4
Heard, John, detective	437	Justices, Districts of, 1869	238
Hedden, Capt Henry	321	Justices increased to five	76

INDEX.

	PAGE
Justices, List of, in 1841	84
Justices of the Peace appointed	58
Juvenile Asylum, View of.	238
Kealy, Capt James	397
Kelso, James J , Supt	102, 245
Kelso, James J , appointed supt	240, 241
Kennedy, Police surgeon James	175, 232
Kennedy, John A , appointed	151
Kennedy, Supt , beaten by a mob	166
Kennedy, Supt , resigns	241
Kieft, William	4
Killilea, Capt Thos .	379
Kipp, Capt Wm H	460
Kloppermannen, or bellmen	41
Knickerbockers and the Battery	110
Knights of the Golden Circle	161
Koopman, or secretary, Office of	8
Kush, Chas , detective	436
Lamb, Alexander .	52
Lamps erected, in 1762	43
Land-grants, Conditional	7
Langan, Jas. J , detective	424
Lanthier, George detective	434
Lawrence, Mayor	81, 98
Leary, Capt. James M	386
Lee, Mayor	78
Legislature appoints commissioners	157
Leisler assumes control	28
Leonard, Jas , appointed inspector	151
Leonard, Inspector Jas , Sketch of	210
Leroy, Thomas H , burglar	310
Lewis, Commissioner W. B	157
License fees of saloons .	221
Lighting of city by night	20
Liquor law of 1866	221
Liquor selling regulated .	6
Liquor-selling regulated in 1864	211
Livingstone, Edward, mayor	63
Lock and key of Old Bridewell	47
Locust wood the best for clubs	209
Long Island, Battle of .	45
Lord, Capt B G , of Sanitary squad	237
Lowndes, Olin M	80
McClave, John, Commr	495, 500
McClusky, George W , detective	435
McCullagh, Capt John	318
McCullagh, Capt John H .	333
McDermott, Inspector John	270
McDonnell, Capt Chas	349
McElwain, Capt John .	357
McFarland, Daniel, the murderer	325
McLaughlin, William W , detective	431
McLean, Charles F , appointed Commr.	286

	PAGE
McLean, John, of Phila	95
McMurray, Commissioner W..	157
McNaught, Robert, detective..	430
McQuire, James	424
Macready, James, the actor	115
Madison Sq Garden accident	369
Manhattan Island, Indian name of	2
Manierre, Commr Benj F	228, 230
Manifesto of Gov Stuyvesant .	6
Mangin Francis, Jr , detec	17
Manual of department issued	27
Marine court	17
Mars, the negro, executed	32
Marshals in 1833.	89
Marshal's office set on fire	164
Martine, Randol, Jr	505
Mason, Commr J W	458
Mason, Joel W appointed Commr	286
Matsell, George W	100
Matsell, Geo W appointed Commr	263
Matsell, Geo W appointed sup	256
Matsell, Geo W , Shield of	91
Matsell's letter to Capt Walling	124
Matsell's report of April, 1849	115
Matthews, David, Mayor	47
Matthews, Commr James	452
Matthews, James, appointed comm.	152
Mealim, Capt Wm	326
Medical assistance, Coming of	301
Memorial to legis', in 1811	60
Message of Committee of 1843	87
Metropolitan act amended	211
Metropolitan Board re organized	231
Metropolitan district defined	212
Metropolitan force in 1858	140
Metropolitan headquarters, Broome St	145
Metropolitan Police act, 1857	101
Metropolitan police district	137, 202
Metropolitan Police, Table of	463
Metropolitan shield	227
Middle Dutch Church	86
Military aid	203
Military attack	1
Military Hall	128
Military in Washington square	1
Military-watch of 1746	40
Miller, Chas P	369
Minuet, Peter, Gov	2
Mob attacks city hospital	45
Mobs handled by Jacob Hays .	63
Montgomerie charter	34
Morris, Mayor	89
Morrison, James E appointed Commr	286

INDEX.

	PAGE
Mount, Capt John J.	176, 376
Mulberry St headquarters	154
Mulry, Thos W., detective	423
Municipal Police Act, 1844	101, 104
Murphy, Capt Michael J	332
Murray arrested in Phila.	95
Murray, Col. James B, in London	98
Murray, Thomas, detective	437
Murray, Superintendent Wm	308
Nathan murder, 1870	369
Negro hanged and burned by mob	175
Negro Plot of 1740.	38
New Amsterdam in 1664	18
New Amsterdam incorporated.	8
New Amsterdam, Naming of.	2
New Court-house, View of	260
New York says "Stop!"	273
Niblo's Garden burned, 1872	332
Nichols, Sidney P appointed Commr	264
Nichols, Sidney P, Death of	499
Nichols, Sidney P, removed	286
Nicoll, Delancey	506
Night posts on North River	444
Night-watch abolished	102
Night-watch, Captains of the	56
Night watch of 1741	40
Nineteenth Precinct described	375
Nineteenth Sub-precinct described	378
Nineteenth ward created	115
Ninth Precinct described	351
Noah, Major, assists Jacob Hays	95
North River day and night posts.	443
North River piers and ferries.	444
Nugent, Colonel, provost-marshal	162
Nursing wounded policemen	196
O'Brien, Col H J beaten to death	184
O'Brien, John J	460
O'Connor, Charles, detective.	432
O Connor, Richard, detective	428
O'Connell Guard riots	80
Offences against property in 1867	235
Offences against the person in 1867	235
Officers and salaries in 1844	103
Officers beaten by rioters in 1863	170
Officers killed in 1864	215
Old Brewery, Five Points.	86
Old Sugar-house as a prison	86
Opium pipe.	521
Opium smoking—The pipe.	517
Opdyke, Mayor, his house attacked	186
Opdyke, Mayor, Proclamation of	199
Orange County bank	95
Orange riots in 1850	124

	PAGE
Orange riots of 1871	244
Orphan Asylum, Colored, burned	161, 172
Orphan Asylum, View of	278
Panic of 1857	137
Park, City Hall, in 1808	60
Parkinson, the locksmith	94
Parris, Edward L	506
Patrol district in each ward.	108
Patrol ordered for day and night	118
Patrolman's shield	150
Patrolmen of telegraphic system	304
Pawnbrokers, Supervision of	295
Pay-rolls See Salaries.	
Peace of 1674	18, 22
Peck, Ellen E, the confidence-woman	420
Penney, William N	506
Pension Fund, Law of	302
Pension Fund, Sketch of	489
Perit, Commissioner Pelatiah	142
PERSONS MENTIONED	
Acton, Thos C, supt.	151, 202
Adams, Thos F, detective	437
Allaire, Capt Anthony J	322
Andros, Governor	18
Bailey, Isaac H	139
Barr, Commr. Thos J	240
Bedford, Gunning S	505
Beebe, Commissioner	128
Belton, Thomas, the thief	310
Bennett, Capt. Theron R	170, 391
Bergen, Commr. John G 158, 168, 204, 227	
Berghold, Capt Wm C F	363
Blatchford, R M	96
Bogart, Capt James Z	190
Bosworth, Commissioner J S	157
Bowen, James	139, 151
Bowne, Robert	40
Bowyer, Bob.	127
Brady, Mayor	108
Brennan, Commr Matthew T 228, 239, 262	
Brockhotts, A	24
Brogan, Capt. John J	353
Brooks, Sergeant Nicholas	450
Brouwer, Jan J	2
Brown, Gen Harvey	198
Burnham, James.	129
Bush, Architect Nath'l D	452
Bylvelt, Peter..	2
Byrnes, Inspector Thomas.	404
Caffrey, Capt Chas W.	314
Cameron, Capt. John	171
Canby, General..	183
Carpenter, Daniel 139, 151, 172, 208, 210	

INDEX.

Persons Mentioned—*Continued*

Name	Page
Cherry, Capt. Thos	326
Clinchy, Capt. Wm H	336
Colve, Governor Anthony	18
Cochrane, Dr	45
Coman, John M	506
Conlin, Capt Peter	372
Conner, Roundsman	173
Conover, Daniel D	141
Cooper, Richard	34
Copeland, Capt Theron S	193, 197, 351
Cortright, Capt M W	388
Cosgrove, Frank, detective	432
Crannoll, Robt	36
Crowley, James, Supt	439
Crowley, Michael, detective	428
Cunningham, Capt. Wm	42
Cusack, Thomas the murderer	310
Davis, Minnie, the fire-bug	357
Davis, Vernon M	506
Decker, Engineer	166
Delamater, William	456
Delaney, Sergt John	481
Devlin, Charles	141
Devoursney, Sergeant	174, 183
Dickson, Capt. John F	182
Dilks, Geo. H, detective	433
Dilks, Inspector Geo. W	151, 187, 370
Dipple, Officer	190
Disbecker, Abram	263
Dolan, Patrick, detective	426
Dongan, Governor	25
Dorsey, Joseph M, detective	426
Doyle, Thos, detective	435
Draper, Commissioner	139, 142
Dunn, John J, detective	429
Eakins, Capt Joseph B	347
Elliot, Andrew	47
Ellison, Sergeant	168
Erhardt, Capt Joel B	162
Field, Officer	192
Finch, Sergeant	166
Fitzgerald, James	506
Fogarty, Dennis J, detective	435
Folk, Inspector John S	151, 174
Forrest, Edwin	115
French, Stephen B	286, 454
Frink, Wm E, detective	432
Gardner, Hugh H	264
Garland, Capt. Ira S	361
Gastlin, Captain George W	441
Gay, Edmund C	456
Gerard, James W	127
Gibbons, J. S	190
Gillisen, Jan	5
Gott, George P	500
Grant, Charles E	456
Gunner, Capt. John	382
Haley, Owen, detective	428
Harmensen, Reynert	2
Harper, James	101, 104
Harrington, William	120
Hart, Ely	81
Hasbrouck, Surgeon-general	136
Havemeyer, Wm F	101
Hawley, Seth C	168, 204
Hays, Jacob	73, 92
Hays, William H	93
Heard, John, detective	437
Hedden, Capt. Henry	321
Heidelberg, Chas, detective	426
Helme, Capt. John C	186
Hendrick, Obe	20
Hickey, Thos, detective	427
Hollgate, the cracksman	95
Hooker, Capt Henry D	374
Hopcroft, George	449
Hudson, Henry	1
Hyer, Tom, the pugilist	123
Jameson, Inspector W	127, 245, 250
Johnson, Mrs., the Swede	356
Johnson, the murderer	96
Jones, Maj.-gen Daniel	46
Jourdan, Supt John	176, 193, 240
Kealy, Capt James	397
Kelso, James J	102, 240
Kennedy, Police surgeon James	175, 232
Kennedy, Supt John A	151, 166, 241
Kieft, William	4
Killilea, Capt Thos	379
Kipp, Capt. Wm H	460
Kush, Chas, detective	436
Lamb, Alexander	52
Langan, Jas J, detective	424
Lanthier, George, detective	434
Lawrence, Mayor	81, 98
Leary, Capt James M	386
Lee, Mayor	77
Leonard, Inspector James	151, 178, 210
Leroy, Thomas H., burglar	310
Lewis, Commr W B	157
Livingstone, Edward	63
Lord, Capt B G	237
Lowndes, Olin M	80
McClave, Commr John	495, 500
McCluskey, George W, detective	435

Persons Mentioned—*Continued*

Name	Page
McCullagh, Capt. John	318
McCullagh, Capt. John H	333
McDermott, Inspector John	271
McDonnell, Capt Chas.	349
McElwain, Capt John	357
McFarland, Daniel, the murderer	325
McLaughlin, W W , detective	431
MacLean, Charles F	286
McLean, John	95
McMurray, Commissioner Wm	157
McNaught, R., detective	430
McQuire, James	424
Macready, James, the actor	115
Mangin, F., Jun , detective	422
Manierre, Commr Benj F	228, 239
Mars, the negro slave	32
Martine, Randolph B	505
Mason, Commr. Joel W	286, 458
Matsell, George W	100, 263
Matthews, David	47
Matthews, Commr James	286, 452
Meakim, Capt Wm	360
Minuet, Peter	2
Morris, Mayor	89
Morrison, James E	286
Mount, Capt John J	176, 376
Mulry, Thos W , detective	423
Murphy, Capt. Michael J	332
Murphy, Thos , detective	437
Murray, Superintendent Wm	308
Murray, Col James B	98
Murray, the bank-robber	95
Nichols, Sidney P	264, 286, 499
Nicoll, De Lancey	506
Noah, Major M M	95
O'Brien, Colonel H J.	184
O'Brien, John J	460
O'Connor, Charles, detective	432
O'Connor, Richard, detective	428
Opdyke, George, mayor	199
Parkinson, the locksmith	91
Parris, Edward L	506
Peck, Ellen E , the confidence-woman	420
Penney, William N	506
Perit, Commissioner	142
Petty, Captain Jeremiah	186, 189
Pigot, Maj -gen R T	46
Pilsbury, Amos	139
Porter, Fitz John, Commr	458
Porter, Captain G. T.	164
Pos, Symen D	2
Post, Capt Ludowyck	12, 14
Purdy, Ambrose H	506
Quinn, Sergeant	193
Radford, Geo, detective	424
Redmond, the hotel-keeper	95
Reed, Jack, the cracksman	95
Reed, John, the detective	121
Reilly, Philip, detective	425
Richard, Paul	38
Robbins, Capt. John M	394
Robertson, Maj gen James	45
Rogers, Silas W , detective	435
Rutland, John, detective	430
Ryan, Capt Thos M.	337
Sanders, Capt John	380
Schultz, Capt William	378
Seymour, Governor	197
Shadbolt, Detective	121
Siebert, Capt Jacob	385
Slauson, Edgar S	434
Sleven, Edward, detective	431
Slowey, Detective	195
Smith, Capt Elbert C	396
Smith, Commr Henry	231, 239, 263, 445
Smith, the bank-robber	94
Smith, Wm. F	286
Speight, Inspector F C	164, 230, 271
Steenwyck, Cornelis	17
Steers, Inspector Henry V	339
Stephens, the cracksman	95
Stevens, Colonel	80
Stillman, Thomas B	139
Stillwell, Alderman	96
Stranahan, James S T	139
Stuyvesant, Peter	6
Tallmadge, Fred. A	139
Taylor, Commissioner	102
Thorne, Inspector T. W	128, 174, 342
Tillou, Alderman	87
Tooker, Jacob, detective	423
Twiller, Wouter van	3
Tynan, Capt. Edward	398
Ulshoffer, Michael	139
Vallely, Jas. F , detective	436
Van Buren, Officer	169
Van Clapperclip, Bobus	4
Vanderbilt, Commodore	98
Van Schellyne, Dirk	11
Varley, Mary	309
Von Gerichten, Jacob	436
Voorhis, John R	236, 286
Wade, John, the detective	122, 423
Wade, Sergeant	168
Waldron, Resolverd	20

INDEX.

	PAGE
Persons Mentioned—*Continued*	
Walling, Supt Geo. W.	100, 120, 188
Washburn, Capt. Geo	360
Webb, Capt. Robt O.	317
Westervelt, Jacob A	118
Williams, Capt Alex S.	364
Williams, the negro	182
Williams, the pickpocket	354
Williams, Alvan H, detective	430
Wilson, the cart-thief	357
Wissinck, Jacob E	2
Wolfe, Sergeant	169
Wood, Albertus, detective	435
Wood, Fernando	101, 141
Wood, Robt L	460
Wood, General J E	199
Yankee Sullivan	223
Young, Mrs Johanna	33
Young, Chief John	168, 197
Yule, Capt Peter	395
Petty, Captain Jeremiah	186, 189, 328
Physicians appointed	112
Physicians, Summoning of	300
Pigot, Maj-gen R. T	46
Pillory introduced	28
Pilsbury, Amos, gen supt	139
Pistols, Carrying concealed	215
Places of confinement	53
Police Act, Metropolitan	101
Police Act, Municipal	101
Police committee, Report of	67
Police courts of 1845	103
Police districts laid out	55
Police, Military use of the	47
Police office in City Hall	54
Police orders in 1673	21
Police stations in 1844	91
Police surgeons, List of	180
Police system, First trace of	3
Police system, Marked advance of	52
Policemen killed in riots	199
Political influence stopped	130
Poor-house, First	34, 39
Poor relief law of 1699	65
Population figures, 1790–1830	73
Porter, Commr Fitz John	458
Porter, Captain G T	164
Posts, night, on North River	444
PORTRAITS	
Allaire, Capt Anthony J	323
Bennett, Capt Theron R.	391
Berghold, Capt. Wm C. F	363
Brennan, Matthew T	262

	PAGE
Brogan, Capt. John J	354
Brooks, Sergeant Nicholas	450
Caffrey, Capt. Chas W	316
Clinchy, Capt Wm. H	336
Conlin, Capt Peter	373
Copeland, Capt. T. S	352
Crowley, James	439
Garland, Capt Ira S	362
Gastlin, Capt Geo W	441
Gott, George P.	500
Gunner, Capt John	383
Hedden, Capt Henry	321
Hooker, Capt. Henry D	375
Jameson, Inspector W	250
Kealy, Capt James	397
Kelso, James J	247
Leary, Capt Jas M	386
McClave Commr John	495
McCullagh, Capt. John	319
McCullagh, Capt. John H	334
McDonnell, Capt Chas	349
McElwain, Capt John	358
Martine, Randolph B	505
Matthews, Commi. James	453
Mealim, Capt Wm	360
Mount, Capt. John J	377
Mullen, Sergt. Washington	462
Petty, Capt. Jeremiah	328
Porter, Commr Fitz John	459
Robbins, Capt. John M	394
Ryan, Capt. Thos. M	338
Sanders, Capt. John	381
Schultz, Capt Wm	378
Siebert, Capt. Jacob	385
Smith, Capt Elbert O	396
Speight Inspector	230
Steers, Inspector Henry V	340
Voorhis, Commr. John R	458
Washburn, Capt. Geo	360
Webb, Capt. Robt. O	317
Yule, Capt Peter	395
Post Office, View of	299
Potter building burned	318
Pound for cattle opened	7
Precincts created	138
Precincts, List of, in 1863	200
Precincts *See* First, Second, etc	
Printed rules first issued	114
Prison-houses of the Revolution	86
Prisoners, sufferings of, 1787	50
Prisoners to do the chores	112
Processes, Serving of	294
Proclamation of Maj.-gen Jones	46

570 INDEX

Entry	Page
Proclamation of Maj.-gen. Pigot.	46
Proclamation of Maj.-gen. Robertson	46
Proclamation of Mayor Opdyke	199
Promotions, how made	292
Property, lost or stolen, 1869	233
Property of arrested persons	297
Proportions to population	144
Provost marshal's office, Sixth Ave	165
Punishments of criminals	30, 33
Purdy, Ambrose H	506
Quakers exempted from duty	40
Qualifications of appointment	126
Qualifications of candidates	149
Quarantine hospital guard	140
Quarantine riots and Capt. Waling	121
Questions asked of applicants as patrolmen	280
Quinn, Sergeant	193
Radford, George, detective	424
Rattle watch appointed	8
Rattle-watch begin drawing salaries	12
Reapportionment of 1846	109
Receivers of stolen goods	154
Recorder, Office of, created	27
Records of early court cases	16
Redmond falsely arrested	95
Reed, John, the detective	121
Reed, the cracksman, taken	95
Regattas, Rules for	298
Registration and election expenses	224
Reilly, Philip, detective	425
Reorganization in 1843	86
Reorganization report of 1832	76
Report of Chief Matsell, April, 1849	115
Resolutions on death of Commr. Bergen	228
Resolutions to Supt. Kelso	241
Revenue from liquor licenses	222
Revolutionary War begins	45
Richard, Paul, mayor	38
Richmond county, Action against	239
Richmond county provided for	220
Riot, Doctors, in 1788	44
Riot in Third Ave., 1863	165
Riots of 1834	80
Riots of 1837	81
Riots of July, 1863	156, 160
Riots of 1871 (Orange)	244
Riot of Astor place, 1849	115
Riot of the Dead Rabbits	142
Rioters addressed by Engineer Decker	166
Rioters convicted	199
Rioters marching down Second Ave	169
Rioters, Number of, killed	196
Rioters surprised during escape	191
River thieves surprised	525
Robbins, Capt. John M	394
Robertson, Maj.-gen. James	45
Rogers, Silas W, detective	435
Rogues' gallery and curiosities	408
Roll of Honor	485
Rosewood not good for clubs	209
Rotunda erected in 1818	79
Roundsmen and postmen	69
Ruland, John, detective	430
Rules and regulations of 1859	148
Rules of Chief Matsell in 1848	114
Rules of Feb., 1684	26
Rules of the Rattle watch	8
Rules of the Watch, 1673	22, 23
Rural districts appoint police	219
Ryan, Capt. Thos M	337
Sabbath regulations	5
St. Francis Xavier panic, 1877	369
St. Luke's Hospital, View of	285
Salaries in 1844	103
Salaries of 1859	151
Salaries of 1864	215
Salaries in April, 1866	218
Salaries in 1867	236
Salaries in 1880	296
Salaries, Jan., 1885	305
Salaries increased in 1853	130
Salaries paid in 1845	106, 109
Salaries under Metropolitan act	136
Salary ordinance of 1851	117
Saloons, Number of, in 1866	221
Sanders, Capt. John	380
Sanitary Company, The	461
Sanitary condition of stations	133, 146
Scales for weighing opium	520
Schepens or early Aldermen	8
Schout, Duties of the	9
Schout Fiscal, Duties of the	2
Schultz, Capt. William	378
Seal of the city, First	27
Second Dist. Police Court	509
Second Inspection District	342
Second Precinct described	372
Sentence for drawing a knife	6
Sergeant's shield	425
Seventeenth Precinct described	333
Seventh Avenue arsenal occupied	163
Seventh Precinct described	320
Seventh Regiment at City Hall	142
Sextons called dog-whippers	10
Seymour, Gov., Appointments of	157
Seymour, Gov., praises the police	197

INDEX.

Sh? lbolt and Capt Walling	121
Shield of captain and sergeant	424
Shield of Chief Matsell	101
Shield of Metropolitan police	227
Shield of the Star-police	106
Siebert, Capt Jacob	385
Sixteenth Precinct described	356
Sixth Precinct described	318
Sixty-ninth Regt. armory	211
Sketch of Commr T. C Acton	202
Sketch of Commr John G. Bergen	204, 227
Sketch of Inspector Carpenter	210
Sketch of Seth C. Hawley	204
Sketch of Inspector Leonard	210
Sketch of the draft-riots of 1863	160
Shuson, Edgar S	434
Slave Insurrection of 1740	38
Sleven, Edward, detective	431
Slowey, Detective, beaten by a mob	195
Smith, Capt Elbert O	396
Smith, Commr Henry, appointed	231
Smith, Henry, Death of	263
Smith, Henry, In Memoriam	445
Smith, Wm F, removed and re-appointed commr.	286
Smith, the bank-robber	94
Speight, Francis C, Inspector	271
Speight, Captain, handles a mob	164
Stadt Huys erected	5
Standing committee of police	64
Star police of 1845	106
State prison, Old	55
Station-houses condemned	155
Station-houses, Condition of	133
Stations, List of	249
Stations, List of, in 1844	91, 103
Stations, List of, in 1848	113
Stations, List of, in 1851	117
Stations, List of, in 1857	143
Stations, List of, in 1858	147
Stations, List of, in 1863	200
Stations, List of, in 1866	223
Stations, List of, in 1867	237
Station-houses, Table of, 1884	401
Station lodging room	468
Stations repaired and renovated	225
Statistics for 1867	226
Statistics of arrests, etc, 1838-57	158
Statistics of arrests in each year, 1847-58	144
Statistics of British police	144
Steam boiler inspection	302
Steenwyck, Cornelis	17
Steers, Inspector Henry V.	339
Stephens captured by Jacob Hays	95
Stevens, Col, quells a riot	80
Stillman, Thomas B	139
Stillwell, Alderman	96
Stolen goods, Custody of	298
Stone cutters' riots	80
Stranahan, James S T	139
Street-cleaning Committee, 1873	262
Street cleaning Dept created	276
Street-cleaning in 1860	154
Strike of the Burgher-watch	10
Stuyvesant, Peter	6
Superintendent of the watch	83
Superintendent's uniform of 1864	213
Surgeon's certificate, Form of	281
Surgeons, Rept of Board of	232
Surgical bureau	133
Surgical districts defined	179
Surman murder case	325
Table of convictions, 1838-57	158, 159
Table of lost children, 1860-72	253
Table of Metropolitan Police	463
Tables of offences in 1867	235
Table of Police Captains	400
Table of Station houses, Augt, 1884	401
Tallmadge, Fred A., Gen Supt	139
Taylor, Commissioner, Death of	102
Telegraph office at headquarters	439
Telegraph operators commended	195
Tenth Precinct described	322
Theft punished by whipping	15
Thief with red hair caught	96
Third Avenue riot of 1863	165
Third Inspection District	370
Third Precinct described	440
Thirteenth Precinct described	327
Thirtieth Precinct described	384
Thirty fifth Precinct described	395
Thirty-first Precinct described	386
Thirty-fourth Precinct described	394
Thirty-second Precinct described	387
Thirty-third Precinct described	390
Thorne, Inspector T. W	128
Thorne, Inspector, Death of	342
Tillou, Alderman	87
Time lost by sickness	216, 232
Tombs, The, built	90
Tooker, Jacob, detective	423
Town crier appears	12
Treasurer of Police created	290
Tribune building attacked	123, 173
Tweed charter of 1870	239
Twelfth Precinct described	373

	PAGE
Twentieth Precinct described	359
Twentieth ward created	115
Twenty-eighth Precinct described	381
Twenty-fifth Precinct described	361
Twenty first Precinct described	337
Twenty-ninth Precinct described	364
Twenty second Precinct described	379
Twenty seventh Precinct described	363
Twenty-sixth Precinct described	339
Twenty-third Precinct described	380
Twiller, Wouter van	3
Two departments at work	141
Tynan, Capt. Edward	398
Ulshoffer, Michael	139
Uniform, Change in	133
Uniform for summer, in 1864	214
Uniform of Harbor police, 1864	213
Uniforming of peace officers	68
Uniforms defined for 1864	212
Uniforms finally adopted	128
Uniforms introduced	28
Uniforms of 1844	103
Uniforms of 1853	126
Uniforms in 1877	278
Uniforms opposed by a mob	127
Vagrant children	76
Valleli, Jas F, detective	436
Van Buren, Officer, wounded	169
Van Clapperclip, Bobus	4
Vanderbilt, Com, and his steamboat	98
Vandergriff, the forger, re-captured	98
Van Orden, Sergeant, occupies arsenal	163
Van Schellywne, Dirk	11
Van Wart appointed captain	54
Varley, Mary	309
Von Gerichten, Jacob	436
Voorhis, John R appointed Commr	263, 286
Wade, Sergeant, attacks the mob	168
Wade, John, the detective	122, 423
Waldron, Resolverd, made constable	20
Wall St City Hall built	29
Wall St, the north limit	9
Walling, Supt Geo W	100, 120
Walling appointed Captain	120
Ward distribution of 1845	105

	PAGE
Washburn, Capt Geo	360
Watch committee investigation	72
Watch district of 1843	90
Watch districts bounded	69
Watch house of 1731	36
Watch-house of 1789	51
Watch, Military, of 1746	40
Watch, Night, of 1741	40
Watch, Superintendent of the	83
Watch system declines	49
Watchman's hat	83
Watchman's rattle introduced	8
Watchman's song	42
Watchmen become dissatisfied	74
Watchmen calling the hour	41
Watchmen increased in 1835	81
Watchmen, Pay of, in 1844	91
Watchmen, Petition for, 1811	60
Watchmen's Mutual Benefit Assoc	84
Watch posts in 1844	91
Way of the Transgressor	503
Webb, Capt. Robt. O	317
Weehawken ferry-house burned	189
Westervelt, Jacob A, mayor	118
Whipping-post, Early use of	3
Whipping-post in use	33
Williams, Capt Alex S	364
Williams, the negro, assaulted	182
Williams, the pickpocket	354
Williamson, Alvan H, detective	430
Wilson, the cart thief	357
Wire factory attacked	186
Wissinck, Jacob E	2
Witnesses, Detention of, House for	214
Wolfe, Sergeant, attacks the mob	169
Women as rioters	190
Wood, Albertus, detective	435
Wood, Fernando, mayor	101, 141
Wood, Mayor, opposes the new act	140
Wood, Robt L	460
Wool, Gen John E, Rept of	199
Yankee Sullivan and Tom Hyer	123
Young, Chief John	168
Young, Mrs Johanna, flogged	33
Yule, Capt. Peter	395

OUR ADVERTISING PATRONS

Acker, Edgar & Co., Grocers	7
Acker, Merrill & Condit, Grocers	7
Albany and Troy Steamers, Day Line	37
Albemarle Hotel	100
American Express Co	45
American News Company	33, 63
Ammidown & Smith, Dry Goods	62
Amsinck, G., & Co., Liquors	49
Appleton, D., & Co., Publishers	34
Arnold, Constable & Co., Dry Goods	15
Atlas Line of Mail Steamers	53
Baeder, Adamson & Co., Glue	42
Bank of the Manhattan Company	92
Baremore & Co., Hops	9
Barnes, A S., & Co., Publishers	54
Beadleston & Woerz, Ales, etc	20
Beck, Fr., & Co., Wall Papers	65
Behning, Pianos	88
Belvedere House	56
Bernheimer, Jacob S., & Bro., Cotton Goods	53
Best & Co., Lilliputian Bazaar	16
Bliss, Fabyan & Co., Dry Goods	65
Bodega, The	68
Brewster & Co., Carriages	31
Brower House	10
Brown Brothers & Co., Bankers	11
Brown, Martin B, Printer	88
Brown, R C., & Co., Cigars	113
Brunswick-Balke-Collender Co., Billiard Tables	28
Brush Electric Illuminating Co.	112
Buchi, L., & Son, Timber	12
Buckingham Hotel	100
Burke, E. & J, Ginger Ale, etc	9
Cary & Moen, Steel Wire, etc	92
Central Cross town R R Co	39
Central National Bank	65
Central Trust Company of New York	28
Chemical National Bank	55
Christy, Wolcott & Co., Paper Hangings, etc.	112
Clansen, H., & Son, Brewing Co.	47
Clausen & Price Brewing Co	102
Clyde, Wm P., & Co., Steamers	26
Collamore, Davis & Co., Crockery, etc	70
Collamore, Gilman & Co., Bric-a-Brac	42
Colwell Lead Co	85
Conover, J S, & Co., Grates, etc	42
Cornell, J B & J M, Iron	2
Cunard Line Steamers	8
De Castro, D., & Co., Ship and Com. Merchants	64
Decker & Rapp, Yellow Pine	98
Devoe, F. W., & Co., Paints, etc	5
Doelger's, Jos., Sons, Lager Beer	46
Doelger's, Peter, Brewery	109
De La Vergne Refrig Mach Co	66
Dick & Meyer, Sugar Refiners	96
Durkee, E. R., & Co., Indigo and Spice Importers	53
Duryea's Glen Cove M'f'g Co., Starch	14
Du Vivier & Co., Champagnes	13
Eagle Brewery	60
Ebling, Ph & Wm, Ale, etc	55
Ehret, Geo., Lager Beer	50
Eighth Avenue Railroad Co	107
Everett's Hotel and Grand Dining Rooms	46
Fall River Line, Steamers	86
Farmer, Little & Co., Type Founders	80
Fifth Avenue Hotel	1
Fleitmann & Co., Dry Goods	32
Frederick's Family Portrait Gallery	75
Gallatin National Bank	65
Gall & Lembke, Opticians	15
Gillott, Joseph, Steel Pens	62
Gilsey House	56
Gold's Heater Manufacturing Co	77
Gorham Manufacturing Co., Silversmiths	18
Great West Disp. and So. Sh Line	52
Great Western Steamship Line	5
Harlem Gas Light Company	69
Harriman, A. Person & Co., Dry Goods	19
Havemeyer Sugar Refining Co	80
Havemeyers and Elder, Sugar Refiners	94
Hawkins, C P., Sons, Ales, etc.	13
Herring & Co., Safes	54
Herrman, H, Sternbach & Co., Dry Goods	26
Hermann Lager Beer Brewery	58
Higgins, A E, Soap	76
Hoboken and New York Ferries	89
Hodgman & Co., Rubber	68
Hoe, R, & Co., Printing Presses	51
Home Insurance Co of N Y.	55
Horsman, E I, Bicycles, etc.	13
Horton's Ice Cream	70
Hotel St. Marc	56
Hupfel, A, Sons, Brewery	93
Hupfel, J., Chr. G, Brewer	32
Harper & Brothers, Publishers	35
Ingersoll Rock Drill Co	76

OUR ADVERTISING PATRONS

Inman Steamship Co., Limited	95
International News Company	77
John Stephenson Company, Limited, Street Cars, etc.	22
Joy, Langdon & Co., Agents	16
Judge, The.	108
Kinney Tobacco Company	44
Knabe, Wm., & Co., Pianofortes	4
Kuhn, Loeb & Co., Bankers	59
Langham, The.	66
Lanman & Kemp, Merchandise	72
Lincoln Safe Deposit Company	54
Lion Brewery	84
Ludwig, E., Imp and Com Merchant	73
Luttgen, Fred'k Wm., Champagne	75
Lyman, T. C., & Co., Ales and Porter	71
Manhasset House	66
Manhattan Brewery	61
Manhattan Gas Light Company	25
Matthiessen, F. O., & Wiechers, Sugar Refiners	21
McAlpin, D. H., & Co., Tobacco	60
Meert, C. F., Champagnes	10
Mercantile National Bank	52
Meyer-Sniffen Co., Limited, Plumbers.	75
Miller & Huber, Flour	16
Morgan's Louisiana and Texas R. R. and Steamship Co	27
Mumm, G. H., & Co., "Cordon Rouge"	108
Municipal Gas Light Company.	99
Munro's Publishing House	70
Murray Hill Hotel	3
Mutual Life Insurance Company of New York	40
Naphey, Geo C., & Sons, Lard	108
National Express Company	81
New Haven Steamers and Connecticut River R. R. Line.	30
Newman, A. G., Hardware	42
New York Belting and Packing Co	101
New York Brass Furniture Co	15
New York Cab Company.	52
New York Clipper	73
New York Gas Light Company	110
New York Mutual Insurance Co	62
Ninth National Bank	55
Norwich Line, Steamers	6
Old Dominion Steamship Co	103
Oppermann & Muller, Brewers	33
Pacific Mail Steamship Co	83
Park & Tilford, Grocers	74
Peck & Snyder, Sporting Goods	78
Pennsylvania Railroad	82
Peters & Calhoun Co., Saddlery, etc	68
Philadelphia and Reading R. R.	23
Piper Heidsieck	91
Providence and Stonington S. S. Co	97
Puck	104
Pyle, James, Pearline	67
Quintard Iron Works.	91
Red Star Line, Steamers	79
Reed & Barton, Electro plated Ware	77
Rendrock Powder Company	43
Richardson, Geo C., Smith & Co., Selling Agents	30
Roebling's, John A., Son's Co., Wire Rope	104
Royal Insurance Company	29
Ruppert's, J., Brewery	24
Schastey, Geo A., & Co., Woodwork	67
Schieffelin, W. H., & Co., Drugs	18
Scribner's, Charles, Sons, Publishers	67
Simmons, John, Wrought Iron Pipe, etc	9
Simpson, Spence & Young, Steamship Agents	52
Singer Manuf'g Co., Sewing Machines	48
Sixth Avenue Railroad Co	105
Slawson, J. B., Fare Boxes.	106
Sloane, W. & J., Carpeting..	15
Sohmer & Co., Pianofortes	36
Southern Freight and Passenger Lines	87
Starr, Theodore B., Diamonds, etc.	53
St. Denis Hotel and Taylor's Restaurant	63
Steinway Pianofortes.	57
Stevenson, D., Brewer.	17
Straiton & Storm, Cigars..	54
Strong, W. L., & Co., Selling Agents	43
Teft, Weller & Co., Dry Goods	36
Union Trust Co. of New York	78
United States Express Company	38
United States Hotel	10
United States Illuminating Co	76
United States Mut. Acc. Association	29
Vaseline.	66
Vermilye & Co., Bankers and Brokers	10
Victoria Hotel	56
Walker & Bresnan, Printers' Furnishers	63
Wallace, William H., & Co., Iron and Steel	19
Wall's, Wm., Sons, Cordage, etc.	16
Ward, James E., & Co., Steamers	90
Warren, Fuller & Lange, Wall Papers	8
Weber Pianos.	111
Wheeler & Wilson Sewing Machines	3
Williams & Guion, European Steamers	41
Willimantic Spool Cotton	62
Windsor Hotel	100
W. J. Wilcox Co., The, Lard Refiners	79

Fifth Ave. Hotel,

MADISON SQUARE, NEW YORK.

The Largest, ✣ Best Appointed,

—AND—

Most Liberally Managed Hotel in the City,

—WITH THE—

Most Central and Delightful Location.

HITCHCOCK, DARLING & CO.

WHEELER & WILSON'S

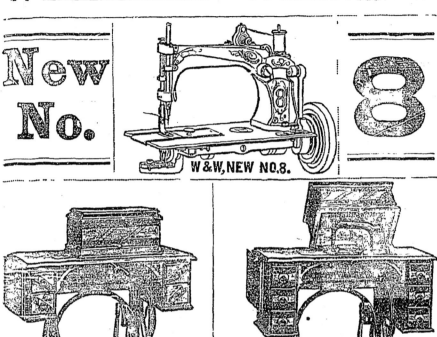

New No. 8

UNRIVALLED FOR FAMILY USE,

AND THE No. 6 AND NEW No. 10

FOR ALL GRADES OF MANUFACTURING IN

CLOTH OR LEATHER.

ADDRESS:

Wheeler & Wilson Manufacturing Co.

Factory and Chief Office, Bridgeport, Conn.,

New York City Office, 44 East 14th St. (Union Square).

NEW YORK:
112 Fifth Avenue.

BALTIMORE:
Cor. Eutaw & West Sts.

BALTIMORE:
204 & 206 W. Baltimore S

MANUFACTURERS OF

GRAND, UPRIGHT AND SQUARE
PIANO-FORTES.

FOR NEARLY FIFTY YEARS BEFORE THE PUBLIC THESE INSTRUMENTS HAVE, BY THEIR EXCELLENCE ATTAINED AN UNPURCHASED PRE-EMINENCE, WHICH ESTABLISHES THEM THE UNEQUALLED IN

TONE, TOUCH,

WORKMANSHIP & DURABILITY.

ESTABLISHED 1852.   ESTABLISHED 1862.

F. W. DEVOE & CO.

MANUFACTURERS OF

Pure Colors, ✢ Fine Varnishes,

Brushes,

ARTISTS' MATERIALS,

Mathematical Instruments.

OFFICES:

Fulton Street, cor. William, New York.

THE MURRAY HILL HOTEL,
NEW YORK CITY.
Located on Park Avenue, extending from 40th to 41st Sts.

The Highest and Healthiest Ground on the Island of Manhattan

The Hotel is now open to the public on both the American and European plans. The location is exceptionally desirable as a permanent residence for families, or for tourists, travelers or business visitors to the metropolis. It is but one minute's walk from the Grand Central Depot, where trains depart for, and arrive from, all the chief cities and towns of the United States; accessible to all elevated and surface lines of railways and stages, the theatres, retail stores, churches and places of interest.

{ Nat L Hunting }   HUNTING & HAMMOND, Proprietors.
{ D. S Hammond. }

GREAT WESTERN STEAMSHIP LINE.
Bristol and New York.
SAILING WEEKLY FROM AVONMOUTH DOCK, BRISTOL.

The Cheapest and Most Direct Route from the West of England, and South Wales, Cornwall, Somerset and Devon, Monmouth and Gloucester.

REDUCTION IN RATES:

STEERAGE.   { Bristol, Cardiff, Newport or Swansea to New York $20 00
PREPAID   { Any Railroad Station in England or Wales, Belfast, Dublin,
CERTIFICATES {   Waterford or Queenstown, to New York.. . . . . . $22 00
             Children between 1 and 12 years, Half Price   Infants, $3 00

SALOON.—PREPAID.—Bristol to New York..... .... $60 00

NORWICH LINE

BETWEEN
NEW YORK, BOSTON, WORCESTER,
And all Points EAST.

NORWICH LINE *Steamers leave Daily, except Sundays,*
— At 5 p.m. —
From PIER 40, NORTH RIVER, Foot WATTS STREET,
Adjoining Desbrosses Street Ferry of Pennsylvania Railroad.

THE NEW IRON STEAMER
CITY OF WORCESTER,
Without any exception the
FASTEST, MOST ELEGANTLY FINISHED and FURNISHED STEAMBOAT on LONG ISLAND SOUND,

Will Leave NEW YORK on TUESDAYS, THURSDAYS, SATURDAYS,

And the well-known Steamer
CITY OF BOSTON,
From NEW YORK, MONDAYS, WEDNESDAYS and FRIDAYS

Connecting with Express Trains that

— Leave —		— Leave —	
NEW LONDON	4 05 a m	NEW LONDON	5 00 a.m.
— Arrive —		— Arrive —	
BOSTON	7 50 a m	PALMER	7 50 a.m.
WORCESTER	6.55 "	AMHERST	9 00 "
NASHUA	9 25 "	BRATTLEBORO	10 26 "
PORTLAND	1 25 p m	BELLOWS FALLS	11 25 "
MANCHESTER	9 48 a.m	WHITE RIVER JUNC.	1 30 p.m.
CONCORD	10 55 "	NORTHFIELD	3 44 "
PLYMOUTH	12 37 p m	BURLINGTON	5 20 "
BETHLEHEM	5 12 "	ST. ALBANS	6.00 "
FABYAN'S	5 35 "	MONTREAL	8 30 "

NO TRANSFERS BY THIS LINE.

LIMITED TICKETS AT REDUCED RATES.

STATEROOMS ENGAGED IN ADVANCE.

G. W. BRADY, Agent, Pier 40, N. R., New York.

ACKER, MERRALL & CONDIT,

57th Street and Sixth Avenue,

Broadway and 42d Street,

130 and 132 Chambers Street,

NEW YORK.

---

39 Rue de Chateaudun,

PARIS.

ACKER, EDGAR & CO.

YONKERS.

CUNARD LINE.

ESTABLISHED 1840.

Between LIVERPOOL, BOSTON and NEW YORK.

From NEW YORK, every Saturday and alternate Wednesdays after April 29.
From BOSTON, every Saturday.

RATES OF PASSAGE: $60, $80 AND $100.

Return Tickets on Favorable Terms

Between BORDEAUX, NEW YORK and BOSTON.

Steamers leave BORDEAUX, every Thursday, connecting at Liverpool for New York and Boston.

Special facilities for through freight at low rates. For freight and passage apply

In Bordeaux to	VERNON H BROWN & CO.,
S. R. OGSTON, Agent,	4 BOWLING GREEN,
5 Cours de Pavé des Chartrons	NEW YORK

WALL PAPERS.
WARREN, FULLER & LANGE,
Manufacturers,

Invite an inspection of their extensive collection of NEW DESIGNS in AMERICAN, ENGLISH, GERMAN, VELVET, FRENCH, HIGH RELIEF, REAL JAPANESE LEATHER PAPERS; Also Designs and Colorings by THE ASSOCIATED ARTISTS, at the Retail Department,

129 EAST 42d STREET,
Near Grand Central Depot

We manufacture all our own Colors and Guarantee our Papers to be Free from Arsenic

JOHN SIMMONS,

Manufacturer and Dealer in

Wrought Iron Pipe and Fittings for Steam, Water, Gas and Oil.

BRASS AND IRON VALVES AND COCKS.

FITTER'S AND ENGINEER'S TOOLS AND SUPPLIES OF EVERY DESCRIPTION.

Nos. 106, 108 and 110 Centre St., New York.

PIPE AND CAST IRON RADIATORS

BAREMORE & CO.,

No. 43 BROADWAY, NEW YORK.

Agency in London, Eng.,

J. H. PETRIE, 2 East India Ave., E C.

Direct Shipments from Country. — **Choice Hops a Specialty.**

BEWARE OF IMITATIONS

"CANTRELL & COCHRANE" DUBLIN & BELFAST.

E. & J. BURKE, General Agents, NEW YORK.

MOËT & CHANDON CHAMPAGNES.

GOLD SEAL. WHITE SEAL. GREEN SEAL.

Total Sales, Three Million Bottles a Year! The Richest Champagnes in the World!

Messrs Chandon & Co possess 1,017 acres of the most renowned vineyards in France. They keep constantly on hand in cellars ten to twelve million bottles of wine, none of which is sold until it has been in bottle four years, during which time it undergoes the manipulation necessary to clear and prepare it for consumption.

☞ The yearly shipments of Moët & Chandon Champagnes are larger by several hundred thousand bottles than those of any other establishment in the trade.

☞ A steady favorite with club connoisseurs.

FOR SALE BY ALL GROCERS.

C. F. MEERT, Sole Agent for the United States, 49 Broad St., New York.

United States Hotel,
Cor. Fulton, Water, and Pearl Sts.,
J. B. Truman, Proprietor.

EUROPEAN PLAN

Rooms for one person from 50c. to $1.50.
Rooms for two persons, $1.50 to $3.00.

The New York Elevated Railroad has a depot in the hotel, cars run every three minutes. Time to Grand Central Depot, twenty minutes. Five minutes walk to New Haven, Hartford, and Bridgeport steamboats.

VERMILYE & CO.,
16 and 18 Nassau St., New York City,

BANKERS AND BROKERS,
Dealers in Investment Securities.

Buy and Sell on Commission, and carry on appropriate margins all Securities listed at the New York Stock Exchange.

INTEREST ALLOWED ON DEPOSITS SUBJECT TO DRAFTS AT SIGHT.

BROWER HOUSE,
Cor. 28th St. & Broadway, New York.

EUROPEAN PLAN.

This Hotel is situated in the centre of the up-town business part of New York, and near all the principal Hotels and Theatres.

Good Rooms at $1.00 per day and upwards, for Gentlemen only.

A first-class Restaurant is attached for Ladies and Gentlemen. Entrance on 28th Street,

THOS. D. WINCHESTER, Proprietor.

Brown Brothers & Co.,

59 WALL STREET, NEW YORK,

209 CHESTNUT ST., PHILADELPHIA,   No. 66 STATE ST., BOSTON,

— AND —

ALEXANDER BROWN & SONS, cor. Baltimore and Calvert Sts., Baltimore,

Buy and Sell Bills of Exchange

— ON —

Great Britain and Ireland, France, Germany, Belgium, Holland, Switzerland, Norway, Denmark, Sweden, and Australia.

ISSUE COMMERCIAL AND TRAVELERS' CREDITS

In Sterling,

Available in any part of the world, and in Francs, for use in Martinique and Guadaloupe.

Make Telegraphic Transfers of Money

Between this Country and Europe.

MAKE COLLECTIONS OF DRAFTS DRAWN ABROAD

On all points in the United States and Canada,

And of DRAFTS DRAWN IN THE UNITED STATES on all Foreign Countries.

BROWN, SHIPLEY & CO.,　　　**BROWN, SHIPLEY & CO.,**
26 Chapel Street, Liverpool　　Founder's Court, Lothbury, London

L. BUCKI & SON,

Successors to

DREW & BUCKI,

Manufacturers of

Plank and Flooring,

OFFICE AND YARDS:

Foot of West 13th Street

New York.

PROPRIETORS OF THE

Suwannee Steam Saw Mills,

ELLAVILLE, FLORIDA.

G W. Hawkins.   R. C Insley   E F. Hawkins

C. P. HAWKINS' SONS,

BREWERS OF FINE

INDIA, PALE and AMBER STOCK,

CANADA AND AMBER ALES. ALSO FINE PORTERS,

→ Ashuelot Brewery, ←

Nos. 343 and 345 West 41st Street,

NEW YORK.

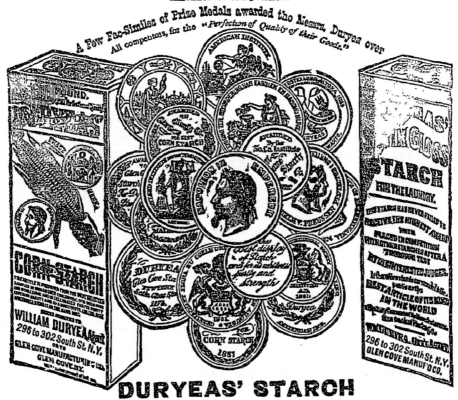

GALL & LEMBKE,
PRACTICAL OPTICIANS,
21 Union Square, New York.

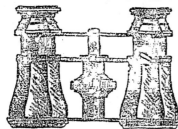

MARINE and FIELD TELESCOPES
Perfectly achromatic, sharp definition and power at long distances

OPERA GLASSES AND LORGNONS,
Handsomely mounted, great illuminating and magnifying power

BAROMETERS AND THERMOMETERS,
Mercurial and Metallic, of absolute accuracy

SPECTACLES
Scientifically adjusted to the various defects of the eyes.

W. & J. SLOANE,
FINE CARPETINGS
AND UPHOLSTERY GOODS.

BROADWAY, 18TH AND 19TH STS., NEW YORK.

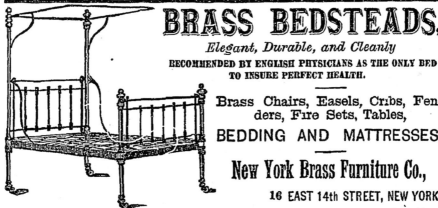

BRASS BEDSTEADS,
Elegant, Durable, and Cleanly

RECOMMENDED BY ENGLISH PHYSICIANS AS THE ONLY BED TO INSURE PERFECT HEALTH.

Brass Chairs, Easels, Cribs, Fenders, Fire Sets, Tables,

BEDDING AND MATTRESSES.

New York Brass Furniture Co.,
16 EAST 14th STREET, NEW YORK.

ARNOLD, CONSTABLE & CO.
SPRING NOVELTIES.

ARE now prepared to exhibit their SPRING Selection of HIGH CLASS NOVELTIES in Silks, Velvets, Dress Goods, Laces and Embroideries Dress and Cloaking Cloths, Suits, Cloaks, Furs, Ladies,' Misses' and Children's FURNISHING GOODS. Shawls, Gentlemen's OUTFITTING GOODS, Hosiery, Underwear, Gloves, Umbrellas, etc., together with an extensive assortment of HOUSEHOLD and FAMILY LINENS, Foreign and Domestic White Goods, Blankets, Flannels, etc., etc. Also, a fine selection of RARE and ARTISTIC DESIGNS in CARPETS, ORIENTAL RUGS, UPHOLSTERY GOODS, FURNITURE COVERINGS, INTERIOR DECORATIONS, etc., etc.

BROADWAY, COR. 19TH ST., NEW YORK.

IF YOU HAVE ANYTHING TO PURCHASE FOR CHILDREN
YOU CAN DO SO TO THE BEST ADVANTAGE AT THE

Because we keep every article of wearing apparel from Hats to Shoes for all ages up to 16 years

Because Our unequalled facilities in this specialty enable us to furnish the most desirable goods at low prices

Because the Garments we make have a style, fit and finish far superior to the goods usually sold ready made. We employ only first-class, skilled workmen

We also make to order Boys', Girls', and Infants' Clothing in the best manner at moderate prices

We take back for Exchange or Refund of Money all Goods that are not satisfactory in every particular In fact the superior facilities we offer only require to be known to make the "LILIPUTIAN BAZAAR" indispensable to all who have children to provide for

BEST & CO., 60 and 62 West 23d St., New York.

WM. WALL'S SONS,
MANUFACTURERS OF
Manila Sisal, Jute and Tarred
CORDAGE & OAKUM.

OFFICE:
113 WALL STREET, NEW YORK.

EDWARD L MILLER FRED. T HUBER

MILLER & HUBER,
FLOUR MERCHANTS,
15 Water Street & 18 Front Street,

Near Broad Street, *NEW YORK.*

JOY, LANGDON & CO.,

99 Chauncy St., BOSTON.   108 Worth St., } NEW YORK.
                          544 Pearl St.,

——AGENTS FOR——

Hamilton Manufacturing Co.	Knickerbocker Prints, Fabriques, &c.
Hamilton Prints and Percales.	Tycoon Reps, 3-4 & 6-4 Alpacas
New Market Manufacturing Co.	Poplins, Cashmeres, &c.
Hooksett Manufacturing Co.	Winnipissiogee Hosiery Mills.
Hamilton Woolen Co.	Pitman Manufacturing Co.
Essex Mills.	Hodgson's Mills.

Hamilton and Essex Fancy Cassimeres and Over Coatings,
HOSIERY, SHIRTS AND DRAWERS,
Crash, Cambrics and Suitings.

D. STEVENSON,

Brewer,

Pale and Stock Ales and Porter.

501 TO 509 WEST 39TH STREET,

Cor Tenth Avenue.   **New York.**

Gorham Manufacturing Co., Silversmiths.

STANDARD OF SILVER.

As a rule the quality of Government Coin has been the standard on which Silversmiths have based their quality. The standard of United States Coin is 900-1000 pure silver to 100-1000 copper or other alloy. The standard of Great Britain is 925/1000 pure silver to 75-1000 alloy.

Our leading Silversmiths, the **GORHAM COMPANY**, adopted the English standard many years ago, and so careful has been the surveillance over the quality of their ware, that not a single piece has been known to leave their Factory under the standard. So well is this now understood that their trade mark is as well known to all purchasers of Solid Silver in this country, as is the STERLING Hall Mark of England, as a sure guarantee for pure metal.

BROADWAY AND 19th STREET, NEW YORK.

W. H. Schieffelin & Co.,

Importers, Exporters, Jobbers and Manufacturers,

170 & 172 WILLIAM ST. NEW YORK. 40 & 42 BEEKMAN STREET.

Imported and Indigenous Drugs, Staple Chemicals, Foreign and Domestic Medical Preparations, Fine Essential Oils, and Select Powders. New Pharmaceutical Remedies, Sponges, Druggists' Sundries, etc., etc., etc.

PURE DRUGS,

Sulphate Quinine, Sulphate Morphine, of Guaranteed Purity.

MANUFACTURERS OF STANDARD PHARMACEUTICAL PREPARATIONS,

INCLUDING FLUID AND SOLID EXTRACTS, ELIXIRS, SYRUPS, Etc, Etc.

Sole Manufacturers of SOLUBLE COATED PILLS and GRANULES,

Comprising all the officinal pills of the Pharmacopœia. They have received the unqualified indorsement and commendation of the Medical Profession, and are unequaled for PURITY OF COMPOSITION, SOLUBILITY OF COATING, UNIFORMITY IN SIZE, AND PERFECTION OF FORM AND FINISH.

THESE PILLS HAVE BEEN AWARDED THE FOLLOWING PRIZES:

1878.—Paris.—The Only Silver Medal—The Highest Recompense Awarded to Pills
1879.—Sydney.—New South Wales—First Award
1879.—New York, American Institute—Medal of Superiority
1880.—Melbourne, Australia—First Award.
1881.—Matanzas, Cuba.—Silver Medal
1881.—London.—The only Award of Merit for Pills alone at the International Medical and Sanitary Exhibition
1881.—Brighton, England.—Only Award for Pills at the Scientific and Sanitary Exhibition.
1883.—Amsterdam, Holland.—Gold Medal.

A. PERSON HARRIMAN & CO.,

457 & 459 Broome Street,

NEW YORK,

IMPORTERS
—AND—
Commission Merchants.

FOREIGN AND DOMESTIC

DRY GOODS.

PARIS. — LYONS. — ZURICH

WILLIAM H. WALLACE & CO.
SELL

IRON AND STEEL

Of every description wanted by

RAILROADS, STEAMSHIPS, MANUFACTURERS, BOILER AND MACHINE SHOPS,

For Boilers, Tanks, Bridges, and all Fire-proof Construction

—ALSO—

Horse Shoes, Shafting, Rivets, Nails, Angles, Tees, &c.

131 Washington St., New York.

Beadleston & Woerz,
Ales, Porter,
and Lager Beer,
Empire Brewery,
291 West 10th Street, New York.

F. O. Matthiessen & Wiechers,

Sugar Refining Co.,

No. 106 Wall Street.

John Stephenson Company, Limited,

47 EAST 27TH STREET,

NEW YORK CITY,

— Manufacture —

STREET CARS

Of Every Description.

LIGHT, ELEGANT, DURABLE.

Best Materials,

MINIMUM PRICES

Orders Quickly Filled.

CAREFUL ATTENTION TO SHIPMENTS.

PHILADELPHIA & READING R.R.

BOUND BROOK ROUTE.

DOUBLE TRACK.   **STEEL RAILS.**   **STONE BALLAST.**

NO SOFT COAL SMOKE.   **NO DUST.**

EXPRESS TRAIN TIME

☞ **2 HOURS 2** ☜

New York and Philadelphia.

SHORT LINE AND QUICK TIME
—TO—

Reading, Harrisburg, Pottsville, Williamsport,

AND ALL POINTS IN

EASTERN and CENTRAL PENNSYLVANIA.

STATION IN NEW YORK:

FOOT OF LIBERTY ST., NORTH RIVER.

STATIONS IN PHILADELPHIA:

Ninth and Green Sts., Columbia Ave., and Third and Berks Sts.

J. E. WOOTTEN,	H. P. BALDWIN,	C. G. HANCOCK,
GENERAL MANAGER	GEN. EAST. PASS. AGT	GEN. PASS. AND TICKET AGT.
	119 Liberty St., NEW YORK.	PHILADELPHIA.

MANHATTAN

Gas Light Company.

Office, No. 4 Irving Place.

WORKS:

Foot West 18th Street,
Foot East 14th Street.

Supply Gas in the district between Grand and Thirty-fourth St.

DIRECTORS:

PERCY R PYNE,	WILSON G. HUNT,
SAMUEL SLOANE,	JAMES H YOUNG,
JNO. J. CISCO,	BENJ CLARKE,
MASON YOUNG,	HY. A. C TAYLOR,

CHARLES ROOME

CHAS. ROOME,
President.

JAS. W. SMITH,
Secretary.

H. Herrman, Sternbach & Co.,

466 and 468 Broadway,

✤IMPORTERS✤

OF

SEALSKINS,
PLUSHES,
VELVETS,
WORSTEDS,
CLOAKINGS.

BRITISH DRY GOODS.

✤CLYDE'S✤

COASTWISE AND WEST INDIA STEAM LINES

BETWEEN

NEW YORK
And SANTO DOMINGO W. I.
CHARLESTON S. C.
WILMINGTON, N. C.
PHILADELPHIA Pa.

PHILADELPHIA
And CHARLESTON, S. C.
NORFOLK and RICHMOND, Va.
ALEXANDRIA, Va., and
WASHINGTON, D. C.

WM. P. CLYDE & CO.,
General Agents,

35 Broadway, New York.   12 South Wharves, Philadelphia, Pa.

MORGAN'S
Louisiana and Texas R.R. and Steamship Co.,
— FOR —
NEW ORLEANS and TEXAS, ARIZONA, NEW MEXICO and CALIFORNIA,

The A1 Iron Steamships

CHALMETTE,	**LONE STAR,**	**EXCELSIOR,**
MORGAN CITY,	**ALGIERS,**	**NEW YORK.**

On Wednesday and Saturday for New Orleans.

THROUGH BILLS OF LADING signed to **Galveston, Houston,** and all points on **Galveston, Harrisburg and San Antonio, Houston and Texas Central Railroad,** and all other **Railroads in Texas,** as also to **Indianola, Corpus Christi, Brazos Santiago, and Brownsville, Mobile,** and to all Mississippi River Points; and to all points on the lines of **Galveston, Harrisburg and San Antonio,** and **Southern Pacific Railways** and their connections. A 1 Iron Steamer "WHITNEY," sailing semi-monthly from **New Orleans** for **Vera Cruz, Mexico;** A 1 Iron Steamers "HUTCHINSON" and "MORGAN," sailing weekly from **New Orleans** to **Cedar Keys, Key West** and **Havana,** and carry both passengers and freight

BOGERT & MORGAN, General Agents,

Pier 36, North River, foot of North Moore Street, New York.

E. E. CURRIER,	A. SHOTWELL, Agent,	FRED'K SHRIVER, Agent,
192 Washington St.,	2 Chestnut St.,	3 Light St. Wharf,
BOSTON.	PHILADELPHIA.	BALTIMORE.

THE MOST EXTENSIVE MANUFACTURERS OF BILLIARD and POOL TABLES IN THE WORLD.

Importers and Dealers in all Billiard Materials.

THE BRUNSWICK-BALKE-COLLENDER CO.,

SOLE PROPRIETORS AND PATENTEES OF THE

Monarch Quick Cushions, and the Celebrated Collender Combination Cushions,

PRINCIPAL OFFICES, SALESROOMS AND MANUFACTORIES.

NEW YORK: Ware-rooms, 860 Broadway, cor. 17th St., and Union Square. Office and Manufactory, 8th Street, and East River.

CHICAGO, ILL.: Office, Salesrooms and Manufactory, Market and Huron Streets, North Side. Branch Salesroom 47 and 49 State Street, South Side.

CINCINNATI, OHIO, 8, 10 and 12 W. Sixth St.   **ST. LOUIS, MO.,** 211 Market St.

Western Branches—CHICAGO, Market and Huron Sts, North Side   ST LOUIS Mo, 211 Market St. KANSAS CITY, Mo 406 Delaware St   ST JOSEPH Mo, 119 North Third St   SAN FRANCISCO, Cal, 653 and 655 Market St   MILWAUKEE, Wis, 108 West Water St   ST PAUL Minn, 292 Jackson St. MINNEAPOLIS, Minn, Boston Block   OMAHA Neb, 503 South Tenth St   DALLAS Texas, 407 Main St DENVER, Col, 371 Lawrence St   DAVENPORT, Iowa, 309 West Second St.   SALT LAKE CITY, Utah, Third South St

Eastern Branches—NEW YORK, 724 Broadway   SYRACUSE, N Y, 91 South Salina St   BUFFALO, N Y, 597 Main St.   BOSTON, Mass., 42 44, 46, 48 Hanover St   PHILADELPHIA, Pa, 1134 Market St PITTSBURGH, Pa, 117 Fifth Avenue   BALTIMORE, Md, 367 West Baltimore St

Central Branches—CINCINNATI, Ohio, 8, 10 and 12 West Sixth St   CLEVELAND, Ohio, 174 Seneca St. INDIANAPOLIS, Ind, 59 South Illinois St.   DETROIT, Mich., 20 and 22 Michigan St   ATLANTA, Ga., 22 Decatur St

Canada Branches—WINNIPEG, Manitoba, P. O Box 1056   WINDSOR, Ont., Opera House Block TORONTO, Ontario, Box 273

Central Trust Company of New York.

No. 15 Nassau Street, Corner of Pine Street.

CAPITAL, $1,000,000 in U. S. Bonds.   SURPLUS, $1,300,000.

Allows interest on deposits, returnable on demand or at specified dates

Is a legal depository for money paid into Court   Is authorized to act as Executor, Administrator, Guardian, or in any other position of trust

Also as Registrar or Transfer Agent of Stocks and Bonds, and as Trustee for Railroad Mortgages

FREDERIC P OLCOTT, President.
GEORGE SHERMAN, Vice-President.
C. H P. BABCOCK, Secretary

EXECUTIVE COMMITTEE.

HENRY F SPAULDING, Chairman

JACOB D VERMILYE,	BENJ B SHERMAN,	SAMUEL D BABCOCK,
CHARLES LANIER,	FREDERIC P OLCOTT,	FREDERICK H. COSSITT,
ISAAC N PHELPS,		EDMUND W CORLIES

BOARD OF TRUSTEES.

Class of 1885.	Class of 1886.	Class of 1887.
Sam'l D. Babcock,	David Dows,	A A Low,
Isaac N Phelps,	Benj B Sherman,	Fred'k H Cossitt,
Jonathan Thorne,	J Pierpont Morgan,	Jacob D Vermilye,
Amos R Eno,	Chas Lanier,	Wm Allen Butler,
Gustav Schwab,	Chas G Landon,	Percy R. Pyne,
James P Wallace,	Wm H Webb,	Wm H Appleton,
Josiah M Fiske,	Frederic P Olcott,	Edmund W Corlies,
Henry F Spaulding,	Henry Talmadge	Geo MacCulloch Miller,
John S. Kennedy		Cornelius N Bliss

STATEMENT OF THE UNITED STATES BRANCH
OF THE
Royal Insurance Company

OF LIVERPOOL, ENGLAND.

JANUARY 1st, 1884.

ASSETS:

U. S. Government Bonds, Market Value.	$2,331,873 75
Real Estate	1,115,649 42
Cash in Banks and in Offices	450,208 94
Accrued Interest	48,100 00
Uncollected Premiums and other Admitted Assets	241,847 69
	$4,187,679 80

LIABILITIES:

Unpaid Losses, Unearned Premiums, and other Liabilities.	$2,292,803 95
Surplus	$1,894,875 85

HEAD OFFICE, Metropolitan District, 50 WALL ST., NEW YORK.

E. F. BEDDALL, MANAGER.   WM. W. HENSHAW, ASSISTANT MANAGER.

POLICEMEN CAN PROCURE
FROM THE
United States Mutual Accident Association
320 and 322 Broadway, New York,

$3000 In case of Death by Accident, and **$15** a week while disabled by Accident.

(Not exceeding Twenty six weeks on account of any one Accident),

At a Cost of $4.00 for Membership Fee, $1.00 per Annum Dues, and Assessments costing about $16.00 per Annum.

These Assessments are made for $2.00, each, at intervals as required to pay losses through the year.

CHARLES B. PEET (*of Rogers, Peet & Co.*), PRESIDENT

JAMES R PITCHER, SECRETARY.

New Haven Steamers and Connecticut River R. R. Line.

PIERS 25 and 26 EAST RIVER (Peck Slip).

ONLY STEAMERS Running To and Connecting with RAILROADS at NEW HAVEN.

FREIGHT Received and Way-Billed Through, under Joint Freight Tariffs, to Stations on

N. Y. NEW HAVEN & HART. BOSTON & N. Y. AIR LINE BOSTON & ALBANY, leased lines
Above New Haven   New Haven to Willimantic   Between Springfield & Boston.

CONNECTICUT RIVER,   ASHUELOT,   VERMONT VALLEY,
CENTRAL VERMONT, CONNECTICUT & PASSUMPSIC RAILROADS, Etc., Etc.

RATES AS LOW AS ANY OTHER ROUTE.
GREAT DESPATCH AND UNEQUALLED FACILITIES.

Steamers leave at 3 and 11 p.m., daily except Sundays.

GENERAL OFFICE, PIER 25 EAST RIVER.

RICHARD PECK, *Superintendent.*   **WILLIAM SCOTT,** *Agent.*

GEO. C. RICHARDSON, SMITH & CO.,

178 Devonshire St., Boston.   115 and 117 Worth St., N. Y.

SELLING AGENTS FOR

LOWELL MANUFACTURING CO.

EVERETT MILLS.

BOOTT COTTON MILLS.

YORK MANUFACTURING CO.

LAWRENCE MANUFACTURING CO.

LEWISTON MILLS.

TREMONT & SUFFOLK MILLS.

MASSACHUSETTS COTTON MILLS.

G. S. M. 6-4 WOOL SACKINGS.

BREWSTER & CO.
(OF BROOME STREET),
＊NEW ＋ YORK＊

Carriages and Road Wagons.
THE LEADING HOUSE IN AMERICA.
Family Carriages for Town and Country use.
SULKIES, DRAGS AND SPORTING TRAPS OF EVERY DESCRIPTION.

ONLY PLACE OF BUSINESS,

BROADWAY, 47TH TO 48TH STREET.

NOTICE.

We have no connection with a stock company advertising a name similar to our own.

FLEITMANN & CO.,

489, 491 AND 493 BROOME STREET.

IMPORTERS
AND
COMMISSION MERCHANTS

SILKS, VELVETS,
DRESS GOODS,
RIBBONS.

J. CHR. G. HUPFEL,

LAGER BEER BREWER,

223 to 229 East 38th Street,

AND

234 to 240 East 39th Street,

NEW YORK.

OPPERMANN & MÜLLER,
TURTLE BAY LAGER BEER BREWERY,

44th and 45th Sts., between 1st & 2d Aves., New York.

MANHATTA.

This popular brand of Cigars has been in the Market over **SIX YEARS**, during which time we have sold about 23 million.

The "Manhatta" is on sale in every State in the Union, and the increasing demand undoubtedly proves that the **FINE QUALITY STOCK** used in its manufacture is **APPRECIATED** by a large majority of consumers.

Send for illustrated descriptive price-list to

The American News Company,

39 & 41 Chambers Street,

NEW YORK.

Appleton's Guide-Books.

Appleton's General Guide to the United States and Canada.

In entirely new type, partially re-written, and wholly revised for the Season of 1884. In three separate forms.
ONE VOLUME COMPLETE, pocket-book form, roan, $2.50
NEW ENGLAND AND MIDDLE STATES AND CANADA, one volume, cloth, $1.25.
SOUTHERN AND WESTERN STATES, one volume, cloth, $1 25.

With numerous Maps and Illustrations

Appleton's European Guide-Book.

Containing Maps of the Various Political Divisions, and Plans of the Principal Cities Being a Complete Guide to the Continent of Europe, Egypt, Algeria, and the Holy Land With numerous Maps and Illustrations, and a Vocabulary of Travel-Talk in English, German, French and Italian. In two volumes, morocco, gilt edges, $5 00.

The present edition of APPLETON'S EUROPEAN GUIDE is the twenty first, and appears carefully revised and with various improvements

Appleton's Hand-Book of Summer Resorts.

Revised each Season to date of issue. With Maps and numerous Illustrations. Large 12mo, paper cover, 50 cents

Appleton's Dictionary of New York and Vicinity.

An alphabetically arranged Index to all Places, Societies, Institutions, Amusements, and other features of the Metropolis and Neighborhood, upon which Information is needed by the Stranger or the Citizen. Revised and corrected for the present Season. With Maps of New York and Vicinity. Paper, 30 cents

New York Illustrated.

A Pictorial Delineation of Street Scenes, Buildings, River Views, and other Picturesque Features of the Great Metropolis. With One Hundred and Forty-three Illustrations from drawings made specially for it, engraved in a superior manner. With large Maps of New York and Vicinity. Large 8vo, illustrated cover, 75 cents

Appleton's Guide to Mexico.

Including a Chapter on Guatemala, and an English-Spanish Vocabulary. By ALFRED R CONKLING, Member of the New York Academy of Sciences, and formerly United States Geologist. With a Railway Map and Numerous Illustrations. 12mo, cloth, $2.00.

The Hudson River Illustrated.

With Sixty Illustrations engraved in best style on Wood from original drawings. Square 8vo, paper, 50 cents

Appleton's Railway Guide.

Containing Maps and Time-Tables of the Railways of the United States and Dominion of Canada. Revised and published Semi-Monthly. Paper, 25 cents

---

D. Appleton & Co., Publishers.

THE BEST PERIODICALS FOR FAMILY READING.

HARPER'S MAGAZINE.
"The Giant of the Monthlies."

The circulation of HARPER'S MAGAZINE has always been greater than that of any other periodical of its class in America while in England it has outrun all the English magazines of its price

Its serial and short stories, its poems, essays, and richly illustrated articles, cover every subject of interest in travel, biography, history, literature, art, and industry

Notable novels are first printed in its pages as serial stories The most brilliant writers of America and Europe, in every department of letters are its contributors, while its illustrations are the best work of the most skilful artists and wood-engravers of our time

The editorial departments are abreast of the age in every human interest The "Easy Chair" chats wisely and wittily of subjects on which everybody is thinking, the "Historical Record' gives a comprehensive summary of the world's progress, the "Literary Record" presents a critical review of current literature, and the "Drawer," with its exhaustless supply of good stories, is a source of perpetual amusement

A like variety of equally good literary and art work cannot be bought in the form of books for many times the price of the Magazine

Subscription Price, $4 per Year

HARPER'S WEEKLY.
"A Picture History of our Own Times."

HARPER'S WEEKLY is the best illustrated paper in America It presents, week by week, in faithful and graphic pictures, the noteworthy events of the day, portraits of men of the time, reproductions of the works of celebrated native and foreign artists, cartoons by eminent pictorial satirists, and humorous illustrations of the ludicrous aspects of social and political life

HARPER'S WEEKLY always contains instalments of one, usually of two, of the very best novels of the day, with fine illustrations Its short stories are bright and entertaining Poems, sketches, and papers on important topics of the day, by the most popular writers, and columns of humorous and personal paragraphs, make it interesting to everybody

Its pages are kept free from everything which would unfit it for the family circle In art and general literature it always appeals to, and cultivates good taste in the field of politics it holds country above party, and while it upholds the grand fundamental principles of the Republican Party, it maintains its right to criticise and dissent

Whoever wants a Cosmopolitan, Independent Illustrated Newspaper should subscribe for HARPER'S WEEKLY

Subscription Price, $4 per Year.

HARPER'S BAZAR.
No Family should be without it.

HARPER'S BAZAR, published weekly is the woman's paper. Its Pattern Sheet Supplement alone, of which between twenty and thirty are issued each year, will enable any lady of moderate means to dress tastefully and fashionably, and to save much more than the price of subscription, by furnishing her with the latest patterns of ladies' and children's dresses, wraps, etc Each Supplement contains a dozen, or more, patterns for which no extra charge is made

All subjects that pertain to the realm of domestic economy are treated from time to time in the columns of HARPER'S BAZAR Cookery for the well and the sick, the management of servants, the best methods of regulating the necessary expenses of the family, social etiquette and usages, gardening, etc Ladies will find in it practical instructions which will aid them materially in remodeling their dresses, refurnishing their houses tastefully and cheaply, and in economizing in various other directions

Its stories, sketches, and other articles being furnished by the best writers of America and Europe, while its superb wood engravings are marvels of perfect execution

Subscription Price, $4 per Year.

HARPER'S YOUNG PEOPLE.
"The best Periodical for Juvenile Readers."

HARPER'S YOUNG PEOPLE, published weekly, is the best help of the parent and teacher, exerting a refining influence through its entertaining stories, anecdotes of travel, biographical sketches scientific articles, etc The engravings and typography are unsurpassed in merit, attractiveness, and artistic finish

A leading journal says "The villainous trash, the penny dreadful 'boys' and girls' papers' at one time so popular and so numerous, have nearly all, thank fortune, been driven from the field by the introduction of publications for the young which are just as cheap, and perfectly healthful and wholesome This good work of reform was led by the Harpers of New York, with their handsome YOUNG PEOPLE"

Boys will find in its pages entertaining descriptions of different athletic sports and popular out-door amusements, and girls will be interested in the directions for making dolls, dolls' clothing embroidery, crocheting, etc A valuable feature of the Post-Office Box, which affords to the young readers an opportunity to correspond with the Post-mistress and with each other, thus giving them ease and familiarity in the use of language Specimen copy sent on receipt of three cents

Subscription Price, $1.50 per Year.

NOTICES OF THE PRESS.

The superb periodicals published by Harper & Brothers, in one way or another, in politics, events, fashions, inventions, trades, new and standard interests in the arts, sciences, travel, discovery, criticism, instruction illustration, amusement, offer a complete epitome of the year.—*Philadelphia Ledger*

One or the other of these journals should find its way into every family —*Southern Planter, Richmond, Va.*

There can be no more acceptable Holiday gift than a subscription for HARPER'S MAGAZINE, HARPER'S WEEKLY, HARPER'S BAZAR, or HARPER'S YOUNG PEOPLE, or, better still, for the entire four publications —*Philadelphia News*

These publications are among the best of the kind in the country, or, in fact, in the world —*Springfield Republican.*

HARPER'S MAGAZINE, HARPER'S WEEKLY, HARPER'S BAZAR, and HARPER'S YOUNG PEOPLE are welcome and familiar visitors in thousands of households all over the country A year's subscription to one of them would make a decidedly welcome Christmas present for adults or children.—*Baltimore American*

Each of these publications in its own field has become as familiar as a household word, and is regarded almost as a household necessity.—*Boston Journal*

Subscriptions will be commenced with the Number of each Periodical current at the time of receipt of order, except in cases where the subscriber otherwise directs.

Remittances should be made by Post-Office Money Order or Draft, to avoid risk of loss.

Address **HARPER & BROTHERS, Franklin Square, N. Y.**

THE SOHMER CELEBRATED

Grand, Square and Upright Pianofortes are preferred by Leading Artists.

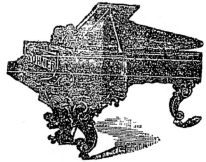

The demands now made by an educated musical public are so exacting that very few Pianoforte Manufacturers can produce instruments that will stand the test which merit requires. SOHMER & CO., as Manufacturers, rank amongst this chosen few who are acknowledged to be makers of standard instruments. In these days, when many Manufacturers urge the low price of their wares rather than their superior quality as an inducement to purchase it may not be amiss to suggest that, in a Piano, quality and price are too inseparably joined to expect the one without the other.

Every Piano ought to be judged as to quality of its tone, its touch and its workmanship; if any of these is wanting in excellence, however good the others may be, the instrument will be imperfect. It is the combination of these qualities in the highest degree, that constitutes the perfect Piano, and it is this combination that has given the "SOHMER" its honorable position with the trade and the public.

Musical authorities and critics prefer the "SOHMER" Pianos and they are purchased by those possessing refined musical taste and appreciating the richest quality of tone and the highest perfection generally in a Piano. The "SOHMER" Pianos are used in the following Institutions: *N. Y. College of Music; Loyt's Conservatory of Music, Villa Maria Convent*, Montreal, *Villa de Sales Convent*, Long Island, N.Y.; *Normal Conservatory of Music; Philadelphia Conservatory of Music*, and all the leading first-class theatres in NEW YORK and BROOKLYN.

RECEIVED FIRST PRIZE AT CENTENNIAL EXHIBITION, PHILADELPHIA, 1876.
RECEIVED FIRST PRIZE AT EXHIBITION, MONTREAL, CANADA, 1881 and 1882.

SOHMER & CO., Manufacturers of Grand, Square and Upright Pianos,
Warerooms, 149, 151, 153, 155 E. 14th St., New York.

TEFFT, WELLER & CO.,

SUCCESSORS TO

TEFFT, GRISWOLD & CO.,

Importers and Jobbers of Dry Goods.

FOREIGN AND DOMESTIC DRESS GOODS,

WOOLENS, HOSIERY, FLANNELS,

NOTIONS, WHITE GOODS, SHAWLS,

STAPLE DOMESTIC GOODS,

CARPETS AND OIL CLOTHS.

326, 328 AND 330 BROADWAY, NEW YORK,

Between Worth and Pearl Streets.

HUDSON RIVER BY DAYLIGHT.

THE FAVORITE STEAMERS
"ALBANY" AND "C. VIBBARD."

GOING NORTH.		GOING SOUTH.	
Leave	A M.	Leave	A M.
BROOKLYN (by Annex)	8 00	SARATOGA (Special train)	7 00
Leave	A M	Leave	A M
NEW YORK, Vestry St	8 35	ALBANY	8 30
NEW YORK, 22d Street	9 00	HUDSON	10 40
WEST POINT	11 50	CATSKILL	11 00
NEWBURGH	12 25	RHINEBECK	12 25
POUGHKEEPSIE	1 15	POUGHKEEPSIE	1 20
RHINEBECK	2 10	NEWBURGH	2 15
CATSKILL	3 25	WEST POINT	2 50
HUDSON	4 45	NEW YORK, 22d St	5 30
ALBANY	6 10	NEW YORK, Vestry St	5 50
Arrive	P M.	Arrive	P M
SARATOGA (Special train)	6 10	BROOKLYN (by Annex)	6 15
Arrive	P M	Arrive	P M

Meals on the European Plan.	Dining Saloons on Main Deck.

Connecting at Albany with New York Central & Hudson River Railroad

—FOR—

BUFFALO, NIAGARA FALLS, SUSPENSION BRIDGE

Thousand Islands and all Western Points.

With Delaware & Hudson Canal Company's Railroad for

BINGHAMTON, ELMIRA, WATKINS' GLEN, BALLSTON, SARATOGA,

MONTREAL AND NORTHERN POINTS.

ALSO,

Central Vermont Route for St. Albans, St. Johns & Montreal.

At NEW YORK with Trains for

PHILADELPHIA, BALTIMORE, WASHINGTON

And Points in the SOUTH, WEST and EAST.

A CHOICE OF TWO ROUTES TO THE

RESORTS OF THE CATSKILLS.

Through Tickets Sold and Baggage Checked to Destination.

C. R. VAN BENTHUYSEN, Gen Ticket Ag't. C T. VAN SANTVOORD, Gen. Manager.

VESTRY STREET PIER, NEW YORK

SAFETY and DISPATCH
BY THE
UNITED STATES
EXPRESS COMPANY.
BETWEEN
ALL THE PRINCIPAL CITIES
IN THE
Middle, Western, Northwestern and Southwestern States
AND THE TERRITORIES AND PACIFIC SLOPE.

In Direct Connection, and under Through Rates, with Connecting Lines extending throughout the entire country, East and West

MERCHANDISE and VALUABLES

Forwarded to All Parts of the Country on

FAST EXPRESS TRAINS in the QUICKEST POSSIBLE TIME
AT EXTREMELY LOW RATES.

Also Connecting with FOREIGN EXPRESS LINES and STEAMERS for All Parts of the World.

Unexcelled Facilities for the Transportation of

CURRENCY, GOLD, SILVER and JEWELRY,

In Fire-Proof Safes in Charge of Special Messengers

Particular Attention given to the Collection of

Notes, Drafts, Accounts, etc., the Recording of Deeds, Mortgages, etc.

And the Execution of all sorts of Commissions.

By Giving and Taking Receipts and keeping Complete Records of all Articles THE UNITED STATES EXPRESS COMPANY are at all times prepared to Prove the Delivery of Every Package entrusted to their care.

REDUCED RATES given on Small Money Remittances, also on Packages of Printed Matter and other Articles known as Third Class Mail Matter

For further information and Rates, apply to any of the Company's Agents.

GENERAL OFFICES:
82 BROADWAY, NEW YORK CITY.

CENTRAL Cross-Town R.R. Co.

JOHN B. SLAWSON, President.
M. I. MASSON, Actuary.

Capital, - - - - $600,000

ROUTE:

From foot East 23d Street to Avenue A to East 18th Street to Broadway to East and West 14th Street to Seventh Avenue, to West 11th Street to West Street to Christopher Street. Returning through West Street to West 11th Street to Seventh Avenue to West and East 14th Street to Union Square to East 17th Street to Avenue A to East 23d Street.

FARE, 5 CENTS.

◁ Assets over One Hundred Million Dollars. ▷

THE ✢ MUTUAL ✢ LIFE

INSURANCE COMPANY,

OF ✢ NEW ✢ YORK.

F. S. WINSTON, President.

◁ The Largest and Best in the World. ▷

TO EUROPE
IN SEVEN DAYS.

TAKE THE
ALASKA
OR
ARIZONA
OF THE
GUION LINE.

THE FASTEST STEAMSHIPS IN THE WORLD.

Apply to
WILLIAMS & GUION,
29 Broadway, N. Y.

A. G. NEWMAN,
1108 Broadway, New York,
MANUFACTURER OF

DECORATED AND PLAIN BRONZE
HARDWARE.

PATENT ELEVATOR DOOR FIXTURES.   HOTEL ANNUNCIATORS.   **PATENT**
BURGLAR AND FIRE ALARMS.   APARTMENT INDICATORS.

Brass and Bronze Railings made to order from Drawings.
ANTIQUE FURNITURE TRIMMINGS.

Factory: 157-163 West 29th Street,   *New York.*

BAEDER, ADAMSON & CO.,
No. 67 Beekman Street, New York,
MANUFACTURERS OF

CURLED HAIR.   # GLUE.   **FLINT PAPER.**

Emery Paper and Emery Cloth, Ground Flint and Cow Hide Whips,

WASHED CATTLE, SADDLERS' AND PLASTERERS' HAIR, MOSS, Etc.

HAIR FELT, FOR COVERING BOILERS AND PIPES, AND FOR LINING REFRIGERATORS.

STORES:
NEW YORK, 67 Beekman Street   PHILADELPHIA, 730 Market Street   BOSTON, 143 Milk Street.
CHICAGO, 182 Lake Street   CINCINNATI, 8 and 10 West Pearl Street

---

GILMAN COLLAMORE.      JOHN J. GIBBONS.

IMPORTERS OF

Rare China,   Rich Cut Glass,
Artistic Faiences,   Plates,
Oriental Porcelains,   And Bric-a-Brac.

19 UNION SQUARE, WEST, NEW YORK

ESTABLISHED 1844.   **J. S. CONOVER & CO.**   ESTABLISHED 1844.
DESIGNERS and MANUFACTURERS of

GRATES AND FENDERS,
OPEN FIRE PLACES,

ANDIRONS, FIRE SETS, HODS, SCREENS, Etc., In all Metals, and Newest Designs.

TILES IMPORTED DIRECTLY FROM THE MOST RENOWNED MAKERS   **30 WEST 23d ST.**

Special Designs and Estimates furnished when desired.

J. R. RAND, President.   N. W. HORTON, Secretary.   A. C. RAND, Treasurer.

RENDROCK POWDER COMPANY,

MANUFACTURERS OF

The Ingredients of the Patent

Rackarock Blasting Powder,

AND DEALERS IN

Electric Blasting Machines, Electric Fuzes, Leading Wire, Blasting Caps, Safety Fuze, &c.

These Ingredients are not explosive until combined. Can be forwarded by express or fast freight if desirable. Approximate Nitro Glycerine in strength.

RAND DRILL COMPANY,

MANUFACTURERS OF

Rock Drills, Air Compressors,

AND GENERAL MINING MACHINERY, BLASTING BATTERIES, FUZE AND CAPS.

240 BROADWAY, NEW YORK.

A. C. RAND, President.   N. W. HORTON, Sup't   J. R. RAND, Sec'y and Treas.

W. L. STRONG & CO.,

New York, Boston and Philadelphia,

Selling Agents

FOR THE PRODUCTIONS OF THE FOLLOWING MILLS

BALLARD VALE MILLS.   C. H. & F. H. STOTT.   WAUMBECK CO.
NORWAY PLAINS CO.   ELIAS TITUS & SONS.   B. LUCAS & CO.
NIANTIC MILLS CO.   CLINTON MILLS CO.
SAMUEL GREENWOOD & SONS.

CALIFORNIA FINE WHITE BLANKETS.

CONESTOGA STEAM MILLS'

FINE BROWN COTTONS AND SATTEEN JEANS.

New England Bunting Co.

SPECIALTIES IN DRESS GOODS.

PURE TOBACCO
PURE PAPER

SWEET CAPORAL,

CAPORAL,

CAPORAL ½,

ST. JAMES, &c.

Straight Cut in Full Dress Package,

THE FINEST CIGARETTE IN THE WORLD.

KINNEY TOBACCO COMPANY,

SUCCESSORS TO

Kinney Bros.

New York, Baltimore and Danville.

Each Cigarette bears *Kinney Bros.* facsimile signature.

Sold by Dealers throughout the World.

AMERICAN EXPRESS CO.

NEW YORK CITY OFFICES

65 Broadway, near Wall St	27 East 14th St., near Union sq.
40 Hudson St., near Duane	940 Broadway, Cor. 22d St
302 Canal St., near Broadway	30th St., H. R. R. R. Depot.
696 Broadway, cor. Fourth St.	45th St opp Grand Central Depot.

407 Madison Ave., Cor. 48th St

Forwarders by the Fastest Passenger and Special Express Trains

BETWEEN ALL THE PRINCIPAL CITIES IN THE

New England, Middle and Western States.

FROM NEW YORK CITY
—VIA—

New York Central and Hudson River R. R.

TO THE WEST BY

SPECIAL AMERICAN EXPRESS TRAINS,

Which carry NO PASSENGERS, and make better time than passenger trains—Running nearly 40 miles per hour, N Y to Buffalo, Cleveland, etc

American Express Company **Money Orders** Cheap, Safe and Convenient, issued for any amount from $1 00 to $50 00, payable either to Order or to Bearer at 6,500 places in the Eastern, Middle, Western and Southwestern States, the Territories, Pacific Coast, Mexico, and the Canadas RECEIPTS GIVEN, AND IF ORDERS ARE LOST, MONEY REFUNDED. Orders are also negotiable at banks Orders sold at all Offices of the Company in the United States **Rates**—$5, 5c | $10, 8c | $20, 10c. | $30, 12c. | $40, 15c | $50, 20c

American Express Company **Transfers Money by Telegraph** between all its important city and village agencies Low Rates and Prompt Service Payment of money made, when requested, at local addresses **Rates**—In addition to the cost of telegraph service, for sums of $100 or less, one per cent Over $100 to $200, $1 25 | $200 to $300, $1.50 | $300 to $400, $1 75 | $400 to 500, $2 00. Rates for larger amounts, apply to Agents

American Express Company. **Reduction in Rates for Currency or Gold Coin Remittances** between nearly 5,000 places reached direct by the American Express Company, in the Eastern, Middle and Western States, and the Canadas; also to offices of nearly all connecting lines **Lowest and Highest Charges, according to Distance Carried—**

$20 or less,	15c	$70	25 to 30c	$125	25 to 50c.	$200	25 to 85c	$250.	25c to $1 00
40	20c	80	.25 to 40c	150	25 to 60c.	225	25 to 90c	300	.25c. to $1.25
50	25c.	100	25 to 45c	175	25 to 75c				

☞ LARGER SUMS IN MUCH SMALLER PROPORTION

N. B.—Money Packages are delivered, as addressed, within the Company's delivery limits of every city and village agency, FREE OF CHARGE

Merchandise Parcel Rates.—The attention of shippers is respectfully called to the following table of approximated rates for the carriage of small packages of merchandise. These rates are the LOWEST and HIGHEST charges made, according to the distance packages are carried, and apply between nearly 5,000 places reached DIRECT by this Company in the United States

1 lb 25c | 2 lbs 25 to 30c. | 3 lbs 25 to 45c | 4 lbs 25 to 60c | 5 lbs .25 to 75c.
7 lbs . 25c. to $1 00

By agreement, and arrangements made for Through Way Billing, the above rates also apply to places reached by nearly every connecting express company in the Northern States and Territories

EVERETT'S HOTEL and GRAND DINING ROOMS

(ON THE EUROPEAN PLAN),

102, 104 and 106 Vesey Street,

Through to 98 Barclay St.   Opposite Washington Market   Between Washington and West Sts.

ENTIRE HOUSE OPEN DAY AND NIGHT,
And lighted in its entirety by the Edison System for Isolated Lighting

200 Rooms—50 cents, 75 cents and $1.00 per day; $2.00, $3.00 and $3.50 per week, and upwards, according to location, etc.

THE LARGEST DINING ROOMS IN NEW YORK—PERFECT VENTILATION.

Samuel H. Everett, Proprietor

H. Clausen & Son Brewing Co.,

 NEW YORK CITY.

BREWERS OF

Superior Pale Amber Ales and Porter,

East India Pale Ale and American Stout,

ALSO

CHAMPAGNE ✧ LAGER ✧ BEER,

For Draught and Bottling Use

Shipping Orders Solicited and Promptly Executed if covered by Draft on N. Y. City Bank, or accompanied with Satisfactory References.

WE MAKE A SPECIALTY OF BREWING

The Celebrated Export Champagne Lager Beer, East India Pale Ale and American Stout,

BOTTLED BY THE

→∗ PHŒNIX BOTTLING COMPANY, ∗←

886 to 890 Second Avenue, New York.

We Received FIRST PRIZES at

CENTENNIAL EXHIBITION, Philadelphia, 1876,
PARIS EXPOSITION, 1878,
CARACAS, VENEZUELA, EXHIBITION, 1883,
SAN FRANCISCO EXHIBITION, 1803,
And at the AMERICAN INSTITUTE FAIR for the last four successive years

---

Shipments of our Bottled Beer to Central and South America, West Indies, Australia, and other Foreign Countries, also all parts of the United States, attest to the reputation and keeping qualities of our Beers.

Genius Rewarded;

OR,

THE · STORY · OF · THE · SEWING · MACHINE.

A handsome little pamphlet, illuminated cover, with numerous engravings,

WILL BE

GIVEN AWAY

to any adult person calling for it, at any branch or sub-office of the

Singer Manufacturing Company,

or will be sent by mail, post-paid, to any person living at a distance from our offices.

The Singer Manufacturing Co.

Principal Office, 34 Union Square,

NEW YORK.

G. AMSINCK & CO.

148 and 150 Pearl Street, New York.

SOLE AGENTS IN THE UNITED STATES AND CANADA FOR

WIDOW DE X. HARMONY & CO.	Cadiz.
THOMAS HINE & CO.	Cognac.
A. PELLEVOISIN	La Rochelle.
PAGÉS & CO	Tarragona.
JOAQUIN RIUS MONTANER	"
LEACH, GIRO & CO	Alicante.
TREYERAN FRÈRES	Bordeaux.
PAUL EMILE THOMAS	Mèze.
PAULIN ARNAUD	"
L. ALBRAND	Narbonne.
ESTÈVE & SINOT	Cette.
MIGUEL DE SOUZA GUEDES	Oporto.
FORTO, CHAMICO, SON & SILVA	"
P. J VANDERBURG	Schiedam.

HOLDERS OF

A. GUCKENHEIMER & BROS., Pure Rye Pennsylvania Whiskies.

PENNSYLVANIA DISTILLING CO., "Montrose" Pure Rye and Bourbon Whiskies.

THE NEWCOMB BUCHANAN CO., Louisville, Ky.

NELSON, ANDERSON, BUCHANAN, Bourbon and Rye Whiskies.

R. HOE & CO.,

MANUFACTURE

Patent Printing Presses

WHICH PRINT FROM A ROLL OF PAPER,

Either from Type Forms or Stereotype Plates,

AT A SPEED OF 30,000 PERFECTED COPIES AN HOUR,

With or Without Folding Apparatus

Also Less Expensive Machines of same description, where such great speed and Large production are not required.

PATENT DOUBLE AND SINGLE CYLINDER PRESSES,
For Newspaper, Book and Job Work.
PATENT STOP CYLINDER PRESSES, For Book Work.
PATENT SINGLE CYLINDER PRESSES, For Book Work.
PATENT STOP CYLINDER LITHOGRAPHIC PRESSES.
PATENT SINGLE CYLINDER TWO-REVOLUTION PRESSES, For Book Work.
PATENT SINGLE LARGE CYLINDER, For Job Work.
ADAMS' BED AND PLATEN BOOK PRESSES.

Printing Machinery and Printing Materials of every description, all manufactured in our own Works, under our own immediate supervision from improved designs, at prices in accordance with their quality and the times, and warranted in every case to be of superior design, best material and excellent workmanship.

Illustrated catalogues with prices may be had on application, and the machines may be seen at our works in operation and in process of construction.

R. HOE & CO.,
504 Grand Street, - - New York City.

SIMPSON, SPENCE & YOUNG,

Steamship Agents and Ship Brokers,

78 and 80 Broad Street, New York. | 12 Great St Helen's, London.
Guildhall Chambers, Newcastle-on-Tyne.

AGENTS FOR

ARROW LINE,	Steamers to	Leith.
FURNESS LINE,	"	Newcastle-on-Tyne and Dundee.
CAMBRIAN LINE,	"	Portishead Dock and Swansea.
BLAIR'S LINE,	"	Brazil.
STETTIN LLOYD LINE,	"	Stettin and Copenhagen.
DIRECT SWEDISH LINE,	"	Stockholm, Gothenburg and Malmo.

New York Cab Company, Limited,

SUCCESSORS TO

RYERSON & BROWN,

Nos. 19 to 25 East 12th Street,   Nos. 116 to 130 West 32d Street,
Fifth Avenue, Corner 44th Street,   Nos. 2, 4 and 6 West 45th Street,
American Horse Exchange, B'way cor. 50th St.,   Nos. 221 and 223 West 53d Street,
And at the Windsor Hotel.

In addition to the regular Livery Business as heretofore carried on by RYERSON & BROWN, this Company has established a

CHEAP CAB SERVICE FOR THE CITY OF NEW YORK.

These Cabs have proved a **success**, and already many of the Old City Cabs have been painted to imitate ours.

Be sure that the TRADE MARK of our Company is on the back Panel of the Cab. All others are Bogus.

Wm P St John, President Chas P Burdett, Vice-President Fred'k B Schenck, Cashier

THE MERCANTILE NATIONAL BANK
OF THE CITY OF NEW YORK,
No. 191 BROADWAY.

CAPITAL, - - - $1,000,000.

Great Western Despatch and South Shore Line
Via Erie Railway,

TO ALL POINTS WEST, NORTH-WEST and SOUTH-WEST.

For Rates of Freight and Bills Lading, apply to

H. R. DUVAL, Gen'l Manager,   T. S. DUMONT, Gen'l Agent,
6 Bowling Green, N Y   236 Broadway, N Y.

ATLAS LINE OF MAIL STEAMERS
—— TO THE ——
West Indies and South America, Jamaica, Hayti,
Porto Rico, United States of Columbia and South America.

PIM, FORWOOD & CO., Agents. 22 & 23 State St., New York.

E. R. DURKEE & CO.,
Indigo and Spice Importers,

SPICE GRINDERS,   MUSTARD MANUFACTURERS

135, 137 & 139 Water Street, New York.

JACOB S. BERNHEIMER & BRO.,
MANUFACTURERS AND

CONVERTERS OF COTTON GOODS,
For Home and Export Trade,

COR. WHITE & CHURCH STREETS,

JACOB S BERNHEIMER
MAYER S BERNHEIMER   *NEW YORK.*

THEODORE B. STARR,
206 Fifth Avenue, MADISON SQUARE, New York,

IMPORTER AND MANUFACTURER.

CHOICE DIAMONDS,
RARE PEARLS,
RUBIES,
SAPPHIRES,
EMERALDS,
GOLD
JEWELRY

WATCHES,
SOLID SILVERWARE,
DECORATIVE PORCELAIN,
ARTISTIC BRONZES,
MANTEL SETS, CLOCKS.

Original Designs of Rich Jewelry.

*Special attention given to the remounting of family jewels.
Goods sent on approval, satisfactory references being given.*

FREE INSPECTION OF STOCK INVITED.

STUBBORN FACTS

are that the justly famous cigars made by the celebrated manufacturers,

Straiton & Storm,

are better than those produced by any other manufacturers. For the following reasons:—

They aim at the highest standard, and when reached they never allow them to deteriorate under any circumstances. The consumers' wants are always in view. The dealer has only to keep the goods in stock to insure to himself a steady reliable trade. We

CHALLENGE THE WORLD

to produce goods BETTER, more RELIABLE, and REGULAR. Dealers supplied by

R. C. BROWN & CO.,

94 and 96 West Broadway,   NEW YORK.

HERRING'S SAFES.

THE WORLD'S CHAMPIONS!

MEDALS AWARDED AT INTERNATIONAL EXHIBITIONS.

1851, 1853, 1867, 1876, 1878, 1879, 1880,

London, Paris, New York, Philadelphia, Sydney, N. S. W., Melbourne, etc.

HERRING & CO., 251 and 252 Broadway, New York.

A. S. BARNES & CO.,

PUBLISHERS OF THE

National Series of School Books, and Wholesale Booksellers and Stationers

111 AND 113 WILLIAM STREET, COR. JOHN, NEW YORK.

Lincoln Safe Deposit Company and Fire-Proof Storage Warehouse,

32 to 38 East 42d St., opposite Grand Central Depot.

BURGLAR AND FIRE-PROOF BOXES, $10.00 to $300.00 PER YEAR
Packages of Silver, Plate, etc., stored under guarantee. Unrivalled Fire Proof Storage for Furniture, Works of Art, Theatrical Properties, etc. TRUNK STORAGE A SPECIALTY. Building approved by Fire Commissioners and Inspector of Buildings

THOMAS L. JAMES, President.

CHEMICAL NATIONAL BANK,
270 BROADWAY.

CAPITAL, $300,000.   **SURPLUS AND PROFIT, $3,750,000.**

GEO. G. WILLIAMS, President.   W. J QUINLAN, Jr, Cashier

NINTH NATIONAL BANK,

CAPITAL,	$750,000.
SURPLUS AND PROFITS,	203,207.

JOHN T. HILL, Pres't.   GARDNER R. COLBY, Vice-Prest.   H. H. NAZRO, Cash'r.

HOME
INSURANCE COMPANY OF NEW YORK,
Office, No. 119 Broadway.

SIXTIETH SEMI-ANNUAL STATEMENT,

Showing the Condition of the Company on the First day of

JULY, 1883.

CASH CAPITAL,	$3,000,000 00
Reserve for Unearned Premiums,	2,212,267 00
Reserve for Unpaid Losses and Claims,	209,711 21
Net Surplus,	1,749,292 61
CASH ASSETS,	**$7,171,270 82**

J. H. WASHBURN, Secretary.   CHAS. J. MARTIN, President.

T. B. GREENE, } Ass't Sec's.   D. A. HEALD, Vice-Pres't.
W. L. BIGELOW, }

PH. & WM. EBLING,

ALE, LAGER BEER BREWERS, AND MALSTERS,

Corner 156th St. and St. Ann's Avenue,

MORRISANIA, NEW YORK CITY.

Special Attention Given to

BOTTLING AND SHIPPING TRADE.

GILSEY HOUSE,

Cor. Broadway and 29th St. - New York.

J. H. BRESLIN & BRO., PROPRIETORS.

VICTORIA HOTEL,

Fifth Ave., Broadway and 27th St., New York.

FRANK WRISLEY & CO., PROPRIETORS.

HOTEL ST. MARC,

EUROPEAN PLAN.

Fifth Avenue, cor. 39th St., - New York.

DEVINE & GILLIS.

Belvedere ∴ House,

Cor. Fourth Ave. and 18th St.,

NEW YORK.

JOS WEHRLE, PROP.

Centrally located near Union Square, convenient to all Railroads, Cars, Stages, and all principal places of Amusement.

A first-class Restaurant and Café attached to the house.

All modern languages are spoken by the Proprietor and attendants.

(56)

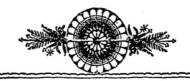

Steinway

PIANO-FORTES,

The Standard Piano of the World.

WAREROOMS:

Steinway Hall, Nos. 107, 109 and 111 E. 14th St.,

NEW YORK.

HERMANN

Lager Beer Brewery,

BURR, SON & CO.,

Proprietors,

221, 223, 225, 227, 232 AND 234 W. 18TH ST.,

NEW YORK.

KUHN, LOEB & CO.,

Bankers,

No. 31 NASSAU STREET,

NEW YORK CITY.

EAGLE BREWERY

L. H. ROEMER & CO.,

—SUCCESSORS TO—

JOHN F. BETZ,

Ale and Porter Brewers,

347-355 WEST 44th STREET, NEW YORK.

D. H. McAlpin & Co.

MANUFACTURERS OF

VIRGIN LEAF AND NAVY

FINE CUT CHEWING and SHIELD PLUG

TOBACCOS.

150 Avenue D, corner Tenth Street,

NEW YORK.

DAVID G. YUENGLING, Jr.,

Manhattan Brewery,

128TH STREET AND TENTH AVENUE,

NEW YORK.

JOSEPH GILLOTT'S Steel Pens,

GOLD MEDAL — **PARIS 1878.**

THE MOST PERFECT OF PENS.

For Fine Writing,
Nos. 1-303-170-
(Other Styles to Suit All Hands.)

For General Writing,
Nos. 332-404-390,
Falcon 878-908

For Broad Writing,
Nos. 7-294-389
Stub Points -849-

SOLD BY ALL DEALERS THROUGHOUT THE WORLD

WHOLESALE WAREHOUSE, 91 JOHN STREET, NEW YORK.

ASK for SIX CORD WILLIMANTIC — THE BEST THREAD for SEWING MACHINES. — SPOOL COTTON. TRY USE BUY

For Sale by all Leading Dealers.

AMMIDOWN & SMITH,
Dry Goods Commission Merchants,
87 & 89 LEONARD STREET, - - NEW YORK.

EDWARD H AMMIDOWN   ALBERT D SMITH

NEW YORK MUTUAL INSURANCE CO.
No. 61 William Street, New York.

ASSETS, JANUARY 1st, 1885, - - - $708,433.64.

Marine Insurance on Favorable Terms.   Certificates Issued Payable Abroad.

EDWARD LARAQUE, Secretary   THEO B BLEECKER, Jr, President.

☞ This Company issues Certificates of Insurance, losses payable in London, at the Banking House of DENNISTOUN, CROSS & CO. Originally Chartered as a Stock Company in 1798. Stock paid off and Mutual System Adopted in 1851.

NOTICE.

When you want a choice smoke, ask your dealer for one of the American News Company's

MANHATTA 5c. CIGARS.

You will find the flavor equal to most of the 10c., and superior to any of the 5c. cigars sold in your section.

THE AMERICAN NEWS COMPANY, 39 and 41 Chambers St., N.Y.

"GET THE BEST," The only LARGE TYPE Edition of

CHARLES DICKENS' WORKS.

EXCELSIOR EDITION.

Price per volume, in cloth binding	$1 50	Price per set, full Russia, gilt edges	50.00
" per set (in neat box)	22 50	" " " half calf or half morocco	50.00

This edition in size of type, page, and general style, excels all others. In fact it is, in the words of Charles Dickens **"The Best Edition of my Books."**

See specimen page, showing style of type, size of page, etc.

THE EXCELSIOR EDITION OF STANDARD TWELVEMOS.

In large 12mo Volumes of uniform thickness, printed from New Plates, on good paper fully illustrated, and handsomely bound, extra cloth, black and gold side and back dies. The volumes in this series are Complete and Unabridged, and are issued at the low price of $1.00 per volume, retail.

LIST OF ABOVE SENT ON APPLICATION

THE AMERICAN NEWS COMPANY, 39 and 41 Chambers St., N.Y.

ST. DENIS HOTEL and TAYLOR'S RESTAURANT

✳ EUROPEAN ✦ PLAN. ✳

Central Location.

Broadway and 11th Street, New York

WILLIAM TAYLOR, Proprietor.

WALKER & BRESNAN,

Successors to R. F. COLE & CO.,

Printers' Furnishing Warehouse,

201-205 William Street, 15 and 17 Frankfort Street,

NEW YORK.

Leads, Brass Rules, Galleys, Metal Furniture and Quotations   Boxwood for Engravers' Use,
Blocking Mortising, etc.

D. DE CASTRO & CO.

SHIPPING

— AND —

𝕮𝖔𝖒𝖒𝖎𝖘𝖘𝖎𝖔𝖓 𝕸𝖊𝖗𝖈𝖍𝖆𝖓𝖙𝖘,

54 WILLIAM STREET,

NEW YORK,

Importers of Coffee,

Cocoa, Cochineal, Dyewoods, Indigo,

𝕴𝖓𝖉𝖎𝖆 𝕽𝖚𝖇𝖇𝖊𝖗, 𝕴𝖛𝖔𝖗𝖞 𝕹𝖚𝖙𝖘, 𝕻𝖊𝖗𝖚𝖛𝖎𝖆𝖓 𝕭𝖆𝖗𝖐, 𝕳𝖎𝖉𝖊𝖘 𝖆𝖓𝖉 𝕾𝖐𝖎𝖓𝖘,

AND ALL OTHER PRODUCTS OF

Central America, United States of Columbia,

VENEZUELA, BRAZIL and the WEST COAST OF SOUTH AMERICA.

Fine Wall Papers

Before you Decorate your house, see the New Series of Designs of

FR. BECK & CO.,
MANUFACTURERS OF

FINE ✦ PAPER ✦ HANGINGS,

→✳ Also, Special Novelties in Wall Papers ✳←

GIVING RICH AND ARTISTIC EFFECTS AT MODERATE PRICES.

[From the New York Tribune, Dec 24, 1884.]
"Messrs FR BECK & Co are the only firm in a position to guarantee Wall Papers *free from Arsenic*"

L·INCRUSTA-WALTON.

Water-Proof. Durable. Sanitary.

The refinement of all Wall Decorations   The combination of
Lincrusta-Walton and Wall Papers now in universal use

FR. BECK & CO.,
Manufactory and Showrooms.

5th Ave. and 30th St., NEW YORK. 7th Ave. and 29th St.

N.B —Panels, Plaques, Medallions and Borders, forming beautiful Art Works in Lincrusta.

GALLATIN NATIONAL BANK,
NEW YORK.

| CAPITAL, | $1,000,000. | SURPLUS, etc., | $954,600. |

OFFICERS

FRED'K D. TAPPEN, President   ALEX H STEVENS, Vice-President   ARTHUR W. SHERMAN, Cashier.

DIRECTORS

| FRED'K D. TAPPEN | ADRIAN ISELIN, Jr | FRED'K W. STEVENS. | ALFRED ROOSEVELT. |
| WM. W. ASTOR | THOMAS DENNY. | ALEX H STEVENS | M BAYARD BROWN |

BLISS, FABYAN & CO.,

DRY ✦ GOODS ✦ COMMISSION ✦ MERCHANTS,

32 TO 36 THOMAS STREET,
117 TO 119 DUANE STREET,

NEW YORK.

WILLIAM M. BLISS, President.   WILLIAM L. STRONG, Vice-President.   EDW SKILLIN, Cashier

THE CENTRAL NATIONAL BANK OF THE CITY OF NEW YORK,
320 and 322 Broadway.

CAPITAL, - - - - - $2,000,000 | SURPLUS FUND and PROFITS, $566,834.46

DIRECTORS.

William A Wheelock	James W Smith	Elias S Higgins	Edwin F Knowlton
Simon Bernheimer	John Byers	Morris Franklin	Edward C Sampson
James M Dunbar	William M Bliss	William L. Strong	

JOHN C. DE LA VERGNE, Pres't.   CHAS. A. STERLING, Vice Pres't.   HENRY W. GUERNSEY, Sec'y and Treas.

The De La Vergne Refrigerating Machine Co.,

MANUFACTURERS OF

Refrigerating and Ice Machines

AND

ANHYDROUS AMMONIA.

153, 155, 157, 159, 161 Bank St.,

Telephone, Spring 85.   NEW YORK.

PETROLEUM VASELINE JELLY

Grand Medal at the Philadelphia Exposition. Silver Medal at the Paris Exposition. Highest Award at the London Medical Congress.

Used and Approved by the Leading Physicians of Europe and America.

THE MOST VALUABLE REMEDY KNOWN

For the treatment of Wounds, Burns, Sores, Cuts, Catholicism, Skin Diseases, Rheumatism, Catarrh, Hemorrhoids, Sunburn, and for every purpose where an ointment is needed Also for Coughs, Colds, Sore Throat, Croup and Diphtheria, Dysentery, etc.

PRICE OF PURE VASELINE REDUCED

Size No 0—1 ounce bottle, ... 10 Cents
    "   " "   "   " 15
    "   " "   "   " 25
1-2 lb.—8 ounce bottle, ... 35
1 lb.—16 ounce bottle, ... 50

VASELINE CONFECTIONS.

An agreeable form of taking Vaseline internally

THE TOILET ARTICLES FROM PURE VASELINE,

Such as POMADE VASELINE,

The purest and best dressing for the hair extant It is elegant, healthful and clean, will cure and prevent dandruff, contains no animal matter, and will never become RANCID Will make the hair grow when nothing else will

PRICE OF POMADE VASELINE REDUCED

Size No 1—2 ounce bottle, ... 20 Cents
    "   " "   "   " 25

VASELINE COLD CREAM.

Will allay all Irritation of the skin and keep the complexion smooth, soft and clear Superior to all Cosmetics For use after shaving, and chafing of infants it is unequalled—25 and 50 Cents.

VASELINE CAMPHOR ICE.

For the lips pimples, blotches, chapped hands, skin, and local Irritation—25 Cents

FOR SALE BY ALL DRUGGISTS.

❧ THE LANGHAM. ☙

FIFTH AVENUE AND FIFTY-SECOND ST., NEW YORK.

THE FAVORITE FAMILY HOTEL OF THE METROPOLIS.

Perfect in all Appointments.   E N WILSON, Proprietor.

❧ MANHANSET HOUSE. ☙

SHELTER ISLAND, L. I., N. Y.

One of the Largest, most Attractive and Fashionable Summer Resorts along the Atlantic Coast

E N WILSON, Proprietor

CHARLES SCRIBNERS' SONS

AND

SCRIBNER & WELFORD,

Nos. 743 & 745 BROADWAY, NEW YORK,

HAVE FOR SALE EVERY IMPORTANT

American and English Book

RECENTLY PUBLISHED, AND

Standard Works in Cloth and Fine Bindings

IN GREAT VARIETY

ALSO, RARE AND UNIQUE VOLUMES, EXTRA ILLUSTRATED WORKS, AND BIBLIOGRAPHICAL TREASURES OF EVERY ORDER

THE PRICES ARE MODERATE, AND THE ASSORTMENT INCLUDES THE CHEAPEST AS WELL AS THE FINEST EDITIONS   CATALOGUES SENT FREE ON APPLICATION.

SCRIBNERS', 743 & 745 Broadway, New York City.

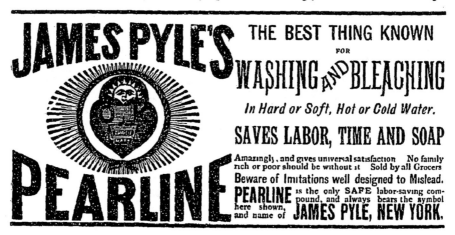

GEO. A. SCHASTEY & CO.,

DESIGNERS AND MANUFACTURERS OF

Interior Wood Work and Decorations,

FACTORY AND WAREROOMS,

BROADWAY AND 53D STREET.

"The Bodega"

81 CEDAR ST.
East of Broadway,

7 New Street, New York.

Fine Port, Sherry and Madeira Wines,

Generally acknowledged to be the best ever offered in this market.

TIMOTHY STEVENS, Proprietor.

PETERS & CALHOUN CO.,

MANUFACTURERS AND IMPORTERS OF

Saddlery and Harness

FOR HOME AND FOREIGN MARKETS.

Salesroom, New York, 691 Broadway,

One Block above Grand Central Hotel.

⇜ Factories, Newark, N. J. ⇝

CONTRACTORS TO THE U. S GOVERNMENT.

HODGMAN & CO.,

MANUFACTURERS OF

INDIA RUBBER GOODS OF EVERY DESCRIPTION.

CLOTHING, BOOTS AND SHOES, BALLS AND TOYS.	RUBBER	SPORTING OUTFITS, FANCY GOODS, Etc. Etc. Etc.

FULL LINE OF EVERYTHING MADE OF INDIA RUBBER.

Cor. of Broadway and Grand St., New York.

ESTABLISHED 1838.

Harlem Gas Light Company,

Office, 2084 Third Avenue,

North-West cor. 114th Street.

Works, First Avenue, 110th & 111th Sts.

District, from 79th St. to Kings Bridge.

HORTON'S
ICE CREAM

Is made from PURE ORANGE COUNTY CREAM, and is the BEST and most popular Ice Cream in the World. TRY IT, AND YOU WILL USE NO OTHER!

PATENT SUPER-FROZEN BRICKS OF ICE CREAM FOR

CHURCHES, FAIRS, FESTIVALS AND TO CARRY HOME, A SPECIALTY.

WILL KEEP HARD ONE HOUR.

Depots:
305 Fourth Avenue, 1288 Broadway, 75 Chatham St., 110 E. 125th St., New York,
And 453 FULTON STREET, BROOKLYN.

DAVIS COLLAMORE & CO.,
921 BROADWAY, cor. 21st STREET and 151 FIFTH AVENUE, connecting.

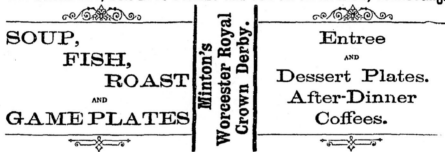

SOUP, FISH, ROAST AND GAME PLATES

Minton's Worcester Royal Crown Derby.

Entree AND Dessert Plates. After-Dinner Coffees.

Pure Cut Crystal Glass in Sets or by the Piece.
Rich Cut Berry Bowls, Fruit Stands, Olive Dishes, &c.
IN NEW AND ELEGANT FORMS. QUALITY UNEXCELLED.

FANCY VASES, BOHEMIAN GLASS, HAVILAND CHINA.

DAVIS, COLLAMORE & CO.,
BROADWAY, corner 21st Street, NEW YORK.

The following serials, published in pamphlet-form, are presented to all purchasers of
NEW YORK FAMILY STORY PAPER FROM 582 UPWARD.
Leave your order with your Newsdealer, and he will obtain the paper and the entire list of eighteen books for you. Remember that there is no extra charge for the books.

Mrs. McVEIGH MILLER'S WORKS.		MISCELLANEOUS WORKS.	
A Dreadful Temptation,	with No. 582	Called Back, by Hugh Conway,	591
An Old Man's Sweetheart,	with No. 583	The Loom Girl of Lowell, by Turner,	592
A Young Girl's Strange Fate,	with No. 584	The Romance of a Poor Young Man,	593
The Outlaw's Bride,	with No. 585	Led Astray, by Octave Feuillet,	594
The Dream of Her Lifetime,	with No. 586	Camille, by Alexandre Dumas, Jr.,	595
Love Wins Love,	with No. 587	In Cupid's Net,	596
The Oath of Vengeance,	with No. 588	A Terrible Crime, by Emma G. Jones,	597
Winning the Heir,	with No. 589	Old Hawkeye's Greatest Trail,	598
Her Mother's Secret,	with No. 590	Wedded and Parted,	599

THE NEW YORK FAMILY STORY PAPER, beginning with 582 up to 599, as above, with eighteen complete novels, will be sent to any address for $1.00, postage paid. Address

Munro's Publishing House,
Box 3643. 24 and 26 Vandewater St., N. Y.

T. C. LYMAN   H. L. GREENMAN.

T. C. Lyman & Co.

BREWERS OF

Pale, Burton and East India

ALES & PORTER,

420 to 428 West 38th St., Bet. 9th and 10th Aves.

NEW YORK.

LANMAN & KEMP,

William St., cor. Cedar St.,

NEW YORK

IMPORTERS

OF

East India and South American

MERCHANDISE.

Wholesale Druggists

FOR

Spanish, South, and Central American

COUNTRIES.

E. LUDWIG,

469 AND 471 BROOME STREET, COR. GREENE,

NEW YORK,

AGENT FOR LES SUCCESSEURS

D'ARLÈS-DUFOUR & CIE.,

Importers and Commission Merchants,

Silks, Velvets, Dress Goods, Shawls, Upholstery Goods, &c.

C. J. BONNET'S BLACK SILKS

PARK & TILFORD

Fifth Avenue and 59th Street,

(CENTRAL PARK)

NEW YORK.

Superlative "ECLIPSE" Extra Dry

A HIGH GRADE, DRY, PURE CHAMPAGNE.

The only true American Champagne, all others are either sparkling Catawbas or charged
Being free of duty, offers an advantage of about $10 per case to consumers, over foreign wines of approaching quality.
Compare it with the finest qualities of the different foreign brands
Honors awarded over most imported Champagnes at both private and public comparisons,
and Medals of Superiority over native Champagnes

"The 'ECLIPSE' EXTRA DRY may be opened by any gentleman at his table with credit to himself, and without displeasing the most fastidious of his guests."—*New York Journal of Commerce*
"In California, Champagnes are made as good as any in the world"—*New York Herald*

Quarts, $14.85. Pints, $16.65. Sample Case, containing three Quarts and two Pints, Champagne, $5.00.
Sold by all responsible dealers. Price List to the trade upon application

FRED'K WM. LUTTGEN, Sole Agent, 51 WARREN ST., NEW YORK.

"GRAND PRIZE" MEDIUM DRY, Quarts, $13.00, Pints, $15.00. Choice California Still Wines in Cases only
Sample Case, containing 2 bottles each "ECLIPSE" Brandy, Port, Burgundy, Claret and Hock, $8.00.

FREDERICK'S
KNICKEBOCKER
Family Portrait Gallery,

No. 770 BROADWAY, Corner NINTH STREET

IMPERIALS, - - - - $6.00 per Dozen.
DUPLICATES, - - - - 3.00 per Dozen.

INSTANTANEOUS PHOTOGRAPHS.

☞ All sittings superintended by Mr. Fredericks personally. ☜

NATURAL EXPRESSIONS AND PLEASING PICTURES.

S F SNIFFEN, President   F R SMART, Treasurer

The undersigned manufacture

FINE PLUMBING MATERIALS,

such as are required and used in work where quality and not price is the consideration. Among the specialties manufactured and controlled by them may be mentioned

The "ROYAL" Porcelain Baths,
         The "BRIGHTON" and "HELLYER" Water-Closets,
The "MODEL" Slop Sinks,   The "TUCKER" Grease Traps,
The "DOHERTY" Self-Closing Cocks, and The "FULLER" FAUCETS.

They have handsome Show-rooms in New York, Boston, and Chicago, where these appliances may be seen fitted up with water connected. A visit to these rooms will prove suggestive and instructive to those who contemplate building, or remodeling their plumbing

THE MEYER-SNIFFEN CO. (Limited.)

46 and 48 Cliff St., New York   1 Pemberton Square, Boston.   91 Adams St., Chicago.

INGERSOLL ROCK DRILL CO.,
10 PARK PLACE, NEW YORK.

MANUFACTURERS OF
"ECLIPSE" ROCK DRILLS.
"Straight Line" Air Compressors,
Machinery for Mining, Tunneling, Grading, Quarrying, etc.
BOILERS, STEAM AND HORSE POWER HOISTS,
Electric Batteries, Fuse, etc.
COMPLETE PLANTS FURNISHED.
For Catalogue, Estimates, etc., Address
INGERSOLL ROCK DRILL CO.,
10 Park Place, New York.

ELECTRIC LIGHTS,
ARC and INCANDESCENT.

BEST IN USE.

ON EXHIBITION AND FOR SALE BY

THE UNITED STATES ILLUMINATING CO.,

CAPITAL, $1,000,000.

59 and 61 Liberty Street, N. Y.

EUGENE T. LYNCH, President.   JOS W. HARTLEY, Secretary

A. E. HIGGINS,
SUCCESSOR TO HIGGINS AND FOWLER,
MANUFACTURER OF

HIGGINS' "HORSESHOE" LAUNDRY, AND OLD FASHIONED PURE FAMILY SOAPS,

OFFICE AND FACTORY, 232, 234 AND 236 CHERRY STREET NEW YORK.

THE INTERNATIONAL NEWS COMPANY,

29 & 31 Beekman Street, New York.

Importers and Exporters of Newspapers, Periodicals and Books.

Special Authorized Agents in the United States and Canada, for the
ILLUSTRATED LONDON NEWS, GRAPHIC and PUNCH, CONTEMPORARY REVIEW, NINETEENTH CENTURY, FORTNIGHTLY REVIEW and the other Leading European Periodicals.

Subscriptions received for every Newspaper and Periodical published in Great Britain, Germany and France. Books imported in Quantity or by Single Volume.

THE BEST HEATERS IN THE WORLD.

GOLD'S PATENT HEATERS.

THE PERFECTION OF HOUSE WARMING.

GOLD'S PATENT
"HEALTH,"
"TUBULAR,"
"HYGEIAN,"
AND
"PERFECT"
HEATERS.

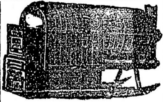
Gold's Patent "Health" Heater.

The only Heaters that produce Pure, Healthful, Pleasant, Moist, Warmed Air without Evaporation of Water.

Send for Illustrated Descriptive Catalogue containing References and Testimonials to

GOLD'S HEATER MANUFACTURING CO.,

*Office and Manufactory, 624 to 642 East 14th Street,
Salesroom, 237 Water Street, New York.*

Sole Manufacturers, also, of the Celebrated Keyser "Peace-Maker" Heaters

---

REED & BARTON,
MANUFACTURERS OF FINE

Electro-Plated Ware,

FORMERLY AT 686 BROADWAY,

REMOVED TO

37 UNION SQUARE, NEW YORK.

Union Trust Company of New York,

No. 73 BROADWAY, cor. Rector St., NEW YORK.

Capital, - - - - - - - - - - $1,000,000 00
Surplus, - - - - - - - - - - 1,660,548 23

Authorized to act as Executor, Administrator, Guardian, Receiver, or Trustee, and is

A LEGAL DEPOSITORY for MONEY.

Accepts the transfer agency and registry of stocks, and acts as Trustee of mortgages of corporations.
Allows interest on deposits, which may be made at any time and withdrawn on five days' notice with interest for the whole time they remain with the Company
For the convenience of depositors this Company also opens current accounts subject, in accordance with its rules, to check at sight, and allows interest upon the resulting daily balances. Such checks pass through the Clearing-house.

TRUSTEES:

JAMES FORSYTH,	R G REMSEN,	JAMES N PLATT,
I H FROTHINGHAM,	WM. F RUSSELL,	JAMES M McLEAN,
G G WILLIAMS,	E B WESLEY,	WM WHITEWRIGHT,
HENRY A KENT,	SAMUEL F BARGER,	AMASA J PARKER,
GEORGE CABOT WARD	A A. LOW	D C HAYS,
GEORGE A JARVIS,	J B JOHNSTON,	HENRY STOKES,
ABRAM DUBOIS,	C D WOOD,	JAMES H OGILVIE,
R J WILSON,	JAMES A ROOSEVELT,	S T FAIRCHILD,
EDWARD KING,	D H McALPIN	ROBERT LENOX KENNEDY.
C VANDERBILT	AUGUSTUS SCHELL.	

EXECUTIVE COMMITTEE:

WM WHITEWRIGHT,	G G WILLIAMS,
JAMES M McLEAN,	E B WESLEY,
AUGUSTUS SCHELL,	C D WOOD,
GEORGE CABOT WARD,	D C HAYS.

EDWARD KING, President.   JAMES M. McLEAN, First Vice-President,
JAMES H OGILVIE, Second Vice-President   A O RONALDSON, Secretary

---

The Largest House in the World for Sporting Goods

BURNT CORK, GREASE PAINTS, COLORED FIRES, MAKE-UP BOXES,
SONG & DANCE and CLOG SHOES, SILK, WORSTED and COTTON KNIT GOODS.

The undersigned keep constantly on hand a full line of FALSE BEARDS, WHISKERS, WIGS, MOUSTACHES or make to order any style of HAIR GOODS for Detective's Use, Theatrical or Private Parties Also, POLICE CLUBS, BILLYS, NIPPERS, HANDCUFFS, LEG IRONS, BELTS, BADGES, WHISTLES, BALLOT BOXES, GAVELS, GYMNASIUM, BOATING and FIREMEN OUTFITS FISHING TACKLE, BASE BALL, ARCHERY, LAWN TENNIS, CRICKET, BOXING GLOVES, INDIAN CLUBS, QUOITS, DUMB BELLS, MAGIC TRICKS, FOOT BALLS, PLAYING CARDS, CHESS, DOMINOES, CRIBBAGE, DICE, MODEL TOY ENGINES, LOCOMOTIVES, and all the latest and best novelties We send by mail, on receipt of 25 cents, our New Catalogue of 325 pages, over 3000 Illustrations.

PECK & SNYDER,
No. 126, 128, 130 NASSAU STREET, NEW YORK.

ONLY ONE CHANGE BETWEEN NEW YORK AND PARIS

BY TAKING THE

RED STAR LINE

Belgian, Royal and United States Mail Steamers, sailing every Saturday between NEW YORK and ANTWERP.

The following Full-Powered, First-Class Steel and Iron Steamers have been specially constructed for the requirements of this trade and combine the latest improvements to insure **safety, Comfort and speed**:

S.S. Westernland, 5500 Tons Reg.	S.S. Noordland, 5000 Tons Reg.	S.S. Waesland, 5000 Tons Reg.
S.S. Belgenland, 4000 "	S.S. Rhynland, 4000 "	S.S. Pennland, 4000 "
S.S. Nederland, 3000 "	S.S. Zeeland, 3000 "	S.S. Switzerland, 3000 "
	S.S. Vederland, 3000 "	

Average time between New York and Antwerp 10 to 12 days

For persons desiring to visit **Paris, Belgium, Holland, the Rhine Provinces, Germany, Italy,** the Red Star Line will be found most advantageous

Through Railroad Tickets issued to all points on the Continent in connection with Red Star Ocean Tickets at lowest rates

The First Cabin Saloons, Sleeping, Ladies', Bath, Smoking Rooms, etc., are located amidships, above the main deck (removed from the engines, screw, and all other objectionable points), where there is the least motion They are fitted with all the latest improvements which can be conducive to comfort and safety. Particular attention is paid to the cuisine, which is unsurpassed

The Second Cabin accommodations are adjoining those of the First Cabin The rooms are all commodious, and with the exception of not being as elegantly or expensively furnished are in every respect equal to those of the First Cabin An excellent table, also all requisites for the voyage are provided

The First and Second Cabin Staterooms are thoroughly lighted and ventilated, and with few exceptions, all outside rooms.

Steerage.—The accommodations are spacious and are divided into rooms, insuring an amount of privacy hitherto unknown to the third-class passenger

Beds and Tinware are also supplied free of charge. The food is varied abundant, and of the very best quality

Experienced surgeons, stewardesses and stewards accompany these steamers

Neither Cattle, Sheep, Horses or Pigs are carried on these steamers

The steamers leave every Saturday promptly at the advertised hour of sailing from the Red Star Docks, foot of Grand Street, Jersey City, adjoining the railroad terminus from the South and West, reached from New York by the Cortlandt or Desbrosses Street Ferries

First Cabin Rates—From $60 to $90, Excursion, $110 to $160, according to location

Second Cabin Rates—$55, Excursion, $100.

Steerage Passage at the Lowest Rates.

For information or passage apply to

PETER WRIGHT & SONS, General Agents 55 B way, N Y, 307 Walnut St, Phila, 119 Randolph St, Chicago.

C. L BARTLETT & CO., New England Agents 115 State Street, Boston

VON DER BECKE & MARSILY, General European Agents, 2 Rivage, Antwerp

---

Organized 1862.   *Incorporated 1874.*

THE W. J. WILCOX CO.,

Lard Refiners,

FOOT OF WEST 59th STREET,

Sales Office:

41 BROAD STREET, NEW YORK.

Award of GOLD MEDAL at Paris for

"SUPERIORITY IN MANUFACTURE FOR EXPORT TO ALL COUNTRIES."

W A COLE, Pres.   JNO. P. TOWNSEND, Vice Pres.   S. E. HISCOX, Sec. and Treas.

HAVEMEYER Sugar Refining Co.,

No. 112 Wall Street,

NEW YORK.

— MANUFACTURERS OF PERFECTLY PURE REFINED SUGAR —

New York Type Foundry and Printers' Warehouse,

Established in Hartford, Conn., 1804   Removed to New York, 1812

FARMER, LITTLE & CO.,

Nos. 63 & 65 Beekman St., cor. of Gold St., New York,

BOOK, NEWS, **TYPE** JOB, and ORNAMENTAL

PERSONS DESIRING TO ORDER FROM US WILL PLEASE SEND FOR SPECIMEN BOOKS.

PRINTING PRESSES OF ANY MAKER.

PAPER CUTTERS, CASES, GALLEYS, ETC., ETC.

SPECIMENS AND ESTIMATES GIVEN ON APPLICATION.

ALL SALES MADE SATISFACTORY.

National Express Company,

GENERAL FORWARDERS

To all Points in Northern and Eastern New York, Northern Massachusetts, Vermont and Canada, and through connecting Express Companies, TO ALL PARTS OF THE UNITED STATES.

COIN, BANK NOTES, VALUABLES, and MERCHANDISE
Forwarded with Safety and Despatch,

AND ESPECIAL ATTENTION PAID TO THE

Collection of Checks, Coupons, Notes, Drafts, and Bills.

Among the important points now reached by this Company are the following, viz.—

Amsterdam, N. Y.	Kingston, N. Y.	Rochester, N. Y.
Buffalo, N. Y.	Little Falls, N. Y.	Rome, N. Y.
Burlington, Vt.	Lyons, N. Y.	Rondout, N. Y.
Canastota, N. Y.	Middletown, N. Y.	Rutland, Vt.
Canajoharie, N. Y.	Montreal, P. Q.	Saugerties, N. Y.
Catskill, N. Y.	Newburgh, N. Y.	Schenectady, N. Y.
Cazenovia, N. Y.	North Adams, Mass.	Stroudsburgh, Pa.
Cornwall, N. Y.	Norwich, N. Y.	St. Johns, P. Q.
Fonda, N. Y.	Oneida, N. Y.	Utica, N. Y.
Fort Plain, N. Y.	Oswego, N. Y.	Weedsport, N. Y.
Hackensack, N. J.	Ottawa, Ont.	West Point, N. Y.
Herkimer, N. Y.	Paterson, N. J.	Whitehall, N. Y.
Jersey City, N. J.	Plattsburgh, N. Y.	

NEW YORK, ALBANY, BOSTON, SARATOGA, SYRACUSE, TROY.

By Special joint tariff arrangement with connecting companies the Company are enabled to forward packages of Merchandise weighing from 1 to 7 lbs., also packages of money at the low rates as per the annexed tables

MONEY.
CURRENCY OR GOLD NOT EXCEEDING

$20....... 15 Cents. | $40 . .20 Cents. | $50 .. ..25 Cents.

PRINTED MATTER.
Books and other matter wholly in print, ordered from or sent by manufacturers or publishers, and prepaid

PACKAGES OF
2 lbs.. 15 Cents. | 3 lbs 20 Cents. | 4 lbs .. 25 Cents.

MERCHANDISE.
Lowest and highest charges, according to distance   Packages not exceeding

1 lb ... 25c.	3 lbs . 25c. to 45c.	5 lbs 25c. to 75c.
2 lbs 25c. to 30c.	4 lbs 25c. to 60c.	7 lbs. 25c. to $1.40

NOTE—Packages as above described, destined to places reached by Northern *connecting* Expresses carried for a *single through charge*

Pennsylvania Railroad

THE GREAT TRUNK LINE OF THE UNITED STATES.

The Most Direct Route Between

NEW YORK AND THE PRINCIPAL COMMERCIAL CENTRES OF THE WEST, and all Points on the Pacific Coast, in the North-west, South, and South-west.

The Pennsylvania Railroad in its construction, equipment, and operation embraces all the improvements known to modern science. The time of its trains is the fastest made consistent with absolute safety.

THE FAMOUS NEW YORK AND CHICAGO LIMITED EXPRESS, *composed exclusively of* Pullman, Hotel, Parlor, Dining, *and Sleeping Coaches, leaves New York daily at 9 00 A.M., arriving at Chicago at 10 40 A.M., and Cincinnati at 8.00 A.M., the next day.*

Superior Meals served on the Train at the uniform rate of $1.

Tickets over the **Pennsylvania Railroad** and Connecting Lines can be obtained by passengers, at the following offices:

849 Broadway, N. Y.	8 Battery Place, N. Y.
435 Broadway, N. Y.	Foot of Cortlandt Street, N. Y.
944 Broadway, N. Y.	Foot of Desbrosses Street, N. Y.
No. 1 Astor House, N. Y.	Annex Office, Brooklyn.
No. 4 Court Street, Brooklyn.	Pennsylvania R.R Station, Jersey City

CHAS. E. PUGH,
GENERAL MANAGER

J. R. WOOD,
GENERAL PASSENGER AGENT

SAMUEL CARPENTER, Eastern Passenger Agent, 849 Broadway, N. Y.

Pacific Mail Steamship Co.

Regular Mail Line.

NEW YORK TO SAN FRANCISCO

Via The ISTHMUS of PANAMA,

CONNECTING FOR

South Pacific, Central American and Mexican Ports.

SAN FRANCISCO to JAPAN and CHINA,

San Francisco to Sandwich Islands, New Zealand and Australia.

First Class Accommodations for Passengers and Freight

For Freight, Passage, or general Information,

APPLY AT THE

Office on the Pier, foot of Canal St., North River,

NEW YORK.

COLWELL LEAD CO.,

63 Centre Street, New York,

MANUFACTURERS OF

American Standard Shot,

OF SUPERIOR FINISH,

DROP SHOT,

CHILLED SHOT,

BUCK SHOT,

BAR LEAD,

SHEET LEAD and LEAD PIPE.

DEALERS IN

PLUMBERS',

STEAM AND GAS-FITTERS'

SUPPLIES,

OF ALL KINDS

Sole Agents for the United States for

SILENT ACTING COCKS.

ALSO AGENTS FOR THE

Norristown Iron Works.

FALL RIVER LINE.

Old Colony Railroad and Steamboat Co.'s
Fall River and Newport Steamers
From Pier 28, North River,
NEW BEDFORD STEAMERS
From Pier 39, East River,
NEW YORK.

GREAT PASSENGER AND FREIGHT SYSTEM
BETWEEN
NEW YORK
AND

Boston, Fall River, Newport, Taunton, New Bedford, Cape Cod, Martha's Vineyard, Nantucket, Fitchburg, Lowell, Lawrence, Nashua and all Northern and Eastern Points.

STEAMERS IN THE PASSENGER AND FREIGHT SERVICE:

"Pilgrim," "Bristol," "Providence," "Newport," "Old Colony."

STEAMERS IN THE FREIGHT SERVICE EXCLUSIVELY:

"City of Fall River," "City of New Bedford," "City of Fitchburg," "Albatross."

CARRYING, TERMINAL AND SHIPPING FACILITIES UNEQUALLED
BY ANY OTHER SOUND LINE.

In addition to Daily Service of Steamers carrying Freight and Passengers, Nine Freight Steamers per week are regularly dispatched in each direction between EASTERN and WESTERN Termini, insuring to Shippers

PROMPT AND RELIABLE MOVEMENT.

Information cheerfully and promptly furnished on application

S. C. PUTNAM, Gen'l Freight Agent,   J. R. KENDRICK, Gen'l Manager,
BOSTON.

F. H. FORBES, Freight Agent,   GEO L. CONNOR, Gen'l Pass. Agent,
NEW YORK.

BORDEN & LOVELL, - - New York Agents.

THE GREAT
Southern Freight and Passenger Lines

— TO —

CHARLESTON, SAVANNAH, FLORIDA,

— AND —

All Points in the South and South-west

— VIA —

CHARLESTON, S. C.,

From Pier 27, North River (foot Park Place), Wednesdays and Saturdays, or oftener, at 3 P.M.

— VIA —

SAVANNAH, GA.,

From Pier 35, North River (foot Spring Street), Wednesdays and Saturdays, or oftener, at 3 P.M.

Rates Guaranteed as Low as by Other Lines.

☞ The Steamships of these Lines have been handsomely fitted up for the convenience of Passengers, and are unrivaled on this coast for **SAFETY, SPEED,** and **COMFORT.**

The attention of Tourists and Travelers, who contemplate visiting **Charleston, Savannah, Aiken, Florida,** and other favorite resorts in the South, is invited to the superior facilities offered by these Lines to the close connection made at **Charleston** with the **South Carolina, Charleston and Savannah Railroads,** and "**City of Palatka,**" and at **Savannah** with the **Central,** and the **Savannah, Florida and Western Railroads,** and the popular **Inside Line** of Steamers for all points in the South and South-west, and **Florida.**

JAMES W. QUINTARD & CO., Agents New York and Charleston Steamship Co.,
Pier 27, North River (foot Park Place), N. Y.

H. YONGE, Agent Ocean Steamship Co., of Savannah,
Pier 35, North River (foot Spring Street), N. Y.

A. D. W. SAMPSON, North-Eastern Agent, 201 Washington Street, Boston, Mass.

W. H. RHETT, General Agent, 317 Broadway, N. Y.

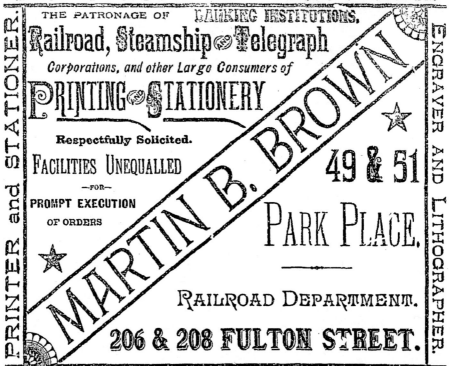

BLANK BOOK MANUFACTURER.

PRINTER and STATIONER. — **ENGRAVER AND LITHOGRAPHER.**

THE PATRONAGE OF BANKING INSTITUTIONS, Railroad, Steamship & Telegraph Corporations, and other Large Consumers of PRINTING & STATIONERY Respectfully Solicited.

FACILITIES UNEQUALLED —FOR— PROMPT EXECUTION OF ORDERS

MARTIN B. BROWN

49 & 51 PARK PLACE.

RAILROAD DEPARTMENT.

206 & 208 FULTON STREET.

"BEHNING" PIANOS

Have universally received the HIGHEST HONORS and Awards wherever exhibited for greatest

**PURITY and EVENNESS OF TONE,
ELASTICITY OF TOUCH,
SIMPLICITY OF ACTION,
SOLIDITY OF CONSTRUCTION,
EXCELLENCE OF WORKMANSHIP,
and ELEGANCE OF FINISH,**

And are pronounced by Leading Pianists and Musical Authorities,

THE BEST NOW MADE.

Warerooms, 3 West 14th St.

FACTORY, 124th ST. and FIRST AVENUE.

Hoboken and New York

FERRIES

BELONGING TO THE

HOBOKEN LAND
AND
IMPROVEMENT CO.

OF NEW JERSEY.

W. W. SHIPPEN, President. S. B. DOW, Treasurer.
CHAS. W. WOOLSEY, Superintendent.

General Office of the Company,

No. 3 NEWARK STREET, - - HOBOKEN.

FERRY LANDINGS:

Foot of Barclay Street, N. Y., to Ferry St., Hoboken.
Foot of Christopher St., N. Y. to Ferry St., Hoboken.
Foot of 14th Street, N. R., N. Y., to 14th St., Hoboken.

WARD'S LINES TO THE TROPICS!

FOR HAVANA.

LIFE IN THE WEST INDIES;

The Only Weekly Line of American Steamers.

Speed and Comfort Combined with Absolute Safety.

The following Steamers of this Line leave New York every Saturday at 3 P.M.

For Havana:

Steamship "NEWPORT,"	3,000 Tons,	Capt. T. S. CURTIS.
Steamship "SARATOGA,"	2,500 Tons,	Capt. McINTOSH.
Steamship "NIAGARA,"	2,300 Tons,	Capt. J. B. BAKER.

Connecting at HAVANA with first-class Foreign and American Steamers for

Florida, New Orleans, Mexico, Puerto Rico, Hayti, St. Thomas and other West India Islands.

For full particulars apply to

JAMES E. WARD & CO., 113 Wall St., New York.

Send for copy of "WINTER MONTHS IN CUBA"

FOR NASSAU, N.P., DIRECT, SANTIAGO DE CUBA and CIENFUEGOS.

The Favorite Excursion this Winter to the Famous

"ISLE OF JUNE"

(The Oldest City in the West Indies),

And Through the INTERIOR OF CUBA.

The First-Class Palace Steamships

"CIENFUEGOS" (new),	3,000 Tons,	Capt. F. M. FAIRCLOTH.
"SANTIAGO,"	2,600 "	Capt. L. COLTON.

Will sail every other Thursday

For NASSAU, N.P., and CIENFUEGOS, calling both going and returning, at SANTIAGO DE CUBA.

Connects at SANTIAGO DE CUBA with first-class Lines for JAMAICA, HAYTI, PUERTO RICO, etc.

For full particulars and illustrated pamphlet, apply to

JAMES E. WARD & CO., 113 Wall St., New York.

American Connoisseurs

AFTER FIFTY YEARS' TEST

PRONOUNCE

"PIPER HEIDSIECK"

TO BE THE ONLY RELIABLE

Champagne.

Quintard Iron Works,

N. F. PALMER, JR., & CO.

ENGINES, BOILERS

—: AND :—

MACHINERY.

Avenue D, 11th and 12th Sts., E. R.,

NEW YORK.

Chartered 1799.

D. C. HAYS, President.　　　　　　　　　　　　J. T. BALDWIN, Cashier.

BANK

OF THE

Manhattan Company,

NEW YORK.

Capital,	$2,050,000
Surplus,	1,025,000

CARY & MOEN,
Manufacturers of
STEEL WIRE FOR ALL PURPOSES, AND
STEEL SPRINGS OF EVERY DESCRIPTION.

Market Steel Wire, Crinoline Wire, Tempered and Covered.
ROUND, FLAT, OVAL AND SQUARE WIRE.
For Lock Springs, Machinery, Drills and Needles, Tempered and Untempered
—ALSO—
PATENT TEMPERED STEEL FURNITURE SPRINGS CONSTANTLY ON HAND.

232, 234, 236, and 238 West Twenty-ninth Street,
225, 227, 229, 231, 233, 235, 237, and 239 WEST TWENTY-EIGHTH STREET.
NEW YORK.

ADOLPH G HÜPFEL.

A. HÜPFEL'S SON'S

ESTABLISHED 1854,

Lager Beer Brewery

161st Street and Third Avenue,

Morrisania,   *NEW YORK.*

We Hereby Inform the Public that Our

CONSIST SOLELY of the PRODUCT of

RAW SUGARS REFINED,

NEITHER GLUCOSE, MURIATE OF TIN, MURIATIC ACID,

NOR ANY OTHER FOREIGN, DELETERICUS OR FRAUDULENT SUBSTANCE WHATEVER IS, OR EVER HAS BEEN, MIXED WITH THEM OUR

SUGARS AND SYRUPS

ARE ABSOLUTELY UNADULTERATED.

HAVEMEYERS & ELDER,

(The DeCastro & Donner Sugar Refining Company),

OFFICE, 117 WALL STREET.

ESTABLISHED 1850.

INMAN LINE.

Royal Mail Steamers.

NEW YORK TO LIVERPOOL EVERY THURSDAY.
LIVERPOOL TO NEW YORK EVERY TUESDAY.

Calling at Queenstown each way.

	TONS		TONS
CITY OF CHICAGO	6,000	CITY OF RICHMOND	4,780
CITY OF BERLIN	5,491	CITY OF CHESTER	4,770
	BALTIC	4,000	

The First Transatlantic Line to adopt Lieut. Maury's Lane Routes, taking the Southerly Course between the months of January and August.

These Steamers are built especially to meet the requirements of the Admiralty, and are fitted with water-tight compartments.

They are among the strongest, largest and fastest on the Atlantic, reducing the passage to a minimum, giving thereby especial comfort to passengers.

RATES OF PASSAGE.

FIRST CABIN.

To Queenstown and Liverpool, - - - $60, $80 and $100

INTERMEDIATE.

To or From Queenstown and Liverpool, - - - - - $35

STEERAGE.

To or from Liverpool, Queenstown, Glasgow, Belfast, Cardiff, Londonderry, London or Bristol at Reduced Rates.

For passage or further information apply to

GEO. A. FAULK	104 South Fourth St., PHILADELPHIA.
L. H. PALMER	3 Old State House, BOSTON.
F. C. BROWN	32 South Clark Street, CHICAGO.
J. J. McCORMICK	Cor. 4th & Smithfield Sts., PITTSBURG.
JOSEPH P. WHYTE & CO	Sixth and Pine Streets, ST. LOUIS.
JOHN CLANCY	408 Chestnut Street,
GILMORE & CO	110 West Fourth St., CINCINNATI.
BEPLER & CO	6 West Third Street,
JOHN E. WALSH	122 Exchange Street, BUFFALO.
CIPPERLY, COLE & HAZLEHURST	11 First Street, TROY, N.Y.
FLETCHER VOSBURG	645 Broadway, ALBANY. Or to

THE INMAN STEAMSHIP COMPANY (LIMITED),

WASHINGTON BUILDING,

No. 1 BROADWAY, NEW YORK.

Agencies in all parts of the United States and Canada.

WM. DICK.   CORD MEYER.

DICK & MEYER,

Sugar Refiners,

No. 110 WALL STREET,

NEW YORK.

REFINERY, Foot North Seventh Street,

BROOKLYN, E. D.

PROVIDENCE & STONINGTON S. S. CO.

Providence Line { From Pier 29 N. R., foot Warren St. 4.30 P. M. in Winter; 5 P. M. in Summer.

Stonington Line { From Stonington Line Pier, N. R. 4.30 P. M. in Winter; 5 P. M. in Summer.

NEW YORK.

PASSENGERS AND FREIGHT TAKEN FOR

BOSTON, PROVIDENCE, WORCESTER,

NASHUA, LOWELL, MANCHESTER, PORTLAND,

And all Northern and Eastern Points.

PASSENGER AND FREIGHT STEAMERS:

Massachusetts, Rhode Island, Narragansett, Stonington.

FREIGHT STEAMERS:

Frances, Pequot, Electra, Doris, A. C. Barstow.

Carrying facilities greater, and Passengers and Freight transported quicker than on any other Sound line.

FAST FREIGHT A SPECIALTY.

THROUGH BILLS OF LADING given between all Points East, West, South and South-west.

THROUGH TICKETS to all Eastern and New England Points, via both Lines can be obtained at all Principal Ticket Offices.

STATEROOMS can be secured at 3 Astor House; 257, 397, 785, 942, Broadway, and Fifth Avenue Hotel; also at Piers.

Information promptly furnished on application.

F. W. POPPLE, Gen'l Passenger Agt.   D. S. BABCOCK, President,
ISAAC ODELL, General Freight Agent, Providence Line, New York.
E. A. DEVEAU, General Freight Agent, Stonington Line, New York.
W. H. MORRELL, Agent for both Lines, B. & P. R. R. Station, Boston.

DECKER & RAPP,

WHOLESALE AND RETAIL DEALERS IN

GEORGIA AND FLORIDA

YELLOW PINE

YARDS AND OFFICE,

FOOT OF BETHUNE ST.

— NORTH RIVER, —

NEW YORK.

Telephone, 119 Twenty-first St.

MUNICIPAL

Gas Light Company,

OFFICE:

358 and 360 Fourth Avenue,

NEW YORK CITY.

Works, foot West 44th, 45th, and 46th Sts., N. R.

CHAS. G. FRANCKLYN, *President.*

        H. E. GAROTY, *Vice-President.*

PHILIP ALLEN, *Secretary.*

        SAMUEL J. YOUNG, *Treasurer.*

BUCKINGHAM HOTEL,
Fifth Avenue and Fiftieth Street,

(Opposite Cathedral.)   NEW YORK.

Conducted on the European Plan, with a Restaurant of Unsurpassed Excellence.

WEDDINGS, RECEPTIONS, DINNERS AND LUNCHES A SPECIALTY.

WETHERBEE & FULLER, Proprietors.

ALBEMARLE HOTEL,
MADISON SQUARE,   NEW YORK.

Most centrally located, at the Junction of Broadway, Fifth Avenue and 24th Street.

CONDUCTED ON THE EUROPEAN PLAN.

JANVRIN & WALTER, Proprietors.

WINDSOR HOTEL.

Fifth Avenue, 46th and 47th Streets, New York.

ONE OF THE MOST PERFECT AND COMFORTABLE HOTELS IN THE WORLD.

HAWK & WETHERBEE, Proprietors.

NEW YORK BELTING AND PACKING CO.

The Oldest and Largest Manufacturers In the United States of 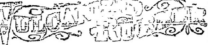 IN EVERY FORM adapted to MECHANICAL PURPOSES.

MACHINE BELTING, with Smooth Metallic Rubber Surface.

This Company has manufactured the Largest Belts made in the world for the principal Elevators at Chicago, Buffalo and New York.

STEAM AND WATER HOSE.

RUBBER "TEST" HOSE, made of Vulcanized Para Rubber and Carbolized Duck. Four ply and Five ply Capped ends. 400 pounds pressure to square inch

Made expressly for and recommended 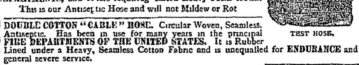 by over 300 FIRE DEPARTMENTS, and others requiring Extra Heavy FIRE HOSE. This is our Antiseptic Hose and will not Mildew or Rot

DOUBLE COTTON "CABLE" HOSE. Circular Woven, Seamless, Antiseptic. Has been in use for many years in the principal FIRE DEPARTMENTS OF THE UNITED STATES. It is Rubber Lined under a Heavy, Seamless Cotton Fabric and is unequalled for ENDURANCE and general severe service.

TEST HOSE.

CABLE HOSE.

CORRUGATED RUBBER MATS AND MATTING.

FOR HALLS, FLOORING, STONE AND IRON STAIRWAYS, Etc.

NEW YORK BELTING AND PACKING CO.

Warehouse: 15 Park Row, New York.

JOHN H. CHEEVER, Treasurer.

BENEDICT'S TIME.

A SPECIALTY.

IMPORTERS AND MANUFACTURERS OF

Watches, Diamonds, Chains, Rich Jewelry AND SILVER WARE.

Having enlarged our store and made extensive improvements, we are the better enabled to display our large and choice stock

West Side Elevated Trains stop at Cortlandt Street, near rear of Benedict Building. Ten minutes from Fourteenth Street

BENEDICT BROTHERS, KEEPERS OF THE CITY TIME,

Benedict Building, Broadway and Cortlandt St.

ESTABLISHED 1821

CLAUSEN & PRICE

Brewing Co.,

New York Brewery.

ALE

AND

 **PORTER.**

59TH ST. AND 11TH AVE.,

New York.

OLD DOMINION
STEAMSHIP COMPANY.

W. H. STANDFORD, - - - - - Secretary.

STEAMSHIPS OF THIS COMPANY SAIL FROM

PIER 26 North River

EVERY

Tuesday, Thursday and Saturday, at 3 P.M.

FOR

Norfolk, Portsmouth, Richmond, Petersburg,

AND

OLD POINT COMFORT AT NEWPORT NEWS,

Connecting with Railroad Systems to the West, South and South-west for White Sulphur, Virginia Springs, and all health, mountain and pleasure resorts of Virginia; also, for Cincinnati and all important Western points, via

The Chesapeake & Ohio Railway.

The Magnificent Steamships of this Company will, on inspection, be found to offer a delightful change to the Traveling Public from the heat, dust and crowded trains so objectionable and unavoidable on Railroads during the Excursion Season.

Time between New York and Norfolk, 24 Hours.

TABLE EQUAL TO FIRST-CLASS HOTELS.

All First-Class Through or Local Tickets by the Main Lines of the Company include Meals and Stateroom accommodation on Steamers

TICKETS FOR SALE At all the prominent Hotels and Ticket Offices throughout the East and North-east and at the

General Offices of the Company,

235 WEST ST. (cor. Beach), NEW YORK.

Everybody knows PUCK!!
Everybody talks about PUCK!!

21, 23 and 25 Warren Street, New York.

Everybody knows that PUCK is 10c. per copy or $5.00 per year.

Published every Wednesday.

For Sale by all Newsdealers.

THE JOHN A. ROEBLING'S SONS CO.

Manufacturers of

IRON AND STEEL

OF EVERY DESCRIPTION AND FOR EVERY PURPOSE.

WHEELS AND ROPE FOR TRANSMISSION OF POWER.

Manufacturers of WIRE of every description.

AGENTS FOR

FIRE PROOF LATHING, WIRE SCREEN CLOTH, BUCK THORN BARB FENCING.

N. Y. Office and Warehouse, 117 and 119 LIBERTY ST.,

Works—TRENTON, N. J.   H. L. SHIPPY, Manager.

Sixth Avenue RAILROAD COMPANY.

✻ 756 SIXTH AVENUE. ✻

OFFICERS.

FRANK CURTISS, - - - - President.

HENRY S. MOORE, - Secretary and Treasurer.

CAPITAL, $750,000.

SLAWSON'S PATENT FARE BOXES, ETC.

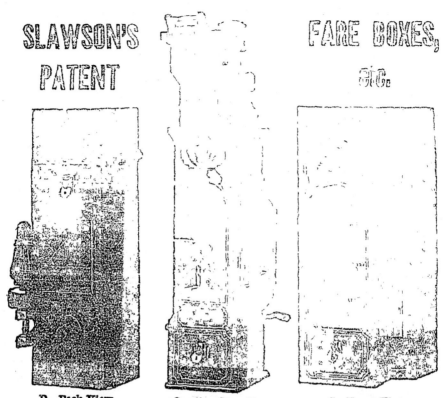

D. Back View.   Omnibus Fare Box.   C. Front View.

Boxes marked C and D have two rests or stops for inspection of fare, on the first of which the fare remains on its edge.

Box marked E is adapted for omnibus use, and is arranged for outside passengers to pay, as well as those inside. Said boxes are of the latest and most approved pattern and contain a front door, by opening which all of the glass inside can be conveniently cleaned. This is a late patent, and is a very valuable improvement over the old method of taking the boxes apart for that purpose. They are well made and not liable to get out of order, cannot possibly be picked, and, even if all the glass is broken, no fare can be extracted from the drawer.

Change Gate. Inside View.

Change Slide. Outside View.

Drivers' Change Box.

The undersigned originated the "FARE BOX SYSTEM," and all of said Boxes, Change Gates and Driver's Change Box are protected by several patents, and parties using them are not liable to claims for infringements.

These Boxes, etc., are now in use not only in the United States and Canada, but in Mexico, South America, Europe, Asia, Africa and Australia—in fact, nearly all places where street cars are used. The prices have been greatly reduced and are made to fit the times.

Orders will be promptly filled by addressing the undersigned at **16 W. FORTY-SIXTH ST.**, or the

JOHN STEPHENSON CO. (Limited), 47 E. Twenty-Seventh Street, New York.

J. B. SLAWSON, Proprietor and Patentee.

Eighth Avenue Railroad Company.

820 EIGHTH AVENUE.

OFFICERS.

WILLIAM H. HAYS, - - - *President.*
JAMES AFFLECK, - *Secretary and Treasurer.*

Capital, $1,000,000.

"CORDON ROUGE."

ONLY AND ORIGINAL BRAND.
GEO. C. NAPHEY & SON'S PURE LEAF LARD.
NEW YORK, PHILADELPHIA, LONDON and BRISTOL.   New York Office, 20 WATER ST.

Liveliest and Sauciest Illustrated Paper Published

10 Cents a Number. $5.00 Per Year.

FOR SALE BY ALL NEWSDEALERS

THE JUDGE PUBLISHING COMPANY,
Franklin Square, New York.

THE
New York Gas Light
COMPANY.

Office: 157 and 159 Hester Street.

Works: 501 East 20th Street.

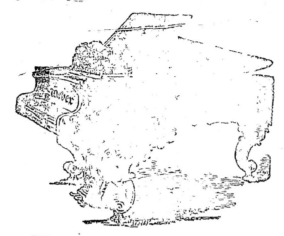

The Weber Pianos.

ARE CONSTRUCTED from the musician's standpoint as well as that of the mechanic, hence these instruments are distinguished from all others by that pure and sympathetic quality of tone that contains the greatest musical possibilities; that consummation of mechanical excellence that admits of the

Most Delicate and Impressive Effects,

while insuring the durability of the instrument, and that uniform superiority that enhances the pleasure of both performer and listener. Constructed from the very best materials and employing only the most skillful workmanship, these instruments combine the highest achievements in the art of Piano making, and *are comprehensively the best now manufactured.*

WAREROOMS ·

Fifth Avenue, cor West 16th St.

NEW YORK CITY

W. L. STRONG, President. C M ROWLEY, Vice-President.

The BRUSH ELECTRIC ILLUMINATING COMPANY

OF NEW YORK.

208 ELIZABETH STREET.

I C ALLEN, Secretary R. W ABORN, Treasurer

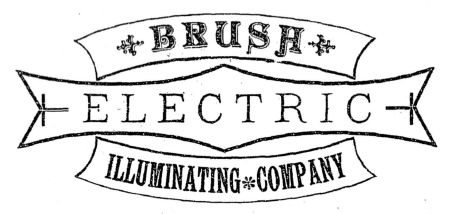

Established in 1835 by Thomas Christy.

Christy, Walcott & Co.,

Manufacturers of Paper Hangings and Paper Window Shades.

Factory 510 to 534 West 23d St. between 10th & 11th Aves.

Office 510 W. 23d St., New York.

(112)

STUBBORN FACTS

ARE THAT THE ⋅⋅⋅ Justly ✦ Famous ✦ Cigars ⋅⋅⋅ MADE BY THE ⋅⋅⋅ Celebrated ✦ Manufacturers, ⋅⋅⋅

STRAITON & STORM,

Are better than those produced by any other manufacturers.
For the following reasons:

They aim at the highest standard, and when reached they never allow them to deteriorate under any circumstances.

THE CONSUMERS WANTS ARE ALWAYS IN VIEW.

The dealer has only to keep the goods in stock to insure to himself a steady reliable trade.

WE ✦ CHALLENGE ✦ THE ✦ WORLD

To produce goods Better, more Reliable, and Regular

DEALERS SUPPLIED BY

R. C. BROWN & CO.,

94 and 96 West Broadway,   NEW YORK.

Josiah Macy's Sons,

COMMISSION

MERCHANTS,

189 & 191 Front St.,

NEW YORK.

MANUFACTURERS OF

**"MACY'S" LARD OILS, PRIME LARD,
AND GREASE STEARINES.**

DEALERS IN ALL GRADES OF

Cylinder, Machinery and Lubricating Oils,

MANUFACTURERS AGENTS,

CLEMENT'S + CORN + STARCH,

CANDLES,

OXIDE + ZINC, + "LZO" + BRAND.